# TODAY'S MARRIAGES AND FAMILIES

*A Wellness Approach*

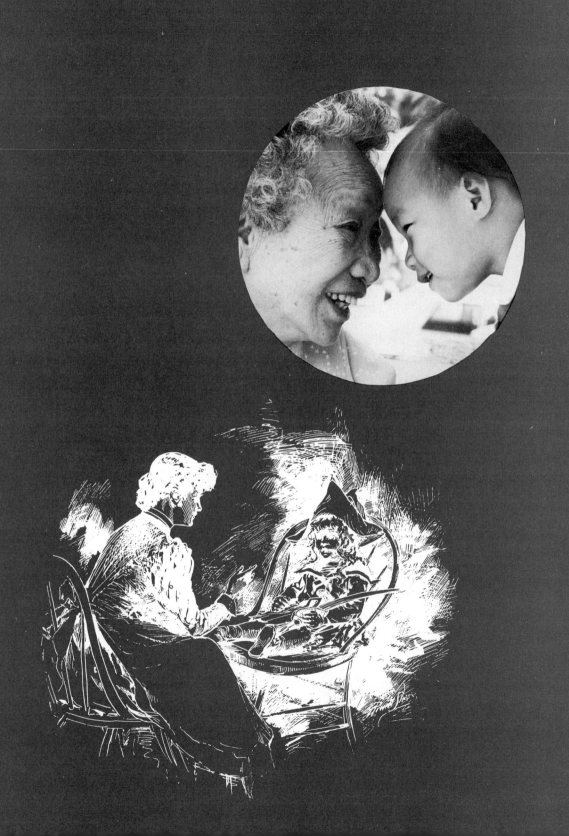

# TODAY'S MARRIAGES AND FAMILIES

## *A Wellness Approach*

**Thomas P. Gullotta**
*Eastern Connecticut State University*

**Gerald R. Adams**
*Utah State University*

**Sharon J. Alexander**
*American Association for
Counseling and Development*

Brooks/Cole Publishing Co.
*Pacific Grove, California*

Brooks/Cole Publishing Company
A Division of Wadsworth, Inc.

Printed in the United States of America

10   9   8   7   6   5   4   3

**Library of Congress Cataloging-in-Publication Data**

Gullotta, Thomas, [date]
    Today's marriages and families.

    Includes index.
      1. Family life education.   2. Family—United
States.   3. Marriage.   I. Adams, Gerald R.
II. Alexander, Sharon J.   III. Title.
HQ10.G85   1986         306.8         85-19051
ISBN 0-534-05520-6

Sponsoring Editor: *C. Deborah Laughton*
Editorial Assistant: *Mary Tudor*
Marketing Representative: *Rich Giggey*
Production Editor: *Phyllis Larimore*
Manuscript Editor: *Rephah Berg*
Permissions Editor: *Mary Kay Hancharick*
Interior and Cover Design: *Jamie Sue Brooks*
Cover Illustration: *Pauline Phung*
Art Coordinator: *Judith Macdonald*
Interior Illustration: *PC & F/Maggie Stevens/Wayne
    Clark*
Photo Editor: *Judy Blamer*
Photo Researcher: *Lindsay Kefauver*
Typesetting: *Bi-Comp, Inc., York, Pennsylvania*
Printing and Binding: *R. R. Donnelley & Sons Co.,
    Crawfordsville, Indiana*
Title Page Photos: *Frank Keillor*

Credits continue on page 503.

**Tom Gullotta** is the executive director of one of the nation's oldest and most respected family service agencies, the Child and Family Agency of Southeastern Connecticut. Holding academic appointments at several state colleges in Connecticut, he is a nationally recognized expert in the fields of primary prevention and adolescence. In addition to being the founding editor of the *Journal of Primary Prevention,* Tom holds editorial board positions on the following publications: *Family Relations, Journal of Early Adolescence, Journal of Adolescence,* and is a general series editor for *Advances in Adolescent Development: An Annual Book Series.* This is Tom's second published textbook. His first, co-authored with Gerald Adams and entitled *Adolescent Life Experiences,* has received critical acclaim nationwide.

**Gerald Adams** is a professor of Family and Human Development and Psychology at Utah State University. A nationally recognized expert in the fields of adolescence and family relations, he has consulted with such diverse organizations as the National Science Foundation, the Boy Scouts of America, and the District Court of Utah on adolescent and family issues. Gerald has co-authored several previous textbooks, including *Physical Attractiveness: A Cultural Imperative* (1978), *Adolescent Life Experiences* (1983), and *Understanding Research Methods* (1985). In addition he holds editorial board positions on the following publications: *Family Relations, Journal of Adolescence, Journal of Adolescent Research, Developmental Psychology, Journal of Primary Prevention,* and is the senior general series editor for *Advances in Adolescent Development: An Annual Book Series.*

**Sharon Alexander** is the director of professional development and research for the American Association for Counseling and Development. A nationally recognized expert in the fields of human sexuality and family life education, she is on the boards of the American Association of Sex Educators, Counselors, and Therapists, and the National Family Life Education Network. She has been an active participant for many years in the affairs of the National Council on Family Relations, serving on a number of important committees, and represented the council at the White House Conference on Families in 1980. In addition to her active participation in several professional associations, Sharon has a strong research interest in the subject area of adolescent sexuality and holds an editorial board appointment to the journal *Family Relations.*

## *Dedication*

To Pasquale, Tom, Big Bernie, Margie, Chris, and Little Bernie, but especially to Rosa and Marietta—I dedicate this work to you for your support and love over these many years. While death may have separated us prematurely, never could it dissolve the bonds of love that bind us together as a family.

*Thomas P. Gullotta*

To my mother and father, Florence and Arthur Adams, for showing me the meaning of commitment in marriage. And to my four daughters, Elizabeth, Shawnelle, Shelli, and Sheryl, who have suffered through my learning how to parent, for having helped me grow as a father, and for having given me such love and attention.

*Gerald R. Adams*

To my husband, Bob, for all his encouragement, support, and love; to my mother, Evelyn Jaramillo, who did a splendid job of socializing me; to my siblings, Richard, Pixie, Rita, and Roger, from whom I learned so much about family living; and to Derek, who is adding daily to my understanding.

*Sharon J. Alexander*

# PREFACE

*This is a textbook* about marriage and family life. Having made that statement we suspect some of you are already grumbling, "Oh no, not another one." And in some ways you are correct. This book, like other marriage and family textbooks, is written from a functional perspective; but in other ways it is different. It is those differences that we feel make this work not only distinct, but unique.

This book is different in that Gerald, Sharon, and I, coming from our own respective disciplines of psychology, family studies, and social work, have strived to integrate our individual understandings of marital and family life into a comprehensive, interdisciplinary, applied overview. The two thousand sources that were used to write this volume are drawn not only from our own fields, but also from history, sociology, psychiatry, education, law, child development, and medicine, in an effort to provide the reader with as thorough an overview of this subject area as possible.

A second difference is that this book combines a functional perspective with an issues approach. Reviewing the table of contents, the reader will notice that the book is divided into five parts. The first consists of three chapters that deal with a historical introduction to the family, major theories of family behavior, and, briefly, how to understand research on marriage and the family.

Part Two, "In the Beginning," reviews the precursors to marital and family life. Part Three traces family life across the life span and explores the plasticity that has always characterized family life. Notice that we have chosen to include the topics of divorce and remarriage in this section in order to examine them as a part of "normal" family life.

Part Four, "Family Matters of Concern," is unique in family textbooks. From our own experiences in teaching this subject, from our conversations with other family life experts, and from our conversations with students over the years, we have chosen five family matters of concern. We explore each of these in depth, providing flexibility for instructors in tailoring a course to meet the needs of their students. For example, Chapter 14 examines family economics not only in good times of employment but in bad times of unemployment. Chapter 15 explores the insidious nature of discrimination on minority families and how those families have survived. Chapter 16 analyzes the effect alcohol, marijuana, and cocaine have on family life. Chapter 17 investigates the factors that contribute to child, spousal, and elder abuse in the family. Chapter 18 examines a subject that, surprisingly, has been ignored in most other family textbooks: death and grief, and how they affect the family. We explore the feelings and emotions of individuals as they struggle to make sense of the loss of a child, spouse, or parent. Finally, the book concludes with a historical reevaluation of the "good old days" and a projection of what family life at the turn of the next century might be like.

To assist students in understanding the material in this book, we have provided several helpful study aids. These include study questions at the beginning of each chapter, discussion questions throughout the chapter, and a comprehensive list of major points to remember at the end of each chapter.

Another unique aspect of this work is the inclusion in most chapters of a section called "Promoting Family Wellness." This book is designed to encourage students to take active roles in promoting their own emotional health, and that of their families and the wider society. As one astute reviewer observed in an early draft of this work, wellness (or primary prevention) is not value free. And on more than one occasion students and instructors may disagree with us. We encourage that behavior and urge you to take us to task when you feel we are incorrect. Learning, we feel, occurs during such discus-

sions and we have tried throughout the book to include discussion questions that will inspire a critical examination of the subject material.

Also, there is nothing sacred about the order in which the chapters in this book appear. While more than half of our reviewers follow the format of this book in teaching their own courses, others do not. We recognize that there are probably as many ways of ordering the material in this text as there are family variations. And as we are firm believers in the strength of a pluralistic society, we encourage instructors to pick and choose and to design a course that meets the needs of their students.

We have tried in this work to reflect the many contributions and viewpoints of scholars from different disciplines to the study of marriage and the family. We have tried to blend theory, research, and practice in a way that students and teachers will find enjoyable and stimulating to read. We have tried to encourage the student to use the principle of wellness (primary prevention) to promote health and prevent illness. We have been assisted in these efforts on several levels and would like to acknowledge the valuable contribution of the following individuals to the creation of this manuscript.

First, we would like to thank the typists who struggled to decipher the crude hieroglyphics we call writing: Ann Hurley, Vicki Luther, and April Boyer. We would also like to acknowledge the important role the reviewers of this manuscript and other professional colleagues played in developing this work: Elaine Anderson, University of Maryland; Paul Aschenbrenner, Hartnell Community College; Clifton Barber, Colorado State University; John Bellfleur, Oakland Community College; Betsy Bergen, Kansas State University; Gregory Brock, University of Wisconsin, Stout; Kathleen Campbell, Bowling Green State University; Rodney Cate, Oregon State University; Ken Davidson, University of Wisconsin, Eau Claire; Roberta Felker, Marymount College; Harold Grotevant, University of

Texas, Austin; Marilyn Ihinger-Tallman, Washington State University; Justin Joffe, University of Vermont; Sally Lloyd, University of Utah; Ann Marie Orza, Eastern Connecticut State University; Arnold Orza, University of Connecticut; Judy Rosenbaum, Director of National Board of Certified Counselors; Rita Phylliss Sakitt, Suffolk County Community College; Eugene Thomas, University of Connecticut; and Jerry Shepperd, Austin Community College. Finally, we would like to express our appreciation to the staff at Brooks/Cole, particularly C. Deborah Laughton, Mary Tudor, Phyllis Larimore, Judy Blamer, Jamie Sue Brooks, Mary Kay Hancharick, and the editor, Rephah Berg, for their good humor, patience, and support in seeing this manuscript grow from a simple little book of 14 chapters to an encyclopedia . . . which is missing, much to our chagrin, a brilliant description of the medical practice known as a craniotomy.

*Thomas P. Gullotta*
*Gerald R. Adams*
*Sharon J. Alexander*

# BRIEF CONTENTS

# CONTENTS

## Chapter 5
# Human Sexuality    88

## Chapter 6
# Communication: The Essence of Relationships    125

## *Part Three*
# FAMILY LIFE ACROSS THE LIFE SPAN    150

## *Chapter 7*
# Intimacy, Love, and Maybe Marriage    152

## *Chapter 8*
# The Developing Marital Relationship    177

# TODAY'S MARRIAGES AND FAMILIES

*A Wellness Approach*

## Part One

# SETTING
# THE STAGE

*1*

# MARRIAGE AND FAMILY LIFE: A HISTORICAL OVERVIEW

1. Has society's understanding of the terms *marriage* and *the family* changed?

2. What is a monogamous marital relationship? Is it the only marital form?

3. What do the terms *binuclear family* and *single-parent family* mean? When do these two terms mean the same thing? When do they mean different things?

4. What is swaddling?

5. In premodern family times, if a horse and a wife fell sick at the same time, which one was left to the healing powers of nature?

6. How did semen loss contribute to men's resentment of women?

7. What factors moved the family from its premodern to its modern form?

8. Was family life in colonial America premodern or modern?

9. Why were women "junior partners" in the age of "the family in harmony"?

10. How did industrialization contribute to the "cult of domesticity"?

11. How did the "move toward equity" diminish the contribution of children to the family but at the same time increase their value?

12. How did the Moynihan Report stimulate a reassessment of the effects of slavery on Black families?

13. Were slave families routinely ripped apart to be sold to other slaveowners?

*To hear that* the American family is changing should surprise no one. What may surprise some is that its changes date back hundreds of years and across oceans to our ancestral homelands. In this chapter we shall examine those changes and, in so doing, paint an impressionistic picture of the family. We shall discern several general trends that moved it from its premodern to its modern form. We will make generalizations and identify trends, but the reader is cautioned to remember that there are exceptions to each generalization. The changes that we identify cannot be tied to absolute historical dates, nor did they occur everywhere at the same time. Change tended to occur first among the upper classes and in urban areas and then slowly spread, at times taking centuries, to the general populace and into less urban areas. These changes were not fully accepted by everyone at the time (or now, for that matter). However, our purpose in this chapter is to show how the family evolved from medieval times to the present, and such exceptions do not alter the direction that family life has taken.

## DEFINING MARRIAGE AND THE FAMILY

Defining the words *marriage* and *family* used to be straightforward. A marriage was a union, institutionalized and publicly recognized, between a man and a woman. Accompanying this union was a set of traditional societal assumptions that the couple would share economic resources, produce offspring, and stay married. A family provided the structural setting in which these assumptions were carried out. It offered a framework by which married individuals shared a residence and economic resources and reproduced. Further, it was in the family that children were raised, socialized, instilled with values, and protected.

Times have changed, however, and many of the traditional assumptions about marriage and family life no longer seem to apply in every instance. For example, suppose a man and woman go through a marriage ceremony but decide to remain childless or are unable to reproduce. Should this couple consider themselves a family? Or what about a couple who marry, have children, but live apart because of job demands? Are they and their children a family? Finally, if a homosexual couple exchange marital vows in a church ceremony, are they married even though civil authorities have not issued them a license?

As you can see, the issues are complicated. In this text we define a **marriage** as an institutionalized and publicly recognized union between individuals who intend to stay married. We consider a **family** to be a group of at least two persons who live together (at least some of the time) and are related by blood, marriage, or adoption.

## Marital Forms

Monogamy, polygyny, polyandry, and group marriage are four ways in which women and men can live together. **Monogamy** is the most common form of marriage in Western society today. It is the joining of one woman and one man to form a family unit. **Polygyny** is the uniting of two or more women to one man to form a family. Though rare in Western society today, polygyny was not uncommon in the past. It was most often found in agricultural societies (Murstein, 1974). In the United States, the only widespread form of polygyny occurred among the Mormons, who briefly permitted this marriage form in the mid-19th century.

**Polyandry** is the marriage of one woman to more than one man. Murstein (1974) describes societies practicing this marriage form as economically struggling communities seeking to keep agricultural lands intact by tracing land ownership through the wife (matrilineal inheritance). Although it may seem as though polyandry is equivalent to polygyny, in practice it was not. While it is true that in both polygynous and polyandrous marriages a male or female could have several marital partners, it was only in polyandrous societies that women were routinely put to death to reduce the number of marriageable women.

The fourth marriage form, **group marriage,** is the union of several men to several women. This marriage form was even rarer than polyandry. The one example most closely approximating group marriage in the United States was the Oneida community of New York (1848–1900).

## Family Forms

Families can take several forms. The most familiar form is the **nuclear family,** which consists of two parents and biological or adopted offspring and in its most idealized state is exemplified by such old time television shows as "Father Knows Best" and "Leave It To Beaver." The rise in divorce rates has contributed to the growth of a second family form that is properly called **binuclear** (meaning two living, divorced, single parents) but is more commonly called the **single-parent family.** A single-parent family may consist of a never-married, widowed, or divorced parent and biological or adopted children. The marriage of a widowed or divorced person to another is called a **remarriage.** Should either remarried spouse bring children from a prior relationship to the new one, the resulting family structure is called a **blended, reconstituted, merged,** or **stepfamily.**

An **extended family** consists of three or more familial generations all living and working together in one household. Although such households are rare today, many families do remain in contact, exchanging information by mail or phone, visiting when possible, and extending

*While we doubt the nuclear family ever existed as depicted in such television shows as* Leave it to Beaver, *a generation of Americans (1950–1965) grew up expecting their families to mirror the images portrayed on the screen.*

help when needed. A family maintaining this continued contact between generations is called a **modified nuclear** or **modified extended** family.

If on marriage the wife (or wives) takes up residence at her husband's home, the family structure is called **patrilocal.** The term **patrilineal** applies when family descent is traced through the father. If on marriage the wife, with or without her husband(s), returns to her own home to live, the family structure is considered **matrilocal.** When family descent is traced through the mother, the term **matrilineal** is used.

Now, armed with some of the words of the trade, let's return to a time in history that has

been termed the "bad old days" of premodern family life (Shorter, 1977).

*Do you agree with our "liberal" interpretation of the terms* marriage *and* family*? How would you define these terms? Does today's "modern" family still meet the needs of all family members?*

## PREMODERN FAMILY LIFE

Studying family history involves trying to understand the relationship of children, women, and men to one another and to the greater society surrounding them. By understanding the position of each in premodern medieval society, we will be able to identify the changes that moved the family into modern times.

### Children in Past Times

We all remember the story of the infant Christ, wrapped in swaddling clothes and laid in a manger. What images does that story suggest to you? An image of a newborn infant wrapped in a clean linen cloth for warmth and yet able to move his arms freely inside that cloth? And your image of the stable—is it clean, with barn animals pressed tightly together, providing warmth for the infant? If those are your impressions, few infants in Europe before the 18th century enjoyed such luxury. For most, being swaddled meant that a strip of cloth some two inches across was passed around the infant's legs, arms, torso, and head until only a small part of the face remained exposed. Encased in its cocoon, the infant mummy was then hung from a peg, laid on a table, or left on the floor near the hearth while mother worked. Left in its excrement for hours, an infant was lucky if the peg did not break, the wrappings were not ignited by a stray spark, or a barnyard

## BOX 1-1
*A Swaddling Update*

Karen Schaper (1982) reintroduces the subject of swaddling in a more positive light than the description provided in our text. She notes that the practice was widespread in early times, extending far beyond the boundaries of Western Europe to include the Indians of North and South America and nations such as Japan and Iran. The popularity of swaddling declined, she believes, with the rise of individual freedom around the time of the French Revolution.

Dick (1847), a 19th-century version of Dr. Benjamin Spock, Mr. Wizard, and Joyce Brothers combined, represented this position of individual freedom when he advised American parents not to wrap their infants tightly in clothing:

A child [should] have no more clothes than are necessary to keep it warm, and that they be quite easy for its body. In conformity to this rule, the dress of children should be simple, clean, light, and cheap—free, wide and open, so as neither to impede the vital functions, nor the free and easy motions of the body, nor prevent the access of fresh air, and be easily put on or taken off. . . . During the first months [of an infant's life], the head and breast may be slightly covered; but as soon as the hair is sufficiently long to afford protection, there appears little necessity for either hats or caps, unless in seasons of rain or cold. By keeping the breast and neck uncovered, they acquire more firmness, are rendered hardier, and less susceptible of being affected with cold. Besides, a child has really a more interesting aspect, when arrayed in the beautiful simplicity of nature, than when adorned with all trappings which art can devise [Dick, 1847, p. 43].

Today, Dick's advice is less heeded, and there appears to be a return to wrapping infants snugly in their clothing. Even so, current swaddling practices are a far cry from those of the past. The encouragement to stroke an infant, "patting his back, gently massaging his arms and legs" (Schaper, 1982, p. 412), signifies a bond between parent and child that was almost totally absent in the past.

hog did not supplement its diet with an infant morsel (Shorter, 1977; see Box 1-1).

Until recent times children have existed at the bottom of the family hierarchy. Not coming into existence, figuratively speaking, until sometime between their fourth and seventh birthdays, many were treated no better than, and most worse than, barnyard animals (Ariès, 1962; Shorter, 1977). Two explanations for the nonexistent position of the child in the family have been put forth.

The first is that high child mortality discouraged parents from attaching much importance to children until they were old enough to have a reasonable chance of survival. Until the mid-19th century, with unspeakable sanitation conditions and with medical care that more often hastened death than prolonged life, many young individuals fought a losing battle to such illnesses as diphtheria, typhoid, measles, and mumps (McLaughlin, 1971; Shorter, 1977). Even as late as the 1700s, 33% of French children died before reaching their first birthday, and only half of those remaining lived to reach 21 (Shorter, 1977).

The second argument is that parental indifference, more than natural conditions, explains the lack of value attached to children in premodern times. This view proposes that parents regarded their offspring as greedy, gluttonous creatures sucking mother's substance from her breast. Hunt (1970, p. 120) suggests that parents saw an infant "prosper at the expense of his mother, from whose body he sucked the precious substance he needed for his own survival." In a society that held the similar view that a woman's intake of a man's vital fluids (semen) into her body weakened him, resentment rather than love may have been nurtured.

In support of this second position, consider the life situation of women during those times. Pregnancy was a near-universal constant, with the possibility of death for mother, as well as infant, ever present. Poverty and famine were constant companions except for the wealthy, and a woman's work responsibilities did not vanish with the birth of a child. She was expected to return to work as quickly as possible.

Evidence of gross indifference abounds. For instance, rocking an infant to sleep in days past more resembled a televised wrestling match than a soothing lullaby. Before the 18th century, *rocking*, it is reported, meant knocking a child unconscious (Shorter, 1977).

Two additional examples suggest not mere indifference but real resentment toward children. The first was the common practice of sending away infants to be wet-nursed (breast-fed) by strangers. As late as 1777, evidence shows that one sixth of the infants residing in or around Paris were nursed this way (Shorter, 1977). Wet nursing sealed for many infants a premature death warrant. Many wet nurses were "desperately poor, harried creatures who generally lived in rural hovels," with milk too scarce to nurse one child, let alone two or three (Shorter, 1977, p. 179):

"Several [wet nurses] have only a single room, in which are crowded together a number of beds and chests. Some have but a single bed, and three nurslings. . . ." [Wet nurses] most often just dumped their water on the dirt floor [of their cottage], "unable to take the trouble to throw it outside." The domestic livestock of pigs, goats, sheep, and poultry lived right with the family. . . . Right at the door was the fertilizer pile, and rotting straw was stuffed around the place in nooks and crannies [as insulation from the cold]. Underfoot there squished, "a sort of black water, greenish, and fetid." Just the place for a baby, in other words [Shorter, 1977, p. 179].

For a period lasting up to two years the infant would be left with a wet nurse out of the sight and care of its parents. The mortality rate, as one might suspect, was high. Wet-nursed infants were at least twice as likely to die as infants who remained home. In some parts of France, mortality rates of wet-nursed infants approached 90% (Shorter, 1977).

And yet, the wet-nursed infant might be considered better off than the infant abandoned to a garbage heap or street gutter to perish. This last example of gross indifference can again be explained by the poverty and famine that periodically swept across Europe. It can also be seen, as in Jean Jacques Rousseau's abandonment of his five children to a foundling home, as an indication of gross indifference that suggests to us a resentment of children (Murstein, 1974).

How many of the approximately 33,000 children abandoned in France each year as late as the mid-19th century were abandoned for reasons of love, indifference, or resentment cannot be determined. Poverty, famine, and war certainly separated parents from children who, if times and conditions had been different, would have remained with them. Still, these conditions alone do not adequately account for the treatment many young children received at the hands of their parents. Did this uncaring attitude result from high infant mortality? From gross indifference, even resentment? Examples supporting each explanation can be found in history, but certainly one generalization can be made—that young children held little value in premodern times.

**?** *In your opinion, was it indifference, resentment, or high child mortality that most strongly influenced premodern parental attitudes toward children?*

## Women in Past Times

In the hierarchy of the premodern family, a woman occupied a position slightly above that of a child but far beneath that of a man. A woman was prized but, more often than not, prized less than a cow. She had no formal recognition by society. She could not hold property, bring matters to court for settlement, or decide whom to marry. A woman's position in the family is well summed up by the following observation:

> The wives are the first servants in the household: they plow the soil, care for the house, and eat after their husbands, who address them only in harsh, curt tones, even with a sort of contempt. If the horse and the wife fall sick at the same time, the . . . [husband] rushes to the blacksmith to care for the animal and leaves the task of healing his wife to nature [Hugo, 1835, cited in Shorter, 1977, p. 56].

We believe there were four factors that created this intolerable set of circumstances. The first is the nature of the marriage contract. In premodern times men and women had little to do with the establishment of their own marriages. The decision was made by the couple's fathers and was based on property and class. The notion that affection might enter into the arrangement was never considered. Love was an unaffordable luxury for individuals engaged in a struggle for survival (Murstein, 1974; Shorter, 1977; Stone, 1977).

Second, religion subjected women to a far inferior position to men. While man was made in the image of God, women were constructed from a few leftover parts. It was Eve who tempted Adam with the fruits of sexual knowledge, leading to their banishment from Eden. Church teachings by scholars like Augustine created an image of women as "lecherous temptresses" possessing "feeble intellects" who could be inhabited by spirits and demons[1] (Murstein, 1974). From that point of view, these contemptible individuals deserved treatment inferior to that given a barn animal, and they needed to be broken, as Katherina was in *The Taming of the Shrew,* of any idea of equality. A woman's role was to bow to her husband as "thy lord, thy life, thy keeper, thy head, thy sovereign" (Shakespeare, 1969, p. 113).

Next, women, until recent times, have been the victims of their own bodies. Physical sex differences exposed women to a host of diseases, injuries, and other dangers that males could escape. For example, men could escape the responsibility of a sexual liaison that produced a child. Women suffered the pains, hazards, and effects of childbirth and suffered through the medical treatments afforded them at that time. And women suffered from a host of organisms, such as vaginal parasites, that did not plague men (Shorter, 1982, p. 263).

A final factor, mentioned earlier, concerns ancient beliefs about vital bodily fluids. Man's vital fluids were contained, in part, in his semen. And until the 20th century he was warned to conserve those precious fluids lest he experience a plague of misfortune. Tempting him to spill his seed and waste his health was the lecherous

---

[1] Those spirits and demons could enter and exit through a woman's hair. Hence, the explanation for why women, until recently in Christian churches, were expected to keep their heads covered while in church.

creature, woman—another reason for him to resent her.

Is this to say that all marriages were forged in a sort of hell? No; many examples of caring relationships in premodern times can be observed. However, even these relationships lived within the context of a time that placed very little value on the female.

*Do you agree that women were seen as inferior in premodern times? Can you think of other reasons than the ones given here to explain a woman's position in premodern society? Which of the reasons given here make the most sense to you? Which make the least?*

## Men in Past Times

"Thy husband is thy lord, thy life, thy keeper, thy head, thy sovereign" (Shakespeare, 1969, p. 113). Assuming that a male survived childhood, he was assured of sitting atop the hierarchy of his family. Though not able to arrange his own marriage (this was his father's task), he was assured of the dowry that his wife would bring to their marriage. Should she be unpleasing to the eye, he could seek outside female companionship. She had no recourse to such behavior. Rather, he viewed her as a baby machine with little other value (Murstein, 1974; Shorter, 1977, 1982; Stone, 1977).

Of course, exceptions existed in which the ruler of the household did show appreciation, concern, and care for other family members. Nevertheless, he did so always within the context of his recognized position as family leader.

*Why do you think men have been able to sit on top of the family hierarchy? Do they still maintain that position?*

## Families in Past Times

Given the roles that children, women, and men fulfilled in premodern families, it is not surprising that, by modern standards, family life left much to be desired. Children were treated with, at best, indifference. Women held a position nearly equivalent to a slave's, and men ruled the roost. Intimacy and romanticism were given short shrift.

Additionally, the premodern family is described by family historians as more community-centered than family-centered. Shorter (1977) provides several examples of community control over behavior. For example, townsfolk might hold demonstrations around a family's cottage to bring public attention to the man's failure to control his wife. The hooting and hollering and burning of straw figures in effigy were attempts to maintain community standards of approved behavior (norms). In parts of Bavaria, marriages arranged by families could be halted by the community. In parts of Scandinavia, community control of courting was powerful enough to permit maidens (who traditionally slept in barns with the domestic animals) to receive suitors in their beds with little fear that coitus would ensue.

Community power over family life might be understood to derive from the isolation of communities from one another. With poor transportation, virtually no communication network, and a protective guild system that prevented craftsmen from easily relocating to different communities, the premodern family was insulated from the outside world. Villagers, tenant farmers, and landholders came to create their own small societies. Because these societies feasted or starved, failed or succeeded together, community agreement on sanctioned and unsanctioned behavior was high. Yet, by the 15th century, beginning with the wealthy and gradually trickling down to the poorer classes, fundamental changes in this family structure began to occur.

## The Transition from Premodern to Modern Family Practices

As trade, communication, and travel between communities increased in the 15th century, three gradual changes altered the behavior of the family. The first was a movement away from family-arranged to individually arranged marriages. As couples acquired more decision-making power, the influence of property and lineage declined and that of intimacy, romance, and love rose. In this new marital arrangement, the value of a wife increased beyond that of a servant or a slave.

The next change involved the value attached to children. Maternal indifference to (perhaps resentment of) the infant was replaced by recognition. Do not confuse this recognition, however, with the acquisition of full human status. The child was still the property of its parents and still at tremendous risk of cruelty. Nevertheless, the common ill treatment of infants gradually gave way to feelings akin to motherly love.

The final change was a movement away from an identification with the community to a closer, more intimate bonding with other family members. Community involvement and control over family life weakened, to be replaced with an image of the family as a "haven in a heartless world" (Lasch, 1977).

From indifference between spouses to mutual affection, from nonattachment to infant bonding, and from community life to a private world—these are the changes that altered family life. Why did these changes occur? Because of changing economic conditions that increased trade and communication between communities? Because of improved public health practices, such as sewers and clean drinking water, that reduced an individual's risk of life-threatening illness? Or because of a growing public recognition and acknowledgment of a feeling called love? Historians argue about which of these forces moved the premodern family to its modern form. We suspect that all of them contributed.

In the next section we shall examine the modern family in America. The American family, Shorter (1977) believes, arrived "modern" and wanting to sever its ties to the Old World, desirous of privacy and intimacy. But again a word of caution is in order, because the movement of families to modern standards of behavior took place gradually and indiscernibly. Thus, we shall see examples of both premodern and modern family behavior in the New World.

 *Why do you think changes in the value attached to children and women were so long in coming?*

# FAMILY LIFE IN AMERICA

The families that disembarked from the *Mayflower* were very different from a typical family gathered around its table today. Three crude time frames can be constructed to demonstrate the changes that happened to children, women, and men to alter family life.

## The Family in Harmony: 1620 to 1820

A clear sign that the colonists who settled in America had reached modern status was the value they attached to children. As early as 1642 the Massachusetts Bay Colony passed legislation requiring that children be instructed. Discipline, nonetheless, could be harsh. In fact, one Puritan law stated that a habitually disobedient youngster could be put to death. However, it was never enforced (Adams & Gullotta, 1983). Rather, children in Plymouth colony were described by visitors as "precocious" and very "frank" (Demos, 1973). Indeed, settlers in America were often accused of overindulging their children, as this conversation suggests:

> "Johnny, my dear, come here," says his mamma.
>
> "I won't," cries Johnny.
>
> "You must, my love, you are all wet, and you'll catch cold."
>
> "Come, my sweet, and I've something for you."
>
> "I won't."
>
> "Oh! Mr. _____, do, pray, make Johnny come in."
>
> "Come in, Johnny," says the father.
>
> "I won't."
>
> "I tell you, come in directly, sir—do you hear?"
>
> "A sturdy republican, sir," says his father to me, smiling at the boy's resolute disobedience. [Marryat, 1839, cited in Bremner, 1970, p. 344].

And yet, for all this indulgence, the chances that a child would survive to adulthood remained slim. Nearly half of those born before 1800 never reached 20 (Grabill, Kiser, & Whelpton, 1973; Scott & Wishy, 1982). In contrast to the indifference in premodern families to the deaths of children, parents mourned the loss of their offspring to the illnesses that periodically swept the household, striking down those not immune:

> October 18, 1713. The Measles coming into the Town, it is likely to be a Time of Sickness. . . .
>
> November 4, 1713. In my poor family, now, first my wife has the Measles appearing on her; we know not yet how she will be handled. My daughter Nancy is also full of them. . . . [as is] Lissy . . . Jerusha, [and my servant maid]. Help Lord; and look mercifully on my poor, sad, sinful family. . . .
>
> [November 9, 1713] On Monday . . . my dear, dear, dear [wife] expired.
>
> November 14, 1713 [my maid servant has died]. The two newborns are languishing in the Arms of Death.

> November 17–18, 1713. About midnight, little Eleazar died.
>
> November 20, 1713. Little Martha dies, about ten o'clock a.m.
>
> November 21, 1713. This Day, I attended the Funeral of my two: Eleazar and Martha. Betwixt 9h. and 10h. at night, my lovely Jerusha expired. She was two years, and about seven months, old . . . Lord, I am oppressed; undertake for me! [Cotton Mather, 1713, cited in Bremner, 1970, pp. 46–48]

As these diary entries suggest, children were clearly acquiring more importance in the family. But their value did not yet entitle them to legal standing in the community. Children remained, as before, the property of their parents, and they could be cared for or mistreated as their parents saw fit.

The status of women in the New World (as well as in Europe) continued to improve slowly. In the colonies this increased appreciation can be attributed partly to their scarcity. Not only did fewer women than men settle in the New World, but those who did faced sizable hardships. A woman's life expectancy in 1789 was about 36 years (Grabill et al., 1973). Before her death she would have conceived an average of eight children. This is a remarkable number when one considers that menarche did not occur until age 17 or thereabouts and that marriage for most women occurred at about age 20 (Bane, 1976; Grabill et al., 1973; Marcy, 1981).

While women and children saw their lot improving slowly, the evidence is clear that authority continued to reside with the man. It was expected that the family would defer to his judgment, would obey his commands, and would cooperate to establish a harmonious family (Scott & Wishy, 1982). Punishment for violating this code of conduct frequently involved community censure of not only the wife but also her husband:

*Surprising as it may seem, women were so scarce in the "new world" that advertisements routinely appeared in English newspapers offering money and property to women willing to travel there to be married.*

> January 1678. Bridget, wife of Thomas Oliver, presented for calling her husband many opprobrious names; as old rogue and old devil, on Lord's days was ordered to stand with her husband, back to back, on a lecture day in the public market place, both gagged for about an hour with a paper fastened to each of their foreheads, upon which their offence should be fairly written [Scott & Wishy, 1982, p. 94].

Evidently Thomas Oliver was to be punished for his failure to preserve harmony and maintain control as head of the family. For our early forefathers, the family was not only the "guardian of public and private good" (Laslett, 1979, p. 246) but also the foundation of church and government (Demos, 1979). Thus, Oliver was to be punished for his failure to protect these virtues. He was, however, in this still decidedly male-ruled world, not punished. His daughter, Mary West, paid for *his* release (Scott & Wishy, 1982).

This is not the only example of the failure to apply justice in an evenhanded manner. Morgan (1973) notes that because eligible women were scarce, rape and adultery were not uncommon in the bay colony. The strict standards that we have come to attribute to the Puritans (see Box 1-2) again proved to be flexible enough to modify the penalties that the laws ordered. Morgan (1973) finds evidence that the death penalty was exercised only three times for adulterous behavior. Except in the instance of sodomy, crimes such as adultery and rape were handled by a whipping or a fine, occasionally by branding, or by being placed on public display and there humiliated.

We observe in this time period both a continued attachment to certain premodern family practices and the rise of new behaviors. Until the early 1700s and diminishing thereafter, the community maintained a fair degree of control over the behavior of individuals. Children continued to gain in importance as a valued resource that, if cared for, could assist in cultivating land, tending farm animals, and caring for their elderly parents. Greven (1973), for instance, notes that parents in the 1600s in Andover, Massachusetts, delayed transferring farmland to their heirs until they were assured of adequate care in their semiretirement. Women, too, saw their lot improving during this period. The task of conquering a large, expansive new land filled with challenges contributed to a need for unity. To achieve the cooperative relationship necessary to succeed in the New World, men increasingly saw their wives as *junior* partners in conquest. Responsibility for the home front in this predominantly agricultural society continued to rest with the male. His responsibility was to bring order not only to the frontier but to the domestic scene as well.

 *What effect do you think the scarcity of women had on advancing women's rights in colonial times?*

## BOX 1-2
### *The Swinging Puritans*

Despite the Puritans' bad press, their attitudes toward sex were far more open than the Victorians'. In the following selection Increase Mather writes to a fellow minister, Michael Wigglesworth, expressing his concern over rumors that the "pious" Wigglesworth (nearing the then ripe old age of 50) is ready to leap into marriage with his teenaged housekeeper. This letter is particularly interesting for several reasons. It not only reflects a healthy interest in women by the elite of the church, a fear of embarrassment, and the position of women in society but also refers to the issue of vital fluids and whether old Wigglesworth's days on earth will be shortened:

Reverend Sir,—Since I saw you last in B. one that doth unfeignedly desire your welfare hath bin with mee, expressing grief of heart with reference unto a matter wherein yourselfe is concerned. I owe you that respect as to informe you what I have bin told. The report is, that you are designing to marry with your servant mayd, [and] that she is one of obscure parentage, not 20 years old, [and] of no

Church, nor so much as Baptised. If it be as is related, I would humbly entreat you to consider these arguments in opposition: 1. For you to doe this, which will be a grief of heart to your dear Relations, if it be not a matter which God doth command to be done is not advisable . . . considering her youth, [and] your age, [and] great bodily infirmities, such a change of your condition, if that which is intimated by the Holy Apostle, 1 Cor. 7, 3, should be attended, your days will be shortened, [and] consequently the 5th Commandment broken. 3. Such general Rules as those, Phil. 4, 8, doe concern as all christians, so eminently Ministers of Christ. And doubtless it will *male audire* for you to do this thing, yea, I fear it will leave a blott upon your Name after you shall cease to be in this world. 4. The ministry will be blamed, which wee should be very careful to prevent. 2 Cor. 6, 3. The mouths of carnal ones will be opened, not only to censure you but your brethren in the ministry will be condemned also. The world will say, theres such an one Hee was as justified a

man as any of them, [and] yet wee see unto what affections have carried him. 5. I am afraid that if you should proceed, that Rule, 2 Cor. 6, 14, will be transgressed. It useth to be said *nube pari,* but to marry with one so much your Inferior on all accounts, is not *nubere pari.* And to take one that was never baptised into such neerness of Relation, seemeth contrary to Gospell; especially for a Minister of Christ to doe it. The like never was in [New England]. Nay, I question whether the like hath bin known in the Christian world. 6. Doth not that Script. 1 Tim. 3, 11, with others of the like importance, prohibit such proceedings. . . . Though your affections should be too far gone in this matter, I doubt not but if you put the object out of sight, [and] looke up to the Lord Jesus for supplies of grace, you will be enabled to overcome these Temptations. The Lord be with you, I am.

March 8, 1679
Yours unfeignedly,
Increase Mather

(Scott & Wishy, 1982, pp. 40-41)

## *The Cult of Domesticity: 1820 to 1920*

The preindustrial American family sought to first tame and then cultivate a new world. The family and the church were believed to be the roots holding all other branch institutions together. The importance of cooperation for a single directed effort cannot be underestimated. Beginning with the growth of urban areas, industrialization, and the influx of immigrants, the role of the family shifted to emphasize security from the outside. Looking at each of these factors, we see that in 1790 only 24 colonial communities had populations exceeding 2500. Sixty years later, in 1850, the urban population had mushroomed so that it nearly exceeded the entire population of the country in 1790 (Bushman, 1981). This growth in the urban-dwelling population was accompanied by the rapid industrialization of the Northeast.

Many authors have written of the effects industrialization had on society. There is general agreement that as industrialization grew the independence of the family unit weakened. No longer was the family a self-sufficient unit, determining its own work hours or schedule. No longer was the male head of the household its sole ruler. The tamer who had shaped the frontier became, in turn, shaped by and tamed to the needs of a new society. The division of labor accompanying industrialization signaled a redistribution of power, with a family's future prosperity dictated by external rather than internal factors (Ariès, 1979; Bremner, 1970; Gordon, 1973).

Associated with the rise of the urban center and the movement of individuals into nonfarming occupations was the influx of new immigrants. The almost 5 million settlers, mostly Protestant and of British descent, who lived in the United States in 1800 watched in fear as "hordes" of "heathen" Irish Roman Catholics moved into the new urban centers to meet the demand for labor (Mennel, 1973; Scott & Wishy, 1982). It seems only appropriate that, in an era of institutional responses to situations (the growth of schools, the textile industry, and reformatories), the family would become an institution. The loosely connected, poorly defined unit of man, woman, and child(ren) called a premodern family no longer existed by 1820. In response to a rapidly changing order, families began to be

seen as a stable element of society, one that was capable of exerting a positive influence on other parts of society. In response to a loss of decision-making power in the labor force, men began to define the home as their castle. At that point each family member came to have a well-defined, institutionalized role as either provider (father), obedient caretaker (mother), or obedient offspring (child).

Through the institutionalization of the family, children and particularly women improved their places in society and became recognized as individuals (Stannard, 1979). Women shedded their tainted image and acquired such virtues as "piety, purity, submissiveness, and domesticity" (Welter, 1973, p. 225). From their prior status as sources of temptation and evil, women came to be seen as naturally pious. Their behavior in the literature of the day came to resemble less that of Eve and more that of some saintly creature as pictured in a Currier and Ives print. This piety, whether real or imagined, "was the core of woman's virtue, the source of her strength" (Welter, 1973, p. 225). Unlike a soiled Eve, a woman in the cult of domesticity exuded purity. In the cult of domesticity, this new Eve, rather than tempting Adam, resisted his lechery. Welter (1973) goes on to point out that women sought not the active life but one of obedience and submission. From 1820 to 1900 or so, woman's idealized role was that of fire tender, religious guide, comforter, nurse, and mother. In short, she was the perfect golden retriever of her day, willing to respond affectionately and submissively to a pat from her benevolent master's hand.

Whether this submissive position was desired or imposed is uncertain. We suspect most women were willing to accept any position to escape the hell of prior times. But why were women, and indirectly their homes, endowed with these particular characteristics? Demos (1979) and Laslett (1979) have both pointed out that the family pulled out of the community and retreated into itself during the early 1800s. Why did the home become "highly sentimentalized . . . pictured as a bastion of peace, of repose, of orderliness, of unwavering devotion to people and principles beyond the self" (Demos, 1979, p. 51)?

The answer can be found in the changes reshaping the male's role in society. As men surrendered their position of independence for a position of dependence, they attempted to create a refuge safe from outside intruders. In his imaginary castle, the male sought sanctuary from a world that no longer treasured young Johnny's republican defiance but his passive submission instead:

> From the age of ten or twelve months . . . every parent ought to commence the establishment of authority over his children. . . . This authority is to be acquired—not by passionately chiding and beating children at an early age—but by accustoming them to perceive that our will must always prevail over theirs. . . . The Rev. Mr. Cecil . . . related an experiment of this kind which he tried on his own daughter, a little girl of about three or four years old. She was standing one day before the fire, amusing herself with a string of beads, [with] which she appeared to be highly delighted. Her father approached her, and said, "What is this you are playing with, my little dear?" "My beads, papa." "Show me these beads, my dear." She at once handed them to her father, who immediately threw them into the fire. "Now," said he, "let them remain there." She immediately began to cry. "You must not cry, my dear, but be quite contented." She then sat down on the floor, and amused herself with some other toys. About two or three days after this, he purchased another string of beads much more valuable and brilliant, which he immediately presented to her. She was much delighted with the appearance of the new set of beads. "Now," said her father, "I make a present of these to you, because you were a good girl, and gave me your beads when I asked for them." . . . Children trained in this way, with firmness and affection, soon become happy in themselves, and a comfort to their parents [Dick, 1847, p. 46].

The cult of domesticity represented a search for order in a time seemingly without order. The retreat toward privacy and domestic bliss was a way of adapting to the change brought on by the industrial age.

 *Do you agree with our assessment of the factors that contributed to the rise of the "cult of domesticity"? What other factors may have been at work?*

## The Move toward Equity: 1920 to the Present

By the time the Roaring Twenties began, the American family was a far different entity from its colonial ancestor. The average number of persons per household had declined from 5.79 in 1790 to 4.34 in 1920 (see Table 1-1), the percentage of large families (six or more members) declining sharply while smaller families experienced a corresponding rise. In 1790, 49% of all families had six or more members; by 1930 this proportion had declined by more than half, to 18.5%. By 1930 there were three times as many

**TABLE 1-1.** *Average number of persons per family household in the United States, 1790–1980*

| Year | Persons per Household |
|------|----------------------|
| 1790 | 5.79 |
| 1850 | 5.55 |
| 1860 | 5.28 |
| 1870 | 5.09 |
| 1880 | 5.04 |
| 1890 | 4.93 |
| 1900 | 4.76 |
| 1910 | 4.54 |
| 1920 | 4.34 |
| 1930 | 3.67 |
| 1940 | 3.67 |
| 1950 | 3.37 |
| 1960 | 3.33 |
| 1970 | 3.14 |
| 1980 | 2.75 |

**TABLE 1-2.** *Percentage distribution of households by size, 1790–1980*

| | Year | | | | | | |
|---|---|---|---|---|---|---|---|
| | **1790** | **1890** | **1900** | **1930** | **1950** | **1970** | **1980** |
| Number of households | 558,000 | 12,690,000 | 16,188,000 | 29,950,000 | 42,826,000 | 62,874,000 | 80,874,749 |
| Percentage of households having: | | | | | | | |
| One person | 3.7 | 3.6 | 5.1 | 7.9 | 10.8 | 17.0 | 22.6 |
| Two persons | 7.8 | 13.2 | 15.0 | 23.4 | 28.8 | 28.8 | 31.3 |
| Three persons | 11.8 | 16.7 | 17.6 | 20.7 | 22.6 | 17.3 | 17.4 |
| Four persons | 13.8 | 16.8 | 16.8 | 17.5 | 17.8 | 15.8 | 15.4 |
| Five persons | 13.9 | 15.1 | 14.2 | 12.0 | 10.0 | 10.4 | 7.8 |
| Six or more persons | 49.0 | 34.6 | 31.3 | 18.5 | 10.0 | 10.7 | 5.5 |

two-person families as in 1790 and nearly twice as many three-person families (U. S. Bureau of the Census, 1975, 1982; see Table 1-2).

These data dispute the contention of some historians that the birth-control pill *alone* has affected population growth. As Table 1-1 clearly demonstrates, birthrates in the United States (as in other developed Western nations) have been declining for 200 years. The synthesis of progesterone in the late 1930s from Mexican yams (Djerassi, 1984) and the development of that chemical into an effective contraceptive—the pill—in the late 1960s did not singly reduce family size. Other factors over the last 200 years, such as the economy and woman's growing control over her own body, explain this decline.[2]

Accompanying these changes were forces that have moved today's families toward an equitable relationship. The term *equitable* is borrowed from Rapoport and Rapoport (1975), who used it to describe ideal dual-career marriages (two-wage-earner marriages). The term connotes the need for accommodation and compromise in to-

day's family life. It suggests a fairness in the division of family responsibilities and flexibility to achieve individual satisfaction within family life. Equity calls on all family members to be aware of and sensitive to other members' needs and to make appropriate sacrifices if necessary. The concept implies that family members have achieved, at least in theory, an equal footing. Although such equality may not yet be a reality, the vertical ranking of family members of yesteryear has toppled.

In the forefront of this change was the women's movement, a movement that Smith (1973) believes began with the era of the flappers. That brief decade sandwiched between World War I and global depression saw the initial erosion of the cult of "piety, purity, submissiveness, and domesticity." Women consolidated past gains and moved forward on several fronts. First, they obtained the right to vote. Second, they increased their small number in the labor force; the Second World War enlarged this small employment beachhead, and the second step in the women's

---

[2] This is not to say that "the pill" has not had a significant effect on society. It has, particularly in giving women the opportunity to become the sexual peers of men. Whether this freedom will continue into the next decade, what with concern over new and currently incurable venereal diseases, such as genital herpes, is uncertain.

movement was achieved (Bane, 1976). The third step was woman's acceptance, without guilt, of her own sexuality.

By loosening the strings of economic dependence, women achieved greater standing in the family. The outcome was greater equality, but whether women initiated this movement or were merely its beneficiaries is less certain. Capitalism, most family historians agree, gave a strong impetus to the nuclear family (Ariès, 1979; Bane, 1976; Bremner, 1970). The nuclear family has been described as ideally suited for the demands of an industrial economy requiring a mobile labor force (Gordon, 1973). Contrary to Engels' (1910) view that capitalism held women in servitude, we suspect that it provided a powerful economic incentive for women and men to redefine their personal relationships. For many families barely managing to survive in mill

*Beginning at the turn of the century and continuing today, women have redefined their roles in American society. Have men been as successful in redefining their roles in this new age of equity?*

or other factory work, this decision was a matter of practical necessity.

In other areas it is clear that women took an active role in gaining improvements in their lot. Beginning with the passage of the Married Women's Property Act, women began to achieve legal standing in the mid-19th century. Bane (1976) views this piece of legislation, establishing women's rights to make legal contracts, hold separate property, and acquire employment, as one of the first steps in the women's rights movement. Likewise, the suffrage movement was a struggle by women for recognition. Finally, the growing acceptance in the 1920s of female sexuality completed a cycle begun in premodern times that saw women undergo a transformation from corrupters to saints to individuals.

While women rose to a more equal footing, young people too, though still liabilities, increased in value. Until late in the last century, young people working on farms or in mills added to a family's wealth. Early (1982, p. 183), writing about the movement of French-Canadian families to the mills of New England, found that by early adolescence most young people worked away from home, with "seven in ten children, ages 11 through 15, [holding] jobs in 1870." For many of these families, as Table 1-3 shows, the number of employable children spelled the difference between poverty and a decent standard of living. Children as young as 4 years could be found in the mills working 14 hours a day as doffers, exchanging empty bobbins for ones filled with thread (Bremner, 1970; Reynolds, 1977).[3]

Around 1900 the participatory role of children declined. They were replaced on farms by machines and in factories that no longer experienced labor shortages by older workers. Child labor laws, more rigid enforcement of compulsory education laws, and the greater costs of feeding and clothing children drove household size down from 5.7 in 1790 to 2.75 in 1980. The remaining children, more likely to survive childhood illnesses and fewer in number, appreciated in value. Each succeeding generation of families strived to provide a better life for its offspring and expended increasing amounts of money per child.

In this new family order, men gained a partner in exchange for a loss of power. No longer the sole ruler of the roost, man now needs the skills of negotiation and compromise to manage family life. Although we believe men are slowly coming to practice a more equitable family lifestyle, others warn of male retreat into activities like sports in an attempt to establish a sanctuary from the modern world. On an increasingly violent playing field, males reassume mythic roles as gladiators striking forth to vanquish imagined foes, and women, represented by cheerleaders, reacquire the traits of an earlier submissive age (Sabo & Runfola, 1980). The failure of some men to accept the new order of equity, Sabo and Runfola (1980) suggest, has led to the continued, often violent exploitation of women.

The changes of the past 60-some years continue and give rise to new situations that demand attention. For example, women's rise to political, sexual, and economic equality has produced a shift in power between the sexes. The issue needing resolution is: How does society, how do you and your significant other, handle that redistribution of power? Children, despite having grown in importance, are increasingly entering alternative care arrangements as both parents are employed. How should society, how should you and your significant other, handle day care,

---

[3] Although most of us would react in horror at the thought of children so young working, let alone working 14 hours a day, the position of doffer involved being on task about 15 minutes out of each hour. The rest of the time, the children sat or played quietly, awaiting the next changing of bobbins.

**TABLE 1-3.** *Number of children needed to escape poverty according to father's occupation and family size*

| Occupation of Father | Number of Working Children Needed | | |
| --- | --- | --- | --- |
| | Families of 4–5 | Families of 7–9 | Families of 10–12 |
| *Unskilled* | | | |
| Common laborer, cotton-mill worker | 2 | 3 | 5 |
| *Skilled* | | | |
| Painter, mason | 1 | 2 | 4 |
| Carpenter, blacksmith, machinist | 0 | 2 | 3 |

and whose responsibility is day care? As the number of elderly people continues to grow, whose responsibility is it to care for them? Is it society's? Is it the family's? Or does the ethic of "rugged individualism" apply in this instance? This book will explore these and other issues that are important in the new order gradually emerging as family size continues to decline, technology revolutionizes the home and workplace, and families search for some new sense of order.

> **?** *Do you agree with the authors' contention that the women's movement is responsible for the move toward equity in American society over the last 60 years? What are your thoughts about Sabo and Runfola's contention that many men are using sports to escape the new order of equity in American family life?*

# THE BLACK EXPERIENCE IN THE UNITED STATES

So far we have told the story of European immigrants who left their native lands willingly to settle in America. There is, however, another history of a group of individuals that cannot be ignored. It is the story of Black women, men, and children captured in Africa, pressed onto ships, and sold in the New World as property.

Separating popular belief from reality is never easy. Though there is complete agreement that slavery was a barbaric and repulsive practice, historians have disagreed about the impact of slavery on the Black family. Two different viewpoints have been put forth. The disagreement can be traced to a 78-page report written by Daniel Moynihan for the Johnson administration in 1965, *The Case for National Action: The Negro Family*.

## The Moynihan Report

The Moynihan Report began as an internal government document, suggesting a role that government might take in assisting Black economic progress after passage of the Civil Rights Act of 1964. This report became the focal point of a heated disagreement about the history of the Black family when Moynihan described that family as a "tangle of pathology" (p. 29).

Moynihan based this description on the available historical works on the effect of slavery on the Black family. Using the work of several eminent historians and social scientists, Moynihan observed that slavery in North America was uniquely different from slavery elsewhere. While slaves in Spanish Catholic Brazil "had a legal and religious tradition which accorded [them] a place as human beings in the hierarchy of soci-

*In 1965 some scholars saw the matriarchal structure of many Black families as contributing to some of the problems these families faced. Do you think the belief was valid either then or now?*

ety . . . [slaves in North America] were . . . reduced to the status of chattels" (Moynihan, 1965, p. 15). Slaves in North America had no religious recognition. They were ignorant of their past. Their families could be bought, sold, traded, divided, molested, abused, or neglected with no recourse to any earthly authority (see Glazer, 1963). Reconstruction after the Civil War, Moynihan believed, delivered liberty but not equality to the Black family. The Black male, in particular, experienced continued humiliation before his family. Never able to assume a position of family leadership, whether slave or free man, he entered the 20th century as he had left the 18th

century—unemployed, poorly paid if employed, with tenuous ties to his family (see Frazier, 1939).

Holding this family group together in both past and present times were women. The matriarchal structure that had evolved from slavery needed to be replaced with a patriarchal structure if Blacks were to make progress:

> The Negro community has been forced into a matriarchal structure which, because it is so out of line with the rest of the American society, seriously retards the progress of the group as a whole, and imposes a crushing burden on the Negro male and, in consequence, on a great many Negro women as well [Moynihan, 1965, p. 29].

Moynihan concluded his report with a suggestion that the United States should endeavor to "bring the Negro American to full and equal sharing in the responsibilities and rewards of citizenship. To this end, [federal] programs . . . shall be designed to have the effect, directly or indirectly, of enhancing the stability and resources of the Negro American family" (p. 48). This "positive" approach offered by a well-meaning official of a concerned administration provoked a firestorm of controversy and a slightly different view of slavery and its impact on the Black family (Rainwater & Yancey, 1967).

 *Do you agree with Moynihan's contention that a Black matriarchal structure has retarded Black advancement in our society? In your opinion, is White American society today matriarchal or patriarchal?*

## A Revisionist View

From the writings of revisionist scholars published after the Moynihan Report, a slightly different (though no less horrifying) picture of slavery emerged. For instance, on the origins of slavery in the United States, Twombley and Moore (1969) identify the North as being as active as the South. They suggest, as does Fox (1969), that slavery faltered in New England because it was unprofitable, not because it was inhumane. There is also evidence that slavery was uncommon in North America until the 18th century (Degler, 1969) and that not until the late 18th century in New England were Blacks deprived of equal justice before the law (Twombley & Moore, 1969).

Evidence accumulated in the years following 1965 moderating historians' contentions that Black families were ripped apart as a rule rather than as an exception. Examining the records of 51 plantations in eight southern states, Steckel (1980) found evidence that slave marriages were not ripped apart or unstable. His work and that of Genovese (1974) and Guttman (1976) show that at least some plantation owners did respect the unity of slaves' families.

Additionally, D. G. White (1983) has assembled data to support a finding that slave families were not completely matriarchal. Black female and male slaves worked, lived, and shared family power, albeit always in an environment that permitted women to exercise greater family authority than men.

### A Reappraisal

There is evidence that some slaves were cared for kindly, that their medical needs were met quickly (Fisher, 1969), and that slavery did not preclude marriage. This evidence does not sway the authors from a conclusion we share with Scott and Wishy (1982, p. 608), that "the Negro family in the urban ghettos is crumbling. A middle-class group has managed to save itself, but for vast numbers of the unskilled, poorly educated city working class, the fabric of conventional social relationships has all but disintegrated." The "tangle of pathology" in our view is

astronomical unemployment rates that keep those who want work from getting any, housing unfit for habitation, and segregation as enslaving as any camp. There are problems in Black families—divorce, illegitimacy, delinquency, and so on—but these problems also exist in White families, especially *poor* White families. *The problem that is unique to Black, Hispanic, and Native American families as we see it is prejudice and discrimination.*

## SUMMARY

As this book unfolds, we shall examine in greater detail the families, White and of color, briefly sketched in this chapter. We shall examine their triumphs and failures with an eye, when possible, toward correcting or avoiding the latter. We shall continue to look back at history to provide a reference point for the many variations of family life that exist in this country today.

## MAJOR POINTS TO REMEMBER

1. Marriage is an institutionalized and publicly recognized union between individuals who intend to stay married. A family is a group of at least two persons who live together and are related by blood, marriage, or adoption.
2. There are four marital forms (monogamy, polygyny, polyandry, and group marriage) and several family forms (nuclear, binuclear, single-parent, blended, modified nuclear, and extended).
3. Before the 15th century, children existed at the bottom of the family hierarchy. Two explanations have been put forth of the lack of value attached to children in premodern family times: (1) high infant mortality and (2) parental indifference, even resentment.

4. In premodern family times, women were not formally recognized by society. Reasons included the nature of marriage contracts, religious prejudices, the hazards befalling women's bodies, and male fears regarding the loss of semen.

5. In premodern times, males sat atop the family hierarchy.

6. In the 15th century, the premodern family began the gradual transition to its modern form. Encouraging this change were an increase in individually arranged marriages, the placing of greater value on children, and a weakening of community control.

7. We can divide family life in the United States into three time periods: the family in harmony, 1620 to 1820; the cult of domesticity, 1820 to 1920; and the move toward equity, 1920 to the present.

8. The age of harmony saw women achieve the status of a "junior partner" and children acquire more importance in the family. Still, the community exercised a fair degree of control over family life, and society expected husbands to maintain family order.

9. The rise of industrialization and the influx of immigrants into the United States brought changes to families between 1820 and 1920. The family came to be seen as a haven from the outside world. The cult of domesticity represented a search for order in a time seemingly without order. The retreat toward privacy and domestic bliss was a way of coping with change brought on by the industrial age.

10. The authors see the women's movement as the major force in the move toward equity.

11. The impact of slavery on the Black family is a heatedly debated topic. Some historians believe that slavery damaged the Black family by encouraging a matriarchal structure, while others disagree.

## ADDITIONAL SOURCES OF INFORMATION

Ariès, P. (1962). *Centuries of childhood*. New York: Knopf.

*Journal of Family History,* National Council on Family Relations, 1219 University Ave. SE, Minneapolis, MN 55414.

*Journal of Social History,* Carnegie-Mellon University, Pittsburgh, PA 15213.

Shorter, E. (1977). *The making of the modern family*. New York: Basic Books.

Shorter, E. (1982). *A history of women's bodies*. New York: Basic Books.

# 2

# UNDERSTANDING FAMILY BEHAVIOR

1. What can we learn from the experiences of Einstein and Galileo about theory and about truth?

2. Does early psychoanalytic thinking provide an understanding of family behavior?

3. Which of the theories in this chapter places a heavy emphasis on self-concept, symbols, and interaction? What is a symbol?

4. What do steel girders have to do with structural-functionalism?

5. Is ecological theory an offshoot of general systems theory? For that matter, what is ecological theory and what is general systems theory?

6. How does the Broadway comedy *Never Too Late* illustrate the principle of being "off time"?

7. How might an understanding of stress theory help someone toward a healthier emotional life?

8. Are the terms *primary prevention* and *wellness* synonymous?

9. How do primary, secondary, and tertiary prevention differ?

10. What are the four tools of prevention?

**The year is** 1915. Albert Einstein pushes back his chair and stands. He has just put the finishing touches on his theory of gravity. But instead of smiling, he appears disturbed. He mumbles to himself, "This cannot be correct." Einstein has predicted that the world exists in a universe that is ever changing. Such a notion is, unquestionably, pure poppycock. Since the time of Aristotle, the idea that the heavens are stationary has been accepted as truth by all. Contrary ideas are clearly incorrect. And so Einstein dutifully reworks his theory to correspond with accepted knowledge. For 12 years his original version lies untouched, until the astronomer Edwin Hubble shakes the world with his observation that the universe is expanding. Einstein had been right after all (Lightman, 1983).

Einstein was the victim of something we call **constituent validity,** which means simply that an idea may be defined as true by a group of people whether it is true or not. History is littered with similar mistakes made by greater and lesser figures alike. This fact illustrates well a uniquely paradoxical human situation. Humans have a great need to understand, to fashion models of how things work, and to comprehend why they work the way they do. These understandings lead to explanations that are called **theories.** Theories seek to predict how something might respond in a given circumstance. For a theory to be useful, it must be applicable over many varying circumstances.

And yet, despite all this theoretical inquisitiveness, humans have a consistent track record of narrow-mindedness. Consider Galileo's experiences with the Inquisition. His scientific curiosity led him to the observation that the earth was not the center of the universe, that the earth revolved around the sun. Galileo's proclamation was greeted with scorn and disapproval, and eventually he was tried by the church as a heretic and banished. Einstein's and Galileo's experiences illustrate the one certain truth contained in this chapter—that truth is to hold no explanation sacred. Theory, like truth, evolves. Its shape changes as curious human beings question and explore further how the world behaves.

In this chapter we examine several explanations of how families behave. Further, we explore how theory can be used to construct a model for preventing family dysfunction and promoting family health. Such an understanding will serve as a foundation in comprehending much of the material in the remaining chapters.

# UNDERSTANDING FAMILIES: THREE THEORETICAL FRAMEWORKS

The sheer number of theories that have been offered to explain human behavior is (in the vernacular) "truly awesome." Some of these focus on the individual and view behavior as emerging from within a person. These explanations we will call **psychological theories.** Other explanations focus on the interaction between the individual and his or her environment. These explanations we will call **social-psychological theories.** Still others examine the influence of social structure and society on behavior. We will call these explanations **sociocultural theories.**

Legitimate criticism can be directed against explanations that focus solely on the individual in explaining family behavior. Nevertheless, it is important to have some understanding of two major psychological theories. As this book unfolds and we examine the family over the life span, we will draw, in an eclectic fashion, on many explanations. Each offers a unique view of how people and families function.

## Psychological Theories

Psychological explanations of behavior involve an understanding of the internal drives and motivations that influence behavior. Two of the most widely used psychological explanations are psychoanalytic and social-learning theories.

*Early psychoanalytic theory.* This theory attempts to explain social development from infancy to adulthood. Early childhood experiences are regarded as leaving a lasting impression on the child's developing personality. As young children move from one psychosexual stage to another, they come to grips with two instinctual urges, the sexual and aggressive drives (see Table 2-1). Both these urges are thought to create a constant state of tension in which the body seeks pleasure and satisfaction. Psychoanalytic theory conceptualizes this tension as resulting from the interaction of three forces—the id, the ego, and the superego.

The **id** can be imagined as unbridled passion reflecting a desire to satisfy instinctual behavior. The **ego** evolves to satisfy the id's instinctual gratification but in ways that avoid punishment. The ego's major function is to attempt to satisfy the demands of the id while observing the dictates of the third component of personality, the superego. The **superego** is the judge of all behavior. It is our internalized moral code. It is thought to develop through a child's interactions with parents, who communicate standards of acceptable and unacceptable behavior (Freud, 1947).

The family is viewed as the societal force that creates and models a set of desirable characteristics that is internalized by the child and is called the **ego ideal.** The parents also facilitate sex-role identification through a psychodynamic process (see Chapter 4). Thus, the family is thought to provide the societal conditions that encourage self-regulation through superego mechanisms, ideals of conduct, and sex-role identification.

Individuals who subscribe to early psychoanalytic theory place a heavy emphasis on a child's first several years of life. Behavior occur-

**TABLE 2-1.** *Freud's first four psychosexual stages*

| Stage | Period of Life | Description |
| --- | --- | --- |
| Oral | Infant | Sexual instinct is satisfied through autoerotic stimulation of the mouth. |
| Anal | Toddler | Sexual instinct moves from mouth to anus; child experiences pleasure and displeasure expelling and withholding feces. |
| Phallic | 4–7 | Child wishes to possess other-sex parent as a sexual partner. |
| Latency | Preadolescent | The ego is thought to be freed from sexual instincts for a brief period before these issues reemerge in adolescence. |

ring in late adolescence or in adult life is traced, in this model, back to an earlier childhood psychosexual stage and unresolved issues related to that stage. Psychoanalytic theory, while rich in intrapsychic understanding, offers little help in understanding families. Focusing on individual behavior, this theoretical perspective cannot totally explain the complex interaction that occurs in families or between families and the society.

**?** *One might argue that influences on the childhood psychosexual development of each family member provide an explanation for the present behavior of that individual within the family, so that early psychoanalytic theory* does *explain family behavior. What is your opinion?*

*Social-learning theory.* Learning theory views human development as the cumulative effect of a multitude of learning experiences that are integrated to form a personality. This happens in a social-learning model in two ways.

The first way is through **reinforcement.** Reinforcement is any event that occurs after a response and affects the chances that the response will occur again. In **positive reinforcement,** a desirable stimulus follows the response, increas-

ing the chances that the response will recur. In **negative reinforcement,** an unwanted stimulus is removed following the response, also increasing the chances that the response will recur. In **punishment** an undesirable stimulus (for example, pain) is presented after the response, or a desirable stimulus is removed, decreasing the chances that the response will recur.

The second way that learning occurs is through **modeling.** In modeling, people imitate the behavior of others whom they admire or respect (Bandura, 1969).

Those who subscribe to social-learning theory emphasize the rewards, negative sanctions, and punishments we have received over our lives that shape our behavioral responses to external events. Further, learning theorists are very interested in the role models whom individuals select to emulate. Although social-learning theory acknowledges that learning (and therefore personal growth) occurs over the life span, it focuses on an individual's reaction to some discrete event. It too lacks the power to explain intrafamily and interfamily interactional patterns.

## Social-Psychological Theories

Social-psychological theories of behavior examine the relationship of individuals to their social

*What aspect of social learning theory does this small boy's behavior illustrate?*

theory proposes that families *interact* through *symbols*. These interacting family members together develop roles (such as father, husband, son, mother, wife, and daughter) and assign those roles to individuals in the family, who then "play" the assigned role (Hill & Hansen, 1960).

This model relies heavily on one's sensory experiences and perception of the environment. Self-concept is of major importance to symbolic interactionists. It involves processes of how we are seen by others, how we imagine ourselves to be seen, and how we feel (pleased or displeased) about those outsiders' view of us (Ritzer, 1983). Cooley (1964) has termed this the "looking-glass self." This self is a conscious process that Mead (1962) describes as having two parts. The first part, "me," is the one we are aware of. It is similar to the superego in that it reflects society's standards of social order, control, and conformity. The second part, the "I," is the part of which we are unaware until some act has been completed.

The symbolic interactionist sees human beings as capable of thought, which is shaped by social interaction. Social interaction permits people to learn symbols and their meanings. The symbols permit human beings to carry out human behavior. Moreover, individuals have the ability to change the meanings attached to symbols or to vary the meanings of symbols for different places, people, and times (Ritzer, 1983). You can probably think of symbols that hold special meaning for your family. Gestures or statements may exist in your family that mean something different within the family than outside it (Burr, Leigh, Day, & Constantine, 1979).

Symbolic interaction holds that people do not merely react to their environment but act on it as well. Life is in a constant state of flux in which individuals interpret what is happening and apply a meaning to it. Events that challenge the role an individual plays or suggest a loss of role may bring pain if so defined by the individual (Burr et al., 1979; Dager, 1964; Stryker, 1964).

environment. These explanations of behavior are broader than psychological theories in that they extend beyond intrapsychic factors to include other individuals, groups, and organizations. Representatives of this type of theory are symbolic interaction and social exchange theories. Both are widely used to explain family functioning.

*Symbolic interaction theory.* A useful way to understand the remaining theories to be described in this chapter is to dissect the label attached to the explanation and examine its components. For example, symbolic interaction

For example, a young person's entrance into college can create several changes in family roles. The student begins to think of himself or herself in a new way: independent and adult. But the student's parents may not agree. One or both may be unwilling to assign an adult role to the child. What happens? At semester breaks and holidays, when students occasionally travel home to check in with the family, students and parents may find themselves arguing about curfews and friends. And when parents end a fight with "As long as you live under this roof, young man (lady), you'll abide by my rules," they are really saying "You're still a child in my eyes."

Although several authors have identified symbolic interaction as the most influential family theory of recent times (Holman & Burr, 1980; Klein, Calvert, Garland, & Poloma, 1969), this approach has weaknesses. Critics contend that it is inappropriate for the study of social organizations. It ignores the use of power in human relationships, and it fails to take into account the unconscious processes at work in human relationships (Manis & Meltzer, 1978). These critics add that families function in a more complex world than symbolic interaction can assess.

*Social exchange theory.* The word *social* in the name of this theory implies the interaction of the individual and the group. *Exchange* is commonly understood to mean the giving of one thing for something else of about equal value. People who subscribe to social exchange theory believe that individuals trade, as in a marketplace, emotions in exchange for other emotions. The business of exchange is transacted among family members and also between family members and others in society.

The rate and nature of exchange depend on four elements. The first is **rewards**—the satisfactions, pleasures, or attainments collected during exchanges. For example, suppose a student in this class were to approach someone and whisper in his or her ear "I love you." If the

other person should respond with a smile, a hug, and a kiss, the student would have received a reward (Nye, 1979).

The second element involves the concept of alternatives and is often called "weighing costs." **Costs** are actions, feelings, or interactions that (1) are unpleasant or (2) are rewards lost. For example, if you are married, falling in love with someone other than your spouse will result in costs to you in the form of painful experiences, perhaps including social ostracism, decline in social status, and divorce. Similar costs will befall the third party in this relationship, as well as your spouse, who may experience feelings of depression, anger, or powerlessness. The second kind of cost, lost rewards, can be understood in terms of the idea that *choice entails loss.* Let's imagine that the price of a meal includes one dessert, either pudding or ice cream. To choose the pudding "costs" the consumer the ice cream. Moving in with your lover would cost you your spouse (Nye, 1979).

It would appear that everything in life costs something. Nothing is free. However, some things cost less, and on some emotional or social investments, a **profit** can be made—that is, one can maximize gain and limit loss. For example, one high school girl we know passed up the opportunity to attend her junior prom because her invitation had come from a rather unattractive boy. By choosing not to attend the prom, she had incurred a cost, but she felt that she had profited by not losing stature in the eyes of her peers. Thus, she had minimized her loss. Had she accepted, her date would have gained in prestige at her expense, or at least so she thought.

The fourth element involved in determining the rate and nature of exchange is the **norm of reciprocity,** the principle that receiving should approximately equal giving. Another way of saying this is that "people should help those who help them, and people should not injure those who have helped them" (Nye, 1979, p. 4).

In short, social exchange theory suggests that "humans avoid costly behavior and seek rewarding statuses, relationships, interaction, and feeling states to the end that their profits are maximized, or losses minimized" (Nye, 1979, p. 2). In this theory, humans are rational; they are actors as well as reactors; all behavior costs something, and people will usually choose the least costly behavioral option. One might also view this process of choice as a striving for equity—that is, seeking appropriate rewards for equal costs.

Social exchange theory has gained tremendous popularity in recent years among family scholars. Yet, as Holman and Burr (1980) have noted, it too has weaknesses. This "approach seems to be most useful in understanding precarious human relationships . . . in more complex relationships the exchange processes become more complicated, subtle, long term, unconscious, and frequently irrelevant. Thus, the theory loses much of its utility" (p. 732).

 *Are social-psychological theories more complex than psychological theories? What are the similarities and differences between social exchange theory and social-learning theory?*

## Sociocultural Theories

Sociocultural theories focus on social structures or systems to explain family behavior. Theories in this group tend to view the family as it reacts to such societal influences as culture and social institutions. Two such theories in this tradition are structural-functionalism and general systems theories.

*Structural-functional theory.* The word *structural* suggests that something is arranged in a definite pattern, or organization, and that this arrangement is related to other parts of the structure and is dominated by the general char-

acter of the whole. The word *functional* means that each element in a group contributes to the development or maintenance of the whole. Structural-functionalism suggests that society is made up of a number of *structures,* each serving a useful *function* that maintains and/or further develops the whole. How might we understand this last somewhat tautological statement? Think of a steel girder. Alone, it is nothing more than one building part. However, when it is assembled with other girders, it creates a structure and serves the function of supporting the walls or roof of a building. To the structural-functionalist, the family is similar to the girder. It serves, with other girders such as schools and churches, the function of supporting society.

The structural-functionalist position is that the social system is the basic unit for study, rather than either the family, as social-psychological theory would suggest, or the individual, as strict psychological theory would argue. Maintaining this position means that family members are not actors but reactors (Hill & Hansen, 1960; Pitts, 1964).

Let's look again at our earlier example of a college student whose parents disapproved of his or her late-night activities or friends. The symbolic interactionist would argue that this incident occurred because of shifting roles and the meaning each player attached to those roles. The student wanted to be treated as an adult, with the privilege of setting his or her own standard of behavior. The parents disagreed and wished to maintain this person's role as a child. The parents' motivations for opposing this role change may have ranged from disapproval of the student's behavior and peer group to reluctance to surrender their parenting roles.

Structural-functionalists would view this situation differently. They would argue that society needs to have people grow up, separate from their parents, and establish their own lives. The structures of college and the peer group in this example serve the function of helping this happen. Away from home and in the company of peers, students are separated from their parents and are engaged in the process of establishing their own lives. These school experiences and peer relationships contribute to the development of a new possible structure (that is, the college student is able to leave the family and form a new family) that helps maintain the whole (that is, the continuation of society). Notice that nowhere in this explanation did we include ideas that humans determine their own destiny or that their interactions or exchanges matter very much. The structural-functionalist position ignores these variables.

Structural-functionalist theory, in proposing that structures serve the function of maintaining and developing society, suggests that the whole—that is, society—strives to maintain a level of homeostasis. It is logical that this theory would express the view that society needs to maintain a balance of functions through a state of equilibrium, so as not to be torn apart (Hill & Hansen, 1960).

At one time, structural-functionalism was a major school of thought in explaining how families operate (Klein et al., 1969). Gradually through the 1970s and into the 1980s, many have abandoned this theory (Holman & Burr, 1980), largely because it fails to view humans as something more than just the raw material that makes up one building block of society.

**?** *Structural-functionalism suggests that humans do not act independently but only react to situations. Do you agree?*

*General systems theory.* What can we learn from examining the words *general* and *systems*? Well, the word *general* is commonly understood to mean "applicable to every member of a group." A system is defined as a group of interrelated parts forming a collective unit. General systems theory suggests that society is composed of many interrelated parts.

Rather than an object like a girder that cannot act, imagine in this case a chip within a personal computer. This chip can perform certain functions with no input at all. It can perform other functions if a program is inserted. It can do still more if it is linked to other chips within the computer. It can act or react, depending on what it is called to do. The chip alone does not make a usable computer system. Other elements, such as a keyboard, monitor, disk drive, and printer, are needed to have a system. The chip, in our example, is analogous to the family and the computer components to society.

The world is filled with systems. Each can operate independently. For example, it can rain or not. Food crops can grow or not. Trading between humans can occur or not. But if we are to have a society, these parts (systems) must come together. Without rain there is desert, and in a desert food cannot be grown. Without food, humans cannot survive. Fortunately, humans have usually established themselves where it is possible to at least eke out an existence. Whether a family operates as successfully as a system depends on several factors.

Systems theorists use several terms when speaking of families. One of these is *boundaries*. **Boundaries** define a system by establishing what elements belong to it. An *open boundary* suggests that the family has much interaction with the outside world—friends, clubs and organizations, church activities. A *closed boundary* implies that the family keeps to itself, with a minimal amount of outside interaction—few if any friends, little if any involvement in civic or community affairs.

The chip in our earlier example, despite its small size, is not one part but many. A family, too, is not one part but is made of two or more units. A **unit,** in systems language, is a component of a system. Unlike computer chips, families can grow in parts (by adding children or other family members) and shrink in parts (by losing family members) over their life span.

A family is a system, made up of units, that has established a more or less open or closed boundary with other systems. But how do families interact with other systems? Systems theorists suggest that an incoming stimulus, or *input,* is mediated within the family and a response, or *output,* returned. This process of mediation is called **transformation.** The process of transformation involves interrupting the input and either *amplifying* or *dampening* the significance of the input. Imagine the loss of a close family friend as the input. A family might amplify this loss and become very despondent and unable to function; or it might dampen this loss by rationalization and, though saddened, go on with its normal activities. Transformation also involves what systems theorists call **cybernetic control,** which means that the response a family makes to some given input is measured against family rules. If the family does not have a satisfactory response for some input, it will engage in **morphogenesis**—a family's search for and/or creation of new responses to that input. These changes may be minor, leaving intact basic family rules, or they may be major, changing the family and its values dramatically (Broderick & Smith, 1979).

Holman and Burr (1980), in their review of family theories, cite the claims of many authors that general systems theory "may be the wave of the future, providing generalizations useful for understanding not only family systems, but other systems as well" (p. 732). And yet, as they point out, general systems theory has not evolved beyond a descriptive theory, unable at present to predict family behavior (see Box 2-1).

 *Using our earlier example of the college student's visit home, try to explain this situation from a systems perspective. Can you identify the inputs and outputs in this example? Does a transformation occur? Does a morphogenesis occur?*

## DEVELOPMENTAL THEORY: AN INTEGRATION

Is it possible to integrate the theories presented so far in this chapter? Can one perspective encompass the variations among these theoretical camps? Developmental theory has tried to bridge these different schools of thought to create a unified explanation of family behavior.

The developmental approach is an attempt to create a comprehensive model capable of explaining family behavior across the **life cycle.** From a developmentalist's perspective, a life cycle begins with the formation of the marital couple and progresses through a series of stages, ending in the death of one of the marital partners (see Table 2-2). Accompanying each of these stages is a series of **tasks** that need to be accomplished in order for the family to progress to the next stage. This overall process is referred to as a **family's lifetime history** or **career** (Aldous, 1978; Hill & Hansen, 1960).

As an illustration, consider a newly married couple. Using Table 2-2, we would place this couple at stage 1 of the family's lifetime career. In order to proceed to the second stage, this couple will engage in a certain set of behaviors, or tasks. These might include establishing a household, generating revenues to maintain that household, and developing a sense of intimacy and marital commitment that makes children desirable.

## BOX 2-1
*The Ecological Perspective*

In recent years interest has grown in an offshoot of general systems theory, the ecological approach. This perspective has captured the imagination of many in the disciplines of social work and community psychology who see it as a theoretical framework capable of explaining the relationship of humans and their environment.

The ecological approach emphasizes the need to understand the relationship of individuals, families, and other groups of people in a natural setting. It holds that all living and nonliving elements in nature are mutually sustaining and interdependent, so that all human behavior is dependent on and influenced by the surrounding environment. An ecological perspective assumes that "resources are shared" (Kelly,

1968, p. 80); that is, no human being has a monopoly on the environment. This perspective proposes that favorable environmental conditions encourage human interaction and development, while an unfavorable environment discourages interaction and development. Further, an ecological perspective suggests that communities evolve—that is, change is inevitable and occurs because the environment can no longer sustain the original relationship (Kelly, 1968).

Kelly and Levin (personal communication, 1984) outline the key concepts of the ecological perspective as follows:

1. Persons are resources.
2. Social settings are integrative—that is, open to all groups and unifying.

3. Social settings and persons have reciprocal influences on each other.
4. Ongoing change is a necessary ingredient to initiate and sustain the development of persons and social settings.
5. Persons and social settings have predictable life cycles.
6. Induced change efforts have radiating effects.
7. Induced change efforts have unintended side effects.
8. Induced change efforts adapt to local social settings.
9. Induced change occurs when local resources and social settings are empowered.
10. Sustained development of persons and social settings occurs when empowered resources contribute to the evolution of the community.

As one stage is completed, another begins, and additional demands (tasks) are made on the family. For example, as the child reaches school age, parents must adjust their roles and open the family's boundaries to permit nonfamily members to enter the family's environment to contribute to the child's education and socialization. This process continues until the last child has left the family. In the final stage of a family's life history, the couple are again alone. Their children have begun family histories of their own, continuing the **lineage family** established by their parents, grandparents, and so on.

As we have already seen, evolution is an im-

portant concept within this framework. The family evolves over the years, facing and accomplishing a number of tasks that mark off each stage in the life cycle of the individual that begins with birth and ends in death (Hill & Rodgers, 1964). Further, it is assumed that the life-cycle stages outlined in Table 2-2 happen for everyone at approximately the same time. Thus, a family can be "on time" or "off time" in regard to the life cycle. The Broadway comedy *Never Too Late* illustrates this last point. This show was about a late middle-aged couple with a grown, married daughter who discover they are to become parents again. The story line of this entertaining

**TABLE 2-2.** *Seven life-cycle stages*

| | |
|---|---|
| Stage 1 | Married without children—45 years old or less. |
| Stage 2 | Childbearing families—oldest child less than 2. |
| Stage 3 | Families with preschoolers—oldest child 2 to 6. |
| Stage 4 | Families with schoolchildren—oldest child 6 to 14. |
| Stage 5 | Families with teenagers—oldest child 14 or older, living at home. |
| Stage 6 | Families in middle years—from youngest child's leaving home until retirement ("empty-nest families"). |
| Stage 7 | Aging families—retirement until death. |

comedy deals with the "off time" nature of having a child in one's late forties and society's reactions to that event.

The astute reader has probably already noticed the use of terms like *roles* and *boundaries* that were used earlier in this chapter in reference to other theories. Developmentalists, like symbolic interactionists, view the family as consisting of a group of interacting actors filling assigned roles. Like the structural-functionalist, the developmentalist believes that the family has several vitally important functions to serve in society, including meeting needs for food, clothing, and shelter, biological reproduction, socialization, and maintaining social order (Rodgers, 1964).

From general systems theory, developmentalists borrow the concept of boundaries and propose that families are neither totally open nor totally closed but respond to the demands placed on them by family members and society (Rodgers, 1973). For example, imagine a couple with their first newborn. Initially, this infant and its parents will have limited contact with the outside world, save grandparents, the family doctor,

and a few close friends. As the child and the family age, contact with the outside world increases, so that by adolescence the child may be spending more time outside the family than in it.

Developmental theory attempts to be flexible but fails on some accounts. As Nock (1979) has pointed out, developmental theory assumes an unbroken, steady movement of the family through a sequence of life events. It assumes that couples will not divorce and will have children. In fact, the stages of development across the life cycle are geared to the ages of the children in the family. Given the numerous variations of family lifestyles that exist today, some have accused developmental theory of reflecting a middle-class nuclear-family bias.

 *In your opinion, is developmental theory successful in creating a "grand" theory capable of explaining all family behavior?*

# UNDERSTANDING FAMILY CRISES: STRESS THEORY

If one understands **stress** to mean *any change in life,* then Rodgers' (1973, p. 218) statement that stress theory is "a special case of general developmental theory" is essentially correct. The life events that mark off the life cycle carry with them positive stress (eustress) and negative stress (distress). Life can be filled with boredom and a lack of challenge (hypostress), or it can be filled with excessive demands on time, labor, and energy (hyperstress; see Figure 2-1). These stressful situations mark transition points that, if coped with successfully, facilitate a healthier family environment.

An initial understanding of how stress affects organisms must be credited to Cannon (1939) and Selye (1974). Selye's laboratory work with

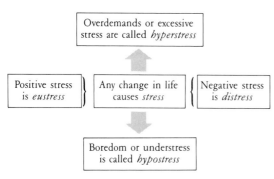

**FIGURE 2-1.** *Four types of stress.*

animals found that stress-producing agents (called "stressors") create a reaction that Selye called the **general adaptation syndrome.** When stress exceeds some threshold, Selye found, laboratory animals enter into a **stage of alarm.** During this stage the organism is on alert, calling on its defensive systems to combat the stressor. The period during which the body fights the noxious stressor is called the **stage of resistance.** If the body cannot defeat the noxious stressor, it enters the **stage of exhaustion.** Unable to overcome the damaging virus, bacterium, or other adverse stimulus, the body surrenders to the stressor and expires.

### *The ABCX Model*

Drawing on this rich vein of research activity, Hill (1949, 1958) developed a model of how families function under stress, the ABCX model. The letter *A* represents some event that brings discomfort, such as death of a family member, a job promotion, relocation, or unemployment. *B* stands for the internal and external resources the family can use to fight the discomfort— wealth, friends, level of self-esteem, internal locus of control, coping abilities, and so on. *C* is the meaning the family attaches to the event. *X* is the crisis. Together, A, B, and C result in X. That is, the magnitude of the crisis, its duration, and

the family's level of reorganization after the crisis are determined by the sum of A (the event) + C (its meaning) − B (the available resources).

The second part of Hill's model predicts how most families will react in a crisis. As Figure 2-2 illustrates, the crisis (X) trips the family into a period of disorganization in which the family marshals its resources, both those already existing and those created in response to the event, to meet the crisis. The angle of recovery reflects the time necessary for the family to find a solution to its distress; the level of reorganization reflects the family's success in returning to a precrisis state.

Now let's take a closer look at the ABCX model by examining its components individually.

*A, the stressor.* A, the event that causes discomfort, can also be called the "stressor." Stressors are events "of sufficient magnitude to bring about change in the family system" (McCubbin et al., 1980, p. 857). In line with our earlier definition of *stress* as any change in life, a stressor may be either a good or a bad event.

Life is filled with stressors. Some of these are sudden changes, such as an unexpected relocation or loss of employment. Others can be more insidious, slowly sapping a family's energy over a period of years, such as poverty, alcoholism, or chronic physical or emotional illness. Still others mark the flow of family life. These include the addition of family members, entry into school, adolescence, dissatisfaction over a marriage, possibly divorce and remarriage, and the loss of family members.

*C, the meaning.* C in Hill's model represents the meaning the family attaches to the event. Events are not stressors unless the family perceives them to be, and the degree of positive or negative disruption is again determined by the family. Suppose a job promotion has been of-

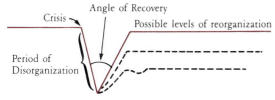

Crisis — Angle of Recovery

Possible levels of reorganization

Period of Disorganization

**FIGURE 2-2.** *The family's reaction to crisis.*

fered to a family member. At first glance this would seem to be a positive event for the family, but it may not be. It may mean the promoted member's extended absence from the home to meet increased job responsibilities, or it may mean a move to a new community. A promotion may then become a negative event in this family's life and acquire the status of crisis (Gullotta & Donohue, 1981b).

*B, resources.* The *B* in Hill's ABCX equation stands for the strengths that the family calls on in time of need. Those B factors, as McCubbin et al. (1980) describe them, include personal resources, a family system's internal resources, social support, and coping. *Personal resources* include financial resources, high self-esteem, and an internal locus of control.

A family system's *internal resources* are its integrative abilities. We use the term *family integration* to mean the degree of unity existing in the family. Where there are common family interests, a common family agenda for the future, and affection for one another, there is a high degree of family integration. Social support involves people outside the family who, in time of need, lend their strength to the family. This is accomplished by helping the family to feel loved, cared for, valued, and worthy, and by communicating to the family that it belongs.

The last factor, *coping,* involves the adaptive ways families use their B resources to handle a crisis. A family's adaptive capability is judged by its ability to mobilize its resources to confront a challenge and adjust to overcome that challenge.

*X, the crisis.* The *X* in Hill's model represents the state of disorganization after a crisis-producing event. There are two types of crisis events. The first are called **developmental** or **normative crises** and are considered a normal part of living life. The birth of a child, a child's entry into school, and the death of an aged family member are illustrations of normative crises. These events confront the family with developmental tasks that, if coped with successfully, move the family on to another life stage.

The second type of crisis is called **situational** or **catastrophic.** These are events that affect only some families and are considered tragic, sometimes ruinous. For example, whereas the death of an aged parent after several months' illness could be considered a normative crisis, the accidental death of a healthy child would most likely be considered a catastrophic crisis. The surviving family members had probably expected the aged parent to die. Although this death causes the family pain, the loss was expected; the developmentalist would say it was "on time." However, the sudden loss of a healthy child was not expected. This death was "off time." No one in the family or society expected that this child would die before his or her parents. The suffering associated with this loss would be intense and long-lasting.

Many situational, or catastrophic, crises, such as natural disasters, are sudden and unexpected, but some are not. Problems such as alcoholism, family violence, racism, and unemployment are also ruinous in their impact on family life and are considered nonnormative events in a family's lifetime history.

*In your opinion, is divorce a normative or a situational stressor? Under what circumstances might the birth of a child be considered a catastrophic stressor?*

## The Double ABCX Model

In recent years, stress theorists have come to realize that the ABCX model focuses primarily on family variables that precede a crisis. Its two-variable design (B and C) does not always explain why over time some families survive distressful situations and others do not.

In response to this theoretical deficit, McCubbin and his associates offered a double AaBbCcXx model of family adaptation (see Figure 2-3 and Table 2-3). In this model Aa is understood to include (1) the initial stressor event, (2) family changes over time, and (3) stressors resulting from the family's efforts to cope. Bb includes not only the family's initial resources but also new sources of strength gathered in response to the stressor. The Cc variable includes not only the family's perception of the stressor but also, as McCubbin has described it, the perception of the "pile-up" of additional life events. Finally, the Xx includes both crisis and adaptation (McCubbin, Cauble, & Patterson, 1982; McCubbin & Patterson, 1983).

## Functional and Dysfunctional Responses to Crisis

Some adaptations in response to a crisis prove to be dysfunctional. For example, overuse of alcohol or other drugs may numb the pain associated with the death of a child, but most of society would find unacceptable this means of coping with loss. Most of us would judge it destructive to the individual, the other surviving family members, and the society at large.

Other adaptations can be considered functional. For example, if the grieving parent turned to friends and family for emotional support and found that support so that the relationships among these individuals were strengthened, most of us would judge this coping process leading to adaptation as constructive—that is, beneficial to the health of the individual, that individual's family, and the greater society. Such constructive, or functional, methods of coping and adaptation in mental health are called "primary prevention" or, in lay terms, "wellness." In the rest of this chapter we'll look at the primary

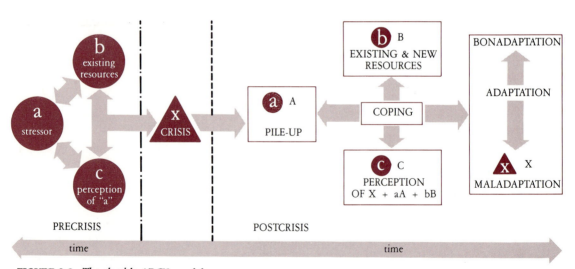

**FIGURE 2-3.** *The double ABCX model.*

**TABLE 2-3.** *Dimensions of the family crisis framework: Double ABCX model*

| Family Precrisis Factors | | Family Postcrisis Factors | |
|---|---|---|---|
| A | Stressor event and related hardships | A | Family "pile-up"<br>• Unresolved aspects of the stressor event<br>• Unmanaged hardships associated with the stressor event<br>• Intrafamily role changes precipitated by stressor<br>• Changes in the family and its members over time<br>• Residual hardships and demands precipitated by family efforts at coping<br>• Social ambiguity |
| B | Family resources available | B | Family resources—modified, strengthened, or developed as part of family adaptation<br>• Coping by managing resources within the family to facilitate adaptation<br>• Coping by developing, stimulating, and controlling resources outside of the family<br>• Social support |
| C | Family perception of the stressor and available resource | C | Family perception of the crisis situation and resources<br>• Redefining the situation<br>• Endowing the situation with meaning |
| X | Family crisis | X | Family adaptation—system–environment fit through process of:<br>• Stimulus regulation<br>• Environmental control<br>• Balancing:<br>Assimilation<br>Accommodation<br>Compromise |

prevention movement and the important role each of us has in enhancing his or her own emotional health and that of others in society.

*Select some life event and use the stress model to examine that event.*

*Do you find that when B (resources) and C (meaning attached to the event) vary, the intensity of the crisis changes?*

*Can you think of ways in which the stress model could be used to promote health and prevent illness?*

# PRIMARY PREVENTION AND ITS TECHNOLOGY

The concept of prevention is far from new. The thought that emotional distress might be avoided and mental health encouraged can be traced back to the ancients. However, the idea of prevention as an attainable goal emerged only recently as the result of the failure of the treatment model to reduce the ever-growing number of seriously emotionally ill individuals in our society (Albee, 1980, 1985). Prevention has evolved since the early 1960s, when Gerald Caplan (1961, 1964, 1974) introduced a model suggesting that emotional illness could be prevented. That three-tier model of primary, secondary, and tertiary prevention, similar to the prevention model found in public health, has been pruned and refined. **Secondary prevention** activities—attempts to reduce the length of time an individual or family experiences an emotionally distressful situation—are now called "treatment activities." **Tertiary prevention** activities—attempts to prevent the recurrence of a debilitating problem and to restore as high as possible the level of individual and family reorganization—are now called "rehabilitation activities." Prevention has emerged in a hybrid form called **primary prevention.**

The goal of primary prevention remains basically unaltered from Caplan's (1974, pp. 189–190) original purpose of reducing "the incidence of new cases of mental disorder in the population by combating harmful forces which operate in the community and by strengthening the capacity of people to withstand stress." Parameters for this goal have now been established. Primary prevention focuses on groups (not individuals) and the specific problems those groups experience (Klein & Goldston, 1977). Prevention is proactive; that is, it builds new coping resources and adaptation skills and thus promotes emotional health (Albee & Gullotta, in press). Finally, prevention activities are planned interventions that can be observed, recorded, and evaluated for effectiveness (Cowen, 1982b; Klein & Goldston, 1977).

From this general conceptualization, different strategies emerge. They all involve each of us as an active participant in preventing illness and promoting health. Prevention advocates reject the claim "that major [emotional] illness is probably in large part genetically determined and is probably, therefore, not preventable, at most modifiable" (Lamb & Zusman, 1979, p. 1349). Rather, prevention takes the position, as Albee has so eloquently expressed it, that emotional problems are not diseases that can be traced to some microorganism or DNA thread. Rather, they are "problems in living, problems often created by blows of fate, by the damaging forces of a racist, sexist, ageist society" (Albee, 1980, p. 70). Prevention views dysfunctional behavior, whether individual or family, as an outgrowth of multiple factors interacting to place groups of individuals at risk. One of these factors is the impact of stress on each person's life. From stress theory, the idea emerges that harmful stress (distress) might be managed, avoided, or eliminated. Thoughts also develop that you and I, our family, and our friends can gather strength to first cope with and then adapt to circumstances that cruel twists of fate fling across the path that humans walk (Hollister, 1977). How might we enrich Hill's "B factor" of family coping strength? The answer is found in the technology that preventionists use to promote emotional health and to discourage emotional illness in society.

The technology of prevention consists of four tools that are used to fashion a healthier environment (Adams & Gullotta, 1983; Gullotta, 1982, in press). These tools are education, community organization/systems intervention, competency promotion, and natural caregiving. These tools have overlapping boundaries, and well-planned prevention programs practice elements of all four (see Table 2-4).

## *Education*

Of all the tools of prevention, education is the most widely used. The belief behind education is that by increasing our knowledge we can change attitudes and behavior that hurt ourselves or others. Education can be used to ease the passage from one life event to another; information can be given to individuals to enhance their well-being. Whether in the form of the spoken word, a visual image, and/or printed material, education has three uses as a prevention tool.

**TABLE 2-4.** *The tools of prevention: Selected examples and desired outcomes*

| Tool | Examples | Desired Outcomes |
|---|---|---|
| Education | | |
| • Public information | Public service announcements, printed material, films, curricula | Avoid harmful stressors, manage stressors |
| • Anticipatory guidance | Preretirement planning, death education, childbirth preparation classes | Manage stressors, build resistance to a stressor, avoid harmful stressors |
| • Behavioral approaches | Biofeedback, yoga, Transcendental Meditation | Manage stressors, avoid harmful stressors |
| Community organization/ systems intervention | | |
| • Modification/removal of institutional practice barriers | Institution of new practices, such as birthing rooms, or a change in old practices, such as permitting fathers in the delivery room | Eliminate stressors |
| • Community resource development | Neighborhood associations, rehabilitation of housing stock | Eliminate stressors, manage stressors, avoid stressors |
| • Legislative or judicial action | Civil rights legislation, taxpayer groups, consumer protection laws | Avoid stressors, eliminate stressors, manage stressors |
| Competency promotion | | |
| • Active approaches | Wilderness schools, art theater programs | Build resistance to a stressor |
| • Passive approaches | Affective education, assertiveness training | |
| Natural caregiving | | |
| • Indigenous caregivers | Lawyers, hairdressers, bartenders, friends | Manage stressors, build resistance to a stressor |
| • Trained indigenous caregivers | Clergy, teachers | Manage stressors, build resistance to a stressor |
| • Mutual self-help | Parents Without Partners, widows/ widowers | Manage stressors, build resistance to a stressor |

The first of these is *public information*. This information awakens, alerts, and sensitizes us to hazardous situations that can affect our lives. For example, public service announcements about cigarette smoking are attempts to enlighten the public and to promote health. Education also includes books (like this one) that encourage you to take responsibility for your own life while sharing with you the findings that the social sciences can offer about individuals, relationships, and the family. Here, the intention is to alert you not only to potential hazards but to health-promoting activities as well. Public information can include films, roleplays, and classroom activities to impart to the learner new or improved skills for handling life.

Research is very clear on the point that all animals, including humans, desire some warn-

*SMOKING SPOILS YOUR LOOKS*

*How does this poster discourage smoking? To whom is this message directed? Why didn't the American Cancer Society simply present the fact that smoking is hazardous to your health? Do you think this poster was trying to contradict the media image of smokers?*

ing about an event before it happens (see Elliott & Eisdorfer, 1982). The time between the warning and the actual occurrence permits us to gather emotional resources to handle the event. Preventionists call the educational technique that builds these resources *anticipatory guidance*. Anticipatory guidance may take as simple a form as printed material that explains an upcoming life event, like the booklet *Caring About Kids* (1981) by the National Institute of Mental Health (NIMH), which explains divorce to young chil-

dren. Or it may involve a mixture of print, film, and lecture material, like that used by health organizations teaching expectant parents about childbirth and the infant.

Finally, some educational approaches use *behavioral techniques* to promote increased self-awareness. This category includes such approaches as biofeedback, progressive relaxation, and Eastern meditational philosophies. These techniques provide informational feedback that permits individuals to acquire the skills to cope with life.

**?** *List the educational messages you have seen or heard recently that encouraged behavioral change to promote health or prevent illness. Share this list with your classmates. What are the issues of concern in these messages?*

## Community Organization/Systems Intervention

The ability to live life effectively is sometimes impeded by forces beyond one's personal abilities. Such forces impede or limit access to life options and opportunities. The second tool of prevention is used to redress these inequities. Obstructions can be removed in any of three ways.

Where obstructions exist because of the institutional practices or policies of an organization, individuals can work to *modify or remove institutional barriers*. One example that has been successful is the pressure exerted by expectant parents and some medical professionals to permit the husband to accompany his wife into the delivery room and witness (or assist in) the birth of their child.

A second area for community organization/ systems intervention (CO/SI) behavior is *community resource development*. Here the activity is focused on achieving a more equitable distribution of power to improve the standard of living of a group of people within a community. Neighborhood associations and community-owned, community-directed operations to rehabilitate housing stock are two examples.

The third activity within the domain of CO/SI activity is *legislative or judicial action*. This is the most controversial of the three approaches because it involves a change in the balance of political power in the direction of empowering the weak. And lately the buzzword *empowerment* has fallen on hard times. Those who need to be "empowered" have fallen even harder. The preventionist recognizes that the families who fill the rosters of clinics and hospitals come predominantly from the leagues of the powerless, the disenfranchised, the helpless, and the hopeless. Lack of power itself has been suggested as a major stress in these people's lives: "Every research study we examined suggested that major

sources of human stress and distress generally involve some form of excessive power [over the powerless] . . . it is enough to suggest the hypothesis that a dramatic reduction and control of power might improve . . . mental health" (Kessler & Albee, 1977, pp. 379–380). If one of the keys to explaining dysfunction is a lack of power, then organizing and mobilizing a group for the purposes of acquiring power in a free society is a necessary and legitimate function of prevention activity (see Box 2-2). Such initiatives have been undertaken by the American Civil Liberties Union, Mothers Against Drunk Drivers, the National Organization for Women, and the National Association for the Advancement of Colored People, among others. These organizations are attempting, through legislative and judicial means, to put teeth into the phrase *equality of opportunity*.

 *Do you think each of us has a responsibility for promoting equality of opportunity?*

## Competency Promotion

Competency promotion activities promote a feeling of being a part of, rather than apart from, society. They encourage feelings of worth, care for others, and belief in oneself. Encouraging such "pride" promotes increased self-esteem, an internal locus of control, and community interest rather than self-interest. Activities such as affective education and assertiveness training are both education and competency promotion tools. They are also examples of *passive approaches* to competency promotion. Passive approaches involve group activities of a classroom nature. They differ from the activities typically undertaken by wilderness schools, Scouting, 4-H, and arts programs. These programs teach skills like climbing, canoeing, or stage-set construction and acting but emphasize, first and

*Legislative action to produce social change is one of prevention's most important tools.*

# Misconceptions about Community Organization/Systems Intervention

The following passage is taken from a paper by George Albee and Thomas Gullotta (in press) entitled "Fallacies and Facts about Primary Prevention." We have included it to further place into perspective the important role that community organization/systems intervention plays in reducing distress and promoting competence.

## MISCONCEPTION

Preventionists really are trying to radicalize the political and economic system under the guise of efforts at prevention. Just because there is a correlation between the level of poverty and the rate of emotional disturbances, and between powerlessness and depression, and between marginal status in society and high rates of disturbance, these correlations do not prove causation (see Lamb & Zusman, 1979). Both poverty *and* mental disorder may be due to common causes: genetic, constitutional, biochemical, and/or other internal defects.

## CLARIFICATION

One of the most frequent arguments heard from those who oppose efforts at primary prevention denies the importance of social factors in causation. The higher rates of psychopathology observed among poor people are shrugged off as correlations that do not prove causation.

Several epidemiological observations, however, support the importance of poverty and/or powerlessness as a major causative factor in emotional disturbance. One of these arguments is apparent from historical fact. As each successive immigrant group occupied the impoverished ghettos of our central cities, that particular group had the highest rates of mental retardation and mental disturbance (once called idiocy and lunacy). As each successive immigrant group moved up into the middle-class world, its rate of distress began to decline to the traditional middle-class rate, while the new arrivals in the slums showed excessively high rates. So at first there were the Irish, and then the Scandinavians, and then the Eastern European Jews, and then the Southern Italians. Today it is the Blacks, Chicanos, and Puerto Ricans who occupy the deteriorating cities. As each immigrant group, in turn, occupied the lowest rung on the economic ladder, its rate was highest. As it left the ghettos and joined the middle class, its rate fell. No changes occurred in group members' genes—but changes *did* occur in their economic security, self-esteem, coping skills, educational competence, and support systems. Is it too radical an idea to suggest that powerlessness is a cause of distress and that a redistribution of power may be preventive?

---

more important, interpersonal and community relationships. Because these activities involve action and are usually directed toward accomplishment of some task, they are called *active approaches*.

 *How do you think competence might be promoted for women, Blacks, children, the elderly, and Hispanics?*

## Natural Caregiving

On almost every issue, adults and youth turn not to professionals but to friends or others (bartenders, hairdressers, the clergy, gas-station attendants, and so on) for advice and guidance. Natural caregiving recognizes the ability within each of us to help a fellow human being. Natural caregiving extends beyond activities like those of helping another in similar straits (mutual self-help groups) to acknowledge the responsibility each of us has to fellow human beings (Cowen, 1982a). Natural caregiving involves behavior such as the sharing of knowledge, the sharing of experiences, compassionate understanding, companionship, and, when necessary, confrontation. Such caregiving is a reference point for people to acknowledge that they are an important part of an emotional network (system) that extends beyond family members and friends to all people.

Some of us may choose professions in which we become **trained indigenous caregivers,** such as teachers and the clergy. Others of us will sometime in our lives join a **mutual self-help group** to give and receive help from others who find themselves in similar straits—for example, as a widow or widower, as a divorced parent, or as an individual recovering from a serious physical or emotional illness. Regardless of the circumstance, it is vital to remember that each of us is an **indigenous caregiver** with a responsibility to assist his or her fellow human beings.

 *Do you think that each of us has a responsibility for assisting a fellow human being in need?*

### Wellness and You

The scope of prevention extends from the individual to the family and to society at large. The ways you cope with stress and help others to cope with stress have an effect that reaches well beyond your family and friends.

In your lifetime, you will be touched by many stressful events. Here we try to lay the groundwork for how you will respond, to teach you how to identify and strengthen your resources. At the end of each of the remaining chapters in this book is a section called "Promoting Family Wellness." In each of these sections we give you a task: to design a personal, family, or at-risk[1] prevention program to promote health and reduce stress. Each exercise will increase your ability to cope with stress, your own and that of others.

Box 2-3 contains a worksheet than can help you accomplish each task. Use it as a guide, but don't be limited by its form. The worksheet is only a jumping-off point, a first stop on your journey to individual and family wellness. It will help you to brainstorm ways of handling stresses that will accompany events yet to come in your life. Use it creatively to find means of strengthening "B" factors beyond those we suggest. Incidentally, we would be most interested in hearing about your approaches to problems in living, and we encourage you to forward your ideas to us through our publisher.

## SUMMARY

The family is a complex system. The theories that try to explain that system—its internal and external interactions—focus on different aspects of the family unit. Some claim family behavior can be analyzed and predicted in terms of the individual; others, in terms of the family environment; still others, in terms of the social environment. Developmental theory tries to integrate key elements from other theories into a single explanation of family behavior.

Stress theory looks at the family in terms of its reaction to critical events. It suggests that family members have the resources to manage stress or

---

[1] *At risk* means that a group has a significantly greater than average chance of experiencing some dysfunction. For example, research shows that unemployment disproportionately affects certain socioeconomic groups in the United States. Those groups would be considered at higher risk for the various mental health problems that often follow unemployment.

## BOX 2-3
*A Primary Prevention Worksheet*

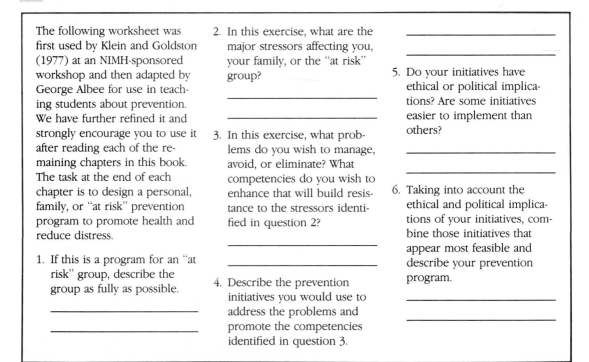

The following worksheet was first used by Klein and Goldston (1977) at an NIMH-sponsored workshop and then adapted by George Albee for use in teaching students about prevention. We have further refined it and strongly encourage you to use it after reading each of the remaining chapters in this book. The task at the end of each chapter is to design a personal, family, or "at risk" prevention program to promote health and reduce distress.

1. If this is a program for an "at risk" group, describe the group as fully as possible.

_____

_____

2. In this exercise, what are the major stressors affecting you, your family, or the "at risk" group?

_____

_____

3. In this exercise, what problems do you wish to manage, avoid, or eliminate? What competencies do you wish to enhance that will build resistance to the stressors identified in question 2?

_____

_____

4. Describe the prevention initiatives you would use to address the problems and promote the competencies identified in question 3.

_____

_____

5. Do your initiatives have ethical or political implications? Are some initiatives easier to implement than others?

_____

_____

6. Taking into account the ethical and political implications of your initiatives, combine those initiatives that appear most feasible and describe your prevention program.

_____

_____

even to eliminate it entirely. That belief forms the basis of the prevention movement. With education, intervention, competency promotion, and caregiving, we can not only manage emotional disturbance but prevent it. We all have the ability to promote our own emotional health and the emotional health of those we love. And we have a larger responsibility as well: to promote a healthy societal environment.

## MAJOR POINTS TO REMEMBER

1. Theories are not facts, but assumptions about how something operates. For a theory to be useful, its assumptions for predicting or analyzing behavior must be applicable over many varying circumstances.

2. Explanations of behavior that focus on the individual and view behavior as emerging from within the person are called psychological theories. Two examples of this school of thought are psychoanalytic and social-learning theory.

3. Explanations of behavior that focus on the interaction between the individual and his or her environment are called social-psychological theories. Two examples are symbolic interaction and social exchange theory.

4. Explanations of behavior that focus on the influence of social structure and society on behavior are called sociocultural theories. Two examples of this school of thought are structural-functionalism and general systems theory.

5. Developmental theory attempts to create a comprehensive model capable of explaining family behavior. It does this by borrowing several theoretical concepts from other theories.
6. *Stress* can be understood to mean any change in life. Some life events (stressors) produce stress that is beneficial (eustress). Other life events produce stress that is harmful (distress).
7. The general adaptation syndrome is a three-stage model of the effects of overwhelming stress on an organism. The stages are alarm, resistance, and exhaustion.
8. The ABCX stress model attempts to explain how families function under stress. In this model, *A* is the life event causing the stress, *B* is the family's resources for dealing with the stress, *C* is the meaning attached to the event, and *X* is the crisis.
9. Primary prevention is synonymous with wellness. It is concerned with lowering the incidence of family problems in society and with promoting family health.
10. Prevention uses four tools to prevent dysfunction and promote health: education, community organization/systems intervention, competency promotion, and natural caregiving. Each of these tools has subcomponents.

# ADDITIONAL SOURCES OF INFORMATION

The proceedings of the annual Vermont Conference on the Primary Prevention of Psychopathology (VCPPP) are highly recommended. The series is available from the University Press of New England, located in Hanover, New Hampshire. Also recommended is the conference itself, held each year in Burlington, Vermont. Information on the conference can be obtained by writing to VCPPP at Dewey Hall, Department of Psychology, University of Vermont, Burlington, Vt. 05045.

Each fall the National Council on Family Relations offers a family-theory development institute before its annual meeting. Those interested in this topic area can write to the council at 1219 University Ave. SE, Minneapolis, Minn. 55414 for information.

## *Publications*

Fields, S. (1978). Gloucester: An epitaph for adolescent apathy. *Innovations, 5*(2), 16–22.

Gottlieb, B. H. (1981). *Social networks and social support.* Beverly Hills, CA: Sage.

Gullotta, T. P. (Ed.). (in press). *Prevention's Technology.* New York: Human Sciences Press.

*Journal of Primary Prevention,* Human Sciences Press, 72 Fifth Ave., New York, NY 10011.

Kay, R. (Ed.). (1983). *Plain talk about mutual help groups.* NIMH, DHEW Pub. No. (ADM) 83-1138. Washington, DC: U. S. Government Printing Office.

Klein, D. C., & Goldston, S. E. (Eds.). (1977). *Primary prevention: An idea whose time has come.* NIMH, DHEW Pub. No. (ADM) 77-447. Washington, DC: U. S. Government Printing Office.

## *Organizations*

National Self-Help Clearinghouse
33 West 42nd St., Rm. 1227
New York, NY 10036
212-840-7606

# 3

# UNDERSTANDING RESEARCH ON MARRIAGE AND THE FAMILY

***Several years ago*** one of the authors took a course from a well-known expert on social perception. One day, at the beginning of class, two men burst into the room, one evidently chasing the other at gunpoint. As the two men ran in front of the students, the one in front looked very frightened, while the one behind him looked very threatening. As you might imagine, all of us in the classroom were more than a little unnerved as the two left the room. Our professor, by now having stopped his lecture, quieted the class down and asked us "What have you just seen?" Over 65% of the class were willing to testify that they had just seen a man being threatened by another man with a gun. Of that 65%, approximately 80% would have been willing to testify to that observation in court. However, the object that was perceived to be a gun was in fact a banana! This little classroom experiment powerfully illustrated how observations can mislead. Nonetheless, observation is the basic process from which social facts are derived. In fact, it is the foundation of science itself.

Each of us, throughout life, has many opportunities to observe naturally occurring events, and from our observations we formulate notions about human behavior. Although these experiences provide us with a wealth of information about human behavior, we tend to be selective in what we see, hear, taste, or touch—ignoring or missing things that are not of interest to us.

Babbie (1979) comments that the keen perception we all imagine ourselves to have may be imperfect because of our human limitations. Personal bias, beliefs, or stereotypes can cause us to see only what we wish to see. Human observers also have a tendency to overgeneralize. From one or two observations we often assume that the observed behavior occurs more frequently than it actually does. To minimize such errors in

And these observations and conclusions provide the social facts that were used in writing this textbook. Let's continue next by reviewing some of the basic principles of all social science research.

*What do you see in this drawing? While each of us has his or her own unique frame of reference, scientific research is based on certain assumptions that try to bring a unified view to an issue of study. Incidentally, do you see an old woman or a young woman in the drawing?*

*In interacting with your own family, how do you try to reduce or eliminate perceptual biases or misperceptions about other family members? How might professionals (such as family therapists or family researchers) try to minimize perceptual errors in gathering data?*

observation, family relations specialists turn to the scientific process and its basic research methodology.

Because this book is based on social facts, we have prepared this brief chapter to outline the most common techniques of observing and studying social behavior. The chapter gives you a general background on the most used methods of studying family and social relations. These methods (commonly called "data-collection techniques") are the scientific foundation on which social and family relations experts have developed their observations and conclusions.

## FOUR PRINCIPLES OF SOCIAL SCIENCE

The social scientific process is the application of logic to the collection of social facts considered to reflect behavior. The reasoning used in this process is based on four assumptions.

### *Social Regularity*

All human behavior is thought to be lawful. *Lawful* means that when all things are equal, people will behave in identical ways under the same social conditions. Thus, behavior is subject to scientific inquiry—the process of establishing laws, which are descriptive statements of the causes of events. A simple example is that if one drops an apple, it will fall to the ground. It will not fall up or sideways but always down. Just as objects obey the laws of physics, human behavior is thought to obey laws based on genetic and social conditions.

In the search for the laws of human behavior, the process of scientific inquiry assumes that human behavior has a type of social regularity and therefore that repeated experimentation will result in replicable findings if the experiments are performed under the same conditions. Repeated testing under the same conditions should, if social regularity exists, result in similar effects in human behavior. Thus, experimental replication, based on the belief in social regularity, is a fundamental technique underlying the scientific process.

## Cause and Effect versus Association

Social regularity exists in two basic forms. It appears in the form of a simple association or in the form of cause and effect. When two behaviors are repeatedly found to occur together, but neither has been shown to cause the other, social regularity is said to exist in the form of an association (sometimes called a "correlation"). For example, one commonly reported association is that divorce is associated with psychological distress. Divorce does not necessarily mean distress, but the two do often go together. Typically, associations, or correlations, reflect the occurrence of two behaviors because of some unknown third factor that accounts for their joint manifestation. For example, divorce may be associated with distress because of the financial problems that follow divorce, or it may be due to any of a number of other factors, such as conflict, moving, new identity formation, or child-care demands.

The second and more complex form of social regularity is cause and effect. What is the actual cause of a behavior? What factor must precede the occurrence of a behavior? In social behaviorist terms, what is the "stimulus" (S) that temporally precedes the "response" (R)? Associations are based on a temporal form of regularity. That is, all we can really say when we speak of an association is that two variables (such as divorce and distress) occur at about the same time; we cannot speak to their cause. However, in causality the antecedent/consequence (cause/effect) relation is based on the assumption that the cause (antecedent) must always precede the ef-

fect (consequence). For example, to prove that a causal relation exists between divorce and distress, we would have to show that a divorce always precedes (comes before) distress. It is unfortunate but true that much of our current understanding of social behavior is based on evidence for associations rather than for cause and effect. For obvious ethical reasons, we are unable, where human beings are involved, to create experimental conditions that allow us to measure cause and effect.

Two types of causation are acceptable in contemporary social science. **Material causation** is causation of behaviors by internal forces—for example, neurological, genetic, or physiological factors. We know, for instance, that some venereal disease, if left untreated, can cause severe emotional dysfunctions. **Efficient causation** is causation of behaviors by forces in the environment. For example, social conditions in the family, sensory stimulation, or other aspects of one's social or physical environment can elicit, inhibit, or facilitate various social behaviors. We believe, for instance, that societal sexism can be a major contributing factor to depression in women; unemployment can contribute significantly to family violence and stress; and grief and loneliness may motivate suicide. In each of these examples the cause is some social environmental condition. It is to efficient causation that much of our attention in this textbook is turned.

## Operationalization

Fundamental to the scientific process is the assumption that all behaviors and social processes can be clearly defined, or operationalized. **Operationalization** refers to a clear and concise definition of (1) the research variable, (2) its basic elements, and (3) its measurability. To test predictions about behavior, the researcher must define each research variable by using clear and concise definitions in a way that allows accurate measurement.

In the operationalization process, the researcher typically begins by formulating a **hypothesis.** A hypothesis is a statement about the relation between two or more variables in the form of either an association or cause and effect. That is, the researcher can either predict an association without making reference to causation or predict that the occurrence of one variable is necessary for the occurrence of the other. The next step is experimentation, in which the researcher studies the effect of an **independent variable** on a **dependent variable.** Typically, the independent variable, in the context of experimentation, takes the form of some type of experimental stimulus. Many times it consists in a contrast between a treatment group and a control group; in this case the stimulus is the treatment. Other times it involves comparing two levels of the experimental stimulus treatment (for example, low support versus high support). The dependent variable is the behavior that is thought to change or occur because of the effects of the independent variable (experimental stimulus treatment). The following example illustrates the use of independent and dependent variables in experimentally testing a hypothesis. Family therapists generally assume that communication skills enhance marital satisfaction. Therefore, it could be hypothesized that improved communication skills for couples in marriage counseling will result in higher perceived marital satisfaction. The independent variable in an experiment to test this hypothesis would be communication skills training for one group of couples (the "experimental group") and no treatment for the other group (the "control group"). The dependent variable would be a measure of marital satisfaction. The experimental group would be expected to show improved marital satisfaction, while the control group would not be expected to improve on the dependent-variable measure.

## Reliability and Validity

The scientific process requires that both the independent and the dependent variable be measured with acceptable levels of reliability and validity. **Reliability** is the trustworthiness of the measures we use to assess the levels of the variables. For instance, in the experiment just described, marital satisfaction might be assessed by a questionnaire that the spouses complete. If people's answers tend to be very similar or identical when they fill out the questionnaire on different occasions, the questionnaire is said to have high reliability, but if their answers differ greatly from one time to the next even though other conditions remain the same, we say the measure has low reliability.

**Validity** concerns whether a measure actually measures what it is supposed to. Two kinds of validity must be considered, internal and external. If our questionnaire turned out not to measure marital satisfaction very well, it would have low **internal validity. External validity** means that the measure applies, or "generalizes," to the whole population we are interested in. Perhaps the questionnaire assesses marital satisfaction well for couples with young children but not so well for couples with no or grown children. Then its external validity would be inadequate for drawing conclusions about the latter kind of couples.

Internal and external validity are characteristics of whole research studies as well as of measures of variables. They are assured by designing studies carefully. The internal validity of a study assures us that the independent variable, rather than some unknown third variable (called a "confounding variable"), causes the effect. External validity tells us that what we learn from an experiment is generalizable to the whole population of interest. It is obtained by using random samples of known population groups—in the

## BOX 3-1
## *Transhistorical History?*

Kenneth Gergen (1980) argues that many research findings reflect a type of "historical relativity": researchers find patterns in child development or family relations that are not generalizable to other places or times. He proposes, for example, that "developmental trajectories may be largely traced to the accidental composite of existing circumstances" (p. 37). Thus, a unique set of social, economic, cultural, and per-sonal conditions influences the behavior of each generation of families, and no similar set of conditions can be present for another generation. Therefore, we can never replicate our findings. If Gergen is right, our understanding of human behavior is *historically situated.*

Gergen's argument can be seen as placing the social scientist into the primary role of historian. We can describe behavior, but we can only spec-ulate on its explanation. Replication is difficult if not impossible. Social regularity or lawfulness may exist, but social/cultural change makes stability and replication unlikely. Can you think of other significant problems that arise from Gergen's argument that might make it difficult to understand families? For further reading on this issue we recommend Gergen (1973, 1976, 1980).

experiment just described this would be certain types of couples.

*Explain how you would operational-ize your favorite theory from Chapter 2 to examine the question "How do family communication problems neg-atively influence family relations?" Develop a hypothesis and determine whether it addresses a cause-and-effect assumption.*

### *Summary*

The process of scientific inquiry is built on the belief that there is social regularity, which results in consistent (replicable) association and cause-and-effect relations. To test for these regularities (or laws), the researcher must operationalize the hypothesized relations through the use of inde-pendent and dependent variables. To do so, one must measure the variables with concern for the reliability and validity of the measurement.

*Why is social regularity important to understanding behaviors in families? If social regularity does not exist, can one be certain of reliability? Lawful-ness? Replicability? Why or why not?*

## THEORIES AS FRAMES OF REFERENCE

Good scientific inquiry is ideally conducted within the guidelines of a particular theory, or frame of reference. How does a theory provide a frame of reference for researchers? Foremost, a theory defines meaningful behaviors, the social processes that predict those behaviors, and the central concerns of study. Further, a theory pro-vides direction for how "truth" should be sought by telling us what research methods should be used to seek social facts to support the theoreti-cal predictions. Thus, a theory provides the crite-ria for establishing facts that support or refute hypotheses. More specifically, a theory establishes the appropriate methodology (or data-collection technique) for testing hypotheses that emerge from a research problem.

Of the numerous theories that apply to the study of families, each has not only particular independent and dependent variables of interest but also preferred research methodologies for gathering social facts. For example, psychological theories emphasize the importance of drives and motivational states. To study such aspects of personality, clinical research methods are used to detect individual differences in internal drives and motivations. These personality differences are then used to predict differences in family behaviors and interactions. Conversely, the family may be studied to assess the effects of socialization on personality.

In social-psychological theories, the focus is on social relationships in the family. For example, subscribers to social exchange theory study social interactions with an eye to exchange of resources. A common research methodology is to study family members' perceptions of rewards and costs in family relations and interactions. When personal costs and rewards are in balance, personal satisfaction results. However, when one person perceives that he or she is giving more than the other, a sense of inequity occurs. Researchers focus on how individuals try to regain equity in these inequitable conditions.

A final illustration of how theories serve as frames of reference is the highly complex theoretical perspective of general systems theory. Systems theory looks at the complex interrelationships within the family. It focuses on the general boundaries established by the family and on communications within the family system. Marriage and family therapists frequently draw on this framework in working with positively and negatively functioning families. Through direct observations of family behavior and self-report questionnaires or clinical interviews, families may be categorized as belonging to one of various types. Particular aspects of the family system, such as cohesion and adaptability (Olson, et al. 1983), are assessed to identify communication styles, interpersonal demands, or family resources. Family types are then compared on their effectiveness in meeting members' needs.

In summary, the role of theory is to provide a frame of reference that focuses the researcher on relevant social processes and research variables. Each theoretical frame of reference defines researchable problems and specifies appropriate ways to collect social facts (data).

 *Can good research be done without a theoretical perspective? When?*

# RESEARCH METHODS FOR STUDYING FAMILIES

But how do researchers actually test their theories of how families work and assess their prevention efforts? To avoid the problems associated with casual observation, such as observer bias and the tendency to generalize too readily from a small number of observations, researchers turn to the scientific process and its basic research methods. Thus, family relations specialists gather data systematically and, if possible, assess them experimentally. The four most common general strategies for gathering data are questionnaires or interviews, direct observation, experimentation, and evaluation. Each technique has its strengths and limitations.

## Questionnaires and Interviews

Most data about families are collected through surveys or interviews. A survey questionnaire is typically a series of prearranged questions to which a person is to respond. Questions are ei-

*What are some of the advantages and disadvantages of using interviewers to collect data for study?*

ther "open ended" or "closed ended" (Adams & Schvaneveldt, 1985). Open-ended questions ask subjects to respond in their own words—for example, "What activities do you see yourself most responsible for in the daily care of your children?" The open-ended question has the advantages of allowing free expression and encouraging the respondent to provide breadth and depth in a response. The primary disadvantages are that unless motivation to respond is high, the response rate may be low or the questionnaire may be only partly completed.

The closed-ended questionnaire is more common. Each question consists of a "stem" followed by two or more choices, such as "yes/no," "true/false," or "agree/disagree/no opinion." Adams and Schvaneveldt (1985) list the major advantages of the closed-ended format: (1) it is easy to complete, (2) it can be finished quickly, (3) it is specific, (4) it can provide more objectivity, and (5) it is easier to score, code, and tabu-late than the open-ended survey. The primary disadvantage is that the respondent may respond without carefully contemplating each alternative.

The interview, in contrast to the questionnaire, brings the researcher and the subject face to face. The interviewer becomes an important component of the research process. This person needs to be warm and friendly, socially skilled, accurate, and sensitive in asking questions and must avoid giving cues that influence the respondent's answers (experimenter bias). As in the survey, interview questions may be open- or closed-ended.

There are two basic types of interview. The focused interview seeks very specific information. Typically, certain types of respondents are sought out because of their experience with some event or function. For example, a focused interview might be used to compare marital relations in traditional families in which wives stay home with those in families in which wives work outside the home. Another format is the nondirective interview, in which the process is fluid and open. The areas of discussion are controlled by the respondent, who provides feelings, ideas, and information on any topic associated with the general research area.

Advantages of interviewing include the opportunity to discuss the purpose of the study with the respondent, the opportunity to establish rapport and trust, the opportunity to probe and clarify, and a higher probability of obtaining sensitive and personal information.

Questionnaires and interviews can be used in combination to study family relations issues. One study that used both was the *National Statistical Survey on Runaway Youth* (1976). Approximately 14,000 homes containing adolescents aged 10–17 were studied to obtain data on child-rearing patterns, schooling issues, psychological characteristics of family members, and so on. Comparisons were then made among youths who had run away from home and were still on the run or at a runaway shelter, runaways who had returned, and youths who had never run away. Problems associated with family relations, supervision, conflict, and peer relations, were found to be more common in the homes of adolescents in the first two categories.

## Observation

Interviews and questionnaires provide self-reported information about behavior, but what people say they do isn't necessarily what they actually do. In the study of many behaviors (particularly more public or common behaviors), observational studies may provide the most direct objective information. Indeed, many classic studies of the family have included direct observation. One need only turn to such work as Margaret Mead's *Coming of Age in Samoa* (1928), Ruth Benedict's *Patterns of Culture* (1946), Masters and Johnson's *Human Sexual Response* (1966), or Oscar Lewis' *Five Families: Mexican*

*Case Studies in the Culture of Poverty* (1959) to find excellent illustrations of observational research.

When direct observation is possible, it is always preferred. If the behavior the researcher wishes to study is likely to occur in public places, or if semicontrolled conditions can be developed to observe the natural occurrence of the behavior, then observation can and should be used to study family members and the behavior. Four types of observation have been used in studying the family—participant, naturalistic, field, and laboratory observations.

*Participant observation.* **Participant observation** research, one of the earliest forms of observational data collection, emerged from ethnography. Researchers using this strategy enter the social world of their subjects, live with them, listen to them, and ask questions, seeking the dynamics underlying human behavior, family relations, norms, and more. The observers either announce their intent openly or infiltrate a group much as a spy would. Generally, an open statement of research intent is preferred. However, the study of deviant or socially undesirable behaviors makes it impossible to openly state a research intent, because the subjects would not then manifest the behavior.

Participant observers develop an intimate and intense relationship with their subjects. Adams and Schvaneveldt (1985) describe the major phases of such research: (1) a surface encounter in which initial contacts are made, (2) the development of rapport, (3) an acceptance of meaningful roles and interpersonal exchange, and (4) a phase of trust and sharing.

Laud Humphreys' (1970) classic study of homosexual behavior is an excellent example of the participant-observer method. Humphreys used this technique to study impersonal sexual exchanges between men in public restrooms. In so doing he was able to provide a sensitive description of the psychodynamics of sexual behavior between men. We recommend reading his work to appreciate the complexity of participant observation. We also recommend Freeman's (1983) *Margaret Mead and Samoa* for an appreciation of the difficulty of completing such research with sensitivity, reliability, and validity. The author reexamines Mead's early work to illustrate how invalid conclusions may be drawn even from the work of this century's most notable participant observer. Although many of Freeman's criticisms can be questioned, his book is an excellent source for appreciating the strengths and limitations of this observation method.

*Naturalistic observation.* Another technique of observation study is **naturalistic observation.** The researcher, avoiding any tampering with the family's normal environment, observes the subjects' particular behaviors. This technique differs from participant observation in that the researcher follows a detailed observational rating form. Behaviors are counted, their duration is timed, the latency between events or behaviors is measured. Generally, formal hypotheses are constructed and observations used to confirm or disconfirm the proposed relation between an event and a behavior.

For example, one could use naturalistic observation to study communication patterns between family members during family reunions. It might be hypothesized that siblings would make more frequent and longer contacts with one another than with other family members and thus represent the strongest social support within an extended kin network. Through observing interactions between relatives at several family reunions, one could compare frequency and duration of social contact between siblings and other relatives to test the hypothesis.

*Field observation.* The observer/researcher may at times need to manipulate subjects' environment in a field setting to test a hypothesis.

For example, the researcher may vary the physical setting to create differing psychological effects. Two or more environments might be created to provide differences in the physical distance between two family members. The researcher would record the type of communication that occurred in the distant and the close home environments.

*Laboratory observation.* In the **laboratory observation** study, different environments are created in a research laboratory. Subjects are then brought to the lab and observed in a controlled environment. Often couples or parent/child dyads (pairs) are given communication tasks and observed for particular behaviors. An ongoing study in our own labs illustrates this technique. Children who have been observed in preschool are identified as popular, moderately popular (average), or unpopular (isolated). To determine whether parental socialization styles may contribute to children's popularity, we bring the parents to our laboratory. In an observational setting we ask them to solve a puzzle task and to spend some unstructured play time with their child. Play styles and communication patterns are being analyzed to determine whether popular, average, and unpopular children come from homes where the mother and father use different parenting styles.

Observational data collection is limited by ethical constraints. In particular, the home has been considered a refuge from outside observation. Further, many behaviors within the family are so infrequent that it is far too expensive to use observational research. Nonetheless, many of the findings, principles, and conclusions offered throughout this book are based on research studies derived from observation.

## Experimentation

A much less frequently used technique in the study of families is **experimentation.** The basic experimental design involves a direct comparison of an experimental group and a control group. Although there are several variations, the basic strategy is as follows (see Figure 3-1).

Subjects are randomly placed in either the experimental group or the control group. Each group is given a pretest on the behavior of interest. Then the experimental group is given the research treatment, and the control group receives no such attention. After the experimental manipulation, both groups are given another (posttest) assessment. The logic is that if the experimental treatment actually causes a change in behavior, then the experimental group's posttest scores should exceed both its pretest scores and the control group's posttest scores.

A study of loneliness and its relation to social communication skills illustrates the use of experimentation. We have recently designed a study to test the hypothesis that if lonely people are given help in improving their social skills, they will develop expanded social networks and report less loneliness. We identified a group of lonely individuals. Half were randomly selected for a social skills training program, and the others were left on their own. Each subject was pretested on reported social relations and lone-

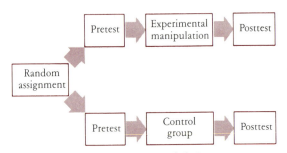

**FIGURE 3-1.** *Basic experimental design.*

liness. At the end of the training period, both groups were retested. If improving social skills does affect social relations, the experimental group should report increased social networks and decreased loneliness, while the control group should show no change.

The main strength of experimentation is its ability to directly test for cause-and-effect relations. Its major weaknesses are that it is expensive and that finding families willing to volunteer is sometimes difficult.

## Evaluation

Application of the scientific method to program management is called **evaluation.** Scientific ap-

CONTROL GROUP          OUT OF CONTROL GROUP

Although evaluating research reports can be very difficult, there are several simple things a reader can look for to estimate the quality of the research. We recommend asking the following questions:

1. Is there a conceptual or theoretical basis for the study? Are the objectives, hypotheses, or goals consistent with the theory or conceptualization?

2. Do the researchers provide information on the reliability and validity of their measures (observations, tests, scales)?

3. Is the sample representative of a larger population? Were subjects acquired through random selection from a population? Or were the subjects used only because they were available?

4. Are the conclusions consistent with the evidence (data)? Did the researchers actually test their hypotheses?

5. Do the researchers indicate their own limitations?

plications of interviews, questionnaires, observations, and experimentation are undertaken to improve program effectiveness, management, and cost effectiveness. Program evaluation of prevention or intervention efforts can be used to justify support through verifying program effects.

Social scientists design evaluation methods to determine whether program goals are being reached. They commonly use three types of evaluation. Some programs hire an evaluator to engage in continuous evaluation, in which both the outcome and the impact of the program are assessed to determine its success. Sometimes, when a quick decision is required, a one-time evaluation can provide the necessary assessment, as in judging cost effectiveness or management practices. In addition, one-time evaluation can assist in making informed decisions on eliminating programs of high cost and low results or expanding low-cost, high-yield programs. Finally, policy research helps identify, through the evaluation process, new program directions. Policy research is usually undertaken to convince a legislature or funding source of need. Policy research reports frequently result in the formation of new agencies or the foundation of new prevention or intervention programs.

There is no single method used in evaluation. Any method can be adapted to evaluation research. However, three general conditions are needed if any method is to be effective: the program structure, operation, and management style must be known; the specific goals and proposed effects of the program must be clear; and the link of the program structure and operation to goals and effects must be stated. Unless these three conditions are met, it is unlikely that any connection between the program and its outcome can be correctly evaluated.

*When should a scientist draw on data from several methodologies to answer questions about family relationship problems?*

## LIMITS IN STUDYING FAMILIES

### *Access*

Although families abound on almost every street in America, access to them is difficult. The notion that the family is a haven, a refuge from the outside world, makes it difficult to study the family and its members. Further, unusual types of families are hard to locate and often sensitive about their uniqueness and uncertain about social scientists' intentions. For these and other reasons, the study of the family is frequently a hard and time-consuming task. Another problem is that we often become aware of family dynamics and relations through dysfunctional families who seek therapeutic help. Because they come out from behind their walls, we are able to observe and directly study their problems. However, well-functioning families seldom seek help. Therefore, we may at times know more about the limitations of a dysfunctional family than the strengths of a functionally well family.

### Ethics

Many important issues in social science remain unaddressed because of ethical constraints. Family relations specialists work under research codes of ethics that morally constrain their conduct and help to minimize psychological and physical risks for subjects. Subjects must be assured of confidentiality, freedom to withdraw at any point if they wish to, and a right to be informed of the intent of study. These factors limit the probability that multiple members of a family will complete any given study and that complete data sets will be obtained on a family.

Codes of ethics are a necessary and important part of research. They assure honesty and integrity in the research process. The constraints on a researcher are outweighed by the assurance of an open, fair, and safe experience for research participants.

### Implications

Our understanding of marital and family behavior has expanded dramatically in the recent past. Anthropologists, sociologists, psychologists, developmentalists, social workers, clinicians, and family life specialists all study the family. However, limited access to various types and forms of families creates gaps in our understanding, and ethical constraints make it impossible to address certain research questions. At times, consequently, we know less than we should. However, the creative application of research techniques to private issues such as child abuse, incest, divorce, and courtship is expanding our understanding and minimizing the limitations associated with problems of access and ethical constraints.

**?** *How might researchers minimize problems of access in the study of the family?*
*Why are ethics important to the scientific process?*

## SUMMARY

This brief introduction to how we study families is intended to establish an awareness that this text is founded on social science research. Research hypotheses are developed from varying conceptual and theoretical perspectives. These hypotheses are then assessed using one of the many available research methods (for example, questionnaire, interview, observation, or experiment). When findings are replicated, a scientific principle is proposed. This principle is presented either as the association between two or more behaviors or social constructs or as a cause-and-effect relation between an independent and a dependent variable.

In the preparation of this text, we have drawn on hundreds of published studies to describe, analyze, and explain individual and family behavior. These studies provide the social facts that we use to draw our conclusions. Therefore, our efforts are limited by the available research data and the strengths and limitations of each method. To gain deeper understanding of the research process in the study of the family, we provide at the end of this chapter a list of additional readings for further study.

## MAJOR POINTS TO REMEMBER

1. Each of us can err in our perceptions during direct observation experiences. Perceptual errors can arise from personal biases, beliefs, or stereotypes.
2. In the scientific process we gather social facts by using research methods that minimize errors in perceptions.
3. Social science is based on the assumptions that human behavior is lawful and regular, that cause-and-effect relations can be established, that all theoretical notions can be operationalized and measured, and that reliability and validity are underpinnings of good science.
4. Theory provides a useful frame of reference, important research variables, major research questions, and useful research methods.
5. Questionnaires are useful in gathering survey information. They can be presented in an open-ended format to gather respondents' ideas or in a closed-ended format to find out whether respondents agree with prestated opinions, perceptions, attitudes, or values.
6. Interviews require well-trained, socially competent interviewers. Like the open-ended questionnaire, the interview is useful in obtaining responses with breadth and depth. Interviews have the added strength that the researcher can prompt or question for clarification or elaboration.
7. Observation methods are available for use in families, social settings, and laboratory contexts. Observation is the preferred scientific method when circumstances allow. Observation techniques include participant, naturalistic, field, and laboratory observation.
8. Experimentation is necessary when studying questions of cause and effect. Unfortunately, it is the least used method in the study of the family because of ethical constraints.

## ADDITIONAL SOURCES OF INFORMATION

Adams, G. R., & Schvaneveldt, J. D. (1985). *Understanding research methods.* New York: Longman.

Babbie, E. (1979). *The practice of social research* (2nd ed.). Belmont, CA: Wadsworth.

Cook, T., & Campbell, D. (1979). *Quasi-experimentation: Design and analysis issues for field settings.* Boston: Houghton Mifflin.

McCain, G., & Segal, E. (1982). *The game of science* (4th ed.). Monterey, CA: Brooks/Cole.

Miller, B. (1985). *Family research methods.* Beverly Hills, CA: Sage.

Schulsinger, F., Mednick, S. A., & Knop, J. (Eds.) (1981). *Longitudinal research: Methods and uses in behavioral science.* Boston: Martinus Nijhoff.

Webb, E. J., Campbell, D. T., Schwartz, R. D., Sechrest, L., & Grove, J. B. (1981). *Nonreactive measures in the social sciences.* Boston: Houghton Mifflin.

*Part Two*

# IN THE BEGINNING

# 4

# SEX ROLES,
# THE FAMILY,
# AND SOCIETY

***Time was when*** women wore dresses—dresses that fit over corsets that enforced a stiff posture, impeded breathing, and made their wearers faint in the summer heat. Men wore pants. Time was when women spent their days and nights laundering, cleaning house, and cooking. Men wore that clean clothing, slept in those clean houses, and ate that cooking. Time was when women never aspired to greatness, struggled to be attractive but not seductive, and "knew their place." Notions of equity or equality were unthinkable.

Fortunately for all of us, times have changed. Signaling this change have been changes in our language, our attitudes, and our behavior. Terms like *male chauvinist, sexist,* and *feminist,* unknown a few years ago, are today in widespread use. Beliefs that women and men can aspire only to certain occupations have been soundly disproved. From women in space, on the U. S. Supreme Court, and at the wheels of trucking rigs to male homemakers, secretaries, and nurses, this decade is embarking on a new definition of what it means to be female or male.

What meaning do these changes have for families? How will family members be shaped by these new—and, to some, disturbing—mores? How should parents deal with their children's sex-role development? How does sex-typing occur and what effect does it have on social relations within the family? In this chapter we will explore such questions and more, beginning with a historical overview of sex roles.

## HISTORICAL DEVELOPMENT OF SEX ROLES

### Masculinity and Femininity

Where have our concepts of sex roles come from? Notions of femininity and masculinity have

*In the 1800s a woman's role in the family was to be firetender, nurturer, cook, and spiritual model. How have women's roles changed today?*

their foundation in historical concepts of womanhood and manhood. Womanhood during the 18th and 19th centuries meant purity of heart, soul, and body. "Impurity" in a woman was seen as unnatural and unfeminine. In fact, nonvirginal unmarried women were considered fallen.

Women were also portrayed as holding virtuous expectations of submission and dependency in marriage. The religious order proclaimed man to be independent, the authority, the leader, and thus woman's superior. It was thought that, by God's design, a truly feminine woman needed a protector, for she was naturally weak and timid. In public addresses of the 1800s, male leaders urged women to recognize their inferiority, submit to it freely, and be grateful for the support of their men. To behave or even to think otherwise would lead others to believe a woman was not pure of heart. A woman was

expected to submerge herself and her talents in labors of love solely for her husband and children. At times that could mean the attempted reformation of her husband's occasional immorality (for example, drunkenness), but even here only through her grace and her role as spiritual model.

In the 1700s and 1800s a woman was to be a guardian of the home. She was to fulfill her feminine function through beauty, love, gentleness, cheerfulness, and mercy. She was expected to avoid knowledge from books that would corrupt her. In order to fulfill this role, she was expected to enter into marriage and maintain a total commitment to her husband; while he governed the home by law, she was expected to assist by gentle persuasion. Thus, womanhood has been associated with nurturance, intimacy, and expressiveness. Manhood has been associated with

PART TWO  IN THE BEGINNING

*Known by such names as the Deerslayer, La Longue Carabine, Hawkeye, and Pathfinder, James Fenimore Cooper's character* Natty Bumppo *is the archetypal American hero to American literary critics. Bumppo, in books published in the 1800s, defined the American male role. What does this scene from* The Last of the Mohicans *tell us about that role?*

independence, authority, and instrumental competence.

But how have social scientists actually studied the psychological side of such cultural norms and expectations? Culture-based expectations of sex-role characteristics have been documented and summarized in numerous ways (for example, Huston, 1983; Shepherd-Look, 1982). Extensive investigations have been completed using such measures as the Bem Sex Role Inventory (Bem, 1974) and the Personal Attributes Questionnaire (Spence, Helmreich, & Stapp, 1975). Early studies focused only on the socially desirable aspects of masculinity and femininity, ignoring the undesirable characteristics associated with each. In recent years this oversight has been addressed, and the resulting studies provide a

more accurate assessment of sex-typed behavior.

To illustrate, the adjectives on the Personal Attributes Questionnaire provide six general categories associated with masculinity and femininity. An overall masculine/feminine scale measures reported identification with or preference for a masculine or feminine sex-typed focus. For example, a masculine sex-typed person is likely to identify with such adjectives or phrases as *aggressive, dominant, worldly,* or *feelings not easily hurt.* However, masculinity and femininity have both socially desirable and undesirable components. Masculine characteristics include not only *active, independent,* and *self-confident* but also *egotistical, arrogant, boastful, hostile,* and *greedy.* Feminine characteristics include attributes such as *expressive, gentle, kind, hopeful,* and *empathetic* and negative ones such as *servile, spineless, gullible, whiny, nagging,* and *fussy.*

In summary, individuals internalize cultural expectations of womanhood or manhood as part of their sex-role concepts. Men and women can internalize varying degrees of masculine or feminine traits. In general, men have traditionally been strongly encouraged to identify with masculine traits, while women have been encouraged to identify with feminine traits. (See Box 4-1 for an illustration of how sex-role concepts can affect behavior in marriage.)

## *Androgyny*

As the old view of sex-role concepts has come to be challenged by the women's movement (Huston, 1983), new and broader definitions of sex-typing have emerged. Arguments have been advanced that the traditional concept of instrumental/task competence associated with maleness and emotional/expressive competence associated with femaleness need not be rigidly defined by gender. Rather, both men and women may internalize psychological attributes that are associated with both instrumental and expressive competence. Some individuals will assume a highly masculine or feminine sex-typing, and others will internalize some of both characteristics. Most researchers agree that internalization of the socially desirable attributes associated with masculinity and femininity, in the form of **androgyny,** results in a healthy and adaptive sex-role concept for men and women.

# SOCIETAL CHANGES IN SEX ROLES

Early historical views of womanhood and manhood were defined by very narrow sex-role expectations, but times have changed. As more and more people have deviated from traditional sex-

role expectations, society has become more tolerant of these deviations, as we shall observe in this section.

## *The Movement toward Role Sharing*

Is society moving toward a more **egalitarian** structure? One way to find out is to examine demographic changes in the general population. In the past, women were grounded in marriage and their work in the home. Their "duty" was to be homemakers and wives. A close look at a woman's "job description" would find the "traditional" wife cooking, washing, caring for the children and husband, providing a taxi service, and performing assorted domestic tasks (Bernard, 1974). Although none of these activities is demeaning, their low prestige value has generated the belief that "women's work" is inferior to "men's work." If all women are still expected to engage in only these behaviors, then clearly we have progressed no further than our 18th-century ancestors toward equity and egalitarianism in sex-role behavior.

Fortunately, the evidence points to the broadening of women's roles in modern society. As one example, women are marrying later, thus giving themselves more time for schooling and work experience (Lewis, 1978). With more education and greater work experience, women are likely to enter marriage with the expectation of sharing in decision making with their spouses.

Changes in societal expectations about sex-role behavior can also be determined by interview and survey techniques. For example, one recent study (Albrecht, Bahr, & Chadwick, 1979) found that adults (aged 18 to over 65) are more accepting of a wife's earning extra money for the family than earlier respondents. Even so, the working wife is still expected to fill the role of homemaker, child-care provider, and, to a somewhat lesser extent, maintainer of kinship ties. Though retaining some "traditional" practices, younger respondents are more accepting of

## BOX 4-1
### *Sex Roles and Division of Labor in Early Marriage*

A study by Jean Atkinson and Ted Huston (1984) illustrates how sex-role orientations influence division of labor in marriage. The researchers assessed the sex-role attitudes of 120 recently married couples and obtained information about household-task participation during nine phone calls to each participant. Tasks associated with shopping/errands, indoor maintenance, financial management, food preparation/cleanup, and outdoor chores were predetermined as feminine, masculine, or undifferentiated. Correlations were made between sex-role attitudes, employment patterns, and household activities. It was found that a traditional division of household labor went with (1) traditional employment patterns (husband employed, wife homemaker) and (2) traditional sex-typing of partners (masculine males, feminine females).

Can you see any strengths in the behavioral pattern that Atkinson and Huston found? Any limitations?

changes in family lifestyles than older respondents surveyed at the same time—more accepting of communal family arrangements, egalitarian dual-career families, part-time employment and/or part-time child-care duties for both spouses. These attitudes bear on the emotional health of married women, because working improves women's mental health and psychological well-being. A man who disapproves of his wife's employment can reduce the beneficial effects of employment for her, but a man who supports his wife's work and can contribute to child care promotes family well-being (Kessler & McRae, 1982).

Other studies have compared the attitudes and beliefs of parents and their children over the decades. Roper and LaBeff (1977), for example, sampled the views of adolescents and their parents in 1934 and in 1974. In 1974 both adolescents and parents accepted feminism or egalitarian role-sharing ideals for husbands and wives. Strong changes occurred on issues associated with economic and political/legal matters: women had made substantial gains through acceptance of equal rights. However, less movement toward egalitarianism was noted on the issue of household responsibilities. Roper and LaBeff suggest that while women are more likely than men to endorse the egalitarian role-sharing ideals of the feminist movement, *both* sexes remain relatively traditional in their beliefs about a woman's responsibility for home management and child care. As other studies have yielded similar findings, it must be concluded that only modest change toward egalitarianism can be found from such survey data (for example, see Scanzoni, 1976; Scanzoni & Fox, 1980; Tomeh, 1978).

A cautionary note should be inserted here. It is quite possible that we can learn more about changing sex roles in society by studying young people than by studying their parents (Carter & Patterson, 1982). Adults have already gone through their socialization process and are more likely to be committed to hard-and-fast sex-role notions. Children, however, are still experiencing intense socialization forces from family members, teachers, television, peers, and social institutions. Hence, comparing different generations of youths might provide more accurate information on changes in attitudes toward sex roles.

In fact, there is some support for this assumption. For example, in a recent comparison of high school seniors' responses between 1964 and 1975 on sex-role orientations in occupational choices, Lueptow (1981) concludes that 10–20% of these adolescents have liberalized their notions in an egalitarian direction. Although many adolescents remain highly traditional, the orientation of girls toward a limited number of traditionally female sex-typed occupations has lessened. Additional evidence gathered by Kreidberg, Butcher, and White (1978), Kenkel and Gage (1983), and Herzog and Bachman (1982) corroborates this conclusion.

Using a longitudinal data source, Thornton, Alwin, and Camburn (1983) found a definite trend toward egalitarian sex-role concepts among women during the 1970s and 1980s. They found that egalitarianism correlates with being younger, having more education, and having spent more time in the labor force, while church attendance and a fundamentalist Protestant religious identification enhance the maintenance of traditional sex-role attitudes. Further, mothers' sex-role attitudes are important in shaping the attitudes of their children. Egalitarian mothers are likely to have egalitarian children.

Several studies have shown that very young children (aged 3–5) hold extreme sex-stereotyped occupational preferences (for example, Riley, 1981), so that sex-role preferences are thought to be acquired very early in life. Sex-role orientations of young children at various historical times therefore provide a sensitive index of societal changes toward egalitarianism. In a classic study of vocational aspirations, children of preschool and early elementary school age were asked what they wanted to be and also what they expected to become in adulthood (Looft, 1971). In 1971 boys named larger numbers of job choices than girls. Girls chose primarily sex-typed feminine occupations, such as nurse or teacher. These findings suggest that children are restricted by sex-typed vocational choices at a very early age. But do these findings still hold today? Recently, Adams and Hicken (1984) partially replicated this study and compared children's responses a decade later to the same

questions. They found little change in boys' ideal and expected vocational choices from 1971 to 1981. However, the number of vocations that girls were interested in pursuing had increased by 9.1%. Further, girls were interested in professional career choices. But even this encouraging note was tempered by certain negative expectations. For example, girls who were interested in the most prestigious and highest-paying occupations expected, in reality, to be unable to fulfill their occupational aspirations. This evidence suggests that although changes in our society are gradually broadening young girls' vocational preferences, there remains a sizeable gap between hope and reality.

In summary, demographic, survey, and interview data from children, adolescents, and adults suggest society is slowly moving toward egalitarianism in sex-role orientation. Perhaps changes that hit so close to the duties and roles of family members are unlikely to occur rapidly. The research reported here shows that although most Americans remain relatively traditional in their sex-role orientation, increasing numbers are seeing the need for change and support an egalitarian orientation (see Box 4-2 for a simple measure of traditional versus liberated self-concepts). However, we must caution that attitudinal change doesn't necessarily mean a corresponding change in behavior. Only the future will tell whether both attitudinal and behavioral change will continue to emerge as society changes.

## Shifts in Motives and Values

Along with the gradual change in sex-role orientation among Americans, is there evidence of a change in related motives or values? Further, is this gradual change associated with any changes in men's and women's reported psychological well-being?

Some evidence can be found that addresses those questions. Examining data from two national surveys on motivation taken in 1957 and

*From the seats of corporate power, to representation in Congress and on the Supreme Court, to outer space, women are challenging and changing the stereotypes of yesteryear.*

1976, Veroff, Depner, Kulka, and Douvan (1980) compared men's and women's responses on four basic motives: (1) the need for achievement, or the importance of meeting standards of excellence, (2) the need for affiliation, or the importance of maintaining emotional connections with others, (3) fear of weakness, or concern about maintaining one's status through another person, and (4) the hope of power, or the importance given to having an impact through one's own actions. Items 1 and 4 are associated with traditional views of masculinity, items 2 and 3 with femininity.

Four important conclusions emerge from this study. First, reported achievement motivation increased from 1957 to 1976 for women but not for men. Second, men diminished in their affiliation motivation, while women remained stable over the two decades. Third, both men and women showed significant increases in their concerns about weakness. Finally, men showed

an increase in hope for power, but women did not.

This study suggests that the gradual change toward egalitarianism is associated with parallel changes in men's and women's motives. Women are clearly showing changes in their need for achievement. Their patterns of employment and reported motives reveal more interest in long-term professional careers. They report increased interest in contributing to society and in the standards of excellence that underlie their intentions. Men, by comparison, show no substantial changes in such motivations. Further, both men and women are fearful of being perceived as weak in work and family settings. Unfortunately, while women are increasing their achievement needs and making employment gains, men are showing increased interest in power while decreasing their affiliative needs. Possibly these latter findings reflect perceived threat from the changes in women's needs; by increasing one's

## BOX 4-2
## *A Traditional/Liberated Self-Concept (for Females Only)*

Recently, Rosalind Cartwright and her colleagues (1982) have developed a checklist that distinguishes self-concepts developed on a traditional and on a liberated premise. Read the following word list and check the items that describe yourself.

1. absent-minded _____

2. good-natured _____

3. careless _____

4. independent _____

5. dependent _____

6. initiating _____

7. dreamy _____

8. insightful _____

9. shy _____

10. pleasure-seeking _____

11. tense _____

12. sharp-witted _____

13. touchy _____

14. sophisticated _____

Count the even items you checked. Now count the odd items. The odd items reflect a traditional sex-role-based self-concept. The even items reflect a liberated orientation.

---

power over another and decreasing one's desire to affiliate, one may be able to maintain control without emotional costs. Or possibly men are reacting to the perceived loss of authority and superiority resulting from egalitarianism by showing an increased need for power. Given that the need for power can be incompatible with the need for affiliation and closeness, it is possible that the social movement toward egalitarianism will have an increasingly negative impact on interpersonal relations. Some problems that result from men's need for power in a human relationship are discussed later in this chapter and in the chapter on family violence.

Bryant and Veroff (1982) performed additional analyses using the same data set as Veroff et al. to measure changes in the respondents' self-evaluations between 1957 and 1976. Men's and women's responses were compared within each of the two surveys as well as between 1957 and 1976. For both sexes, marital conflict (or unhappiness) was less important as a contributor to general unhappiness in 1976 than in 1957. Further, for women only, a negative attitude toward children was associated with unhappiness—but primarily in 1957, not in 1976. These findings suggest that in 1976 both men and women felt happier if they did not base their conceptions of happiness on traditional family role expectations. A man's future orientation was less important in predicting happiness in the 1970s than in the 1950s. This finding is consistent with the earlier report that the male need for achievement had stabilized. Other findings suggest that men are becoming disillusioned with the value of work while women remain hopeful that work may contribute to a sense of personal worth and adequacy.

These studies suggest that the egalitarian movement is accompanied by shifts in motives, values, and perceived psychological well-being. Collectively, the research points to a conclusion that women are profiting from the move toward egalitarianism, while men are adjusting in somewhat more defensive ways. Only time and additional research will tell us whether the gradual changes in our society will benefit both sexes.

### Benefits and Problems

As society moves toward egalitarian sex roles, increasing numbers of role-sharing families will emerge. Will these families escape the occasional turmoil we find in traditional family life?

Will marital relationships improve?

One survey of dual-career marriages offers some insight into these questions (Haas, 1980). Role-sharing spouses said that egalitarianism gives husbands and wives more freedom. In fact, one third of the respondents in this study reported that they perceived their parents as constrained by the traditional division of family labor. Haas concludes that egalitarian marriages offer individuals a greater opportunity to pursue personal interests, an opportunity for the wife (in particular) to gain personal fulfillment outside the home, relief from the stress of assuming sole responsibility for particular tasks, and greater independence. Overall egalitarian behaviors encouraged the participants in this study to perceive their marriage partners as better spouses. Some even reported a major improvement in parent/child relations.

Problems did occur in implementing a role-sharing family structure. For example, some spouses lacked the inclination to do some nontraditional tasks. Frequently, husbands said their wives could complete a household task more easily and quickly. Often a spouse who felt overworked would complain that the partner was lazy and threaten to stop completing the assigned nontraditional task. Differing standards of appropriate housekeeping created occasional conflict between the spouses. Conflict also occurred over employment issues, location of employment opportunities, and meeting the time demands of work.

How were these problems resolved? Many of the tedious or unsavory tasks (such as cleaning the bathroom) were completed on a rotating basis. When standards of housekeeping differed, one spouse usually tried to lower his or her expectations. Agreements would be made on minimal standards. When a lack of skills created a problem, often the more skilled person would teach the other one. When job demands created conflicts, creative solutions developed to allow for professional fulfillment.

Although husbands can clearly benefit from role sharing, societal forces discourage it (Pleck, 1979). Traditional values assume that men are valued in accordance with their work outside the home, while women are expected to assume the role of domestic caregiver. From an exchange perspective (Scanzoni, 1970), a husband assumes the breadwinner role and exchanges his success for his wife's love, household services, and companionship. From resource theory (Blood & Wolfe, 1960), it can be argued that husbands contribute less time to household duties because they have fewer resources to contribute (particularly time) to such tasks.

Others have been less kind toward husbands and have argued a straightforward "exploitation" view. They point out that, according to time and budget studies (for example, Walker & Woods, 1976), husbands spend much less time in domestic duties than wives even when both work. Thus, men are simply exploiting women.

Neither view, Pleck (1979) suggests, recognizes the gradual change that is appearing in marital relationships. Pleck proposes that men are lagging behind women in sex-role and attitudinal changes. Supporting this position, Lein (1979) notes that men who want to assume more participation in the family can find few if any natural support groups to encourage them. Men's ambivalence about or resistance to change may be due in part to the absence of such support. Indeed, men's peer groups may actively criticize or ostracize members who assume more so-called feminine behaviors in the home. Perhaps in the near future, however, men will begin finding in society at large the support for role sharing that's missing in their peer groups. This may have begun with such films as *Kramer vs. Kramer* and *Mr. Mom*.

Some evidence indicates that fathers are showing more interest in such home duties as infant care, showing more emotional involvement with their children, spending more time in social and recreational caregiving with children, and developing strong child-care competencies (Stevens, 1980). Perhaps the day will soon arrive when it will be as acceptable for fathers to speak of child care and family-life interests as it is for mothers.

 *Do you approve of the changes that are occurring in family relations? What do you think are the desirable and undesirable aspects of egalitarianism and role sharing?*

## SEX-ROLE DEVELOPMENT IN CHILDREN

Child psychologists are interested in how boys and girls develop a sense of gender, internalize notions of "boyness" or "girlness," and come to identify with masculine or feminine behaviors based on social conventions. Several excellent summaries of this psychological research describe the intricacies of **sex-role development** (for example, Huston, 1983; Kagan, 1964; Mussen, 1969; Shepherd-Look, 1982). Although considerable disagreement exists on what the major dimensions of **sex-typing** are, most researchers do agree on several sex-typed characteristics.

### Dimensions of Sex-Role Development

In early work on sex-role development, child psychologists (for example, Kagan, 1964) argued that a major distinction needed to be made between children's knowledge of cultural *expectations* for males and females and their sex-role *identity*—their internalization of or conformity to cultural expectations. A child's understanding of social norms surrounding masculinity and femininity is one thing, and the degree to which the child assumes these sex-typed characteristics is another. Social scientists have used five dimensions of sex-typing to study sex-role devel-

opment: (1) biological gender or gender constancy, (2) sex-role concepts (sex-stereotyped attitudes, activities, or interests), (3) sex-appropriate personal/social attributes or behaviors, (4) gender-based social relations, and (5) nonverbal and verbal styles and symbolic content (Huston, 1983). These five major constructs have each been valuable in studying children's and adults' notions of womanhood and manhood.

Our knowledge of sex-role development and behavior, obtained using the five constructs, has emerged in the form of three basic research directions (Biller, 1970). First, we have a growing understanding of an individual's **sex-role orientation.** We are coming to understand how children and adults individualize their perceptions of themselves as masculine or feminine—or, as some have suggested, as androgynous, a combination of the two. Second, sex-role behaviors are associated with a **sex-role preference,** as measured by the degree to which the individual wishes to have certain masculine or feminine characteristics. A final research direction has focused on **sex-role adoption,** using all five dimensions of sex-typing to study the degree to which an individual conforms to a particular sex-role orientation.

### Three Theories of Sex-Typing

One of the major roles of the family is to assist in socializing the next generation. In particular, the family is thought to be the key agent influencing sex-role development. Three major theories have been widely used to explain the social process that underlies sex-typing.

*Psychoanalytic theory.* One of the oldest theories of sex-typing was proposed by Sigmund Freud, who suggested that children experience feelings of hostility and sexuality toward their parents. For example, according to psychoanalytic theory, a boy sexually desires the mother and envies the father for his possession of her time and attention. Thus, the father is the target of the boy's hostility and the mother the target of his sexual impulses. Recognizing, however, that his impulses must go unfulfilled, and aware that an expression of those feelings could result in the loss of either or both parents' love, the boy represses his impulses. As a defense against the threat of these sexual and hostile impulses, the child engages in an identification process. The child is thought both to internalize the moral standards of the more threatening parent and to transform his personality through a socialization process that works by way of identification (see Figure 4-1).

Although many psychologists still use this theory to explain sex-typed identity, very little empirical evidence can be found to support it (Da-

mon, 1983). Perhaps its weakest component is the belief that a child passively and holistically internalizes sex-typed behavior. Research shows that children are more than passive "puppets" of social experience. Children (and adults) are active organizers of their life experiences and maintain selective attention to personally relevant information (see Damon, 1983).

*Social-learning theory.* There are several social-learning-based theories of sex-role development. The major process is thought to be associated with simple reinforcement principles (see Figure 4-1). For example, a boy becomes attached to his father because the father is a reinforcing person in the child's life. This reinforcement/attachment process results in the boy's identification with appropriate sex-typed behav-

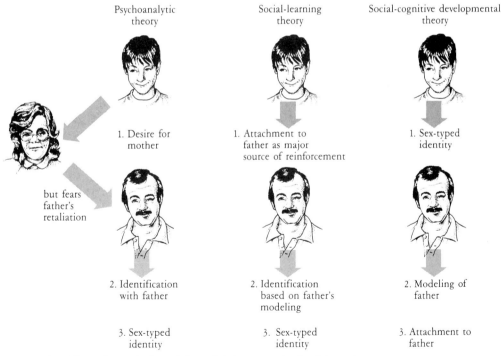

**FIGURE 4-1.** *Three theoretical models explaining sex-role development.*

iors that the father models. Thus, the identification process, based on reward rather than sexual or hostile impulses, results in a sex-typed identity. Jerome Kagan is best known for an early social-learning theory of sex-typing. He argues that the identification process is motivated by the child's desire for resources and rewards that the model possesses, including mastery and love. The child assumes, through a process of similarity, that by identifying with the parent, he too will acquire the resources of mastery and love. The reinforcement principle emerges in two ways. First, by showing how the child behaves similarly to the parent, the parent reinforces the child for imitating him/her. Second, through adopting the model's behaviors, the child acquires the mastery and love he perceives in his parent. Once again, because this identification process is based on hypothetical constructs such as love or mastery, only limited direct empirical evidence supports this social-learning identification theory (Damon, 1983).

*Social-cognitive theory.* The most recent and perhaps most radical theory of sex-typing has been suggested by Lawrence Kohlberg. Kohlberg differs radically from psychoanalytic and social-learning theorists in arguing that children do not merely adopt sex-typed behavior from a parent but, rather, actively acquire it on their own. Thus identification is not the underlying process; rather, it is a by-product of sex-typed identity.

Damon (1983) has provided a most useful synthesis of Kohlberg's theory. Kohlberg proposes that children are constantly trying to make sense of the world around them. As Damon has written,

> Part of the child's cognitive effort is the search for identifying features of the self. . . . The important point is that Kohlberg's theory places this cognitive effort prior to the process of identification with others. In other words, Kohlberg

believes that before the child establishes an identification with another person, the child must make some judgments about the nature of his or her own distinguishing characteristics. Gender, according to Kohlberg, is the most cognitively accessible characteristic of self, since it is detectable in several overt physical attributes (dress, hair length, genitals) [1983, p. 176].

Thus, once a child has developed a stable gender identity, he or she will spontaneously seek out and develop sex-appropriate values and standards. Further, because children perceive that which is similar to themselves as good, they will most likely identify with the same-sex parent as a model. This identification process is completed when the child develops a strong and lasting emotional attachment to the same-sex parent. This attachment encourages conformity to that parent's standards and role-modeled behaviors.

Damon (1983) argues that Kohlberg's social-cognitive theory is superior because it recognizes the active role that children themselves play in sex-typing. This theory avoids many of the problems associated with psychoanalytic and social-learning theory. Although many of Kohlberg's theoretical assumptions are not yet fully understood, some scholars view his theory as the best overall explanation of sex-typing (Damon, 1983).

**?** *How do sex roles affect your social relations? What behaviors do you engage in that are related to femininity? Masculinity? Have your parents affected you in providing the socialization underlying such behaviors? How? Are there other forces?*

## Influences on Sex-Role Development

Most theories of sex-role development agree that the family plays a critical role. According to psychoanalytic theory, for example, a child acquires the appropriate sex role through identifying with the same-sex parent. In learning theory, imitation, modeling, and reward encourage specific sex-role behaviors. Boys or girls tend to be rewarded for imitating behavior modeled by adults of their sex and punished for imitating behavior modeled by adults of the other sex. In the social-cognitive model, the child is thought to seek out either "masculine" or "feminine" behaviors (depending on his or her gender), which parents then reward (see Flake-Hobson, Skeen, & Robinson, 1980, for an extended description).

Each of these theories recognizes socialization as an important contributor to sex-role development. The family, along with other environmental agents, performs an important role in this socialization process. But just how does this process work?

*Parent/child interactions.* One body of research finds that parent/child interactions are colored by stereotypic assumptions about masculinity and femininity (Bardwick, 1971; Maccoby & Jacklin, 1974). For example, Rubin, Provenzano, and Luria (1974) found that parents were likely to view their sons as firmer, larger-featured, more alert, and stronger than their daughters. In comparison, daughters of equal body weight and dimensions were typically seen as softer, more delicate, and more awkward. Other research shows mothers to be more likely to reward aggressiveness in sons and interpersonal skills in daughters (Moss, 1967; Rebelsky & Hawks, 1971). Parents are more inclined to respond to a daughter's cries (Lewis, 1972) and maintain a more protective stance toward their daughters (Hoffman, 1972). Still other investigations document that mothers speak more often to their daughters (Cherry & Lewis, 1976), touch them more (Goldberg & Lewis, 1969), and maintain closer proximity to them (Lewis & Weinraub, 1974). Further, Hoffman (1972) ar-

gues that differential treatment based on traditional sex-role notions can undermine a girl's confidence in her ability to cope assertively and independently with her environment.

*The media.* Two items found in almost every home encourage traditional sex-role adoption and thereby restrict individual choice. Both reading material (Bereaud, 1975; Feminists on Children's Media, 1971; Women on Words and Images, 1972) and television (DeFleur, 1964; Sternglanz & Serbin, 1974) reflect a strong stereotypic bias in their representation of social life. Television, in particular, tends to portray women as passive, unskilled, and ineffective and men as dominant, independent, and assertive. In *Growing Up Free,* Pogrebin (1980) summarizes numerous studies of cartoons, soap operas, and commercials and concludes that TV programmers' overuse of a traditional sex-role perspective has a profound negative effect on sex-role adoption by young people.

*Toys.* In a review of the literature, Kacerguis and Adams (1979) find that most toys intended for girls restrict occupational role choices for them later in life. They argue that toys offer "experimentation with future roles and present an opportunity on the child's level. Therefore, continuous presentation of stereotypic toys may deny a child freedom to explore, discover, and express potential" (p. 372). Because toys provide not only a medium for rehearsal of future roles but also information about future occupations, Kacerguis and Adams conclude that present practices encourage the continuation of traditional sex-role behaviors.

 *Can you think of other socialization factors that contribute to sex-role stereotypes and sex-role development? How do these factors positively or negatively influence women? Men?*

## BOX 4-3
*Television Viewing and Adolescents' Sex-Role Stereotypes*

The analysis of content on television has repeatedly shown that women are underrepresented, overvictimized, and trivialized. Does extensive exposure to such images of women during childhood encourage sexist attitudes? To assess this possibility, Michael Morgan (1982) studied television viewing and adolescents' sex-role stereotypes over a two-year period, beginning with samples of sixth- and tenth-graders. Extensive television watching was associated with increased sexism in the stereotypes held by adolescent girls. No parallel finding was observed for boys. However, highly sexist attitudes for boys were predictive of greater television viewing. Given that females have been found to be typically less sexist, these results suggest that television viewing may have its greatest influence on individuals who are least likely to hold traditional sex-role attitudes.

## SEX ROLES AND COMPETENCE

As indicated earlier, an androgynous person is one who has characteristics of both the masculine and the feminine sex roles (see, for example, Bem, 1977; Bem, Martyna, & Watson, 1976; Downing, 1979; Orlofsky, Aslin, & Ginsburg, 1977; Spence & Helmreich, 1979). Individuals with more traditional sex-role orientations are called either masculine or feminine. Perhaps the most important aspect of masculine, feminine, and androgynous characteristics is their significance for social behavior. An individual can maintain either a self-assertive or an integrative pattern of interacting with others. **Self-assertion,** the traditional masculine pattern, involves assertiveness, independence, and dominance. **Integration,** the traditional feminine pattern, is a more expressive role that promotes intimacy, nurturance, and cooperation (social unity). An individual can possess both self-assertive and integrative patterns of behavior and therein be androgynous.

In recent years some have argued that androgynous men and women are more competent than traditionally sex-typed persons. In an extensive review of the research addressing the androgyny/competence hypothesis, Ford (1981) proposes six major criteria of competence: self-esteem, mental health and psychological adjustment, physical health, psychological development, achievement motivation, and social competence. His review leads us to four conclusions:

- Androgynous persons generally score high on self-esteem—but not much higher than self-assertive (masculine) persons. Both these groups generally have higher self-esteem than the integrative (feminine) group.

- Androgyny and self-assertion are stronger predictors of positive mental health and psychological adjustment than integration is.

- Androgyny and self-assertion are predictors of mature identity development, sexual maturity, and achievement motivation.

- Androgyny and self-assertion are strong predictors of assertiveness, independence, dominance, positive marital adjustment, social poise, and certain aspects of leadership, while androgyny and integration are associated with other competence criteria such as nurturance and solidarity.

## BOX 4-4
### *The World of Sports: A Critical Perspective*

Donald Sabo and Ross Runfola, in their book *Jock: Sports and Male Identity* (1980), argue that sports train boys to be "men" and to fulfill societal expectations of masculinity. In fact, they believe that society "cuts off the penis" of boys who are enrolled in dance, while placing it on girls who engage in competitive sports. These authors argue:

Men who survive the attrition of our culture's highly competitive, star-oriented sports system for the most part have personalities that conform to the traditional male stereotype: high in achievement need, respectful of authority, dominant among peers, self-controlled, and low in sensitivity to other people [Ogilvie &

Tutko, cited in Sabo & Runfola (1980), p. 47].

As women continue to enter "jockdom," will they take on similar personality characteristics? Is the move toward equality in the sports arena a positive expression of changing sex roles?

---

We conclude from this review and other research that androgynous individuals are more flexible and adaptive to changing social conditions in the family and the work world (Ford, 1981; Taylor & Hall, 1982; Whitley, 1983). For example, androgynous females are more accepting of nontraditional job changes, they are more supportive of persons in nontraditional jobs, and they are more active listeners (Lamke, 1982; Motowidlo, 1982; Wells, 1980). Highly traditional sex-typed females, by contrast, are inhibited in their individuality and expression of autonomy and achievement behaviors (see, for example, Block, Von der Lippe, & Block, 1973). Strongly masculinized males are reported to be more prone to neurotic and high-anxiety behaviors (Harford, Willis, & Beabler, 1967). In addition, it appears from the literature that androgynous persons are more competent, confident, spontaneous, and self-accepting and have greater capacity for intimate contact (see, for example, Bailey & Prager, 1984; Ickes & Barnes, 1979).

The real strength of androgynous persons is their capability for both self-assertive behaviors and integrative behaviors, as the situation demands (Bem, 1975; Bem et al., 1976). Bem (1975) has shown that androgynous persons

are able to engage in "masculine" independence in a pressure-to-conform setting and "feminine" playfulness in other interpersonal situations.

The ultimate meaning of egalitarianism and androgyny is found in the social relations of dyads or the family itself. Androgynous men and women appear to have a stronger capacity for establishing and maintaining intimate relations. However, androgyny has still other implications. Falbo and Peplau (1979) found that sex-role orientation has a direct implication for the type of power or persuasion technique a person will use in romantic or intimate relations. Their study suggests that masculine persons employ more direct strategies, such as telling their partner to do something—which is consistent with a self-assertion interpretation of masculinity. Feminine persons are more likely to use indirect and subtle techniques of an integrative type. Androgynous persons are more likely to use persuasion, bargaining, or positive affect—a combination of self-assertion and integration.

How, then, does androgyny affect the family? We have seen in our discussion of egalitarian role sharing that it encourages role diversification and allows greater role flexibility, compro-

## BOX 4-5
## *A Male Chauvinist Quiz*

Shirley Rombough and Joseph Ventimiglia at the University of Texas at Arlington have devised a 20-item test to assess one's sex-role orientation. To take the test, write down whether you strongly agree, agree, have no opinion, disagree, or strongly disagree with each item.

1. The job of plumber is equally suitable for men and women.

2. It's all right for the woman to have a career and for the man to stay at home with the children.

3. Men make better engineers than women.

4. Working women are too independent.

5. Women should not be discriminated against in getting manual labor jobs.

6. Driving a truck is equally suitable for men and women.

7. It is more important for a wife to help her husband than to have a career herself.

8. A woman should willingly take her husband's name at marriage.

9. The husband should make the major decisions.

10. The husband should handle the money.

11. A woman should wait until her children are out of school before she goes to work.

12. A woman's purpose in life should be to take care of her family.

13. Women should stay home and care for the children.

14. The major responsibility of the wife is to keep her husband and children happy.

15. Women should have the same sexual freedom as men.

16. Men are more emotionally suited for politics than are women.

17. Young girls are entitled to as much independence as young boys.

18. Men are better leaders than women.

19. Women are more envious than men.

20. Women have more intuition than men.

Score as follows: For items 1, 2, 5, 6, 15, and 17, score 1 point for "strongly agree," 2 points for "agree," 3 points for "no opinion," 4 points for "disagree," and 5 points for "strongly disagree." For all other items, score 1 point for "strongly disagree" through 5 points for "strongly agree." You are designated as a *feminist* if your total score is in the 20s, a *liberal* for the 30s, *average* for 40 through 69, *traditional* for the 70s, and a *chauvinist* for 80 or above.

mise, and negotiation. But egalitarianism may be less suited for other types of lifestyles and therefore may be less functional for some families. To illustrate, Abrahams, Feldman, and Nash (1978) argue that some life situations may heighten androgynous role-sharing tendencies while others may minimize such tendencies. Comparing several types of families, the authors speculated that having a baby would increase the division of labor among couples. They believed that the husband would feel compelled to emphasize his career and financial responsibilities, while the wife would quickly assume responsibility for care of the child. Indeed, the findings supported the researchers' expectations. Thus, varying family-life contexts can create tremendous pressure for husbands and wives to assume traditional roles in the family.

One final comment: There are no published data to suggest that androgynous parents are any more or less effective parents. Research indicates that they are likely to be "child centered" but not more likely than sex-typed parents to have socially competent children (Baumrind, 1982). Baumrind therefore argues against promoting androgyny as a sex-role trait associated with some new American ideal for parents. Even so, there are benefits to be derived from encouraging androgynous behavior in society. These benefits will be made clear in the final section of this chapter.

 *Is there a time or place when masculinity is preferred for males and femininity for females? When might androgyny result in ineffective social behavior?*

## SEX-ROLE DIFFERENTIATION, MARRIAGE, AND PARENTING

Sex roles are thought to influence both marital relationships and parenting behaviors. In a marital relationship sex roles may influence a couple's division of labor. Meissner, Humphreys, Meis, and Scheu (1975) suggest two basic theories of division of labor for dual-career married couples. In the **adaptive-partnership theory,** as the wife increases the family's resources through her paid employment, the husband will respond by assuming more responsibility for household duties. According to the **dependent-labor theory,** because women's labor-force participation (particularly in traditionally "feminine" occupations) is seen as secondary to men's and is valued less, division of labor is unaffected by wives' employment. Time-sample studies clearly show that the dependent-labor theory

better predicts division of labor in the home. However, a recent study (Atkinson & Huston, 1984) suggests that this finding holds primarily for couples having traditional employment patterns. Less traditional couples were more flexible and adaptive in their division of labor. Further, husbands who perceived their skills at "feminine" household tasks as adequate or good and wives who perceived their "masculine" household skills as adequate were more likely to assume nontraditional household responsibilities.

Some research has suggested that sex roles also affect parenting behaviors. For example, Russell (1978) has reported that masculine men tend to be more involved in child care if married to feminine women than if married to masculine or androgynous women. More recent research by McHale and Huston (1984) likewise shows that men's sense of competence and their desire to become involved in child care before becoming fathers are both very good predictors of actual involvement once the child is born. Further, these social psychologists show that mothers must be willing to step back from the role of primary child-care provider if they want fathers to become more involved. This may not be easy, given women's socialization history and cultural expectations of caregiving for young children in particular.

 *Sex-role typing, in the form of flexibility and skill development, directly affects a couple's division of household chores. What other behaviors of spouses might be influenced by sex roles?*

*What kinds of problems can you envision between fathers who want to spend more time caring for their children and mothers who have difficulty giving up their caregiving time?*

Traditional sex-role orientations, as social conventions, contribute to the problem of sexism. According to George Albee (1981, p. 20), **sexism** means "ascribing superiority or inferiority, unsupported by any evidence, in traits, abilities, social value, personal worth, and other characteristics to males or females." Albee argues that women as a group have been treated in a prejudicial and sexist manner, resulting in economic and social exploitation of them as a cheap labor force and high rates of psychopathology, including depressive disorders, for women. Albee comments:

> Whether the woman's defect—her fatal flaw—is explained on the basis of Freudian chauvinism (penis envy), on observable physical differences (the weaker sex), or on historical guilt (Eve caused the Fall), the result is the same. We see profound and debilitating suffering in the victims, acceptance by some of them of the values and beliefs of their oppressors . . . and widespread learned helplessness and despair [p. 21].

Sexism, whether deliberate or not, can restrict women and men to confining roles and limit their opportunities, experiences, and personal development. We assume that egalitarianism and role-sharing behavior are desirable for family members, and we propose that the prevention of sexism is a healthy and desirable goal. But more than sexism is at issue. There are immediate implications for social behavior and personality development. For example, egalitarian attitudes generate more flexible options for personal growth. Likewise, several studies find egalitarian attitudes associated with enhanced identity formation and higher levels of ego development (for example, Bailey & Prager, 1984; Stein & Weston, 1982).

Evidence associates instrumental (masculine) and expressive (feminine) orientations with vocational and interpersonal identities, respectively (for example, Grotevant & Thorbecke, 1982; Thorbecke & Grotevant, 1982). For both men and women, self-reported masculinity and personal mastery are likely to be expressed behaviorally in an active search for self-direction and a commitment to a chosen occupation. In contrast, psychological femininity is correlated with interpersonal identity exploration. The emotional sensitivity and expressiveness of psychological femininity are attributes that facilitate friendship and dating behavior. Androgynous individuals have the psychological wherewithal for a personal striving for mastery, balanced by sensitivity and interpersonal expressiveness.

What suggestions do we advance for the prevention of sexism? We argue that one positive direction (among many) is to promote choice. Therefore, applying prevention technology in this context includes an effort to ensure that individual choice, rather than society, dictate a person's decision to be feminine, masculine, or androgynous. The focus must be on freedom to select and internalize any combination of sex-role characteristics independent of gender.

## EDUCATION

Endorsement and acceptance of sex roles in the form of masculine, feminine, or androgynous psychological traits or egalitarian role-sharing attitudes are learned behaviors. Cultural messages are communicated through newspapers, radio, television, film, magazines, and books. If freedom of choice is to increase, then the media must offer portraits of men and women in both

# BOX 4-6
## In a Different Voice?

Carol Gilligan (1982), writing on feminist psychology, argues that women have been systematically misunderstood. Theories of psychological growth and development have been constructed around the lives of men and have been incorrectly applied to our understanding of women. Further, because the standard of maturity for men is based on individualism, when women, who traditionally focus on a world of relationships and social connections, are judged against the male standard, they indeed appear less mature. But different standards of growth do not reflect differences in level of maturity. If the standard of maturity were based on intimacy, men would fare no better. Rather, different yardsticks may be needed to measure men's and women's psychological and social development. How might this be particularly true for sex-role development? Identity? Intimacy? Work and family life?

masculine and feminine roles. One of our favorite illustrations of how this can be achieved is a television commercial in which an attractive woman is called to work at the last moment for a flight with an airline. Dressed in a flight uniform and heading into the airplane, she turns out to be the copilot, not an attendant. Such a commercial, by exploiting the stereotype itself, sensitizes the public to the realization that the ability to succeed in a vocation is a function not of gender but of intelligence and skills.

Other important means of informing the public include workshops, seminars, editorials, and conferences designed to educate businesspeople, professionals, and other men and women of changes in work and family patterns, of attitudes, stereotypes, and expectations about females, and of sociocultural influences on women's life patterns (Huston-Stein & Higgins-Trenk, 1978). Major changes in work roles have occurred since 1940, when only 15% of married women were employed outside the home. In recent years this figure has grown to over 50%. Clearly, many women are successfully combining employment with family roles of mother, homemaker, and/or wife. Unfortunately, the social status of women has not changed substantially. Many husbands still expect their working wives to assume primary responsibility for homemaking and child care. Many professional women appear to be dealing with this dilemma by delaying marriage, postponing childbearing, or remaining childless. Huston-Stein and Higgins-Trenk (1978) argue that few men accept a career-oriented wife. Broad-based education of the general public is a first step to help men understand the nature of women's sex-role development and to sensitize them to the need for personal choice. Finally, sociocultural barriers such as the demands of time, travel, and the assignment of priorities to job over family need to be addressed by women and employers alike. As this dialogue continues and customs change, both sexes can be expected to profit from such societal changes as paternal child-care leave, flexible work hours, and company-provided day care.

On an individual basis, each of us can educate, sensitize, and inform his or her own children about socially acceptable sex-role behavior. The following are possibilities:

- Allow a child to experience and express his own sex-role preferences and discuss these preferences.
- Encourage a child to think about the meaning of the behavior behind her sex-role ori-

entation and whether that preference is suitable to her goals.

- Discuss how one could treat others in both traditional and nontraditional ways.

- Explore the meaning of sex-stereotyping information that comes from personal experiences, television, reading, and so on.

- Introduce a child to varying sex-role models who represent masculine, feminine, and androgynous perspectives.

- Avoid sexism in discussing occupations, family roles, psychological characteristics, and acceptable conduct. For example, don't say "Big boys don't cry—be a man" or "Only girls become nurses."

## COMMUNITY MOBILIZATION/ SYSTEMS INTERVENTION

At the societal level, sexism can be combated by community action. Progress has been made through lobbying for laws assuring women of equal access to training and equal employment opportunities.

Three general activities can be pursued through community organization (Gullotta, 1983, in press). First, *institutional practice barriers* that limit equal access or pay can be eliminated. For example, affirmative action is specifically designed to eliminate sexist biases. Likewise, employers can be encouraged to use flextime, give maternity *and* paternity leave, and develop day-care services near the job site. Second, organizational activities can work toward *community resource development.* Uniting neighborhood service programs, politicians, and business in a collaborative effort, steering committees can be developed to promote women's rights and changes in family patterns and employment. Finally, women and men can lobby

for *legislative and judicial action* that represents the best interest of all family members. The passage of laws to prohibit sexual harassment at the workplace, affirmative action, and equal pay for equal work exemplifies possible goals.

## COMPETENCY PROMOTION

Certain talents and skills accompany masculine, feminine, and androgynous sex-typing. The self-assertiveness of masculinity and the integrativeness of femininity provide the foundation for differing interests and skill development through early socialization experiences with parents, peers, relatives, and teachers.

Socialization experiences of a masculine orientation are those that encourage the development of competitiveness, a need for achievement, assertiveness/aggressiveness, skill development, and industriousness. Socialization of a feminine orientation focuses on cooperation, sharing, understanding, caring, helping, and emotional expression. Both orientations provide skills needed in work and social life.

Promotion of both sets of competencies can be accomplished by providing opportunities to develop achievement and competition skills and, at the same time, to learn a broader social perspective, cooperation, and the skills of leading and following. Numerous youth and adult organizations promote such a combination of skills. Many programs that promote pertinent masculine and feminine competencies are cited in this book. One of these programs, Creative Experiences, is an excellent example of how the arts can be used to promote androgynous behavior in young people. This intergenerational program in the arts brings together children, adolescents, and adults (including whole families) who work together in activities ranging from producing a cable television program to theatrical performances to civic projects. By giving the initiative for organization, planning, analyzing, and developing programs to young people, the program enhances pride, a sense of accomplishment, the opportunity to develop a nontraditional sex-role perspective, and, above all, responsibility (Smith, Goodwin, Gullotta, & Gullotta, 1979).

For couples, premarital and marital enrichment programs that encourage spouses to communicate, appreciate, and clarify roles and expectations in meeting work, home, and child-care duties promote competence in handling the increased complexity of an egalitarian life. Such discussions lead to the recognition that new nontraditional sex-role skills need to be developed. A wife may need to develop some new mechanical skills; a husband may need to learn to cook or clean effectively, or develop better personal skills associated with child care.

We believe that the development of both masculine and feminine competencies and of an accompanying egalitarian role-sharing attitude encourages flexibility in behavior, a wider range of skills, and improved mental health. Such competencies permit men, in particular, to find value within themselves, not in their exercise of power over family members. The surrendering of such power should relieve the depression many women suffer and may be a major step forward in reducing the incidence of spousal abuse in our country.

## NATURAL CAREGIVING

Sex-role-related psychological characteristics are acquired mainly from those who care for us during our childhood. As caregivers, we must recognize that the best single tool at our disposal for encouraging androgyny in our children is our own personal conduct and example. When we model competitiveness, nurturance, caring, and instrumental and industrious behavior, our children observe how both masculine and feminine characteristics can be acceptably displayed by the same person. When we practice role sharing in home duties, children develop an acceptance of egalitarian attitudes. Self-help groups can encourage these behaviors. One example of the success such groups can have is Parents Without Partners, created to respond to the increase in single-parent families. Its members, women and men raising children alone, exchange emotional support and guidance. Such groups give individuals the support they need in developing new nontraditional sex-role-related skills and talents.

 *What ideas do you have for preventing sexism and promoting choice in sex-role adoption?*

# SUMMARY

Sexism abounds in our society (for example, see Guttentag, 1977). It can be traced to traditional cultural expectations and sex-role concepts. In this chapter we have argued that a gradual social departure from this traditional sex-role perspective is emerging, but the traditional perspective still dominates. Until sexism and rigid sex-role concepts are changed, both women and men will be denied the opportunity to develop to their fullest potential as human beings.

# MAJOR POINTS TO REMEMBER

1. Cultural notions of womanhood and manhood dating back two centuries have set the foundation for our concepts of femininity and masculinity. Womanhood, as reflected in femininity, was associated with nurturance and caring. Manhood, as reflected in masculinity, was associated with independence and mastery.
2. A sex-role identity that includes both masculine and feminine characteristics is called *androgyny*. Androgyny is the psychological manifestation of an egalitarian attitude and role-sharing perspectives.
3. Society is gradually changing toward egalitarian attitudes reflecting role-sharing behaviors. The accompanying changes in motives and values include a decrease in men's affiliative needs and an increase in women's achievement needs.
4. The benefits of increased role sharing include greater freedom of choice, personal opportunities, personal fulfillment, and independence. Problems can include difficulty in resolving task duties, differential standards in completing household tasks, and employment issues.
5. Researchers use five categories of sex-typed characteristics in studying individuals' sex-role development: gender constancy, sex-role concepts, personal/social attributes or behaviors, gender-based social relations, and communication style or content.
6. Research into sex-role development has focused on sex-role orientations, preferences, and adoption. Each area provides important information on conformity to cultural expectations of sex-role concepts.
7. Three major theories of sex-role development draw on the identification process in explaining sex-typing. The psychoanalytic perspective views sexuality and hostility as major underlying forces. The social-learning viewpoint recognizes similarity, love, and mastery as motives for identification. Social-cognitive theory views identification as the by-product of innate sex-typing tendencies.
8. Parent/child interactions, availability of toys, and the media are influential in forming a child's stereotyped sex-role self-concept.
9. Androgynous individuals have the advantage over traditionally sex-typed individuals of being more flexible: they are capable of using either self-assertive (masculine) or integrative (feminine) behaviors to meet the demands of various situations.
10. There is evidence that sex roles influence both marital and parenting behavior.

# ADDITIONAL SOURCES OF INFORMATION

Gilligan, C. (1977). In a different voice: Women's conceptions of self and morality. *Harvard Educational Review, 47,* 481–517. [Adults]

Gilligan, C. (1982). *In a different voice.* Cambridge, MA: Harvard University Press. [Adolescents, adults]

Hole, J., & Levine, E. (1971). *Rebirth of feminism.* New York: Quadrangle Books. [Adults]

Mead, M. (1949). *Male and female.* New York: Dell. [Adolescents, adults]

Pogrebin, L. C. (1980). *Growing up free.* New York: McGraw-Hill. [Children, adolescents, adults]

# 5

# HUMAN SEXUALITY

***This chapter is*** about sex—a topic that keenly interests most of us. Little is known about the early sexual evolution of the human species. Although sexual expression, sexual experiences, and interpersonal relations have always been an integral part of family life, it is generally believed that early humans had no realization of the relationship between **coitus** (sexual intercourse) and **conception** (the beginning of pregnancy). Some have even argued that incest was common among primitive humans and that only as nomadic tribes came to interact on a more frequent and friendly basis did the taboo against incest emerge.

As one might expect, the failure to recognize the connection between sexual intercourse and pregnancy meant that women spent most of their adult lives bearing children, and as we saw in Chapter 1, those lives were shortened by a host of dangers accompanying childbirth. Tannahill (1980) estimates that 86 of every 100 of our Neanderthal ancestors died before age 30. When we consider that as late as the 18th century a woman's life expectancy was only 36 years, with most deaths attributable to childbirth or its consequences, we can understand the dread women must have felt, conceiving, as they did (on the average), eight children before their death.

According to anthropologists, during the Neolithic Age nomadic tribespeople became farmers, new observations occurred, and a second sexual taboo emerged. These people observed that blood was essential for life and came to believe that it possessed magical powers. Therefore, menstrual blood assumed an intrinsic power of its own. Tannahill (1980) writes: "Blood magic and simple bafflement could have been enough to make man wary of woman during her periods. Isolating her may have appeared as sensible insurance against the unknown. And woman herself may not have objected" (pp. 44–45). In all likelihood, then, the avoidance of intercourse during menstruation derived from fear of the unknown. Some people believe that men have used fears about menstruation in a variety of ways against women over the centuries.

As time advanced, religion gained more influence over sexual conduct. Within our own Judeo-Christian heritage, the early church condemned several sexual behaviors. Generally, adultery was rejected. Abortion and infanticide were sometimes opposed but at other times allowed. Homosexuality and masturbation were abhorred. Some religions went so far as to make recommendations on the suitable frequency for marital intercourse: "'Every day for the unemployed,' said the Jewish Mishnah [oral law]; 'twice a week for laborers, once a week for ass drivers.' . . . The Church [Catholicism] said never, unless children were the object" (Tannahill, 1980, p. 161). Today many churches forbid all forms of sex, except penile-vaginal intercourse in privacy between spouses, as unnatural. And many churches still encourage sexual acts exclusively for procreation.

In this chapter we shall explore human sexuality as it applies to the family. To begin, we shall review the history of sexuality in marriage and then the anatomy of human sexuality. We do so in the belief that the fundamentals of human sexuality begin with basic physiology, but first, a little excursion into history.

## RELIGIOUS HISTORY AND SEXUALITY IN MARRIAGE

Historians believe that the formal institution of marriage arose with the reciprocal exchange of women between tribes and the elaboration of kinship systems (Levi-Strauss, 1969). It is thought that giving away sisters and daughters served as insurance against attack by developing recipro-

cal tribal bonds through marriage. But what were the implications for sex and marriage? Because women were exchanged, they were treated as property. Their status as property produced sanctions against trespassing (for example, violating a virgin or committing adultery) in the religious and legal codes of the time. As Williams (1980, p. 96) writes,

> The unchaste maid was no longer marriageable, thus worthless to her father; the violator had to marry her and pay money to her father (Exodus 22:17). Adulterers could be put to death (Leviticus 20:10), the woman for her sin, the man for violating the property of another man. The sexual behavior of women was carefully guarded in order to ensure that legal offspring would inherit property. Women were unclean and required ritual purification in connection with the natural events of their bodies, such as menstruation and childbirth. If a woman gave birth to a son, the period required for her purification was thirty-three days. If the child was a daughter, the time required was sixty-six days (Leviticus 12:4–5).

As Christianity emerged, the value of marriage and women actually declined. Chastity was a sign of holiness; marriage and sexuality impeded such a lofty pursuit. According to Williams (1980, p. 96), Ephesians 5:22–23 says:

> At best, the woman was a silent submissive wife; at worst she was the instrument of damnation, exciting lust and luring man from his holy mission. . . . The man was not made for the woman, but woman for man. Wives, submit yourselves unto your own husband . . . as unto the Lord. For the husband is the head of the wife, even as Christ is the head of the church.

It was during the Reformation that attitudes began to change. The religious reformer Martin Luther thought celibacy an unobtainable goal for the masses and viewed sex and marriage as a gift from God. The theologian John Calvin did not

WILLIAM J. GLACKENS: *NUDE WITH APPLE*, 1910

*Compare this painting entitled* Nude with Apple *with the drawing below it. How do you think these artists have interpreted women's roles in their day?*

agree completely. Although he accepted sex, he renounced pleasure and worldliness. His thinking gave rise to the shadows of sin and guilt that continue to surround sex in the Western world.

The Victorians brought yet another embellishment to human sexuality. They idealized women, particularly mothers, as spiritual and moral leaders. Formerly viewed as a temptress, woman was now to be the regulator of passions and sex in a relationship. With time and for a myriad of reasons (not least of which is women's growing control over their own bodies—see Shorter, 1982), society has cast off in the last 60 years many of the constraints that religion placed on sexuality.

# THE ANATOMY OF HUMAN SEXUALITY: A BRIEF REVIEW

Human sexuality consists of two related systems. One involves the human **sexual response,** and the other **reproduction.** Together they form the basis for understanding human sexuality.

The reproductive system consists of the external and internal sex organs. Human life results from the interplay between male and female reproductive systems through sexual intercourse. During intercourse, the male ejaculates semen, which contains sperm, through his penis into the vagina of the female. The sperm cells travel through the female's reproductive system. If one of the sperm cells contacts an ovum (egg cell) and penetrates its wall, conception occurs and a new life begins. Some nine months later (approximately 266 days), if all proceeds well, the original two cells will have multiplied to more than 200 billion cells in the form of a baby.

## Male Reproductive Organs

The male reproductive system (Figure 5-1) has three major components (Katchadourian & Lunde, 1972): the testes, or organs for producing sperm; a system of ducts that store and transport sperm (epididymis, vas deferens, urethra); and the penis, the organ for delivering the sperm. The external organs are the penis and scrotum. The penis consists of spongy tissue and contains the urethra. The urethra serves a dual function of conveying urine from the bladder and, during ejaculation, semen from the testes. When a man is sexually aroused, the penis enlarges and stiffens as the blood vessels in it become engorged (filled). The glans, the tissue at the tip of the penis, is particularly sensitive to stimulation. The scrotum is a pouch that contains the testes (the male gonads) and the tubes that carry sperm from the testes into the penis. The testes produce sperm and a male hormone, testoster-

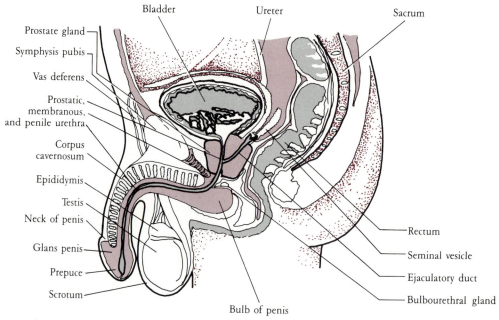

**FIGURE 5-1.** *Male reproductive organs.*

one. Sperm production (spermatogenesis) takes place inside the testes within a series of tubules (called "seminiferous tubules"). The remaining structures are for the delivery of the sperm to and out of the penis during stimulation.

## Female Reproductive Organs

Figure 5-2 shows the female reproductive system. The external organs, collectively referred to as the vulva, are the mons pubis, the major and minor lips, the clitoris, and the vaginal opening. The mons is covered with hair after puberty. The major and minor lips are elongated folds of skin that surround the vaginal opening. The minor lip encloses the clitoris, which, like the penis, is highly sensitive and becomes engorged with blood during sexual excitement.

The internal sex organs include a pair of ovaries, which produce ova (eggs) and two female sex hormones, estrogen and progesterone. The ovarian ligaments hold the ovaries in place. During each menstrual cycle, one mature ovum leaves the ovary and enters the fallopian tube, which carries the ovum to the uterus. Unlike sperm cells, which have locomotor abilities, the ovum is carried to the uterus by the cilia (small, hairlike projections) lining the tube. Most fertilizations occur in the fallopian tube. The uterus is a muscular organ where the fertilized ovum (zygote) lodges itself, matures into an embryo and then a fetus, and eventually becomes a baby. The vagina is the canal leading from the vulva (external genitals) to the uterus.[1]

## The Sexual Response System

Thanks to the bold and pioneering work of Masters and Johnson (1966), our knowledge of the human sexual response cycle has increased dra-

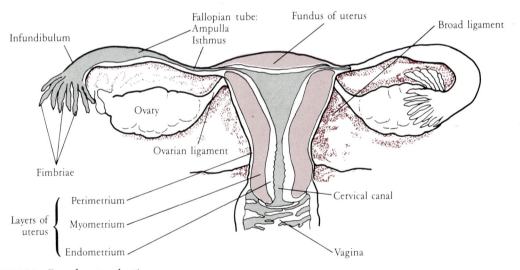

**FIGURE 5-2.** *Female reproductive organs.*

---

[1] Although breasts are not part of the reproductive system, they have erotic significance for many males and females. The nipple and areola (pigmented area around the nipple) are highly sensitive.

**TABLE 5-1.** *Human sexual response cycle: Genital reactions*

| Male | Female |
|---|---|
| *Excitement phase* | |
| Penile erection (3 to 8 sec) as phase is prolonged | Vaginal lubrication (5 to 15 sec) as phase is prolonged |
| Thickening, flattening, and elevation of the scrotum | Thickening of vaginal walls, flattening and elevation of labia majora as phase is prolonged |
| Moderate testicular elevation and size increase | Expansion of inner 2/3 of vaginal barrel and elevation of cervix and body of the uterus |
| *Plateau phase* | |
| Increase in penile coronal circumference and testicular tumescence ($\frac{1}{2}$ to 1 × enlarged) | Orgasmic platform in outer 1/3 of vagina |
| Full testicular elevation and rotation (30 to 35 degrees) | Full inner 2/3 vaginal expansion; uterine and cervical elevation |
| Purple cast to corona of penis (inconsistent, even if orgasm is to ensue) | "Sex skin" discoloration of labia minora (constant, if orgasm is to ensue) |
| Mucoidlike emission from Cowper's gland | Mucoidlike emission from Bartholin's gland |
| *Orgasmic phase* | |
| Ejaculation | Pelvic response |
| 1. Contraction of accessory organs of reproduction (vas deferens, seminal vesicles, ejaculatory duct) and prostate | 1. Contractions of uterus from fundus toward lower uterine segment |
| 2. Relaxation of external bladder sphincter | 2. Minimal relaxation of external cervical os |
| 3. Contractions of penile urethra at 0.8-sec intervals for 2 to 3 contractions (slowing thereafter for 2 to 4 more contractions) | 3. Contraction of vaginal orgasmic platform at 0.8-sec intervals for 4 to 8 contractions (slowing thereafter for 2 to 4 more contractions) |
| 4. External rectal sphincter contractions (2 to 4 contractions at 0.8-sec intervals) | 4. External rectal sphincter contractions (2 to 4 contractions at 0.8-sec intervals) |
| | 5. External urethral sphincter contractions (2 to 3 contractions at irregular intervals) |
| *Resolution phase* | |
| 1. Refractory period with rapid loss of pelvic vasocongestion | 1. Ready return to orgasm with retarded loss of pelvic vasocongestion |
| 2. Loss of penile erection in primary (rapid) and secondary (slow) stages | 2. Loss of "sex skin" color and orgasmic platform in primary (rapid) stage |
| | 3. Loss of remainder of pelvic vasocongestion in secondary (slow) stage |

matically. Table 5-1 lists the genital reactions of sexual response for females and males. The response cycle is divided into four basic phases—excitement, plateau, orgasmic, and resolution. In the first phase, excitement, the body responds to sexual stimulation. This stimulation need not be physical touch alone; it may include images, thoughts, sights, or odors. For males this phase causes an erection of the penis; females experience the secretion of fluids lubricating the vagina. In the plateau phase, blood gathers in the sex organs and other erogenous areas, causing further excitement and pleasurable sensations. The orgasmic phase follows, in which the pleasurable feelings climax and a series of muscular contractions—an orgasm—occurs. During the resolution phase, the tensions subside and the body systems (blood pressure, breathing, pulse) return to normal rates. After a period of relaxation (called the "refractory period") the person can respond to new stimulation. For males this period can vary from a few minutes to several hours. For females the resolution period is typically very short, lasting only minutes, although it may lengthen as the female ages.

## FORMS OF SEXUAL EXPRESSION

Humans express their sexuality in a multitude of ways, ranging from touching, kissing, and masturbation to oral sex, anal stimulation, and coitus. Each form provides a pleasurable expression of intimacy when *both* partners find the act pleasing and enjoyable. Stimulating oneself or another by touching or rubbing the genitals (masturbation) has been condemned or supported, depending on the era and the authority, by the religious and medical communities. In contemporary society increased acceptance of masturbation is found in sex-therapy books, where it is viewed as a way of learning about one's sexual functioning. For example, Read (1979) writes that masturbation leads to "a freeing of one's sexual feelings and a releasing of one's sexual energy and needs. To be able to masturbate without guilt is to say, 'I accept and enjoy my sexual feelings'" (p. 81). However, some people believe masturbation is morally wrong. The choice is based on one's personal moral perspective.

Masturbation is more common among males than females—although it is increasing among women. Both sexes often fantasize while masturbating. Erotic photographs, movies, novels, or thoughts can lead to sexual arousal and often accompany self-masturbation. Stimulating a part-ner's genitals can enhance the excitement or plateau phase. Indeed, many couples engage in mutual masturbation in lieu of intercourse. Others find that manual stimulation of the clitoris during intercourse enhances the likelihood of orgasm. Having both partners experience an orgasm (not necessarily simultaneously) enhances intimacy for many couples.

A somewhat less common but increasingly accepted form of sexual expression is oral sex. **Fellatio** is oral stimulation of the penis, and **cunnilingus** is oral stimulation of the female genitals. Many people view oral sex as unclean, but others find it highly pleasurable.

Sexual intercourse is the most common form of intimate sexual activity between adults. The act involves inserting the penis into the vagina and moving it back and forth with pelvic thrusts. When intercourse is sustained, both partners may experience great pleasure and orgasm.

Some couples engaging in further sexual experimentation attempt anal intercourse—a practice that we strongly discourage. Not only infectious bacteria but also the deadly HIV virus that causes AIDS (acquired immune deficiency syndrome) are transmitted readily in this manner from an infected individual to a noninfected individual. Because the health risks from this sexual practice are extremely high, anal intercourse is more than simply an unwise sexual expression—it is downright foolish.

## SEXUAL PREFERENCE AND RESPONSIBLE SEXUALITY

Sexual preference, or orientation, may be more complex than originally believed. Maier (1984) indicates that there are four recognizable levels of sexual orientation. At the two extremes are exclusive **heterosexuality** and **homosexuality.** Heterosexuality, preference for the opposite-sex partner, is by far the most common sex-

## BOX 5-1
### *A Victorian View of Masturbation*

*The imagined results of masturbation, circa 1895. Pictures and descriptions, such as these, of the crippling effects of masturbation on young people appeared in all 19th-century medical books in a fruitless attempt to stop the practice.*

insanity. No wonder that conscience and fear become tormenting inquisitors, and that the symptoms are changed into imaginary spectres of stealthily approaching disease.

"There is no future pang Can deal that justice on the self-condemned He deals on his own soul."

**Why Emissions of the Vital Fluid Debilitate.** The seminal fluid consists of the most vital elements in the human body. It not only assists in maintaining the life of the individual, but communicates the essential, transforming principle which generates another mortal having an imperishable existence. Its waste is a wanton expenditure, which robs the blood of its richness and exhausts the body of its animating powers. No wonder that its loss enfeebles the constitution, and results in impotency, premature decline, St. Vitus's dance, paralysis, epilepsy, consumption, softening of the brain, and

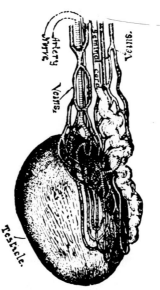

The Testicle in a healthy condition.

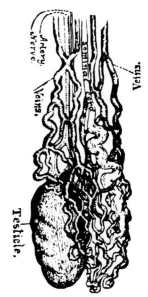

A Testicle wasted by Masturbation.

ual orientation. Homosexuality is a preference for the same sex. General estimates are that 2–3% of the total population is homosexual (Maier, 1984). At the midpoint is **bisexuality,** an equal preference for the same- and opposite-sex partners. The fourth category is **asexuality**—that is, little or no interest in sexual activity with either sex.

Arguments have been made about issues of morality and normality of sexual preference, but the central issue is responsible sexuality. Although defining responsible sexuality is no easy task, we agree with Gordon, Scales, and Everly (1979):

> Normal sexuality is voluntary, genuinely pleasurable, and inclined to enhance the personalities of the people involved. Abnormal or immature sexuality tends to be involuntary. People engage in it not because they want to, but because they can't help it. Immature sexuality is generally exploitative, rarely enjoyable, and often degrad-

ing. Responsible sexuality, by contrast, is characterized by respect for oneself and by genuine caring for another human being [p. 28].

Cassell (1983) describes responsible human sexuality, regardless of sexual preference, as including several dimensions. It is based on a balance between an objective view of human sexuality and a sensitivity to the awareness of human needs; on caring and respect; and on a commitment to humane and humanistic values in intimate relationships.

## PATTERNS OF SEXUAL BEHAVIOR DURING THE LIFE SPAN

Sexual behavior begins as a social process unfolding from birth. We arrive in and depart from this world as sexual beings, and all family members—children and adults—are involved in and concerned about sexuality.

### *Childhood and Early Adolescence*

Learning about the physical differences between the sexes and the social mores that define acceptable sexual behaviors is part of everyone's childhood. In late childhood or early adolescence, issues of sexuality increase in importance. About the time when endocrinological changes occur in young people's bodies, heralding the onset of puberty, increased interest in human sexuality emerges.

At puberty some of the endocrine glands—namely, the hypothalamus, pituitary, and gonadal glands—initiate body changes by secreting hormones (internal chemicals) into the bloodstream or lymphatic system. Though functional at birth, these glands remain dormant (at least for females), owing to an inhibitory effect of the hypothalamus, until a critical body weight of about 106 pounds or a proportion of 17%

body fat is attained. Metabolic rates that accompany this critical weight or fat level trigger the hypothalamus to disengage the inhibitory mechanism, and puberty begins (Higham, 1980). One aspect of puberty is major somatic (body) development. A major growth spurt occurs for girls around the 11th birthday, on the average, and about two years later for boys. This pubertal growth spurt includes lengthening of the trunk, development of greater muscle mass in boys, and broadening of shoulders in boys and of hips in girls (Petersen & Taylor, 1980). The reproductive system begins to mature, and adultlike secondary sex characteristics (pubic hair, breasts, and so on) develop.

NORMAN ROCKWELL. *THE SATURDAY EVENING POST* COVER FOR MARCH 6, 1954

*From day to day the body changes. Think back for a moment to when your body started changing. Can you remember how awkward you felt as you practically watched yourself grow?*

The family can serve an important role during this time in helping the early adolescent prepare for somatic changes. Evidence suggests that some but not much family assistance is forthcoming (see Adams & Gullotta, 1983). For example, most information to prepare girls for menstruation comes either from informal social networks such as girlfriends or from mothers (Logan, 1980; Ruble & Brooks-Gunn, 1982). Generally, fathers are unaware or uninformed about the menstruation experience (Ruble & Brooks-Gunn, 1982). Further, most parents have done little to inform their adolescent boys about erections or nocturnal emissions ("wet dreams"). Boys acquire most of their information from peers. Many boys and girls react to the first nocturnal emission or menstruation with a mixture of excitement, gratification, and perhaps fright (Shipman, 1968). However, this confusion need not occur. The experience of one adolescent girl shows how pleasurable this natural and normal step in growing up can be when the parents work together to ritualize it:

> When I discovered it, I called my mother and she showed me what to do. Then she did something I'll never forget. She told me to come with her and we went to the living room to tell my father. She just looked at me and then at him and said, "Well, your little girl is a young lady now." My Dad gave me a hug and congratulated me, and I felt grown-up and proud that I was really a lady at last [quoted in Shipman, 1968, pp. 6–7].

This kind of experience can help children appreciate their growing sexuality, and such occasions are opportunities to convey information about the human body at a point when interest is high and information is likely to be well received.

Parents need to be sensitive to how young adolescents may feel or think about themselves during the initial stages of change. In one study, for example, sixth-grade girls had a less positive body image than sixth-grade boys or older girls (Petersen, 1979). Petersen reports that girls have considerable difficulty in even acknowledging any feelings about their changing bodies. Thus, it appears that for many girls pubertal change creates considerable stress associated with body image. Several important psychological changes emerge during and after the onset of pubertal change (Adams & Gullotta, 1983). As puberty begins, girls are more distressed than boys. However, after onset girls become less distressed about their appearance, and pubertal change appears to stimulate greater psychological maturity. So although some anxiety may accompany the onset of pubertal change, the outcome of this maturational process may be a highly integrative one (Rierdan & Koff, 1980).

The sexual behavior of most early adolescents focuses on acquiring sexual information, beginning dating, and concern about delayed or precocious physical development. Findings are mixed on who is more reluctant to discuss human sexuality with each other—parents or adolescents. Some researchers find that parents are (Sorenson, 1973), while others find that adolescents are (Alexander & Jorgensen, 1983). In any event, adolescents invariably turn to other young people rather than adults for information and advice. Adolescents express many interests about sexuality in turning to their peers. For example, at an early age adolescents want information about sexual intercourse (Alexander, 1984; Rubenstein, Watson, Drolette, & Rubenstein, 1976), and they show a clear interest in comprehending the meaning, ethics, and issues surrounding human sexuality.

We may not think of dating and romantic love as central issues for late childhood or early adolescence. However, one survey of more than 1000 young people aged 5–18 shows that many young persons perceive themselves as having had a romantic relationship with a person of the other sex (Broderick, 1976). This researcher

## BOX 5-2
### An Experience with Nocturnal Emission

Judy Blume gives a compelling account of a boy's confusion when he is unprepared for his first wet dream:

> That night I dreamed about Lisa. My dream went on and on. It started out at the football game where Lisa put her arm around me. Only in my dream she didn't stop there and Corky was in it too. She was sitting on the football field and Lisa kept saying, "you see, Corky—here's what to do—to do—to do—."
>
> I woke up suddenly. It was morning. I felt wet and my pajamas were sticky. Oh God! There is something wrong with me. *Really wrong.*
>
> Wait a minute. Wait just a minute. Maybe I had a wet dream. Yeah—I'll bet that's it. How about that? I thought they'd be different though. I thought a lot more stuff would come out. And anyway, I wasn't sure I'd ever have one. At least not yet.
>
> What am I supposed to do? Maybe I should stay in bed all day. But then my mother might call the doctor and he'd probably tell her the truth. I better get up.

found that, from the fifth grade on, between 40% and 60% of both boys and girls reported having been in love or currently being in love. Other work suggests that most people experience their first major infatuation at age 13 (Kephart, 1973). Thus, early dating relations and sensations of romantic love are important components of sexuality in late childhood and early adolescence.

Another major concern for young people during this period of life is the timing of pubescence. Precocious (early) puberty comes to some children as young as 8 or 9. For others, delayed maturation perpetuates a childlike image or stature. Both conditions can create tremendous concerns for children. The major problem with atypical development is the discrepancy it causes between a young person's chronological age and expectations associated with bodily appearance (Feinman, 1979). A youth who looks very young for his or her age will be treated as a child. One who looks older will be expected to behave in more mature ways. A physical appearance discrepant from one's actual age can make one feel different from one's peer group and at a disadvantage in comparisons with peers.

### Middle and Late Adolescence

During postpubescent adolescence and the college-age years that follow, young people in Western culture gradually establish independence and autonomy from their families, and a search for intimacy emerges that leads adolescents to seek new mutuality with others outside the family and to build strong emotional ties with friends and dating partners.

The traditional standard placed on emerging romantic relationships is intimacy without intercourse until marriage. However, with gradual changes in moral and sexual standards, many young people are coming to accept intercourse outside marriage. Reiss (1967) observes that many contemporary youths support sexual intimacy when the partners share a meaningful degree of affection. In fact, Reiss (1967) and others (for example, Jurich & Jurich, 1974) have proposed that there are at least four basic codes of sexual conduct. Some adolescents subscribe to the **traditional code**—that sexual intercourse should not occur for either sex until marriage. Others hold a **double standard,** accepting intercourse outside marriage for males but expect-

*Interest in the opposite sex often develops, by early adolescence, into a clear desire to understand the meaning, ethics, and issues surrounding human sexuality.*

ing abstinence from females. Reiss argues that two new standards are coming into vogue. One standard, **permissiveness with affection,** condones sexual intercourse before marriage if the couple believe they are "in love." The other standard, **permissiveness without affection,** accepts sexual intercourse for mere physical pleasure; love is not a prerequisite. Jurich and Jurich (1974) suggest that a corollary of this last standard is "nonexploitative permissiveness": sexual intercourse with or without love is acceptable if both partners maintain a shared understanding of the act.

There is evidence that contemporary adolescents and youths may be adopting more liberal standards. Summarizing several research reports on changes in sexual behavior during the 1970s, Shah and Zelnik (1980) conclude that not only are more unmarried adolescent females having intercourse, but the age of initial intercourse is dropping (see Table 5-2). These shifts are consistent with Reiss' (1967) notion that we are experiencing a general relaxation in sexual standards. Shah and Zelnik suggest that within a stable relationship (such as an engagement) most adolescents accept premarital intercourse. One cannot conclude that contemporary adolescents are promiscuous. Indeed, adolescents are engaging in intercourse at earlier ages—but most confine themselves to one significant partner. Furthermore, even though 16.2 years is now the median

age for first sexual intercourse for females (see Table 5-3), 45% of 19-year-old females remain virgins.

Zelnik and Shah (1983) have found some notable sex differences in data drawn on a sample of youths in 1979. The average age at first intercourse was 16.2 years for females and 15.7 years for males. Females experienced their first intercourse with males approximately three years older than themselves, but males tended to have their first intercourse with a partner very close to their own age. Black adolescents tended to have their first intercourse at a younger age than Whites. Females were more likely than males to have had their first intercourse with either a steady or engaged partner, while males were more likely than females to have had their first intercourse with a friend or recent acquaintance (see Table 5-4). As Table 5-5 shows, for both male and female adolescents aged 15–17, going steady substantially increases the probability of experiencing coitus with one's romantic partner.

Of course, sexual behavioral patterns are unlikely to begin with coitus. Usually they start with masturbation, kissing, or petting. Survey and interview data indicate that by age 19 approximately 80–90% of males and 20–30% of females engage in self-manipulation of the genitals to orgasm (for example, Dupold & Young, 1979; Kinsey, Pomeroy, & Martin, 1948; Ramsey, 1943; Sorensen, 1973). Kissing is usually the first sex-

**TABLE 5-2.** *Percentage of never-married females aged 15–19 who have ever had intercourse, by age and race, United States, 1971 and 1976*

| | 1971 | | | 1976 | | |
|---|---|---|---|---|---|---|
| Age | Total | Black | White | Total | Black | White |
| 15–19 | 26.8 | 52.4 | 22.7 | 34.9 | 62.3 | 31.7 |
| 15 | 13.8 | 31.9 | 10.8 | 18.0 | 38.4 | 13.8 |
| 16 | 21.2 | 46.4 | 17.5 | 25.4 | 52.6 | 22.6 |
| 17 | 26.6 | 56.8 | 21.7 | 40.9 | 68.4 | 36.1 |
| 18 | 36.8 | 59.6 | 32.8 | 45.2 | 74.1 | 43.6 |
| 19 | 46.8 | 79.2 | 41.2 | 55.2 | 83.7 | 48.7 |

**TABLE 5-3.** *Percentage of females aged 15–19 who have ever had intercourse before marriage, by marital status and race, United States, 1971, 1976, and 1979*

| Marital Status and Age | 1971 | | | 1976 | | | 1979 | | |
|---|---|---|---|---|---|---|---|---|---|
| | Total | White | Black | Total | White | Black | Total | White | Black |
| All | 30.4 | 26.4 | 53.7 | 43.4 | 38.3 | 66.3 | 49.8 | 46.6 | 66.2 |
| Ever married | 55.0 | 53.2 | 72.7 | 86.3 | 85.0 | 93.9 | 86.7 | 86.2 | 91.2 |
| Never married | | | | | | | | | |
| Total | 27.6 | 23.2 | 52.4 | 39.2 | 33.6 | 64.3 | 46.0 | 42.3 | 64.8 |
| 15 | 14.4 | 11.3 | 31.2 | 18.6 | 13.8 | 38.9 | 22.5 | 18.3 | 41.4 |
| 16 | 20.9 | 17.0 | 44.4 | 28.9 | 23.7 | 55.1 | 37.8 | 35.4 | 50.4 |
| 17 | 26.1 | 20.2 | 58.9 | 42.9 | 36.1 | 71.0 | 48.5 | 44.1 | 73.3 |
| 18 | 39.7 | 35.6 | 60.2 | 51.4 | 46.0 | 76.2 | 56.9 | 52.6 | 76.3 |
| 19 | 46.4 | 40.7 | 78.3 | 59.5 | 53.6 | 83.9 | 69.0 | 64.9 | 88.5 |
| Age at first intercourse (all) | | | | | | | | | |
| Mean | 16.4 | 16.6 | 15.9 | 16.1 | 16.3 | 15.6 | 16.2 | 16.4 | 15.5 |

**TABLE 5-4.** *Percentage distribution of females aged 15–19 and of males aged 17–21, by relationship with their first sexual partner, according to race, United States, 1979*

| Relationship with First Partner | Females | | | Males | | |
|---|---|---|---|---|---|---|
| | Total | White | Black | Total | White | Black |
| Engaged | 9.3 | 9.6 | 8.2 | 0.6 | 0.5 | 1.0 |
| Going steady | 55.2 | 57.6 | 46.5 | 36.5 | 39.2 | 21.9 |
| Dating | 24.4 | 22.2 | 32.6 | 20.0 | 20.2 | 19.0 |
| Friends | 6.7 | 6.0 | 9.4 | 33.7 | 30.2 | 52.4 |
| Recently met[a] | 4.4 | 4.6 | 3.3 | 9.3 | 9.9 | 5.7 |

[a] Among females in this table and Table 5-5, this category includes a small number who reported some other relationship.

**TABLE 5-5.** *Percentage distribution of females aged 15–19 and of males aged 17–21, by relationship with their first sexual partner, according to age at first intercourse, United States, 1979*

| Relationship with First Partner | Females | | | Males | | |
|---|---|---|---|---|---|---|
| | <15 | 15–17 | >18 | <15 | 15–17 | >18 |
| Engaged | 3.9 | 8.8 | 18.7 | 0.4 | 0.8 | 0.0 |
| Going steady | 44.4 | 61.9 | 46.1 | 20.0 | 46.2 | 47.9 |
| Dating | 28.9 | 21.6 | 29.0 | 18.6 | 22.4 | 12.6 |
| Friends | 13.2 | 4.3 | 5.4 | 54.4 | 20.0 | 26.7 |
| Recently met | 9.6 | 3.4 | 0.8 | 6.6 | 10.6 | 12.8 |

ual experience with a partner. By middle adolescence nearly everyone has had at least one experience in kissing a person of the other sex (Dupold & Young, 1979). As relationships grow, the next stage in sexual involvement is usually petting. Approximately 60% of 15-year-olds have been involved in light petting (stimulation outside a partner's clothes) and approximately 30% in heavy petting (caressing a partner's body) (Dupold & Young, 1979).

## Adulthood

The most credible studies to date on sexual relationships between adults both inside and outside marriage are by Blumstein and Schwartz (1983), Hunt (1974), Kinsey et al. (1948), and Tavris and Sadd (1977). Despite sampling and measurement problems in all these reports, these researchers provide the best available data on sexuality inside and outside marriage.

Summarizing these works, Williams (1980) notes that the frequency of sexual intercourse has not increased dramatically from the 1940s to the 1970s. For example, in the 1940s males aged 26–35 reported a weekly median frequency of 1.9 times. During the 1970s (depending on the report) this increased by 10% (Tavris & Sadd, 1977) to approximately 2.1 times weekly. Of course, these figures are averages, and there is a wide range of variability. Some couples engage in sex less than twice a month, others three or more times a day.

Evidence suggests that neither educational nor occupational status affects frequency of coitus in marriage. However, religion may. In the early 1940s, Kinsey reported that less religious husbands had intercourse 20–30% more frequently than more religious husbands. Hunt (1974), writing in the 1970s, reports that religious females report a lower frequency of sexual intercourse than either religious males or nonreligious males and females.

Marital adjustment and sexual compatibility are related. Partners may vary in their desire for physical closeness and touching and in their preferences about the extent and nature of foreplay, the frequency and length of intercourse, and various practices. Similarly, what stimulates them may differ. Learning what one's partner likes adds to one's excitement and pleasure. Many spouses make changes to accommodate and please their partners throughout marriage. Where sexual incompatibility exists, a spouse may seek sexual liaisons outside of marriage. Williams (1980) recognizes two basic forms of extramarital affairs. In a "conventional affair" the activity is kept hidden by secrecy and deception. The other spouse does not consciously recognize the affair and would not condone it. In other cases the affair is openly known and consented to, as both spouses have agreed to extramarital sex—an arrangement that some call "open marriage" (O'Neill & O'Neill, 1972). (However, O'Neill does state that an open marriage doesn't necessarily mean consent between the couple for extramarital sex. It may merely mean acceptance of platonic heterosexual friendships.)

It is estimated that about half of all married men have sexual intercourse with someone other than their wives at some point during the marriage (Kinsey, cited in Williams, 1980). Men at lower educational levels have a higher incidence of extramarital intercourse in their twenties; college-educated men have a higher incidence in their thirties. For females the frequency of extramarital relations is roughly half that for males, so that only 25% of married women have extramarital sexual relations (Hunt, 1974; Williams, 1980). However, comparisons of the various data sources suggest that extramarital sex is increasing, and increasing faster for females than for males.

Why do people seek extramarital sexual experiences? Several studies suggest that the primary reasons are unhappy marriages and unfulfilled sexual needs (Williams, 1980). Other reasons include a partner's physical handicap, unfaithfulness, or unloving, unclean, or unattractive nature; curiosity; desire for variety; uncertainty about one's sexuality; need for escape; fear of aging; revenge; and lack of inhibitions.

Recent estimates suggest that a very small number of persons engage in consensual adultery—adultery with the consent of one's spouse (Williams, 1980). Smith and Smith (1974) describe consensual extramarital relations as appearing in three basic forms: adultery toleration, comarital relations, and group marriage. Adultery toleration involves recognized freedom by both spouses to engage in extramarital sex. In comarital relations, extramarital relations are incorporated into the marriage itself. Sometimes this activity is called "mate swapping" or "swinging." In group marriage there is unrestricted access to all couples within the group for sexual activity.

### Late Adulthood

It is not uncommon for younger persons to imagine that "old" people don't have sex. Although the frequency of coitus may decline with age, the need for sexual companionship and expression does not. Changes in sexual physiology occur with age for both sexes. Body responses are slowed and the intensity of sexual responses diminishes. However, both males and females remain capable of orgasm and can find great fulfillment in sexual activities. As many as one third of all men past 70 are still sexually active (Comfort, 1976). Further, for both men and women, regular sexual activity enhances the probability of continued sexual capability. Indeed, Masters and Johnson (1966) say that the three essential factors for continued sexual activity in the later years are good health, interest in a sexual partner, and continuing sexual experience.

As individuals age, several physiological changes alter basic sexual responses. For males,

a full erection may occur less readily, diminished expulsive pressure during ejaculation is likely, a reduced volume of seminal fluid is produced, and sexual intercourse may become less frequent. Further, men experience a decline in testosterone levels, which results in a decline in sperm production. Occasionally this hormonal shift is associated with an enlargement of the prostate. Because prostate enlargement results in urinary problems, surgery may be needed. Psychological problems accompanying these changes for men can include depression and anxiety about a loss of virility.

Parallel physiological changes occur in women as they age. Lubricating fluid diminishes in volume, the vaginal walls become less elastic, and more time is needed to elicit arousal. Menstruation ceases and menopause occurs. A general hormonal imbalance at menopause can create headaches, dizziness, hot flashes, and heart palpitations. Some women become depressed, anxious, or irritable, and sometimes estrogen replacement therapy is needed.

One final problem in regard to sexuality in old age is that women, on the average, outlive men. Although appreciation for physical closeness and caressing increases with age (Maier, 1984), most women over 75 are widowed, and many live in nursing homes or retirement centers with mostly female residents. Therefore, there is limited opportunity for sexual expression with a partner during the last few years of women's lives.

## SEXUAL DYSFUNCTIONS

Adequate sexual functioning is an important component in an intimate relationship. Numerous reviews indicate that 50–80% of couples in marital therapy have reported struggles with sexual problems (Scharff, 1976; Stuart & Hammond, 1980).

These dysfunctions can be categorized into four broad groups (Levine, 1981). **Gender-identity disorders** are disturbances in self-image based on discrepant perceptions of masculinity and femininity. Such disorders are variously labeled as gender dysphoria syndrome, transvestism, or transsexualism. Another form of sexual dysfunction is **perversion.** Perversions such as masochism, sadism, pedophilia, rape, voyeurism, or exhibitionism are thought by many psychiatrists and sex therapists to be erotic expressions of aggression toward a victim (rather than a partner). Though relatively rare among both sexes, both gender-identity disorders and perversions are more common among men than women. **Homosexuality,** a sexual attraction to the same sex, is not a sexual dysfunction when chosen freely as a lifestyle. However, it can be considered a dysfunction when a person experiences pain and dissatisfaction with this sexual preference. The fourth category, **dysfunctional symptoms,** involves the inability to experience satisfying sexual arousal to orgasm with an intimate partner. Because the last category is the most common sexual dysfunction found in marital life, we will briefly explore this area further.

Table 5-6 summarizes the five most common components of sexual dysfunctions and the primary symptoms for males and females. Many of these symptoms can be reduced by dealing with sexual fears and anxieties through sexual skill acquisition, systematic desensitization (gradual exposure to anxiety-provoking thoughts and actions), reinforcement techniques, and other techniques used in sex therapy and marital counseling (see, for example, Levine, 1981; Stuart & Hammond, 1980; Wince, 1981).

Any couple may have an occasional adjustment problem resulting in a temporary sexual dysfunction, but many couples are at "high risk" for sexual problems from the very beginning. One study comparing sexually dysfunctional with functional couples has found a profile of behaviors and personal history that suggests early socialization experiences can place an individual or couple at risk (Hock, Safir, Peres, & Shepher, 1981). These researchers have found that the potential for developing sexual dysfunctions is high:

1. If, as a child, one experienced familial disruptions such as divorce or death of a parent.
2. If the male was raised in a traditionally religious household and continues to maintain a traditional value system.
3. If the couple have little correct knowledge of human sexual response and needs.
4. If there is little empathy or communication between the couple.
5. If the couple hold prejudices or myths about sexual behavior or performance.

Collectively, these factors suggest that individuals who get little sex education during childhood are at risk for developing sexual dysfunctions. Further, overinternalization of highly traditional sex-role values, limited interpersonal social skill development, and the establishment and maintenance of sexual myths place adult intimate relations at risk for sexual dysfunctions and dissatisfaction. Early sex education may be important in preventing many of the factors underlying dysfunction from occurring in the first place.

# SEXUALLY TRANSMITTED DISEASES

When any two individuals come into contact, the possibility exists that bacteria or viruses can be transmitted. This likelihood increases when the individuals are sexual partners. Sexually transmitted infections (venereal diseases) can be

**TABLE 5-6.** *Classification of sexual dysfunctions by component symptoms*

| Component | Sex | Symptoms | Common Terminology |
|---|---|---|---|
| Desire (libido) | Male and female | Absent desire<br>Infrequent desire<br>Excessive desire | None |
| Arousal | Male | Inability to obtain erection<br>Inability to maintain erection | Impotence or erectile dysfunction |
| | Female | Inability to become aroused<br>Inability to stay aroused | Frigidity or excitement phase dysfunction |
| Orgasm | Male | Rapid, uncontrolled ejaculation<br>Ejaculation too difficult to achieve<br>Inability to ejaculate with partner<br>Inability to ejaculate in the vagina | Premature ejaculation<br>Retarded ejaculation<br>Ejaculatory failure or ejaculatory incompetence |
| | | Ejaculation without orgasm<br>Orgasm without ejaculation<br>Orgasm with no apparent ejaculation (semen in bladder) | Pleasureless orgasm<br>Dry orgasm<br>Retrograde ejaculation |
| | Female | Orgasm too rapid<br>Orgasm too difficult to achieve<br>Inability to achieve orgasm with partner<br>Inability to achieve orgasm during intercourse<br>Pleasureless orgasm | Orgasmic phase dysfunction<br><br>Coital anorgasmia<br>Pleasureless orgasm |
| Satisfaction | Male and female | Little or no emotional satisfaction | None |
| Other problems | Male | Penile anesthesia during coitus<br>Penile pain during coitus or with erection | None<br>Male dyspareunia |
| | Female | Vaginal anesthesia during coitus<br>Vaginal or pelvic pain during coitus<br>Intolerance of intromission | Dyspareunia<br>Vaginismus |

passed during sexual activity to the oral, anal, or vaginal orifices (body openings). The organisms that cause most sexually transmitted diseases thrive in darkness, moisture, and warmth. The human body provides the perfect environment for these organisms. Thus, venereal disease finds a comfortable home in the mucous membranes of the genitalia, mouth, throat, anus, or eyes. If left untreated, many venereal diseases can cause serious and permanent damage, including death. Of equal concern is that all venereal diseases can be passed on to unborn children unless precautions are taken.

Four sexually transmitted diseases concern us in this chapter: syphilis, gonorrhea, herpes, and acquired immune deficiency syndrome (AIDS).

## Syphilis

There is reason to believe that syphilis originated in the New World. We have no evidence that syphilis existed in Europe before Columbus'

All too often, we at VD clinics emphasize the importance of the infected patient. While this is a major concern of ours, we also recognize that too little emphasis is given to the infected person's partner(s).

If we only concern ourselves with the patient who is the source of the infection, we deal with *just half of the problem*. Many times the source of the infection is identified, but others who may have been exposed never learn of their relation to the chain of infection.

If you have any symptoms of VD, get them checked out at our VD clinic or by your own private physician — But, in either case, it's *your responsibility* to let your sexual contacts know that they too, need a check-up. Whether male or female, *symptoms aren't always present*, so don't assume they'll seek medical help on their own.

Both you and your partner(s) should *be aware* of any changes in the genital area, or specifically:

(1) Any Discharge   (2) Burning upon Urination   (3) Rashes
(4) Sores   (5) Genital Itching

But remember, you may NOT have any symptoms, so if suspicious, *get a complete VD check-up* — a syphilis blood test and a gonorrhea culture.

So, next time when you visit, take care of your partners and bring a date to the clinic. We'll serve you well!

SAN FRANCISCO CITY CLINIC
356 SEVENTH STREET
SAN FRANCISCO, CALIFORNIA 94103

VD Information Hotline 495-OGOD!
(495-6463)

*What tool of prevention does this poster illustrate? What might this poster say if it were aimed at primary prevention of VD?*

voyage, but by 1497 the disease was running rampant there, causing many deaths. Columbus himself is thought to have died of syphilis. Called by various names (*pox, bad blood, Neapolitan disease*), this disease received its present name in the 16th century when an Italian physician, Girolamo Francastoro, wrote a poem in which a shepherd named Syphilus was struck by this plague.

Syphilis is caused by a slender, corkscrew-shaped microorganism called a *spirochete*. It is most commonly spread by direct contact during sexual intercourse. Once infected, an individual, if left untreated, goes through three stages of the disease and a latent period.

The first ("primary") stage emerges three to four weeks after being infected. One or more hard, sometimes painless open sores called *chancres* emerge, each ranging from one-eighth inch to one inch in diameter. In men, chancres appear on the shaft of the penis; in women, on the vulva, the vaginal walls, or the cervix. After a few weeks the chancres disappear but the disease does not. The disappearance of these chancres reflects the evolution of the disease into the second ("secondary") stage.

Symptoms of the secondary stage, appearing some two to six months after exposure, are headaches, loss of appetite, sore throat, sometimes a fever, and one of two types of skin rash—

macular or papular syphilide. In macular syphilide, small, round, shiny red spots appear on the arms and/or upper body. Papular syphilide appears as raised red spots covering the whole body. Hair loss can occur.

After several weeks syphilis enters a latent period. In this period all symptoms disappear, as the disease becomes spontaneously cured, remains latent, or invades other organs such as the eyes, heart, brain, or spinal cord. During the latent period, the disease is no longer contagious during intercourse, but a pregnant woman can transmit it to the fetus.

After one or several years, if the disease has been invading other body tissues, the final (third, or "tertiary") stage occurs. In this stage, extremely serious health problems appear. Depending on which body organ has been attacked, they may include blindness, insanity, paralysis, or severe heart problems. It is the heart problems that most frequently cause death (Morton, 1976).

## Gonorrhea

Gonorrhea, caused by the bacterium *Neisseria gonorrhoeae,* affects the mucous membranes of the throat, rectum, or genitalia. Slang terms for gonorrhea include *drip, clap, dose,* and *strain.* The first symptom is a yellowish, puslike discharge from the penis or a yellowish-green vaginal discharge. Males may also have a burning sensation when urinating and an itching sensation within the urethra. As many as 80% of infected females have no early symptoms.

In more advanced stages, gonorrhea can cause chronic infection of the urethra, resulting in inability to urinate. In women the disease can spread throughout the uterus and fallopian tubes, causing incorrectable sterility. Infections resulting from gonorrhea can cause heart problems, blindness, or arthritis. Formerly, infants became infected at birth in their passage through the diseased birth canal, resulting in blindness. To avoid this possibility, silver nitrate drops or penicillin ointments are put in newborns' eyes.

Before the discovery of penicillin, syphilis and gonorrhea were treated with arsenic, mercury, and other unsuccessful remedies. Now a variety of antibiotics can be taken during the early stage of these infections to treat and eliminate them.

## Herpes

Herpes takes its name from *herpein* (Greek), "to creep." In its latent stage, the herpes virus most often resides at the base of the spine or recessed in the fifth cranial nerve. When the carrier's resistance is lowered by fatigue, stress, or illness, the virus "creeps" down the nerve fibers at the rate of one inch in 16 hours and erupts in a painful sore that appears most often on the lips, inside the mouth, or on the genitals. The venereal forms of the virus are herpes simplex virus type 1 (HSV 1) and herpes simplex virus type 2 (HSV 2) (Gregg, 1983). There are more than 50 kinds of herpes viruses (Langston, 1983). The most common are herpes simplex types 1 and 2, which infect genitals, skin, eyes, the mouth, and the brain; herpes zoster, which causes shingles and chicken pox; cytomegalovirus, which causes blindness or mental retardation in babies; and Epstein-Barr virus, which causes mononucleosis (kissing disease) and some forms of cancer.

It was once incorrectly believed that herpes type 1 occurred only above the waist and type 2 only below the waist. Because of oral contact with various parts of the body, both types are increasingly found almost anywhere (see Table 5-7).

Not to be confused with cold sores or fever blisters, herpes simplex type 2 blisters (often accompanied by a fever and chills) appear anywhere from one day to about three weeks after

**TABLE 5-7.** *Estimated frequency and location of herpes simplex type 1 and type 2 infections*

| Location of Primary or Recurrent Disease | Most Frequent Herpes Type | Estimated No. Cases/Year in United States |
|---|---|---|
| Primary | | |
| Mouth | 95% type 1 | 500,000 |
| Eye | 95% type 1 | Unknown |
| Recurrent | | |
| Mouth | 95% type 1 | 98 million |
| Eye | 95% type 1 | 280,000–300,000 |
| Primary | | |
| Genitals | 60–90% type 2 | 20,000–500,000 |
| Fingers | 80% (?) type 2 | Unknown |
| Recurrent | | |
| Genitals | 70–85% type 2 | 3–9 million |
| | 15–30% type 1 | |
| Fingers | Often type 2 | Unknown |

contact. (Figure 5-3 shows the most common locations.) The sores and flulike symptoms disappear over the course of a few days to several weeks, as the virus retreats along the nerve fibers to wait to erupt again at some future date. During an outbreak of HSV 1 or 2 the disease is highly contagious because the sore or sores are constantly shedding the virus. Caution needs to be exercised at this time because one can inadvertently give the virus to others or spread it to other parts of one's own body. For example, inserting contact lenses after touching a cold sore without washing one's hands with soap and water may transmit billions of active viruses to one's eyes (Bettoli, 1982).

Unlike other venereal disease organisms, which cannot live outside the body, HSV 1 and 2 can survive for several hours on such surfaces as the human skin, clothing, and plastic (Turner, Shehab, Osborne, & Hendley, 1982). In fact, the National Institutes of Health recently reported that three elderly women had contracted the disease while soaking in a hot tub. Although viruses cannot live in the chemically treated water in a hot tub, they did survive long enough on the tub rim to infect these three individuals ("Highlights," 1984).

Additional concern is warranted for pregnant women who have genital herpes. For instance, genital herpes increases the risk of spontaneous abortion or premature delivery. There is also a risk of 40–60% that a woman delivering vaginally who is experiencing an outbreak of genital herpes at the time of delivery will infect her infant (Bettoli, 1982).[2] Finally, evidence is accumulating that women with genital herpes run eight times the normal risk of developing cervical cancer.

---

[2] A woman with genital herpes need not fear infecting her unborn infant provided she fully informs her physician of her condition. Should an outbreak of HSV occur near or during the birth process, the child can still be safely delivered by a caesarean section.

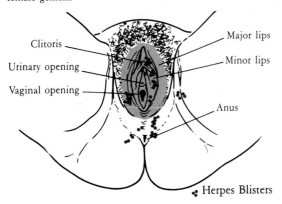

Most common area of herpes blistering on external female genitals

Clitoris

Urinary opening

Vaginal opening

Major lips

Minor lips

Anus

Herpes Blisters

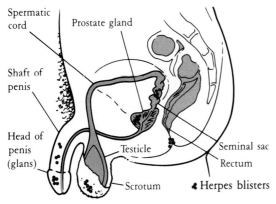

Most common locations of herpes virus in internal and external male genital system

Spermatic cord

Prostate gland

Shaft of penis

Head of penis (glans)

Testicle

Seminal sac

Rectum

Scrotum

Herpes blisters

**FIGURE 5-3.** *Areas of female and male genitals commonly infected with herpes simplex type 2.*

Although genital herpes cannot be cured at this time,[3] it can be managed. The drug acyclovir has been approved for topical application and has been shown to be effective in speeding the healing of HSV sores. This same drug in an oral form is presently undergoing clinical trials to determine its safety and effectiveness as an oral medication. Studies continue, and preliminary results are encouraging (Corey & Holmes, 1983).

Meanwhile, the following suggestions will minimize discomfort for the herpes sufferer and reduce the probability of spreading the disease to others. During an outbreak of genital sores, avoid intercourse (oral, anal, or vaginal) for 14 days. There is some debate over whether condoms may help prevent the spread of genital HSV. Although condoms are effective in protecting against other venereal diseases, concern has been expressed that the HSV may pass through the condom and infect a partner. Our advice is to play it safe and avoid intercourse. When the HSV is active, take particular care not to touch the sores. Should you touch a sore, wash your hands immediately and do not touch your eyes. To prevent recurrences, get ample rest and good nutrition and engage in stress reduction techniques. We urge women sufferers to receive an annual medical exam that includes a pap smear. Herpes, though painful for one's body and soul, can be lived with successfully with some care and effort (Englebardt, 1982; Lenard, 1982; Randal, 1982).

## Acquired Immune Deficiency Syndrome (AIDS)

The story of this last venereal disease begins in March 1981, when a group of epidemiologists[4] at the Center for Disease Control in Atlanta, Georgia, noticed something unusual. In California, in the Los Angeles area, five male homosexuals had

---

[3] A research team from the National Institute of Dental Research and Allergy and Infectious Diseases has recently reported success in developing a genetically engineered vaccine that is effective in preventing mice from developing HSV. This vaccine also appears to prevent recurrent outbreaks of HSV in mice. Whether this vaccine will prove safe and effective is unknown at this time. Clinical trials with human subjects are a few years away (Crener, MacKett, Wohlenberg, Notkins, & Moss, 1985).

[4] An epidemiologist is a person who studies epidemics.

died during the previous 18 months of a rare protozoan infection that causes pneumonia. Intrigued by their finding, the researchers were also surprised, on further investigation, to discover that an unusually large number of homosexuals had died from a very rare skin malignancy called Kaposi's sarcoma. Both diseases had been known to strike individuals undergoing immunosuppressive therapy (typically to prevent the body's rejection of a transplanted organ). But why would this disease attack these individuals and, as time went on, other persons who were not homosexual? The answer to this riddle, called "acquired immune deficiency syndrome" (AIDS), can be found in a virus that destroys the body's ability to ward off disease (*AIDS Information Bulletin,* 1983; Culliton, 1984; *Facts about AIDS,* 1983; West, 1983).

Despite the intensive efforts of hundreds of research centers around the world, there is no cure or preventive vaccine that has yet been developed to control the deadliest disease that humankind has ever encountered. The HIV virus that is responsible for AIDS has been reported in over 80 countries. As of March 9, 1987, almost 32,000 individuals in the United States have been diagnosed as having AIDS and more than half of that number have already succumbed to the disease. It is estimated that as many as 1.5 million U.S. citizens have been infected by the HIV virus. Of this 1.5 million, it is thought that by 1991 approximately 300,000 persons will have been diagnosed as having AIDS, with 72,000 new cases diagnosed in that year alone. Although the risk to heterosexual individuals is increasing as the disease moves out of formerly high-risk populations (some fear rapidly), the majority of reported AIDS cases remain either homosexual or bisexual men (73%) or male or female intravenous drug users (17%). The remaining 10% include the heterosexual partners of AIDS carriers, recipients of contaminated blood transfusions, and infants born to infected mothers.

The HIV virus is passed in the following ways: by sexual intercourse from an infected individual to another person, by the sharing of unsterilized needles between drug users, through contaminated blood transfusions, and from an infected mother to an unborn child. The disease appears to progress through three stages. In the first stage, the individual tests positive for AIDS antibodies but otherwise remains asymptomatic and appears healthy. Currently, there is no estimate of how many individuals in this first group will develop AIDS. The next stage is called AIDS-related complex or ARC for short. Individuals in this stage experience noticeably swollen glands, near constant fevers in excess of 100 °F, persistent diarrhea, and fatigue. It is also unclear at the present time how many of these individuals will go on to develop AIDS. The final stage is AIDS. The body's immune system has been severely weakened or destroyed, and the body is vulnerable to any number of opportunistic diseases. It is these opportunistic infections that kill an AIDS carrier.

Disturbingly, there may be a "latent period" from a few months to several years between contracting AIDS and the onset of symptoms. Individuals may therefore be transmitting the disease without realizing that they are carriers (Centers for Disease Control, 1983a, b). Aside from infants *in utero* or sexual partners of AIDS carriers, *no evidence exists that AIDS can be transmitted by casual or even close daily contact with AIDS victims.* Various experimental drugs, such as AZT and peptide T are being used to provide some help to individuals struggling with AIDS. Until such time as a cure or vaccine is developed, we urge sexually active individuals to take the following steps to help prevent the spread of this fatal disease.

1. Avoid sexual contact with persons who have AIDS.
2. Avoid engaging in sex with multiple partners or with others who have multiple partners.
3. Avoid sex with illegal intravenous drug users.

4. *Insist that both you and your sexual partner use condoms and spermicidal foam.*

5. Homosexuals should *not* use amyl nitrite to facilitate lovemaking. This drug is an immunosuppressant—the worst possible agent to have in your bodies!

# BIRTH CONTROL

The most effective way to prevent pregnancy is abstinence. However, if a couple decide to have sexual intercourse and do not currently want a child, they should adopt a method of birth control.

## Contraception

**Contraception** is the use of a device or method to prevent pregnancy. Table 5-8 describes the major contraceptive methods.

Perhaps the most effective and widely used method today is the **oral contraceptive pill,** or birth-control pill. The "pill" is taken orally by the female. It contains a combination of progesterone and estrogen that prevents the release of an ovum and thereby prevents fertilization. Generally, the pill is taken for 21 days, beginning on day 6 after the start of menstruation. (Some brands also provide 7 placebo pills to be taken following the 21 hormone-containing pills, in order to simplify the on-and-off regimen to one of taking a pill daily.) During the next seven days, menstruation occurs. This method is 97–99.7% effective. The pill is simple and easy to use and does not require special preparation before intercourse. Some women experience side effects. The most common problems are reported nausea, weight gain, headaches, and depression. To obtain the pill, the woman must have a physical examination and get a prescription.

Others prefer to use an **intrauterine device** (IUD). An IUD is typically made of plastic, sometimes containing small amounts of copper. The device, placed by a gynecologist into the uterus, prevents the fertilized egg from becoming implanted. Reported effectiveness is 97–99%. A small percentage of users expel the IUD without knowing it. There is also a risk of approximately 1 in 1000 that the uterus will become perforated by the IUD and require surgical removal (Boston Women's Health Book Collective, 1976).

Because of side effects of the pill and the IUD, some women prefer to use a **diaphragm.** Requiring a medical prescription and fitted by a doctor, a diaphragm is a concave disk with a flexible springlike rim. To use the diaphragm, the female coats it with a spermicidal jelly and inserts it into the vagina, where it fits snugly over the cervix and serves as a type of seal to prevent sperm from entering the uterus. When used properly, the diaphragm is approximately 97% effective. Although there are no major side effects, many couples find it awkward to stop foreplay to insert the diaphragm. Further, some women report that the cream or jelly used with the diaphragm causes irritation (Boston Women's Health Book Collective, 1976).

Two other choices are **spermicide,** which comes in foam, jelly, or cream form, and **condoms.** Spermicides are sold over the counter without a prescription. They kill sperm on contact and are inserted into the vagina, using an applicator, before intercourse. Effectiveness ranges between 70% and 80% and depends on how conscientiously it is used. To be most effective, the cream or foam must be inserted no more than 15 minutes prior to intercourse. Hence, many men and women perceive it as somewhat inconvenient.

The condom ("rubber," "prophylactic") is a rubber sheath that fits tightly over the erect penis. Ejaculated sperm are retained inside the condom (unless it ruptures). When used properly, it is about 97% effective. Because the condom is sold over the counter, the ease of obtaining it, along with its low cost, makes it a very useful contraceptive.

**TABLE 5-8.** *Major contraceptive methods*

| Method | Birth-Control Pills | Minipills | Intrauterine Device (IUD) |
|---|---|---|---|
| **What is it?** | Pills with two hormones, an estrogen and progestin, similar to the hormones a woman makes in her own ovaries. | Pills with just one type of hormone: a progestin, similar to a hormone a woman makes in her own ovaries. | A small piece of plastic with nylon threads attached. Some have copper wire wrapped around them. One IUD gives off a hormone, progesterone. |
| **How does it work?** | Prevents release of egg from ovaries, makes cervical mucus thicker, and changes lining of the uterus. | It may prevent release of egg from ovaries, makes cervical mucus thicker, and changes lining of uterus, making it harder for a fertilized egg to start growing there. | The IUD is inserted into the uterus. It is not known exactly how the IUD prevents pregnancy. |
| **How reliable or effective is it?** | 99.7% if used consistently but much less effective if used carelessly. | 97–99% if used perfectly but less effective if used carelessly. | 97–99% if patient checks for threads regularly. |
| **How would I use it?** | Either of two ways: 1. A pill a day for 3 weeks, stop for 1 week, then start a new pack. 2. A pill every day with no stopping between packs. | Take one pill every day as long as you want to avoid pregnancy. | Check threads at least once a month right after the period ends to make sure your IUD is still properly in place. |
| **Are there problems with it?** | Must be prescribed by a doctor. All women should have a medical exam before taking the pill, and some women should not take it. | Must be prescribed by a doctor. All women should have a medical exam first. | Must be inserted by a doctor after a pelvic examination. Cannot be used by all women. Sometimes the uterus "pushes" it out. |
| **What are the side effects or complications?** | Nausea, weight gain, headaches, missed periods, darkened skin on the face, or depression may occur. More serious and more rare problems are blood clots in the legs, the lungs, or the brain and heart attacks. | Irregular periods, missed periods, and spotting may occur and are more common problems with minipills than with the regular birth-control pills. | May cause cramps, bleeding, or spotting; infections of the uterus or of the oviducts (tubes) may be serious. See a doctor for pain, bleeding, fever, or a bad discharge. |
| **What are the advantages?** | Convenient, extremely effective, does not interfere with sex, may diminish menstrual cramps. | Convenient, effective, does not interfere with sex, less serious side effects than with regular birth-control pills. | Effective, always there when needed, but usually not felt by either partner. |

*continues*

Finally, a recently introduced contraceptive device is the **vaginal sponge,** a soft, disposable circular device that is inserted into the vagina and covers the cervix. It prevents pregnancy by blocking the entrance to the uterus so that sperm cannot enter and by releasing a spermicide. The vaginal sponge is effective for 24 hours and should be left in place for at least 6 hours after intercourse (Aznar, 1979; Edelman, 1980; Vorhauer, 1980).

**TABLE 5-8.** *Continued*

| Method | Diaphragm with Spermicidal Jelly or Cream | Spermicidal Foam, Jelly, or Cream | Condom |
|---|---|---|---|
| **What is it?** | A shallow rubber cup used with a sperm-killing jelly or cream. | Cream and jelly come in tubes; foam comes in aerosol cans or individual applicators. All are placed into the vagina. | A sheath of rubber shaped to fit snugly over the erect penis. |
| **How does it work?** | Fits inside the vagina. The rubber cup forms a barrier between the uterus and the sperm. The jelly or cream kills the sperm. | Foam, jelly, and cream contain a chemical that kills sperm and acts as a physical barrier between sperm and the uterus. | Prevents sperm from getting inside the vagina during intercourse. |
| **How reliable or effective is it?** | About 97% effective if used correctly and consistently but much less effective if used carelessly. | About 90–97% effective if used correctly and consistently but much less effective if used carelessly. | About 97% effective if used correctly and consistently but much less effective if used carelessly. |
| **How would I use it?** | Insert the diaphragm and jelly (or cream) before intercourse. Can be inserted up to 6 hours before intercourse. Must stay in at least 6 hours after intercourse. | Put foam, jelly, or cream into your vagina each time you have intercourse, not more than 30 minutes beforehand. No douching for at least 8 hours after intercourse. | The condom should be placed on the erect penis before the penis ever comes into contact with the vagina. After ejaculation, the penis should be removed from the vagina immediately. |
| **Are there problems with it?** | Must be fitted by a doctor after a pelvic exam. Some women find it difficult to insert, inconvenient, or messy. | Must be inserted just before intercourse. Some find it inconvenient or messy. | Objectionable to some men and women. Interrupts intercourse. May be messy. Condom may break. |
| **What are the side effects or complications?** | Some women find that the jelly or cream irritates the vagina. Try changing brands if this happens. | Foam, cream, or jelly may irritate the vagina or the penis. Try changing brands if this happens. | Rarely, individuals are allergic to rubber. If this is a problem, condoms called "skins," which are not made of rubber, are available. |
| **What are the advantages?** | Effective and safe. | Effective, safe, a good lubricant, can be purchased at a drugstore. | Effective, safe, can be purchased at a drugstore; excellent protection against most sexually transmitted infections. |

**TABLE 5-8.** *Continued*

| Method | Condom and Foam Used Together | Periodic Abstinence (Natural Family Planning) | Sterilization |
|---|---|---|---|
| **What is it?** | | Ways of finding out days each month when you are most likely to get pregnant. Intercourse is avoided at that time. | Vasectomy (male). Tubal ligation (female). Ducts carrying sperm or the egg are tied and cut surgically. |
| **How does it work?** | Prevents sperm from getting inside the uterus by killing sperm and preventing sperm from getting out into the vagina. | Techniques include maintaining charts of basal body temperature, checking vaginal secretions, and keeping calendar of menstrual periods, all of which can help predict when you are most likely to release an egg. | Closing of tubes in male prevents sperm from reaching egg; closing tubes in female prevents egg from reaching sperm. |
| **How reliable or effective is it?** | Close to 100% effective if both foam and condoms are used with every act of intercourse. | Certain methods are about 90–97% if used consistently. Other methods are less effective. Combining techniques increases effectiveness. | Almost 100% effective and *not* usually reversible. |
| **How would I use it?** | Foam must be inserted within 30 minutes before intercourse and condom must be placed onto erect penis prior to contact with vagina. | Careful records must be maintained of several factors: basal body temperature, vaginal secretions, and onset of menstrual bleeding. Careful study of these methods will dictate when intercourse should be avoided. | After the decision to have no more children has been well thought through, a brief surgical procedure is performed on the man or the woman. |
| **Are there problems with it?** | Requires more effort than some couples like. May be messy or inconvenient. Interrupts intercourse. | Difficult to use method if menstrual cycle is irregular. Sexual intercourse must be avoided for a significant part of each cycle. | Surgical operation has some risk, but serious complications are rare. Sterilizations should not be done unless no more children are desired. |
| **What are the side effects or complications?** | No serious complications. | No complications. | All surgical operations have some risk, but serious complications are uncommon. Some pain may last for several days. Rarely, the wrong structure is tied off, or the tube grows back together. There is no loss of sexual desire or ability in vast majority of patients. |
| **What are the advantages?** | Extremely effective and safe; both methods may be purchased at a drugstore without a doctor's prescription. Excellent protection against most sexually transmitted infections. | Safe, effective if followed carefully; little if any religious objection to method. Teaches women about their menstrual cycles. | The most effective method; low rate of complications; many feel that removing fear of pregnancy improves sexual relations. |

## BOX 5-3
## *Abortion Rights for Minors*

Dear Dr. Gottesman: There is much confusion about current law regarding the right of an adolescent to obtain an abortion without her parents' consent. We know that last term the U. S. Supreme Court heard such a case. What are the implications for minors?

D.W., Duluth, Minn.

Dear D.W.:

Abortion rights, especially those of minors, remain a major topic of controversy across the United States. Debates between right-to-life and abortion-rights groups are hot and heavy, and often turn into shouting matches. Feelings run especially high in these circles when teenage girls seek abortions without telling their parents. Several Supreme Court cases have held that minors do not need parental consent to obtain abortions.

The first major judicial deci-

sion concerning an *adult* woman's right to an abortion was the Supreme Court decision of *Roe v. Wade*. In this case, the Court held that the right of privacy in the U. S. Constitution is broad enough to encompass a woman's decision about whether to terminate her pregnancy. . . .

In addition, the Court ruled that the state may place increasing restrictions on abortion as the period of pregnancy lengthens, so long as those restrictions are tailored to recognized state interests. . . .

The Supreme Court last term stood firmly behind its 1973 *Roe v. Wade* decision legalizing abortion for adult women, and ruled 6–3 that government cannot interfere with this "fundamental right of women" unless such interference is already justified by "accepted medical practice." It struck down as unconstitutional laws requiring (1) hospitals rather

than clinics to perform abortions after the first three months of pregnancy; (2) 24-hour waiting periods; (3) elaborate informed-consent procedures; (4) decent burial for disposal of the fetus.

The Court squarely faced the issue of a pregnant minor seeking an abortion in *Planned Parenthood of Central Missouri v. Danforth* in 1976. There, the Court stated that minors, as well as adults, are protected by the Constitution and possess constitutional rights. It then ruled that the state may not impose a blanket provision requiring the consent of a parent or guardian as a condition for an unmarried minor to obtain an abortion during the first 12 weeks of her pregnancy.

The Court again confronted the issue of a minor's right to privacy with regard to abortion in *Bellotti v. Baird* in 1979. In this case, it declared unconstitu-

All these contraceptives are relatively effective in preventing pregnancy. Each has advantages and disadvantages. It should be noted that the effectiveness levels reported in this section include individuals who used the contraceptive device improperly. Contraceptive devices are effective only when used properly.

For people who want no (or no more) children, **sterilization** provides a means of permanent contraception. Medical procedures are available for males and females.

For males, the operation is called a **vasec-**

**tomy.** Typically completed in a doctor's office under local anesthesia, it involves making a small incision on the side of the scrotum and then cutting and tying off the vas deferens. This prevents sperm from leaving the testicles. Consequently, during ejaculation, only seminal fluid without sperm is emitted. The sperm remain in the testicles and are absorbed by the body (Johnson, 1983).

For females, sterilization involves disconnecting the fallopian tubes either by tubal ligation or by the endoscopic technique. **Tubal ligation** is

## BOX 5-3
*Continued*

tional a Massachusetts statute requiring the consent of both parents—or, in their absence, the consent of a court of law— before an unmarried woman under age 18 could obtain an abortion. The Court held, however, that parents might be consulted by the courts in determining what is in the minor's best interest.

Thus, once again, parents were not totally ruled out of the picture.

In the latest case, *City of Akron v. Akron Center for Reproductive Health, Inc.,* the Supreme Court reiterated the position it took in *Bellotti* that laws requiring parental consent to a minor's abortion are constitutional as long as (1) the minor may appeal to a local court if "she is unable to obtain her parents' permission, and (2) a specific mechanism is provided for appeal." . . .

In this case, the city of Akron

enacted a provision prohibiting a doctor from performing an abortion on a pregnant minor under the age of 15 unless the doctor obtained the "informed written consent of one of her parents or her legal guardian" or unless the minor obtained "an order from a court having jurisdiction over her that the abortion be performed or induced."

The district court struck down the ordinance because it did not provide an opportunity for the minor to show she was mature enough to make that determination herself; rather, the ordinance required parental consent or a court order in all cases. The court of appeals affirmed the district court's ruling.

The U. S. Supreme Court found that the Akron ordinance did not expressly create the alternative procedure required in the *Bellotti* case to give the

girl a chance to show she was mature enough to decide to obtain an abortion on her own. The Court said Akron could not make the blanket determination that all minors under age 15 were too immature to make such a decision or that an abortion would *never* be in the minor's best interest. . . .

In conclusion, the Supreme Court held that although a state has a legitimate interest in protecting immature pregnant minors by requiring parental or judicial consent to abortion, the state must provide an alternative procedure whereby a pregnant minor may demonstrate that she is sufficiently mature to make the abortion decision herself or that despite her immaturity an abortion would be in her best interest.

done under general anesthesia. Through an abdominal incision, the fallopian tubes are cut and the ends tied off. Ovulation and menstruation continue, but the ova, instead of reaching the uterus through the fallopian tubes, are absorbed by the body. Fertilization cannot occur.

More recent medical advances have drawn on **endoscopy,** the use of a needlelike tube that contains a light and camera to locate the fallopian tubes. A small incision is made in the navel (laparoscopy) or entry is made through the vagina (culdoscopy or hysteroscopy) to cauterize

(sear) and seal off the cut ends. Typically, only local anesthesia is needed for this procedure (Johnson, 1983).

## Abortion

About 13% of pregnancies end in miscarriage, or spontaneous abortion. Natural forces in a woman's body trigger a miscarriage when the embryo is grossly defective or other abnormalities exist. An induced **abortion** is the deliberate termination of a pregnancy. (Technically, abortion is not a contraceptive method. Rather, it is a remedy for terminating a pregnancy. We suspect that very few women habitually use abortion as a birth-control technique. However, some people do view it as one.) In 1973 the U. S. Supreme Court ruled that abortion during the first trimester (12 weeks) of pregnancy is legal for all adult-age women in all states (see Box 5-3). Recent statistical reports indicate that the number of abortions almost doubled between 1974 and 1980 for both Whites and non-Whites and that significantly more unmarried than married women choose abortion (see Table 5-9).

An abortion typically involves one of two methods. In a **dilation and curettage** the physician anesthetizes the patient and then dilates (enlarges) the opening of the uterus. The uterus is then gently scraped with a curette (a long-handled instrument with a metal loop at one end). On loosening the fetus, an intravenous chemical is frequently given that induces expulsion of the fetus. An alternative technique, which can be used only during the first trimester, is the **suction method.** A suction apparatus is used to gently evacuate the contents of the uterus.

It is recommended that an abortion be performed during the first trimester because health risks increase after that. In most cases, once the fetus is 12 weeks old, the state may place restrictions on the right to abortion.

Public outcry has claimed that women who have induced abortions place themselves at risk for problems in future childbearing or even breast cancer, but there is actually little evidence supporting such statements (Cates, 1982). Rather, the choice to have a legal abortion remains primarily an ethical and moral question.

**TABLE 5-9.** *Pregnancies terminated by abortion, by marital status, United States, 1974–1980*

| Measure | Year | | | | |
|---|---|---|---|---|---|
| | 1974 | 1977 | 1978 | 1979 | 1980 |
| **Number of abortions** | | | | | |
| Married | 248,150 | 299,710 | 330,630 | 322,210 | 319,880 |
| Unmarried[a] | 650,420 | 1,016,990 | 1,078,970 | 1,175,460 | 1,234,010 |
| **Percentage distribution of abortions** | | | | | |
| Married | 27.6 | 22.8 | 23.5 | 21.5 | 20.6 |
| Unmarried[a] | 72.4 | 77.2 | 76.5 | 78.5 | 79.4 |
| **Percentage of pregnancies terminated by abortion** | | | | | |
| Married | 8.3 | 9.8 | 10.4 | 9.9 | 9.8 |
| Unmarried[a] | 59.9 | 66.0 | 65.4 | 66.0 | 64.9 |

[a] Includes separated, divorced, widowed, and never-married women.

This chapter has covered a broad expanse of material dealing with the topic of human sexuality. Our interest in this chapter is the promotion of sexual responsibility in oneself, in one's family, and in society. Each of the four tools of prevention can be applied to this task.

## EDUCATION

One way of promoting sexual responsibility is basic sex education. Although sex education has not been shown to diminish premarital sexual activity (for example, Spanier, 1978), without some basic knowledge about human sexuality, one cannot make educated decisions. And informed decision making is a goal of prevention.

To promote sexual responsibility, the following values should be recognized:

1. The value of receiving correct and factual information that can aid in responsible decision making or actions.
2. The value of personal responsibility for one's own actions with the recognition that it is irresponsible to act without regard for the consequences.
3. The value of control, where sexuality and the sex act are not seen as means of controlling another.
4. The value of consideration for the welfare and needs of the other.
5. The value of each individual as a worthy person.
6. The value of communication, where partners openly discuss their needs, interests, and desires to learn about each other's feelings (Calderone & Johnson, 1981).

Parents, teachers, members of the clergy, and peers can promote sexual responsibility through their actions and the information they provide. Whether in a structured setting, such as a class, or an informal one, such as an unplanned discussion of a television program, opportunities to convey values about responsible behavior are numerous. These values can be discussed in the context of sexual behavior or in other contexts such as getting along with others.

 *How else might education be used to promote sexual responsibility?*

## COMMUNITY ORGANIZATION/ SYSTEMS INTERVENTION

This preventive tool involves mobilizing people to make society's structures (laws, institutions, courts, and so fourth) more responsive to their needs. It has been used extensively to promote sex education in schools, churches, and community service organizations. The prevailing attitude 100 or even 50 years ago was that knowledge about sexual matters was inappropriate and perhaps dangerous for children. People were not likely to learn about topics such as intercourse before it was necessary—that is, shortly before marriage. Gradually, attitudes changed, and people began requesting that courses be provided. For example, nearly 100 years ago, the Parent-Teachers Association suggested that sex education should be part of the school curriculum. This recommendation elicited the kind of attention, not all of it favorable, still seen today as controversy continues to surround sex education in schools.

In the 1970s, most sex education programs avoided the issue of values, but today programs

*If parents expect their children to be sexually responsible individuals then they need to become actively involved in promoting that behavior.*

incorporate discussion of parental, societal, and personal values. The rationale is that youth need to understand that sexual behavior is inevitably influenced by values. Educators try to promote sexual responsibility by discussing values.

Like schools, churches have responded to youth's need for sex education. Catholicism, Lutheranism, Methodism, Judaism, and Unitarianism are only a few of the denominations that have sex-education curricula. Some have developed programs not only for youth but also for parents. Similarly, Girls' Clubs, Boy Scouts, and other youth-serving groups have developed programs to provide information about sexuality and an opportunity to discuss this topic. Typically, these programs deal with values, decision making, and sexual responsibility.

These community efforts are based on the premise that information is preferable to ignorance and that it is appropriate for these groups to provide (or assist parents in providing) this information. They have often been designed in response to parent and student requests. Thus,

numerous groups have accepted some responsibility for promoting responsible behavior.

*Who should be primarily responsible for providing information about sexuality? Why? What barriers make meeting this responsibility difficult? How can these barriers be overcome?*

## COMPETENCY PROMOTION

The goal of competency promotion is to increase an individual's self-esteem, to promote an internal locus of control, and to foster community-interested rather than self-interested individuals. These issues are integral to decision making, which is the basis for responsible sexual behavior.

Parents can promote decision-making skills among their children by allowing them to make some decisions starting in early childhood. Selecting a toy, choosing milk or juice, and hundreds of other decisions are within the capabilities of young children. Helping them learn that their choices have consequences and that we have to think of others as well as ourselves is important in developing responsibility. Continually expanding their opportunities for making decisions as they grow older will enhance their decision-making abilities.

Making decisions gives people a feeling of empowerment—that is, a sense that they have some control over their lives. Such an internal locus of control is essential if people are to be able to think independently and act on their own convictions.

In some schools, teachers and counselors provide training in decision making, often using case illustrations about people who have to make choices. They discuss what options are possible, the pros and cons of each, and what impact a decision would have in the short and the long term. By analyzing the potential benefits and liabilities of the choices, by asking how a particular choice fits with one's personal values and long-range goals, and by assessing how a choice will affect self and others, youths learn to apply the decision-making process to any choices they have. This skill is particularly useful when making decisions about sexual behavior. Thus, if children are given structured opportunities to make choices and to analyze choices faced by others and the implications of each choice, they gain in decision-making competence.

 *Two teenagers who have been dating spend several hours alone at the girl's house. After kissing and snuggling for a while, they become sexually aroused and have to decide whether they will "pet" for the first time. What should they do? What factors would you consider in deciding what they should do? What else would you want to know before deciding?*

# NATURAL CAREGIVING

The fourth tool of prevention encourages us to extend ourselves in a caring fashion to other human beings. This caring is the essence of responsible sexual behavior because it requires that we consider the needs and wants of the other person as important as our own. We have a responsibility for treating one another not as sex objects to be manipulated but as human beings with feelings that should be respected.

Everyone needs natural caregiving, and young adolescents, who are often preoccupied with their changing bodies and new feelings, are in particular need. Parents, older siblings, teachers, health-care professionals, and members of the clergy can help by providing information and opportunities for discussion. Letting adolescents understand that they are not alone, that others have similar concerns, and that all their questions can be discussed is part of natural caregiving.

Adolescents' concerns include values. Young people want to know what is right and wrong, what principles should guide them, how others have made decisions about sexual behavior, and what the outcomes have been. Ideally, discussions of sexual responsibility will occur before a young person ever faces such choices. Choices about sexual behavior, contraception, or abortion are easier when people have explored their beliefs in advance. Discussions about "What should X do if . . ." provide opportunities to explore choices and values and help prepare people for future choices they may face.

*Give some examples of irresponsible sexual behavior. Why are they irresponsible? Why do people behave irresponsibly? What do you think is the most common kind of irresponsible sexual behavior?*

# SUMMARY

We have covered a wealth of material in this chapter. We have provided you with the information necessary to act on the basis of an educated choice. We hope that you will, in turn, extend that right to others.

# MAJOR POINTS TO REMEMBER

1. Primitive peoples' views of sexuality were associated with notions of magic power, religious beliefs, and strong moral sanctions. Contrasted with today's mores, these perspectives were very conservative and constraining.
2. The reproductive system consists of physiological components that provide both sexual pleasure and the means of producing offspring.
3. Sexual expression takes many forms. At the simplest level it involves touching, hugging, and kissing. At more complex levels it includes sexual intercourse and other behaviors such as oral sex.
4. There are four basic sexual orientations—heterosexuality, homosexuality, bisexuality, and asexuality.
5. Sexual behavior begins in childhood, expands in adolescence, matures in adulthood, and may decline gradually in old age.
6. Sexual dysfunctions can impair sexual behavior and intimacy in a relationship. Disorders can be categorized as gender-identity disorders, perversions, homosexuality, and dysfunctional symptoms. Sexual dysfunctions are most likely if a person has experienced childhood family disorganization, knows little about human sexuality, and has poor communication skills.
7. A number of diseases can be transmitted during sexual intercourse. Syphilis and gonorrhea were the major ones until herpes and acquired immune deficiency syndrome became common in recent years. The likelihood of contracting such diseases increases with the number of sex partners.
8. Pregnancy is most effectively prevented by abstinence. However, other reliable and effective contraceptive techniques can be used: pills, condoms, diaphragms, spermicides, intrauterine devices, and vaginal sponges. Sterilization and abortion are other means of preventing birth. Each technique has its own rate of effectiveness, side effects, and unique implications with regard to one's own beliefs and values. Some people have major moral and ethical concerns about one or more of them.
9. A sound sex education should include, among other topics, information on reproduction, birth control, disease, morality, values, and responsible decision making.

# ADDITIONAL SOURCES OF INFORMATION

## *Publications*

Andry, A. C., & Schepp, S. (1968). *How babies are made.* New York: Time/Life Books. [Early childhood]

Bernstein, A. (1978). *The flight of the stork.* New York: Dell. [Adults]

Calderone, M. S., & Ramey, J. W. (1982). *Talking with your child about sex.* New York: Random House. [Adults]

Carrera, M. (1981). *Sex: The facts, the acts and your feelings.* New York: Crown. [Adolescents]

Comfort, A., & Comfort, J. (1979). *The facts of love.* New York: Ballantine Books. [Adolescents]

Gittelsohn, R. B. (1980). *Love, sex and marriage: A Jewish view.* New York: Union of American Hebrew Congregations. [Adolescents]

Kaplan, H. S. (1979). *Making sense of sex.* New York: Simon & Schuster. [Adolescents]

Maier, R. A. (1984). *Human sexuality in perspective.* Chicago: Nelson-Hall. [Adolesents, adults]

McCary, J. L. (1973). *Human sexuality* (2nd ed.). Princeton, NJ: Van Nostrand. [Adults]

Nagler, B. (1972). *Daddy's first baby book.* North Palm Beach, FL: Kanrom. [Parents]

Nilsson, L. (1975). *How was I born?* Stockholm: Delacorte Press. [Children, adolescents]

Sheffield, M. (1978). *Where do babies come from?* New York: Knopf. [Ages 3–8]

## Organizations

### AIDS and gay issues

In addition to the following national organizations working on AIDS, many state and city health departments have established local task forces or committees. Usually these groups are within the health department or the governor's/mayor's office and serve to coordinate state or city services on AIDS.

There are also church-affiliated organizations set up to counsel and minister to persons with AIDS, as well as to gay men and lesbians. Two of the more widely known groups are Dignity (Catholic) and Integrity (Episcopalian).

U. S. Public Health Service
AIDS Hotline: (800)342-AIDS (toll free); from Washington, DC, call 642-8182; from Alaska and Hawaii, call collect (202)254-6867

U. S. Public Health Service
Office of Public Affairs
Humphrey Bldg., Rm. 721H
Washington, DC 20201

Taped message 24 hours a day, 7 days a week; staff available to answer questions 8:30 A.M.–5:30 P.M. Eastern time, Monday through Friday

National Gay Task Force
80 Fifth Avenue
New York, NY 10011
Crisisline: (800)221-7044 (toll free); from New York, Alaska, or Hawaii, call (212)807-6016.
Open 3–9 P.M., Monday through Friday
The Crisisline is set up to respond to a variety of gay and lesbian concerns, including AIDS. It provides information on AIDS risk reduction and symptoms and referrals to other local hotlines or organizations. In addition, health professionals can receive information packets discussing where to obtain in-depth medical reports, NGTF policy statements on AIDS, and a national listing of local AIDS resources.

Federation of AIDS-Related Organizations
c/o Vachon
110 East 23rd Street
New York, NY 10010
This is a national coalition of AIDS service groups, clinics, gay/lesbian organizations with AIDS concerns, and local AIDS networks. Among other activities, FARO offers a clearinghouse and conferences on AIDS.

Gay Rights National Lobby
Box 1892
Washington, DC 20013
(202)546-1801
This group offers information on AIDS.

National Coalition of Gay STD Services
P.O. Box 239
Milwaukee, WI 53201
(414)277-7671
The coalition is a membership organization that coordinates all STD/AIDS resources nationwide. It provides a regular newsletter with medical updates, clinic information, regional reportage, and counseling forums.

## Birth-control information

Planned Parenthood Federation of America
810 Seventh Ave.
New York, NY 10019

## Herpes information

American Social Health Assn.
260 Sheridan Ave.
Palo Alto, CA 94302

Veneral Disease Control
Center for Disease Control
Atlanta, GA 30333
(404)329-3311

# 6

# COMMUNICATION: THE ESSENCE OF RELATIONSHIPS

1. When do human beings begin to communicate?

2. Is it possible to be with another person and not communicate?

3. What is nonverbal communication? How much of our message does it carry? What are the various nonverbal means of communication?

4. What are the major blocks to effective communication?

5. What interpersonal needs does communication fulfill?

6. What is self-disclosure? Why is it important in close relationships?

7. What are some major differences between communicating with friends and communicating with family members? Between communicating with an adult and communicating with a child?

8. What factors can interfere with couple communication?

9. What can people do to improve their communication skills?

10. How does who "owns" a problem affect communication about the problem?

**When was the** last time you communicated with someone? Not talked, but communicated—that is, your listener understood what you were trying to say, and you, in turn, understood your listener. Most of us have no problem talking, but are the words we speak clearly understood? And, in return, do we really hear what others are saying—not just their words but their meaning?

Communication is the essence of all relationships and therefore is an essential ingredient in families. It is a skill that is not acquired easily but can be nurtured, as we'll see in this chapter. Before we can analyze communication in intimate relationships, we have to understand this process among people in general. The chapter therefore begins by explaining the principles of communication, describing what experts have learned about communication, and detailing how to communicate clearly. A discussion of what makes effective communication so difficult and the special features of family communication will follow. Thus, this chapter combines theory and practice to help you apply this information to your own life.

## THE ELEMENTS OF COMMUNICATION

For our purposes, we will define **communication** as the sharing of information, including facts, ideas, values, expectations, feelings, and opinions. Sometimes people communicate about things that are widely known, such as current events, and sometimes about things that are known by few others, such as secrets. **Self-disclosure** is defined as revealing personal information about ourselves (Jourard, 1971). It may concern our dreams, fears, feelings, secrets, or anything else we would not share with most people. As such, it is a particular kind of interpersonal communication.

The three components of communication are simple: a **sender,** a **message,** and a **receiver.** The complexity arises because we cannot read minds. If we could connect two persons' brains to transmit thoughts directly from one to the other, much as we do with computers, many problems associated with understanding would be alleviated. However, even if such technology were available, we might be quite reluctant to have our most precious commodity, our "mind," invaded in this way.

Problems may arise in each of the three components of communication. For example, the sender may be unclear about what message to send, may be uncertain how to word it, or may have difficulty transmitting it accurately. Thus, the message may be ambiguous or obscure. The receiver may have difficulty interpreting the message accurately or, as frequently happens, may not be listening at all! To understand the communication process better, let's look at how we convey our messages in person.

Suppose we decide to send a spoken message. We must first determine what is to be communicated and then find the words to say what is meant. This process is called **encoding.** If we are uncertain or ambivalent about the message, we will have difficulty encoding it accurately. Once a message is sent, the listener hears and decodes it. If words are slurred, mispronounced, or misused, if their meaning is unclear, or if they have different meanings for the sender and the receiver, it is difficult for the listener to interpret the message accurately. If the listener is not concentrating on the message, he or she may miss its meaning entirely. These are some of the problems that take place when we try to communicate. Sometimes, of course, the two parties have understood the same idea: clear communication has taken place.

How the listener interprets the message depends on more than just the words used. A lis-
tener, like a detective, searches for all possible clues to make an accurate interpretation. For example, the listener listens to the way the communicator speaks—his or her tone, voice inflection, and emphasis. Consider the differences in the messages below:

"*I* like that chair" (although you may not).

"I *like* that chair" (a lot).

"I like *that* chair" (compared with other chairs).

If a four-word message can be this variable depending on how the message is said, imagine the complexity of other exchanges, most with more complicated ideas to communicate!

Messages are transmitted simultaneously on many channels through nonverbal behavior. These channels include all the unspoken means we have of communicating, such as tone, inflection, emphasis, eye contact, facial expression, gestures, touching, and proximity to the listener (Fast, 1970; Verderber, 1978). Whenever we communicate in person, nonverbal clues carry much of our message. One student of gestural communication estimates that 65% of the meaning is transmitted nonverbally (Birdwhistell, cited in Schramm, 1973). Another (Mehrabian, 1972) thinks it might be as high as 90%!

Let's examine just one aspect of nonverbal communication—proximity. Very different messages are conveyed simply by the distance between two persons. Picture a park bench with two persons seated on it. The distance between them and their relative body positions give us good clues about the degree of closeness or distance they feel. If they are at opposite ends, facing away from each other, it is obvious that they are trying to avoid contact. If they are turned toward each other, it indicates that they share a relationship (acquaintances, friends, lovers). Finally, if they are leaning toward each other, with their faces less than 18 inches apart, they are in

GEORGE SEGAL: *THREE PEOPLE ON FOUR BENCHES*, 1980

*What are some of the nonverbal messages the sculptor is trying to convey here?*

the intimate personal-space zone, which indicates that they share a special closeness (Hall, 1963).

Frequently, we become aware of proximity when we feel uncomfortable because the message we want to send is incongruous with our distance from the other person. When we want the other person to back up, our personal space is being violated. When we want the other to be nearer, we are trying to increase closeness. Whether between strangers or between intimates, proximity is one means of communication. Imagine the complexity of understanding a message when other channels such as eye contact, gestures, and words are used as well!

Nonverbal communication has three distinguishing characteristics (Verderber, 1978). Unlike speech, it is continuous, lasting as long as people are together. Even when they aren't talking, their actions and demeanor send a message—perhaps reflecting hostility, comfort, or exhaustion. Whereas verbal communication uses only one channel (words), nonverbal communication is multifaceted, using signals that can be received by many senses. Facial expressions may be accompanied by gestures, touching, and body movement, and each channel conveys a message that can be decoded. Finally, unlike verbal content, which is usually under the sender's control, nonverbal communication is often unconscious. Consequently, nonverbal messages, in conveying our real feelings, may conflict with our verbal message, leaving it up to the listener to interpret what we really mean. Not surprisingly, listeners frequently pay more attention to the nonverbal content because they believe it is more accurate (Verderber, 1978).

As we've already indicated, when two or more persons are together, they cannot avoid communicating. Even if they choose not to talk to each other, the very behavior of not speaking conveys a message. "I'm too tired to talk or listen," "I don't talk to people I don't know," and "I'm angry at you" are just a few possible interpretations. Knowing the situation and the individuals involved would help in translating this behavior accurately, but only the parties involved can explain what their silence means—and they may not agree! Obviously, one problem with nonverbal messages is that they are open to broad interpretation and therefore are frequently misunderstood. While the sender, by being silent, may mean "I want to think this problem through by myself," the receiver may interpret this behavior as "He doesn't even know I'm around."

Verbal messages are always accompanied by nonverbal messages, and these two may conflict. To help our listeners understand us, it is important to assess feelings and opinions as much as possible before communicating. How do I really feel? Am I reluctant to express what I mean? Why? The more we become conscious of our "gut level" responses, the more complete information we will have when encoding our messages and the more successful we may be in making the verbal and nonverbal messages consistent with each other. Later in this chapter we will look at some ways to express feelings accurately so that verbal and nonverbal messages match and listeners are more likely to understand what is really meant.

Communication is rarely a one-way process from sender to receiver. Only when the sender cannot get any feedback, verbal or nonverbal, from the receiver is the process one-way. Movies, books, newspapers, videos, and records are examples of one-way communication. Most of our communication is interpersonal. Throughout a conversation, the two parties take turns sending and receiving messages. Even while listening, receivers transmit nonverbal messages about their interest, attention, and understanding of what is being said. Thus, interpersonal communication is a reciprocal, interactive process, necessitating encoding and decoding by both parties (Gordon, 1970; Gottman, Notarius,

Gonso, & Markman, 1976; Knapp, 1984; Schramm, 1973). When more than two persons are involved, it can be even more complex.

Why is communication so important? Because it satisfies our needs (1) to include others and feel included, (2) to influence and be influenced by others, and (3) to give and receive affection (Knapp, 1984). These three needs are basic *interpersonal* needs. People vary in their levels of these needs, and fluctuations within individuals are normal. For example, today we may want to be included in social activities, tomorrow we may prefer solitude. Whatever our interpersonal-need levels, communication provides opportunities for us to feel valued. It is not surprising, then, that it is an essential ingredient in our lives.

 *Give the following sentence different emphases, tones, and inflections to convey various meanings: "He looks great." Discuss these differences. Then try "He looks great?"*

## BARRIERS TO EFFECTIVE COMMUNICATION

As communicators, we encode a message and transmit it on several channels—verbal and nonverbal. But how does it get encoded? Most basic, of course, is the language spoken. Language and our knowledge of it can limit or enhance our ability to express ourselves. For example, the English language has 4 common words for snow—*snow, sleet, blizzard,* and *slush*—while the language of native Alaskans has over 20. How precisely the individual speaks the language also influences the message. "The interview was funny" is ambiguous; "The interview was peculiar" or "The interview was humorous" is much clearer.

Many other factors affect the process of encoding. Time, place, and situation are a few external influences (Verderber, 1978). When senders feel pressed for time, they send abbreviated messages and assume that their listeners comprehend fully. If the climate is uncomfortable or the noise level is high, the sender and the listener may have difficulty concentrating. Is privacy lacking? Interruptions fragment a message and often confuse the receiver. These are only a few of the external factors that can inhibit accurate transmission of a message.

## Self-Concept and Relationships

Many internal factors also influence the encoding of a message. A person's self-concept is important in preparing any communication (Satir, 1972). If people feel competent and secure, they are more likely to assess and encode their messages accurately, providing their listeners with consistent information. If, however, they are feeling bad about themselves or their situation, they may be distracted, and the messages they send may be ambiguous.

Let's analyze one example. Carol has just learned that Ellen has been accepted into graduate school, and she wants to congratulate her. On seeing Ellen, however, Carol reflects on her own poor academic performance and the impact it will have on her employment. When Carol speaks to Ellen, she is ambivalent and her wishes for success sound hollow. Ellen tries to interpret the real meaning of the message: "Does she really want me to fail? Does she think I won't be able to cope? Does she think graduate study is foolish given the current job market? Is she envious? What's wrong?" Depending on the two students' relationship, the circumstances, and their communication skills, these conflicting signals will be discussed, wondered about, or ignored. The likelihood of misinterpretation is high.

Imagine the additional complexity if Carol and Ellen are sisters. Are they competing for recognition from their relatives? Is Carol's reaction influenced by her perception that Ellen always was the favored child? Is Ellen insensitive to the financial drain graduate school will be on the entire family? These questions illustrate just a few of the additional dynamics of communication between relatives. The history of the relationship, the current family dynamics, and the actual relationship (for example, mother/daughter, mother/son, husband/wife) all contribute to the way communication is perceived.

## Perceptual Filters

Self-concept and relationships are not the only elements that influence how messages are encoded. Many other factors can influence the sender in formulating messages. We will call them "filters" because they screen how messages are produced. Expectations of self and others, personal values, and stereotypes can distort a person's perception of what message to send. The person's past history in communicating with family members, friends, acquaintances, and so forth may be significant (Bach & Deutsch, 1970; Satir, 1972). If the persons involved have a history of interacting with each other, it may influence how well they are able to communicate at any given time (Knapp, 1984). Each of these potential filters (and this list is not exhaustive) may distort the message as it is encoded.

The influence of these filters changes with different situations. For example, our stereotype filter may be minimal in most situations but significant when talking with elderly people, police officers, or foreigners.

Equally important, these filters exist within listeners as well, affecting how they decode the message. Even if the sender is very clear, the receiver can misinterpret the message because his or her own filters distort perceptions. Furthermore, people receive little explicit training in listening. Courses in reading and speaking are readily available across the country—but courses in listening are rare. Because many people think listening is a passive activity, they let their attention wander. Perhaps they listen only long enough to have the sender stimulate an idea for them to discuss. Then they are busy preparing what they want to say and awaiting a pause by the speaker, meanwhile missing much that has been said. Or listeners cannot concentrate on what is being said because they are struggling with some of their own concerns ("I have to get that report done," "I wonder when the meeting is") or they are distracted by the environment just as the speakers are.

Figure 6-1 illustrates the process of communication. The "message" is depicted as an iceberg, with the words explicit and the nonverbal communication resting beneath them. The filters vary in size because their influence varies among individuals and even for the same individual in different situations. For example, Roger may have a stereotype about fat people that is activated only when he is interacting with someone fat or talking about fat people. His filter about men doing housework is relevant in other situations, such as when Kathy, his wife, asks for help. Similarly, how Kathy decodes his message will depend on which filters of hers (for example, the roles of wives and husbands) are relevant to the situation. Like Roger, she is often unconscious of these filters (Bach & Deutsch, 1970).

We all have filters that distort the messages we send and receive. Such problems occur even among family members who know each other well and communicate regularly. For example, the interpretation of the question "When are you coming home?" may be influenced by the roles of the sender and receiver (such as mother/son, brother/brother, or wife/husband) as well as how they are getting along and the context of the question. This simple inquiry may be interpreted (among many possibilities) as a straightforward request for information, an intrusion into one's activities, or an expression of distrust. Filters about family roles and relationships often make it more difficult to understand our relatives.

## Communicating Feelings

One particularly important type of communication in personal relationships is expression of feelings. Our society often gives boys the message that males keep their feelings to themselves: "Big boys don't cry," "Don't let them know you're hurt," "Face it like a man" (without showing emotion). As a result, many males come to believe that expressing emotions is not masculine. Girls, in contrast, are typically allowed to express their feelings and to be emotional. Eventually, since young women who are expressive

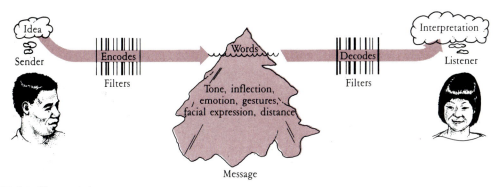

**FIGURE 6-1.** *Transmitting a message.*

date young men who are inexpressive, communication difficulties are common.

Inexpressive males (those who cannot express feelings) can be categorized as follows: the "cowboy," who has feelings but is unable to express them; the "playboy," who does not have feelings (Balswick & Peek, 1971); and the "little boy," who is overwhelmed with insecurity. John Wayne is the prototype for the cowboy, James Bond for the playboy, and Woody Allen for the little boy. It is hard to imagine any of these men in a conversation expressing their fears, hopes, or desires on an adult level.

When the major role of the husband/father was to provide security and the basic necessities for his family, inexpressiveness was less a problem. Today, as the companionate and affectionate aspects of marriage and parenting gain importance, inexpressiveness is more dysfunctional (Balswick & Peek, 1971). In a survey of working-class families, Rubin (1976) found that inexpressiveness in husbands was a major source of frustration for both husbands and wives. Wives complained that life seemed empty, that they were dissatisfied with just a house and children, that they wanted more. Their husbands who provided all the essentials were frustrated and confused: "I give her a nice home, a nice car . . . three nice kids. . . . And with all that, she's not happy. I worry about it, but I can't figure out what's the matter, so how can I know what to do?" (p. 114). It isn't just working-class families that experience these frustrations, although Rubin believes that middle-class families have had more role models and opportunities to integrate expressiveness into their relationships.

Of course, some women are inexpressive. Who is inexpressive in a relationship is less important than that the partners are different in communication style. Problems result when one partner wants to communicate but the other partner cannot respond.

? *What can we do to minimize communication distortions caused by filters, interpersonal relationships, and low self-concept? Using a fictional or real example, analyze a communication problem created by one of these influences.*

# COMMUNICATION IN DIFFERENT TYPES OF RELATIONSHIPS

When we encounter someone we will interact with on an ongoing basis—an employer, a colleague, a fellow student, a new neighbor—we try to listen effectively and learn about him or her. When we are uncertain what he or she means, we may ask for clarification. If we disagree with what the person says, we may avoid that topic in the future or express our opinion in a nonthreatening way. Usually we avoid insulting friends, neighbors, and peers, because such behavior strains or breaks a relationship.

Yet, those we are closest to—spouse and other family members—often do not get such consideration. "Your hair looks atrocious," "That color is putrid," "What a dumb suggestion," and other putdowns reverberate through households across the country. Similarly, complaints that "My spouse (or parent) doesn't understand me the way you do" are commonly heard outside the household. Why is it so hard to communicate with those we care about most? Because intimate relationships differ from other relationships in several important respects. Let's look at these differences, first for couples, then for parents and children.

## *The Intimate Pair*

An intimate relationship usually begins with a special attraction, followed by a "courtship" period during which each person tries to learn as much as possible about the other. Frequently, there is an enchantment with the other person—his or her thoughts, attitudes, and behavior. Tennov (1979) calls this total preoccupation with the other person **limerance,** that falling-in-love stage of ecstasy that moderates with time. Both parties may be on their best behavior, overlooking small irritations by the other person or interpreting them as "cute" or "too insignificant" to mention (Bach & Deutsch, 1970).

Because the partners live in different locations, they arrange time to be together to enjoy each other's company. They typically spend a great amount of time together communicating about themselves and their goals, feelings, and desires, and they may devise fantasies for their life together. They may communicate about their communication: "I feel so attractive when you look at me that way," "I felt important when you asked for my opinion," "I like it when we can spend time just talking," or "When we talk about our dreams for the future, I feel close to you." This kind of communication is called **metacommunication.**

All these behaviors—concentration on the other person, efforts to be together, intense feelings, self-disclosure, metacommunication—help to build the relationship. The level of self-disclosure increases as the individuals feel more secure, further building the level of trust (Knapp, 1984). Communication, then, is the basis for the relationship.

Over time, each partner may be able to guess how the other will respond in situations. This ability to "predict" can often be deceptive, however, and frequently one or both partners unconsciously begin to assume things about the other person that are incorrect (Bach & Deutsch, 1969, 1970, 1979; Lederer & Jackson, 1968). Each one may mentally transform the other into what he or she wants the other to be. She thinks: "He'll like my friends after he gets to know them

better," and he thinks: "After we're married, she'll make new friends and we won't have to socialize with these creeps." Because the partners are reluctant to discuss their differences and their disagreements, they deceive each other, and an unproductive communication process becomes part of their pattern.

As these two individuals evolve into a "couple," other unconscious processes may influence their relationship. Because our first understanding of couple relationships comes from living with our parents, we may unconsciously respond to our partner on the basis of this "understanding" of husband/wife relationships. For example, she may think that husbands should be home by 6:00 P.M. because her father always was, while he may want to avoid complying with such requests because his father always acquiesced to his demanding mother. Her expectations, which are based on her parents' pattern, are thwarted by his need to avoid repeating his parents' pattern. Yet, both may be unaware that their behavior is based on reactions to their parents' relationship.

Even people who grew up in households without two parents learned about couples from society. We are bombarded with examples of couple relationships, from Snow White and Prince Charming to the President and the First Lady to Elizabeth Taylor and her latest. Friends, neighbors, relatives, peers, and the media all shape our views. However, only rarely do we get a close view of an intimate relationship; usually we learn about only the best or worst aspects. Yet, these other models influence how we think couples should or shouldn't be and help shape our view of ourselves and our partner, sometimes leading to disillusionment when we learn that the reality differs from the image (Bach & Deutsch, 1970).

Whether married, living together, or just spending time together, an intimate couple begin their relationship by acknowledging that the partners are special to each other. They form bonds that make it harder to separate from each other than from others with whom they associate. A married couple have more ties than most other pairs: financial, sexual, legal, emotional, and possibly parental (Blumstein & Schwartz, 1983; Bohannon, 1970). When employees decide that their relationships and rewards (financial and otherwise) on the job are not worth it, they can simply gather their belongings and quit. The relationship is terminated. Spouses, however, even if they gather their belongings and walk out, are still married until they legally terminate the relationship—and then, too, there may be children to consider, jointly owned property, and other ties.

The more levels on which the pair are linked, the more difficulty there is in terminating the relationship. This difficulty in breaking the bond provides a measure of security for both partners (Blumstein & Schwartz, 1983). Each knows that the other has made a commitment to the relationship. Thus, although we may lose a friend by saying "I have never seen anyone do anything so stupid," saying that to a spouse is not likely to end the marriage (although it won't help it). Consequently, we may feel free to say things to a spouse that we would never say to a friend.

Intimate pairs differ from other relationships in several ways. First, the partners, in getting acquainted, often behave differently because they want to attract each other and because their feelings are so intense. Second, they arrange to meet frequently. Third, they are susceptible to thinking they know what the other person means, wants, or feels. They often fail to check out their perceptions although frequently those perceptions are wrong (Bach & Deutsch, 1979; Gordon, 1970; Gottman, 1979). Fourth, they tend to have many expectations of the role their partner should play, many of them never expressed and some of them unconscious. Fifth, because partners have ties on so many levels, they cannot

easily end the relationship. Sixth, over time many partners begin to take each other and their relationship for granted.

These factors are potential barriers to communication. How frequently is communication a problem for married couples? A survey of 266 family counseling agencies in the United States (Beck & Jones, 1973) found that communication was a problem area for almost nine out of ten couples who sought counseling (see Figure 6-2). This finding was corroborated in a survey of 730 marriage counselors, who listed a breakdown in communication as the most frequent reason couples pull apart (Safran, 1979).

Researchers have compared communication patterns within happy and unhappy couples (Gottman, 1979; Gottman, Markman, & Notarius, 1977). When these couples were asked to solve an existing or fictitious marital problem, unhappy couples expressed more negative feelings to their partners than happy couples did. They also showed more negative nonverbal behavior. Another interesting finding was that distressed spouses spent more time than nondistressed spouses expressing their own viewpoints rather than acknowledging the viewpoint of the partner. In short, these unhappy couples had developed a communication pattern that was more negative than positive and that was defensive

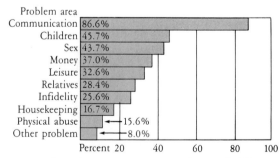

**FIGURE 6-2.** *Most common areas of marital difficulty among couples with marital problems seeking help from family service agencies.*

rather than receptive. This pattern was very difficult to escape, and distressed couples were often unable to solve problems (real or fictional) as a result (Gottman, 1979; Gottman et al., 1977).

 *Using social exchange theory, discuss why negative or positive patterns of communication between a couple would tend to be self-perpetuating.*

## The Family Group

All the factors that affect communication between couples can be influential in family interaction as well. Many characteristics of married couples' relationships apply to parent/child relationships. For example, family members spend much time in the same place and interact daily. Many of their interactions focus on the elements of daily living—shelter, food, clothing, and schedules. They share a history and emotional ties. They have expectations of one another, based on experience, comparison with others, and societal norms. These bonds help meld the family together and may facilitate or impede clear communication.

Families with children living at home differ from other groups in two other significant ways that affect communication. First, they are composed of members with widely varying power, expertise, and abilities (Satir, 1972). The age and maturity of the children, their ability to express their needs and wants, and their ability to contribute to maintaining the family have a profound impact on the way the family works together. Of necessity, parents interact much differently with a toddler than with an adolescent. Second, sometimes family members have different goals and needs. At school, at work, and at play, one's goals are generally shared and accepted by others. When they aren't, it is frequently possible to dissolve the group or limit the amount of interaction. In families, it is not easy to dissolve the group or avoid interaction. For example, Dad's goal may be to transfer to a job in a new city so the family will have more money. His daughter, Nancy, may not support this goal because she doesn't want to move. Even if they express the same goal—for example, a better family life—Father may interpret this goal to mean working longer hours to earn more money for the family, while Nancy means she wants to spend more time with her father.

The role of communication in families is significant, for it is here that we learn to express ourselves. Parents are expected to teach their children how to speak their native language, how to interpret verbal and nonverbal messages, and how to interact with others. Researchers who subscribe to symbolic interaction theory note that parents are very influential in shaping their children's self-concepts and views of individual family members' roles. "Father" has a role and position distinct from "son," "daughter," or "mother," and the interaction of the others with him is influenced by what "father" symbolizes. Social interaction within the family contributes to children's understanding of themselves, their family, and others. All this information is imparted by verbal and nonverbal communication.

Communication is essential in families in nurturing children, helping them grow, and building relationships. Although we do not know exactly when communication begins (see Box 6-1), we do know that learning about language, building a self-concept, and establishing interaction patterns all begin in the family.

Yet, often family communication is harmful and leads to negative reactions to self and others. What causes such exchanges? Why does familiarity seem to strain, rather than help, a relationship? We have already discussed how differences in skills, needs, and understanding in families hinder communication. Additional factors also influence how family members communicate.

BOX 6-1
*When Does Communication Begin?*

When do humans begin to communicate? When they can formulate sentences? When they can speak a few words? As soon as they learn to point? Actually, children begin communicating long before they have any concept of language. They are born with an ability to communicate. Their first cries send a message of displeasure: perhaps they are uncomfortable, in pain, hungry, or afraid, as the world outside the uterus is a completely new experience for the newborn. Maybe infants communicate

even before birth. Kicking and thrashing when uncomfortable, the fetus often elicits a patting or soothing response from the mother, who rubs her enlarged abdomen. If the kicking stops, perhaps the mother's message was received.

Several problems arise in trying to understand these actions. Did the fetus mean to send a signal? If so, what was its meaning? Did the mother decode the message correctly? Was her response appropriate?

Could the fetus interpret this response correctly? If mother and baby seem more satisfied after this exchange, effective communication actually may have taken place. If they seem less satisfied, there may have been a communication breakdown in the encoding or decoding process. Of course, it may be that the baby is not sending any message at all! So can a fetus and mother actually communicate? We're not sure. Maybe.

For example, many parents were raised when "Children should be seen and not heard" was a popular principle of child rearing. Not only were children to be quiet, their wishes and views were not to be indulged lest they become "spoiled." Today, however, experts recommend that children participate in meaningful ways in their families, expressing their opinions on a regular basis as well as in family meetings called for that purpose (Dreikurs, 1964; Gordon, 1970; Satir, 1972). Parents who choose to follow this philosophy may have no personal experience to draw from and few role models to emulate. Counteracting this change is the approach they learned firsthand when they were growing up. It is challenging to change a system of communication, especially with so little direct assistance.

Family members may develop negative patterns of interaction that are difficult to overcome. Virginia Satir (1972), a leading family therapist, has identified four typical negative interaction patterns: blaming, placating, comput-

ing, and distracting. She suggests that people readily fall into one of these patterns whenever they have low-self-esteem. The **blamer** is critical of everything and puts responsibility on other people. The **placater** tries to eliminate conflicts and differences by smoothing things over. The **computer** assesses the situation and responds on a factual basis with no recognition of feelings. And the **distracter** tries to divert attention from the issues.

We can find prototypes for these styles of interaction in literature, movies, and television. Consider the following characters from television series. Archie Bunker spends much of his time blaming others for problems, avoiding responsibility, and hiding his feelings. Edith Bunker is a perfect foil for this blamer, because she placates Archie most of the time rather than express her own feelings. The blamer is a boss, while the placater is a servant. When Archie and Edith use a different style of interacting, when they take responsibility and express their feelings, they become sympathetic characters as well as more effective communicators. Mr. Spock of "Star Trek" is the consummate computer. He analyzes everything dispassionately and occasionally is perplexed by the emotions displayed by others on the crew. Of course, since he is not a human being, he has a perfect excuse for not displaying any emotion. Jessica Tate of "Soap" personifies the distracter. If someone were to tell her that her house was on fire, she might respond with "There's a fire sale at Schultz's Department Store, and everything is half price. How can we resist going?" The blamer, the placater, the computer, or the distracter—none communicates effectively.

Whatever our communication style, it is clear that we can (and often do) love someone without understanding him or her. Many factors may interfere with our understanding—expectations, personal needs, assumptions—and affect our ability to communicate satisfactorily.

**?** *Select a television program about a family and analyze their communication patterns. How do filters, self-esteem, and perceived roles interfere with effective communication? Give some examples. What examples can you find of clear communication?*

# IMPROVING COMMUNICATION BETWEEN ADULTS

By now, you may be thinking that clear, effective communication is an impossible task. Although it is difficult, it is possible—and rewarding. But how does one learn to communicate in an open, clear, effective way with partners and family members? Four elements are essential in developing a pattern of effective communication: (1) a positive self-concept, (2) time for personal communication, (3) assessment of the purpose of the message, and (4) appropriate skills (responses).

## *Developing a Positive Self-Concept*

Many of us, in the course of growing up, focus on the things we can't or don't do well. As babies, we are limited in our actions, and as we grow, we compare ourselves with older, more able people. Sometimes we internalize the resulting feelings of inadequacy. The messages we give ourselves (for example, "I am smart," "I am clumsy," "I am likable") are very important in the development of our self-concepts.

Others, particularly those closest to us, also have a significant impact. For example, our self-concepts may have been influenced by adults who thought praising us might make us conceited or complacent, so they pointed out our limitations, hoping we would try to correct them. Rather than making us feel better, this approach typically makes us feel worse. When we feel inadequate and unworthy, it is difficult to be supportive of others. Feeling negatively about ourselves affects our communication with others, perpetuating a cycle of distorted communication (Satir, 1972). But what can we do about low self-esteem?

We can decide to focus on our positive qualities, rather than our negative ones. If no positive ones come to mind, what strengths would a friend, partner, or relative point out? If we don't typically appreciate those aspects of ourselves, we need to pay more attention to them. Complimenting ourselves, acknowledging our value, and appreciating ourselves build our self-esteem. This process is called **cognitive restructuring** because we rebuild ("restructure") what we think ("cognition") about ourselves. The better we feel about ourselves, the more likely we are to appreciate and accept other people.

To help increase our self-esteem, we can read books that have addressed the theme of self-understanding and appreciation, such as *How to Be Your Own Best Friend,* by Mildred Newman and Bernard Berkowitz (1971), *I'm OK, You're OK,* by Thomas Harris (1967), and *Your Erroneous Zones,* by Wayne Dyer (1976).

A personal development group with a trained leader may be helpful. Participating in groups that focus on interpersonal communication can help us reassess our evaluations of self and others.

Helping others can make us feel good about ourselves. It can give us a new perspective on ourselves and others and demonstrate that we can make a contribution.

Learning something new can give us a feeling of accomplishment. We took a risk, tried something, worked at it, and have grown as a person. To gain from such endeavors, it is not necessary to become the best or even to master the area. Even if we learn that astronomy, small-engine repair, or backpacking is not something we enjoy or do well, we have learned more about ourselves in the process and have grown as a result.

This list of self-esteem builders is not comprehensive. We present it to highlight the diverse types of activities people can engage in to raise their self-esteem.

 *What other ideas can you suggest for building self-esteem? How is positive self-esteem different from conceit?*

## Making Time for Communication

The second element in effective communication is arranging time to share feelings and discuss the relationship. After an intimate relationship is well established, partners tend to communicate less about their feelings and focus more on the functional aspects of their lives—schedules, meals, bills, and so on. These topics certainly do need to be discussed, but not to the exclusion of discussions about feelings and the relationship. Unfortunately, couples tend to slip into this different emphasis without realizing it. When couples fail to discuss issues that are integral to their relationship, they are less satisfied with their communication and their marriage (Gottman, 1979). Researchers have noted that many financially secure couples with a workaholic husband are good at doing (exchanging information and services) and having (acquiring money and goods) but have trouble with being (communicating feelings) (L'Abate & L'Abate, 1981). They find it difficult to communicate "deep" or "soft" feelings, thereby inhibiting intimacy in the relationship.

This tendency to deal exclusively with the functional aspects of life is increased when partners live together. Whereas in the past they had to make arrangements to see each other, now that contact is a part of their daily routine. Because they spend a great deal of time together, it seems less necessary to focus on their feelings, their goals, and what they want and need from their partnership.

Yet we know from research that the quality of communication in a marriage depends on the exchange of personal and private information—that is, self-disclosure (Montgomery, 1981). In studying how important self-disclosure is in marriage, Jorgensen and Gaudy (1980, p. 286) conclude that "communicating about fears, problems, self-doubts, feelings of anger or depression, and aspects of marriage perceived to be bothersome to one or both partners, as well as openly sharing positive feelings about the self and other, are of central importance in fulfilling the 'therapeutic function' of marriage." These researchers found that the more frequently partners engaged in self-disclosure, the more likely they were to feel fulfilled in the marriage.

Quality communication can be attained if couples make arrangements to be alone together, without distractions like children and television, to talk about themselves, their feelings, and their relationship. This simple step is often overlooked. Relationships, like gardens, have to be cultivated continually, not just at the outset. Just as planting a seed in soil does not ensure a healthy plant, being linked by law or by living quarters is no guarantee that a meaningful, intimate partnership will result.

 *Is it possible to have an intimate relationship without self-disclosure? Is it possible to have friendships without self-disclosure? Why is self-disclosure difficult?*

## Assessing the Purpose and Responding to the Message

The third and fourth critical elements of effective communication are assessing the purpose of the message and responding appropriately. Because these two are inextricably linked, we will discuss them together in this section.

Communication has many purposes—to give or get information, to share opinions, and to express feelings and overcome problems, among others. Listeners give speakers **feedback**—an indication of their level of understanding and interest. A quizzical look, a blank stare, or a nod of the head is nonverbal feedback about how well a message is understood and how interested the listener is. There are three types of feedback response patterns (Watzlawick, Beavin, & Jackson, 1967). **Confirmation** shows acceptance of the speaker and the message. **Rejection** shows that the listener understands the speaker and the message but disagrees with one or both of them. **Disconfirmation** responses ignore

the existence of the speaker or the message. These responses say "You do not exist" (Watzlawick et al., 1967). As speakers, we are sensitive to the feedback (both verbal and nonverbal) we receive from listeners. We may clarify, restate, or emphasize part or all of our message in response to a listener's reactions.

The listener has a complex job. In order to respond appropriately to a sender, the listener must determine what the purpose of the message is. We have all experienced the frustration that results when we just want someone to understand our feelings and our listeners instead give us advice. Meaningful exchanges are virtually impossible when the two persons are talking about different things. It is up to the listener to try to interpret the *purpose* of the message in order to respond appropriately. The listener should scrutinize all verbal and nonverbal clues to determine what is really meant.

It is probably easiest to respond to messages that focus on providing or seeking information. "The dog got out," "The price of gas went up," and "What program do you want to watch?" are straightforward. The factual content is high and the emotional content is low. As the balance between facts and feelings changes, however, it becomes more difficult to interpret the message. "I just don't know what I'm going to do" sounds like a request for advice or information, but the sender frequently just wants someone to listen. "She hurt my feelings" often gets a response of "Don't take it so personally" (giving advice and discounting the feeling) when the person only wants to be understood. These miscommunications are dissatisfying to both parties. The sender feels misunderstood and the listener feels ignored.

When the purpose of the message is to express opinions, letting speakers explain themselves is effective. It may be helpful to verify your perceptions of what they mean, indicate your understanding, and clarify their position. In

these circumstances, it is important to respect their right to have an opinion different from yours. You may express disagreement openly, but personal attacks ("What a stupid idea!" or "Where did you learn to think?") are counterproductive.

If the purpose of the communication is to share positive feelings, the appropriate response is to show an understanding of those feelings and encourage them: "No wonder you feel relieved. That was quite a job you did," "That's wonderful," "You must feel ecstatic," "You certainly deserved that recognition." Avoid negative statements, even if they reflect reality. "That B+ is nice, but it's not an A" or "That accomplishment isn't going to make a difference in the end" is discouraging. Other people usually recognize that their feelings are transient and simply want to enjoy the moment. If you want them to share feelings with you in the future, let them enjoy theirs now.

When the purpose of the message is to indicate some emotional distress, the listener must determine who "owns" the problem. Thomas Gordon (1970) developed this approach in train-

ing parents to communicate more effectively with their children, and his principles are appropriate for all age groups. According to Gordon, the problem is "owned" by the person whose needs are not being met. If two of us are talking about a situation that is upsetting, there are three possible "owners" of the problem: you, me, or both of us. The appropriate response depends on who has the problem. Let's look at each of these possibilities.

*If the other person owns the problem.* When the other person has the problem, we should not try to take it away by giving advice, dismissing its importance, changing the subject, or any other tactic. The sender simply needs to know that his or her feelings are understood. We can convey our understanding by focusing on what was (or is) felt and verbalizing these emotions. This type of response is called **reflective listening** (we reflect the other person's feelings) or **active listening** (we listen participatively rather than passively). "You sound so frustrated," "That's awful," and "You must be furious" are examples. Tone, inflection, and emphasis are critical in delivering such feedback. We indicate our **empathy** (understanding of feelings) through such comments. Our role as the listener is to let the sender talk, interjecting comments only to convey that we understand and care. If we try to provide solutions (and most of us do in the hope that they will lessen the distress), they may be rejected because our response is not relevant to the purpose of the communication. Such suggestions are often interpreted to mean "She thinks I'm too stupid to figure out what to do" or "He doesn't think I should feel this way." The sender seeks understanding, not information.

Gordon (1970, pp. 41–44) developed a list of types of responses that inhibit further conversation. Avoiding them can substantially improve the effectiveness of conversations. He calls them the "Typical Twelve" because they are the ways people frequently respond:

1. Ordering, directing, commanding
2. Warning, admonishing, threatening
3. Exhorting, moralizing, preaching
4. Advising, giving solutions or suggestions
5. Lecturing, teaching, giving logical arguments
6. Judging, criticizing, disagreeing, blaming
7. Praising, agreeing
8. Name-calling, ridiculing, shaming
9. Interpreting, analyzing, diagnosing
10. Reassuring, sympathizing, consoling, supporting
11. Probing, questioning, interrogating
12. Withdrawing, distracting, humoring, diverting

Many people think they have to give advice or direction to be good listeners. In fact, quite the opposite is true. Human beings have a strong need to be understood and accepted as they are. People pay therapists at least partly because therapists are skilled listeners. Therapists create a climate where clients feel they are understood and accepted with all their feelings and shortcomings. When someone else has the problem, and we choose to listen (we *do* have a choice), we are filling the role of a natural caregiver, accepting those feelings and allowing the other person to develop solutions.

Being a listener when the other person owns the problem might seem simple, but it is quite difficult. We must set aside our own feelings, ideas, and recommendations to understand and accept the other person. His or her needs and feelings, not ours, must be foremost.

*If we own the problem.* If we have a problem that we want to talk to someone about, it is important to try to express ourselves as clearly as possible. Our first step is to study our feelings. What do we feel? (Usually more than one emotion is present.) What seems (or seemed) to arouse those feelings? By answering those questions, we will be able to encode our message more accurately. It is not necessary to rehearse what we want to say—only to understand some of our feelings.

Then we begin explaining our feelings with "I" statements: "I felt . . . ," "I was hurt when . . . ," "I wanted to bang my fist," and so on. Understanding and expressing feelings to someone who listens often provides an emotional release and helps us work through our problem. Of course, we can explain the situation in the course of talking about our feelings, but our emphasis falls on how we feel about the situation.

Tuning into feelings is difficult for some people. This problem is not surprising when we consider how much of our socialization emphasizes not expressing what we feel: "That's not worth crying about," "Of course you love your sister," and "Pretend you like your birthday present" are typical messages we get from others about "correct" feelings. Many of us have been conditioned to think that positive feelings are "corny" or that negative feelings are immature or unacceptable. Some people believe that feelings are acceptable only if they are rational—which is a quite irrational idea!

Actually, all feelings are acceptable. It is essential for our development that we learn how to express verbally both positive and negative feelings. Practice helps. As we learn to express our feelings and actually do so, it gets easier. We begin by trying to identify what we are feeling at the time and then expressing it. Frequently, as we talk about the problem, the feelings become clearer.

Often in relationships the behavior of one person upsets the other. For example, suppose that we "own" the problem and it is caused by the behavior of our listener. How can we convey our feelings without making our listener defensive? So often we respond with "you" messages: "You make me so mad," "You are inconsiderate," "You are a slob." Such messages are counterproductive. First, they blame or insult the other person, which tends to generate defensiveness. Second, they are not specific; in fact, the person may not know what particular behavior has caused our reaction (Gordon, 1970).

Both these problems can be overcome if we use an "I" message that describes the problem in a nonblaming way and explains its tangible effect on us. Gordon (1970) has developed the following formula: "I feel [give the feeling] when [describe the behavior] because [explain its impact on you]." Let's look at each of its components.

In the first part of the formula we assess and express our feelings. By doing so, we take responsibility for our feelings and for explaining them to the other person. Caution should be exercised in expressing anger, because it is a secondary feeling. It blames the other person ("I am angry at you") and often masks other feelings—worry, fear, or hurt (Dreikurs, 1964; Gordon, 1970; Satir, 1972). When we are angry, it is best to look for our other feelings and express

them. Another difficulty with the first part of the formula is that we sometimes substitute thoughts for feelings. "I feel *that* . . ." will not describe a feeling despite the use of the word *feel.* It leads to **intellectualizing**—explaining things by reasoning, rather than by feelings.

The second part of the formula describes the upsetting behavior in a nonblaming way. Emphasize the result of the behavior ("when the clothes are left lying around") rather than blaming the other person ("when you throw your clothes on the floor").

In the third part of the formula we explain the impact of the behavior on us. This impact should be real and tangible (Gordon, 1970). For example, if I get irritated because the other person doesn't get enough sleep, I need to be able to explain how that gives me a problem (he falls asleep when we're together, he doesn't have enough energy to do the things we planned). Otherwise, it is really his problem (*if* he perceives it as a problem) and not my concern.

Now let's construct two examples using Gordon's formula. In the first we're unhappy about clothes on the floor, and in the second about tardiness.

> "I get irritated when I see clothes lying on the floor because I don't like to pick them up. I would rather spend my time doing other things."

> "I feel frustrated when I have to wait for you because it wastes my time."

Of course, we are not limited to just one statement. We may want to talk about other feelings and their effects on us. What is important throughout this series of messages is that we focus on ourselves rather than blaming the other person. When we explain how and why a behavior distresses us, the person is more likely to be understanding and responsive. "I" messages aren't magic—they cannot change the other person's behavior—but they often lead to a mutually beneficial discussion.

*If we share the problem.* Often people share a problem. Sometimes the other person responds to an "I" message by indicating a problem of his or her own. Let's continue with the second example, in which we stated our frustration with someone's tardiness. She may respond: "You always suggest things at the last minute." (Note: This is not an "I" message. She is defensive and blames us for her lateness.) Notice that the ownership of the problem has shifted—she has negative feelings about this situation as well. How can we formulate a response to this statement?

First, we must assess the purpose of the message. Although she is giving us some information (she's unhappy), the overriding reason for this message is to express her negative feelings. So we respond the way we would any time the other person has a problem—by listening reflectively: "These last-minute suggestions are very frustrating to you" or "It sounds like you feel pressured because you don't have enough warning." She is likely to go on at some length expressing her feelings and giving examples of problem situations. After we indicate our understanding, we can send some additional "I" messages. It should be clear to both of us that we share a problem.

Problem solving is the approach to use in this case. It is a creative process for finding a mutually agreeable solution to a problem. It may be implemented formally by following a structured six-step process or informally by using the same steps flexibly. Each method is explained below.

In method 1, we follow a structured problem-solving process. The six steps are:

1. Identify the problem.
2. Brainstorm possible solutions (all ideas, no matter how silly, are acceptable at this point).
3. Evaluate the possible solutions for acceptability and feasibility.
4. Select the solution(s).
5. Implement the solution(s).
6. Evaluate the effectiveness of the solution(s).

When the problem is complex, this method is often best because the structure helps focus the discussion. Because reaching acceptable solutions to complex problems may take some time, it is wise to set aside a specific time to problem-solve (Gordon, 1970). Trying to reach a solution when time or other constraints limit our ability to focus on the task jeopardizes the outcome. Of course, some problems have to be addressed immediately, but many can wait until the climate is more conducive to solutions. Any solution selected must be acceptable to all parties, or it will not work.

When the problem is relatively simple (as in our example), it is possible to problem-solve informally, flexibly using the steps outlined in method 1. Let's illustrate this process with our tardiness example. After we have sent our "I" messages and listened reflectively (thereby identifying the problem), either one of us simply suggests a change in either person's behavior that would help solve the problem:

"I'll try to give you more warning."

"Why don't I set the time to meet? That way I'll be responsible for having enough time."

"Could you call me when you know you're going to be late?"

Brainstorming for solutions and reaching an agreement is a positive way to solve shared problems. Here are some recommendations for conducting problem-solving discussions:

1. Avoid past history. Focus on the present. You can't correct what went wrong in the past. Figure out what you can do differently

to avoid the problem in the future (Gordon, 1970; Lederer & Jackson, 1968).

2. Take responsibility for expressing your feelings clearly and accurately.
3. Verbalize your understanding of the other person's feelings. You do not have to agree with those feelings, but you must accept the person's right to them.
4. Remember, you share this problem. Both of you must "win" for the solution to work.

Although it takes time and practice to problem-solve, the results are well worth the effort.

In dealing with communication issues within couples, we have discussed three types of responses: reflective listening, "I" messages, and problem solving. Simply assess the purpose of the message to determine which one to use. Although using these skills may be difficult at first, practice enhances our ability.

> **?** *Select a partner and practice the communication techniques we have described to solve the following problems: A is distressed because B is boisterous in public. B is frustrated because A frequently agrees to do things together but then backs out at the last minute.*

# IMPROVING COMMUNICATION BETWEEN PARENTS AND CHILDREN

Let's review the requirements for effective communication: a strong self-concept, the time to communicate, an assessment of the purpose of the message, and an appropriate response. Which of these apply to communication between parents and children? It is conceivable that the gaps in power and ability between parents and children call for a different approach to communication in families.

## Fostering a Positive Self-Concept

Parents play an essential role in the development of self-concept. Every child needs to feel loved, and parents need to express these feelings verbally and nonverbally. Smiling, cuddling, and stroking communicate positive feelings even to very young children who cannot understand spoken words and help build their sense of worth.

As children grow, they gain some control of their environment, which gives them a sense of competence. These positive feelings may be fostered or destroyed by messages from parents. Children who are told they are "stupid," "bad," or "nothing but trouble" will begin to believe these messages and feel bad about themselves. However, children who are told their *behavior* is unwise or troublesome will learn to distinguish between their actions and themselves and will be less likely to have low self-esteem.

No adult wants to stay in a relationship where most of the messages are negative. The same is true, perhaps even more so, for children. It is important to focus on the positive when dealing with children (as with adults). This emphasis helps create a supportive environment, encouraging children to feel good about themselves and making them more responsive to requests for change.

## Making Time for Communication

Often communication within families, just as within couples, focuses on the tasks of maintaining the household. These exchanges, though necessary, should not constitute most or all of the interaction. Time is needed to talk about feelings, concerns, and the relationship. Emphasis should be on the quality of the interaction rather than on the quantity of time spent. Children readily recognize the difference between spending time being with someone and spending time in the same room. One mother with several children found that if she spent 15 minutes a day alone with each child, friction among the children decreased and all family members got along better. (By suggesting that parents set aside special time to communicate with each child, however, we do not mean that they should ignore him or her the rest of the time.)

## Assessing the Purpose and Responding to the Message

Communication between parents and children follows the same process we have described for adults: assess the purpose of the message and respond by listening reflectively, sending "I" messages, or solving a shared problem. Because adults have more experience than children, they often forget that if the child "owns" the problem, they probably should not suggest a solution. In fact, once children are able to articulate their concerns, they need practice solving their own problems in order to learn how and to increase their sense of mastery and control in their lives. Parents should be watchful but not intrusive.

An example illustrates how able and ready children are to solve their own problems if given the chance. A mother who was learning to listen reflectively in a parenting course reported her experience to the class. Several days before, her 6-year-old son had gotten a haircut. He hated it and, most of all, was afraid of being ridiculed at school the next day. When he expressed his fears to her, she suppressed her inclination to reassure him how nice he really looked or suggest that he stop being so concerned about it. Instead, she reflected his feelings: "You're really upset about your haircut." "You're afraid the other kids are going to tease you." After a few exchanges, he seemed to feel understood and ended the conversation—but without any solution to the problem! She felt she had failed him. The next day she was genuinely surprised when he returned from school and reported his story. He had kept his jacket on with his hood up when he took his seat in class that morning. When the class began, as usual, with "Show and Tell," he volunteered to share something. He walked to the front of the room, proudly pulled back his hood, and showed off his haircut for all to see. The children applauded (they applauded all "Show and Tell" stories). His haircut was a hit! Both mother and child learned from this experience. He solved his own problem quite creatively, which built his self-esteem and confidence, and she learned that trusting her 6-year-old to solve his own problems was good for both of them.

A fundamental difference between parents and children is their power and autonomy. As a result of this gap, parents tend to overlook the integrity of the child as a separate individual, capable of learning and making decisions. When adults solve a problem that the child owns, they send an important, hidden message: "You are incapable of managing this by yourself." Rather than gaining feelings of competence, the child feels inadequate. Hence, adults should assess who "owns" the problem and, when the child owns it, should listen reflectively, rather than try to solve it.

*A teenager wants to drive to the homecoming game, but the parents, concerned about drinking, drugs, and rowdy friends, prefer to do the driving. Apply the communication skills we have described to solve this problem. You may want to form pairs to play the roles of the teenager and the parent.*

Alfred Korzybski, an expert on semantics (cited in Hayakawa, 1979), theorized that communication is the fundamental survival mechanism of the human race. He suggested that beyond breathing and eating, communicating is the most important thing human beings do. Unless we withdraw from society and live as hermits, we will spend a great deal of our time communicating with others. It is to our benefit, then, to learn to communicate well.

## EDUCATION

Communication is the skill we use when we interact with others. It can make life more difficult or more rewarding, depending on our expertise. Most important, it is a *learned* skill. If we are dissatisfied with our style, we can change it. We can benefit greatly by learning more about communication. Feedback from others about our verbal and nonverbal behavior can teach us a great deal. Statements like "You don't seem like you mean it" or "You say everything is OK, but you don't sound OK" mean that our verbal and nonverbal behaviors are contradictory. Tuning in to our feelings and expressing what we truly mean are essential.

Using the communication techniques described in this chapter may improve our communication skills further. Although reflective listening or "I" messages may seem awkward at first, with practice they will become natural. Learning to assess quickly who "owns" the problem and knowing what kind of response to formulate is important too. The more we understand and practice our communication skills, the more effective we will become (Gordon, 1970).

Throughout this chapter we have discussed the elements of effective communication and have briefly described some effective patterns. But we have only touched the surface; entire books are devoted to communication! Reading more about communication can improve one's skills. A few books we recommend are *Communicate!* (Verderber, 1978), *A Couple's Guide to Communication* (Gottman et al., 1976), *Peoplemaking* (Satir, 1972), and *P.E.T.: Parent Effectiveness Training* (Gordon, 1970). Each of these books gives examples of ineffective communication and suggests how to avoid these pitfalls. This list is not comprehensive. The point is that we can improve our communication skills by learning more about the subject.

*Have you ever studied communication before? Did you put into practice anything you learned? What other educational approaches might be used to understand communication better?*

## COMMUNITY ORGANIZATION/ SYSTEMS INTERVENTION

This prevention tool focuses on changing the community or system to be more responsive to people's needs. One change that would foster communication is to socialize boys to be more expressive. To do so, intervention is necessary at the family, school, and community levels. Family members, particularly parents, need to understand how their attitudes affect children's development. If we socialize boys to be tough and aggressive and girls to be emotional and submissive, they naturally will have trouble understanding each other. Many changes have been made to allow people more flexibility (for example, girls are now encouraged to compete in athletics), but more changes are needed.

Another change that could be helpful is providing more male role models for young children. Typically, young children spend most of their time with women—their mothers, babysitters, child-care personnel, and elementary school teachers. Young boys and girls might benefit from more opportunities to interact with adult males.

**?** *What are the benefits and liabilities of socializing boys to be more expressive? Should we change the way we socialize girls to make them less expressive? What would be the benefits and liabilities of that change?*

## COMPETENCY PROMOTION

This prevention tool emphasizes the acquisition and use of skills. Practice in using effective communication skills in our daily lives is very useful. We should not expect perfection, only improvement. It may even help to work on our skills with another person who gives us feedback about how well we understood him or her and how clearly we expressed our own feelings. Such feedback should be accurate and supportive. Its purpose is to build (not deflate) self-esteem and to improve communication skills.

You and another student in your class can work together on your communication skills. Take turns listening reflectively, sending "I" messages, and deciding who owns a problem. You can use your own experiences or those of

*Urie Bronfenbrenner (1974) once observed that adults could start helping young people by doing "nothing more radical than providing a setting in which young and old can simply sit and talk" (p. 61).*

people you know or create a story. The purpose of the exercise is to practice communicating effectively. It may be helpful for a third person to play the part of observer. The observer notes the interaction between the speaker and the listener and gives them both feedback when they have finished their communication exercise. This technique is often used in training counselors and therapists.

 *Should we train children to use the communication skills described in this chapter? How might such training change their relationships with friends and family members?*

## NATURAL CAREGIVING

This prevention tool focuses on the care we provide to those close to us. Whenever we communicate warmth, caring, and concern, we are natural caregivers. When we help others meet their needs for inclusion, influence, and affection, we are using this tool. It is a pervasive aspect of our lives with people with whom we are intimate.

One purpose of friendship is to listen, to understand, and to make the other person feel understood. We fulfill this purpose through communication. Thus, effective communication and natural caregiving are two sides of the same coin.

One program that has been very successful in providing natural caregiving is the Foster Grandparents program. Older people interact with young children, providing love, building self-esteem, and teaching children new things. In providing this nurturance, these adults not only help young children, they also gain respect and love as the children communicate their appreciation. This program, like all other natural caregiving endeavors, is based on communication.

*What are some nonverbal ways of providing natural caregiving?*

# SUMMARY

The subject of this chapter has been the complex, fluid process called communication that is a part of our daily lives. It is the basis for all interpersonal relationships, within and outside families. Communication is usually interactive, with senders and receivers constantly changing roles. Communication can be clear or confused, supportive or detrimental, encouraging or discouraging—or anywhere in between.

Because communication has different purposes, it is essential to determine the reason for the message before responding. When the message is about a problem, one should determine who owns the problem and respond appropriately with active listening, "I" messages, and/or problem solving. Because communication is such a complex process and one in which we have received little formal training, we often develop ineffective and counterproductive patterns, but they can be overcome with practice and effort.

# MAJOR POINTS TO REMEMBER

1. We cannot avoid communicating when we are with other people.
2. Verbal and nonverbal aspects of communication contribute to our understanding of messages.
3. Nonverbal behavior includes tone, inflection, emphasis, eye contact, facial expression, gestures, touching, and proximity.
4. Blocks to effective communication include misuse of language, an inappropriate environment, low self-concept, perceptual filters, and an inability to express oneself clearly and accurately.
5. Communication between intimate partners may be distorted by limerance and the assumption that one can read one's partner's mind.
6. Early in relationships, couples may make special efforts to communicate effectively by making efforts to be together, concentrating on each other rather than on themselves, being self-disclosive, and providing positive feedback.
7. Communication in the family differs from that in most other groups because the power and abilities of its members may differ greatly and because it is a "permanent" group, not easily dissolved.
8. Negative patterns of interaction include blaming, placating, computing, and distracting.
9. The appropriate type of communication will vary depending on who "owns" the problem.
10. To foster effective communication, the following elements are essential: develop a positive self-concept, make time for communication, and assess the purpose of the message and respond appropriately.

# ADDITIONAL SOURCES OF INFORMATION

Blume, J. S. (1970). *Iggie's house.* Scarsdale, NY: Bradbury Press. [Early adolescents]

Castle, S. (1977). *Face talk, hand talk, body talk.* New York: Doubleday. [Children]

Conta, M. M., & Reardon, M. (1974). *Feelings between brothers and sisters.* Chicago: Raintree. [Children]

Gottman, J. M., Notarius, C., Gonso, J., & Markman, J. (1976). *A couple's guide to communication.* Champaign, IL: Research Press. [Adults]

Norris, G. B. (1971). *If you listen.* New York: Atheneum. [Early adolescents]

Schwarzrock, S., & Wreen, C. G. (1973). *You always communicate something.* Circle Pines, MI: American Guidance Service. [Adolescents]

Stolz, M. S. (1964). *A love, or a season.* New York: Harper & Row. [Adolescents]

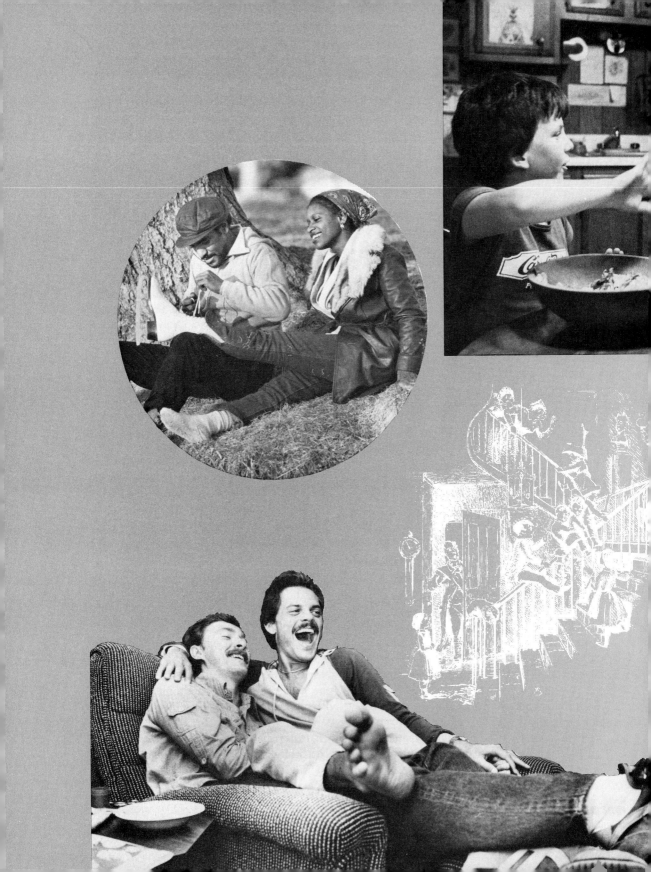

*Part Three*

# FAMILY LIFE ACROSS THE LIFE SPAN

151

7

# INTIMACY, LOVE, AND MAYBE MARRIAGE

*You may not* remember when the lyrics "Love and marriage, love and marriage, go together like a horse and carriage" were on the lips of most young people. Actually, neither do we. But we do recall any number of songs in which the singer pledged eternal, or at least temporary, love for someone. There can be little doubt that human beings need other human beings. Companionship, intimacy, love, caring, and sharing are natural parts of a healthy personal life. In this chapter we examine how individuals come to discover others, explore relationships with them, and decide whether to commit themselves to a relationship or dissolve it.

## DISCOVERING RELATIONSHIPS

### Developing Heterosexual Interests

The discovery of intimate relationships and an interest in the other sex are thought to emerge at puberty. Before that, children consistently prefer same-sex friends. Some scholars have attributed this preference largely to the organizational structure of children's environments, such as schools (Karweit & Hansell, in press). Intimacy evolves gradually through a series of social transitions. One notable change, well documented in the research literature on adolescence (for example, see Adams & Gullotta, 1983, for a review), is that, beginning in early adolescence, young people spend more time with peers than with adults. The movement toward heterosexual contact is preceded by maintenance of small same-sex social cliques (Dunphy, 1963). As adolescents mature, these cliques begin group-to-group interactions with opposite-sex social cliques. Gradually the leaders (or more mature adolescents) begin to develop additional cliques that include both sexes. Eventually the newly formed heterosexual cliques come to replace (though not totally) the same-sex cliques. These same small heterosexual cliques associate with others in larger crowd activities such as parties. Finally, in late adolescence the crowd begins to lose its utility and disintegrates into small groups of couples who spend most of their social time together. The couples begin to bond together and make longer-range commitments than those held during the larger heterosexual clique phase (see Figure 7-1).

Montemayor and Van Komen (1983) confirmed this gradual transition from same-sex to opposite-sex friendships in a study of 13- through 19-year-old adolescents. They found that mixed-sex groups increased from 7.1% for 13-year-old girls to 53.9% for 19-year-old girls and from 10% for 14-year-old boys to 55.6% for 19-year-old boys. Clearly, young people move from same-sex to mixed-sex groups as they grow older.

While interaction patterns with peers are changing, adolescents are also experiencing transitions in social relations within their families. Both these transitions in peer and family social relations reflect a changing individual in changing social structures. Although one goal of adolescence is to increase independence from the family, it is also a period of life when the young person needs to maintain an affectionate and supportive relationship with parents. This paradox is often confounded by parents' lack of enthusiasm for the adolescent's readiness for independence and autonomy. An adolescent's first attempts at increased independence from parents are usually associated with some degree of conflict. However, such conflict is likely to result eventually in a major improvement in family relations.

Addressing this very issue, Sullivan and Sullivan (1980) compared male adolescents who lived at home after high school and commuted to college with those who boarded at school. They found that those who stayed home had

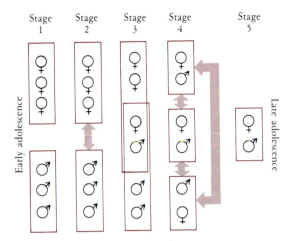

**FIGURE 7-1.** *Development of heterosexual cliques, crowds, and couples in adolescence. Individual sets without arrows do not interact. Sets with arrows are interacting groups. In overlapping sets, only the included figures interact.*

more direct conflict with their parents. Absence from home facilitated these young people's achievement of independence, while those remaining home found their efforts to establish a separate identity impeded by arguments with their parents.

Thus, transformations in social relations that are pertinent to personal development begin within both the peer group and the family long before committed heterosexual relationships emerge. These early social transitions within the family may not be totally smooth. However, once the transition in social relations begins, the movement toward heterosexual activities and dating soon follows.

## Falling in Love

Remember sitting in class in high school and pining with lovesickness for someone across the room? What attracted you to that person?

Levinger (1974; Levinger & Snoek, 1972) provides a simple and straightforward model of the way adolescents (and adults) identify potential dating partners. His premise is that attraction toward another person (or perceived shared attitudes with another) provides pleasant sensations that enhance the probability of developing an intimate relationship.

In Levinger's model the adolescent begins unaffiliated with a significant other (partner) but involved in a same-sex friendship group. Next, through social contacts a male and a female become unilaterally aware of each other. This **unilateral awareness** is based on limited information and impressions about each other—mostly on external characteristics such as looks, race, or general appearance. This level of human relatedness includes evaluations of each other but little interaction.[1] As reciprocal contacts develop, a new phase called **surface contact** begins. The two individuals briefly interact, sharing such casual remarks, as "Nice day," "This Jell-O tastes like rubber," or "Great music." This communication is often sterile and nonintimate. However, as individuals recognize their shared interest in each other, they move toward sharing a more intimate relationship called **mutuality.** Mutuality is most likely to occur after several dates and becomes evident in such behaviors as mutual gazing, touching, helping, disclosing, and statements of liking and loving. A shared commitment to marriage may even develop, and an engagement may be announced.

Do you remember what attracted you to your first love? Numerous studies reveal that people are attracted to others similar to themselves. Some studies (for example, Pursell & Banikiotes, 1978) show that similarity of sex-role characteristics attracts; that is, androgynous persons are (at least initially) more attracted to other androgynous persons than to traditionally masculine or feminine sex-typed persons. Other studies of friendships reveal that friends often share atti-

The need for closeness and a sense of emotional feeling for another are two attributes of mutuality.

tudes and values. Some research finds that the most important attributes in interpersonal attraction are those that readily define recognizable groups, such as sex and race, and those that determine physical proximity, such as age or grade in school. Kandel (1978) finds that similarity in the use of illegal drugs is a more accurate predictor of friendship patterns than similarities in attitudes or personality. She concludes that similar behavior patterns are more predictive of attraction than attitudes are.

---

[1] This stage is much like the "meat market" bar scene of examining other patrons and trying to decide whether to "make a move" on some good-looking person.

Social psychologists argue that attraction comes largely from mutually satisfying interaction (for example, Latané & Hothersall, 1972). Laboratory work with animals (Latané, Meltzer, Joy, Lubell, & Cappell, 1972; Sloan & Latané, 1974) and humans (Insko & Wilson, 1977) shows that enjoyable social experiences influence attraction. Persons who experience a pleasant interaction with someone tend to perceive that person as more similar to themselves and to like the person more than if they have not had such an interaction. At social gatherings we are likely to be attracted to those who share our interests, values, and attitudes. It is therefore reasonable to speculate (Sutherland & Insko, 1973) that interactions involving uninteresting dialogue will not increase interpersonal attraction. Indeed, most of us can remember an exchange with someone that was so unenjoyable that we dreaded ever seeing the person again.

Without question, the single most studied variable in interpersonal attraction has been physical attractiveness (see Adams, 1977, 1982; Berscheid & Walster, 1974a; Patzer, 1985, for reviews). In one of several notable studies highlighting the strong influence of physical appearance on interpersonal attraction, Dion, Berscheid, and Walster (1972) found that people expected attractive individuals to lead better lives and to possess more socially desirable personality traits than unattractive individuals. However, another study (Dermer & Thiel, 1975) showed that attractive individuals may also be viewed as more vain and egotistical and as more likely to have an extramarital affair or to divorce.

The effects of physical attractiveness on dating and marital choice are enormous. Numerous studies find that attractive individuals are preferred as dating choices (for example, Brislin & Lewis, 1968; Byrne, Ervin, & Lamberth, 1970; Curran & Lippold, 1975; Walster, Aronson, Abrahams, & Rottman, 1966). Mathes (1975) found that physical attractiveness maintained its influence over liking a date through at least five separate encounters even though additional information about the person (for example, level of anxiety, interests, and values) became available with each contact. The reasons for this strong effect remain unclear. Nonetheless, we know that attractiveness is related to perceived sex appeal, sensations of love, and emotional arousal (Cavior, Jacobs, & Jacobs, 1974; Critelli, 1975; Peplau, 1976; Shea & Adams, 1984). We also know that being associated with an attractive person raises one's own social status (for example, Bar-Tal & Saxe, 1974; Sigall & Landy, 1973). We must therefore conclude, with Dion et al. (1972), that beauty is good and is in the eye of the beholder.

Besides similarity, satisfying social interactions, and physical attractiveness, other factors are also important in attraction. One of them is propinquity. That is, we tend to like people who are physically close to us more than those who are physically distant. Another factor is complementarity of needs: under certain conditions we are attracted to people whose characteristics satisfy our own needs. And we are attracted to competent people, people who are pleasant or agreeable, and people who simply like us.

It is perhaps an oversimplification, but much of the research literature suggests that we like people who bring us personal gratification. Thus, many of the findings on interpersonal attraction are explained by the hypothesis that people value and seek out characteristics that are rewarding to them.

*What factors were significant when you first fell in love? What factors are most important now?*

# DATING AND COURTSHIP

## *Dating Patterns*

Benson (1971) proposes that dating and courtship are two distinct phases, each with its own set of rules. As adolescents leave the later stages of dating, they begin the early, informal stages of courtship. Benson says four new conditions accompanying industrial development have encouraged dating among ever younger adolescents. First, the industrial revolution in the United States contributed to the creation of adolescence as a distinct life stage and of an adolescent youth culture. This culture has been fueled by the media's emphasis on youth fads, music, dancing, dating patterns, and other leisure interests. "A big part—in some ways the most important part—of youth culture is the dating complex" (Benson, 1971, p. 54). Second, dating has become the means by which an individual finds a loving partner, in the first phase of the courtship process. Third, as society moves toward greater sexual equality, boys and girls spend more time together, making it likely that adolescents will begin to date at an earlier age and will date more partners. Indeed, Broderick and Weaver (1968) present data suggesting that romantic attraction between boys and girls begins around age 10. Finally, no longer living under the watchful eyes of one's parents produces freedom in mate selection and enhances the search for a mate.

*Definition of a date.* What do we mean by the word *date*? At one time the term meant that a male asked a female to accompany him to an activity and she accepted with the approval of her parent(s). He would pick her up at her home at an arranged time, pay for all expenses while out, and return her to her porch at the specified hour. According to the reports of modern-day parents, this version of dating is rare. Many parents have commented to us that they are never really sure when their adolescent is having a date. Murstein (1980) has spoken about recent changes in dating:

In high schools and colleges, according to informal reports by students, they tend to congregate

in groups from which the majority gradually evolve into pairs, although retaining some allegiance to the group. There is less structure as to appropriate male-female behavior, expenses are often "dutch treat," and highly structured dating protocol has largely disappeared [p. 780].

This lack of structure has made it difficult for researchers to observe the dating process.

We do know, however, that dating and courtship develop commitment to a relationship (Johnson & Shuman, 1983). As a couple move from occasional dating to regular and then steady dating, they strengthen their commitment to each other, and the behaviors that reinforce the commitment make it difficult to withdraw from the relationship.

*Two views of dating.* Historically, there have been two dominant views of dating (Gordon, 1981). Waller, in 1937, wrote on the **rating and dating complex,** using his observations of dating patterns at Pennsylvania State University. He argued that the formal period of courtship was declining, that emphasis had shifted to thrill seeking, exploitation, and dating several partners. Waller used the term *rating* because the dating system stressed prestige. Waller warned that this rating-dating complex would create antagonism between the sexes and undermine sound mate selection.

There is serious doubt, however, that Weller's rating-dating complex actually represented dating patterns across America (Gordon, 1981). Observations by Newcomb (1937) suggested that the majority of college students still practiced more traditional dating and courtship behavior. It was likely that in colleges where Greek societies (fraternities and sororities) set standards for social acceptability, the ethic of rating and dating was common, but the millions of youths not in college or not in Greek societies probably never followed the rating and dating pattern. Although some studies have supported a rating and dating complex (for example, Smith, 1952; Winch, 1943), much recent research suggests that students have moved away from the competitive and materialistic aspects of dating toward interest in dating others with pleasant personalities and in expanding personal experience with others (for example, Blood, 1955, 1956; Kraine, Cannon, & Bagford, 1977).

 *If you reject the rating-dating complex, how would you explain the influence of physical appearance on attraction?*

*Dating expectations.* Perhaps you remember your first (and maybe last) blind date. Remember the waves of anxiety that swept over you as you wondered what the stranger would look like and what would happen on your date? These anxieties reflect a person's expectations about dating.

What expectations do adolescents have? When 432 Los Angeles–area adolescents were asked to describe a desirable dating partner, both males and females mentioned intelligence, physical appearance, and shared background, religious preference, values, and interests as key desirable attributes (Zellman, Johnson, Giarrusso, & Goodchilds, 1979). Females were more likely to mention personality and sensitivity; males were more likely to mention physical appearance.

This same study asked a variety of questions about sexuality—for example, whether wearing a particular article of clothing meant the person wanted to have sex. It was thought that girls' low-cut tops, shorts, tight jeans, or see-through blouses might serve as cues for boys, while boys' open shirts, tight pants, or jewelry might cue girls. Girls were not inclined to see dress as a signal of wanting sex, but boys were. Clearly, this finding points to a possible problem. Adolescent girls may unknowingly be viewed by boys as inviting sexual advances when in reality they are merely being fashionable.

What about the reputation of one's date? Does being told that one's current date has had frequent sex with others imply that one will experience a "come-on" from that date? Both male and female respondents thought it would for a boy. For a girl, both thought she would probably make advances, and female respondents held this belief more strongly. In addition, "female respondents were significantly more likely to feel that the male . . . had a right to expect sex from his date when she had a 'tarnished reputation'" (Zellman et al., 1979, p. 8). One must conclude from these findings that reputation counts.

Does the location of a date signal an interest in having sex? Both males and females perceived going to the boy's house when nobody was home as a strong cue that the boy wanted sex. Another cue that the other person was interested in sex was behavior during the date. However, there were strong sex differences in the findings. Females generally were unaware of behavior as a primary cue, while males were greatly influenced by it. They perceived talking about sex, playing with a date's hair, tickling, and so on as cues of sexual interest.

These findings suggest that adolescent girls have a less sexualized view of their dating world. In contrast, boys are easily cued and use social cues to suggest to their dates that they are interested in having sex. Such findings suggest that girls' behavior can convey an unintended sexual message to their dates.

*Dating among college students.* A larger body of research exists on dating patterns for college-age youths. One recent study is of particular interest. Knox and Wilson (1981) wanted to find out how students met, where they went, and what they did on dates. They asked a sample of

## BOX 7-1
### *First the French Kiss and Now the French Feel*

Most of us know what a French kiss is: the thrusting of one's tongue into another's mouth. But what is the "French feel"? Actually, there is no such term. We made it up to describe an extension of French-kissing behavior that Dr. Marcel Baudovin (cited in Shorter, 1977, p. 106) claims was prac- ticed in the west of France before World War I.

The French kiss, Baudovin reports, was commonly ex- changed between the sexes as pecks on the cheek between friends are today. Those more intimately involved went be- yond kissing to mutual mastur- bation (or, as we call it, the "French feel"). Baudovin con- tends that this practice was so widespread that special clothing was designed to enable partners to stimulate each other without having to undress.

We have only two comments to offer our readers: first, the clothing industry rose to the occasion, and, second, fiction pales in the face of history.

---

334 East Carolina University students how they had met the people they dated. About one third of the sample had met their date through a friend's introduction. The next most probable places for meeting a date were parties and work. One of the least likely places was in class.

The most common dating activity was to go to a public event (such as a football game), attend a party, and then return to the man's or the wom- an's dormitory room. The most frequent topic of conversation during dates was "our relation- ship." School matters and friends arose less of- ten (but more often than other topics). Talking about sex occupied less than 5% of dating time.

The survey also asked respondents about their sexual values and encouragement or dis- couragement of sexual intimacy. Men and women responded differently to questions about when kissing, petting, and intercourse were acceptable. Kissing was acceptable on the first date to more than half the women and close to three quarters of the men. By the third date, kissing was acceptable to almost everyone. Heavy petting (with hands anywhere) was not acceptable to most respondents until the fourth date or later. However, a sizable percentage of men (31%) felt that petting should occur on the first date, and more men expected sexual inter- course to occur earlier in the dating sequence. Greater emotional involvement with a date in- creased the level of sexual intimacy that respon- dents regarded as appropriate. This was particu- larly true for women.

How would these college students encourage sexual intimacy? Many reported they would just say they wanted to make love (Knox & Wilson, 1981). Others would create a conducive atmo- sphere (hints, close physical contact, music). Women were more likely than men to use the tactics of moving closer to the person and hint- ing. In addition, alcohol and marijuana were fre- quently used on dates, possibly to lessen inhibi- tions. (Dawley, Winstead, Baxter, and Gay, 1979, review several reports that users of marijuana believe it enhances sexual pleasure. In a survey of 84 graduate students, these investigators found that 61% believed marijuana functioned as an aphrodisiac.)

And what if the individual wished to discour- age sexual advances? In most cases, he or she would just tell the other person to "cool it." Other techniques included ignoring the behav- ior and keeping some distance between oneself and one's date.

*What problems might arise between dating partners as a result of males' and females' differing expectations about sexual behavior? How might the partners resolve these problems?*

## Courtship Development

If the relationship doesn't cool but instead continues to heat up, when does the dating process turn into courtship?

*Changing roles.* We can say that when two individuals begin to think of marriage, rather than leisure-time or recreational activities, a courtship has begun. McDaniel (1969) found that there was a formal sequence in the dating and courtship pattern that began with random dating, progressed to going steady, and culminated in becoming pinned or engaged. Changes in role behavior accompanied these increased levels of involvement. Drawing on research by Winch, Ktsanes, and Ktsanes (1955), McDaniel found that girls were more assertive during the period of occasional dating, assertive but open to suggestions when going steady, and more compliant and passive once engaged. (Assertiveness in this study was measured by the degree to which the person manipulates and maintains control, while receptiveness focused on admiration, accepting another's decisions, and dependence.) This early study clearly suggests that as individuals pass through the various phases of courtship, behaviors and expectations evolve through several stages.

*Communication patterns.* Recent work on dating and courtship shows that communication patterns change over the course of the relationship. Kraine (1975), for example, compares communication styles in early-dating, going-steady, and marriage-bound couples. His basic assumption is that as couples evolve through the three

stages of dating and courtship, their communication style will change from one that is destructive of relationship formation to one that is facilitative. Indeed, he finds that early-dating conversational styles range from mildly impeding communication to severely disrupting it. Later, when individuals are confident of their partner's good will, conversational styles are communication-enhancing. Kraine argues that early egocentric communication impedes the interpersonal processes necessary for the establishment, maintenance, and repair of romantic relationships, whereas the more empathic communication patterns of committed couples support the processes that build and maintain romantic relationships.

*Relationship enhancement.* What factors beyond a general communication pattern facilitate or impede the development of a romantic relationship? For one, level of involvement appears to influence interpersonal satisfaction (for example, Eidelson, 1980). In a developing relationship, interpersonal satisfaction increases as the involvement between the couple intensifies (Huston & Surra, 1981; Huston, Surra, Fitzgerald, & Cate, 1981; Johnson & Shuman, 1983). In addition, as a couple become closer, their network of joint friends expands (Milardo, 1982), and this friendship network stabilizes the closeness of the relationship. Therefore, as individuals are rewarded by their mate or date and by the social friendship network, they grow more satisfied with their relationship (see, for example, Cate, Lloyd, Henton, & Larson, 1982). Finally, interpersonal attraction can be enhanced by the perceived power of another. Power can assume many forms (French & Raven, 1959) and is derived from many sources (Huston, 1984). Attraction to another can be based on the **legitimate power** of attitudes, behaviors, or beliefs, on the positive effect of **reward power,** or on the negative effect of **coercive power. Expert power** can influence others through superior knowledge or skills or informational value. And because, as noted earlier in our discussion of identification, the desire to be similar to another person is a strong motivator of behavior, another source is **referent power,** based on identification with another person.

Similarity in physical attractiveness between partners may influence the progress of courtship. White (1980) found that similarity of attractiveness predicts progress from casual or serious dating to cohabitation or engagement: when the partners are approximately equally attractive, intimacy is likely to intensify over time.

Numerous social and psychological variables have been suggested as contributors to relationship enhancement (Huston & Levinger, 1978, provide an extensive review). Two appear particularly important. First, several investigations have suggested that self-disclosure of personal information is particularly important (for example, Rubin, Hill, Peplau, & Dunkel-Schetter, 1980). Sharing one's self at a level of intimacy facilitates the courtship process. Second, some evidence indicates that the man's need for power (need to have an impact on others) interferes with relationship formation. Stewart and Rubin (1974) found that among dating couples the man's hope (or need) for power predicted dissatisfaction and problems in relationships.

Couples that included men high in hope for power were very likely to break up and highly unlikely to marry.

*Theoretical perspectives.* Early research on courtship proceeded from a social-process perspective, which focuses on the interchange between partners at a given point in the courtship. Such research is a static examination of courtship at a fixed point in time. It asks merely what the social factors are that influence mate selection. More recently a developmental theoretical perspective has emerged. The focus is on change in the social process as a couple move through the courtship and identification of different developmental patterns during courtship.

According to a recent overview of research on courtship (Huston et al., 1981), much of the early research focused on **compatibility models** of mate selection. These early social-process models generally revealed that persons with similar personal and social characteristics, such as age, social class, religion, and values, were most likely to choose each other as marriage partners. A classic example of this early compatibility research is Winch's (1954) work on complementarity of personality needs. As a natural extension of these compatibility studies, Kerckhoff and Davis (1962) proposed a **filter theory** of

# cathy

### BOX 7-2
## *Courtship American Style: Let's Make a Deal*

If you were unable to meet desirable candidates for marriage, what would you do? Increasing numbers of Americans are using a broadening number of resources to meet possible mates. Davor Jedlicka (1980) has described several available options. The first is a newspaper network. One can place an advertisement in a newspaper. Responses are sent to the publisher, who forwards them to the advertisers. Another resource is the copublisher network. A copublisher purchases matrimonial magazines from a publisher. For a fee, interested parties can acquire the addresses and/or phone numbers of the persons in the advertisements. Yet a third possibility is computer dating. Information about each participant and his or her preferences in a partner is entered into the computer, and possible matches are selected. A more recent option is the videomate selection process. A person videotapes a short self-description, which is shown to other clients. Tapes are viewed by both parties, and, for a fee, arrangements are made for the two individuals to meet.

Two recent research reports provide highly interesting findings about these innovations. Harrison and Saeed (1977) analyzed the content of 800 lonely-hearts advertisements and found that each individual was willing to offer something for something else in return. The authors summarize: "Women were more likely than men to offer attractiveness, seek financial security, and seek partners who were older than they were themselves. Men were more likely than women to seek attractiveness, offer financial security, and seek partners who were younger than they were themselves" (p. 259). Thus, each advertiser appeared to be interested in obtaining some form of equity. Work by Cameron, Oskamp, and Sparks (1977) reveals that the newspaper ads represent a pattern of offers and requests "reminiscent of a heterosexual stock market" (p. 27). Advertisers sought to maximize their "profit" by presenting a positive image of themselves.

For a personal look at the buyer and seller proposals of the advertisements, we suggest you look at a copy of such magazines as *Singles Critiques, Singles Press, Singles News Register, Swingers World Magazine,* or *Modern People.*

courtship selection: "Persons compare themselves first in terms of social characteristics; later, filtering proceeds with regard to similarity in values; and finally, for those couples still together continued progress towards marriage depends on the complementarity of needs" (Huston et al., 1981, p. 55). More recently, Murstein (1974, 1977) has reinterpreted previous research on filter theory from a social exchange perspective. He proposes that couples decide whether to continue an intimate relationship on the basis of compatibility of stimulus, value, and role characteristics. Initially, people select each other on observable characteristics, such as physical attractiveness. Once dating, the partners evaluate the degree to which they are similar in values, attitudes, opinions, and the like. Only in the later stages of courtship do couples begin to assess role fit and compatibility of life expectations.

As theorists recognized the useful foundation of the social-process perspective but also realized that courtship is a gradual transformation leading toward commitment to marriage, increased interest in a developmental perspective emerged. For example, Robert Lewis (1972, 1973) proposed that the following six developmental tasks are necessary in forming a commitment to marriage. These tasks are thought to occur in a fixed sequence; that is, success on the first stage determines likely success on the second, and so on.

1. First the individuals must perceive some degree of similarity between themselves in values, interests, opinions, appearance, or needs.
2. This perceived similarity enhances the couple's rapport and interest in communicating or ability to communicate.
3. Next, both partners begin to engage in self-disclosure when talking.
4. Through self-disclosing, the couple begin to understand each other, gaining an accurate perception of each other's interpersonal role and desires.
5. Through role-sharing activities the couple identify the appropriate fit for themselves within the relationship.
6. Finally, if the perceptions are that both individuals are compatible with the roles expected within the relationship, the process culminates in a commitment, or crystallization, resulting in marriage.

Theoretical formulations such as Lewis' are instrumental in stimulating researchers to include in their study of courtship both social, or interpersonal, process and the notion of stages, or phases. For example, Braiker and Kelley (1979) compared casual daters, serious daters, engaged couples, and married couples on four major dimensions of relationship development: love, conflict, self-disclosure (or maintenance), and ambivalence (hesitation about the relationship). They found that love and maintenance behaviors increase as one becomes more committed and involved, while ambivalence generally decreases. Conflict tends to increase from casual to serious dating but levels off with stronger commitment. This study clearly shows that the interpersonal processes occurring at different stages of the courtship change in response to new demands placed on the relationship.

But do all courtships follow an identical pattern of stage development? The answer is found in two studies with similar methodologies (reported in Huston et al., 1981). The researchers traced the development of premarital relationships into marriage, using retrospective (recall) interviews. In Study I, using a graphing technique, participants outlined the course of their relationship, indicating the points when they were casually dating, seriously dating, and committed to marriage. The researchers identified three types of courtship styles: accelerated, intermediate, and prolonged (see Figure 7-2). In the **accelerated courtship** relationships there was a significantly higher chance of marriage early in the premarital involvement phase, with a rapid climb in the probability of commitment to marriage. Commitment emerged early, and partners spent relatively little time in the early dating stages. In the **intermediate courtship** there was a smooth and continuous movement toward commitment. These couples moved toward marital certainty with moderate speed and little conflict or reported downturns in the probability of marriage. Finally, the **prolonged courtship** style was characterized by a slow, up-and-down ascent to marital commitment.

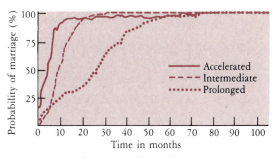

**FIGURE 7-2.** *Three courtship styles: average trajectories to marriage for relationship types in Study I.*

Study II found an additional pattern—an **accelerated-arrested courtship** style. As in the accelerated style, subjects reported a higher-than-average probability of marriage during the casual dating phase and a rapid movement to even higher probabilities of marriage. However, in contrast to the accelerated style, the accelerated-arrested courtship has a significant downturn for a period of time just before making final marital commitments. Between the two studies, we can see that at least three and possibly four patterns of courtship development occur.

Do these styles reflect social-process differences? To look for differences in interaction, in Study II couples were asked to indicate on a checklist the degree of affectional, leisure, and instrumental (work) activities that were shared at each stage of involvement. Overall, the researchers report that the frequency of affectional activities increased significantly between lower and higher involvement levels. Further, as couples moved into higher levels of involvement, they reported sharing more and more of the practical instrumental tasks of life (cleaning house, washing the car, and so on). As involvement increased, couples also reported spending more leisure time together and less with friends. Additional analyses revealed that different social interaction patterns distinguished the courtship styles. Partners in intermediate courtships were the least involved with each other in affectional and instrumental activities. These couples spent more time apart and generally segregated their roles on instrumental variables. Instrumental activities in prolonged-courtship couples were highly segregated along sex-role dimensions: males did "male" things and females did "female" things. Affectional activities were less frequent in the prolonged than in the accelerated group and about as frequent as in intermediate-courtship couples. The accelerated-arrested style was distinguished by close affiliation and cohesiveness between the partner and others. Finally, the accelerated relationships were, among other things, the most highly affiliated: couples reported sharing both female and male instrumental activities.

Collectively, findings such as these show that the discovery of courtship patterns from a developmental perspective can provide clues about corresponding shared or nonshared couple behaviors. Thus, a theoretical link can be established between developmental patterns in courtship and social behaviors.

Developmental theory has, however, been hampered by the lack of adequate measures of the phases of relationship formation. Recent efforts by King and Christensen (1983) address this gap by providing a new assessment device to measure courtship progress. Their 19-item Relationship Events Scale is a hierarchically arranged six-level measure of progress in courtship that reflects increasing intimacy, interdependence, and commitment. King and Christensen found that engaged or married couples obtained higher scores on the Relationship Events Scale than couples who were dating or going steady. Higher scores also correlated with greater affection and relationship satisfaction and with more frequent sexual relations. The six levels and their corresponding scale items are as follows:

*Level 1 (pass 2 or more)*
My partner has called me an affectionate name (sweetheart, darling, etc.).

I have called my partner an affectionate name (sweetheart, darling, etc.).

We have spent a whole day with just each other.

We have arranged to spend time together without planning any activity.

We have felt comfortable enough with each other so that we could be together without talking or doing an activity together.

*Level 2 (pass 1 or more)*
We have received an invitation for the two of us as a couple.

My partner has referred to me as his/her girlfriend/boyfriend.

I have referred to my partner as my girlfriend/boyfriend.

*Level 3 (pass 2 or more)*

My partner has said "I love you" to me.

I have said "I love you" to my partner.

My partner does not date anyone other than myself.

I do not date anyone other than my partner.

*Level 4 (pass 1 or more)*

We have discussed the possibility of getting married.

We have discussed living together.

*Level 5 (pass 2 or more)*

I have lent my partner more than $20 for more than a week.

My partner has lent me more than $20 for more than a week.

We have spent a vacation together that lasted longer than three days.

*Level 6 (pass 1 or more)*

We are or have been engaged to be married.

We have lived together or we live together now.

Studies such as those reviewed here show that the courtship process is associated with a variety of significant changes in social interaction and communication styles. Of course, each courtship is unique. Nonetheless, these groundbreaking developmental studies suggest that all courtships fall into a few relationship styles, associated with certain behavioral patterns. It is, however, yet to be determined to what degree the various courtship patterns predict fulfillment, longevity, and behavior in marriage itself.

 *How have dating patterns changed in your lifetime? Do you think dating and courtship behaviors will change in the future? How? Why?*

# INTIMATE RELATIONSHIPS

## *Defining Intimacy*

It is thought that the changes in the dating and mate selection process are due in part to the changing psychological needs of adolescents and young adults. Erikson (1963) has theorized that cultural and social forces in our society require young adults to resolve a growing need for intimacy against the danger of personal isolation. Erikson proposes that the major task of young adulthood is to establish committed intimate relationships through the development of close friendships and the selection of a marriage partner. Erikson defines *intimacy* accordingly, as "the capacity to commit [oneself] to concrete affiliations and partnerships and to develop the ethical strength to abide by such commitments, even though they may call for significant sacrifices and compromises" (1963, p. 263). The alternative to intimacy is isolation, the fate of the young adult who is unable to establish intimate relations with others.

But what are the characteristics of intimate behavior? For Erikson intimate relations include mutual trust, sharing, and openness. In a summary of several scholars' work, Fischer (1981) has mentioned a growing capacity for closeness, empathic sharing, self-disclosure, interdependency, and ease in communication between partners. McAdams (1982; McAdams & Powers, 1981) has further shown that intimacy motivates one toward enjoyment in mutual delight, reciprocal dialogue, sincerity in communication, liking, and loving. Other evidence indicates that mutual self-disclosure within an intimate relationship enhances relationship satisfaction (for example, see Hendricks, 1981). Finally, Falbo and Peplau (1980) have shown that intimate relations that include direct rather than indirect communications (such as self-disclosing processes) are more satisfying. These research studies and many others suggest that intimacy is characterized by strong nurturant and affiliative behavior that enhances closeness between two individuals.

How, then, might we define differing levels or types of intimate relations? Two research studies provide useful illustrations. Orlofsky, Marcia, and Lesser (1973; Orlofsky, 1976) have proposed three major criteria for assessing a person's level of intimacy: Does the person have close relationships with male and female friends? Does he or she have an enduring heterosexual relationship? And are the person's close relationships deep or superficial? Depth includes openness, affection, respect, loyalty, a capacity to accept and resolve differences, and mutuality.

Using these criteria, these researchers have been able to define five relationship categories. At the two extremes are the intimate and isolated relationships. The **intimate relationship** involves love and an enduring commitment. In the **isolated relationship,** the person is withdrawn and has no close personal associations. Between these two extremes are three other types. The **preintimate relationship** is a loving relationship but with no enduring commitment. A **stereotyped relationship** is an association with male or female friends that lacks depth and closeness. The **pseudointimate relationship** is artificial; it only *seems* to have depth and caring.

From a developmental perspective, Fischer (1981) proposes that four relationship styles emerge between high school and college. She identifies them using the two dimensions of intimacy and friendship. As Figure 7-3 shows, the style of highly friendly relations with little intimacy is labeled *friendly.* A style with little friend-

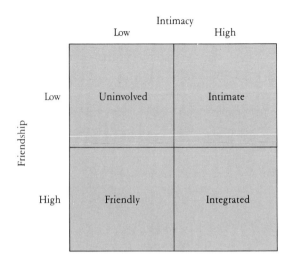

**FIGURE 7-3.** *Four relationship styles.*

ship or intimacy is called *uninvolved.* The highest, or most complex, relationship style is called *integrated* and includes high levels of friendship and intimacy. Finally, a highly intimate relationship with a low level of friendship is labeled *intimate.* On a developmental continuum from lowest to highest intimacy, a person would move from uninvolved to friendly to intimate to integrated.

In a study of 300 high school and college students, Fischer (1981) shows that individuals can be categorized according to these four relationship styles. She finds that women are more often categorized by intimate styles and men by uninvolved styles. Thus, high school- and college-age females may well be more advanced than males in their affiliative and intimacy needs and functioning.

## Identity and Intimacy

Erikson (1963) writes that the development of intimacy is most likely in young adults who have formed a healthy identity during adolescence. In essence, Erikson says that we must know ourselves before we can merge our identity with another's. Is a positive identity in fact a requirement for establishing an intimate relationship? Several studies have addressed this important question.

Orlofsky et al. (1973) examined the relations between four types of identity status and five intimacy types. Two criteria defined a subject's identity status: (1) whether the person showed a search for an identity, and (2) whether he or she reported a commitment to a set of values and goals. Using these criteria, Orlofsky et al. categorized individuals as either (1) diffused (no exploration, no commitment), (2) foreclosed (no exploration, with a commitment), (3) moratorium (exploration, no commitment as yet), and (4) identity achieved (history of exploration, reported commitment). They hypothesized that higher levels of identity, such as moratorium and identity achieved, would predict higher levels of intimacy (for example, preintimate or intimate relationships). They found that a mature identity usually but not always preceded more mature intimacy levels. A mature identity made a mature relationship style more likely; occasionally, however, individuals with a less mature identity were found to have mature intimacy styles. On the basis of several additional studies that have addressed this issue (for example, Fitch & Adams, 1983; Hodgson & Fischer, 1979; Kacerguis & Adams, 1980; Marcia, 1976; Tesch & Whitbourne, 1982; Whitbourne & Tesch, in press), we conclude that a positive environment that develops a healthy identity during adolescence provides the foundation for the positive intimacy needs and functioning of young adulthood. Knowing oneself and being committed to values are necessary if one is to merge one's identity with that of another to form a couple.

 *Could intimacy sometimes precede identity, rather than the reverse? Are there differences for women and men?*

## Styles of Loving

Intimate couples frequently exchange verbal endearments: "I love you, honey"; "I couldn't live without you, I love you so much"; "Do you love me today?" But what do they mean by *love?*

Scholars assign various meanings to the word *love.* For Heider (1958), loving is merely intense liking. However, other scholars have argued that liking and loving, though related, are distinctly different things. For example, Rubin (1970) has developed two separate scales that are widely used to measure liking and loving. Agreement with the statement "Most people would react very favorably to _____ after a brief acquaintance" reflects liking, whereas agreement with the statement "It would be hard for me to get along without _____" reflects loving. According to Rubin (1970), loving includes elements of affiliative needs and dependence, attachment, care, responsibility, respect, and absorption in another. By contrast, liking includes aspects of favorable evaluation and respect and the perception that the other person is similar to oneself. As such, liking is very similar to interpersonal attraction.

If we agree that liking and loving are distinctly different and that *love* has various meanings, what can we say about the meaning of *love?* Lee (1977) has arrived at an interesting topology of love. He specifies several types of loving, or "lovestyles," observed in intimate heterosexual affiliations. Lee says that a person may express more than one type and, over time, may evolve from one type to another.

The most common lovestyles are eros, ludus, storge, mania, agape, and pragma. **Eros** is characterized by a search for a partner who fits an image already held of the ideal mate. It is the pursuit of the ideal "beauty." **Ludus** is a playful love that leads to multiple short-lived affairs. Emotional involvement is carefully controlled and jealousy is suppressed. The image of an active playboy or playgirl captures the essence of ludus. **Storge** is a slowly developing affection with emphasis on companionship. In a storge relationship we find a gradual disclosure of self, an avoidance of passion, and an expectation of long-term commitment. **Mania,** a combination of eros and ludus, is associated with obsessiveness, jealousy, and emotional intensity. Because the manic lover lacks confidence in the relationship, he or she is preoccupied with the loved one and constantly needs reassurance of the beloved's love. **Agape,** a combination of storge and eros, is an altruistic form of love. Reciprocity is not demanded in an agape lovestyle, which is characterized by caring, gentleness, and rationality. Finally, **pragma,** a combination of ludus and storge, involves an effort to rate the partner's value. A compatible match is sought through careful examination of numerous demographic characteristics of the partner, such as education, religion, age, and social status.

These six "lovestyles" show us that love is more complex than we might realize. When a person speaks of a loving relationship, it can mean any of six relationship types. Therefore, when two individuals speak of love, it is important that each understand what the other means by *love*. The meaning can vary considerably between two persons in love!

Of all forms of love, romantic love (paralleling Lee's category of eros) has been the most studied. Some research suggests that romantic love has at least three components (Hinkle & Sporakowski, 1975). First and foremost, romantic attitudes include the belief that there is one very special person for each of us, a belief reflected in such statements as "Love comes but once in a lifetime" or "Usually there are only one or two persons in the world you can really love." Second is the belief that love can overcome any and all obstacles, as seen in statements like "As long as two persons love each other, their religious differences do not matter" or "Differences in social class are of little importance in selecting a marriage partner compared with love." Finally, romantic attitudes may include a certain degree of irrationality. This irrationality is shown in such statements as "Love doesn't make sense—it just *is*" or "Daydreaming usually comes with being in love."

Our research efforts (for example, Munro & Adams, 1978) have shown that another form of love can also be measured. The attitudinal statements of some couples reveal a more rational form of love, resembling storge. This form of love is seen as a warm, secure, and sharing experience, reflected in such statements as "Love is feeling warm, close, and involved but not necessarily sexually excited" or "Good companionship is more important than romantic love in making a good marriage."

We can see that love is varied and complex. Nonetheless, it is the very essence of emotional expression between two intimates. Love is the outward expression, in the form of an attitude or sentiment, of intimacy.

## Influences on Romantic Love

*Arousal states and love.* To understand the mechanisms behind romantic love, Berscheid and Walster (1974a) have proposed a 'two-component theory of passionate love." They propose that physiological arousal can be cognitively labeled as love. Thus the two components are (1) a state of physiological arousal and (2) a process of cognitive labeling. If one experiences an arousal state that one believes is associated with one's partner, this arousal state will be interpreted as love. Once the arousal state disappears, the sensation of love will gradually diminish.

Several conditions can create an arousal state that produces feelings of romantic passion. Some are unpleasant—a frightening event, perceived rejection, outside interference with the relationship, or sexual frustration. Others are pleasant, such as need satisfaction or enjoyable excitement during a social exchange (Kendrick & Cialdini, 1977). A good illustration of the effects of aversive states on perceived love is the "Romeo and Juliet effect" (Driscoll, Davis, & Lipetz, 1977). Driscoll et al. found that parental interference in a dating couple's growing relationship promotes rather than diminishes the couple's feelings of love. One might speculate that parental interference creates an aversive arousal state associated with the partner. This state is then associated with the label *couple* and so increases the perception of love. Other experiences also shown to increase reported romantic love include the viewing of erotic material (Dermer & Pyszczynski, 1978) and engaging in exercise. Seligman, Fazio, and Zanna (1980) have shown that as the rewards of a relationship become more extrinsic than intrinsic, reported love tends to decrease.

*Predicting the course of love.* In looking to the future, we suspect that more research will address the process whereby romantic love unfolds. For example, Tesser and Paulhus (1976) have begun to explore causal (predictive) models of love. Drawing from a variety of past research efforts, these social psychologists propose several factors that should predict growth or decline in romantic love. First, because thought tends to polarize attitudes, the more one thinks about one's dating partner, the greater the growth in love. Second, because most people have a period of disillusionment with their dating partner, as the individual begins to see the partner's faults, love will decrease. Further, the more frequent dating is, the greater is the chance of some disillusionment. Finally, increased dating should predict increased romantic love, simply because continued exposure to

another person enhances interpersonal attraction—assuming that the experience is not associated with substantial disillusionment.

In this study, dating couples were tested twice, two weeks apart. Tesser and Paulhus gathered information on thoughts, dating frequency, romantic love, and perceptions of the partner's faults. They tested their predictions and concluded that (1) thinking about one's partner is predictive of a higher degree of romantic love, (2) perceptions of the partner's faults have little impact on reported love, and (3) exposure (frequency of dating) does not necessarily predict increased love. Although this study has been criticized (Bentler & Huba, 1979; Smith, 1978) for certain problems in statistical assumptions, the attempt to integrate several potential causes of romantic love into one comprehensive model provides an important direction for future research efforts.

 *Can you think of additional factors that might predict the growth or decline of love between a couple?*

*Love across the life span.* Love and affection is an essential need for all of us, regardless of age. Indeed, relationships begin, grow, and end at every stage of life. Increasingly, family relations specialists and social psychologists are coming to look at differences in loving styles across the life span. For example, Dion and Dion (1976) compared the reported liking and loving scores of casually dating, exclusively dating, engaged, and married couples. As predicted, casually dating couples reported less love than the three other groups. Thus, reported feelings of romantic love are predictable from a couple's dating, courtship, or marital category. But what of the life span in general? Are there differences in reported lovestyles with age?

Neiswender-Reedy, Birren, and Schaie (1976) have tested the notion that love relationships become less romantic and less physically passionate as people get older. Reasoning from the notion of disillusionment, they predicted that couples become more realistic and practical as they mature. The researchers compared attitudes about love among married and unmarried couples in adolescence, young adulthood, middle age, and old age. Surprisingly, no age differences were observed. In all age groups, subjects were more romantic than realistic (rational) in their conceptions of love. Unmarried men were more romantic than unmarried women, whereas married women were more romantic than married men.

In our own research (Munro & Adams, 1978) we have speculated that role structure ought to be a good predictor of the degree of romantic versus realistic love. This speculation was based on previous research suggesting that interpersonal attitudes, sentiments, or affective-based perceptions toward others are most important when role expectations are simple and loosely defined and are least important when role expectations and obligations are clearly defined or demanding. Accordingly, we predicted that romantic attitudes would be highest early in developing relationships and during the later years of marriage when children have left home. Rational attitudes (or sentiments based on companionship, caring without high excitation or sensuality) should be highest during life-cycle periods when financial responsibilities, work, and child rearing make heavy personal demands on the couple. We compared four types of couples on reported love: high school seniors, married couples without children, married couples with children, and married couples with grown-up children. The major findings support the role-structure theory. The demands of highly complex roles reduced romantic love attitudes and increased rational love attitudes. Over the life span, then, individuals change their lovestyle to adapt to their social roles and situational demands.

## Therapy for Problems in Relationships

Many therapeutic interventions focus on interpersonal conflict, jealousy, and loneliness. Interpersonal conflict is often seen as the cause of breakups. Therapists generally feel that a couple's mode of conflict resolution is especially important for the success of a relationship. Practices that help unmarried and married couples learn how to resolve conflict are central intervention tools for encouraging thriving intimate relationships. It is evident that the psychological realities of the two partners can be markedly different, and marriage counselors can provide interventions to alleviate this problem. In particular, it is important to help couples learn to resolve their conflict by facing the discrepancies in interpersonal perceptions rather than avoiding them (Knudson, Sommers, & Golding, 1980).

Jealousy often creates conflict between partners, and intervention efforts to reduce responses provoked by jealousy are common in therapy with couples. Jealousy might be defined as an emotional reaction to the perceived threat of loss of one's partner. A variety of factors can contribute to this perception. For example, White (1977) has reported that inequality of emotional involvement between partners promotes feelings of jealousy by the more involved person. Jealousy is also likely when a perceived interloper (an old boyfriend, for example) is present. In particular, an attractive interloper creates such responses as jealousy and anger (Shettel-Neuber, Bryson, & Young, 1978). Involvement in extramarital relations evokes the most jealousy (Hansen, 1982). The greatest jealousy is likely to occur for those who are most emotionally involved and who perceive their partner as having another sexual involvement (Buunk, 1982).

Deficient social relations often bring on loneliness. Lonely persons frequently report that their relationships are superficial and that no one understands them (Russell, Peplau, & Ferguson, 1978). Recent research suggests that loneliness may be due to limited social skills (Berg & Peplau, 1982; Jones, Hobbs, & Hockenbury, 1982). Loneliness may have such undesirable results as anxiety, boredom, self-deprecation, or hostility (see, for example, Goldenberg & Perlman, 1984). Jones et al. (1982) find that loneliness may be due mainly to deficient conversational skills and that lonely people may give less attention to their partners. Thus, intervention with lonely individuals may require changing their skills in social communication. Our earlier chapter on communication identified some of the major components in such interventions.

## The End of a Relationship

Ending an intimate and loving relationship can hurt. Many people seek professional help in adjusting to a separation, deciding whether to end a relationship, or reuniting a couple. Individual, group, or couples counseling can help in dealing with the pain of a broken relationship. Other important support networks include friends and relatives. A little sympathy can, at times, do much to make an individual feel less lonely and lost.

We know relatively little about "breaking up," but Hill, Rubin, and Peplau (1976) do provide some insightful findings on this process among unmarried couples. First, they find that a woman's degree of emotional involvement is the best predictor of the long-term viability of a relationship. The stronger a woman's romantic feelings, the greater the commitment to keeping the relationship alive. Second, breakup is more likely when one partner is more involved in the relationship than the other. Third, the greater the similarity in attitudes and values, the more likely the relationship is to continue. Differences in interests, intelligence, or ideas, desire for independence, and interest in others were the reasons most commonly given for breakups. These authors note that the best "divorce" is the one you get before you get married. They suggest that intervention to encourage couples to break up, if several of the factors mentioned above exist in their relationship, may be best for all concerned.

## ON REMAINING SINGLE

We would be remiss to end this chapter with the notion that marriage is for everyone. It would also be an error to assume that not to marry means to be unhappy. For various personal reasons, about 1 in 24 adults does not marry. For some, the freedom to date whomever they choose and to come and go as they please is so important that they reject marriage as interfering with these possibilities. For others, commitment to a demanding career overshadows interest in marriage and a family. Of course, there are others whose singleness is forced on them by financial limitations, physical abnormalities, or poor social skills. Likewise, singlehood may result from a scarcity of possible partners, as frequently happens after a war, or the death of a spouse.

Even though the disadvantages of singlehood by choice do not clearly outweigh its advantages, single people generally experience pressures to marry. They may be denied job promotions (although they may get more opportunity to travel than married employees). It may be difficult to develop friendships with married people. Some

*There are advantages and disadvantages to remaining single. Can you name a few of them?*

spouses see the single friend as a threat to their marriage. However, the greatest pressure toward marriage is likely to come from parents (Stein, 1976). Many parents believe that their adult children will be happiest married, that marriage encourages maturity, or that marriage is the only natural way of living.

However, studies of national samples (for example, Glenn, 1975) have generally shown that singleness is far from being associated with extensive mental or social problems. Indeed, singles are usually the second-happiest group (married couples being the happiest), ranking above homosexual couples, unmarried couples, and others. Thus, to remain single does not imply misery, loneliness, or despair. Singlehood can be as fulfilling as marriage, depending on the needs and interests of the individual. Since singleness in adulthood is relatively rare, we will reconsider it in the chapter on alternative lifestyles.

 *What myths and stereotypes surround singleness? How can singles cope with such myths?*

Because intimate relationships, inside and outside marriage, can reduce stress and provide psychological resources to an individual, family and individual wellness will be promoted by individual competence in such relationships. Our focus will therefore be on the promotion of such competence.

## EDUCATION

An understanding of the social rewards of interpersonal relations enhances individual competence. Recently Buss (1983) has suggested two classes of social rewards. One set of rewards is called **process** and involves social stimulation. The second set is called **content** and involves varying degrees of intimacy in relationships. Process social rewards include (1) the presence of others, (2) attention from others, (3) responsiveness by others, and (4) initiation of contact by others. Content social rewards, which are defined by the particular social responses that are offered, include deference or respect, praise, sympathy, and affection. Individuals can be educated to use both process and content social rewards in their interaction with others in order to develop more rewarding and closer relationships. For example, an individual's responsive and attentive behavior during social exchanges will enhance the other person's attraction to that individual. If the individual demonstrates respect, praise, nurturance, or warmth, the social interaction is likely to lead to further involvement and greater intimacy.

Perhaps the most popular form of primary prevention is group premarital counseling (sometimes called "couples counseling" or "re-lationship enhancement"). A typical premarital counseling program gives a premarital assessment to each couple to determine their instructional needs, to introduce the couple to realistic marital problems, and to explore each person's expectations. The general intent of such programs is to create an awareness of expectations and of discrepancies between the partners and prepare the couple for potential problems. Some premarital groups primarily assess individual expectations and provide awareness training; others educate and provide skills training; still others provide premarital counseling (Bagarozzi & Raven, 1981; Guerney, 1977; Ridley & Bain, 1983). Such programs can help to prevent future problems by exploring the couple's perceived family roles, parental or family expectations, perceived needs, family finances, recreational interests, career goals, desire for children, personal and religious values, sexual preferences, and conflict resolution and communication styles.

Programs that focus on improving communication and/or problem-solving skills can facilitate positive relationships. The efficacy of such programs has been established with couples, children, and adolescents (Avery, Rider, & Haynes-Clements, in press; Guerney, 1976; Rappaport, 1976). Major gains include increased ability to express feelings, respond empathically, disclose needs effectively, and develop feelings of closeness (for example, Ridley & Bain, 1983). Relationship enhancement programs may focus on social skills such as giving and receiving positive *and* negative feedback, conflict resolution and negotiation, resisting pressures from others, empathy and perspective taking, or fighting fairly.

## COMMUNITY MOBILIZATION/ SYSTEMS INTERVENTION

Various groups throughout the country have undertaken community organization efforts to enhance premarital and marital relations. For example, in Utah, recent legislation mandates that all high schools provide a premarital course on family relations and parenting. The course is designed to enhance personal relations, improve social skills, and promote communication within the family.

The Catholic church has developed another community program that mobilizes its members to focus on enriched intimate relations. Married couples are brought together in an encounter format during a two-day period to become reacquainted, refocused, and more aware of each other's needs. Programs such as these are designed to prevent disharmony, conflict, and faulty expectations through education, social skills training, heightened awareness, and improved caregiving.

## COMPETENCY PROMOTION

In order to feel good about someone else, one needs to feel good about oneself. In order to love, one needs to be loved. In order to care, one must be cared for. An individual's family of origin is crucial in providing these experiences to the growing child, and programs that encourage such parental behavior can promote competence in children. Likewise, efforts that adults take to improve their self-image will benefit a couple's relationship. It is no accident that in Erikson's model identity achievement precedes intimacy. In order to share yourself with another, you must know yourself and be comfortable, not embarrassed, with that self. Activities that promote identity achievement also promote competence and improve the evolving relationship between two individuals. Such activities might include enhancing self-esteem, promoting self-efficacy, industriousness, or social awareness, exploring religious, ideological, or political values, and combining individuality with intimacy.

## NATURAL CAREGIVING

We believe intimacy grows from positive and warm natural caregiving experiences during childhood and adolescence. Natural caregivers such as relatives and friends provide important role models of interpersonal and social competence. Children are likely to imitate sharing, caring, affection, positive conflict resolution, mutual self-disclosure, and fidelity and to incorporate such modeled behavior into their own repertoires. Reinforcement by parents, teachers, and other caregivers will encourage these behaviors and foster the child's growing social competence.

We know from research that parental interference in early romantic relations can create an overinvestment between the couple and that a supportive social network will facilitate the dyad's identification as a couple. Therefore, parents of dating adolescents should avoid overinterference because it might extend normally short-lived affiliations beyond their natural course. Conversely, as dating relations progress toward courtship and engagement, family members can enhance the bonding process by conferring the social identity of a recognized couple.

# SUMMARY

Competence in interpersonal relationships emerges during childhood and adolescence, expands during dating and courtship, and matures within intimate contexts such as marriage. Major influences on attraction to a person include physical attractiveness, perceived similarity to oneself, pleasant interactions, propinquity, and complementarity of needs. Sought-after qualities in a dating partner and expectations about what will happen on a date differ between male and female adolescents. Courtship patterns vary from couple to couple, but research has turned up some commonalities, such as changes in communication style and in how the partners spend their time together as the relationship progresses.

Participation in an intimate relationship requires a healthy identity. Even within the same couple, individuals' conceptions of love may be quite different. Intensity and styles of love are influenced by several factors, such as physiological arousal states, parental interference with the relationship, and the roles that the partners must fill.

The capacity for intimacy comes, ideally, from positive experiences with other people during childhood and adolescence. It can be enhanced by training in adulthood.

# MAJOR POINTS TO REMEMBER

1. Early adolescents associate in small same-sex groups. Gradually these give way to mixed-sex groups, which in late adolescence break up into dating couples.
2. As adolescent peer groups change, so do family social relations. The adolescent's strivings for independence and autonomy are initially met by family conflict but eventually result in major improvements in family relations.
3. Interpersonal attraction and heterosexual pairing begin with unilateral awareness, expand to surface contact, and culminate in mutuality.
4. Interpersonal attraction is enhanced by similarity, proximity, satisfying interaction, and physical attractiveness.
5. New patterns in dating have emerged because of the youth culture, sexual equality, and increasing freedom in mate selection.
6. Dating expectations vary between males and females. Males are more likely than females to expect a sexual encounter on a date.
7. As a relationship progresses, communication patterns change from disruptive to facilitative, and the relationship is viewed as more satisfying and close.
8. Similarity of physical attractiveness between partners is predictive of progress toward greater involvement.
9. Four theoretical models are used to understand courtships. The compatibility model focuses on similarity as a basis for mate selection. The filter theory centers on information processing. The social exchange perspective looks to stimulus, value, and role characteristics. The developmental model examines social process as a courtship evolves.
10. Recent research reveals four patterns of courtship development as a couple progress toward commitment: the accelerated, intermediate, prolonged, and accelerated-arrested courtship styles.
11. Intimacy is characterized by mutual trust, sharing, self-disclosure, closeness, loving, and sincerity of communication. Levels of intimacy vary from isolation at one extreme to intimate/integrated at the other.
12. Establishing a strong personal identity enhances the prospect of developing intimate relationships with others.
13. Love is more than liking. There are six common lovestyles: eros, ludus, storge,

mania, agape, and pragma. These styles are expressed in attitudes and sentiments.

14. Relationships don't always go smoothly and can end. When there are problems, interventions can be provided to deal with conflict, jealousy, loneliness, and adjustment.

15. Singlehood is not to be confused with isolation. It is a viable alternative.

## ADDITIONAL SOURCES OF INFORMATION

Adams, G. R., & Crossman, S. (1978). *Physical attractiveness: A cultural imperative.* Roslyn Heights, NY: Libra. [Adolescents, adults]

Blume, J. (1971). *Then again, maybe I won't.* New York: Dell. [Children, early adolescents]

Blume, J. (1974). *Blubber.* New York: Dell. [Adolescents]

Miller, A. (1982). *In the eye of the beholder: Contemporary issues in stereotyping.* New York: Praeger. [Adults]

Miller, S., Nunnally, E. W., & Wackman, D. B. (1975). *Alive and aware.* Minneapolis, MN: Interpersonal Communications Program. [Adolescents, adults]

Stahmann, R. F., & Hiebert, W. J. (1980). *Premarital counseling.* Lexington, MA: Lexington Books. [Adults]

Stuart, R. B. (Ed.) (1981). *Helping couples change.* New York: Guilford Press. [Adults]

# 8

# THE DEVELOPING MARITAL RELATIONSHIP

1. What topics should a couple discuss *before* they decide to marry?

2. What parts do change and life cycle play in marital adjustment?

3. What factors influence who has power in a marriage?

4. How does sexual behavior change during marriage?

5. What is marital satisfaction? What factors are associated with marital satisfaction and dissatisfaction?

6. What impact does income have on the marital relationship?

7. How do marital adjustment, marital satisfaction, and marital stability differ?

8. How is marital stability related to marital satisfaction?

9. How do dual-worker couples distribute household tasks?

### How Do You Keep the Music Playing?

*How do you keep the music playing?*
*How do you make it last?*
*How do you keep the song from fading too fast?*
*How do you lose your self to someone*
*And never lose your way?*
*How do you not run out of new things*
*to say? . . .*

*If we can be the best of lovers*
*Yet be the best of friends*
*If we can try with every day to make it better*
*As it grows, with any luck, then, I suppose*
*The music never ends.*

—Lyrics by Michel Legrand/
Alan & Marilyn Bergman

Our focus in this chapter is one of the most intricate and intimate of relationships—marriage. Marital relationships are as varied as the couples who constitute them. Think for a moment of some famous couples: Lucille Ball and Desi Arnaz, Prince Charles and Princess Diana, George and Louise Jefferson, Ozzie and Harriet Nelson, Archie and Edith Bunker, and Jane Fonda and Tom Hayden. These fictional and real couples are examples of how diverse marital relationships can be.

Despite this variety, there are patterns to marriage that are common. In this chapter we will cover the first 30 years of the marital relationship. (A note of caution: Most research on the marital relationship has examined couples with children. Therefore, much of what we know about couples who have been married 5, 10, or 15 years is based on couples with children—and children have a significant impact on the marital relationship. It is only recently that large numbers of couples have wanted to remain childless and have been able to do so, and little research has been done on them.)

In this chapter we discuss several aspects of marriage: the marriage contract, marital adjustment, marital satisfaction, marital stability, and the impact of work on the marital relationship. We conclude with suggestions on how to foster an understanding of marriage for both single and married people.

## THE MARRIAGE CONTRACT

*I, _____, take thee, _____,*
*to be my lawful*
*wedded husband [wife].*
*To have and to hold*
*From this day forward*
*For better for worse*
*For richer for poorer*
*In sickness and in health*
*To love and to cherish*
*Till death do us part.*

    Traditional wedding vows

In reciting marriage vows, couples enter into a marriage contract, based not just on the vows but on the laws of the state where they are married. During the past few decades, people have changed their view of marriage, and some have changed the vows they recite as well. However, the marriage contract has generally remained the same. Many couples are not aware of the state contract they agree to when they marry.

A marriage contract is unique in several respects. Marriage is a private relationship, and yet it is regulated by the state. The two parties entering into marriage do not develop their own contract to meet their needs and preferences, as other parties to contracts do; rather, the state provides the standard contract, and occasionally the couple modify it through a prenuptial agreement or their own contract (Weitzman, 1981). Most couples would be surprised by state con-

*Marriage at the turn of the century: What are the chances that this couple discussed birth control, family size, her career plans, and dual savings accounts, either before or after the wedding?*

## BOX 8-1
### *Topics to Discuss before Marriage*

Lenore J. Weitzman (1981) suggests that people who plan to live together in an intimate relationship consider developing their own contract. Whether or not such a contract is developed, we believe that it is important for intimates to discuss the following topics to clarify their expectations.

1. *Aims and expectations for the relationship*. What are joint and individual goals for the relationship? Personal and joint priorities? Proposed timing for life events (education, children, and so forth)?

2. *Duration of the relationship*. Is commitment to the relationship time-limited, renewed periodically, or lifelong?

3. *Employment*. What is each party's expectation for employment for self and partner? Employment goals, stopping or starting work, accommodating two workers, and similar topics should be covered.

4. *Income and expenses*. What are each person's assets, income, debts, and obligations? Will income and expenses be pooled, kept separate, or partly pooled? Who will decide how money is spent? Who will keep records on income and expenditures? If one partner is no longer employed, will he or she have any discretionary money to spend? How will any financial obligations to friends or relatives be handled? How does each partner feel about incurring and limiting debts? Who will assume responsibility for managing each partner's current debts?

5. *Property*. What property (material goods, cars, houses, investments) does each partner have now?

How will the couple share it? In whose name(s) will property be acquired in the future? How will it be purchased?

6. *Living arrangements*. Where do the partners plan to live? How will differences of opinion about a move be resolved?

7. *Household tasks*. How will responsibilities be divided? Will there be a schedule for completing tasks or standards for completion?

8. *Surname*. What will be the last name of each party? Of any children? In case of divorce, what will the last name of each party be?

9. *Sexual relationship*. Will this relationship be monogamous? If not, what limits will be established to govern extramarital relations?

10. *Personal behavior*. Do the partners have expectations for their behavior in public?

tract provisions. In most states, marriage contracts specify that the husband will support his wife, the husband is head of the household, the wife is responsible for domestic services, and the wife is responsible for child care (Weitzman, 1981). For many couples, this division of labor works well because it reflects their joint view of marriage. For other couples, it is limiting and they ignore it. Some husbands are better than their wives at child care or housekeeping; some

wives are better decision makers and income earners. Some such couples have chosen to exchange roles. An emerging pattern in the United States is to share these responsibilities, rather than divide them (Blood & Wolfe, 1960; Weitzman, 1981).

When marrying, couples focus on the ceremony, the reception, the honeymoon, the gifts, and the establishment of the household. Rarely do they consider the provisions of the marriage

## BOX 8-1
### *Continued*

In private? Do they want to change any behavior of their own (smoking, exercising, television viewing)? Do they want to establish special time for themselves and their relationship? How much time does each person expect to spend apart?

11. *Relationships with others.* What commitments does each partner have to relatives and friends? Is the other partner expected to participate? What commitments does each partner have to participate in community, social, or work-related activities?

12. *Children.* Do the couple plan to have children? If so, how many, spaced how far apart, and beginning when? Do they agree? If they plan to use birth-control methods, which one(s)? How will they resolve a contraceptive failure? How will child-rearing responsibili-

ties be distributed? If either partner has children from a previous relationship, what role will they play in the couple's family?

13. *Religion.* What denomination, if any, is each partner? What religion do they plan to practice? In what religion will they raise any children?

14. *Inheritance and wills.* Does either partner have a will? How will it be modified, if at all, to reflect the relationship? Do they want a joint will? What provisions, if any, will each make for his or her relatives?

15. *Disagreements.* How will disagreements between the partners be resolved? Are there any rules about expressing disagreements (for example, only in private, no violence)? Will the partners be willing to seek professional help in resolving disagreements?

16. *Making changes.* Recognizing that each partner will change, how do they plan to accommodate these changes? If they cannot do so, what agreements do they want to make about dissolving the relationship? How will their assets and debts be divided? Who will take custody of any children? How will child support be determined?

These topics and questions indicate the scope of intimate relationships, particularly marriage. They may seem overwhelming or too practical, removing the romance from intimacy. Nevertheless, a couple who have discussed these issues and reached consensus know better what to expect from each other and the relationship and have a firmer foundation on which to build.

---

contract. If, instead, they devoted some time to discussing roles, responsibilities, and expectations, career aspirations, and desire for and care of children, they would be better prepared to face the realities of married life. Box 8-1 lists topics to be discussed before marriage. Some couples choose not only to discuss these issues but also to draw up a written contract that addresses them. If couples disagree before marriage on these issues, they may want and need to

reevaluate their compatibility. It is easier to enter into a marriage contract than to break one.

*What would be the benefits and liabilities of changing the legal marriage contract? What changes would you make?*

# LEARNING TO LIVE TOGETHER

Consider these differences:

- David likes to sleep late, while his wife is an early riser.

- Karen wants to spend an occasional evening out with her women friends, but Neal wants her to spend all her free time with him.

- Carlos wants to be responsible for yard and car care, while Rita wants him to help with housework too.

- Ann wants Barry to make the money decisions, while he thinks they should both be involved.

These illustrations suggest some of the adjustments that may be necessary in a marriage. The more the partners differ in their views, the more adjustments they will need to make. Such stresses are common—not just in the newlywed stage but throughout the marriage.

One reality of marriage that is not thoroughly discussed and rarely measured is that people change. In particular, people are likely to change in their twenties when they are adjusting to adult responsibilities and freedoms. The person you marry at age 20 changes by age 30—and so do you. It is encouraging that spouses adapt as well as they do. When we recognize that changes go on in both partners and that their changes are not necessarily in the same direction, it is impressive that so many marriages endure.

Furthermore, each partner experiences the marriage differently. What is satisfactory to one partner may be unsatisfactory to the other. One spouse may be satisfied with the level of communication while the other desires more; partners may want different levels of sexual activity; and so on. Perhaps there are really two marriages—his and hers (Rollins & Feldman, 1970). In fact, Jessie Bernard, a family scholar, notes that "there is by now a very considerable body of well-authenticated research to show that there really are two marriages in every union and that they do not always coincide" (1972, p. 4). Making both her marriage and his marriage satisfying presents a significant challenge, and constant fluctuations are likely. On balance, however, the goal is to reach at least a minimum level of satisfaction for both partners.

Sheehy (1974) discusses the adult life cycle, focusing on the predictable changes and crises that adults face. She emphasizes the continuing human needs to merge with another person (as in marriage or parenthood) but also to search for one's identity as a separate individual. These often conflicting desires vary from person to person in their timing, further complicating couple relationships. He may be in a merging stage while she is in a separating stage, and neither may be aware of these normal differences. Loving someone can be complicated as well as rewarding, and living with someone you love can be even more complex. Couples learn to cope with these variations. The ease of adjustment differs from one marriage to the next and in the same marriage over time. One spouse, in noting the differences in marriage over time, comments at each wedding anniversary "I've been married _____ years, and some have been shorter than others." Said humorously, this statement nevertheless captures the reality that the levels and kinds of adjustment required vary over time.

Obviously, marriage is filled with areas demanding adjustment and readjustment. Some are small, like deciding which side of the bed to sleep on; others are major, like deciding how money will be saved and spent. In this section we will discuss a number of important areas of adjustment: personal habits, separation and togetherness, decision making, sexual behavior, sex roles, and finances. Extensive adjustments are likely when the couple begin living together, and so we will focus on early marital adjustment.

## Personal Habits

He squeezes the toothpaste from the top, she from the bottom. She wipes the sink dry after brushing her teeth; he leaves his whiskers and shaving-cream residue behind. She was taught never to burp out loud; belching is part of his sport-viewing ritual. Habits such as being neat or sloppy, rising early or late, being quiet or sociable, being energetic or lethargic can drive a couple to madness. Some idiosyncrasies, such as gobbling down a meal, might be observed during courtship, but frequently there are surprises in the early days of living together. Although such behaviors are generally minor in the scheme of things, they can turn into a Chinese water torture, slowly driving a partner crazy. Negotiation and tolerance are important during this period to adjust to these differences.

## Separation and Togetherness

> "Bill thinks we ought to do everything together—housekeeping, shopping, fixing dinner. He even thought he should visit my friends with me. But Sue cured him. She talked about her menstrual pains for an hour and he finally left. I love him dearly, but sometimes I just want to be apart."

How much closeness does each partner want? How much separation? These questions are fundamental in the development of the marital relationship, and, as in all other areas of adjustment, a spouse's view may change. In fact, a study of over 3600 married couples found that wives wanted more closeness than husbands early in the marriage but husbands wanted more closeness than wives later in the marriage (Blumstein & Schwartz, 1983). Some couples choose to do almost everything together, from walking the dog to balancing the checkbook, while others choose to do most things separately.

Partners in a marriage typically spend time alone together, thereby establishing the unity of their new family, but they rarely cut ties with everyone else. In dealing with how frequently and under what circumstances they will interact with others, they face the issues of separation and togetherness. Each couple needs to decide how they want to relate to in-laws, friends, colleagues, and neighbors. How frequently will they visit relatives? Will they visit them together or separately? Will each spouse have a night to go out to socialize with friends? Will they see only friends they both like? In short, what are the boundaries of this newly married pair? One issue that may arise is jealousy, either as a result of time spent away from spouse or whom it is spent with.

Clearly, there is a delicate balance between individual identity and couple unity. Neither partner should lose a separate identity, but spouses should merge sufficiently to form a new family unit. Couples differ in the balance they select. And this balance is likely to change throughout the marriage, as the partners change.

## Decision-Making Power

> "My father used to say that he made all the important decisions in the family—like who should run for president, when the country should go to war, and whether taxes should be raised—and my mother made the small decisions, such as buying a house, moving, and having children."

Only 20 years ago, most wives promised to "love, honor, and obey" their husbands (but husbands didn't promise to obey their wives). That vow promising obedience had much to do with power—an important aspect of any relationship, including marriage.

**Power** is defined as "the ability to alter another's choice" (Turk, 1975, p. 82). This ability is influenced by authority and control. **Authority** is decision-making power based on societal norms. In filling certain roles, such as boss, teacher, or police officer, people acquire authority. For example, parents have the authority to establish rules for their children (although children may ignore them). **Control** is pressure or appeal (explicit or subtle) to the other party that succeeds in changing attitudes or behaviors. For example, if John is able to get his wife, Patty, to go shopping when she originally didn't want to, John has exerted control over her. What we don't know about power in this example is what methods John used (persuasion, coercion, bargaining, compromise) or how resistant Patty was.

Even if we knew the method(s) used, we would have an incomplete picture. Who has the power: the person who makes the decision, the person who decides who makes the decision, or the person who decides who decides (Olson & Ryder, 1970)? For example, does the relative who decides to visit have the power to make that decision? Or does the wife who extends the invitation have that power? Or the husband who decides that if his wife wants to see this relative, she may extend an invitation? In fact, each has some power, but in this illustration the husband has the ultimate power. Too often, researchers have asked family members merely who made a decision (in this case, the wife, to extend the invitation) and failed to ask how others played a part in it, thereby getting an erroneous picture of who has power.

Table 8-1 contains some questions to assess marital power taken from a longer inventory developed by Blood and Wolfe (1960). In this example, a score of 36 or more suggests that the husband exercises more power (at least in the areas specified), a score of 21–35 suggests an egalitarian relationship, and a score of less than 21 suggests the wife exercises more power.

Who has authority and for what purposes varies among peer groups, societies, and eras. Only a few centuries ago, under English common law, a wife and children were the property of the husband/father, with little say about their own lives and destinies. That standard evolved, eliminating "ownership" but giving the husband/fa-ther authority in marital and family decisions. In this century, that norm is changing to give authority to both partners in a marriage (see Chapter 1).

Of course, many families still function with the father as authority, while others have the mother as authority and still others have shared authority. The pattern for a particular family is influenced by level of education, religious teachings, socioeconomic status, and peers. Low levels of education and socioeconomic status tend to be associated with the residence of power in the husband, while higher education and socioeconomic status tend to be associated with the egalitarian pattern (Komarovksy, 1962; Scanzoni, 1975).

Most studies assessing marital power have focused on control/influence, rather than authority (Blood & Wolfe, 1960; Blumstein & Schwartz, 1983; Komarovsky, 1962). Researchers have identified three decision-making patterns. In some marriages the husband has greater power (husband-dominant); in others the wife does (wife-dominant); and in still others power is shared (egalitarian). The egalitarian couple can divide power in two ways: each partner can make decisions on separate issues, or they can share in making decisions about the same issues.

It is important to remember that power is not just an outcome (whose wishes prevailed) but a process (how the decision was reached) (Scanzoni, 1979). For example, classifying a couple as wife-dominant because the wife makes all the decisions about household upkeep and furnishings would be erroneous if the husband has decided that he wants her to make these choices.

Power may be derived from social norms (authority), from superior knowledge or persuasive abilities, or from the ability to provide rewards or inflict punishment (Olson & Cromwell, 1975). Power has costs, which vary. The decision maker is responsible for the outcome of the decision. It takes time to make decisions, particularly if many factors must be considered. Dealing with

| Husband Always | Husband More than Wife | Husband and Wife Exactly the Same | Wife More than Husband | Wife Always |
|---|---|---|---|---|
| A. Who usually makes the *final* decision about what car to get? | | | | |
| [5] | [4] | [3] | [2] | [1] |
| B. Who usually makes the *final* decision about whether or not to buy some life insurance? | | | | |
| [5] | [4] | [3] | [2] | [1] |
| C. Who usually makes the *final* decision about what house or apartment to take? | | | | |
| [5] | [4] | [3] | [2] | [1] |
| D. Who usually makes the *final* decision about what job the husband should take? | | | | |
| [5] | [4] | [3] | [2] | [1] |
| E. Who usually makes the *final* decision about whether or not the wife should go to work or quit work? | | | | |
| [5] | [4] | [3] | [2] | [1] |
| F. Who usually makes the *final* decision about how much money your family can afford to spend per week on food? | | | | |
| [5] | [4] | [3] | [2] | [1] |
| G. Who usually makes the *final* decision about what doctor to have when someone is sick? | | | | |
| [5] | [4] | [3] | [2] | [1] |
| H. Who usually makes the *final* decision about where to go on a vacation? | | | | |
| [5] | [4] | [3] | [2] | [1] |

the people who will be affected by the decision may require time, energy, and interpersonal skills. And ensuring that the decision is implemented means additional time and effort or delegation to others and follow-up supervision.

Power pervades all aspects of the marital relationship. Who will make the decisions on jobs, relocating, time and content of communication, having children, child-rearing methods, spending and saving money, individual purchases, sexual activity, relationships with relatives and friends, use of leisure time, and so on? The list is endless because whenever a decision is to be made, at least one spouse will exercise power. How a couple chooses to make decisions is important in marital adjustment. One "best" way does not exist. What is most important is that the partners agree on how decisions will be made and that they recognize that their agreement may evolve as they change.

*Using a fictional couple (from television, movies, or books), analyze who exerts more power. On what do you base your analysis? Apply one theory from Chapter 2 to explain this balance of power.*

### Sexual Adjustment

In "All in the Family," Archie and Edith were reserved in their sexual behavior. They certainly didn't discuss sex, and they had sexual relations only at night, with the lights off. Appallingly to Archie, Gloria and Mike thought sex was an appropriate topic of discussion, and they even had intercourse in the daytime! These two generations within one household illustrate the diversity of sexual attitudes and behavior that exists within marriage.

In our society sexual mores have changed dramatically in this century. In the early 1900s, it was common for experts to recommend that intercourse in marriage (it was strictly forbidden outside marriage) should take place only about once a month. Indeed, women were considered delicate creatures who only "tolerated" intercourse: "The best mothers, wives and managers of households know little or nothing of the sexual pleasure. Love of home, children and domestic duties are the only passions they feel" (Fallows, 1910, p. 142). Although such notions seem absurd to us today, they are important in understanding the evolution of sexual behavior.

What kinds of adjustments may be necessary for couples today? As we saw in Chapter 5, partners may differ in many of their preferences about physical closeness and sexual activity, so that some (not all) couples find they must adjust to each other's desires. Sexual attitudes and behaviors, like all other aspects of marriage, change over time, and so sexual adjustments are appropriate throughout marriage.

Marital adjustment appears to be related, in part, to the degree of sexual compatibility that couples develop (Broderick, 1982). Researchers suggest, for example, that at least five marital styles emerge during lengthy marriages and that each has its own quality of sexual relationship (Cuber & Harroff, 1965). The **total relationship** is the most intense: partners mesh on several levels, including the sexual. The **vital relationship** is less intense than the total relationship; however, romance is alive, sex is frequent, and the couple remain highly communicative with each other. At the other extreme, a **conflict-habituated relationship** is associated with constant quarreling and, frequently, extramarital involvement. In the **devitalized** style, the former vitality is gone, and both spouses miss and resent its absence. Generally these couples are cynical or pessimistic, and sexual activity is infrequent, absent, or confined to discreet affairs. The **passive-congenial** style is a loyal relationship with little intimacy. Although these couples take each other for granted, they are happy and are not bitter about the lack of intensity. This study clearly shows that sexual and marital satisfaction can take various forms.

Several studies provide detailed information on changes in marital sexual behavior. The most credible are those by Kinsey and his associates (1948, 1953), Hunt (1974), Tavris and Sadd (1977), and Blumstein and Schwartz (1983). Each of these studies, though limited by sampling and measurement problems, contributes to our understanding of sexual behavior.

In his pioneering research on human sexuality, Kinsey asked men and women about frequency of marital intercourse. Hunt, in a 1972 survey, again asked about frequency. In both samples, coital frequency decreased with age and length of marriage (see Table 8-2). These findings are supported by the survey by Blumstein and Schwartz (1983) as well. During the first two years of marriage, 45% of their couples reported having intercourse three or more times a week, and an additional 38% reported intercourse between one and three times a week. Among those who had been married more than ten years, 18% reported having intercourse three or more times a week, while 45% reported intercourse between one and three times a week. Thus, it seems that coital frequency decreases among married couples over time.

TABLE 8-2. *Weekly frequency of marital coitus, by age group, in Kinsey's and Hunt's samples*

| Kinsey (1938–1946) | | Hunt (1972) | |
|---|---|---|---|
| Age | Median Frequency | Age | Median Frequency |
| 16–25 | 2.45 | 18–24 | 3.25 |
| 26–35 | 1.95 | 25–34 | 2.55 |
| 36–45 | 1.40 | 35–44 | 2.0 |
| 46–55 | .85 | 45–54 | 1.0 |
| 56–60 | .50 | 55+ | 1.0 |

A difference between the samples is that intercourse was more frequent among those surveyed by Hunt in 1972 than those surveyed by Kinsey from 1938 through 1946. Hunt explained this difference by noting that the sexual mores of the 1970s allowed women more latitude in expressing their desire for intercourse, in contrast to when it was considered their wifely duty. He suggested that this increase indicated women were enjoying coitus more. Data on frequency of orgasm for married White females support that view. In Kinsey's sample, 45% of the women who had been married for approximately 15 years reached orgasm 90–100% of the time; in Hunt's sample, 53% did. (Of course, orgasm is only one measure of sexual satisfaction.)

As reported, the frequency of intercourse decreases over time (Blumstein & Schwartz, 1983; Greenblat, 1983; Hunt, 1974; Petersen, 1983). Jobs, demands on the partners' energy, children, and a decline in interest may decrease the frequency of intercourse, while closeness or greater sexual enjoyment may increase it. Some people explained that their frequency had decreased because during the first year of marriage their rate had been artificially high; others explained that their rate hadn't decreased because they had established a pattern while living together before marriage (Greenblat, 1983). Couples who switched to more effective birth-control methods experienced smaller declines in frequency (Trussell & Westoff, 1980). One study found that the best predictor of frequency of coitus in later years is the frequency during the first year (Greenblat, 1983).

For most couples, a decrease in frequency is not troublesome. However, those who have intercourse infrequently are more likely to be dissatisfied with the entire relationship as well as with the quality of the sexual relationship (Blumstein & Schwartz, 1983). For example, 89% of the spouses who had intercourse more than three times a week were satisfied with the quality of their sex life, compared with 32% of those who

had intercourse once a month or less. What is important in sexual adjustment is not a high level of frequency; rather, it is that the two parties *agree* on frequency and activities. A spouse who wants coitus daily may be an excellent match for one partner but a disastrous match for another who wants intercourse once a week.

Komarovsky (1962), studying working-class families, found that for some unhappy couples their sexual relationship was the only area of satisfaction in the marriage. Conversely, some very happy couples had a poor sexual adjustment. On the whole, however, a satisfactory sexual adjustment contributes to marital happiness, just as a positive adjustment in any other area does.

Sexual exclusivity is central to most marital relationships. In their vows, couples promise to be faithful for the rest of their lives. However, this promise is not always kept. According to numerous studies, in more than half of all marriages a partner will have sexual intercourse with someone other than the spouse at some point during the marriage (Blumstein & Schwartz, 1983; Hunt, 1974; Kinsey et al., 1948, 1952; Petersen, 1983). The incidence and impact of extramarital sex vary (see Box 8-2). For some, extramarital sex is a single episode, while for others it is a lifetime pattern. Adjusting to this aspect of a spouse's sexual behavior may require great effort, and some marriages do not survive.

 *What are the benefits and liabilities of the norm of sexual fidelity?*

### Sex-Role Adjustment

Alicia and Eric, newly married and setting up their household, jointly prepared their first dinner in their apartment. But when it was time to do the dishes, Eric balked: "My hands are the wrong shape to do dishes," he said, hoping this

**BOX 8-2**
*Extramarital Sex*

Extramarital sex—sex with someone other than one's spouse—probably has a history as long as marriage. In studying 185 primitive societies, Ford and Beach (1951) found that fewer than one sixth of those societies limited people to one mate. Monogamy is a relatively new concept and is far from receiving complete compliance.

Monogamy is the norm in most developed countries, although the strength of this norm varies considerably. Most religions teach that extramarital sex is sinful, and laws in the United States prohibit it. Nevertheless, both men and women have extramarital affairs. They may be more common now than centuries ago, but we have no historical data with which to compare current statistics. Even the Puritans had to deal with such affairs; and their punishments, as depicted in *The Scarlet Letter,* were severe: public humiliation and ostracism.

Kinsey estimated that 40–

50% of husbands and about 25% of wives have extramarital intercourse at least once, and Hunt (1974) generally supports that projection with his more recent data. Both researchers found that men at lower educational levels have a higher incidence of extramarital intercourse in their youth, while college men have a higher incidence in their thirties. The rates are equal by the time both groups reach their forties. Based on the results of a survey conducted by *Playboy* magazine, Petersen (1983) estimates that 70% of male and 65% of female respondents to that survey will have had an extramarital affair by age 50. Although *Playboy* readers are not representative of the general population and probably have a higher rate of extramarital activity, what is interesting is that the rates for women are approaching those for men. Blumstein and Schwartz (1983) found similar rates for men and

women: 25% of husbands and 21% of wives had already had extramarital sex. (These percentages are much lower than those in other reports because they include only the actual incidence, not the projected future rate.)

Reasons for affairs vary and often are not directly related to the spouse. The *Playboy* respondents mentioned reassurance of desirability, excitement, love, and friendship, along with sexual variety, change of routine, and better sex. Other researchers have found that unhappy marriages and unfulfilled sexual needs are primary (Williams, 1980). Still others have concluded that men more often are looking for sexual variety while women more often are seeking a special relationship (Blumstein & Schwartz, 1983).

Kinsey reported that extramarital sexual activity is usually kept secret. Only 20% of the husbands and wives who had

ridiculous excuse would be accepted. "Don't you remember?" said Alicia, "They were reshaped when you said 'I do.'" Eric's feeble, tongue-in-cheek excuse showed that he knew the division of chores he was proposing was not fair, but he would certainly accept it if Alicia would! Alicia's retort showed that she too could use humor to convey her expectations. Had either of them gotten angry or had Eric refused to share the chores, their sex-role adjustment regarding household tasks could have been difficult.

In pioneer days, the division of labor for maintaining a household was determined by necessity as well as by sex. The husband hunted for food, tilled the soil (or took care of the cattle), and provided shelter and other necessities. Although the wife may have helped him with some of the tasks, she was primarily responsible for preserving and preparing food, managing the

**BOX 8-2**
*Continued*

had extramarital sex reported that their spouses knew, although another 10% of wives and 30% of husbands said their spouses suspected. Blumstein and Schwartz (1983) found a much lower level of secrecy: 64% of husbands and 65% of wives reported that their spouses knew. Blumstein and Schwartz also asked how many sexual partners had been involved. Among these couples 29% of husbands and 43% of wives had had only one extramarital partner, and another 42% of husbands and 40% of wives had had fewer than six. Of course, we do not know how many of these involvements were single encounters and how many were long-term associations. (Spouses who not only know about a partner's extramarital sexual activity but agree to it are discussed in Chapter 13, Alternative Family Lifestyles.)

Assessing the impact of extramarital sex is difficult. It may have effects, positive or negative, that neither partner recognizes. A trust is violated (unless the spouses have agreed to sexual relations outside marriage), communication may be strained, and the level of commitment may be weakened. However, an affair may lead to greater appreciation of one's spouse, enhancement of one's self-concept, or introduction of new sexual practices into the marriage.

Extramarital affairs are rarely all good or all bad. Rather, they tend to strain emotions, sending the participants on an emotional roller-coaster ride of soaring thrills and devastating lows. Masking these changes from a spouse can be difficult.

How do people react when they learn about a spouse's affair? Many are deeply distressed and decide that divorce is the only option. Approximately 20% of the *Playboy* survey respondents who were divorced said that an affair had been responsible for their divorce. Other spouses, perhaps equally disturbed, gave the relationship another chance, deciding that they were better off with their spouse than without. Almost 50% of the *Playboy* respondents said they would forgive an extramarital affair, with men slightly more forgiving than women. Blumstein and Schwartz (1983) also found that husbands were more forgiving than wives. In some cases, the spouses renew their commitment to each other and find marriage more rewarding than before; in others, the marital relationship never completely recovers. The impact of extramarital sex varies with the circumstances, the intensity, the personalities involved, and many other factors. It's important to remember that extramarital sex does not necessarily mean the end of a marriage.

household, and taking care of the children. But as our society moved from the farm to the factory, the husband left home to work. He provided food and other necessities by purchasing them rather than hunting, fishing, and farming. Wives worked separately, often by producing goods (canned foods, handmade clothes) or providing services (laundry, ironing) for pay while working at home and supervising children. In low-income, city-dwelling families, many wives went to factories, worked 12-hour days, and then returned home to care for their families.

Today the majority of women work because their families need the money. Others work because they enjoy the stimulation it provides. As in the past, they typically return home and take responsibility for daily household tasks. Along with the movement to more sharing among husbands and wives in other spheres, such as decision making and sexual pleasure, wives are starting to seek more assistance from their husbands in household tasks.

Although husbands do participate in household tasks, including child care, the average amount of time they spend is small. In an extensive study of who performs household work, Walker and Woods (1976) found that nonemployed wives work about 8 hours a day at these tasks while their husbands work about 1½ hours a day. Wives who were employed outside the home more than 29 hours a week spent almost 5 hours a day on household tasks, and their husbands spent about 1½ hours a day (Saturdays and Sundays are included in these estimates).

Other norms are changing slowly. For example, expectations for fathers have expanded to include their involvement in all aspects of their children's lives, from attending prenatal classes to being a companion and adviser. These changes are occurring because the costs of adhering to old roles outweigh the rewards of adopting new roles. Like all changes, they are not occurring for everyone, everywhere.

## Finances

She: "I don't believe in layaway or putting things on credit, except big purchases like a car or house. You end up paying a lot more for things if you have to pay interest."

He: "Sometimes it's important to get something right away, even if you have to charge it. Who cares if you have to pay interest if you get to use it right away?"

Both these viewpoints have merit, but imagine the frustration if these two persons were spouses! She would be saving money only to find him spending it. Clearly, managing finances is another major issue in marriage.

Blumstein and Schwartz (1983, p. 51) note that "money is the last frontier of self-disclosure." That is, partners are less likely to know about each other's earnings, debts, and spending habits than about other things such as sexual behavior and ethical values. Yet, managing money is a major responsibility for each couple. How they choose to divide this task will depend on the partners' wants, abilities, and power.

Blumstein and Schwartz found that when couples were dissatisfied with the amount of money they had, they reported that their relationship was less satisfying. An estimated one fourth to one third of the couples surveyed reported that money was their number one problem. Arguments about how money should be managed are more common than those about how much is available. Of these spouses, 49% fight about money at least once every few months, and only 23% never fight about it. Money is important to both spouses, but apparently for different reasons. In analyzing their results, Blumstein and Schwartz concluded that: "To men it represents identity and power. To women, it is security and autonomy" (p. 76).

In recent years, many couples have decided not to combine their money. They keep separate checking accounts, and each may contribute (equally or proportionately to earnings) to joint expenses. Some couples enter into prenuptial agreements that establish the division of property, alimony, and inheritance. These practices are still uncommon. In Blumstein and Schwartz's survey, only 12% of wives and 8% of husbands thought spouses should keep their money separate. Perhaps as more women establish careers and become self-supporting, the frequency of these arrangements will increase.

From couples who have two large incomes to couples who receive subsistence payments, the issue of finances must be faced throughout marriage. Money will continue to be an issue among couples because it really represents "trust, commitment and . . . permanence" (Blumstein & Schwartz, 1983, p. 110).

 *Using social exchange theory, explain how the "exchange" between husband and wife varies depending on who is employed.*

## MARITAL SATISFACTION

*How do you not run out of new things to say? And since we know we're always changing How can it be the same?*

— Lyrics by Michel Legrand/
Alan & Marilyn Bergman

These lyrics capture partners' concerns about how long their relationship will be rewarding and enriching and, by doing so, focus on a major aspect of marriage—**marital satisfaction.** In contrast to marital adjustment, which comprises the accommodations each spouse makes in a marriage, marital satisfaction is the feelings of each partner about the relationship. It is the amount of pleasure a spouse derives from the relationship. As such, it is entirely subjective. A spouse may need to make extensive adjustments and yet be satisfied with the relationship or need to make only a few adjustments and yet be dissatisfied with the relationship. Furthermore, two persons in a marriage may have significantly different levels of satisfaction. No wonder understanding relationships is so complex!

Like power, marital satisfaction has received much attention from researchers, although definitions and terms have varied. Some researchers have spoken of "marital happiness" or "marital quality"; in this chapter, we will use the term *satisfaction* for consistency.

Satisfaction is a subjective measure—what may be satisfying for one person may not be for another. Perhaps satisfaction reflects the relation between what people expect (in this case, from marriage and a spouse) and what they actually receive (Rollins & Feldman, 1970). Or satisfaction may reflect the difference between what people actually receive and the alternatives they have. Let's look at each possibility from one spouse's viewpoint.

Jason spends most of his evenings working late or having fun with his circle of male friends and spends little time with his wife, Jennifer. If her only expectations for him are to support her and be faithful, she may rate her marriage as mostly satisfactory, even though he doesn't spend much time at home. But if Jennifer wants to share some activities with her husband, she is likely to be disappointed in what she is getting from her marriage. Thus, the same marriage may be viewed as satisfactory or unsatisfactory, depending on Jennifer's expectations (and they may change).

The other premise suggests that Jennifer's level of satisfaction is likely to be influenced by the alternatives available. If friends or relatives tell her that men prefer to spend time with one another and she should adjust, she may decide she has no other choice. If her friends' marriages are similar, she may decide that marriage cannot be expected to provide a "best friend." If she doesn't think that she would be better off alone or that she is likely to find a better spouse, she will evaluate her relationship as more satisfying than if she has other alternatives. Satisfaction is not static; expectations, alternatives, and actual behavior are likely to change for both spouses.

According to exchange theory, spouses trade resources such as money, goods, services, affection, sex, status, and information (Foa & Foa, 1974). Satisfaction reflects the acceptability of the exchange. If the exchange is mutually rewarding, both partners will be satisfied. If not, the dissatisfied partner(s) will probably try to alter the exchange so it will be satisfactory. Communication, negotiation, manipulation, and with-drawal are common means used to change the balance of the exchange.

Marital satisfaction may be influenced by four major components: (1) role enactment by self, (2) role enactment by spouse, (3) agreement on these roles, and (4) the costs of enacting these roles (Burr, 1971). Problems may result from dissatisfaction in any of these areas. For example, if David thinks he is an inadequate husband, he may get depressed (#1). If he thinks his wife is not enacting her role properly, he will be irritated (#2). If they disagree on what role each is to play, tensions will result (#3). And if the costs of enacting the role of husband are great, he will be unhappy (#4). Many marriages have problems in one of these four areas, although most are not afflicted with problems in all four at the same time.

## Causes of Satisfaction and Dissatisfaction

It should be clear that marital satisfaction varies from time to time, from individual to individual, and from couple to couple. We do know that certain situations foster satisfaction or dissatisfaction for the majority of couples. Let's turn our attention to these factors.

The more a couple discuss personal feelings and concerns, the higher their level of satisfaction (Jorgensen & Gaudy, 1980)—and marital satisfaction increases communication between the spouses (L. K. White, 1983). In short, couples who are happy communicate more, and more communication leads to happiness. Unfortunately, the opposite is true as well: couples who are unhappy communicate less, and less communication leads to more unhappiness. It is essential, then, for a couple to assess their level of communication and their satisfaction with it and make any necessary changes.

Postponement of children is associated with higher marital satisfaction (Miller, 1976). There may be several explanations. A couple who postpone children have more time to establish the marital relationship, to make necessary adjustments, and to build financial security. Conversely, couples who have a premarital pregnancy have higher levels of marital dissatisfaction (Miller, 1976).

Shared values and goals increase marital satisfaction. One study of military couples found that what mattered was not the selection of traditional or nontraditional sex roles but whether the couple *agreed* on their choice (Bowen & Orthner, 1983). This finding supports Burr's (1971) proposition that when partners agree on their roles, they are more likely to be satisfied with their relationship.

Several factors are related to dissatisfaction in marriage. One is low income (Miller, 1976). White couples who report a traditional division of household chores are less satisfied with their marriages than those who share. In Black families, however, a traditional division of labor is not associated with less spousal interaction or lower marital satisfaction (L. K. White, 1983). More research is needed on racial and ethnic differences in all aspects of marital and family relationships, including marital satisfaction.

When people have more demands placed on them than they can handle comfortably, they experience **role strain,** which is a major cause of dissatisfaction (Feldman, 1971; Miller, 1976). A heavy workload, many children, a new job, or illness in the family can make it difficult to meet the partner's needs.

In summary, communication (particularly about personal issues) and agreement on roles, values, and goals are associated with marital satisfaction, while low income, traditional division of tasks, and many children are associated with marital dissatisfaction. Such dissatisfaction sometimes leads to divorce.

BOX 8-3
## *Pointers about the Marital Relationship*

1. Communication about your feelings and your marriage is essential if you are to have a vibrant relationship.

2. Your partner cannot read your mind; you must explain your views, feelings, needs, and wants. Remember, though, that explaining isn't magic—it doesn't mean that everything will go your way.

3. The two of you don't have to like all the same things (friends, activities), and it is acceptable to enjoy these without your spouse's participation.

4. You can disagree without being disagreeable.

5. Agreements should be acceptable to both partners. If one partner is forced to give in, problems are likely to arise.

6. In general, it is best to bring up problems or concerns when they arise, *if* circumstances permit (for example, if other people are not around). However, if you are too angry to discuss the situation reasonably, wait until you can express yourself without

verbally (or physically) attacking the other person.

7. You do not have to spend all your free time either together or apart.

8. Do something special for the other person, just for the fun of it.

9. Express your feelings of pride and satisfaction about your partner to your partner. Everyone likes positive feedback.

10. Treat your partner with at least as much respect and kindness as you would a friend.

## *Satisfaction over the Life Span*

"When we first got married, we were crazy about each other. It was like playing house. Eventually separate interests and work demanded more attention. We sort of fell into a comfortable pattern—not the ecstasy of the early years but not the hurt or disappointment either. We just understood each other better and were comfortable together. I guess that's what they mean by 'settling down.'"

According to many studies, marital satisfaction varies over the life span. Conflicting findings have portrayed two patterns, shown in Figure 8-1. In pattern A, marital satisfaction decreases slowly over the life span. In pattern B, satisfaction decreases from a high early in marriage to a low during the middle stages of the life span and then increases slightly again after children leave home. The differences in these findings may be

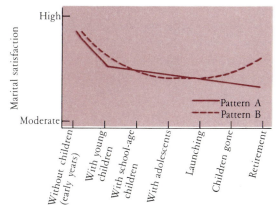

**FIGURE 8-1.** *Two patterns of marital satisfaction over the life span.*

due to the methods of measurement, the populations surveyed, or other research issues (Spanier & Lewis, 1980; Spanier, Lewis, & Cole, 1975). In fact, about 8% of the change in marital satisfaction can be accounted for by the stage of the family life span. Issues such as communication, commitment, age, and years of marriage account for much more of the change (Miller, 1976; Rollins & Cannon, 1974). For those who remain married, marital satisfaction may decrease slightly over time, but this decline is small.

What does seem clear is that the addition of children to the family reduces marital satisfaction (Olson, McCubbin, & associates, 1983). Children add different kinds of strains and satisfactions to the marital relationship, and these may change over time. Some stages are more stress-filled than others. Harry (1976) found that the greatest financial strain was created by preschool-age children, while the greatest time strain was associated with having school-age children. Others report that satisfaction scores were lowest and strains were highest among families with adolescents (Olson, McCubbin, & associates, 1983).

Do these findings mean that if a couple want to stay happily married, they should not have children? The answer is no. There are some indications that satisfaction decreases for couples without children as well, although the decline is

less (Olson & Ryder, 1970). However, couples with children do need to work harder to make their marriages satisfying by doing the things that are associated with marital satisfaction—communicating and sharing activities. They should not let their parental roles replace time for each other.

Argyle and Furnham (1983) found that older persons and men received more satisfaction from marriage. The higher level of satisfaction among men supports actuarial data showing that married men live longer than single men and that single women live longer than married women. This fact has led some people to conclude that marriage is a better support system for men than for women (Bernard, 1972; Rettig & Bubolz, 1983).

In the next section we will look at factors associated with marital stability—how likely a marriage is to last—because they often underlie factors that are linked to marital satisfaction.

 *What forces at the societal and personal levels hinder marital satisfaction, and how can couples overcome them?*

## For Better or For Worse                                   by Lynn Johnston

# MARITAL STABILITY

*The more I love, the more that I'm afraid*
*That in your eyes I may not see forever.*
*If we can be the best of lovers*
*Yet be the best of friends*
*If we can try with every day to make it better*
*As it grows, with any luck, then, I suppose*
*The music never ends.*

—Lyrics by Michel Legrand/
Alan & Marilyn Bergman

These lyrics address the fact that most people want a stable *and* happy marriage. The lyricists propose a formula for achieving "forever": being the best of lovers, being the best of friends, trying to make it better every day, and luck. We agree that these can be important elements in a happy, stable marriage, although not all couples follow this formula.

"Until death do us part" used to mean that a couple remained married regardless of their incompatibility. Thus, although marriages were more stable 50 or 100 years ago, they weren't necessarily happier! Stable marriages range from happy to unhappy, just like unstable ones. **Marital stability** is the term used to describe how likely a couple are to remain married. Marital satisfaction is likely to go with marital stability, but not necessarily so. Although exceptions exist, unhappy marriages frequently end in divorce, while happy marriages tend to endure.

Many of the factors associated with marital stability seem obvious. Couples with a common background (age, religion, socioeconomic status, race, education, and so on) are more likely to have stable marriages. It is common in our society for people to encourage marriage between persons with similar backgrounds. Conversely, people are concerned when a couple differ widely on one or more major background factors. In general, many more adjustments are required if spouses are of different races, are deeply religious but in different faiths, or have different income backgrounds or levels of edu-

cation. Of course, people with widely varying backgrounds can and do stay married. Overall, however, their chances for divorce are higher.

A person's family of origin (the family he or she grew up in) may influence marital stability. First, after a divorce, children are likely to have less economic support and supervision than in two-parent families. Mueller and Pope (1977) found that these factors were associated with marrying younger and with less education, and such couples were more likely to divorce. Second, a person's family of origin may foster or interfere in the marriage. Relatives may help a couple by advising one or both partners, modeling appropriate behavior, or resolutely refusing to take sides—or they may give advice that is disruptive, model inappropriate behavior, and interfere in many aspects of a couple's relationship. How the couple handle this assistance or disruption will influence its impact.

Age at marriage is positively associated with marital stability: people who marry at 30 are less likely to divorce than those who marry at 20. In general, people who are older have a better understanding of themselves, others, and what they want from a relationship.

Marital stability is also influenced by the amount of agreement between husband and wife on such things as their expectations, values, money handling, time spent together, sexual behavior, and work roles (Blumstein & Schwartz, 1983). Significant disagreements in such areas require substantial adjustments and are likely to decrease marital satisfaction. Sharing their view of their life together reduces the amount of adjustment necessary. However, there is a catch to sharing a view: each person's view is likely to change during the marriage!

 *How are marital adjustment, marital satisfaction, and marital stability related?*

# THE WORKING WIFE

One area of major change for many couples in the past 25 years is wives' employment. In 1960 the norm was that a married woman would work only until she had children; in the 1980s the norm is that she will work most of her life.

The U. S. Department of Labor (1982) projects that women who were 16 years old in 1977 (the most recent data available) will be employed for 27.7 years, compared with 38.5 years for men. Women's work patterns differ from men's in two major ways: women are more likely to interrupt their employment for child rearing, and they are more likely to take part-time employment. In addition, most women have not been socialized, as men have, to consider work central to their lives. They haven't necessarily grown up assuming that they must work to support themselves, and even married career women expect to pursue employment at their own pace (Blumstein & Schwartz, 1983). Nevertheless, the average woman will be employed for more than 25 years—a reality that most young men and women do not expect.

Women work for a variety of reasons—income, stimulation, and fulfillment. Research has shown that the likelihood that a woman will be employed is increased by the family's financial need, her attachment to working, her earning potential, and the presence of older (rather than younger) children in the home (Sorensen, 1983). Women who have more education and more "attractive" jobs are more likely to work.

Of course, the tasks normally performed by a full-time homemaker must still be done when a wife is employed. Others may be paid to take on some of these duties, the husband may do more, children may take some additional responsibilities, or wives may continue to perform these tasks on top of their employment workload. The time required for household tasks may be reduced as more prepared foods are used or no-iron clothing is purchased. Standards for housekeeping may be reduced, so that tasks like

*Do you think this husband: is waiting for his wife to clean the house, is upset because her feet are on **his** new sofa, or, has called out for dinner?*

vacuuming and dusting are done less frequently.

How do most families manage their housekeeping when both spouses are employed? Many studies have shown that husbands whose wives are employed perform more household and child-care tasks, though only a small portion of them (Blumstein & Schwartz, 1983; Walker & Woods, 1976). Figure 8-2 documents husbands' participation. The trend toward husbands' performance of these tasks may be increasing as women demand more egalitarian relationships. For the most part, however, women simply have two jobs—employee and homemaker. It is no surprise, then, that employed women, especially mothers with young children, experience strain in fulfilling their many roles.

Of course, if strain were the only result of wives' employment, couples would avoid it altogether. Employment provides many satisfactions for the woman and her family. Most women work for the income. In some families the in-

PART THREE   FAMILY LIFE ACROSS THE LIFE SPAN

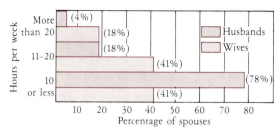

**FIGURE 8-2.** *Time spent on housework by dual-worker married couples.*

come is used to provide things that would otherwise not be purchased (more clothing, restaurant meals, lessons), and in others it is used to provide luxury items (boats, vacations) or increase savings. This additional income can reduce other strains a family may face. Thus, an employed wife and her family may trade increased workloads at home for financial benefits. Women also want to work because it gives them more power, status, respect, and self-fulfillment (Blumstein & Schwartz, 1983).

Being an employee may increase feelings of competence because, unlike homemakers, employees are evaluated and can readily compare their performance with others'. Employment often elicits a sense of personal accomplishment as well as recognition by others (Blumstein & Schwartz, 1983). In general, husbands of successful wives are more satisfied with the marital relationship (Blumstein & Schwartz, 1983).

Employment may ease women's family lifespan transitions as children grow and demand less attention and care. Freudiger (1983) found that employed wives' satisfaction with life increases as they grow older although nonemployed wives' satisfaction does not. This result may reflect a decrease in strain as children grow as well as increased feelings of competence from work, while homemakers may feel less needed as their children grow.

The husband's reaction to his wife's employment status is important to the satisfaction of both spouses. Some husbands have strong views on whether their wives should work. If their wives disagree, conflict and strain are increased. A recent study found that 34% of husbands believed they should be the sole support of the family and their wives should be full-time homemakers and mothers, while only 25% of wives supported this view (Blumstein & Schwartz, 1983). Other husbands prefer that their wives work, in part because it reduces the burden of financial support. Blumstein and Schwartz found that 31% of the husbands they surveyed supported this view, compared with 39% of the wives. They also found that some husbands take pride in their wives' job competence and find that a working wife becomes more understanding of the dynamics and demands of working, which is helpful. Finally, many husbands are flexible on their wives' employment, giving wives the major (though not necessarily exclusive) say in deciding whether to work; 35% of husbands and 36% of wives fall into this category (Blumstein & Schwartz, 1983). Their preferences may change depending on family circumstances such as income, debts, and ages of children—the same factors that enter into women's employment choices.

Clearly, a wife's employment has significant costs and rewards for family members, just as her choice not to enter the labor force does. No best choice exists for all families. In fact, studies have found that marital satisfaction does not depend on whether the wife works but on whether she can realize her preference (Orden & Bradburn, 1968; Scanzoni & Fox, 1980). In other words, if a woman doesn't want to work, she is happiest if she doesn't, and if she wants to work, she is happiest if she can. Her husband's support of or opposition to her choice will significantly affect her level of role strain.

*Should married women be employed? Should mothers of young children be employed? What about married men, and fathers of young children? Explain your responses.*

## PROMOTING FAMILY WELLNESS
### *Understanding the Marital Relationship*

People often assume that they know about the institution of marriage. After all, they have observed the marriages of relatives, friends, and neighbors, read about marriages in books, and seen them in movies and on television. Such observations, though useful in providing a spectrum of types of relationships, do not necessarily provide enough information to help people understand the many aspects of the marital relationship or decide what kind of a marital relationship they want. Consequently, when people begin to consider marriage, acquiring information, understanding, and skills becomes important. The four tools of prevention can help people develop a positive marital relationship.

## EDUCATION

We learn about marriage within our own families. Our parents' behavior shapes some of our ideas about husbands and wives, often without our conscious recognition. Parents who express their likes and dislikes, annoyance and displeasure, love and anger in front of children convey a message that spouses interact with each other. The balance of positive and negative interactions conveys another message: well-adjusted couples demonstrate that being married is generally enjoyable, and poorly adjusted couples show that marriage is often stressful.

Talking with married people to learn about their enjoyable and stressful experiences can be beneficial. Although each marriage is different, couples do share many stages. Learning how others have handled particular problems and getting their ideas on your concerns can help you understand your situation and ways to manage it.

Books, magazines, and television can be helpful. Whether we're studying a fictional couple like Archie and Edith or learning from a real couple on a talk show, we can gain a broader perspective that helps us formulate how we want our marriages to function.

After reading this textbook, you should be better informed about and prepared for marriage. In assessing yourself and your goals, you may choose not to marry, or you may become more thorough in evaluating prospective mates. Whatever your immediate and eventual choices, a better understanding of the marital relationship will assist you.

Throughout this chapter we have emphasized that the most important element in a marriage is not what choice is made but that husband and wife agree on that choice. Some couples prefer a traditional role division; others prefer an egalitarian one. Either is fine, but difficulties will arise if partners disagree. Sex roles, money management, desire for parenthood, interaction patterns with children, communication styles, values, personal habits, and personality are only some of the dimensions to consider when selecting a spouse. Learning about yourself and your prospective partner and, in particular, about your areas of disagreement and how you will handle them is important in choosing and living with a spouse.

*What other educational approaches, formal and informal, can you suggest for increasing your understanding of marriage?*

## COMMUNITY ORGANIZATION/ SYSTEMS INTERVENTION

As a prevention tool, community organization/ systems intervention is concerned with modifying institutions and policies. Numerous efforts have been undertaken locally and nationally. We will focus on one of national scope, often offered in religious settings: marriage enhancement classes.

During the past two decades, a diverse array of marriage enhancement programs has been developed to assist married couples. These programs may be called "Marriage Encounter," "Marriage Enrichment," or something else. The exact activities and philosophies may differ, but the goal is to provide a structure and a setting for spouses to communicate with each other. Typically, a couple will take a weekend or several evenings to focus on their marital goals, their feelings about the marriage and each other, and their communication. Some denominations require engaged couples to participate in a similar program before they can be married.

These programs have interrupted a cycle of relationship neglect and helped thousands of couples enrich their marriages. Each program urges the couple to continue to use the techniques they have learned to communicate on a regular basis.

Marital enhancement programs were developed in response to a void in services for happily married couples. They have become a part of the social support system in many communities and are an excellent example of a prevention effort to promote family wellness.

 *What would be the benefits and liabilities of requiring all couples to complete a marriage enhancement course before obtaining a marriage license?*

## COMPETENCY PROMOTION

Helping people increase their skills and feelings of competence is the goal of competency promotion. Growing up in a family provides many opportunities for acquiring the skills needed in marriage: money management, communication, homemaking tasks, and negotiation. Communication and negotiation skills are learned through interactions with parents, siblings, friends, classmates, and many others. They may be modeled by others or explicitly taught through direction and even practice exercises. However they are learned, they are critical skills in all our interpersonal interactions.

Money management and homemaking tasks can easily be taught in the family. In assigning chores, parents are helping children learn to be self-sufficient. Receiving an allowance, of which part is targeted for special purposes (for example, savings, donations, gifts) and part may be spent in any way, gives children early experience in managing money. They learn quite readily that if they spend all their discretionary money when they get their allowance, they don't have any left for the rest of the week. Learning such lessons when young may help one avoid similar mistakes when older.

 *What other competency promotion strategies could be used to increase an understanding of marriage? To what aspects of marital understanding would they contribute?*

## NATURAL CAREGIVING

This prevention tool addresses the care and nurturance we provide to one another. The support, attention, love, and appreciation that spouses exchange are natural caregiving. Typically, couples focus a great deal of time and attention on each other early in the relationship. Often, however, this fades over time. It's almost as if couples think "We don't have to talk to each other because we live together" or "We know each other so well, we can direct our attention to other matters." But the marital relationship, like any personal relationship, requires time, nurturance, and communication.

Because there are so many distractions and demands on time, it is easy to understand how partners fall into a pattern of noncommunication. After they spend eight hours a day at work, and additional time commuting and doing necessary tasks, they often forget or are too tired to spend time with each other. Equally troublesome, much of the time they do spend together is not focused on themselves or their relationship but on activities such as watching television,

doing chores, or caring for children. These activities can be enjoyable to do together, but they should not be substituted for time for the relationship.

Time, attention, and care—these are the elements necessary to nurture a marital relationship. Of course, they cannot make partners change their views or their behavior. If the partners are not well matched, their struggle will be arduous and their adjustments extensive. Being well matched, however, is insufficient to keep a marriage together. To do so takes natural caregiving—not just in the early years but every year.

*If a friend were to tell you about his or her marital problems, how would you respond? Why?*

# SUMMARY

When a couple marry, they enter into a relationship regulated by the state through the marriage contract and perhaps through their own prenuptial agreements. Spouses must adjust to each other in many areas—personal habits, desire to be together or apart, decision making and power, sexual behavior, division of household tasks, child care, and money management. Moreover, they need to be prepared to deal with change in each other and in themselves on any of these issues.

This chapter has covered marital satisfaction—how happy a person is with his or her marriage—and marital stability—the likelihood of staying married. And, we have seen that an important area of adaptation for many couples is the wife's employment. Women work for personal fulfillment as well as for money, and whether a given woman will be happier working depends on whether she wants to work and her family's attitude toward her work.

# MAJOR POINTS TO REMEMBER

1. Marriage is a contract, specified by each state.
2. Each partner experiences the marriage differently.
3. Three concepts that are helpful in analyzing a marriage are adjustment (how well each partner makes the necessary compromises), satisfaction (how happy a spouse is with the marriage), and stability (how likely the marriage is to endure).
4. Although partners merge to form a new family unit, they must also maintain separate identities.
5. Power is a process as well as an outcome. It may be based on authority and control. Power between spouses is influenced by such factors as level of education, income, religious teachings, personal and peer

values, and personality. Power patterns may be husband-dominant, wife-dominant, or egalitarian.
6. The frequency of sexual intercourse decreases somewhat during marriage. A low rate of intercourse tends to be associated with marital dissatisfaction.
7. Money is a significant issue in marriage. Many couples wed with little understanding of each other's attitudes toward money or spending habits.
8. Dissatisfaction can be viewed as the difference between reality and expectation or as the difference between reality and other options. The greater the gap, the higher dissatisfaction is likely to be.
9. Role enactment by self and partner, agreement on roles, and costs of fulfilling roles may influence marital satisfaction.
10. A wife's employment affects the family in both positive and negative ways. In choosing to work, a woman may gain income and personal satisfaction but also increase her role strain.

# ADDITIONAL SOURCES OF INFORMATION

## *Publications*

Blaine, M. K. (1975). *The terrible thing that happened at our house.* New York: Parents' Magazine Press. [Children]

Colman, H. C. (1975). *After the wedding.* New York: William Morrow. [Adolescents]

Head, A. (1967). *Mr. & Mrs. Bo Jo Jones.* New York: Putnam. [Adolescents]

Platt, K. (1975). *Chloris and the freaks.* Scarsdale, NY: Bradbury Press. [Early adolescents]

Rogers, C. R. (1972). *Becoming partners: Marriage and its alternatives.* New York: Dell. [Adults]

Simon, N. (1976). *All kinds of families*. Chicago: Albert Whitman. [Children]

Smith, G. W. (1971). *Couple therapy*. New York: Collier. [Adults]

## Organizations

National Marriage Encounter
7241 North Whippoorwill Lane
Peoria, IL 61614
One of many groups that encourage couples to explore and enhance their relationship. (Many churches offer similar experiences.)

Association of Couples for Marriage Enrichment (ACME)
P.O. Box 10596
Winston-Salem, NC 27108
Groups led by lay couples (not members of the clergy or therapists) to enhance marital relationships.

# PARENTHOOD: THE FAMILY EXPANDS

1. What criteria should be used in making a decision about having children? What are the poor and good reasons for having children?

2. How does a child affect a couple's relationship?

3. What are the chances of getting pregnant in a given month? What percentage of couples have difficulty conceiving?

4. What is prenatal care? When should it begin? Why is it so important?

5. What types of development do humans experience? Do these types occur simultaneously? At the same pace?

6. What impact do developmental stages have on parenting skills?

7. When should mothers begin interacting with their children? When should fathers? What is different about the ways fathers and mothers interact with their babies?

8. How do cultural differences affect child rearing?

9. How much does the average family spend to raise a child to age 18?

10. Who takes care of children when both parents work? How should parents select caretakers?

As America's most popular career, parenting is the least prepared for occupation, not listed in any index of occupations, but found in the vast majority of homes [Hicks & Williams, 1981, p. 580].

To be a good parent is to achieve one of the most difficult goals in modern life [Gould, 1974, p. 196].

Snow White, Cinderella, and Sleeping Beauty are rescued by daring princes and whisked away to live "happily ever after." We wonder why children are never mentioned. Is this gap an oversight by the storytellers, or did they believe that "happily ever after" means that there are no children? In the past 30 years, researchers have found that the introduction of children into the family changes the marital relationship. In this chapter we will discuss these findings as well as making the decision about parenthood, getting pregnant, giving birth, and raising children.

Should every couple have children? Absolutely not! Children are not possessions to be acquired, like stereos, cars, and homes. They are people with a right to be cared for and loved by responsible adults. With today's birth-control methods, people can choose to have or to forgo having children. But how do you go about making this decision? It is likely to be influenced not only by your personal history, preferences, and priorities but also by your peers, your family, and the values of our society. Your partner is subject to such influences as well. The decision is not a simple one.

## TO BE OR NOT TO BE A PARENT

A cross-cultural study found that children are valued today for the love, happiness, and companionship they are expected to provide (Arnold et al., 1975). The chief drawbacks of children that parents noted were emotional (worrying about the child) and financial. Like any other role, job, or career, parenthood has positive and negative aspects. Yet, in our culture, we have socialized children to assume that with adulthood comes parenthood. Parents assume that their children will have children; they say things like "You'll understand when you have children" or "Someday you can teach your children to ride a bike too." Television, books, school, and friends may contribute to this expectation as well. For example, soap operas (and prime-time dramas) mythologize parenthood through messages that pregnancy will save a marriage and make the wife more important to her husband and that motherhood will fulfill women (Peck, 1974). By the time we are adults, we may have difficulty separating our desires from society's desire for us. Not surprisingly, some of us become parents without carefully examining this choice.

## The Choice

Our society is becoming increasingly flexible about allowing people to make choices—and to change their minds about these choices. For example, we can usually change jobs, employers, or fields of study without reprisals. Goods that we purchase can be traded in, sold, or abandoned. Ending a marriage brings fewer societal sanctions today than 20 years ago, as divorce laws have been liberalized. There is one choice, however, on which society does not accept "changing one's mind": the choice to be a parent. Becoming a parent creates another life—the life of an innocent person. Children cannot be returned or exchanged, and society does not accept abandoning them.

Only two acceptable ways exist for changing your mind about children: abortion, long before a child would be born, and adoption, usually shortly after birth. In our society, adoption is acceptable only if the mother is unmarried. Married couples rarely place a child for adoption, and when they do, they usually incur the disapproval of family and friends.

Because being a parent is a demanding, long-term commitment, ideally it should result from a deliberate, carefully explored choice rather than from chance. Reality, however, is far from this ideal. Millions of unintended pregnancies occur each year. Many of these pregnancies are terminated. Other people who experience an unintended pregnancy choose to continue it and adjust their lives to accommodate a child. Because human beings are creative, flexible, and adaptable, most can integrate an unexpected child into their lives. But not every child has an adult who is willing and able to cope, as evidenced by the thousands of cases of child abuse and neglect each year. We believe that adults who carefully weigh the rewards and liabilities of children will make their choice about parenthood more realistically and, if they choose to become parents, will be better prepared for it.

It seems that during the past 20 years people have started to consider parenthood a choice rather than a requirement. Census data show a slight increase in the percentage of women who say they do not plan to have children. Pohlman (1974) found that even in the short time span of five years more undergraduate women reported a choice to remain childless (see Table 9-1). Whether these women have actually remained childless is uncertain; what is clear is that more women are considering parenthood a choice. (Data on men's attitudes are not available, a gap that reflects society's and researchers' bias that fatherhood is less important to men than motherhood is to women.)

There are many questions one must answer: What are children really like? Can I provide the care they need? Do I want to modify my lifestyle to accommodate them? Do my partner and I agree about having children? If we want to be parents, when do we want to start a family? How many children do we want? Spaced how far

**TABLE 9-1.** *Fertility preferences of college women in traditional and avant-garde colleges, 1965 and 1970*

|  | More Traditional College | | More Avant-Garde College | |
|---|---|---|---|---|
|  | *1965* | *1970* | *1965* | *1970* |
| Number of children wanted |  |  |  |  |
| 0 | 0% | 6% | 10% | 18% |
| 1 | 4% | 1% | 0% | 7% |
| 2 | 27% | 63% | 39% | 55% |
| 3 or more | 68% | 30% | 52% | 19% |
| Number of students sampled | 96 | 95 | 54 | 110 |

apart? What will we do if we can't have children? Answering these questions requires careful evaluation and good communication between partners.

Whatever choice you make, you are likely to experience some regret. Parents may envy nonparents their freedom, while nonparents may envy parents their joys in celebrating special occasions with their children. So occasional regret over either decision is not unusual. The goal is to make the choice with which you will be more satisfied.

 *Most couples want to become parents. Using theories from Chapter 2, explain why.*

## The Issues

Among the issues to consider in deciding to have children are a couple's reasons for wanting or not wanting them, their agreement on their parenting roles and on how to raise children, how children will affect their lives (their relationship, their employment, their lifestyle), and the costs and rewards of having children (Elvenstar, 1982).

There are many poor reasons for having children. Psychiatrist Robert Gould (1974, pp. 193–

196) developed the following list of wrong reasons:

1. Our parents want grandchildren.
2. We can afford to have a baby.
3. If I'm somebody's mother (father), then I'm somebody.
4. I need to be needed.
5. A baby will give me something to do.
6. We think it will help our marriage.
7. It's a way to prove you're a man (or a woman).
8. We don't want to be different.
9. I want my child to get the things I never had.
10. A child is my only claim to immortality.
11. Male: A baby will keep a woman in her place.
12. Female: A baby will keep my husband attached to me and less likely to stray from home.

Appropriate reasons for having children include a desire to help a child grow and develop and to enrich a couple's life by sharing it with a child. In general, the reasons for not having children are rational (costs, demands, restrictions on a couple), while the reasons for having children are emotional (pride, a desire to share, a sense of fulfillment). Each couple must weigh these often competing reasons and base their choice on those that have the most meaning for them.

*Look at the list of wrong reasons for having children. Do you think any of them are actually good reasons? Why? Why are the wrong ones wrong?*

## The Impact of Children

The birth of a child affects a marital relationship in several ways. Research finds, for example, that a birth may be perceived as a crisis (Dyer, 1963; LeMasters, 1957; Wainwright, 1966). Marital satisfaction declines for many couples (Feldman, 1971, 1974; Miller & Sollie, 1980). The marital relationship may change to emphasize the partnership rather than the romantic aspects (Belsky, Spanier, & Rovine, 1983).

One problem with this research is that it generally considers only marital satisfaction and omits personal satisfaction. One study found that parents were more likely to report satisfaction from personal ("feeling of fulfillment") rather than marital ("feeling closer to spouse") sources (Russell, 1974). It seems likely, then, that satisfaction with the marital relationship declines when a child arrives but personal satisfaction may increase.

Sociologist Alice Rossi (1968) notes a number of features of parenthood that may contribute to the adjustments parents face. In contrast to marriage, in which partners have a chance to get to know each other before they marry, it is not possible to select a child's characteristics before getting pregnant. Although partners choose to marry, many couples have pregnancies they did not want. Parenthood begins with an abrupt transition, and training in how to be a successful parent is scarce.

So does having a child add to or detract from personal and marital satisfaction? The answer depends on a broad array of factors. For example, the husband and wife may experience the events of pregnancy, birth, and caring for the child differently (Cowan, Cowan, Coie, & Coie, 1978). Their satisfaction with their parenting roles and the adjustments required of each will vary. Another factor may be income. Low income and low education are related to low satisfaction in marriage (Renne, 1970). Since children are expensive, they are likely to increase concerns about finances.

A child may interfere with a parent's other rewarding activities. Researchers have found that women with more education and commitment to careers tend to report fewer gratifications from pregnancy and parenthood (Gladieux, 1978; Steffensmeier, 1982). Perhaps the most frequently noted problems of new parents are lack of time and inability to control their time (LaRossa, 1983). Babies require a great deal of attention, and their schedules are likely to vary daily.

Role strain is a problem for parents, who must integrate a new role (parenthood) into their existing roles (spouse, employee, friend, and so on). This 24-hours-a-day, seven-days-a-week responsibility is awesome. Yet, most parents manage to adjust. Patience, flexibility, increased organization, and adaptability are coping mechanisms that help them do so (Miller & Sollie, 1980). Like any challenge, children add stress and the opportunity for fulfillment to parents' lives (Miller & Sollie, 1980).

Some adults, deciding that the benefits of children do not outweigh the costs, choose to be "childfree." In a study of voluntarily childfree women, Veevers (1973) found that almost one third had decided not to have children before they married and then had selected a spouse who would accept their decision. The other two thirds simply postponed having children until they finally decided never to have them. In couples who choose this option, the wife is likely to be highly educated, employed, and not identified with a formal religious denomination (Gustavus & Henley, 1971; Houseknecht, 1977, 1979; Veevers, 1973). As increasing numbers of couples choose this option, it is likely that they will receive more support for their choice.

*When couples plan for another child, they must often make major decisions about such issues as schooling, employment, travel, and finances.*

If a couple have decided to have children, other major decisions remain: When and how many? When is the right time to expand the family—this year? next year? in five years? Schooling, employment, travel, and finances may influence the timing. In general, researchers have found that couples who postpone having children have higher levels of marital satisfaction (Miller, 1976). This delay enables the couple to

establish their marital relationship and adjust to each other before introducing a child into their family.

Just as there are wrong reasons for having a first child, there are wrong reasons for having a second, third, or fourth:

1. We want at least one child of each sex.
2. Our first child will have a sibling to play with.

A good reason to have more than one child is because a couple have enjoyed the first child so much they want to share their lives with another one (Elvenstar, 1982). Of course, decisions about having children and timing can be changed, and couples may want to reevaluate their choices as their lives change.

## PREGNANCY AND BIRTH

For many people, getting pregnant is an unwanted accident. For the infertile, it is an ordeal involving failure, uncomfortable medical procedures, and scheduling intercourse to coincide with ovulation rather than with their desires. But for many others, conceiving a child is a conscious choice. Among *fertile* couples who are not using contraception, an average of 20% of women will become pregnant in any given month (Silber, 1980). This frequency decreases with the woman's age, as shown in Table 9-2. Even in their late thirties, however, 65% of fertile women conceive within a year.

Research has found that Blacks begin having children at younger ages than Whites, that Catholics begin bearing children later than other religious groups (perhaps because they are older when they marry), and that the more education a woman has, the older she is likely to be when she has her first child (Rindfuss & St. John, 1983). For economic, educational, employment, and personal development reasons, it is best to

**TABLE 9-2.** *Likelihood of pregnancy in fertile women, by age*

| Age | Probability of Conception per Month | Average Time to Conception (Months) | Probability of Conception within a Year |
|---|---|---|---|
| Early twenties | 25% | 4 | 97% |
| Late twenties | 15% | 6.7 | 86% |
| Early thirties | 10% | 10 | 72% |
| Late thirties | 8.3% | 12 | 65% |

avoid pregnancy during the teenage years (see Box 9-1).

To get pregnant, experts recommend having intercourse when interested, rather than by the calendar (Silber, 1980). This approach diminishes anxiety, which can inhibit ovulation, making pregnancy impossible. After 6–12 months, if a pregnancy has not occurred, then it may be appropriate to become more systematic.

Timing intercourse to coincide with ovulation obviously increases the likelihood of pregnancy. For most women, ovulation occurs 14 days *before* the start of the next menstrual period. To pinpoint ovulation, a woman must take her temperature with a basal body temperature thermometer (which measures tenths of degrees) each morning before she rises and record her daily temperature variation on a chart. If she has a regular, consistent cycle, it is simple to determine when she ovulates. If her cycle is 30 days, she ovulates on day 16. If it is 35 days, she ovulates on day 21. And if her cycle is 27 days, she ovulates on day 13.

## Infertility

Although most couples are fertile, one in six couples have difficulty conceiving (Menning, 1977). Either spouse may have the fertility problem, or the couple may share the problem (Menning, 1977; Silber, 1980). Infertility can become so frustrating that it becomes all-consuming. Guilt ("It's my fault that we can't have children"

or "What have we done to deserve this punishment?"), stress ("Tonight's the night, even though we don't feel like it"), hopelessness ("We're never going to have a baby"), and depression can result, threatening the marital relationship. To assist these couples, self-help groups have developed across the country, often called "Resolve" after the national organization concerned with this problem.

In many women, menstrual cycles are irregular, the timing of ovulation varies, or ovulation may be absent occasionally or completely. A fertility specialist should be consulted when a couple suspect they have a problem in conceiving, usually after a year without success. Surgery and medication have been helpful in overcoming many conception problems. Men have fertility problems as well—low sperm counts, abnormally shaped or slow-moving sperm, or blocked vesicles. Sometimes surgery, medication, or limiting the frequency of intercourse overcomes these problems.

Over 50% of these couples do eventually conceive, often with the help of specialists (Menning, 1977; Silber, 1980). Surgery to correct blocked fallopian tubes and medication to stimulate ovulation or to improve the quality or number of sperm are frequently used. Recently an extraordinary measure has been developed to help infertile couples: "test tube" babies. In this procedure, called "*in vitro* fertilization," ripened ova are removed from the woman and fertilized with her husband's sperm in a petri dish (not a

## BOX 9-1
*Adolescent Pregnancy and Parenthood*

Misinformation about sexuality is prevalent among teenagers in our society. A few examples of failure to understand some aspect of pregnancy or parenthood include misunderstandings about contraceptive methods (infrequent sex or douching prevents pregnancy), babies (they're inexpensive and they give love), and adoption (adoptive parents aren't real parents).

The United States has one of the highest adolescent birthrates among developed countries. On the average, Japan has 3 births per 1000 teenage girls annually, Canada has 33, and the United States has 52 (Alan Guttmacher Institute, 1981).

## EXPLANATIONS FOR TEENAGE PREGNANCY

Why are so many U. S. teenagers having babies? Five reasons have been offered: ignorance about reproduction, peer and societal pressures, the couple's relationship, psychological influences, and lack of meaningful alternatives to parenthood.

### Lack of Understanding about Reproduction

Although parents and children say that parents should be primary in providing information about sexuality and reproduction (Alexander, 1984; Bloch, 1979; Koblinsky & Atkinson,

1979; Yankelovich, Skelly & White, 1979), they are not (Alexander & Jorgensen, 1983; Roberts & Holt, 1980; Thornburg, 1981). Instead, major sources of information for many youth are friends, who are often misinformed, and the media, which are often sensationalistic (Tatum, 1981; Thornburg, 1981). Although school curricula may include human sexuality and reproduction, it is not covered in most grades. In grades where this topic is covered, an average of less than 10 hours a year is spent on it in large-city school districts (Sonenstein & Pittman, 1983). These limitations make it difficult to provide adequate information.

Further, cognitive and emotional development may limit a youth's ability to apply sexual information. Four key steps are essential in avoiding pregnancy for the sexually active. They must (1) exercise self-control, (2) foresee the possible consequences of sexual intercourse, (3) believe that pregnancy could result *in their own case,* and (4) acquire and use a contraceptive method (Polsby, 1974). Some teenagers (and adults!) do not understand or make these connections.

### Peer and Societal Pressures

Many teenagers believe that "everybody is doing it" when in

fact, in 1979, 50% of girls aged 15–19 had *never* had sexual intercourse (Zelnik & Kantner, 1980). Yet, the desire to conform may influence some adolescents to become sexually active. Only 20 years ago the norm for teenaged girls was abstinence, and those who had sexual experience were likely to deny it. Today many teenagers think it is necessary to deny their inexperience.

In our sex-saturated society, advertisements use sexy models, suggestive voices, and provocative messages to sell clothing, mouthwash, tires, cars, and beverages. Songs, movies, books, and television are filled with sex. The pervasiveness of sexual messages may make sexual involvement more enticing and more acceptable to teenagers (Jorgensen & Alexander, 1981). Sex sells, and many youth are "buying."

### The Couple's Relationship

The more committed the partners are to the relationship, the more likely they are to have intercourse *and* to use contraception (Furstenberg, 1971; Jorgensen, King, & Torrey, 1980; Kantner & Zelnik, 1972). The relative power of each partner and the extent of traditional sex roles in their relationship may influence the use of contraception (Scales, 1977). If the female

## BOX 9-1
### *Continued*

has power in the sexual and contraceptive aspects of the relationship, pregnancy risk is decreased because the partners are likely to have sex less frequently and are more likely to use contraception (Jorgensen et al., 1980).

### Psychological Influences

Adolescents may consciously or unconsciously want to become parents. Those concerned about masculinity or femininity may choose parenthood as a means of reassurance. If a mother began childbearing in her teens, her daughters are more likely to do so (Baldwin & Cain, 1980; Furstenberg, 1978; Landy, Schubert, Cleland, Clark, & Montgomery, 1983; "With Help from Families," 1979). If the father is absent or emotionally distant, risk of teenage pregnancy is higher (Jorgensen et al., 1980; Landy et al., 1983). Pregnancy may be an attempt by the teenager to fill the lack of warmth and love in her life (Nadelson & Notman, 1977; Osofsky & Osofsky, 1978).

### Lack of Alternatives

Some teenagers, particularly those in low-income neighborhoods, believe they have few prospects for the future. Poor academic performance and few marketable skills mean they can get only menial, low-paying jobs. They see few role models who have become "successful."

In their environment, adult status for women may be obtained largely by parenthood. This lack of alternatives for obtaining adult status and personal fulfillment places lower-income teenagers at higher risk for pregnancy (Furstenberg, 1976; Klein, 1978).

Clearly, no single answer explains all the reasons for teenage pregnancies.

## OUTCOMES OF TEENAGE PREGNANCIES

Each year there are over 1 million teenage pregnancies in the United States, and most cause stress for the girl, her partner, and her family. There are four options for resolving these pregnancies: abortion, adoption, marriage, and single parenting. No simple, easy answers exist for an unwanted pregnancy. Each woman must choose an option on the basis of her own beliefs and situation. Even failing to choose an alternative—by denying the pregnancy, ignoring the adoption alternative, or postponing any decision—is making a choice. Let's look at the benefits and problems of each choice.

### Abortion

In 1978 about 38% of teenage pregnancies (almost 434,000) were terminated by abortion (Alan Guttmacher Institute,

1981). In 1973 the Supreme Court ruled that abortion was a private matter between a woman and her physician. Ninety-one percent of all abortions are performed in the first trimester (Henshaw, Forrest, Sullivan, & Tietze, 1984). The majority of women who have an abortion feel relieved and positive about this choice (Chilman, 1978; Osofsky & Osofsky, 1972). In one study, 20% of the teenagers surveyed regretted their choice. These girls were more likely to be Catholic, to be Chicano, to hold conservative views on abortion, and to come from low-income homes (Evans, Selstad, & Welcher, 1976).

The financial cost is generally $200–300 for a first-trimester abortion but much higher for a second-trimester abortion, which requires hospitalization. The emotional costs for women who choose this option (rather than being coerced) generally are outweighed by their feelings of relief. Because an abortion is a minor medical procedure, it does not interrupt education, employment, or future goals. Finally, the health risks are less than those of carrying a pregnancy to term.

### Health Consequences of Carrying to Term

Because the next three options (adoption, marriage, and single

*continues*

**BOX 9-1**
*Continued*

parenting) all require carrying the pregnancy to term, health consequences for the teenaged mother and her child are discussed here. Teenaged mothers are 15% more likely to suffer from toxemia (increased blood pressure, swelling, and in severe cases coma, convulsions, and possibly death), 92% more likely to have anemia (a deficiency in red blood cells with decreased energy level), and 23% more likely to have complications from a premature birth than mothers aged 20–24 (Alan Guttmacher Institute, 1981). The risks are even higher for those who are poor or Black. Children of adolescent mothers are 39% more likely to be of low birth weight, a major cause of many serious infant health problems and even death (Alan Guttmacher Institute, 1981). Some studies have found that almost all these risks can be reduced or eliminated by early and regular prenatal care

(Baldwin & Cain, 1980). A teenager who decides to carry her pregnancy to term should therefore seek early prenatal care, eat nutritious food, and follow medical advice.

## Adoption

Today fewer than 10% of unmarried pregnant teenagers choose adoption. These mothers (and often the fathers too) do so because they recognize the impact their limitations would have on their child as well as the impact of the child on their lives. This choice is a wrenching experience as parents struggle to have reason prevail over emotion. It is not a choice made by parents who don't care but one made by parents who care very much.

The birth parent(s) pays no fee to place the child for adoption. The medical costs for pregnancy and delivery may be paid by the adoption agency.

After the mother has recovered from labor and delivery, she can resume her education or employment. An adoption will have little impact on her long-term prospects for education, employment, and marriage. No data are available on the emotional costs, but we do know that most of these women resume their lives and eventually have families. The vast majority of adopted children become an integral part of a family and grow up in a financially more stable environment than the birth parents could have provided (Bachrach, 1983). As a choice, adoption has few if any financial costs, possible short-term interruption of education or employment, and uncertain emotional costs. The long-term outlook for these mothers and children is very positive.

## Marriage

Young women who choose marriage are more likely to

---

test tube!). The fertilized ova are then placed in the woman's uterus, with hope that at least one will implant. Pregnancy occurs in approximately one out of seven cases (Richard Falk, personal communication, October 17, 1983).

Some couples in which the woman cannot conceive have taken another extraordinary measure and hired another woman to conceive and bear a child for them. In this process the **surrogate** (substitute) **mother** is paid to become pregnant (through artificial insemination) with

the husband's sperm, carry the pregnancy to term, and give the baby to the father. The child is then adopted by the wife; the husband is the biological parent, and the wife is the adoptive parent. Occasionally there have been legal problems when the surrogate mother decides to keep the child or when the parents-to-be decide they do not want the child.

These options are expensive—more than $4000 per month for each *in vitro* fertilization attempt, with only a 40% success rate after four

**Box 9-1**
*Continued*

come from homes with either very happy or very unhappy marriages and lower socioeconomic status, to have traditional role values and a low achievement drive, and to have begun dating at a young age (Chilman, 1978). Child rearing while a teenager is likely to interrupt and perhaps terminate the young mother's education, make it harder to find employment, and restrict employment to lower-paying jobs (Alan Guttmacher Institute, 1981).

Economic strain in these newly formed families is likely because either or both partners have less education and skills than those who marry in their twenties (Chilman, 1978; deLissovoy, 1973; Furstenberg, 1976). Divorce and separation are more likely than for those who marry in their twenties (Alan Guttmacher Institute, 1981; Baldwin & Cain, 1980; Furstenberg, 1976). Hence, children of teenaged mothers are more

likely to grow up in a one-parent household, a situation that is also associated with lower income. In summary, if the marriage is stable and income is sufficient, the outlook for parents and the child is generally positive. If the marriage or income is strained, the mother and child are likely to have less favorable outcomes.

**Single Parenting**

Most unmarried teenaged mothers live with relatives, usually parents, who provide financial, emotional, and child-care support and probably share the mother's child-rearing responsibilities and authority. Only 50% of women who had had a child before age 18 had finished high school by age 24, in contrast to 97% of those who had not had children by age 24 (Card & Wise, 1978). This gap in education remained regardless of socioeconomic status, race, academic aptitude, and achieve-

ment. Single teenaged mothers are more likely to be on welfare; 61% of the women who received Aid to Families with Dependent Children in 1975 had begun child rearing while they were teenagers (Moore, 1978).

Support from relatives can offset some of the negative consequences of single parenting, although families may also interfere with the young mother's child rearing. The consequences of teenage single parenting are generally negative, and yet many teenaged mothers manage to complete their education and obtain secure, good-paying, and rewarding jobs. Many learn the necessary skills to be nurturing parents and provide a positive environment for their children and eventually form successful marriages. But reaching these goals is difficult. An unintended pregnancy during adolescence adds stress to an already tumultuous stage of development.

months (Richard Falk, personal communication, October 17, 1983), or up to $25,000 for a surrogate adoption process (Avery, 1983). However, cost may be irrelevant for couples who desperately want a child.

Another option exists for childless couples—adoption. A couple may apply to adopt a child through a licensed adoption agency. After several interviews and visits to their home, their caseworker notifies them of whether they have been approved to adopt a child. If they are ac-

cepted, the waiting begins. If they want to adopt an infant, they may have to wait many months or even years. If they want an older child, a minority child, or a handicapped child or are willing to adopt more than one child from the same family, their waiting period may be short.

Adoption may cost several thousand dollars, depending on the couple's income and their willingness to accept a hard-to-place child. For a better understanding of the experience of being an adoptive parent, see Box 9-2.

**BOX 9-2**
*On Being an Adoptive Parent*

In a textbook crammed with facts intended for the mind, this box is written from the heart. In a textbook where research is intermingled (we hope) with humor, this insert may appear frivolous sentimentality to some. But my co-authors have encouraged me to undertake this exercise—you see, our son is adopted.

It has been no small task for me to write this. I have procrastinated on bringing pencil to paper for over a year. In my own defense, I must say it's not that I haven't wanted to write it; it's just that I've struggled with what to say and to whom I should say it.

Should I share with you our five-year wait before a home study began? (A home study is the determination of whether a couple—or, in other cases, a single person—are suitable for adopting a child.) Do I share with you the hours we spent with our adoption caseworker talking about ourselves, our families, our marriage as she tried to determine whether a child should be placed with us? Or should I tell you about the night, six weeks after we had been approved, when we first learned of our son's birth a few weeks earlier? Should I tell you of the shock, the disbelief, the panic that swept over both of us as we rushed around our community in a frantic drive to prepare for his arrival 48 hours later? Or should I tell you about the day he arrived—so small, so frail, and yet determined, even

then, to express his opinion on the proceedings? (My wife contends I imagined it, but I swear that as we left the agency with our less than 1-month-old son, he said "Nobody told me these guys would be novices!") Or perhaps I should share how my life has changed since his arrival—how the very center of my being has shifted to focus on him.

As I think about it now, what I want to share is a message to his biological mother and to all the other biological mothers who choose to make the sacrifice of permitting their son or daughter a chance at a life they know they would not be able to provide. Chris and I love (y)our son.

In comparing biological, step-, and adopted children, Bachrach (1983) found that adopted children were more likely to live in financially well-off families with older mothers who had more education and to have fewer siblings. Adoptive parents generally have more resources (time, money, education) to share with a child. It is likely that the child of a premaritally pregnant mother has much to gain from being placed for adoption.

We have digressed to discuss what happens when a couple have difficulty conceiving a child. The extensive and costly procedures that such couples undergo illustrate the deep desire many people have to raise children. As medical science progresses, new and more effective treatments will be developed. Let's return now to the typical couple and look at the impact of pregnancy on their lives.

## The Pregnancy Experience

The most obvious effects of pregnancy are on the woman's figure. Some women are troubled by these changes and worry that they are no longer attractive to their husbands (Brazelton, 1981; Russell, 1974). In some couples, sexual interest declines during the pregnancy, particularly during the last trimester (Masters & Johnson, 1966). These changes are less troublesome when couples realize they are common and temporary.

The physical changes that accompany pregnancy are complex. The uterus softens and expands, breasts engorge and prepare for nursing, and hormones flow throughout the body, helping it adjust to the growing fetus. Many women experience nausea, dizziness, tiredness, and swelling during part or all of a pregnancy, but many do not. Women should check with their doctor about any problems they are having and about an appropriate diet.

Pregnant women should not have X rays, should avoid ingesting in any way substances that may be toxic to the fetus, such as breathing paint, and should not take drugs unless they have specifically been shown to *not* affect the fetus. (Unfortunately, the embryo is most vulnerable during the early weeks of pregnancy, before a woman may know she is pregnant.) Cigarette smoking should be avoided because it is associated with delivery of low-birth-weight babies, who are at higher risk for complications. Alcohol consumption should be reduced if not avoided completely. Researchers have determined that two or more alcoholic drinks a day may damage a fetus, but they have not found what level of alcohol consumption is safe (Mukherjee & Hodgen, 1982). They therefore recommend that pregnant women drink *no* alcohol.

Early prenatal (before the birth) care is very important. Most obstetricians (doctors who specialize in delivering babies) think it is so important that they charge the same fee for providing prenatal care (with an average of ten or more office visits) *and* delivering a baby as for only delivering a baby. Doctors recommend that prenatal care begin in the first trimester and continue regularly throughout the pregnancy. This approach enables the doctor to gain an understanding of this particular pregnancy, to monitor the progress of the mother and fetus, and to determine early whether there are problems.

If a hereditary disease or the mother's age (over 35) is a concern, chorion villi sampling or amniocentesis may be suggested—extraction of fluid and villi, or cells cast off by the fetus (from the chorion or the amniotic sac, respectively). In

chorion villi sampling, a small flexible tube is inserted through the cervix to extract villi (hairlike projections) from the chorion. In amniocentesis, a long needle is inserted through the abdomen into the uterus to collect this material. The cells develop in a laboratory, and the genes in them are examined for defects. If there are genetic defects, the couple is faced with a difficult decision: do they want to terminate this pregnancy, or do they want to raise a child they know will suffer from a genetic disorder? There are no easy answers to a problem pregnancy.

Recently medical science has begun to diagnose and even treat some problems of the developing fetus inside the uterus (Fadiman, 1983). In general, these problems are not genetic but are developmental, such as a blocked urinary tract. As fetal medicine progresses, more problems may be treated before the baby is born.

The physical changes that accompany pregnancy are only one aspect of the changes experienced by the parents-to-be. A planned pregnancy is a time of celebration as well as a time of introspection. The parents-to-be may be troubled by many questions: Will our baby be normal? Will we be good parents? How will we manage financially? Are we ready to adapt our lives to a child's needs? Have we made a mistake? These worries are countered by joy and contentment. Changes in mood are common for both husband and wife, and worry may be a coping mechanism to help them prepare to respond to their baby's needs (Brazelton, 1981).

Fathers-to-be have special concerns. They may worry about their wives' health. In fact, an estimated 11% of fathers-to-be experience **couvade**—pregnancylike symptoms such as loss of appetite, headaches, nausea, and insomnia (Trethowan & Conlon, 1965). These symptoms disappear after the baby is born. Men may worry about their ability to support the family or their ability to be good fathers. Such concerns are typical in the transition to parenthood.

In addition to these concerns, partners may

reassess their financial situation. If she is working, how long will she continue? Will she return to work? If so, how soon? If not, what adjustments will they make to a reduced income? Even if she does return to work, they will have new expenses and may need to make financial adjustments. Will insurance cover medical expenses? If not, they need to make arrangements to pay these costs.

Introduction of a child into the family affects the couple's principal resources—time, energy, and money—and adjustments must be made. During pregnancy they begin to make many changes that will help them cope with the arrival of the baby. In addition to those mentioned above, physical preparations need to be made. The baby will need space, a bed, clothing, diapers, food, and diverse supplies. In short, a first baby changes the way the family lives.

 *Among the adjustments that couples have to make when they have a baby, which do you think are the most troublesome? Why?*

## Giving Birth

Childbirth preparation classes have spread across the country during the past 20 years, helping parents-to-be understand the birth process and giving basic information about infants. Accompanying this movement are changes in hospital policies that allow fathers-to-be in labor and delivery rooms (in some cases, even for caesarean sections) and reduce the amount of medication the mother receives during labor and delivery. Some preparation courses, such as Lamaze classes, teach pregnant women techniques to cope with pain during labor. Husbands are taught to coach their wives, helping them get through the pain with a minimum of medication.

Frederick Leboyer, a French physician, has influenced birthing procedures in many communities. Believing that birth is a traumatic experience for the infant, who leaves the moist, warm, quiet, dark environment of the uterus and is squeezed through the birth canal to begin breathing in a dry, noisy, bright, strange environment, Leboyer (1975) suggests that the delivery room be darker and quieter. The newborn is placed on the mother's abdomen shortly after birth to be reunited with the mother and to continue to experience tactile closeness. After a few minutes the baby is gently washed in warm water and returned to the parents. These procedures emphasize making the environment respond to the needs of the infant rather than making the infant respond to the environment.

Some parents are choosing to have their babies at home, often delivered by nurse-midwives, who are specially trained in childbirth and competent to assist in normal deliveries. When midwives suspect complications, they refer their patients to physicians. Midwives may also provide prenatal care and often stay with the parents throughout the labor and delivery process, lending encouragement and advice.

For most women, giving birth is an arduous and painful process that ends suddenly with a baby. Parents are simultaneously exhausted from the struggle and ecstatic with their newborn. The experience is frequently overwhelming, as feelings of pride, joy, elation, and relief flood their senses. One father in the delivery room, trying to tell his wife what sex the child was, reported later: "I looked at the baby and couldn't remember how to tell for a moment! My mind just wasn't working." Perhaps jubilation interferes with thinking. In any case, the birth of a healthy baby is a moment of relief and joy.

Of course, not every delivery is simple, and not every baby is perfect. When there are problems, physicians may ask the father to leave the room, involve other experts in the case, and move quickly. The birth of an at-risk baby is emotionally traumatic. Parents may blame themselves for what they did or didn't do. They need the support of hospital personnel, relatives, and friends in dealing with this crisis. Survival rates for at-risk infants have improved remarkably over the past 20 years. Nonetheless, having a less than perfect child is disappointing and stressful (Featherstone, 1980; Paul, 1981).

# SOME FACTS FOR PARENTS

Although few of us become parents by surprise, the realities of parenthood often surprise most of us. We may construct elaborate fantasies about teaching our children to walk, talk, read, and play games, but few of us daydream about coping with disobedience, emergency-room visits, or petty theft. Tantrums, illnesses, fights, misbehavior, stubbornness, and impossible demands are challenges that children present. Parents of one newborn said, "We knew where babies came from but we didn't know what they were *like*" (LeMasters, 1974, p. 202). Often to our dismay, they continue to surprise us with what they are like as they grow. Of course, there are moments of pure joy with children. To see them progress, to share their triumphs, to receive their thanks and love all add to our lives.

People in general and parents in particular often have mixed feelings about children. They demand a great deal of our time, energy, and caring. In return we get frustration as well as appreciation. This section will outline the types of development children experience and some of the realities of child rearing.

## Aspects of Child Development

Different types of development occur throughout the life cycle at different rates and are particularly evident in children. When parents can recognize these aspects of development, they can appreciate their child's progress on many levels.

*Physical development* is the most obvious, and it receives considerable attention from adults, especially with infants: "How much does she weigh?" "How long is he?" Questions about size and age continue throughout life, and children may become sensitive to their differences from peers. Being taller, shorter, slimmer, or heavier can affect the development of a child's self-image. Most children detest being different physically, and their concerns about these differences vary according to their personalities and the importance of their peer group. Physical development is greatest during the prenatal period, early childhood, and puberty.

*Sensorimotor development* (development of senses and coordination) begins in the uterus when the fetus first learns to find its fist and suck it. Newborn babies can see and hear, although these senses will improve during the first few weeks of life. They will turn toward a soft voice to see where the sound originates, and they prefer women's voices (Brazelton, 1981). If an object comes toward them within 30 centimeters (about three inches), they will raise a hand to try to avoid it (Bower, 1981). If an adult within their field of vision (about eight inches) sticks out a tongue, the newborn will even mimic this behavior! Clearly, the sensorimotor skills of the newborn are much greater than most people recognize. This development continues at a rapid pace as children learn to reach for toys, to crawl, to walk, and to play physical games.

*Personality development* progresses from birth. Research has confirmed what parents have long reported—that children are born with different personalities (Chess, Thomas, & Birch, 1959; Thomas, Chess, & Birch, 1970). Some are quiet, happy, responsive, and regular in their schedules; others are very active, easily upset, unresponsive, and irregular in their schedules. Still others show combinations of traits. Parents often have children with very different personalities, which makes dealing effectively and fairly with them truly a challenge.

*Emotional development* begins as children learn to deal with their feelings. When they realize they cannot always have what they want, they may fuss and cry. Parents who accept these outbursts without giving in teach their children that getting angry doesn't change things. Eventually, children learn that they can have some control over their feelings and that other people have feelings too. Joy, pride, frustration, and anger are normal and contribute to the child's emotional development.

*Cognitive* (intellectual) *development* has a major impact on children's lives. They learn

*Curiosity is a driving force behind the acquisition of knowledge in young children. (It is also the source of many a mess.)*

from birth about their environment and themselves. "Crying brings help" is one of the first lessons. They progress to learning that help is not always available, then to learning that different people treat them differently, then to learning that toys that are dropped will fall. They come to understand that objects have permanence—they still exist somewhere even if the child can't see them. And before they can understand what is being said, they learn to listen to language and to make sounds. As children grow, their ability to think increases in complexity. Their interests expand from wanting to know about their immediate world (neighborhood and friends) to wanting to know about the universe.

Children begin to acquire language skills in the first year of life. Parents should talk to babies, even though they cannot understand. It helps them learn that people make sounds and encourages them to do the same.

Parents are the first and most important teachers of their children. Throughout their children's lives, parents need to transmit a belief that learning is fun. Babies are natural learners and will enjoy learning if not discouraged. Children vary, of course, in the ways they learn best, the kinds of information they absorb easily, and how quickly they understand. These differences challenge parents to build on each child's strengths and provide extra support when learning is difficult.

*Social development* (learning to interact with others) occurs during the first year of life as babies learn to smile and coo first at parents and later at others. Inanimate objects can play an important role in social development at early ages as children teach and mimic each other. One study found that children as young as 18–24 months preferred playing with objects or another child to playing with their mothers (Eckerman, Whatley, & Kutz, 1981). Social development progresses rapidly through learning in the family. It is fostered by interaction with others,

## BOX 9-3
### Guidelines for Parents

There is no one right way to raise a child, any more than there is one way to be a boss or make a friend. There are many styles, some more effective than others. Whatever the approach, building a child's self-esteem and helping the child learn to cope with life are essential. Here are some suggestions for making parenting rewarding.

1. Be flexible.

2. Find ways to enjoy your child.

3. Try to recognize and appreciate each stage of development.

4. Understand the purpose of your child's misbehavior.

5. Spend time (ten minutes or so) alone with each child each day.

6. Listen to your child and let him or her know you understand (although you do not have to agree).

7. Try to view the world from your child's perspective occasionally, to give you a better understanding of the situation.

8. Teach your child—about emotions, development, behavior, rules, and life in general.

including friends and schoolmates. During the teen years, interaction with peers is a major preoccupation of many adolescents.

*Sexual development* begins *in utero* with the formation of the reproductive system. Males may have erections before birth, and newborn females may have vaginal lubrication (Masters & Johnson, 1966). Curiosity about sexual differences, sexual development, and where babies come from is common in preschool children. With the onset of puberty, marked changes occur in internal and external reproductive organs, sparking greater interest in one's own and others' development.

Children are a continuing challenge to their parents as their development progresses. Delightful stages are followed by exasperating ones, all part of the process of normal development. The fact that children do not understand these changes adds to their confusion and frustration. It is important that parents see the pattern in development so they can recognize what is happening to their child and know what to expect.

During adolescence, identity mushrooms and children begin the gradual process of detaching themselves from their parents. They develop the capacity to function as adults, taking responsibility for themselves and their behavior. These changes do not occur easily. Instead, being an adolescent is like driving an old car—it alternately surges forward, backfires, and pokes along.

The following principles about development should be kept in mind. First, children are experiencing many types of development simultaneously, though not necessarily at the same rate. For example, in infancy sensorimotor development is rapid, while emotional development is much slower. Second, not all children develop at the same rate. Some go through a stage earlier and some later. Third, one "correct" way to raise all children does not exist. Because their personalities vary, effective techniques with one child may be ineffective or even counterproductive with another.

It is easy to see why experts have analyzed families from the developmental perspective. Just as children have tasks to master, from learning to walk to choosing a mate, so do parents, from providing total care for a helpless infant to allowing a teenager to make decisions and accept responsibility. The hovering behavior so essential to a newborn is stifling to an older child. In short, the challenges of parenting change as children develop, and parents must change their behavior to be responsive to their children's needs.

Clearly, growing up is a complex process and is often difficult and confusing. Most children and youth do not know that these changes in behavior and outlook are normal. Not surprisingly, children are a continuing challenge. It often seems that just as we adjust to one stage and learn how to help our children grow, they enter a new stage that requires further adaptation. Making this process even more complicated, most parents are coping with more than one child at a time. Being a parent is fascinating and demanding, joyous and frustrating. It is not easy, and it is not for everyone.

? *How could understanding child development influence a parent's behavior? Choose a childhood behavior and analyze it from the different developmental perspectives described in this section.*

## Roles of Parents

Among parental role responsibilities (see Box 9-4) is *socialization,* the process of helping a child become a contributing member of society. It requires providing for children's emotional and physical needs as well as helping them understand limits, comply with rules, and gradually learn acceptable behavior.

Parents who allow their children total freedom do a disservice to themselves, others, and, most of all, their children. Children who think everyone should comply with their wishes are self-centered, ungovernable, and usually disliked—outcomes parents rarely want. At the other extreme, rigid discipline is often counterproductive and results in rebellion. It is important to be reasonable in setting limits, to modify the child's environment when that is appropriate, and to strive for fairness and consistency. Love, respect, and support should undergird all these efforts. Unfortunately, it is much easier to state these objectives than to reach them. Mistakes and misunderstandings are normal.

In contrast to child-rearing books of the recent past (Gesell, Ilg, & Ames, 1956; Ilg & Ames, 1955; Spock, 1961), throughout this chapter we have referred to "parents," rather than to "mothers." Only a few decades ago, fathers were expected to play a minimal role in socializing their children, especially young children. Their responsibility was to support the family. When children were old enough to play games or sports, many fathers began these activities with them. Recent research results, however, document that fathers are very important in their children's development. It was previously thought that men did not know how to deal with children, especially very young children. Researchers now have found that fathers can be just as nurturant as mothers and can be competent caretakers, even of infants (Parke & Sawin, 1976). In fact, fathers interact with their infants differently than mothers (Brazelton, 1983). Fathers poke and stimulate their babies; mothers talk to and stroke them. By age 2, children express a preference for the type of play fathers initiate, which is more physical and less intellectual than that of mothers (Clarke-Stewart, 1978; Lamb & Lamb, 1976). Researchers have also found that fathers spend the majority of their time socializing their children and minimal time providing for their physical care (Parke & Sawin, 1976; Rendina & Dickerscheid, 1976).

Of course, after a death, divorce, or desertion, the father may be the only parent. The movie *Kramer vs. Kramer* illustrated some of the strains a father may experience when he becomes the primary caretaker. Mr. Kramer didn't know how to cook breakfast, had difficulty doing laundry,

*As Dustin Hoffman's character in* Kramer vs. Kramer *demonstrates, sex is not a factor in parental competency. In fact, fathers play an important developmental role in children's lives, recent research has shown.*

and strained to juggle employment and child care. Exploratory research, however, has found that such fathers report coping reasonably well with their new roles (Mendes, 1976; Orthner, Brown, & Ferguson, 1976).

Research shows that fathers can have a significant impact on psychological and social development (Lamb & Lamb, 1976, p. 381). Ideally, both parents play a role in the socialization of their children. To do so effectively requires communication between spouses on child-rearing practices and the child's behavior.

## Differing Parental Behavior

Child-rearing attitudes and behavior are influenced by education, social class, and ethnic group (Bartz & Levine, 1978). These elements may come from diverse sources. For example, the many educational influences on parents may include the advice of experts promoting the latest child-rearing principles through the media, experiences in being with children (dealing with brothers and sisters while growing up, babysitting), and formal training in parenting skills.

Norms in our society generally reflect middle-class values. Other groups typically are measured against these norms, and differences have often been considered deviant or unacceptable (Staples & Mirande, 1980). Recently researchers have recognized that "different" does not mean "bad" and have tried to assess the impact and appropriateness of differences for subgroups.

An example of this approach to research is a study of mothers' aspirations for and socialization of their children and the children's actual achievement (Blau, 1972). Both boys and girls responded more positively to parental warmth and attention than to discipline. White and Black working-class mothers were more likely to encourage and praise daughters and more likely to criticize sons. In these families, girls tended to show intellectual competence earlier than boys. In families where boys and girls were treated alike, their intellectual competence was similar. To explain these differences in child-rearing practices, Blau theorized that working-class fathers want their sons raised strictly, to prepare them for employment. Since initiative, creativity, and outspokenness are devalued and dangerous to continued employment in many working-class jobs, discipline and coercion may contribute to sons' preparation for the work force. Thus, raising sons and daughters differently may have some positive outcomes for sons in working-class families, even though their intellectual competence may suffer.

Minority groups have higher poverty rates than the general population, and many studies are not able to separate socioeconomic status from minority-group membership. Yet, even among lower-socioeconomic-status families,

## BOX 9-4
## *Parental Role Responsibilities*

In constructing a survey instrument on parental role responsibilities, Lucia Gilbert and Gary Hanson questioned 900 working men and women on their views. They asked how important each item was as a parental responsibility, under normal circumstances, during various stages of rearing a child. Using their responses, the researchers identified 13 categories of responsibilities with five to seven items each. The categories and representative items appear here.

| Category | Representative Item |
|---|---|
| 1. Teaching cognitive development | Help child develop reading skills |
| 2. Teaching handling of emotions | Teach child how to be affectionate |
| 3. Teaching social skills | Teach child how to compromise |
| 4. Teaching norms and social values | Help child develop values to live by |
| 5. Teaching physical health | Engage in athletic play with child |
| 6. Teaching personal hygiene | Make sure child bathes regularly |
| 7. Teaching survival skills | Show child what to do in case of fire |
| 8. Basic needs—health care | Arrange routine dental check-ups |
| 9. Basic needs—material (food, clothing, shelter) | Provide adequate shelter for child |
| 10. Basic needs—emotional | Express affection toward child |
| 11. Basic needs—child care | Provide for care when parent absent |
| 12. Assist child in dealing with social institutions | Encourage child to have a sense of civic responsibility |
| 13. Assist child in dealing with other family members | Facilitate the relationships between child and his/her grandparents |

child-rearing behaviors differ across minority groups. We will look briefly at child-rearing attitudes and behaviors in Black and Mexican-American (Chicano) families.

Black parents expect their infants to exhibit certain behaviors (control over body functions and feelings) much earlier than the average child does (Bartz & Levine, 1978). Black parents are highly supportive and encouraging of their children (like White middle-class parents) and yet highly controlling (unlike White middle-class

parents). Some researchers have concluded that this environment is negative for children, but others have found it positive. For example, Baumrind (1972) found that authoritarian Black families raised daughters who were likely to be self-assertive and independent. It seems that the mixture of high control (which often has negative outcomes such as hostility to parents or passivity) and support and encouragement has a beneficial outcome for Black children, particularly females.

Immigrant families' efforts to socialize their children are filled with difficulties. Values taught at school (such as speaking English and becoming Americanized) may conflict with those taught at home (retaining the group's language and culture), creating intergenerational conflict. This stress is found at all socioeconomic levels, even when immigrants are familiar with the new values before arriving (Wakil, Siddique, & Wakil, 1981). Which values should prevail is a dilemma both parents and children face.

Largest among these immigrant groups is the Mexican-American population, which is expected to surpass Blacks as the largest minority group in the United States by 1990 (Maloney, 1981). Researchers report conflicting conclusions on whether Chicano families are male-dominated (Vega, Hough, & Romero, 1983) or egalitarian (Staples & Mirande, 1980). They do agree that children are highly valued in these families and that parent/child relationships are supportive and nurturing. In Chicano families, providing needed help to other family members—not just children but members of all ages—is required (Vega et al., 1983).

Parenting, never an easy job, is made more difficult when the family's values conflict with the culture's. Parenting behaviors are influenced by personal experience and modified by the culture at large. Changes are often difficult, particularly when they conflict with the views of one's subculture. For more on the problems faced by minorities, see Chapter 15.

> **?** *What are the benefits and liabilities of different approaches to raising children, for both parents and children?*

## Some Realities of Raising Children

Much more is involved in raising children than understanding child development. Although learning effective child-rearing behaviors is es-

sential and although these behaviors take up a major portion of parents' time and energy, there is more to the picture. The monetary costs of raising children, dealing with sibling rivalry, coping with illnesses and accidents, and selecting child care are additional realities in most families.

Children are expensive. There was a time in this nation's history when Americans spoke of their children as assets, not as liabilities, but no longer. As the costs of housing, food, and everything else have gone up, so has the cost of raising a child. To some degree this explains the gradual decline in birthrates since the 18th century. A child today, whose total cost often exceeds the median price of a new home, may well be considered a luxury by some.

Depending on their financial resources, most families will spend between $35,710 (on a thrifty standard) and $73,491 (on a moderate standard) to raise a child born in 1980 to age 18 (Edwards, 1981). Those who can afford a liberal (luxury) standard might, depending on their region of the country, spend as much as $121,490 in 1980 dollars to raise their child to age 18. Table 9-3 shows the annual cost of raising a child in an urban area in 1980 on three living standards—thrifty, low, and moderate.

**TABLE 9-3.** *Annual cost of raising an urban child from birth to age 18, at three cost levels*

|  | Thrifty | Low | Moderate |
|---|---|---|---|
| Food at home | $10,444 | $12,899 | $16,151 |
| Food away from home | 597 | 870 | 1,950 |
| Clothing | 2,577 | 3,773 | 5,493 |
| Housing | 11,575 | 15,615 | 24,795 |
| Medical care | 1,903 | 2,508 | 3,870 |
| Education | 303 | 366 | 1,215 |
| Transportation | 5,304 | 7,696 | 11,686 |
| Other | 3,008 | 4,627 | 8,331 |
| Annual average | 1,984 | 2,686 | 4,083 |
| Total | 35,711 | 48,354 | 73,491 |

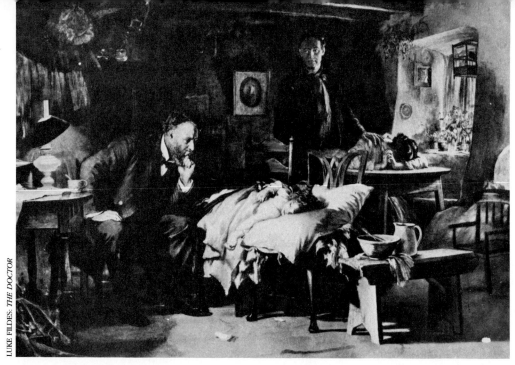

*Fildes' painting of a 19th century physician tending a critically ill child captures on canvas the fears of all parents. Examine the painting carefully. Notice the distance separating the parents from their child and the position of the child's body. What do you think the artist is trying to communicate to his audience in this painting?*

Another reality of raising children for most families is sibling rivalry, the normal conflict that goes on between **siblings** (sisters and brothers). Parents may inadvertently foster such problems by favoring or demeaning one child: "Why can't you be neat like your brother?" or "You never do anything right." Even if parents don't contribute to the problem, children will fuss and fight with one another. They may be vying for parental attention, or they may just irritate one another. It is natural for siblings, like anyone else, to disagree on many things; use of personal possessions, responsibility for chores, and playing together are only a few examples. Establishing rules, staying out of arguments, and recognizing that sibling rivalry is natural may help parents cope.

Another reality of raising children is illness and injury. Most problems are minor—colds, earaches, allergies, cuts, bruises, broken bones. Almost every child has some of these problems. A fussy, sick child may be hard to comfort and may demand extra attention. In general, children are hardy creatures and readily recover from colds, earaches, and broken bones.

Of course, not all illnesses and accidents are minor. Children may be seriously injured or contract illnesses that require hospitalization. Some do not survive. More children die as a result of car accidents than from any single disease (Reisinger et al., 1981). All states now require small children, usually under age 5 or weighing less than 40 pounds, to be restrained in specially designed car seats (Physicians for Automotive Safety, 1985). The heartbreak of losing a child is enormous (Deford, 1983; Gunther, 1971). It does not matter what age the child is. Parents who lose a child during pregnancy or shortly after birth, as well as parents whose child was an adult, are grief-stricken (see Chapter 18).

Another reality of raising children is child care. Virtually all children are cared for part of the time by someone other than their parents—for example, other relatives, babysitters, nursery school teachers, day-care providers. This change in caregivers can be a positive experience for both parents and children, giving each some time to develop separately.

In 1950, only 12% of mothers with children under age 6 were employed; in 1982, 50% were (Burud, Collins, & Divine-Hawkins, 1983). Who cares for these estimated 8.5 million children? Table 9-4 shows that relatives care for 43% of these children. An additional 33% are cared for in home settings by nonrelatives, and 15% more are cared for in group care settings.

What should parents look for to ensure that their children are well cared for? Whether evaluating babysitters, child-care-center personnel, or even relatives, the first concern is the adults' (or teenagers') ability to provide quality care for the child. Do they like children? Do they understand them? Will they play with, encourage, and supervise them? Are there enough adults for the number of children? A minimum of one adult to eight children is recommended for preschoolers.

Additional criteria are suggested for day-care centers (Battiata, 1983), but we think that most should be applied to other caretaker situations as well. Is the environment safe and clean? Are the meals nutritious and tasty? Do children get nutritious snacks in the morning and afternoon? Do children play outside as well as inside? What kind of play and learning equipment are available indoors and outdoors? Is there a balance between structured and free time? Do the children there seem to be enjoying themselves? Are parents kept informed of their child's progress and behavior?

Answers to these questions will help parents evaluate a child-care setting. The best evaluators

**TABLE 9-4.** *Child-care arrangements of working mothers, 1958 and 1977*

| Arrangement | Year | |
| --- | --- | --- |
| | 1958 (percentage) | 1977 (percentage) |
| In the child's own home | | |
| Cared for by the father | 14.7 | 10.6 |
| By another relative | 27.7 | 11.4 |
| By a nonrelative | 14.2 | 6.6 |
| | 56.6 | 28.6 |
| In another home | | |
| By a relative | 14.5 | 20.8 |
| By a nonrelative | 12.7 | 26.6 |
| | 27.2 | 47.4 |
| Group care center | 4.5 | 14.6 |
| Child "cares for self" | 0.6 | 0.4 |
| Mother takes child to work | 11.2 | 9.0 |
| | 16.3 | 24.0 |

of all are the children. If they haven't adjusted after six weeks, if they are withdrawn, cranky, or depressed, this setting is not for them. Selecting another place can make a dramatic difference in their behavior and comfort (Battiata, 1983).

Costs, sibling rivalry, illness and accidents, and child care are by no means all the issues parents face as they raise children, but they do capture the flavor of this role. Being a parent also includes making decisions about television viewing, school settings, teachers, sports participation, learning, and playmates. It is the biggest job most of us will ever undertake, demanding years of commitment and continuing adjustments. It provides a unique opportunity to contribute to the development of another human being—not to mold the child into our "ideal" but, rather, to provide a climate and a learning experience that will allow the child to develop in his or her own way, nurtured by the environment we have provided.

Participants in the White House Conference on Families in 1980 recognized the importance of prevention for promoting happy, healthy families. Among their recommendations, family-life education for children and adults was one of the highest priorities (Alexander, 1981). Unfortunately, such recommendations have not been implemented systematically in most communities, leaving it to each person to acquire this information.

## EDUCATION

Education is an important prevention tool not only in making the decision to become a parent but also after that decision if your choice is to have children. Learning about parenting, about child development and behavior, and about yourself is critical in learning to raise children. In addition to reading about these issues, actual experiences with children can be most informative. Babysitting and volunteer work with children provide opportunities to interact with them. These experiences are not the same as having our own children with total authority and responsibility, but they do help us understand what children are like.

Numerous books on child development and child rearing can be most helpful. *Between Parent and Child* (Ginott, 1969), *Between Parent and Teenager* (Ginott, 1971), *P.E.T.: Parent Effectiveness Training* (Gordon, 1970), *How to Parent* (Dodson, 1970), and *Creative Parenting* (Sears, 1982) are only a few. Libraries offer many more, some focused on children with special problems.

**?** *What other educational approaches might be used to acquire child-rearing competency? What have been your own educational experiences in understanding children and child rearing? Which have been most instructive?*

## COMMUNITY ORGANIZATION/ SYSTEMS INTERVENTION

In recent years a number of structural changes in organizations have been developed to help parents improve their parenting skills. Perhaps the most widespread may be the development of childbirth education classes. Thousands of parents participate in these classes every year, learning not only about labor and delivery but also about infant care. Courses have also been offered nationwide on effective parenting strategies, such as Parent Effectiveness Training (P.E.T.) and Systematic Training for Effective Parenting (STEP).

Many communities have developed special programs to help teenaged parents become effective parents and adults. These programs teach young mothers about child care and development and may also provide a full academic program, health services, employment skills training, or counseling services, all aimed at making the mother a more effective parent.

 *What changes could society make that would assist parents in their child-rearing responsibilities? What would be the benefits and liabilities of these changes?*

## COMPETENCY PROMOTION

Some schools have instituted child-care centers on the premises to provide young children with quality care—and to give older students the opportunity to work with young children. Far better than just reading about child development, students in these programs get to work with many children, learning firsthand about child development, personality differences, and child-rearing techniques. Many of these programs combine child development textbooks and classroom instruction with the laboratory experience, giving students an opportunity to apply theories and strategies to actual situations (Durbin, 1973).

In recognition of the benefits of this approach, a unique project was developed to teach sixth-grade boys about babies. Described in *Oh, Boy! Babies!* (Herzig & Mali, 1980), this project teaches child development and skills in caring for young children. It helps boys become more familiar and comfortable with babies. It is likely that the "graduates" of this program will be more comfortable caring for their children than boys who haven't had this experience.

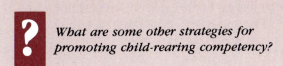

*What are some other strategies for promoting child-rearing competency?*

## NATURAL CAREGIVING

Parenting is natural caregiving—parents give to their children. But who gives to the parents? Often children do. A parent who can say "I've had a bad day—I need a hug" is likely to be showered with affection, even from young children. Parents can, of course, support each other in their roles as parents, expressing appreciation and ad-

miration. The family, then, is the primary unit for natural caregiving. With the efforts of all involved, it can become a nurturing, enriching environment.

The circle of natural caregiving does not end with the family. It expands to include informal or formal advice from other parents. Neighbors, co-workers, and relatives can be rich resources of information and advice on childbearing and child rearing. Talking to others who have been through a stage of development or a particular situation can be most reassuring.

Of course, sometimes our concerns are specific and not easily solved. In such cases, joining a self-help group consisting of people who are experiencing the same concerns can be most beneficial. Diverse self-help groups have developed around parenting issues, such as Resolve, to help couples who cannot conceive; Parents Anonymous, to help parents who abuse their children; and MADD (Mothers Against Drunk Driving), to get drunk drivers off the road. Other groups exist to help discipline unruly children, to cope with handicapped children, and to help substance-abusing children. The many self-help groups that exist emphasize the abilities of adults to help other adults understand and deal with troublesome situations. They are important prevention strategies for parents.

*How can parents stimulate the development of natural caregiving in their children? Why does the development of nurturance contribute to child-rearing competency?*

# SUMMARY

Although most of us have been socialized to assume we should have children, many of us should not. The decision is important and deserves careful thought. There are both poor reasons and good reasons to have children.

Having a child changes the marital relationship and brings stress. But a child also provides an opportunity for fulfillment. For those who have fertility problems, about one in six couples, there are self-help groups and fertility specialists who can provide help. Another choice is adoption.

In this chapter we have seen that couples are rarely prepared for the realities of parenthood and that there is no one right way to raise all children. An important point to keep in mind is that parents need to be flexible.

# MAJOR POINTS TO REMEMBER

1. Parenthood is a choice with benefits and liabilities like any other choice. The benefits include personal fulfillment, the opportunity to contribute to the life of another person, and the joy of watching a child develop. The liabilities include decreased marital satisfaction, increased role strain, and demands on resources (money, time, energy).
2. Ovulation occurs 14 days *before* the start of the next period in most women.
3. Women who begin child rearing during their teenage years are more likely to be on welfare and to have less education and fewer job skills.
4. One of six couples has trouble conceiving. The problem may be the woman's, the man's, or the couple's. Medication, surgery, "test tube" fertilization, surrogate motherhood, and adoption are some options.

5. During pregnancy, it is important to get early and regular prenatal care, to eat a nutritious diet, and to abstain from smoking and drinking alcoholic beverages.
6. Children experience many types of development, including physical, sensorimotor, personality, emotional, cognitive, social, and sexual. The various types of development occur at different rates in the same child, and each type may occur at different rates for different children.
7. The primary responsibilities of parents are to socialize the child and provide for his or her physical, emotional, and security needs.
8. Fathers can be good nurturers. They interact with babies differently than mothers. They make an important contribution to their children's development.
9. How parents socialize their children is influenced by how they were raised, current child-rearing practices, socioeconomic status, and ethnic background.
10. For a moderate-income family, it will cost approximately $73,000 (in 1980 dollars) to raise a child to age 18.
11. Among the realities of raising children are sibling rivalry, illness and accidents, and the need for child care.

# ADDITIONAL SOURCES OF INFORMATION

## *Publications*

Alexander, M. G. (1971). *Nobody asked me if I wanted a baby sister.* New York: Dial Press. [Children]

Brazelton, T. B. (1981). *On becoming a family: The growth of attachment.* New York: Delacorte Press. [Adults]

Child Study Association of America. (1965). *Families are like that: Stories to read to yourself.* New York: Thomas Y. Crowell. [Children]

Ginott, H. G. (1969). *Between parent and child.* New York: Avon Books. [Adults]

Gordon, T. (1970). *P.E.T.: Parent Effectiveness Training.* New York: Peter H. Wyden. [Adults]

Guest, J. (1976). *Ordinary people.* New York: Viking Press. [Adolescents]

Herzig, A. C., & Mali, J. L. (1980). *Oh, boy! Babies!* Boston: Little, Brown. [Children]

Mosel, A. (1968). *Tikki tikki tembo.* New York: Holt, Rinehart and Winston. [Children; Chinese folktale about sibling rivalry]

Nilsson, L. (1966). *A child is born.* New York: Delacorte Press. [Children, adults]

Satir, V. (1972). *Peoplemaking.* Palo Alto, CA: Science and Behavior Books. [Adults]

Winthrop, E. (1975). *A little demonstration of affection.* New York: Harper & Row. [Adolescents]

## Organizations

Resolve, Inc.
P.O. Box 474
Belmont, MA 02178
A self-help group for couples experiencing infertility.

Parents Anonymous
22330 Hawthorne Blvd., Suite 208
Torrance, CA 90505
A self-help group for parents who abuse their children.

MELD
123 East Grant St.
Minneapolis, MN 55403
A self-help group for becoming more effective parents.

Families Anonymous
P.O. Box 344
Torrance, CA 90501
For concerned relatives of youths with behavior problems.

Association for Children and Adults with Learning Disabilities
4156 Liberty Road
Pittsburgh, PA 15234
For families with a learning-disabled child.

# 10

# DIVORCE AND THE SINGLE-PARENT FAMILY

*Have you ever* noticed how people tend to date themselves by the films and television shows they watched when they were growing up? Reluctant as the three authors are to admit it, we belong to the first generation of TV addicts. We grew up watching, in glorious shades of black and white, *The Donna Reed Show, Ozzie and Harriet, Leave It to Beaver, Father Knows Best,* and scores of other programs that depicted the American family as White, middle-class, and, most of all, nuclear. Although these television parents slept in separate beds and mom was clearly less competent than dad, they etched in our young minds an image of what family life should be. Strangely, for reasons we never understood, our families didn't match those on television. In our families, when we misbehaved badly, we were spanked. That never happened on these programs. Those cute little misunderstandings between young people and teachers that were resolved painlessly on television got us suspended and, in the case of one of us, moved by parents to a private school. Consequently, we found it extremely interesting to read, several years ago:

> Word was heard from Billy Gray, who used to play brother Bud in "Father Knows Best," the nineteen-fifties television show about the nice Anderson family who lived in the white frame house on a side street in some mythical Springfield . . . the house at which Father arrived each night, swinging open the front door and singing out, "Margaret, I'm home!" Gray said he felt "ashamed" that he had ever had anything to do with the show. It was all "totally false," he said, and had caused many Americans to feel inadequate, because they thought that that was the way life was supposed to be and that their own lives failed to measure up [*The New Yorker,* 1977, cited in Skolnick, 1979, p. 297].

# Keeping Up

Then she got single and lived happily ever after.

All of us live in a world filled with myths. We cherish beliefs that in the end justice triumphs, that the underdog has a chance of winning, and that, once married, people live happily ever after. Regrettably, life is not like a children's storybook (J. M. Bernard, 1981). The phrase "happily ever after" is used more cautiously today—particularly with regard to marriage.

In this chapter we look at the dissolution of marriage—its history, its demographics, and its impact on individuals and families. We conclude by examining not so much what can be done to prevent divorce but what can be done to promote a child's adjustment to life following the dissolution of a marriage.

## THE HISTORY OF DIVORCE

Before the advent of Christianity, the dissolution of a marriage was a civil affair. The changes in our lifetime that have made divorce easier are really nothing more than a return (for very different reasons) to practices that existed until the sixth century A.D. (Alvarez, 1981).

In Rome, for instance, marriage was a civil contract that could be dissolved by having either spouse declare a bill of divorce in the presence of seven adult Roman citizens (Kitchin, 1912).[1] Alvarez (1981, p. 109) writes that by the fifth century A.D. these laws "were so relaxed that a wife could divorce her husband for any of twelve reasons, ranging from treason and murder to introducing immoral women into his house." Enlightened as the Romans may have been, equality between the sexes was not one of their strong points (see Chapter 17), and while women could divorce for 12 reasons, men could divorce for 15, including a wife's "going to dine with men other than her relations without the knowledge of or against the wish of her husband and frequenting the circus, theater, or amphitheater after being forbidden by her husband" (Alvarez, 1981, p. 109).

It was Christianity, Kitchin (1912) contends, that redefined the nature of marriage in society. From a civil arrangement between two individuals (most often established by parents), marriage became a spiritual affair. The married state came to represent, in the eyes of church leaders, more than the uniting of two mortal beings: it was "a model in miniature of the eternal marriage of the church with Christ" (Alvarez, 1981, p. 111).

Given that the marriage between the church and Christ could never be put asunder, marriages now forged in heaven could not be broken, even by the furnaces found in the hell of marital discord—that is, unless one of the links was proved defective. Divorce was not possible, but annulment did provide a way out. Church

---

[1] The astute reader will wonder later in this book, in the chapter on family violence, how Roman men could in that chapter sell their wives and in this chapter divorce them. The answer is time. In early Roman history, a wife would be sold or put to death. In later Roman history, she would be divorced.

PART THREE   FAMILY LIFE ACROSS THE LIFE SPAN

law permitted annulments for six reasons: adultery, unnatural offenses, cruelty, infidelity, impotence, and entrance into the ministry. These reasons for terminating a marriage were even further restricted for non-Catholics in the 16th century after the Protestant Reformation. Until recently only the wealthiest of Protestants in England could divorce (Alvarez, 1981). Did such restrictions end divorces? The answer is clearly no. Extralegal solutions were devised by the populace—desertion, bigamy, and "wife sale." By a medieval folk custom, a disgruntled husband could bring his wife to market much as one would bring a horse (with a halter around her neck) and there sell her to the highest bidder. Thomas Hardy's *Mayor of Casterbridge* begins with just such a sale:

"For my part I don't see why men who have got wives and don't want 'em, shouldn't get rid of 'em as these gypsy fellows do their old horses. . . . Why shouldn't they put 'em up and sell 'em by auction to men who are in need of such articles? Hey? Why begad, I'd sell mine this minute if anybody would buy her!"

She turned to her husband and murmured, "Michael, you have talked this nonsense in public places before. A joke is a joke, but you may make it once too often, mind!"

"I know I've said it before; I meant it. All I want is a buyer."

[An offer of five guineas is made.] "Now," said the woman, breaking the silence, so that her low dry voice sounded quite loud, "before you go further, Michael, listen to me. If you touch that money, I and this girl go with the man. Mind it is a joke no longer."

"A joke? Of course it is not a joke!" shouted her husband, his resentment rising at her suggestion. "I take the money: the sailor takes you. That's plain enough. It has been done elsewhere—and why not here?"

. . . "Mike," she said, "I've lived with thee a couple of years, and had nothing but temper! Now I'm no more to 'ee; I'll try my luck elsewhere. 'Twill be better for me and Elizabeth-Jane, both. So good-bye!"

Seizing the sailor's arm with her right hand, and mounting the little girl on her left, she went out of the tent sobbing bitterly [Hardy, 1886/1966, pp. 8–11].

Thankfully, times have changed and divorce is no longer the exclusive privilege of the wealthy. Some of the reasons people decide to end their marriages and the growth in their number concern us next.

# DIVORCE: DEMOGRAPHICS AND EXPLANATIONS

## *Demographics*

To gain an appreciation for the numerical magnitude of divorce statistics, it is useful to look at the past. Official records report a divorce rate in 1880 of 1 divorce for every 21 marriages in the United States, rising in 1916 to 1 for every 9 marriages. At the end of World War II (1946) the divorce rate skyrocketed to 1 divorce per 3.7 marriages. By 1950 it had declined slightly to 1 per 4 marriages, and it remained at about that level for several years. However, in the late 1960s rates again began to increase to their present stable levels (see Figure 10-1). In 1968, for example, 1 divorce occurred for every 3.5 marriages; by 1970 this had increased to 1 divorce for every 3 marriages. As we entered the 1980s, for every 2.04 marriages 1 divorce occurred (Hacker, 1983; O'Neill, 1973; U. S. Bureau of the Census, 1975). For the year 1980, this meant that a total of 1,182,000 divorces were granted in the United States (Hacker, 1983, p. 110).

Marriages ending in divorce in 1979 failed, on average, to survive seven years (see Table 10-1). At the time of divorce, the woman's median age was 29.9, her former husband's 32.4 (Hacker, 1983, pp. 109–110). It appears that the presence of children affects marital stability, as 44.6% of

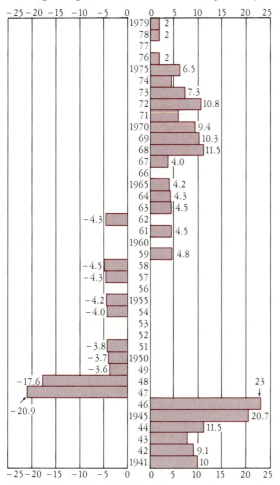

Percentage change in the divorce rate from the previous year

FIGURE 10-1. *The stabilizing divorce rate.*

If divorce rates remain at present levels, estimates are that 38% of White children born in 1980 will be members of single-parent households for some period of time before age 16. For Black youth, the chances of experiencing a single-parent household are significantly greater. By age 16, 75% of Black youth will be members of such families (Bumpass, 1984). Moreover, the number of single-parent households grew by 70.5% between 1970 and 1980, and the number of two-parent households declined by 4% (Spanier & Glick, 1981, p. 330).

> **?** *The divorce rate has stabilized in recent years. Do you think it will remain at this level, or should we expect to see additional change? What might that change be?*

## A Theoretical Perspective: Social Exchange Theory

In recent years many scholars have used a social exchange perspective to explain the increasing incidence of divorce in this country.

Social exchange theory views a marriage as a mixture of rewards and costs. For example, imagine a married couple who find each other sexually attractive, emotionally fulfilling, and good financial providers. On these variables, each partner is receiving and contributing equally to the relationship. The reward variables (attractiveness, companionship, financial security) are equally distributed between the pair. The costs (for example, not having a relationship with someone else) are also equally shared. All of us would probably predict that this relationship will be stable. But as we vary one or all of the three variables, this relationship can change in value for one or both partners.

For instance, let's say that only one partner finds the other sexually attractive. Holding the

divorcing couples had no children, 25.5% had one, 19.7% had two, 7.2% had three, 3.1% had more than three (Hacker, 1983, p. 110). Recent work by Rankin and Maneker (1985) supports this general finding but points out that a child's age has a powerful effect on the decision to divorce. In their sample only parents with children over age 2 appeared to be discouraged from dissolving their marriages.

**TABLE 10-1.** *Length of marriages at the time of divorce, 1979*

| Length of Marriage | Percentage | Cumulative Percentage |
|---|---|---|
| Under 1 year | 4.4 | 4.4 |
| 1 year | 8.1 | 12.5 |
| 2 years | 9.0 | 21.5 |
| 3 years | 9.2 | 30.7 |
| 4 years | 8.4 | 39.1 |
| 5 years | 7.2 | 46.3 |
| 6 years | 6.2 | 52.5 |
| 7 years | 5.7 | 58.2 |
| 8 years | 4.7 | 62.9 |
| 9 years | 4.1 | 67.0 |
| 10–14 years | 13.5 | 80.5 |
| 15–19 years | 8.0 | 88.5 |
| 20–24 years | 5.4 | 93.9 |
| 25–29 years | 3.3 | 97.2 |
| 30 or more years | 2.8 | 100.0 |

Median: 6.8 years

other two variables constant, we now have to say that one individual is gaining at the expense of the other. Or the two may find each other deficient in different areas: he may be seen as unattractive, while she may be viewed as emotionally unfulfilling. The point is that when an imbalance occurs, the shortchanged person typically tries to rectify the situation. If the imbalance is perceived as significant and cannot be corrected, one or both losing partners may decide to end the relationship.

*Try using a different theoretical framework to explain the life event of divorce. What conclusions can you draw by using this different perspective? Do the conclusions drawn from social exchange theory remain valid, or do different theories generate different conclusions?*

## Factors Contributing to the Divorce Rate

Why has there been such a tremendous growth in the divorce rate? There is no one explanation. Some authors argue that the gains women have made over the last few decades have allowed them to end unsuccessful marriages. The ability to work, for example, and thus achieve economic independence is perhaps the single most important step women have taken. But of importance also is the demise of woman's submissiveness to her spouse. The ages of the "family in harmony" and the "cult of domesticity" are long past, and it is no longer shameful for family power and decision making to be shared. Further, changes brought about by our entrance into an age of equity have gradually reshaped cultural attitudes to a conviction shared by an ever-growing majority in this country that marriages that do not bring mutual satisfaction and fulfillment need not be continued (Keniston, 1977).

Other authors do not find answers for the increasing divorce rate to lie solely in a personal context. Crosby (1980), for instance, looking at divorce from a historical perspective, echoes the comments made earlier in this chapter that divorce rates of earlier times have been distorted. How accurate was the recording of marriages that failed in the 18th and early in the 19th century? What influence did the cost of divorce, the grounds required for a divorce, and social attitudes have on holding down official divorce rates? It may well have been in the past that many couples who remained married in the eyes of society and dwelled under one roof were divorced from each other physically and emotionally.

Finally, there is the extremely interesting argument that divorce ends marriages today that death would have ended yesterday (Bane, 1976; Crosby, 1980). Those who offer this observation

## BOX 10-1
*The Future of Marriages Made in 1977*

In 1980 the federal government's Division of Health and Vital Statistics issued a report forecasting the future of marriages established in 1977. Assuming that current trends continue, the report predicts that nearly half these marriages will end in divorce. The following table shows the estimated rates of dissolution for these marriages during five-year periods through the next century.

| Period | Percentage Divorcing | Cumulative Percentage |
|---|---|---|
| 1977–1982 | 19.2 | 19.2 |
| 1983–1987 | 13.7 | 32.9 |
| 1988–1992 | 7.3 | 40.2 |
| 1993–1997 | 4.2 | 44.4 |
| 1998–2007 | 4.0 | 48.4 |
| After 2007 | 1.2 | 49.6 |

are not thinking so much of spousal murder as of past life expectancies. Earlier in this book, you'll remember, we noted that, on average, in the 18th century a woman would not have married until age 22 or later. Given that her average life expectancy in 1790 was 36, her marriage would have lasted, on average, less than 14 years. Marcy (1981) cites estimates that in the early 1880s 30% of English marriages ended just this way, with the death of a spouse before the 16th wedding anniversary. Finally, for a rough comparison, consider the median length of marriages that ended in divorce in 1979 (see Table 10-1) and the fact that 68.5% of women who were granted divorces in 1977 were 34 years of age or younger (Hacker, 1983, p. 110).

 *In your opinion, which factor best explains the present divorce rate—the movement toward equity, statistical distortions, or longer life expectancies? Are there factors we have overlooked? If so, what are they?*

## THE STAGES OF DIVORCE

A number of authors have constructed typologies to describe the events before, during, and after a divorce. Of all the frameworks offered, we find Bohannon's (1970) the most useful. Bohannon views divorce as involving six separate but related life events. First, there is the "emotional divorce," in which each spouse comes to realize that the marital relationship as he or she experiences it is deteriorating. Next is the "legal divorce," which involves the steps necessary to end a marital relationship and to establish a life separate from one's former spouse. Third is the "economic divorce," in which the economic resources of the family are redistributed to the former marital couple.

The "coparental divorce" involves issues of child custody, visitation, and parenting. The "community divorce" involves redefining the relationships the former marital couple held with parents and friends and their standing in the larger community since the dissolution of the marriage. The sixth and final station is the "psy-

## BOX 10-2
### *The Future of Divorce among the Elderly*

Presently, the elderly rarely divorce. In 1975, for instance, only 1% of divorce decrees were granted to persons 65 and over. Peter Uhlenberg and Mary Ann Meyers (1981) suspect, however, that this will change as the American population continues to gray. They believe that—

• The increase in the annual divorce rate for this older population from 1.2 divorces per 1000 married women in the 1960s to 2.2 per 1000 in

1975 forecasts a rise in marital dissolution in future years for this population.

• Increases in future years in the number of older persons in second or third marriages suggest a higher risk potential for divorce.

• As the present generation of young adults ages, there is little reason to believe its members will alter their attitude that divorce is a solution to an unpleasant marriage.

• Because women's increasing financial independence will weaken their financial dependence on men in later life, divorce rates will rise.

• Longer life expectancies will mean that divorce rather than death will end unsatisfactory marital relationships.

Whether these predictions are correct is a question that time will answer.

chic divorce." It is concerned with each spouse's ability to separate from the former marital relationship and to establish an "autonomous self-identity" (Pais & White, 1979, p. 274).

As we look now in greater depth at each of these way stations, we will occasionally widen the parameters of these stages to include topics that we feel deserve examination.

### The Emotional Divorce

As we saw, the factors that lead to an "emotional divorce" have often been explained using the concepts of exchange theory (Edwards & Saunders, 1981; Price-Bonham & Balswick, 1980). In this model each partner assesses the assets and liabilities attached to the marital relationship. Should either partner feel that the costs of the marriage outweigh its benefits, then the marriage is in jeopardy. Although the reasons couples separate are many, they do tend to cluster into certain reappearing explanations.

For instance, Hayes, Stinnett, and DeFrain (1980) found that, in their sample of 138 divorced, middle-aged, mostly middle-class persons whose marriages had lasted at least 15 years, one fourth felt they had married too young. This is an extremely interesting comment from a population whose marriages had exceeded by several years the median length of marriages at the time of divorce (about 7 years). It provides support for the finding that women who marry before age 18 are twice as likely to divorce as those who marry in their 18th or 19th year, and three times as likely to divorce as those who marry between 20 and 24 (Spanier & Glick, 1981). Similar findings exist for men. Men who marry during their teenage years are at least twice as likely to divorce as those who marry later (Spainer & Glick, 1981).

Three quarters of the sample reported serious problems in communication. Sixty percent reported a decrease in activities that the two partners shared. The majority also reported re-

*Why do you think adolescent marriages are more likely to end in divorce than marriages made later in life?*

ductions, before the announcement of the separation, in affection shown and in efforts to enhance the partner's self-esteem.

In more than 50% of the sample, the event that triggered the emotional divorce, which led to the dissolution of the marriage, was an affair by the husband. Weiss (1975) has commented that infidelity is particularly damaging to a partner's self-esteem—especially a woman's self-esteem. Hancock (1980) believes women are especially vulnerable because society makes marriage central to their identity. Although more women than men request divorces (Zeiss, Zeiss, & Johnson, 1980), Goode (1956) believes that by their behavior men instigate a woman's decision to seek a divorce. Some evidence to support Goode's belief is found in studies that reveal women to have an initially poorer psychological adjustment to separation than men (Bloom & Caldwell, 1981). Interestingly, Bloom and Cald-

well found, however, that men fare worse later in the postseparation period as a whole.

But not all separations occur because of infidelity. Hayes et al. found that about 25% of their sample sought freedom from an unsatisfying marital relationship. Other studies find that factors such as personality, values, and a lack of communication contribute to the emotional divorce that precedes the legal divorce (Kitson & Sussman, 1982).

 *Do you agree with one researcher's observation that marriage is central to a woman's identity?*

## The Legal Divorce

After an emotional distancing (which may include a physical separation), one partner may

PART THREE   FAMILY LIFE ACROSS THE LIFE SPAN

bring action to dissolve the marriage. The wheels of the judicial system then begin to turn as a legal notice is served on the other partner that their marriage has gone beyond eroding emotionally to a state of actual legal deterioration.

There are three ways in which a marriage can be ended through civil means. The first is **civil annulment.** An annulment states that the marriage never existed. It is the means by which couples who are underage or closely related typically find their marriage dissolved. The second means is the **no-fault divorce.** Of recent vintage, it permits a couple to end a marriage without declaring one partner guilty on one of the six historic grounds established by canon law (adultery, unnatural offenses, cruelty, infidelity, impotence, and entrance into a religious order).

Often couples pursuing a no-fault divorce enter into a process called **divorce mediation.** By this procedure both partners try to settle peacefully as many outstanding issues as possible before entering the courtroom (Coogler, Weber, & McKenry, 1979; Steinberg, 1980). Fine (1980) describes the purpose of mediation as fostering cooperation between the separating individuals and keeping areas of conflict contained:

> The mediator goes through several areas in order: the assignment of properties and goods to each party; dissolution of the dependency relationships between the marital couple and how, for example, they are going to react to mutual friends, arrange church, clubs, and sports group affiliations; discussion of the caring for the children . . . children over the age of five are seen in groups where the divorce proceedings are described and where they are encouraged to express their feelings [p. 356].

The methods of divorce mediation are similar to those used in labor negotiations. Mediation involves finding a neutral setting in which the parties can meet, defining the issues for mediation (custody, property division, and so on), and processing each issue in order to reach a settlement (Vanderkooi & Pearson, 1983).

If a couple cannot agree to end their marriage without fault, then an **adversarial divorce hearing** is held in a courtroom with a judge presiding. In an adversarial divorce hearing, one or more of the six historic canon laws are said to have been violated by one (or both) partner(s) against the other. Witnesses for both sides may be called, testimony is heard, and a decision is reached finding one or both parties at fault.

 *What advantage might a no-fault divorce and the process of divorce mediation have for families with children?*

### The Economic Divorce

Although we would like to think that child custody decisions are not being based on a parent's gender, most still are. Presently, fewer than 7% of fathers have custody of their children (Spanier & Glick, 1981).[2] The process of divorce, though, involves more than the assignment of children to one or both parents. It involves the redistribution of family assets to each partner. Personal items, community property, and income are divided between the couple.

Payments made from one former spouse to the other for his or her support are called **alimony.** Of the more than 5 million divorced women in this country in 1979, only 9% were to receive alimony payments, and only 6.4% (about

---

[2] It might interest readers to know that this was not always the case. Before this century, custody was frequently awarded to the father. Historians suggest this was done not only because men could better afford the cost of raising children, but also because children were considered the father's property.

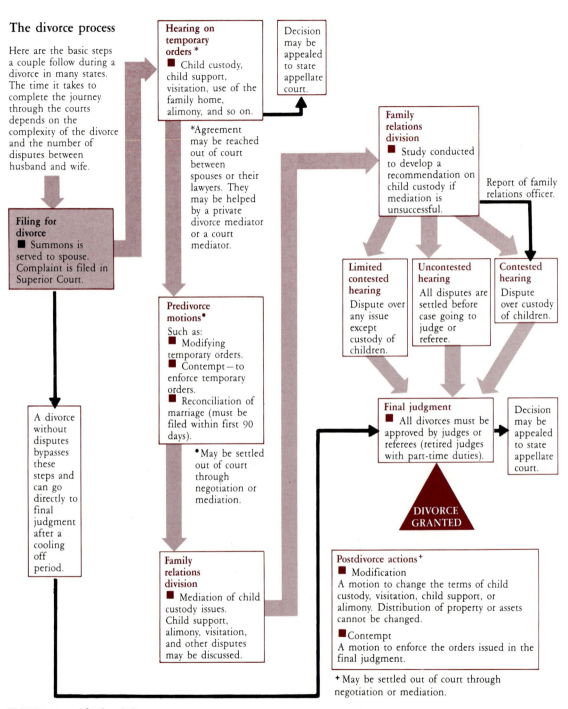

**The divorce process**

Here are the basic steps a couple follow during a divorce in many states. The time it takes to complete the journey through the courts depends on the complexity of the divorce and the number of disputes between husband and wife.

**Filing for divorce**
■ Summons is served to spouse. Complaint is filed in Superior Court.

A divorce without disputes bypasses these steps and can go directly to final judgment after a cooling off period.

**Hearing on temporary orders \***
■ Child custody, child support, visitation, use of the family home, alimony, and so on.

\*Agreement may be reached out of court between spouses or their lawyers. They may be helped by a private divorce mediator or a court mediator.

**Predivorce motions•**
Such as:
■ Modifying temporary orders.
■ Contempt—to enforce temporary orders.
■ Reconciliation of marriage (must be filed within first 90 days).

•May be settled out of court through negotiation or mediation.

**Family relations division**
■ Mediation of child custody issues. Child support, alimony, visitation, and other disputes may be discussed.

Decision may be appealed to state appellate court.

**Family relations division**
■ Study conducted to develop a recommendation on child custody if mediation is unsuccessful.

Report of family relations officer.

**Limited contested hearing**
Dispute over any issue except custody of children.

**Uncontested hearing**
All disputes are settled before case going to judge or referee.

**Contested hearing**
Dispute over custody of children.

**Final judgment**
■ All divorces must be approved by judges or referees (retired judges with part-time duties).

Decision may be appealed to state appellate court.

**DIVORCE GRANTED**

**Postdivorce actions+**
■ Modification
A motion to change the terms of child custody, visitation, child support, or alimony. Distribution of property or assets cannot be changed.

■ Contempt
A motion to enforce the orders issued in the final judgment.

+ May be settled out of court through negotiation or mediation.

**FIGURE 10-2.** *The legal divorce process.*

340,000) actually did receive payments; the average amount was $263.50 a month (Hacker, 1983, p. 96).

Payments made to support a child are called **child support.** Of the approximately 8.5 million families headed by divorced women, slightly fewer than half (48.3%) were granted child support by the court. Of these, fewer than half (48.9%) had former spouses who remitted the full court-awarded amount. Slightly under one quarter (22.7%) received child support payments amounting to less than the awarded amount, while 28.4% received nothing. The latest government survey shows that monthly child support payments in this country averaged $155.08 for Whites and $107.83 for Blacks (Hacker, 1983, pp. 95–96).

These data translate into a cold reality expressed again and again in the literature—that women and (in 93% of the settlements that involved children) their offspring experienced a substantial reduction in their standard of living. McAdoo (1982a, p. 17), for instance, reports that the median income of White two-parent families in 1980 was $21,094. For Hispanic families it was $14,717, and for Black families it was $12,674. Female-headed families with children had significantly lower incomes: $8323 for White families, $5739 for Hispanic families, and $5069 for Black families. It should not be surprising that the rolls of Aid to Families with Dependent Children (AFDC) are filled with female-headed households. In 1980, 69.8% of AFDC households were female-headed (Hacker, 1983, p. 192).

Bane (1979) comments that the economic problems afflicting these households have a multitude of sources, including "loss of economies of scale; greater prevalence of divorce and death among poor families; low and irregular levels of alimony, child support, and public assistance; fewer adult earners; fewer opportunities for female heads of families to work; [and] lower wages than men when they do work" (p. 283). Perhaps most disturbing of all is the well-documented fact that divorce is concentrated among those families with the fewest financial resources (Bane, 1979). As many writers have noted, losing half to two thirds of one's former income or failing to receive support payments is devastating financially and emotionally to the single parent and her offspring (Albrecht, 1980; Desimone-Luis, O'Mahoney, & Hunt, 1979; Hetherington, 1979; Thomas, 1982). Further, it has been estimated that if these trends continue, the "feminization of poverty" will be completed by the year 2000. By that we mean that nearly 100% of the poverty population will comprise female heads of household and their dependent children (National Advisory Council on Economic Opportunity, 1980).

 *Should society take steps to ensure that delinquent child support and alimony payments are made? What actions could be taken?*

## The Coparental Divorce

The "coparental" divorce applies to the by-products of a divorce—the children. In this section we will focus on their attitudes, their behavior, and their reactions to this life event. (We will examine custody and parenting issues later.)

*Effects of divorce on young children.* It is for children of preschool, nursery school, and elementary school age that divorce poses the greatest stress. The emotional state of children too young to understand the events unfolding around them is affected by the emotional states of their parents. These children act like barometers, reflecting their parents' ability or inability to cope with the events surrounding them (Kurdek, 1981).

For children of preschool, nursery school, and elementary school age, the pain is more intense. Feelings that they are responsible for their parents' decision to end the marriage are common, as the continuing work of two groups of researchers finds (Hetherington, 1979; Hetherington, Cox, & Cox, 1978; Wallerstein, 1983; Wallerstein & Kelly, 1974, 1976, 1980a, 1980b). An examination of this work permits an intimate view of families in distress.

Hetherington and her associates' (1978) study of a group of 48 middle-class families with pre-school children documents the tremendous stress families experience in the first year after a divorce. Parents in their study expressed feelings of loneliness, alienation, depression, and inability to care for their children. These expressions of personal and parental inadequacy could be found in their interaction with their children. Divorced parents, for example, were less likely to expect mature behaviors of their children than parents in intact families, resulting in the appearance of dependency behaviors such as whining and nagging in their offspring. The general inability of parents to reestablish self-maintaining behaviors drew their personal resources inward. Struggling to maintain their own identities, they spent less time being with and caring for their children. Parenting styles were also affected: mothers became more authoritarian and fathers more liberal and indulgent. Neither parenting style was particularly successful, and the lack of disciplinary follow-through was evident. The mother/son relationship declined into a power struggle escalated by both sides. Sons became increasingly antisocial and mothers became increasingly punitive, each side increasing the other's unhappiness.

Of sizable importance is that by the end of this two-year study many of these dysfunctional patterns had disappeared. Although the mother/son relationship was still strained, the new family had recovered most of its ability to function as a unit.

Hetherington (1979) sees divorce as not one but several stressful events for a child. Temperamental children, she says, are at greatest risk for adjusting poorly to this event. She and her colleagues (1978) conclude that divorce is not "victimless." Every family in this study experienced a loss of functioning both during and after the divorce.

The work of Judith Wallerstein and Joan Kelly (1974, 1976, 1980a) supports the findings described above. Their initial clinical sample consisted of 60 families with children ranging in age from 3 to 18. According to these researchers, parenting skills deteriorated in the first year after the divorce, and this time was the most stressful for all family members. Age affected children's reactions to the news of a divorce. Preschoolers engaged in denial, while 7- and 8-year-olds showed signs of significant depression. Children aged 9 and 10 felt shame and expressed anger but had more ways than younger children of dealing with these feelings.

Several years after their initial study, Wallerstein and Kelly (1980b) reported that not all these young people had resolved the experience of parental divorce. Those best able to adjust to their new life situation not only possessed strong personalities but had parents who were emotionally healthy and remained involved with their children. The authors report that, for the 37% of the sample who continued to show signs of depression, the divorce process had never been completely worked through.

Other observations and reviews of the literature lend support to an observation that "creative divorce is analogous to creative pneumonia" (Weiss, cited in McCall & Stocking, 1980). Increases in referrals to mental health clinics for acting-out behavior and complaints about such behavior in young children have been noticed (Emery, 1982; Kalter, 1977; Nelson, 1982; Schoettle & Cantwell, 1980). Families experiencing divorce are more disorganized (Felner, Farber, Ginter, Boike, & Cowen, 1980; Goetting, 1981). Young children seem to experience a lower image of themselves (Parish & Dostal, 1980; Parish & Taylor, 1979). And yet, as we shall see shortly, this life event need *not* be crippling for young children.

*Effects of divorce on adolescents.* In a study of the reactions of adolescents to their parents' divorce, Reinhard (1977) found surprisingly few negative feelings. The majority of the sample, though unhappy with the divorce, did not view their parents' decision as senseless or immature but as the correct action. Adolescents in this study saw themselves as assuming more responsibility in the family as a result of the divorce but did not view this responsibility negatively, nor did they express anger or a sense of loss of love. They also did not try to conceal the divorce from peers. Significantly, peers seemed to respond in an accepting fashion, and social relationships were enhanced as a result. Finally, these young people did not report any antisocial behavior, leading one generally to conclude that the divorce of their parents was not a particularly earth-shaking experience.

With a few exceptions, these general findings reappear in the current literature. Even the exceptions that exist suggesting, for example, that female delinquency may be related to broken homes cannot establish causality, for there are confounding variables (mothers with higher rates of emotional illness and alcoholism) that make it extremely difficult to attribute a sample's acting-out behavior to single-parent homes (Offord, Abrams, Allen, & Poushinsky, 1979).

On a variety of measures such as locus of control and ego identity (Grossman, Shea, & Adams, 1980) and androgynous sex-role orientation (Kurdek & Siesky, 1980a), young people from divorced homes have not been found to differ significantly from their peers in intact homes. In fact, Grossman et al. (1980) found these young men to have higher ego-identity scores than peers from intact homes.

*Adjusting to parental divorce.* What facilitates a young person's healthy adjustment to di-

vorce? Wallerstein (1983) believes that young people must resolve six tasks in order to get on with their own lives in a healthy fashion. The first task is to "acknowledge the marital rupture." Ideally, after an initial regression, young people will come to grips with this fact by the end of the first year. The second task is to "disengage from parental conflict" and to resolve for themselves that they cannot save their parents or replace a divorced spouse.

The next task is "resolution of loss." In a divorce all young people feel hurt and rejected, some more than others. Parish (1981) has reported that young people carry into college feelings that divorce is a stigma. Moderating this sense of loss is the ability to share this loss (Kurdek & Siesky, 1980b; Luepnitz, 1979). The ability to reach out to friends for social support is important in accepting a divorce. Equally important is the way the parents approach the divorce. Although we will discuss this aspect at greater length shortly, we need to point out that warm, loving relationships maintained by *both* parents with their offspring after a divorce facilitate adjustment (Emery, 1982; Kurdek, 1981).

The fourth task is "resolution of anger and self-blame." Wallerstein (1983) believes young people do not accept the concept of no-fault divorce. They hold one or both parents or themselves responsible. Their anger, until resolved, may be expressed internally in withdrawal or depression or externally in acting-out behavior in the family, at school, in the larger community. The fifth task involves "accepting the permanence of the divorce," giving up dreams that the divorced couple will reunite. The last task to be accomplished is "achieving realistic hope regarding relationships." Young people need to come, in the end, to believe that *they* are capable of establishing meaningful relationships and not be obsessed with fears over their ability to love and care for another.

Is it possible to cope and adapt after a parent's divorce? There is good evidence to support Nelson's (1982, p. 57) comment that "children's social maladjustment following divorce is a temporary rather than an enduring reaction." Kurdek, Blisk, and Siesky (1981) found, for instance, that four years after the parents' divorce their sample of upper-middle-class young people evidenced little self-blame or hope for parental reconciliation. These young people, the authors wrote, had a high level of interpersonal reasoning and an internal locus of control and were older than children cited in other studies who were less able to cope. Further, because the divorce had not occurred recently, the authors believe, these young people were able to place this event in perspective.

Kulka and Weingarten (1979) examined the long-term effects of divorce on young people. Their interviews of adults who were children of divorce suggested that divorce had had a modest impact on their lives. Among the findings of this study:

- Adults whose parents divorced when they were young do not report greater unhappiness, worry, or anxiety about the future than individuals from intact families.

- Adults from divorced families tend to report their youth as the most unhappy time of their lives.

- Adults from divorced families are more likely to report "having felt an impending nervous breakdown" (p. 58). Kulka and Weingarten caution that this comment was not "interpreted by respondents as a reflection of their own deficiency or pathology" (p. 58). Rather, "these adults have indeed been more frequently confronted by stress inducing events" (p. 59).

- Adults from divorced homes tend to report poorer physical health than adults from intact families. However, these reports seem to diminish with age.

- Adults from divorced homes do not report higher levels of depression than adults from intact families.

- Women from divorced families seem to be better able to cope with stress than men from divorced families.

- Adults from divorced families tend to report more marital dissatisfaction and to have a higher incidence of separation and divorce than adults from intact homes.

As the studies discussed in this section show, many young people, though hurt, have managed to grow beyond that hurt. Other young people are not so fortunate. It seems that parents who are loving, caring, and involved, outside support systems, and individual resilience are essential for youth to cope successfully with divorce. Adequate financial support is also crucial for satisfactory adjustment. Where these elements are lacking, the chances for growing are stunted.

 *Using the studies described in this section, what actions do you believe could be taken to reduce distress for children of divorce? Would you take different actions for adolescents?*

## The Community Divorce

Ending a marriage involves more than money, lawyers, and children. It involves redefining oneself within the community. Some studies find, for instance, that divorced women feel more restricted than widows in their dealings with society. Divorce, even in this enlightened age, carries a stigma that contributes to jealousy and a fear of mate stealing among some individuals (Kitson, Lopata, Holmes, & Meyering, 1980).

The community divorce also extends to one's own family and the level of care it provides to a divorcing or divorced person. In many families the decision of an adult offspring to end his or her marriage is not accepted for many years, if ever (Johnson, 1981). A family that disapproves of the decision to divorce or a family that is itself overextended because of stress is unlikely to give support (Kitson, Moir, & Mason, 1982). This lack of care and social support can have a tremendous influence on the divorced person's ability to handle the personal stress associated with this life event.

 *Do you think relatives should support a family member's decision to divorce even when they disapprove of that decision?*

## The Psychic Divorce

The psychic divorce involves the divorced person's emotional acceptance of "the permanent separation, the giving up of emotional involvement with the spouse and the relegation of the marital relationship to memories, a redefinition and acceptance of oneself as a single person, and the psychological capacity to find a new love object" (Wise, 1980, p. 149). This is much easier said than done.

As we have already seen, separation and the process of divorce throw families into a state of confusion. Household routines are disrupted. Financial problems may force the divorcing person to increase work hours or to enter the work force untrained. Job performance tends to decline as the divorcing individual pulls his or her coping resources inward in an attempt to regain a handle on life (Goetting, 1981). Some pursue emotional/physical relationships with others fast and furiously as they try to confirm for themselves their continued sexual desirability. But reports show that after the first year the so-called romantic singles lifestyle is filled for many with

disappointment over the lack of intimacy in relationships that fail to develop (Goetting, 1981).

It is therefore not surprising that divorce is related to poor health for both men and women on a number of indexes. Holmes and Rahe (1967) rank divorce as nearly as stressful a life event as the death of a spouse. Bloom, White, and Asher (1978), in their excellent review of the impact of marital disruption on health, find considerable evidence to link the erosion of a marriage to a similar erosion in one's health. They report:

- Divorced persons are found in greater proportions in psychiatric hospitals than the nondivorced.

- Divorced persons have more motor vehicle accidents.

- Divorced persons have higher rates of illness, disability, and alcoholism.

- Divorced persons have higher rates of suicide and homicide than the general population.

- Divorced persons express feelings of loneliness, failure, and embarrassment.

These findings continue to be reaffirmed in recent studies that find loneliness a prevalent problem among both men and women (White & Bloom, 1981; Woodward, Zabel, & DeCosta, 1980). Divorce and suicide continue to be significantly related. It appears that the one moderating influence on this relationship is the presence of children in the family, which reduces the risk of taking one's own life (Stack, 1981). Self-concept declines after divorce, and feelings of incompetence and failure increase (Thomas, 1982).

Factors suggesting a positive adjustment involve, as Wise (1980) has suggested, the ability to separate from the marriage (White & Bloom,

1981). Thomas (1982, p. 33) reports that those best equipped to do this have such personality traits as "dominance, self-assurance, intelligence, creativity, social boldness, liberalism, self-sufficiency, greater ego strength, and lower anxiety level." These characteristics, though sought by all of us, are not found in everyone. Weiss' observation (cited in Thomas, 1982) that it may take three to four years to resolve a broken marriage suggests that for most people the mending process is gradual and may be, as Bloom and his associates (1978) observe, dependent on the establishment of a new, satisfying heterosexual relationship.

 *Is a satisfying relationship with another human being essential for mental health?*

## IS DIVORCE GOOD OR BAD?

We have offered what may seem an overwhelming case against anyone's seeking a divorce. It is true that nearly everyone who experiences this life event suffers. And yet we can also state unequivocally that divorce is preferable to marriage in many situations. How can we make such a statement? Recall that social exchange theory suggests that when marital liabilities exceed marital assets in the eyes of one or both partners, divorce may be considered. So long as the marriage remains in this unbalanced state, one or both marital partners suffer. The action that a partner takes to end the marriage is, in reality, an action to put an end to his or her state of suffering.

For example, imagine that a wife wishes to put her skills to use in the workplace, but her husband absolutely insists that she remain home. Although he may have other admirable qualities, his position on this issue may seem so unreasonable to his wife that this liability exceeds the value of the marriage's other assets. She may decide that his position is an attempt to dominate her life that she will not tolerate. After many lengthy arguments and unable to resolve this issue, the couple may decide to dissolve their marriage.

By ending the marriage, the spouses will put to rest an issue that created considerable distress in their lives. They will rejoice in the relief that accompanies the ending of a marriage that brought more pain than satisfaction. And yet, they will grieve too, over the loss of assets that existed in the marriage.

Is it desirable to end an unhappy marriage? From a social exchange perspective, if, after trying, partners cannot balance marital assets against liabilities, the answer is yes. It must always be remembered that the decision about the value of a marital relationship belongs to the partners in that relationship. It is *their* perspective and *their* assessment of the marriage that matters.

After the divorce, if the couple are childless, they may never see each other again. However, when children are involved, the circumstances change. Even though the marriage dissolves, the influence of one partner on a former partner may continue through their children. Divorce severs a marital relationship, but as we shall see next, it rarely dissolves the parent/child relationship.

 *Is divorce preferable to an unhappy marriage?*

## AFTER THE DIVORCE: PARENTING

When Bohannon (1970) described the six stations of divorce, he included in the "coparental divorce" the topic of parenting. We have chosen to separate it because the issue of parenting deserves special attention.

Admittedly, women still win the overwhelming majority of child custody decisions, but the attitudes of society and the courts have moved to view the father's continued role in his children's lives as important.

Studies find that a father's continued relationship with his children helps them adjust to the divorce (Wallerstein & Kelly, 1980c). Children in the elementary grades see their fathers as important figures in their lives and desire their fathers' attention and contact (Hingst, 1981). Given the opportunity to take a role in parenting, fathers can influence their children's lives positively and can avoid the "sugar daddyism" that comes with infrequent visits (Greif, 1979). Joint custody or frequent visitation works best when the former marital partners can support each other's parenting efforts, are flexible individuals, have a clear understanding of custody rules, and live in close geographic proximity (Abarbanel, 1979). Those parents who are best able to believe in each other as parents, who tolerate differences in each other, and who keep their own former marital problems out of the way (Ahrons, 1981; Steinman, 1981), in our experience, tend to—

- Work on resolving their conflicts or at least not inflicting them on their children.

- Work on developing or maintaining a caring, supportive relationship with their children.

- Develop social support systems or take advantage of whatever systems are available (McCall & Stocking, 1980, p. 12).

For example, in a sample of White middle-class divorced parents, Alexander (1980) found that the "child's best interests" determined visitation arrangements. Thus, the divorced couples were able to set aside their own grievances and act in behalf of their offspring.

These positive reports, however, do not mean

*Joint custody works best when the child's best interests determine visitation arrangements. Sometimes, though, even the best arrangements are hard on children and parents alike.*

that joint custody or visitation rights always work. A study of visitation rights for fathers has shown that many situations are strife-ridden:

> Although the majority of parents tried to honor the children's visiting time, 20% of the women saw no use in the father's visits and actively tried to sabotage each meeting. This fighting between parents reached pathological, even bizarre, intensity; one refined mother, for example, smeared dog feces on the face of her husband when he arrived to see his children [Wallerstein & Kelly, 1980c, pp. 1536–1537].

Even families who try to behave in a civilized fashion after the divorce may not escape problems. Futterman (1980) has found numerous examples in his clinical caseload of "friendly, cooperative, mutually agreed upon divorce settlements" (p. 526) in which the children have not worked through the process and experience difficulties at home and in school. Messinger and Walker (1981, p. 431) caution that "to deny the

## BOX 10-3
### *Mothers without the Custody of Their Children*

Slightly more than one-half million mothers live apart from their children. In a society in which 93% of custody decisions favor the mother, these women often experience societal rejection and personal ambivalence and uncertainty about their lives. Fischer (1983) finds that the reasons that these women live apart from their children vary. Some women have decided to leave the home to find themselves. Some couples have chosen to share custody of the children or to have a commuter marriage. For still other women, their children chose to live with their father after a divorce. Finally, in many instances, the courts are awarding custody to fathers who seek it. In 1977, according to Fischer, nearly two thirds of the fathers who asked for custody got it.

pain of separation is the creation of a repressive atmosphere that includes denial of the children's sense of loss." They urge that young people be given an opportunity to express their feelings.

In our experience, problems in the relationship between the parent who has custody and the one who does not are often hardest on the offspring. The divorce process is extremely painful in many families, and young people are sometimes used as pawns in the separation battle. Few of the wounds incurred by the spouses in the divorce struggle are ever completely healed, and many couples continue the struggle for years after the divorce. The young person in this situation continues to be manipulated and used by both parents until the youth learns to use *them*. Our experience suggests that some of these parental relationship problems can be reduced only if the parents agree not to pull their children into the divorce process in an attempt to "get the goods on" or "get even with" the other partner.

What happens when the father is the primary parent? Earlier we noted that only 7% of child custody decisions select the father as the primary parent. Recently our knowledge about these men has grown, and with it an understanding that fathers can be "quite capable and successful in their ability to be the primary parent" (Friedman, 1980, p. 179).

Characteristics of fathers who are successful caregivers include a willingness to give unselfishly of their time and selves to their children. A successful male primary parent is patient and flexible and is a stabilizing influence on the family (Smith & Smith, 1981; Watson, 1981).

And yet being a successful parent does not mean one escapes trouble. Chang and Deinard (1982) report, as others have, that fathers experience problems in role clarity (Nieto, 1982). Fathers have problems in housekeeping and particularly in meeting the needs of daughters. Most fathers assuming the role of sole parent reported trouble in adjusting work schedules to make time for their children. Other problems included restricted opportunities for dating and reports of depression.

Of course, women acting as single parents suffer from the same demands of adjusting work schedules, meeting financial expenses, and trying to fill the roles of both mother and father. They too have reduced opportunities for dating and feel the pains of depression. Although it is possible to be a successful single parent, it is not by any stretch of the imagination an easy task.

 ***Could joint custody be harmful to children? If so, how?***

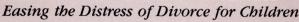

# PROMOTING FAMILY WELLNESS
## *Easing the Distress of Divorce for Children*

We have designed a sample program to illustrate how the technology of prevention can be used to help children live with divorce. We encourage you to take the ideas in the following pages and develop them further. Use the planning tool in Chapter 2 to redesign and elaborate on our proposals and to develop program ideas that could help other family members manage this life event.

## EDUCATION

From the printed word to a visual image, education cannot end the pain resulting from a divorce, but it can help young people cope with that pain. Information that shares the experiences of another provides a model not only of what is to come but also of what might be done. This kind of information, which prepares individuals for events about to unfold or already unfolding for them, is called "anticipatory guidance" (Gullotta, 1981).

In recent years many excellent educational materials have been developed to assist in this role transition. Two such publications for young people are *The Boys' and Girls' Book about Divorce* (Gardner, 1971) and *Two Homes to Live In* (Hazen, 1978). Both explain for young minds, in words and pictures, the events unfolding for them and their families.

To help parents cope with the changes occurring in their lives and understand their children's behavior, many churches and family agencies offer educational programs modeled after the Family Service Association of America's training guides *Separation and Divorce* (Callahan, 1979), *The Single-Parent Experience* (Barnes & Coplon, 1980), and *Parenting Children of Divorce* (Barnett, Gaudio, & Sumner, 1980).

Through discussions, roleplays, and lectures, these courses help participants gain not only cognitive knowledge but insight into the feelings of family members. Preventionists believe that sensitizing parents to their child's emotional needs makes it likelier that those needs will be met. For example, the preventionist hopes that a parent who comes to understand that nagging or whining is often a child's expression of insecurity will act differently when those behaviors appear. Rather than punishing the child, the parent may use newly acquired parenting skills to resolve the situation.

Preventionists also hope that, on learning that children wither in bitter postdivorce struggles, parents will make an effort to alter their behavior. The preventionist does not expect divorced parents to become the best of friends, only to avoid using their children as pawns in their disagreements. Family-life education seminars that provide information like that found in this chapter and encourage discussion and roleplays increase the chances that parents will try to act in the best interests of their children.

But the printed or spoken word is not the only educational tool. Television programs like *One Day at a Time* and films like *Kramer vs Kramer* and *E.T.* that depict single and separated parents "making it" contribute to a much-needed societal reassessment of divorce. Such programming presents young people with role models to emulate. Responsible, sensitive, and intelligent programming conveys more than possible solutions to human dilemmas, it moves viewers to understand that they are not alone. Others share with the child of divorced parents the same dilemmas, the same circumstances.

Finally, recent actions by some churches in several states to delay a couple's marriage in the church hold promise for reducing the divorce rate in the first few years of marriage (and the distress of future children). These churches have asked that those who wish to be married in that religion undergo a series of educational seminars and encounter weekends, stretching over several months. The desired outcome of this educational process is a greater awareness of each partner's strengths and weaknesses. Such a program needs to be explored by other religious faiths, for not only should it bind the parishioner more closely to the church, but it may improve communication skills in those who do marry and help others decide not to marry.

> **?** *What other educational approaches to the problem of divorce can you think of? In what settings (church, school, and so on) would you use them?*

## COMMUNITY ORGANIZATION/ SYSTEMS INTERVENTION

Preventionists believe that children are this nation's most precious natural resource. They believe that every child deserves an adequate diet, adequate clothing and shelter, and a safe environment. Consequently, findings that divorce throws many families into circumstances in which these needs cannot be met are unconscionable to the preventionist.

One of the authors (Gullotta, 1981) has proposed that this set of circumstances can be modified. For example, the procedures by which alimony and child support payments are dispensed can be changed. Rather than continue present practices, which encourage widespread abuse, laws could be altered to have the state or federal government serve as the collection agency and the award distributor. Families would then be assured of receiving payments on time and

would be able to plan their finances and not live anxiously wondering when (or whether) a support payment would arrive.

We know from the literature that many women have to return to work after a divorce. We also know that often they are ill prepared for reentry into the labor market and that their offspring become latchkey children. Steps can be taken to improve these situations and, in so doing, improve the lives of the children. For example, educational opportunities in state colleges and universities could be made available to divorced persons at a reduced cost. Day-care options could be expanded to provide the supervision necessary to prevent the accidents that can occur when children are left alone.

These proposals aimed at changing existing laws and institutional practices merely scratch the surface of possibilities. Each proposed initiative has several possible outcomes—one of which is an improvement in a child's life.

> **?** *Although ensuring that child support and alimony payments are made would ease the anxiety of the parent receiving those payments, it might increase the anxiety of the parent making the payments. What is your opinion of these proposals? Do you believe they have merit? How might they be implemented and financed? Does society have a responsibility to the children of divorce?*

## COMPETENCY PROMOTION

The literature suggests that a parental divorce lowers the self-esteem of some young people. Clinical reports also suggest that children often feel at least partly responsible for their parents' divorce. Preventionists believe that schools, churches, and youth agencies are settings in which these feelings can be confronted and self-esteem promoted.

For example, several authors have described approaches that schools might use to help young people develop a positive self-image and face the reality of their parents' decision to divorce (Benedek & Benedek, 1979; Holzman, 1984; Whitfield & Freeland, 1981). Collectively, these authors encourage that curricula stress the pluralistic nature of family life and that bulletin boards, assigned reading, class projects, and even "parents' day" be refocused to reflect this theme.

Schools, churches, and youth agencies can dispel the mistaken belief of many young people that they are alone and different from others. Through activities such as fellowship groups and weekend retreats, young people can be helped to realize that divorce is not a stigma, that they did not cause their parents' divorce, and that they need to let go of the past in order to live in the present and prepare for tomorrow.

**?** *What other activities might be undertaken to promote a sense of self-worth and pride in young people after a divorce?*

## NATURAL CAREGIVING

Several years ago, one of the authors worked with a 12-year-old whose parents were bitterly ending their marriage. Try as he might, his efforts to offer support and understanding and to secure the girl's trust failed. Despite his failure to engage this individual, she survived her parents' angry divorce and grew from it. This growth occurred as a result of meeting an older female high school student whose parents had divorced several years earlier. It was this student who took the young girl "under her wing" and helped her face and understand the events happening in her life.

This case vignette illustrates in the truest sense the essence of natural caregiving. It reminds us that caregivers are not found exclusively in the ranks of mental health professionals. We suspect that a major reason most adolescents cope so successfully with the divorce of parents is the presence of social support in the form of the peer group. Young children are at a disadvantage in this respect. Their focus has not yet turned away from adults (particularly parents) toward peers, and so the loss of a parent's attention can cause considerable distress. The willingness of this older student to "care" for this young girl illustrates how we all can, by our own actions, meet the emotional needs of another. Preventionists believe that efforts like peer counseling in which older youth work with younger ones or Big Brother/Big Sister programs can help young people cope with the dissolution of their parents' marriage.

Further, because young people are emotionally dependent on their parents, efforts to provide those parents with the necessary social support, if successful, should benefit their children. Mental health professionals have undertaken projects to increase social support from groups of people, such as lawyers, whose work brings them into close contact with divorcing persons (Felner, Primavera, Farber, & Bishop, 1982).

Efforts have also been made to increase social support through such self-help groups as "Parents Without Partners." In this self-help movement, separated and divorced parents come together to support one another, to learn, and to engage in other sharing activities.

Meeting in church halls, schools, or in each other's home, individuals may be both caregiver and care receiver simultaneously while searching for the resources to cope with their life situation.

Programs like *Parents Without Partners* provide a vehicle for the divorced to vent anger, to exchange ideas, to encourage one another and to refind oneself. To the extent that these things happen thus speeding the post divorce process, it helps not only the parent but the child as well [Gullotta, 1981, pp. 361–362].

Recent evidence underscores the contention that social support is a powerful force in ensuring a successful outcome to a distressful life event. For example, one group of researchers report that their efforts to promote natural caregiving and educational awareness among separated individuals significantly reduced their distress (Bloom, Hodges, & Caldwell, 1982; Bloom, Hodges, Kern, & McFaddin, 1985). Stewart (1983) reports similar positive outcomes. Single mothers in her study report "positive changes in self-esteem, personal growth, confidence, motivation, coping skills, and self awareness," as well as increases in leadership skills and the motivation to seek not only jobs but the development of community resources (p. 12).

 *Do you agree with our explanation that adolescents tend to handle a divorce better than children because of peer support?*

# SUMMARY

Ending a marriage, relatively easy in ancient times, became more difficult under Christianity. A few centuries ago, divorce was impossible for Catholics (although annulments were allowed) and for Protestants, except the wealthy.

Divorces in the United States have climbed from about 1 per 21 marriages in 1880 to about 1 per 2 marriages in 1980 and have stabilized at that rate.

In this chapter we have examined the stressor divorce and in so doing have come to realize that this one life event is really several. Divorce affects all family members often in ways that damage the ability of an individual to function successfully in society.

Despite the immense pain that a divorce causes, ending an unhappy marriage is better than continuing it if spouses perceive its liabilities as greater than its assets. The effort of workers in prevention cannot "magically erase a family's anger, but it can ease that hurt. It can ease that anger. It can stop a sad life event from becoming a crippling life event" (Gullotta, 1981, p. 362).

# MAJOR POINTS TO REMEMBER

1. Historical evidence shows that divorce is not a recent phenomenon. Over the centuries, people unhappy with each other have found ways to dissolve their marriages even if the state or the church prohibited such action.

2. The divorce rate has climbed dramatically in recent decades to stabilize at a point where approximately one divorce occurs for every two marriages.

3. Social exchange theory suggests that a couple divorce when one or both partners perceive a significant excess of costs over rewards in their relationship that cannot be corrected.

4. Divorce is not one but several interrelated life events. Each of these events (the emotional, legal, economic, coparental, community, and psychic divorce) can be very stressful.

5. The level of distress a divorcing person experiences is determined by the interaction of such variables as individual psychological characteristics, age of children, family, peer, and community support, financial resources, and the individual's assessment of the marriage.

6. When children are involved in a divorce, the situation becomes more complicated. It appears that young children cannot understand that no one in the family is at fault for the marriage's demise, and they hold either themselves or their parents to blame. Adolescents seem better able than younger children to cope with their parents' divorce.

7. Many families with young children experience a period of turmoil lasting more than a year. It is thought that this turmoil continues until the divorced parents and their offspring learn to accept and assume new roles. Lacking the proper parental support and unable to call on their own psychological resources, some young people appear never to be able to accept this life event.

8. Although divorce is a painful life experience, remaining in an unfulfilling marriage ensures only misery.

9. Regardless of whether the custody decision reached during the divorce proceeding places the children with mother, with father, or jointly, the success of that decision depends on the ex-partners' ability to work together. The ability to set aside past differences and act for the children's best interests is crucial. Even so, being the head of a

divorced household is not easy, and many people express feelings of being overwhelmed by the job.

10. Prevention efforts at easing the distress of divorce for children cannot eliminate the hurt children feel, but those efforts can ease the transition from a nuclear to a binuclear family.

 ## ADDITIONAL SOURCES OF INFORMATION

### *Publications*

Caines, J. (1977). *Daddy.* New York: Harper & Row. [Children; a Black elementary school child visits her father after a divorce]

Galper, M. (1978). *Co-parenting: Sharing your child equally.* Philadelphia: Running Press. [Parents]

Helmering, D. W. (1981). *I have two families.* Nashville, TN: Abingdon. [Children]

National Institute of Mental Health. (1981). *Caring about kids: When parents divorce.* DHEW Pub. No. (ADM) 81-1120. Washington, DC: U. S. Government Printing Office. [Parents]

Okimoto, J. D. (1979). *My mother is not married to my father.* New York: Putnam. [Early adolescents]

Ricci, I. (1980). *Mom's house, dad's house.* New York: Macmillan. [Older children; discusses coparenting arrangements]

Thomas, I. (1976). *Eliza's daddy.* New York: Harcourt Brace Jovanovich. [Children]

Weiss, R. S. (1979). *Going it alone.* New York: Basic Books. [Parents]

### *Organizations*

Divorce Anonymous
P.O. Box 5313
Chicago, IL 60680
A self-help group for divorced persons.

Parents Without Partners
7910 Woodmont Avenue
Bethesda, MD 20814
A self-help group for divorced persons with children.

Big Brothers/Big Sisters
220 Suburbia Station Bldg.
Philadelphia, PA 19103
A nonprofit organization that funds adult role models for children who lack either a mother or a father.

# 11

# REMARRIAGE AND THE BLENDED FAMILY

1. What is new about remarriage today, compared with remarriage in colonial times?

2. Which sex remarries more often and why?

3. What demographic factors influence remarriage?

4. From a symbolic interactionist's viewpoint, what gives meaning to a symbol like remarriage?

5. Why do people remarry? Why do some people divorce after a remarriage?

6. What stage of remarriage involves children?

7. Why is it difficult to be a stepparent?

8. Why is family financial management more complicated for remarried couples than in a first marriage?

*Just a few* years ago, this family form was described as a noninstitution (Price-Bonham & Balswick, 1980). It has been given such names as *reconstituted, merged,* and *blended.* It provides a mind-boggling assortment of possible personal and family variations that include his, hers, theirs, his ex's, her ex's, his children, her children, their children, his parents, her parents—the possibilities seem to go on forever. The noninstitution of which we are speaking is remarriage.

In this chapter we look at whether remarriage is a new marital form and whether stepfamilies are new family structures. We examine the demographics associated with this life event and the developmental tasks that accompany it. We end with prevention efforts that can help families with stepchildren adjust to this increasingly common life event.

## REMARRIAGE: A HISTORICAL VIEW

Assuming that Alvarez (1981) is correct that relaxed divorce laws are simply a return to more sensible practices that existed until the sixth century A.D. (see Chapter 10), the rise in remarriage rates can be viewed in much the same way. The ease with which Romans dissolved marital unions was accompanied by practices that forged new marital unions just as quickly. Until recent times the religious forces that made it difficult to divorce made it similarly difficult to remarry, with one exception—the remarriage of widowed persons. Historical evidence suggests, for example, that in Plymouth colony about one third of men and one fourth of women remarried after the loss of a spouse (Demos, 1970).

It is not remarriage itself that is new; it is the structure remarriage has taken in recent times.

Rather than an alternative to a single life after the death of a spouse, it has become an alternative to a single life after divorce. The growth in this second alternative has been recent and considerable. Remarriages after divorce have increased as a proportion of all marriages from 3% in 1900 to 26.3% in 1979 (Cherlin, 1978–79; Hacker, 1983, p. 102). In the next section we break down these aggregate percentages to learn more about this population.

# DEMOGRAPHICS AND EXPLANATIONS

It is with irony that we observe that the greatest number of first marriages for women occur under the warmth of the June sun (12.3%), while the greatest number of remarriages for women occur in the cold, harsh month of December (10.2%) (Hacker, 1983, p. 103). The paths that lead back to marriage can be viewed numerically, theoretically, and emotionally.

## Demographics

Although roughly equal numbers of men and women remarry, a higher percentage of men do than women. The reason is the large number of women who survive their husbands, providing a larger pool of women eligible for remarriage. Most remarriages occur about three years after a divorce (Spanier & Glick, 1980). The median age at remarriage is 31.9 years for brides and 35.3 years for grooms. Understandably, the median age of widowed persons who remarry is older— 55.2 years for brides and 61.7 years for grooms (Hacker, 1983, p. 104; see Box 11-1).

Age appears to be a significant factor in determining remarriage for divorced women: younger ones are more likely to remarry (Spanier & Glick, 1980, p. 290). Of women who divorced before their 30th birthday, 76.3% eventually remarry. As age increases, this percentage declines. Of women who divorced in their thirties, 56.2% remarry; in their forties, 32.4%; and after fifty, 11.5% (Hacker, 1983, p. 112). Interestingly, in what might be construed as a subtle sign of sexism, the Bureau of the Census collects no comparable data on men.

The data available on men suggest that when they remarry, it is to younger women. In contrast to first marriages, in which the man is, on average, 2.5 years older than his spouse, in later marriages he averages 6.2 years her senior, assuming it is her first marriage (Hacker, 1983, pp. 113–114).

What impact do education and children have on remarriage? It appears that as a woman's educational level increases, her chances of remarriage decrease (Spanier & Glick, 1980). This inverse relationship might be traced to an educated woman's greater ability to be financially independent. One might expect that a large family would adversely affect a woman's chances of remarriage, but the effect is slight. Age emerges again as a very potent intervening variable. Of women under age 30 with no children, 79.6% will remarry; with one child, 75.0% will; with two children, 74.9%; and with three children, 71.5% (Hacker, 1983, p. 112). When we compare any of these figures against the probability of remarriage at older ages, we can see how important age is to the probability of a second marriage for women.

Helpful as figures are in gaining a crude understanding of a subject area, they are never the full story. People remarry for reasons other than age, education, and number of children, as we shall see.

## A Theoretical Perspective: Symbolic Interaction Theory

As a social-psychological theory concerned with the way people endow events, feelings, and actions with meaning, symbolic interactionism

## BOX 11-1
## *Remarriage in Later Life*

If this textbook had been published 30 years ago, the material in this box would have been the primary subject matter of this chapter. Instead, remarriage after the death of a spouse in old age takes a distant second place to remarriage after divorce.

Barbara Vinick (1978), in a study of remarriage in old age, notes that more than 35,000 such marriages now occur each year. Among the 24 couples she studied, most married after the loss of a spouse. Men in her study appeared to be lonelier than women before remarriage and seemed, in spite of the poorer financial condition of women, "to need remarriage more than women" (p. 361). Most remarried couples had met through an introduction by a friend or relative or had known each other previously. Courtship was initiated by the man. Men averaged 5.5 years older than their new wives. Marital satisfaction in this group was high, perhaps understandably so, considering that most of these couples married for companionship. Vinick sees remarriage "as a viable alternative lifestyle in old age" (p. 362). She bases this statement on not only the companionship gained but also the physical care extended to several spouses who otherwise would have needed institutionalization.

does not offer a single explanation for the motives that lead individuals to remarriage. Rather, it suggests that individuals bring their own unique understanding to an event like remarriage. In this theory, remarriage is a symbol endowed by society and the individual with meaning.

As an illustration, let's suppose a man has willingly terminated his marriage. In order to do so, he has had to reconceptualize his marriage in such a way that it no longer holds a significant meaning for him. With time, he may become dissatisfied with the role of single person. It may be that he misses acting in an intimate way toward another or that he feels stigmatized by those around him. In either case, to remarry, he must reevaluate marriage and the role associated with that symbol.

For the symbolic interactionist, remarriage is just one symbol interacting with others that individuals endow with meaning. The reasons for acting in a particular way toward a symbol must be found in a personal context.

 *Try using another theoretical perspective to explain remarriage. Are there similarities between the two explanations? Are there differences?*

### Why People Remarry

In the last chapter we noted the observation of Bloom et al. (1978) that the pain accompanying a divorce may not be resolved until one reestablishes a satisfying heterosexual relationship. In short, this is a quest for love—a quest that Goetting (1982, p. 215) says is a "major goal in life." But love is not unidimensional. The intense, passionate, romantic interludes that often follow a divorce do not bring lasting satisfaction for all. Rather, accompanying the need for "romantic" love is a need for friendship, sharing, and companionship, or "conjugal" love. From the symbolic interactionist point of view, one possible reason for remarriage, then, is to establish or reestablish a meaningful relationship.

*People remarry for many reasons. Look closely at this picture and think about the feelings of each person. Describe what you think the feelings of the bride, groom, and children might be.*

Others have used social exchange theory to explain remarriage. Remember that in a social exchange model individuals balance the costs and benefits of a relationship to arrive at a personally rewarding settlement. At least in the short run, divorce is financially and emotionally costly. Economic resources and family ties are strained. If children are present, whatever personal satisfaction arises out of a divorce may be short-lived if parental responsibilities are conflict-ridden. Remarriage for some individuals, then, may be an attempt to write off some of these losses. The inverse relationship between a woman's education and remarriage (Spanier & Glick, 1980) supports this view. Certainly, those who are well educated and capable of supporting themselves will experience less internal pressure to remarry than those struggling for survival who see marriage as a way to improve their economic standing.

Testing for one part of this argument, Mueller and Pope (1980) assumed that women would slip downward in remarriage, sacrificing social and economic status for marriage. The authors based this assumption on the belief that women entering marriage for a second time were "handicapped." Interestingly, their findings did not substantiate this assumption. Most women remarry at or above the "status level" of their first husbands (exceptions occur for older women). The authors speculate that women who choose not to remarry are those who prefer a single lifestyle over marrying downward. Of course, many couples reenter marriage for the same reasons newlyweds marry, including being in love. For some, loneliness and desire for companionship bind the couple together; for others, the binding force is a desire to raise their children together rather than separately.

Finally, individuals may remarry to fulfill personal or societal expectations (Goetting, 1982). For example, remarriage may be an attempt to resolve feelings of failure carried over from the first marriage. Or (again from a symbolic interactionist's view) remarriage may be a way of resolving the absence of role clarity that exists in our society for singles. The growth of computer dating services and clubs to bring singles together suggests to the authors that the pressure on people past their early twenties to form into couples is intense. The observations Goode (1956) made more than three decades ago continue to ring true. The stress associated with the normlessness of divorce (and, we would suggest, single life in general) pressures individuals toward marriage.

Thus, it is not surprising that roughly four out of five currently divorcing Americans will remarry (Cherlin, 1978–79). And yet, having been through the institution once offers no assurance that a second marriage will be any more successful than the first. About half of remarriages fail, in comparison with about one third of first marriages (Goetting, 1982, p. 213). Why?

## Why Second Marriages Fail

Some authors suggest that remarriages fail because unresolved personal conflicts are carried over to the second marriage (Bergler, 1948). Furstenberg (1979) notes that second marriages are built on the foundation of the first and cites Schlesinger's speculation that the very nature of the marital relationship may be affected. Unquestionably, persons who reenter marriage for no other reason than to succeed where first they failed are likely to be at high risk for failure again.

A second explanation is that having divorced once makes it easier to do so a second time. Although a second divorce is no less an unpleasant task, the remarried person "knows how to get divorced and what to expect from family members, friends, and the courts" (Cherlin, 1978–79, p. 641). Possibly, also, having found the solution for unhappiness once in divorce, a person may have fewer inhibitions against using this same mechanism to end an equally unhappy second marital union.

A third observation is that divorce after remarriage is more likely to occur when children from a previous marriage are present in the new family, while children born to the new couple tend to decrease the probability of marital dissolution. The reasons will be discussed shortly when we look at stepfamilies.

Finally, remarriages may face financial hardships because the economic base may be smaller. Financial uncertainty accompanies many remarriages (Albrecht, 1979; Price-Bonham & Balswick, 1980). Child support, alimony, and the like are highly emotionally charged issues around which arguments easily arise.

In this section we have moved from statistics to explanations and have seen that more than "love" may affect a decision to reenter into marriage and that marriage the second time around is no guarantee of happiness. If there is anything we can learn from this, it is that marriage is complex and people's motivations for acting are equally complex. Finally, the sheer number of remarriages suggests that remarriage is not a departure from "accepted marriage practice" but, rather, an increasing pattern of regularity in a "changing system of kinship" (Furstenberg, 1979, p. 11). Goetting (1982) suggests that the path to remarriage is marked by several developmental tasks. In the following sections we examine that path and the tasks that await resolution.

 *In your opinion, does society pressure people toward marriage? Does it pressure divorced people toward remarriage?*

# THE STAGES OF REMARRIAGE AND THE FAMILY

In recent years several authors have constructed models of the events individuals experience as they enter marriage for a second time (Goetting, 1982; Ransom, Schlesinger, & Derdeyn, 1979; Whiteside, 1982). The most helpful model for us here is that of Goetting (1982), who, using the work of Bohannan (1970), described six stations leading to remarriage.

The first three stations of remarriage focus on the individual in relation to his or her environment. The first station Goetting describes is the **emotional remarriage,** wherein an individual hurt by the loss of a loved one learns to trust and love again. The **psychic remarriage** occurs when the individual is capable of thinking of himself or herself no longer as a single person but as a member of a couple. The third station is the **community remarriage.** Here, not only does the individual see herself or himself as part of a couple, but the nature of the relationship alters to emphasize couple activity at the expense of single friendships.

The second three stations of remarriage focus on couples in relation to their families. The fourth of the six stations, the **parental remarriage,** involves stepparenting. It is this relationship that is fraught with hardship and in the estimation of many authors is the most difficult task associated with remarriage. The fifth station, the **economic remarriage,** involves the melding of economic resources. Including as it does decisions about the allocation of often scarce financial resources, this area is ripe for potential disagreement. The final station, the **legal remarriage,** involves decisions about the future distribution of estate assets. It is concerned with such touchy issues as who should receive assistance beyond that awarded by the legal system—inheritance, support for college, and so on.

As with all typologies, there is nothing that forecasts that an individual will experience each of these issues as outlined. Nor is there any reason to believe they will occur in just this order for everyone. But, much can be learned by examining each of these stations in greater detail.

## The Emotional Remarriage

As we have already learned, the dissolution of a marriage is a painful event. It is particularly shattering to one's self-esteem when infidelity plays a role. In the last chapter we discussed the finding of Hayes et al. (1980) that half the marriages in their study had ended because of the husband's infidelity. Albrecht (1979) reports similar findings. His sample of 500 randomly selected ever-divorced persons ranked infidelity as the number one reason for ending a marriage (see Table 11-1).

Even if the reason for ending a marriage is not infidelity, the event is no less emotionally charged. Whether it is because of a mutual loss of affection, problems with in-laws, or financial difficulties, most divorced persons reenter the single state questioning the institution of marriage. It is therefore not surprising to see them testing their continued sexual desirability (as some authors have reported) both to bolster sagging self-esteem and to self-fulfill their expectations of the excitement of single life (Goetting, 1981). As we noted in the last chapter, this foray into single life brings to many, within a year or two, a dissatisfaction over the shallowness in the quality of their personal relationships. It is out of this dissatisfaction that the search for intimacy and companionship is renewed. Provided the "chemistry" between two persons is right, the process of establishing an intimate relationship, with all the risks for loss and rejection, begins again.

## The Psychic Remarriage

The "psychic divorce" (see Chapter 10) is the process of untying oneself from a couple relationship and establishing a new identity as an

**TABLE 11-1.** *Why marriages fail: Reasons given by 500 divorced persons*

| Reason | Number of Times Listed First | Rank | Total Number of Times Listed | Rank |
|---|---|---|---|---|
| Infidelity | 168 | 1 | 255 | 1 |
| No longer loved each other | 103 | 2 | 188 | 2 |
| Emotional problems | 53 | 3 | 185 | 3 |
| Financial problems | 30 | 4 | 135 | 4 |
| Physical abuse | 29 | 5 | 72 | 8 |
| Alcohol | 25 | 6 | 47 | 9 |
| Sexual problems | 22 | 7 | 115 | 5 |
| Problems with in-laws | 16 | 8 | 81 | 6 |
| Neglect of children | 11 | 9 | 74 | 7 |
| Communication problems | 10 | 10 | 18 | 11 |
| Married too young | 9 | 11 | 14 | 12 |
| Job conflicts | 7 | 12 | 20 | 10 |
| Other | 7 | | 19 | |

individual. The "psychic remarriage" involves reversing one's identity from that of an individual back to that of a couple.

Goetting (1982) notes that for women the ease of this transition depends on their gender identity. She speculates that women holding traditional gender identifications more easily make the move from a single to a couple identity because the "traditional" woman places a higher value on marriage. As Hancock (1980) suggests, society makes marriage central to a woman's identity. An individual who accepts this traditional position would more likely be deeply hurt by the dissolution of a marriage and, the reasoning goes, would adapt positively when returning to a couple relationship. Goetting believes that a nontraditional woman would have greater difficulties in this transition. Loss of the freedom and independence found in singlehood might be harder for such a woman to accept as she reenters couple life.

Central to the psychic remarriage is personal satisfaction in a relationship. As we learned earlier in this book, marital satisfaction is not equally distributed between the sexes. Interestingly, the second time around does little to even the score. Men remain, on average, more satis-fied with marriage than women (Albrecht, 1979; Glenn & Weaver, 1977; White, 1979). Thus, even though researchers find that remarriages are as satisfying as first marriages, sex differences within remarriage remain. For the nontraditional woman who does not hold marriage central to her identity, dissonance arises as she attempts to balance her need for autonomy against her need for companionship. Whether an individual is traditional or nontraditional, the psychic remarriage involves altering one's lifestyle to include another.

 *Do you agree that a "traditional" woman will more easily adjust to a couple relationship than a "nontraditional" woman?*

### The Community Remarriage

Change in a person's circle of relationships often accompanies a divorce. Friendships from the former marriage rarely last. Support from one's family of origin can waver depending on the stresses that family is experiencing at the time and members' approval or disapproval of the divorce.

Adjusting to these changes, the divorced person creates a new circle of friendships, which is vulnerable to disruption when the person reenters a couple relationship. Goetting (1982) suggests that as the couple's relationship evolves, "one may be put in a position of severing the close personally-tailored ties established while divorced, and replacing them with less intimate, couple-oriented relationships" (p. 219). It appears that in reestablishing couple intimacy the person sacrifices intimate relationships with others. The community remarriage also marks the reentry of one person into another person's family. For example, one study on women's kin relationships (Anspach, 1976) finds that a divorce decreases a woman's contact with her former husband's family. With remarriage she is absorbed into the family of the new husband.

> **?** *In your opinion, why do many single friendships end and couple friendships begin when two persons form a couple?*

## The Parental Remarriage

It takes most people a good part of their lifetime to acquire a house, a dog, and a car, to marry, and to have children. Over the years it takes to reach this position in life, they have time to adapt to change. Yet, consider the newly remarried family with children. In some ways it is analogous to a frozen TV dinner. Preparation time is minimal—just marry and combine. The potential for things going haywire in this instant family is high, and many reports support the conclusions of a study by Bowerman and Irish (1962):

> Homes involving steprelations proved more likely to have stress, ambivalence, and low cohesiveness than did normal homes. . . . Stepmothers have more difficult roles than do stepfathers. . . . Stepdaughters generally manifested more extreme reactions toward their parents

Ms. MAGAZINE COVER FOR FEBRUARY 1985

*His . . . hers . . . and now ours. Remarriage often produces the instant family.*

than did stepsons. The presence of stepparents in the home [tended to diminish children's] level of adjustment [p. 121].

And yet, our understanding of remarried life is not as bleak as that depicted in the above passage. Many stresses must be handled and readjustments made, but stepparents and stepchildren can succeed if the new family resolves four somewhat amorphous issues.

*Entry of a new stepparent.* The first issue is the entry of a new stepparent into a family. Several writers have discussed the difficulty many stepparents have in entering a family in which the position of mother or father has been "frozen"—filled by the child(ren) (Goldstein, 1974; Messinger & Walker, 1981; Visher & Visher, 1983; Whiteside, 1982). These authors believe "freezing" happens because the single parent turns to the children between marriages for emotional support, love, and even guidance. Reordering this structure is a delicate and often painful process, during which offspring feel rejected by their natural parent.

*Role ambiguity in stepparenthood.* Roles and boundaries are unclear in newly formed stepfamilies. Some authors have gone so far as to say that "organizational disturbance in stepfamilies is inevitable" (Fast & Cain, 1966, p. 485); others have commented that stepfamilies are "forever scrambling to maintain some semblance of equilibrium" (Visher & Visher, 1978, p. 255). This search for order occurs partly because society has not been able to respond quickly enough to the new variations found within stepfamilies. As Prosen and Farmer (1982) observe, *stepparent* originally meant a new individual in a household who replaced a dead parent, not a living one. In replacing a living parent, a stepparent becomes an "added" parent. Further, the replaced parent rarely disappears (Goldstein, 1974). Thus, the new stepparent not only is initially frozen out of a role but has the additional burden of wondering what that role should be (Kent, 1980; Nelson & Nelson, 1982; Ransom et al., 1979; Whiteside, 1982). Many authors recommend that time, understanding, and tolerance will resolve this issue. A stepparent's role is not ascribed but achieved, and that role can vary from family to family (Messinger & Walker, 1981; Visher & Visher, 1983; Walker & Messinger, 1979).

*Reaction of offspring to the remarriage.* The ability to thaw a family's structure to permit a stepparent to play a role is advanced or retarded by the immediate and long-term reactions of offspring to the remarriage. Young people in a remarriage face some difficult new life circumstances. Not only have they been separated from one natural parent, but they have obtained a surrogate parent, possibly new half-brothers and half-sisters, and other assorted kinfolk. The potential for conflict is certainly present.

Accordingly, it is not surprising that some studies show remarriage has negative effects on young people. More mental health problems are reported for young people in remarried homes than for those in homes broken by death or divorce, although all three groups show more dysfunction than children in intact families (Langner & Michael, 1963; Rosenberg, 1965). Some suggest that a young person's poor adjustment to remarriage may result from wishes that the biological parents would remarry, guilt over imagining the child caused the divorce, or failure to resolve the loss (Prosen & Farmer, 1982). Some authors believe that a child's age is not important in determining a stepparent's success in parenting (Palermo, 1980). Others disagree, suggesting that as young people grow older, it becomes more difficult for stepparents to assume a parenting role (Kompara, 1980).

Finally, some studies find that young people in remarried households with stepfathers commit more delinquent acts (Haney & Gold, 1977). Kalter (1977) underscores this point by adding that, for girls, higher levels of drug use and sexual activity are associated with having a stepfather. Kalter offers the possible explanation that much of this acting-out behavior is due to a "lack of incest barrier between stepfather and daughter" (p. 47). Goldstein (1974) suggests that much of the hostility between adolescent girls and stepfathers may be an attempt to "protect the participants from their sexual impulses" (p. 438). In contrast, others see these problems as emerging from the difficulty daughters may have in accepting their mothers as sexually active beings (Visher & Visher, 1983).

Unquestionably, there is a lowered incest barrier (Fast & Cain, 1966; Schulman, 1972). These feelings are complicated by the stepfamily's struggle for cohesiveness at the same time the adolescent is trying to resolve oedipal issues and to separate from the family. One author suggests the resolution of this situation rests, to a great extent, with the natural mother's ability to "maintain the incest taboo" (that is, to ensure the relationship does not acquire incestuous overtones). If she is successful in establishing the taboo, she relieves her daughter and husband of the need to maintain a mask of "pseudo-hostility" (Goldstein, 1974).

But not all the writings about young people living in stepfamilies are filled with warnings. Several studies have found few, if any, differences between unbroken and remarried families. According to one study, for instance, "The impact of divorce, father loss, and solo parenting [on evaluations of self and parent] tends to be modified when the remaining parent . . . remarries" (Parish & Dostal, 1980, p. 350). The direction of this change depends on which parent remarries—more favorable for fathers, less favorable for mothers. However, the difference for mothers is not significant (Parish & Dostal, 1980). In other work with a sample of 98 female college students who had lost a father to death or divorce, those whose mothers had remarried felt more secure and evaluated themselves more positively than the others (Young & Parish, 1977). Burchinal (1964) compared five family types—unbroken, single parent (mother head of household), remarried (mother–stepfather), remarried (father–stepmother), and remarried (both parents)—for differences in personality characteristics and social relationships. He found no differences in personality characteristics (illness proneness, nervousness, anxiety, mood changes, envy, withdrawal) of the adolescents in these five family types and no particular differences in social relationships, school/community activities, academic average, popularity, or attitudes toward school. These findings led Burchinal to conclude:

It is true that some children will suffer extreme trauma because of divorce or separation and consequent withdrawal of one parent, and for some, their development will be affected deleteriously. However, even in these cases, it is difficult to assess whether the difficulty occurs because of divorce or whether it reflects the conflict preceding the divorce and separation. Nevertheless . . . there is no question that . . . family dissolution and, for some families, reconstitution, was not the overwhelming influential factor in the children's lives that many thought it to be. . . . Acceptance of this conclusion required the revision of widely held beliefs about the detrimental effect of divorce upon children [p. 54].

Burchinal's view that remarriage can be a positive or negative experience for offspring, depending on conditions not directly related to the marriage, is shared by Wilson, Zurcher, McAdams, and Curtis (1975). To see whether differences exist between young people in unbroken homes and young people with stepfathers, these researchers examined 106 social and psychological factors from two large national surveys. Their findings supported Burchinal's. They further questioned the accuracy of such stereotypes as the "evil stepfather" and the idea that having a stepfather is emotionally damaging. They suggested that remarriages (with a stepfather) are not inferior to natural-parent families.

Finally, one group of researchers reported that "the social behavior of children is not necessarily less competent in stepfamilies than in intact families" (Santrock, Warshak, Lindbergh, & Meadows, 1982, p. 480). These researchers set up a laboratory situation in which equal numbers of boys and girls, 6 to 11 years of age, in remarried, divorced, and intact families were observed interacting with their parents. These children and their (step)parents were asked first to plan a weekend activity together and then to discuss "the main problems of the family" (p. 475). These exercises were videotaped and then analyzed for content. Santrock et al. found that boys in stepfather families showed more competent social behavior than boys in intact families. However, girls in stepfather families displayed more anxiety than girls in intact families. No differences were observed between divorced and intact families. Interestingly, and of importance, the authors noted that differences between step- and intact families were compounded by the marital conflict present in those families. In this sample, boys from intact families and girls from stepfather families had more marital conflict in their homes than their counterparts. This report of personal functioning tied to family environment echoes Nye's (1957) observation that young people's behaviors are affected less by the form of their family than by the degree of happiness found there. We would like to emphasize this last point. There is nothing sacred about any family form. Young people wither just as quickly in unhappy and unnourishing nuclear families as in unhappy and unnourishing divorced or re-married families. We will admit that young people prosper more readily in a nuclear family untouched by severe marital turmoil. However, it is not the single-parent or remarried family structure that impedes maturation. Rather, it is the turmoil found in the original nuclear family that contributes to developmental delays—delays that can be reversed in a new family form.

*Parenting issues.* The final issue that the step-family must resolve is parenting. Children's fairy tales are filled with stories of the cruelty stepparents (stepmothers in particular) show to their stepchildren. For example, who among us has not felt anger toward Hansel and Gretel's, Snow White's, or Cinderella's wicked stepmother? Stepfathers have escaped this stigmatization, although it has been suggested that the giant in "Jack and the Beanstalk" symbolizes a stepfather (Visher & Visher, 1978).

One reason stepmothers have fared so poorly in the literature is that they are so intimately connected to children. Stepparenting is no easy task, particularly when the children are adolescents. Lutz (1983) found that adolescents have the greatest difficulty in accepting discipline from a stepparent. Because stepmothers are more likely than stepfathers to have close contact with the children in the new family, a stepmother faces more disciplinary issues, and problems inevitably arise about her authority to discipline her husband's children. Most authors agree that a stepparent should not try to step into the role of natural parent too quickly. Many advise stepparents that it may be better in the beginning to attempt friendships rather than parent relationships with their new stepchildren (Kompara, 1980).

According to Kompara (1980), permitting a young person the time to mourn enables the stepparent to move from friend, perhaps, to parent with a smaller chance of rejection. Settling parenting issues in such a way that the parents are cooperating with each other in a *consistent* fashion reduces the chance that stepmothers (or stepfathers) will be viewed as witches (or evil giants) and will increase the probability that the French term for stepmother, *belle mère* ("beautiful mother"), will be applied (Schulman, 1972).

**?**

*How might a natural parent "unfreeze" a role for a stepparent? Is the cooperation of the other biological parent necessary?*

*Do you think that in time a stepparent's role will be ascribed, not achieved?*

*How might a parent establish an "incest barrier"?*

*Do you agree with the authors that a bad family environment damages the emotional growth of children and that this harm can be reversed?*

*Should a stepparent ever try to fill the role of a natural parent; if so, when?*

## BOX 11-2
### *The Ten Commandments of Stepparenting*

No one ever said living in a stepfamily would be easy. But then, no one in his or her right mind ever said living in any family would be easy. The following words of advice by Sharon and James Turnbill apply not only to stepfamilies but to all families. To live in "peaceful coexistence," Turnbill and Turnbill (1983) suggest:

1. "Provide neutral territory." If a family cannot start over in a new house or apartment, then at least provide the children with some space that is theirs and theirs alone.

2. "Don't try to fit a preconceived role." In short, be yourself.

3. "Set limits and enforce them." Consistency between the marital partners is the rule here.

4. "Allow an outlet for feelings by the children for the natural parent." Natural parents do not disappear from a child's life. Allow the children the right to have feelings for their biological parent.

5. "Expect ambivalence." Parents are loved and hated from minute to minute in nuclear families, and the same occurs in stepfamilies.

6. "Avoid mealtime misery." If war over the meal table can be avoided, it should be.

7. "Don't expect instant love." Children need time to mourn the loss of their divorced biological parent. Time and tolerance will permit a role of friend and/or parent to emerge for a stepparent.

8. "Don't take all the responsibility. The child has some too."

9. "Be patient."

10. "Maintain the privacy of the marital relationship." Parents need to show their children a unified front, and when disagreements occur, they can be settled amicably.

## The Economic Remarriage

As discussed in Chapter 10, divorce significantly reduces a family's financial standing. Remarriage brings an expansion of financial resources, but decisions are no less complicated. In fact, financial problems top the list of the difficulties remarried families face (see Table 11-2). One study, for example, finds that husbands experience considerable trouble in trying to support their new family while maintaining alimony and/or child support payments to their old family (Albrecht, 1979). Just try to imagine the pressures created in these situations. How does one balance limited financial resources? Can you purchase music lessons for your biological children and deprive your stepchildren of those same opportunities?

This dilemma underscores the reality that the first marriage, particularly when children are involved, has a continuing and important impact on the second marriage. Even though the relationship was legally severed by the courts, emotional and/or financial arrangements continue to tie former marital partners together.

The situation is further complicated when a stepfamily fails to receive the child support payments it expects (Goetting, 1982). We know from the last chapter that there is considerable variability in the amount awarded for support and the amount (if any) actually received. The distressing uncertainty is one of cash flow. The stepfamily is never sure what its resources will be. Anger may grow as a result, and considerable pressure may fall in a displaced manner on the stepfather to curtail his monetary support of his biological family. Resolving these issues is exceedingly difficult.

**TABLE 11-2.** *Major problems in remarried families reported by 369 remarried persons*

| Problem | Number of Times Listed First | Rank | Total Number of Times Listed | Rank |
|---|---|---|---|---|
| Financial problems | 55 | 1 | 74 | 1 |
| Emotional problems | 21 | 2 | 49 | 2 |
| Sexual problems | 17 | 3/4 | 30 | 3 |
| Spouse's former marriage | 17 | 3/4 | 25 | 4/5 |
| Problems with in-laws | 9 | 5/6 | 25 | 4/5 |
| Conflict over children | 9 | 5/6 | 15 | 6 |
| Neglect of children | 7 | 7 | 10 | 7/8 |
| No longer love each other | 5 | 8/9 | 10 | 7/8 |
| Infidelity | 5 | 8/9 | 7 | 9 |
| Own former marriage | 1 | 10/11 | 4 | 10/11 |
| Physical abuse | 1 | 10/11 | 3 | 10/11 |

To moderate the impact of such uncertainty, many families organize their finances in one of two ways. Some follow the "common pot" method, pooling all the family's economic resources. Others choose the "two pot" system: the spouses keep their resources separate, and each spouse assumes responsibility for his or her own children but common expenses are shared. Other types of arrangements exist too. According to Fishman (1983), the economic behavior of stepfamilies affects family life. "Common pot" families seem to be drawn closer together by their economic interdependence, while "two pot" families appear to maintain more loyalty to the natural parents. Before marrying, increasing numbers of couples are consulting lawyers and drawing up letters of agreement (Fishman, 1983). Such actions are part of the legal remarriage.

 *What advantages and disadvantages do one-pot and two-pot family economic strategies have?*

## The Legal Remarriage

Walker, Rogers, and Messinger (1977, p. 277) have written that remarriage "begins with a set of legal encumbrances" that involve alimony and (if children are present) custody, child support, and visiting rights. Some 1 million young people begin living in stepfamilies and one-half million adults enter the role of stepparent each year, and society continues to grapple with the responsibilities these family members have to one another (Kargman, 1983).

Legal remarriage involves estate issues. How shall a remarried person divide his or her accumulated life's earnings? Is it given to biological children or stepchildren, to first or second spouse, to all or none? Moreover, what responsibility does a stepparent have to support a stepchild should the second marriage end? Presently, there is no legal responsibility for child support. But with stepparents asking for and receiving visitation rights when a remarriage ends, this situation may change. Whether in future decades society will prescribe rules (through laws) to govern these matters or whether this area will remain undefined is a question that will remain, for now, unanswered.

 *In your opinion, should society be concerned with the legal remarriage?*

Clearly, stepfamilies have to struggle with many difficult issues. Preventionists can offer several ideas for ways stepfamilies can help themselves and be helped to adjust to the inevitable stresses that accompany remarriage.

*Why is the preventionist so interested in providing information and letting the individual decide what to do with it? Why not just tell stepparents what to do and be done with it?*

## EDUCATION

Education is predicated on the belief that human beings are rational creatures capable of learning from their experience and the experiences of others. This tool attempts to enlighten and inform people and to prepare them for potential pitfalls before they remarry. One form of education is the written word. Publications like *Yours, Mine and Ours: Tips for Stepparents* (National Institute of Mental Health, 1978) have been designed to confront the prospective stepparent with the difficult issues that await resolution in a newly merged family (see Box 11-3). This publication encourages future stepparents to recognize that problems may occur and then to work on those areas before trouble starts.

A second form of education for facing and dealing with issues like role ambiguity is a family-life education course. Using films, roleplays, and small-group discussions, such seminars help people define the issues that are most pressing for them. In this setting, myths and feelings that all good stepparents must be close to their stepchildren or are alone in their struggle to create a new family can be faced. Such educational programs can help participants realize that their problems are shared by others. By using the experience of others, preventionists hope, stepparents can develop their own problem-solving approaches.

## COMMUNITY MOBILIZATION/ SYSTEMS INTERVENTION

What structural changes might help remarried families prosper? One would be the prevention of discrimination and the promotion of tolerance. Remarriage after a divorce is relatively recent, and society has evolved few rules for handling this event. To encourage tolerance, one might focus attention on the institutional practices of organizations that stigmatize stepchildren, thus communicating to them a message that their families should be sources of embarrassment rather than pride. For example, does your local school curriculum stress the pluralistic nature of the American family, or does it emphasize only the nuclear family? If its reading materials show only nuclear families, then a subtle message of inferiority is being communicated to children whose families are different. This is a message that can be changed.

To begin to remedy discriminatory practices, one might look at insurance company policies that do not permit a stepchild to be covered by a stepparent's health insurance plan. You might ask yourself what message we are giving stepchildren when an insurance company refuses to cover their health costs but insures the remarried couple and their biological offspring. If you believe that message is stigmatizing, you may

## BOX 11-3
### *Tips on Preparing to Live in Step*

Earlier in this chapter we offered the advice of Sharon and James Turnbill (1983) for living in step. This next selection is taken from the National Institute of Mental Health publication *Yours, Mine and Ours: Tips for Stepparents* (1978). It illustrates well one of the educational tools of prevention—namely, anticipatory guidance. The following advice is intended to help forming families deal with the pressures that confront almost everyone with children who remarries:

- Plan ahead! Some chapters of Parents Without Partners conduct "Education for Remarriage" workshops. Contact your local chapter or write to Parents Without Partners, 7910 Woodmont Ave., Washington, D. C. 20014.

- Examine your motives and those of your future spouse for marrying. Get to know him or her as well as possible under all sorts of circumstances. Consider the possible impact of contrasting life-styles.

- Discuss the modifications that will be required in bringing two families together. Look for similarities and differences in your ideas about child rearing.

- Explore with your children the changes remarriage will bring—new living arrangements, new family relationships, effect on their relationship with their noncustodial parent.

- Give your children ample opportunity to get to know your future spouse well. Consider your children's feelings, but don't let them make your decision about remarriage.

- Discuss the disposition of family finances with your future spouse. An open and honest review of financial assets and responsibilities may reduce unrealistic expectations and resulting misunderstandings.

- Understand that there are bound to be periods of doubt, frustration, and resentment.

- Let your relationship with stepchildren develop gradually. Don't expect too much too soon—from the children or from yourself. Children need time to adjust, accept, and belong. So do parents.

- Don't try to replace a lost parent; be an additional parent. Children need time to mourn the parent lost through divorce or death.

- Expect to deal with confusing feelings—your own, your spouse's, and the children's. Anxiety about new roles and relationships may heighten competition among family members for love and attention; loyalties may be questioned. Your children may need to understand that their relationship with you is valued but different from your relationship with your spouse and that one cannot replace the other. You love and need them both, but in different ways.

- Recognize that you may be compared with the absent parent. Be prepared to be tested, manipulated, and challenged in your new role. Decide, with your mate, what is best for your children and stand by it.

- Understand that stepparents need support from natural parents on child-rearing issues. Rearing children is tough; rearing someone else's is tougher.

- Acknowledge periods of cooperation among stepsiblings. Try to treat your stepchildren and your own with equal fairness. Communicate! Don't pretend that everything is fine when it isn't. Acknowledge problems immediately and deal with them openly.

- Admit that you need help if you need it. Don't let the situation get out of hand. Everyone needs help sometimes. Join an organization for stepfamilies; seek counseling.

want to encourage legislative actions to correct this situation.

Finally, in some states, when a stepparent dies without a will, the stepchildren are automatically excluded from entitlement to any part of the estate. If you believe that this legislation reflects an ancient discriminatory attitude against stepchildren, you might encourage change to correct this practice.

> **?** *Do other institutional practices stigmatize stepchildren? What are they? How might they be changed? Does society have a responsibility for addressing these issues? On a more personal level, do you have a responsibility for addressing issues of discrimination and intolerance?*

## COMPETENCY PROMOTION

How does one promote a feeling of family pride in a stepchild? We suspect that several groups play important roles in generating a child's pride in his or her family. One group is the child's extended family. If stepgrandparents and other relatives act embarrassed or treat the stepfamily with condescension, then messages that this family is somehow defective are being transmitted. If school curricula and teacher behaviors favor one family structure over others, then the opportunity to enhance family pride is lost. The same can be said for church and youth organizations.

If we assume that a stepchild's reaction to a remarriage mirrors, in part, the community's reaction to that marriage, then the importance of accepting remarriage as a legitimate institutionalized structure becomes quickly evident. And yet, experience tells us that discriminatory behavior by relatives, neighbors, schools, and others will continue. Can these harmful actions be neutralized?

The preventionist believes the answer to this question is a qualified yes. The remarried family can internally generate a sufficient sense of unity to negate most of the hostility in the environment. This sense of family unity, leading to pride in one's family, is facilitated, we believe, by communication, mutual support, and the expression of warm positive regard for all family members.

> **?** *One can lobby schools and other community organizations to encourage a pluralistic view of the family; what actions could one take with friends and relatives? What activities, actions, or traditions contributed to a sense of pride in your family? How did they generate that pride?*

*Stepfamilies can and do succeed in environments in which communication, mutual support, and the expression of warm positive regard for all family members are maintained.*

# NATURAL CAREGIVING

The essence of natural caregiving is the provision of social support. For parents, two possible sources of support are the family-life education group and the mutual self-help group. These groups enable stepparents to share the disappointments and the triumphs of stepparenthood (Messinger, Walker, & Freeman, 1978; Pill, 1981). By giving stepparents an opportunity to ventilate their frustrations, these groups can ease the tension between generations. They permit stepparents to draw on the strength, wisdom, and life experience of others in resolving home difficulties.

For children a potential source of support is the classroom teacher. As a trained indigenous caregiver, the teacher is in a position to affect not only a classroom's but a stepchild's attitudes toward remarriage. As a young person approaches adolescence, mutual self-help groups in the form of peer counseling networks offer the friendly ear of a reflective listener that is so often helpful in putting problems into perspective.

Finally, each of us should consider the role we can play as indigenous caregivers. To change society's attitudes toward remarriage, we can begin with our own attitude. We can, by our own behavior toward others, put into practice the principles espoused in this last section.

**?** *A major tenet of the preventionist's philosophy is that each of us has a responsibility for other human beings. This belief is reflected in the preventionist's tool of natural caregiving. Do you agree with this principle? Can you think of instances when such assistance could be harmful or could be construed as meddling interference? What guidelines might govern when assistance should and should not be given?*

# SUMMARY

Remarriage, like divorce, appears to have been easy in ancient times and to have become more difficult as Christianity spread—except that remarriage of the widowed remained common. Today, in contrast, many remarriages occur after divorces. The average age of people marrying after a divorce is in the thirties, and four of five persons currently divorcing will marry again.

The issues we have looked at in this chapter affect more than a half million new adults and 1 million new young people each year. Reentering marriage after the dissolution of a previous marital union is not easy, especially if there are children. The opportunities for failure, as in every other life event, are ever present. But families do make it. They do succeed. We believe those that do are prepared for the challenges that will confront them. They seek and receive social support from their surrounding environment, and they are able to be flexible in adjusting to new and ever-changing family events.

# MAJOR POINTS TO REMEMBER

1. From a historical perspective, remarriage after a divorce is a new occurrence.
2. Roughly equal numbers of men and women remarry. However, when a man remarries, it is typically to a younger woman.
3. For the symbolic interactionist, remarriage is but one symbol interacting with others that individuals endow with meaning. The reasons for remarrying after a divorce are found in a personal context.
4. Roughly four out of five divorced persons remarry.
5. Remarriages occur for many reasons, including the desire to establish a meaning-ful relationship, love, companionship, and fulfillment of personal or societal expectations.
6. Just as remarriages occur for many reasons, they also end for many reasons, including unresolved personal conflicts carried over from the first marriage, the presence of children, money problems, and the greater ease of divorcing the second time around.
7. There are six stations leading to remarriage: the emotional, psychic, community, parental, economic, and legal remarriages.
8. Successful stepparenting involves resolving four somewhat amorphous issues: the entry of the new stepparent into the family, role ambiguity in stepparenthood, the reaction of offspring to the remarriage, and parenting.
9. Some stepfamilies handle their financial affairs using a "common pot" approach, while others use a "two pot" approach. How finances are handled has a bearing on the family's sense of identity.
10. Careful planning before a remarriage and promoting tolerance as two prevention strategies for helping stepfamilies succeed.

# ADDITIONAL SOURCES OF INFORMATION

## *Publications*

### *Remarriage*

Baer, J. (1972). *The second wife: How to live happily with a man who has been married before.* Garden City, NY: Doubleday. [Adults]

Block, J. D. (1979). *To marry again.* New York: Grosset & Dunlap. [Adults]

Flack, F. F. (1978). *A new marriage: A new life.* New York: McGraw-Hill. [Adults]

Greene, C. C. (1978). *I and Sproggy*. New York: Viking Press. [Children]

Okimoto, J. D. (1980). *It's just too much*. New York: Putnam's. [Children]

*Stepfamilies*

Benjamin, C. L. (1982). *The wicked stepdog*. New York: Thomas Y. Crowell. [Children]

Berman, C. (1980). *Making it as a stepparent: New roles, new rules*. Garden City, NY: Doubleday. [Adults]

Duberman, L. (1975). *The reconstituted family: A study of remarried couples and their children*. Chicago: Nelson-Hall. [Adults]

Einstein, E. (1982). *The stepfamily: Living, loving and learning*. New York: Macmillan. [Adults]

Felker, E. (1981). *Raising other people's kids*. Grand Rapids, MI: Eerdmans. [Adults]

Visher, E. B., & Visher, J. S. (1979). *Stepfamilies: A guide to working with stepparents and stepchildren*. New York: Brunner/Mazel. [Adults]

Visher, E. B., & Visher, J. S. (1982). *How to win as a stepfamily*. New York: Dembrer Books. [Adults]

## Organizations

Remarrieds Inc.
Box 742
Santa Ana, CA 92701

The Stepfamily Foundation
333 West End Ave.
New York, NY 10023

# 12

# MARRIAGE AND FAMILY LIFE IN THE LATER YEARS

1. When do we begin aging? What are the benefits and liabilities of aging?

2. What are the developmental tasks of middle age? What factors can influence these tasks?

3. Why do middle-agers have more interaction with relatives than any other age group?

4. What is filial responsibility and who is most likely to exercise it?

5. What are some of the reasons middle-agers change careers?

6. What events typically divide middle from late adulthood?

7. Why are there more widows than widowers?

8. Who is most helpful in the short and long term in assisting the widowed to cope with and adjust to the death of a spouse?

9. How critical are sons and daughters to the well-being of older adults? What percentage of older adults provide help to their grown children? What percentage receive help? What are the most common services exchanged between older adults and their children?

10. What are the most common housing arrangements for older adults? What percentage are in nursing homes at any given time?

I'm middle-aged now. And in some ways—not all—I never had it so good. The terror is gone. Bogeymen don't scare me. I'm a bogeyman myself now and I know how we operate [Elkin, 1981, p. 15].

Between the turn of the century and the present, the number of persons aged 65 and over has increased eightfold; their proportion in the population has increased threefold. The status of old people has increased not at all [Shanas, 1980, p. 14].

The aged are the true pioneers of our time, and pioneer life is notoriously brutal [Plath, 1972, p. 9].

What are middle age and late adulthood like? When we picture people in these stages, we probably don't think about Joan Collins, who posed nude for *Playboy* at age 50, or Bobe Hope, who entertained U. S. troops abroad at age 80.

Our society is becoming aware of a new prejudice—**ageism,** "a systematic stereotyping of and discrimination against people because they are old" (Butler, 1975, p. 12). Just like racism and sexism, ageism means we place people in a negative category (incapable or unworthy due to race, sex, handicap, or age) rather than seeing them as individuals with capacities and deficits, just like everyone else. Ageism may be overt or subtle. For example, people in their fifties or older rarely appear in advertisements for clothing, cosmetics, homes, or food. (Don't people in these age groups use these goods?) Instead, older models sell denture adhesives, dyes to color gray hair, and medicines—products that emphasize the deterioration of the body. It's no wonder so many of us don't want to think about growing older!

To overcome ageism, many biases—conscious and unconscious—must be overcome. First, many people think that getting older means getting stagnant. Most of the people in

*At the time of the American revolution the median age of the colonists was 18, and 50 was old. Today, with the median age well above 30, society's definition of old has changed and women who at one time would have been considered elderly are regarded as sex symbols.*

these stages, however, are involved and interesting. They have a broader perspective on issues as a result of their extensive experience. Second, we sometimes confuse aging with disease and disability (Butler, 1975). Although older adults have a greater incidence of health problems, only 5% are receiving institutional care (in a hospital or nursing home) at any given time (Butler, 1975). The majority are able to care for themselves and for others. Third, we tend to judge people's abilities by their age, when in fact people age at different rates and some adults have become famous for accomplishments in their later years (see Box 12-1). Bernice Neugarten, an

eminent gerontologist (student of aging), believes that our "social clock," which tells us when we should marry, raise children, and retire, is getting more fluid, thereby enabling us to move at our own pace rather than following an arbitrary pattern established by society (Hall, 1983). Thus, stagnation, disability, and incompetence are three erroneous stereotypes associated with aging. Although some older people suffer from these problems, so do people at other stages of development.

Aging may be looked at in many ways. Some people see it as a process of losing what one has, while others see it as an opportunity to gain something new. In fact, both perspectives are correct. For example, in our fifties we may have lost some of the energy we had in our twenties, but we may possess greater perspective and understanding. Our attitudes about aging (losing, gaining, or both) will influence how we feel about this process.

When do we begin aging? Actually, since before we were born, we have been "growing mature or old" (*Funk & Wagnalls Encyclopedic College Dictionary,* 1968). If we think of aging as the natural process of development, it seems less unappealing or frightening. To age also means "to become mellow or mature . . . to acquire a desirable quality" (*Webster's New Collegiate Dictionary,* 1977).

How old is "old"? In the authors' experience, *old* is a highly subjective and relative term. When we were 10, 16 was old. When we were 16, 35 was old. Now that we are in our thirties, 70 seems old. How old will "old" be when we're in our seventies? Perhaps 100? At age 80, Malcolm Cowley (1980) wrote his own book on what it is like to be old because other books on the subject had been written by "lads and lasses" in their late fifties or early sixties! Clearly, "old" is influenced by our personal perspectives.

Much of our language reflects our unflattering view of aging. In developing this chapter, the authors struggled with what to call these stages

**Konrad Adenauer** (1876–1967) was 73 when he became the first chancellor of the Federal Republic of Germany.

**Pope John XXIII** (1881–1963) was chosen pope at 77 and is noted for reforms resulting from the Second

Vatican Council, which he convened.

**Jomo Kenyatta** (c. 1894–1978) was elected Kenya's first president at age 70 and led the country for 14 years.

**Golda Meir** (1898–1978) was named prime minister

of Israel at 71 and served for five years.

**Anna Mary Robertson Moses** (1860–1961) was 76 when she began painting as a hobby. Known as Grandma Moses, she won international fame and staged 15 one-woman shows throughout Europe.

and the people in them. We chose *middle adulthood* and *late adulthood* because they describe the placement of these stages in the life span. We use *middle-agers* and *older adults,* respectively, to refer to people in these stages. These terms are neutral but descriptive. Perhaps in the future our language will change to accommodate these or other positive terms for people at these stages of life.

Middle adulthood is defined as ages 45–64 and late adulthood as over 64. These divisions are arbitrary, based on changes most families face: children leaving home (beginning of middle adulthood) and retirement (beginning of late adulthood). We recognize, of course, that the departure of children or the beginning of retirement occurs earlier for some people, later for others, and not at all for others. Within these stages, many other factors may influence our lives: job changes, unemployment, health problems, and the death of family members or friends, to name a few.

Although research on retirement families was sparse 20 years ago, this age group has received considerable attention during the past two decades. We know a great deal about the lives of older adults—their family and social relationships, their finances and work, their health, and

their housing arrangements. Unfortunately, the middle-agers have received far less attention (Streib & Beck, 1980). Our discussion of this stage will be shorter, not because it is less important but because we know less about it.

## MIDDLE ADULTHOOD

Middle adulthood is a

distinct period in the life cycle that seems to be better defined in terms of social clocking than chronological age. It is a time when many aspects of life are nearing an end. Middle age is a period of self-reflection. For some, it is a rebirth of the self . . . a renaissance . . . a time to plunge ahead with pleasure and opportunity. For others, middle age is a period of stagnation. For still others, it is fraught with unresolved crises [Robertson, 1978, p. 377].

As in any other stage, some people adapt well and others adapt poorly.

### *Psychological Changes*

The goal of any transition from one stage to another—adolescence, parenthood, or middle adulthood—is to end a phase of one's life, accept the end of that phase, and review it to decide which aspects to keep and which to discard (Levinson, Darrow, Klein, Levinson, & McKee, 1978). Researchers suggest that the middle-age transition requires five tasks: (1) recognizing biological limits and health risks, (2) restructuring one's self-concept, (3) assessing work and accomplishments, (4) reassessing important relationships, and (5) accepting death and mortality (Cytrynbaum et al., 1980). These tasks relate to putting one's life into perspective—relationships, accomplishments, and mortality. Although this focus may seem negative, it is not. These tasks require a shift from an idealistic outlook (what I would like in my life) to a realistic one (what I have had in my life and can expect in the future). Completion of these tasks helps us reorder priorities, liberate energy for the future, and increase self-acceptance (Jacques, 1965). Failure to complete these tasks means we may hold unrealistic goals, lack appreciation for what has been accomplished so far, or fail to accept the ultimate reality of life—death.

Perhaps middle age is best understood as a change in temporal orientation from "time since birth" to "time yet to live" (Neugarten, 1968). Brim (1982) has identified several facts about this transition, sometimes called a "midlife crisis." Not surprisingly, they are also true of other transitional stages, such as adolescence and old age. First, events in several spheres (for example, job, marriage, and health) may affect us within a short time, or these influences may stretch over a decade or more. Second, just like other transitions, this one marks the change from one steady state to another. Life was easier before the transition began, and it will be so again after the transition has passed. Third, the challenges we face do not appear in an established order or at a designated time. Fourth, we may be happier after adjustments have been made than before the transition began. Making a successful transition to middle adulthood means

that we will be better able to enjoy our lives and better prepared to cope when the next transition arrives.

In studying changes in men during middle adulthood, Brim (1982) identified seven possible catalysts. We believe they apply to women as well. These potential influences on the transition to middle adulthood are (1) endocrine changes, (2) concern about the gap between aspiration and achievement, (3) a resurgence of "the Dream" (how we hope our life will evolve), (4) the struggle between stagnation and growth, (5) changing relationships within the family, (6) social-status and role changes, and (7) confrontation with death. Let's look briefly at each of these changes.

Hormonal changes in the body signal that we are growing older. During the late forties or early fifties, most women cease menstruating and are no longer able to conceive children. Men have decreased levels of testosterone and take longer to achieve an erection, although their pleasure and fertility are not impaired (Carrera, 1981). These changes are normal, and people who accept them as an expected phase of development cope better than those who interpret them as signs of the end of life or of sexual functioning.

In our parenting or work roles or both, we may be concerned that we have not accomplished what we had hoped. This recognition can be distressing. Children may not have turned out as we hoped. Our job may not be as rewarding as we want. Or we may not have been promoted and now realize that others who are younger and have different skills will be promoted instead. Accepting these realities and restructuring our "Dream" so it remains within our grasp are key steps in coping with this stage of the life cycle.

Researchers have found that the sexes become more alike, perhaps in conjunction with these changes. Men become less aggressive, more social, more interested in love than in power, and more present- than future-oriented (Gutmann, 1969). Women become more aggressive, less sentimental, and more dominating. These changes are true across cultures (Gutmann, 1969). They may be a natural result of our development and may facilitate our ability to cope with this and later stages of life.

During this period a variety of changes may be occurring in family relationships. Children are likely to be leaving home, and both parents must adapt to this change. Parents and children become more equal. Mothers who have stayed home to raise children may return to work. The parents of middle-agers may need increased assistance. Each of these changes can influence the transition to middle adulthood.

Role changes include many of the family changes just mentioned. In addition, differences in jobs, income, and activities may influence social status.

The final major influence on the midlife transition is adjusting to death. Death is no longer a vague concept or something that happens to other people. During middle adulthood, death becomes a concept applied to our own lives. We come to fully recognize our own mortality and to adjust our lives in view of it (Jacques, 1965).

With all these changes influencing middle-age transitions, life during this stage can be quite challenging. Because substantial research has been done on family relationships during middle adulthood, let's turn our attention to this important aspect of life.

> **?** *Two persons, Kit and Lee, age 45, are ambitious in their jobs, committed to their families, and involved in other interests. What differences can be expected in their behavior and outlooks if Kit has adjusted to middle adulthood and Lee has not?*

## Family Relationships

The majority of research studies on people aged 45–64 have concentrated on family relationships—with spouse, children, grandchildren, aging parents, siblings, and other relatives. People in middle adulthood are often the second generation in a four-generation chain: their parents are the first generation, their children the third, and their grandchildren the fourth (Shanas, 1980). Many who are newly freed from child-rearing responsibilities find them replaced with caretaking of a parent (Streib & Beck, 1980), a situation that may be stressful for all involved (Shanas, 1980). Clearly, family relationships are a major influence on middle-agers.

Unfortunately, much of the research on family interaction during this stage focuses on the frequency of visits and the kinds of help exchanged. This information, though instructive, does not indicate what happens during the visits and how family members feel about each other. We may know that parents interact with their adult children periodically, but we do not know whether they enjoy or dislike these exchanges. Interaction between family members may range from joyous and rewarding to frustrating and infuriating. Information about family interaction should be considered carefully with these limits in mind.

Let's consider each of the major family relationships during middle adulthood.

*The spouse.* As we saw in Chapter 8, there is a small but consistent drop in marital satisfaction from a high in the early years to a low when the children are adolescents (Olson, McCubbin, & associates, 1983; Rollins & Cannon, 1974; Rollins & Feldman, 1970). Marital satisfaction seems to increase after children depart, although it does not reach the high point of the early years (see Figure 8-1).

As children leave home (frequently called the "launching" or "empty nest" stage), the parental role diminishes and the marital role may receive more attention. It is not surprising, then, that many couples report an increase in marital satisfaction. Shared interests and activities may multiply. Sexual activity, although it probably has declined in frequency over the years, is still enjoyed by most couples. Increased privacy, reduced time demands, and freedom from pregnancy can contribute to a couple's enhanced enjoyment of sex.

Without the demands of supporting children, many couples have the financial freedom to pamper themselves. They may travel, invest more energy in hobbies, and generally enjoy themselves. Financial planning and preparation for the retirement years may become priorities. If income is low, worries about making ends meet and concerns about the future may inhibit the freedom of these years.

After the children are launched, some couples find that the children were the only thing keeping them together. Some of these marriages continue; the unhappy partners exist together, alienated and disappointed. Others choose to divorce, and their transition to singlehood may be very traumatic. Having matured together, established a "couple identity," and raised children, these partners have invested much time and energy in their life as a couple. Dropping this identity and loosening their ties are difficult after so many years. A study of 310 divorced couples from ages 20 to 70+ found that those over 40 were more unhappy than younger age groups and those over 50 were unhappiest (Chiriboga, 1982). They were more pessimistic about life and seemed to have more trouble than younger people establishing a new social life. Divorce, not easy at any age, seems to be particularly traumatic in the later years. Of course, after adjustment, many find their lives more satisfying and

enriching. They develop new interests or foster old ones, meet new people, and rebuild and nurture their self-concepts.

Only a small percent of couples divorce during middle adulthood. Many find increased marital satisfaction and financial freedom. They exult in the opportunity to do things for themselves and to enjoy their evolving relationships with their children.

*Children.* The transitional phase between adolescence and adulthood is often troublesome to parents and their children. Changing from parents who care for, finance, supervise, and worry about their children to ones who allow offspring to take full responsibility for their own welfare requires dramatic shifts for all concerned.

Teenagers, in the midst of their search for a meaningful place in society, frequently are unaware that their parents may be facing their own identity crisis (Brim, 1982; Hess & Waring, 1982). If teenagers rebel against parental authority, parents are likely to feel unappreciated and may believe they have failed as parents. Although struggles with authority are typical for teenagers, they may threaten parents' self-concepts at a time when other areas are being reassessed as well.

Typically, children are "launched" when they marry or move away from home. Living apart helps parents and their "children" (who are typically in their late teens or early twenties) change their interaction patterns. With separate residences, it is difficult or impossible to enforce curfews, supervise activities, and provide daily care for young adults. In other families, the transition to adulthood is marked by parenthood or full-time employment without necessarily moving away from home. Whatever the case, in time, most parents reduce their worries and accept their children as adults who need to lead their own lives. Some parents begin making adjustments as their children mature, helping them to accept responsibility for themselves and their actions before they leave home.

In recent years, researchers have found that launching the last child is not stressful (Lowenthal & Chiriboga, 1975), that any negative effects on well-being "are slight and have largely disappeared" within two years (Harkins, 1978, p. 549; see also Glenn, 1975), that some women look forward to this time (Lowenthal & Chiriboga, 1975), and that earlier- or later-than-expected launchings are more troublesome to mothers than on-time ones (Harkins, 1978). In fact, in national surveys conducted in the mid-1960s and early 1970s, women in their forties and fifties were more likely to say they were "very happy" if their children were launched than if their children were still at home (Glenn, 1975). As more women are employed, both before and after children leave home, it is likely that launching will be less traumatic, because the work role will become an option.

Launching the last child during middle adulthood is a recent phenomenon (Troll, 1971). With the trend toward having fewer children and spacing them more closely together, today's families finish their child-rearing responsibilities at an earlier age. In the past, grandparents frequently still had young children of their own; today, they typically do not (Troll, 1971).

*Grandchildren.* Some experts believe that the importance of the grandparent role has increased in our country because people live longer (and therefore have more time to develop relationships with their grandchildren) and because people become grandparents at earlier ages (Troll, 1980a). Neugarten and Weinstein (1964) have identified five styles of grandparenting: funseeking, distant figure, formal, surrogate parent, and reservoir of family wisdom. Funseeking and distant-figure grandparents are likely to be younger, while those who are more formal are likely to be older. Younger grandparents may be more playful, engaging grandchildren in a variety of activities they both enjoy (the "funseeker"). Or they may have many interests and activities of their own (Clavan, 1978) and thus have less time for their grandchildren ("distant figure"). "Surrogate parents" are people who are substitute parents, significantly involved in raising someone else's children. Grandparents may be surrogate parents, particularly when the parents (their children) are adolescents, are single or divorced, or lack sufficient income. The "reservoir of family wisdom" grandparent is an adviser to the parent(s) and grandchildren. Clearly, as with other relationships, the amount and kind of interaction influence the relationship.

How important these relationships are to the grandparents, the grandchildren, or the parents, we simply don't know. For many they are vital, adding to the enjoyment of all. For others they are unimportant, offering only occasional (and not necessarily rewarding) contact. Today, grandparents must earn their status as "valued friends" (Troll, 1971), and some do not.

*Siblings.* Most adults have at least one living brother or sister (Cicirelli, 1980). A substantial number of siblings stay in contact. Although they may decrease their contact during the child-rearing years, they frequently become closer again once the children have departed. In fact, in one study, half the sisters reported feeling closer to each other in adulthood than they did in childhood (Adams, 1968). (This finding should be encouraging to parents of growing children who are struggling to reduce their children's sibling rivalry.)

The closeness of the ties varies according to sex. Typically, the sister/sister tie is closest, followed by the sister/brother tie and then the brother/brother tie (Cicirelli, 1980; Troll, 1980b). Older persons who have remained single are likely to maintain closer ties to their siblings (Shanas, 1980).

*Parents.* Although sibling relationships are important to many middle adults, their aging parents are likely to play a more central role in their lives. With increased life expectancies, it is not uncommon for people between 45 and 64 to have at least one living parent. These adults have more contact with relatives than any other age group, because they are likely to interact frequently with two generations—their children and their parents (Troll, 1971). These parents may range from vigorous and healthy, able to provide for their own needs, to partly or completely incapacitated. Of course, the relationship and interaction between these two generations will be strongly influenced by the capacities of both generations.

The kind and amount of care provided to elderly parents depend on diverse factors such as the parents' needs, their marital status and age, their resources, their distance from children, the adult child's resources and feelings of obligation, and the past and current parent/child relationship (Quinn, 1983; Seelbach, 1978). Table 12-1 shows that the help exchanged between these generations reflects their differing needs.

Exchanging gifts, services, and advice can foster the intergenerational bond (Hess & Waring, 1982). In some cases, elderly parents have little ability to help children, owing to financial or physical constraints, yet they themselves may need assistance, ranging from household maintenance to physical care during an illness to

**TABLE 12-1.** *Helping patterns of older adults and their children*

| Pattern of Assistance | Percentage Responding That They Provide Help | |
|---|---|---|
| | Homeowners | Residents of uptown residential hotel |
| *Older person helping child/grandchild* | | |
| When sick | 48 | 21 |
| Help care for children | 45 | 12 |
| Help shop/run errands | 20 | 0 |
| Give gifts | 89 | 76 |
| Help with money | 38 | 24 |
| Help fix things around the house | 26 | 3 |
| Help with housekeeping | 7 | 3 |
| Advice on jobs, business | 18 | 9 |
| General advice | 37 | 21 |
| *Older person receiving help from child/grandchild* | | |
| When sick | 83 | 58 |
| Advice on money matters | 26 | 30 |
| Help shop/run errands | 65 | 46 |
| Give gifts | 98 | 85 |
| Help fix things around the house | 66 | 24 |
| Help with housekeeping | 35 | 9 |
| Help with money | 19 | 42 |
| Provide transportation | 67 | 54 |
| Advice on jobs, business | 19 | 3 |
| General advice | 25 | 15 |

long-term, daily care. In these cases, duty may be the basis of the contact. *Filial* means appropriate to a son or daughter, and **filial responsibility** is an obligation to care for one's parents.

When these two generations live near each other, contact may be an obligation rather than a choice. When they live far apart, the obligation to visit is reduced, and contact may be limited mostly to letters and phone calls. For those who live a moderate distance apart, contact may be based on choice rather than duty (Adams, 1968). The offspring live far enough away to be excused from regular visits but close enough to visit if they choose.

Those who have a sense of filial responsibility and feelings of attachment to their parents are more likely to interact with them, providing companionship, care, and assistance (Cicirelli, 1983).

When widowed parents become disabled, whether for a short or a long time, children are the ones they most frequently ask for assistance (Cicirelli, 1981). Single children are more likely to provide help than married ones (Stoller, 1983), daughters are more likely to give help than sons (Shanas et al., 1968; Stoller, 1983), and children who are employed are slightly less likely to provide help (Lang & Brody, 1983).

In assessing the ability of the family to cope with an elderly parent, Ward (1978) concluded that families are effective in emergency situations and for short-term problems. A family is able to mobilize quickly, seek any necessary assistance from agencies, and help the parent recover. Most families cannot meet the long-term, intensive care needs of the elderly.

The amount of intergenerational interaction is substantial for people in middle adulthood. These exchanges may be characterized by warm, positive communication and sought by all involved, may be charged with negative emotions, or may be a mixture of both. They may reflect the needs of one generation for assistance and thus may result from a sense of duty rather than a choice to interact. Middle-agers may feel squeezed between the needs of two generations. Although we know more about familial relationships during middle adulthood than any other topic, there is still much more to learn.

 *What are the benefits and liabilities of allowing one's children ages 16 and over to make their own decisions? Are there areas in which parents should retain some power? If so, what are these areas and why?*

## Employment

Males are socialized primarily for the role of worker. Increasingly, females are being prepared to assume this role as well—not just as an interlude before marriage or children but as a role for the major part of their lives. In the early phase of middle adulthood, two major changes may occur in the worker role: a change in careers or reentry into the work force. Let's look at each.

Few studies exist on the incidence of midlife career changes. It seems that external forces, rather than personal preferences, play a major role (Parnes, Adams, Andrisani, Kohlen, & Nestel, 1975). Work-force cutbacks, permanent layoffs, abolished positions, health problems, or early retirement (for example, after 20 years' military service) may lead an employee to search for a new career. (See Chapter 14 for more information on employment and unemployment.)

Reentry into the work force is more characteristic of women than men because women are more likely to drop out. Whether returning because they seek new challenges or because expenses require it, many need retraining. We know little about how these women adapt or how rewarding they find their jobs.

The other major change in the employment area that occurs during middle adulthood is preparation for retirement. It is estimated that the average man who retires in the year 2000 will have 25 years of retirement, compared with 14 years for those who retired in 1975 (Butler, 1975). Thus, this life stage will continue to gain in importance. Preparing for the transition from employee to retiree is important during middle adulthood.

One study found that the majority of adults 45 and older view retirement very positively (Atchley, 1974). Financial prospects are critical to their outlook: those with higher expected incomes are even more positive. People at lower occupational levels, though frequently looking forward to the end of an unrewarding job, often dread the prospect of poverty, given their limited retirement income (Atchley, 1983). Thus, financial security and job satisfaction may influence the decision to retire. In addition to preparing for the financial changes that accompany retirement, middle-agers frequently plan other activities to take the place of work. Hobbies, community activities, and volunteering all foster a smooth transition to retirement (B. K. Smith, 1973). Such steps are especially important for males because employment has been a major source of their identity.

Reactions to retirement range from euphoria to depression, and even an initially happy response may give way to an unhappy one (B. K. Smith, 1973). Some people look forward to retirement as a time with fewer demands and more flexibility in how they spend time, while others feel devalued. Our hunch is that one reason for these differences is the meaning that employment and other activities have for the individual. Some people simply continue to work. They may own their own businesses, accept part-time work, or stay with their current employers. Others are not successful in the fight against retirement. The mandatory retirement age is usu-

ally 70, but some people choose to work into their eighties and even nineties.

The meaning of retirement varies from individual to individual. For some it is a well-earned rest, while for others it is enforced uselessness. One of the goals of middle adulthood is to resolve the retirement issue positively.

 *If you were suddenly retired by a "genie" at your current age and on a comfortable income, how would you spend your time? What do you think you would like about this arrangement? What would you dislike?*

# LATE ADULTHOOD — over 64

My grandparents reared me from infancy. My parents separated shortly after my birth, and when I was eleven months old, my mother brought me to live with her parents. . . . My grandfather, then in his seventies, was a gentleman farmer. I remember his blue overalls, his lined face and abundant white hair. He was my close friend and my teacher. Together we rose at 4 a.m. each day to feed chickens, candle eggs, grow oats and tend to the sick chickens in the "hospital" at one end of the chicken house. He would tell me of his younger days in Oklahoma and I would listen eagerly.

He disappeared suddenly when I was seven. I came back from a visit to a neighbor and he was gone. It made no sense. My grandmother said he went to visit relatives in Oklahoma—but he had not told me anything about the trip. With time, I realized I was never going to see him again. Dismay turned to fright and then to grief. I knew before they told me that he was dead.

. . . It was my grandmother in the years that followed who showed me the strength and endurance of the elderly. This was during the Depression. We lost the farm. She and I were soon on relief, eating government-surplus foods out of

*The expression that an individual's most prized possession is his or her health has special meaning for the elderly.*

here, caretakers of others. They are a diverse group. Many are healthy, have positive attitudes, and lead rewarding lives. Others have some impediments to their functioning—perhaps illness or economic limitations. Some are able to overcome hardships, while others withdraw from the world. In short, older adults cannot be easily categorized. We will discuss common elements of late adulthood, but flexibility should be used in applying them to individual cases.

Late adulthood, the last stage of the life span, usually begins with retirement. It ends with death, which may be preceded by a period of disability. Disability may set in at any time, including before retirement—or it may be absent entirely, when death results from accident or sudden illness. Some people become temporarily disabled as a result of accident or illness but, on recovery, are able to care for themselves again. So the statements we can make about late adulthood vary, depending on the capacities of the individuals we are assessing. At any given time less than 5% of this population is being cared for in an institution (Butler, 1975). Others, who are temporarily or permanently impaired, are cared for by relatives. And the vast majority care for themselves.

## Psychological Changes

Researchers have suggested that individuals who give more to others than they receive, who are autonomous, and who are stable are aging successfully (Williams & Wirth, 1965). The psychological well-being of older adults is probably most strongly affected by their health (Quinn, 1983). Their relationships with others and their personality characteristics are also very influential on their well-being.

In an unusual longitudinal study that surveyed parents in their thirties and again in their seventies, Mussen, Honzik, and Eichorn (1982) found that positive marital adjustment and satis-

cans with stigmatizing white labels. Grandmother found work in a sewing room run by the WPA, and I sold newspapers and fixed bicycles for ten cents an hour. We moved into a hotel. When I was eleven, it burned to the ground with all our possessions. We started again. And what I remember even more than the hardships of those years was my grandmother's triumphant spirit and determination. Experiencing at first hand an older person's struggle to survive, I was myself helped to survive as well [Butler, 1975, pp. ix–x].

This personal account illustrates the strength and courage of older adults in meeting crises in life. They are role models and sometimes, as faction with the husband's job during the couple's thirties were correlated with high life satisfaction in their seventies for both husbands and wives. They also found some differences between men and women. For men, the factors in their thirties that predicted high adjustment in their seventies were emotional and physical health and the wife's emotional stability. For women, the factors were a positive, responsive attitude toward life, early marital satisfaction, and adequate income. Internal factors (emotional and physical health), interpersonal factors (marital adjustment and satisfaction), and external factors (adequate income) all influenced later life satisfaction. Conversely, lower income (Hutchison, 1975) and poorer health (Beck, 1982) are associated with dissatisfaction with this stage.

Adjusting to diminished social contacts is important in late adulthood. Friends and relatives may die, employment probably ends, and energy may diminish (Hess & Waring, 1982). People tend to constrict their social circle gradually, perhaps placing more emphasis on contacts with kin.

**?** *Looking at the results of the 40-year longitudinal study, do you think the same factors would be correlated with high life satisfaction for men and women who are in their thirties today? Why or why not?*

## Family Relationships

Relationships among family members tend to remain strong in late adulthood, even over great distances (Troll & Smith, 1976). In general, women maintain closer relationships with their relatives (Vinick, 1978), and minority groups such as Blacks and Mexican Americans have closer family ties than Caucasians (Dowd & Bengtson, 1978).

*The spouse.* The Beatles used to sing: "Will you still need me? Will you still feed me when I'm 64?" We believe the answer to these questions is yes, although we have few data on the spousal relationship during late adulthood. Marital satisfaction is related positively to morale among older adults, particularly women, and marital satisfaction increases after children are launched (Lee, 1978).

Expectations for the sexual relationship in marriage have changed dramatically over the last two decades. In the past, wives, who had been told it was their duty (not their right) to have sexual relations with their husbands, often looked forward to the end of their reproductive capacity as an opportunity to end unwanted sexual activity. Aging freed them from a duty many had not found pleasant. Similarly, some husbands were relieved when they no longer had to perform. Still others felt guilty or abnormal for continuing sexual activity into their later years.

Then, in 1966, Masters and Johnson published the results of their research on the human sexual response and reported that older adults could and should continue their sexual relationship into their later years. They noted that couples who maintained sexual activity had little difficulty continuing it into their sixties and seventies. Thus, the standard for sexual behavior among older adults was reversed, from abstinence to continued activity.

This switch has been perceived positively by some and negatively by others, depending on their attitude about sexual intercourse. Some experts have suggested that older adults may now feel they *must* continue their sexual activity to have a full life. Though pleasurable, sexual activity is not essential for older adults—or for any age group! Data on the frequency of sexual activity among older adults are rare, but it is likely that many are continuing their sexual relationships, probably with less guilt than in the past. Whether the choice is for abstinence or for continued activity, disagreement on the choice will increase stress in the relationship.

During this stage of life the death of a spouse and adjustment to that loss are typical. By age 70, the majority of women are widows, although the majority of men aren't widowers until age 85 (Atchley, 1983). This discrepancy is due to two demographic factors: women live approximately eight years longer than men, and wives average two years younger than their husbands. Thus, most wives outlive their husbands and must adjust, often after more than 40 years of married life, to being single again.

Bankoff (1983) found that widows had two phases of adjustment. The first is the "crisis loss phase," in which the bereaved person's life is in chaos. Life may seem meaningless (Parkes, 1972), and apathy is common. Support from children and many others may be helpful in coping with funeral arrangements, wills, life insurance, and the like, but the children's involvement is often short-lived. Perhaps because children are grieving for their deceased parent, they find it difficult to offer support. Widowed and single friends provide important support and contribute to the widow's personal well-being during this phase (Bankoff, 1983).

In the second phase, the "transition phase," the widow adjusts to being single. Her grief has lessened and she is likely to resume social relationships if she withdrew from them during the crisis loss phase. The opportunity to talk about personal problems with friends is associated with well-being during this stage (Bankoff, 1983; Hess, 1972; Vinick, 1978). Other widows may serve as role models and may offer helpful advice as well as empathy.

Although the loss of a husband can be devastating, the loss of a wife is likely to be even more traumatic. Why is this so? First, most men have less experience with daily homemaking tasks (Vinick, 1978). Performing these tasks may be a painful reminder of their wife's absence or may

be contrary to their view of "men's work." Second, men are less likely to maintain kin and social ties (Troll, 1971; Vinick, 1978). Widowers are likely to be more isolated, and they may have few widower friends who can help them through this crisis, because fewer men outlive their wives (Vinick, 1978).

How do men cope with this loss? While women are likely to expand their ties to family and friends, many men cope by marrying again (Troll, 1971; Vinick, 1978). Since there are far more single women than single men in this age group, men can more easily find a spouse (Vinick, 1978). The reasons men give for remarrying are for companionship, to reduce their loneliness, and to be cared for (Vinick, 1978).

Friends, children, and even society at large may object to remarriage in late adulthood (McKain, 1972). Because norms suggest that older adults are not sexually active, the general public may oppose marriage in these years. Of course, sexual activity is possible and enjoyable in late adulthood. If partners have remained sexually active during middle adulthood, they show only a moderate decline in sexual activity during late adulthood, unless health problems arise (Masters & Johnson, 1966). One study found that the chances for success of these late marriages were increased if the partners had been acquainted for a long time, if friends and children approved, if they had an adequate income, and if they moved to a home that was new to both partners (McKain, 1972).

*Children.* Eighty percent of adults 65 or older have living children (Shanas, 1980). They are likely to exchange gifts, services, and advice, just as they did at earlier stages. In general, parents participate in exchanges as long as they are able and then continue to receive help from their children when they are not (Troll, 1971). Even when they are disabled, they may reward a particular child for services rendered with gifts or in their will (Sussman, Cates, & Smith, 1970). Although children may be important in terms of exchanges of help, they are not as important as friends in facilitating high morale (Arling, 1976; Lee & Ellithorpe, 1982). Clearly, children represent only one resource for parents.

Are people who have never had children unhappy in late adulthood? Studies suggest that older nonparents fare as well as parents. A study of almost 700 married or widowed women over age 60 found that while marital status, religion, and social interaction were important in explaining well-being, children were not (Beckman & Houser, 1982). Other researchers have found little evidence that adult children contribute significantly to their parents' *psychological* well-being (Glenn & McLanahan, 1981). Perhaps older adults without children have found other supports and rewards in their lives. Or perhaps some of the rewards of children are offset by the obligations and stress they bring.

*Grandchildren.*  Of course, if one has children, the possibility of grandchildren follows. We discussed the types of grandparents in the section on middle adulthood, and so our discussion here will be brief. The following comment illustrates the importance of personality in grandparent/grandchild relationships:

*Grandparents can have a great influence on the lives of grandchildren, depending on the situation. What influence did your grandparents have on your life?*

> When I was growing up, I had two grandmothers. Both seemed very old to me. Granny M. didn't like noise, but she let me play outside and she bought me nice presents for birthdays and Christmas. Grandmother S. also gave me presents, but she didn't seem to like children a lot and she told my parents when I misbehaved. So Granny M. was my favorite. She was fun to visit. And I fussed when I had to visit Grandmother S.

Just as this grandchild felt differently about these visits, so grandparents' feelings may vary according to the grandchild. The grandchild's age influences the type of interaction and may affect the grandparents' feelings toward the child. The age, sex, and personality of both individuals influence their interaction.

Among people over age 65, 75% have living grandchildren, and half of them see a grandchild almost daily (Troll, 1980a). Although grandparents may enjoy their interaction with their grandchildren, contact with friends is more important for morale during late adulthood (Wood & Robertson, 1978).

Further research is needed on many aspects of the grandparent/grandchild relationship.

## BOX 12-2
### *Simulating the Sensory Losses of Age*

To help people understand how many older adults experience the world, Leon Pastalan has developed a variety of devices, including glasses and earplugs, that simulate common sensory problems of people in their seventies. Younger people who used these devices to experience the world of the elderly found that an ordinary task such as grocery shopping was a disconcerting, if not disturbing, experience. They were unable to read labels and found that sounds were distorted, sometimes leading them to think others were talking about them. These devices are particularly useful in sensitizing those who interact with older people and in helping architects and urban planners design environments that reduce problems associated with sensory losses. Of course, brief experiences with the devices cannot simulate the long-term frustration, anger, and sadness over a permanent loss of one's abilities.

How does the parents' relationship foster or inhibit the interaction of this pair? How does infrequent visiting influence the relationship? At present, information in this area is sketchy.

*Do you interact with any older adults who are relatives? What goods and services do you exchange? What feelings are associated with these exchanges?*

### Other Relationships

As we've already indicated, friendships are more important than interaction with children or grandchildren for morale in late adulthood (Arling, 1976; Wood & Robertson, 1978). Friendships tend to be based on shared values (Adams, 1968) and to provide emotional support. Perhaps because friends are more likely to have had some of the same experiences, their understanding and advice are more meaningful. Unfortunately, in late adulthood, same-age friends are more likely to die, adding to other losses. Gradually, ties to friends and relatives contract, making the world of social contacts smaller. Neverthe-

less, such relationships enrich the lives and contribute to the well-being of older adults.

### Health

Because health, always one of the most important influences on well-being, is likely to decline in the later years, it takes on particular importance during this stage. It may influence not only psychological and emotional well-being but also housing, family interaction, and spending patterns (Streib & Beck, 1980).

Among the changes that occur as we age are decreases in the power of our senses. We may require glasses (or stronger glasses) or a hearing aid. Our senses of taste, touch, and smell may also be diminished. Many of these sensory losses can be treated.

Proper nutrition may be a problem in late adulthood (Butler, 1975). Figure 12-1 depicts some of the health problems associated with poor nutrition. The "Meals on Wheels" program, which delivers a hot noontime meal and a meal for later in the day to thousands of older adults every day, is invaluable in preventing hunger, fostering good nutrition, and promoting health.

Many physical problems can be treated with medications. Adults over 65 make up 11% of the

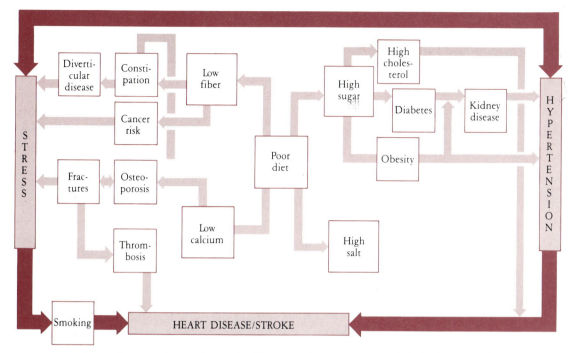

**FIGURE 12-1.** *The influence of poor diet on health: Our culture gives no medals for living to old age. Instead, 86% of our elderly are rewarded by being trapped in a maze of health problems. Above, an illustration of how minor conditions and lifelong habits lead to serious illness on any number of paths.*

population but consume 25% of all medications. In fact, one of every three is taking five or more medicines at the same time (Drummond, 1983).

Occasionally hospitalization is necessary to treat an illness. After a hospitalization period, relatives, friends, or professionals may provide some additional care as the older adult continues to recover. Health problems may affect mobility or reduce the ability of older adults to care for themselves. Daytime or round-the-clock care may be necessary but can be very expensive.

Patients who are too ill to recover may prefer to know that they are dying (B. K. Smith, 1973) and may request that extraordinary measures not be used to prolong their lives. Dying people need to know they are loved and appreciated and have had an impact on others (B. K. Smith, 1973).

## Housing Arrangements

"Dallas," "Dynasty," and "Falcon Crest" (among other TV series) all have three generations living together in one large residence owned by the oldest adult in the family. Although this arrangement facilitates character interaction and program drama, it is not used by most American families. Among older adults only 12% of married couples and 17% of single people (unmarried, divorced, or widowed) live with one or more of their children (Shanas, 1980).

Among those who do live with children, satisfaction with this arrangement depends on characteristics of the older person, particularly his or her level of dependency, and characteristics of the primary caregiver. In addition, the older adult's contribution to household maintenance (services and money) and the inconveniences that result from this arrangement influence the level of satisfaction (Mindel & Wright, 1982).

A large majority (69%) of older adults live in their own homes with the mortgage paid off (Butler, 1975). Because the home is old, it may require maintenance or expensive major repairs. The neighborhood may be deteriorating, property taxes may be rising, and utility costs may be very high (Butler, 1975). Nevertheless, the majority of older adults choose this arrangement, a preference that shows how strongly we value independence (Hess & Waring, 1982).

Even though most older adults do not live with their children, 34% live within ten minutes of at least one child (Shanas, 1980). After retirement, many parents move near one or more children (Troll, 1971). It is evident from this pattern that autonomy *and* a continuing relationship with children are highly valued. The decision to live with a child is generally made only when other options are less acceptable or unavailable (Troll, 1971).

Housing accommodations tailored to the needs of older adults include age-segregated housing, group homes, and nursing homes. We will look at each of these briefly.

Retirement communities are housing developments designed for the needs and wants of older adults. They may be composed of single-family homes, townhouses, condominiums, apartments, mobile homes, special care facilities, or any combination thereof. Young people, particularly children, are not allowed to live there, although they generally are welcome to visit. Studies have found that age-segregated housing encourages socialization (Hochschild, 1973;

Sherman, 1975) and higher morale and activity levels (Teaff, Lawton, Nahemow, & Carlson, 1978). Unfortunately, retirement communities may cost more than the average income of older adults (Butler, 1975), excluding this option for many people. Group homes are described in Box 12-3.

Nursing homes are an option when older adults are physically unable to care for themselves. Varying in quality, services, and costs, they are similar to group homes in that services are provided to meet all the older adults' needs. In addition, residents' physical problems receive medical attention. Nursing homes tend to be specially constructed or adapted for older adults' physical limitations; stairs, dark halls, and dim lighting are generally eliminated. Nursing homes are used by less than 5% of the population aged 65 and older, although as age increases, the percentage using them increases.

One criticism of nursing homes is that they isolate older adults from their families. However, one study of long-term residents of a nursing home found that they were close to and involved with their families (Smith & Bengtson, 1979). Nursing homes are necessary because they can provide essential services to older adults and their families.

*What housing arrangement would you prefer if you were 70 years old and widowed? If you were 80 years old and widowed? What factors should be considered before an older adult moves (or is moved) to a new housing arrangement?*

## Social Services

It is evident that poor health can influence housing arrangements, requiring older adults to ob-

## BOX 12-3
### Group Homes

Group homes are a relatively new phenomenon for older adults. One particularly successful model, developed in Florida, is now spreading across the country. Older adults who are ambulatory and able to bathe and dress themselves are eligible to apply to live in a "Share-A-Home." Living in one of these homes costs an average of $325–400 a month (1978 prices), including utilities, food, and transportation. A salaried manager and staff are responsible for housekeeping, preparing meals, providing transportation, doing laundry, and managing finances. The current members of the home and a prospective

member undergo a 30-day trial period to decide whether he or she fits into this arrangement and "family." No contracts are signed, and a member can withdraw at any time.

The social network formed by this group becomes a family. Members eat together and socialize, but they are able to withdraw when they choose. This group home is responsive to economic, social, and psychological needs. It is cheaper than many other living arrangements, particularly given the services provided. It offers an opportunity for interaction that reduces the isolation and loneliness of many older adults. And it re-

spects the autonomy of each member.

Group homes vary in services and management. Some require residents to do some or all of the housekeeping tasks, and others hire staff to perform these functions. Unfortunately, group homes are not available in most communities. Where they do exist, the demand may exceed the supply, and those who may need such housing most—the poor—may not be able to afford it. Nevertheless, this option presents some intriguing prospects for the future.

tain care not available where they currently live. Services such as homemaking, home health care, nutrition services, day care, and part-time companions enable many older adults to remain in their homes. Because these services can prevent illnesses, hospitalization, and the need for nursing-home care, they actually may be cost-effective (Butler, 1975).

Social Security and Supplemental Security Income (a guaranteed minimum income for older adults) are common sources of support in old age. In 1980 the average retirement benefit from Social Security was $4097 per year for an individual and $6060 for a couple (Atchley, 1983). Few of us would want to manage on such a meager amount. In 1970 about 50% of retired workers were also entitled to benefits from a pension plan (Atchley, 1983). Savings and investments

may make these years comfortable financially, but millions of older adults face these years without financial security.

Many Americans not only grow older, they grow poorer (Butler, 1975). As a result of living longer, they may outlive their savings and need public assistance. Sometimes older adults do not know about or use available services. Seeking outside help means acknowledging that they are less able to care for themselves, an often frightening realization. They may fear that accepting help is a first step toward institutional care (Butler, 1975; Gelfand, Olsen, & Bloc, 1978). It is important to help older adults understand that needing outside support does not mean they are failures. Rather, it reflects the fact that we have become better able to treat illnesses and prolong life (Gelfand et al., 1978).

As with other aspects of our lives, the tools of prevention can help us and our family members deal with growing older and with older people. Mutual understanding and compassion enhance our relationships at all stages of the life cycle, including middle and late adulthood. Let's consider how these tools can be useful during these stages. Remember that the tools of prevention often overlap, even though they are discussed separately.

## EDUCATION

Learning about a subject helps us respond more appropriately to situations. In our society, few opportunities are provided to learn about middle and late adulthood in educational settings. Workshops and courses on these stages of development would be valuable in helping people understand the tasks, responsibilities, and rewards of these stages.

Such education is needed by people at many age levels. Because our society is often age-segregated, children and youth may have few opportunities to learn about and interact with older adults. Activities that bring different age groups together decrease stereotyping and increase appreciation of members of other groups as individuals (Powell & Arquitt, 1978).

Middle-agers need an opportunity to learn about this stage of development and about aging. How do others cope with aging or disabled parents? What roles should grandparents play? How should one prepare for retirement? What are the tasks of this stage of development? Many could enhance their lives and make their transitions easier if they knew more about what is happening to them and their loved ones.

Older adults (65+) need to know about the tasks of this stage and ways to foster their enjoyment of life. They particularly need to learn about services available in their community. Special classes for older adults about these and other aspects of their lives would be particularly useful. Understanding what is happening and how best to deal with life changes decreases stress and enhances the lives of all involved.

*What other educational tools could be used to prevent ageism? Which do you think would work best in your community?*

## COMMUNITY/ORGANIZATION SYSTEMS INTERVENTION

Changes in organizations' policies and programs would be beneficial to middle-agers and older adults. For example, employers need to know that older workers are productive and are a good investment (Butler, 1975). Older does not mean less productive! Employers need to realize that forced retirement is detrimental to workers who do not want to retire. Some workers prefer to reduce their hours or take more vacations rather than retire. Flexibility in this area would enable employers to retain skilled, mature workers and add to the productivity of the economy.

Numerous communities have implemented programs that break down age stereotypes. Some schools have programs in which older adults tutor children or adolescents. These endeavors often teach both age groups about each other's capabilities and diversity, thereby reducing ageism. The Foster Grandparents program, which brings together older adults and youth in foster care, accomplishes the same result. In another encouraging program, high school students assist older adults by repairing and winterizing their homes. These older adults see that teenagers can be caring and helpful, and the teenagers gain a new appreciation of older adults when they get to know them and understand their abilities as well as their limitations.

 *What community organization/systems intervention programs are available in your community to help middle-agers and older adults? Who runs them? What other types of programs would be helpful?*

## COMPETENCY PROMOTION

Middle-agers and older adults need to participate actively in their own development. Their involvement, vigor, and commitment to fostering their own growth is vital. When people of any age feel competent to care for themselves, they gain self-respect. One effort to promote competency among middle-aged women is homemaker retraining (Robertson, 1978). Designed for women who dropped out of the work force to raise children, retraining programs offer counseling, career exploration, job-seeking skills, and sometimes job training. These programs have been successful in building confidence among these women and helping them get jobs.

Similar programs are needed for many older men—not to learn how to obtain a job but to learn homemaking tasks. If their wives are disabled or deceased, they may not be able to cook or manage other household tasks. Encouragement and training may make a vital difference in older men's abilities to care for themselves and

in the quality of their lives. In short, middle and older adults can learn new skills that may be essential to their mental and physical well-being.

Volunteering can be most rewarding, particularly for those who are searching for a meaningful place in society. Whether they work in a political campaign or for a charitable cause, volunteers not only give of themselves but also are rewarded with a sense of being valued. This feeling is an essential component of well-being at any age. And the opportunity to interact with others of different ages provides opportunities to counteract the ageism so prevalent in our society.

*What theories can be applied to explain why competency promotion is so important in our lives?*

## NATURAL CAREGIVING

Middle-agers and older adults are role models to younger generations, demonstrating how they adapt to growing older. One trend in recent years seems to be an increase in the number of prominent people who willingly disclose their correct age. The Jack Benny standard of being eternally 39 is fading. By dropping the stance that adults never get older, these people demonstrate to others that they think it is OK to get older. They accept themselves and model the acceptance of aging to others.

Numerous groups have developed across the country to provide a supportive environment for middle-agers and older adults. The American Association of Retired Persons is a powerful force representing the needs of older Americans. It provides diverse direct services to its members, from refresher courses in driving to international tours. These services alert all age groups that older adults are competent and stimulating,

# The best age
# is the age you are.

*The best age is the age you are . . . that is, if people accept you for what and who you are. How might each of us encourage that acceptance?*

varied in their interests and needs. Many other groups, broad-based or limited to a particular interest, are available to middle-agers and older adults.

Friends are an important source of natural caregiving. Research has found that friends are particularly important to the morale of older adults. Their ability to understand, sympathize, and serve as role models enhances their own and their friends' well-being.

*What are some benefits of being over 45? Over 65? Over 80? What can we do for ourselves and for others to make these stages of life positive?*

296

# SUMMARY

Despite the stereotyping and prejudice of ageism, people in later life are a diverse group of individuals with varying capacities and deficits. Aging, in the sense of maturation, begins before birth, and "old" is a highly subjective concept.

Middle adulthood (ages 45–64) is a time to assess what one has accomplished in life, and to restructure attitudes toward time and death. Middle-agers must be responsive to the changing needs of two groups—children for more independence and autonomy and parents for more dependence and support.

In late adulthood (age 65+) the strongest influence on psychological well-being is probably health; relationships, personal characteristics, and income are also important. Social contacts diminish as employment ends and friends and relatives die. A common trauma in this stage is widowhood, with which women tend to cope by drawing on support from others, men by remarrying. Other issues are housing, poverty, and support from friends and relatives.

As the number of four-generation families increases in our society, research will provide more information on how they interact. Employment and retirement will become increasingly important issues for older adults. As medical science learns more, we will be better able to prolong life and prevent disability. Sufficient housing designed for older adults may be a problem as their number increases rapidly in the next 30 years (owing to the aging of the baby-boom generation). Exciting prospects and challenges await all of us as we age.

# MAJOR POINTS TO REMEMBER

1. A variety of developmental tasks accompany middle and late adulthood.
2. In general, marital satisfaction increases after children leave home.
3. Launching children has only a slightly negative, short-term impact on mothers.
4. Middle-agers are the generation with the highest rate of contact with relatives.
5. After children are launched, parents may increase their contacts with their siblings.
6. Changes in employment may be a major influence during middle adulthood.
7. Health, personal relationships, and attitude toward life are major influences on the functioning of older adults.
8. Older adults who are not parents do not differ in well-being from those who are.
9. The majority of women are widowed by age 70, men by age 85. To cope with the loss of a spouse, widows tend to expand their ties to family and friends, while widowers tend to marry again.
10. Middle-agers and older adults tend to exchange services, gifts, and advice with their adult children.
11. As we age, our senses may decrease in sensitivity and our health may decline. Early medical treatment can often reduce these problems.
12. Housing arrangements vary for older adults. They may live in their own home, in a retirement community, with adult children, or in a group or nursing home.
13. Older adults may receive income from Social Security and Supplemental Security Income, but these sources provide only a subsistence income. Some older adults also have income from pension plans or from investments, which increases their standard of living.

# ADDITIONAL SOURCES OF INFORMATION

## *Publications*

Anders, R. (1976). *A look at aging.* Minneapolis, MN: Lerner. [Children]

Clifford, E. R. (1978). *The rocking chair rebellion*. Boston: Houghton Mifflin. [Adolescents]

Green, P. (1977). *Mildred Murphy, how does your garden grow?* Reading, MA: Addison-Wesley. [Early adolescents]

Levinson, D. J., Darrow, C. N., Klein, E. B., Levinson, M. H., & McKee, B. (1978). *The seasons of a man's life*. New York: Knopf. [Adults]

Raynor, D. (1977). *Grandparents around the world*. Chicago: Albert Whitman. [Children]

Shanks, A. Z. (1976). *Old is what you get: Dialogues on aging by the old and the young*. New York: Viking Press. [Early adolescents]

Sheehy, G. (1974). *Passages*. New York: Dutton. [Adults]

## Organizations

American Association for Retired Persons
1909 K St., NW
Washington, DC 20036
A nonprofit membership organization dedicated to enhancing the lives of older adults.

Gray Panthers
3635 Chestnut St.
Philadelphia, PA 19104
A senior citizens' activist group.

Mended Hearts
7320 Greenville Ave.
Dallas, TX 75231
For people who have successfully undergone heart surgery.

Reach to Recovery
777 Third Ave.
New York, NY 10017
A self-help group for women who have had mastectomies.

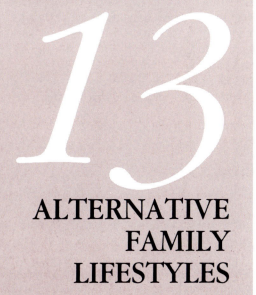

# 13

# ALTERNATIVE FAMILY LIFESTYLES

**A recently published** handbook on contemporary families and alternative lifestyles begins with a prologue on the history of American families (Chilman, 1983). Chilman, writing as a social historian, notes that contemporary society was influenced by the social protest movement of the 1960s and by the "me first" psychological movement that followed. She argues that disillusionment, depression, and alienation over the failure of the protest era resulted in a culturewide psychological reaction that diverted interest from seeking a social utopia to pursuing fulfillment through a search for the liberated self. This new-found focus on self-fulfillment, Chilman says, resulted in the popularity of several "high priests" of the liberated self, such as Rollo May, Abraham Maslow, Carl Rogers, and Fritz Perls. This "period of narcissism" brought expanding exploration in social relations and family relationships and a focus on finding the "real me." Events during this period reflect a narcissistic imbalance in psychological focus. Race riots and student protests flared up, divorce rates accelerated dramatically, the marriage rate dropped, nonmarital intercourse increased, abortion rates skyrocketed, desertions increased, and other nationwide problems expanded (for example, domestic violence, child abuse, child neglect, incest, and rape in the family). According to Chilman, the epitome of morale problems was the spying, bribery, thievery, and lying of those in the inner sanctum of President Nixon's White House.

With this trend, we should not be surprised to find a backlash, the return of some to old-time fundamentalist religion and its values. Many public figures have come to speak of the political need to "save" the traditional family, to return to an absolute standard of right and wrong, to maintain a so-called profamily force within government. Unfortunately, the profamily position, supported by the media-named and evangelistic

Moral Majority, uses the argument that since God is on our side, anyone who is different must be wrong, corrupted, and evil. According to Chilman, the profamily platform of contemporary politicians wishes to return to the "happy homes" of yesterday when wives stayed home and husbands were the breadwinners, when "unnatural types" such as gays and lesbians were seen as unclean, abnormal deviants, when a father was to be feared, to maintain the final say on all significant matters, and to be "boss" in his own little empire—the home.

Although Chilman presents rather strong and direct statements, the perceived turn to the political right in the early 1980s is only partly supported by social facts. Voting patterns have indeed become more conservative, but the general trend toward increasing liberality in personal choice and lifestyle continues. For example, a 30-year analysis of Americans' attitudes shows increasing liberalization on such questions as sexual intercourse outside marriage, cohabitation, and related morals and values (Yankelovich, 1981). With this liberalization in societal acceptance of personal lifestyle choices have come numerous forms of living arrangements that differ from the traditional nuclear family.

 *What other evidence has been presented in this text to support the notion that attitudes and values in the United States have become liberalized?*

# VARIATIONS ON THE THEME OF THE TRADITIONAL NUCLEAR FAMILY

Americans have always held a nostalgic, idealized portrait of the nuclear family. In this picture, father drives off from the family's suburban home to work in the city, mother stays home

NORMAN ROCKWELL. *FREEDOM FROM WANT*, 1943 PROMOTION FOR THE "FOUR FREEDOMS" WAR BOND SERIES

*Does this romanticized portrait of the American family gathered together to celebrate a holiday resemble your own holiday experiences?*

caring for the children and taking care of the house, and the children obtain an education in a neighborhood school. Old television series like "Father Knows Best" or "Ozzie and Harriet" exemplified the American dream of how family life ought to be. Indeed, a "lucky" generation of (now middle-aged) Americans were able to obtain this idealized form of domesticity (Masnick & Bane, 1980) in which residence was in the suburbs, the husband was a breadwinner and the wife a homemaker, both were dedicated to child rearing, and all family members lived a life of high consumption. Indeed, some argue, so pleasant a lifestyle is the nuclear family that those adults now between 40 and 60 years of age who obtained it find it difficult to validate lifestyles that differ from this idealized one (Masnick & Bane, 1980).

Masnick and Bane (1980) have summarized several trends and projections that reveal a pattern of change for the American family, showing that many variations on the nuclear family have existed in the past, currently exist, and are projected to increase in the coming years. For example, Figures 13-1 and 13-2 show the past and predicted frequencies of various types of households and their employment characteristics.

Changes between 1960 and 1975 were concentrated mainly in three household types—young married couples, female-headed homes, and singles. Overall, 8 million more married couples were counted; however, 7.1 million

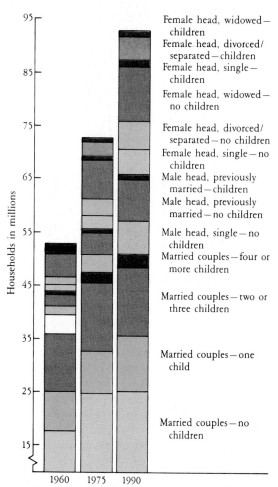

**FIGURE 13-1.** *Types of households, 1960, 1975, and 1990.*

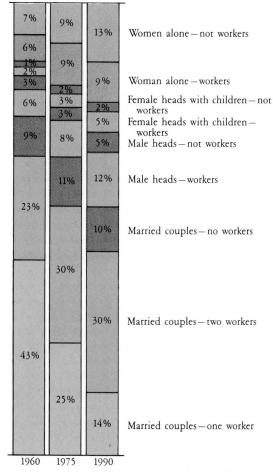

**FIGURE 13-2.** *Employment characteristics of households, 1960, 1975, and 1990.*

were couples who had no children in their home. These findings indicate more young families without children. Substantial increases were also found in female-headed households. These increases included women who were single, divorced or separated, and widowed, with and without children. Likewise, a substantial increase—11.7 million—in the number of single men and women was observed. Two-worker husband/wife households increased from 23% of all households to 30%. One-worker married-couple households decreased because of a drop in one-worker couples and the increase in singleness.

In many ways, the trends projected for the 1980s and 1990s are continuations of those of the 1960s and 1970s. Projections indicate at least 20 million more total households; however, married couples will make up a much smaller proportion of the increase. Further, because of high rates of singleness, divorce, and separation, another 16.8 million persons will live in one-adult households with children or alone. One-worker married couples will continue to decrease, while two-worker married couples will increase slightly.

Projections such as these indicate continuing diversity in American households, family types, and individual social lifestyles. Many people will remain single. Others will marry but depart from the traditional nuclear-family form. Households will change because of divorce. Work patterns will affect relationships in families. Recognizing these demographic trends, we have prepared this chapter to explore a number of lifestyles that are variations on the traditional nuclear family, to review the concept of cultural diversity in the family, to address the relation of employment and family styles, and to discuss variations based on sexual exclusivity/inclusivity. In the belief that every family form has advantages and shortcomings, we will review what family-life profes-

sionals have reported in their research as the strengths and limitations of alternative family lifestyles.

We caution that knowledge of alternative lifestyles is limited by sampling problems, difficulty of access to unique family styles, ethical constraints, and the methodological limitations that accompany the study of unique social groups. Therefore, this chapter should be read as only suggestive, based on our current limited understanding of alternative family lifestyles.

*Are the trends in household composition and employment characteristics likely to create social problems? What might they be?*

# VARIATIONS BASED ON FAMILY COMPOSITION

Variations on family relations can be seen in the composition, or membership, of a household: individuals living alone, as a couple, or as parent and child. We begin with a brief discussion of singleness—a growing form of the family.

## Singleness

Some 55 million American adults over age 18 are unmarried (U. S. Bureau of the Census, 1981). This total consists of never-married, divorced, widowed, and separated persons (see Table 13-1). According to Stein (1983), census data show why this group is growing. For example, the median age for first marriage increased from 20.8 for women and 23.2 for men in 1970 to 22.1 and 24.6, respectively, in 1980; and 50% of women aged 20–24 remained unmarried in 1980, compared with 30% in 1960. The number of persons living alone increased by 60% from the 1970s to

**TABLE 13-1.** *Marital status of the U. S. population (age 18 and over) by sex and age, 1979*

| Marital Status | Total Population (18 and Over) | Percentage of Total Population | Percentage of Age Group | | | | | | | | | |
|---|---|---|---|---|---|---|---|---|---|---|---|---|
| | | | 18–19 | 20–24 | 25–29 | 30–34 | 35–39 | 40–44 | 45–54 | 55–64 | 65–74 | 75 and over |
| *Men* | | | | | | | | | | | | |
| Single | 16,970,000 | 23.3 | 94.9 | 67.4 | 30.2 | 14.9 | 8.2 | 8.4 | 6.9 | 5.2 | 5.6 | 4.9 |
| Separated | 1,513,000 | 2.1 | 0.2 | 1.2 | 2.0 | 3.1 | 2.6 | 2.8 | 2.4 | 2.2 | 2.1 | 1.2 |
| Divorced | 3,471,000 | 4.8 | 0.1 | 1.7 | 5.5 | 7.3 | 6.9 | 7.1 | 5.7 | 4.7 | 3.9 | 2.2 |
| Widowed | 1,945,000 | 2.7 | 0.0 | 0.0 | 0.2 | 0.2 | 0.2 | 0.6 | 1.8 | 3.4 | 9.3 | 24.0 |
| Married | 48,816,000 | 67.1 | 4.8 | 29.7 | 62.1 | 74.6 | 82.2 | 81.2 | 83.2 | 84.4 | 79.2 | 67.7 |
| Total | 72,715,000 | 100.0 | | | | | | | | | | |
| *Women* | | | | | | | | | | | | |
| Single | 13,644,000 | 16.9 | 83.1 | 49.4 | 19.6 | 9.5 | 6.6 | 5.1 | 4.4 | 4.6 | 6.0 | 6.2 |
| Separated | 2,409,000 | 3.0 | 1.2 | 3.1 | 4.3 | 4.3 | 4.1 | 4.6 | 3.3 | 2.0 | 1.4 | 0.4 |
| Divorced | 5,355,000 | 6.6 | 0.9 | 3.2 | 7.8 | 10.2 | 9.8 | 11.1 | 8.2 | 6.5 | 4.0 | 2.2 |
| Widowed | 10,449,000 | 13.0 | 0.0 | 0.1 | 0.5 | 0.8 | 1.6 | 2.8 | 7.6 | 18.8 | 41.2 | 69.7 |
| Married | 48,771,000 | 60.5 | 14.8 | 44.2 | 67.7 | 75.2 | 78.0 | 76.5 | 76.3 | 68.1 | 47.5 | 21.5 |
| Total | 80,628,000 | 100.0 | | | | | | | | | | |

the 1980s. Never-married adults make up more than 23% of the male and 17% of the female population.

No single answer explains why this growing number of young adults is choosing to postpone marriage. Several factors are likely contributors (Stein, 1983)—the effects of social movements such as women's liberation, the conflict between marriage and the desire for a career, the increased use and effectiveness of birth-control methods. We suspect that all these factors, along with the economic problems of our time, contribute to this social pattern.

The complexity of understanding this group is illustrated in an excellent typology of singleness (Stein, 1981). Stein derives four categories of singleness from two polar dimensions, voluntary/involuntary and temporary/permanent. **Voluntary temporary** singles are mostly people who are postponing marriage to achieve a particular goal or aspiration, such as education, work, or self-development. This category may also include couples who are living together to test the relationship before committing to marriage. **Voluntary stable** singles are people who

choose to remain permanently single—those who choose not to marry (or remarry), those whose lifestyles exclude marriage as an option (for example, priests and nuns), and even cohabitators who do not wish to marry. For whatever reason, this group has made a commitment not to marry based on personal choice. **Involuntary temporary** singles, in contrast to the first two groups, are those who wish to marry and are actively seeking a marriage partner. Finally, the **involuntary stable** single is one who will remain single though not by choice. This group includes elderly persons who are noncompetitive in the market, physically or mentally impaired persons, and perhaps divorced or widowed persons who perceive interest by any potential mate as unlikely.

Stein (1976) has shown in his study of voluntary singles that numerous factors are associated with the decision to remain single. He calls them "pushes" and "pulls" because people are "pulled" toward singleness by its advantages (for example, expanded career opportunities, increased number of sexual partners, feelings of autonomy and self-sufficiency, a free lifestyle that

PART THREE FAMILY LIFE ACROSS THE LIFE SPAN

offers variety and excitement) and "pushed" toward singleness by the disadvantages of being married. There are pushes toward marriage too, however: the idealization of marriage and pressure to marry by parents and peers can create tremendous stress on single persons. Relationships developed outside marriage may bring the disapproval of family members and employers. Lack of a long-term emotional attachment with a sense of commitment may create loneliness and isolation. The very freedom that singleness brings also brings, for many, feelings of emptiness and insecurity. Major tasks and issues faced by single adults include problems in maintaining sexual relationships and friendships with couples, health management, and living arrangements (Stein, 1983).

Nonetheless, many enjoy singleness as either a permanent or a temporary lifestyle. It can be filled with highly meaningful and intimate relationships. Friendships with the same and the other sex can provide important psychological and social support. Most of us have been or will be single for some part of our adult life. Although singlehood is for most a temporary or unintended state, it should not be perceived as an undesirable condition. Fulfillment can be found either within or outside a formal marriage. Alternatives exist that can be as satisfying as the traditional romantic marriage.

## Married Childfree Couples

National census data show a recent trend toward more young couples' being childfree (less positively described as childless), and popular media interest in the childfree family has expanded astronomically (McKirdy & Nissley, 1980). The National Alliance for Optional Parenthood has recently mounted a vigorous awareness program promoting childlessness as a viable choice (Veevers, 1983). But childfree couples are not new to this decade. In her review of historical documents, Veevers (1983) shows that rates of childlessness have risen and fallen in the past, mainly following changes in fertility rates. However, recent trends reflect voluntary childlessness rather than fecundity problems. At a recent conference on building family strengths, a workshop model was presented for decision making about the childfree option, based on the notion that "People cannot choose to become parents if they do not perceive an alternative, such as the childfree life style" (Thoen & Russell, 1979, p. 339).

Early writings on the childfree couple were replete with stereotypical perceptions of selfishness, loneliness, immorality, and immaturity (Houseknecht, 1982a, 1982b). In particular, the deliberately childless wife has been viewed as less well adjusted or admired (Calhoun & Selby, 1980). However, a comprehensive review of voluntary childlessness (Veevers, 1983) provides little evidence for these stereotypical perceptions. Indeed, voluntary childlessness appears to be associated with positive social adjustment, independence, and marital happiness.

Unfortunately, most early studies of the childfree couple used small, unrepresentative samples (for example, Silka & Keisler, 1977), and more recent studies have failed to distinguish among involuntary childlessness, voluntary childlessness, and temporary delay in having children. In one of the most comprehensive analyses of childlessness, Mosher and Bachrach (1982) have provided national estimates of the prevalence and correlates of voluntary, involuntary, and temporary childlessness in the United States. Using the National Survey of Family Growth data, they report that about 18% of married women in the 1970s were childless. However, that percentage included 13% who were only temporarily childless—they were delaying having children for personal reasons. Only 2%

(700,000 women) were actually voluntarily childfree. The rest were involuntarily childless because of medical problems. Mosher and Bachrach (1982) also find that about half of the couples who make an early commitment to remain childfree change their minds later in the marriage.

Several basic characteristics distinguish voluntarily childless couples from other types of families. Often one or both spouses have been married before. In particular, when the husband has been married before, there is a greater chance the couple will not have children. Experience with an unsuccessful marriage may reduce a person's willingness to risk having a child, fearing that the second marriage may also be dissolved. Further, the cost of supporting children from a previous marriage may preclude having resources for more children. As one might expect, voluntary childfree couples are more likely to use contraceptives or to include a husband who has had a vasectomy (Mosher & Bachrach, 1982). Voluntary childfree couples tend to be very well educated, to earn high incomes, and to be nonreligious (Houseknecht, 1982a; Mosher & Bachrach, 1982; Veevers, 1983). Often they are professionals or hold managerial jobs in business.

Voluntary childlessness appears to have emerged for several reasons. Increasing opportunities for higher levels of education may result in greater career commitments for both men and women. As Houseknecht (1982a, 1982b) has proposed, those with such commitments may evaluate child rearing as a social cost that is weighed against the personal rewards of their careers (income, self-fulfillment). For others, the economic demands of the time may create the conditions that at least support temporary childlessness. Likewise, a changing society may be creating a norm that accepts childlessness rather than the traditional "mandatory motherhood" norm of the past (N. J. Davis, 1982). Indeed, research reported by Houseknecht (1982a) suggests that voluntary childfree couples may receive more support than couples who choose to marry and have children.

The childfree family has several strengths. Childfree couples are less likely to be sex-stereotyped in their family roles (Houseknecht, 1982b), this family form is based on personal choice and interests (Thoen & Russell, 1979), and support and advocacy are emerging in the belief that such decisions are personal and need to be respected as such (Veevers, 1983). The main limitation of this family type is that childfree couples may miss the joys and fulfillment that come with socializing and caring for the next generation. However, this gap may be readily filled by experiences with children other than one's own. Many couples have little need for or interest in the care and rearing of children, and we believe this attitude should not be seen as unhealthy or maladjusted.

## Never-Married Families

One family form that social scientists have ignored is the never-married-parent family. It is hard to know how many never-married parents there are. However, one report (Masnick & Bane, 1980) indicates that between 0.2% and 0.7% of households in 1960 and 1975 were headed by never-married females with one or more children under age 15. No comparable data can be found for never-married fathers with children in the household. Masnick and Bane predict that in the 1990s households headed by never-married females will increase to 1.3% of the total.

From research on female-headed households (for example, see Adams & Gullotta, 1983), we can speculate that never-married female heads of household are likely to have little education, low income, and financial problems. The children are likely to suffer the effects of poverty but are not likely to be unusual in most personality characteristics.

As more women establish fulfilling professional careers, we might expect more well-educated, successful, older women to join the ranks of never-married parents. We know, for example, of an unmarried university professor who recently became pregnant. She has chosen to keep the child, and the father has decided to provide some financial and personal support. These parents plan to rear the child through sharing their resources but not to marry or live together. The effects that such arrangements have on children and their social development are unclear. However, as this alternative lifestyle becomes more common, we expect more research on it.

## Homosexual Couples

Recently, same-sex relationships have received increasing attention and perhaps even tolerance in editorials, in news articles, and in community acknowledgment and acceptance of "gay" activities and activist organizations. Research during the late 1970s dispelled the myth of the homosexual as disturbed and deviant (Macklin, 1980). In particular, a study by the Institute for Sex Research (Bell & Weinberg, 1978) has shown that the majority of homosexuals are in stable relationships and are leading satisfying and personally fulfilling lives.

As is true of so many alternative lifestyles, little is scientifically known about the quality and nature of gay relationships. A few recent interview studies (for example, McWhirter & Matti-

*In recent years society has become more accepting of individuals' decisions to lead alternative lifestyles. What do you think has encouraged this acceptance?*

son, 1984) and integrative reviews of the research literature (Harry, 1983; Macklin, 1980), however, provide a tentative overview.

More often than not, when heterosexuals write of the gay male relationship, they tend to heterosexualize it by applying a "butch"/ "femme" perspective. One member of the couple is assumed to be the dominant, "masculine" partner (butch) who provides the structure, decision making, financial stability, and orientation to the relationship. The other partner is viewed as a more "feminine," passive partner (femme). However, much of the literature fails to support this sex-typed notion of gay relationships (for example, Bell & Weinberg, 1978). The majority of relationships are not based on a butch/femme sex-typed perspective (Saghir & Robins, 1973; Westwood, 1960). Harry (1983) concludes after a review of several investigations that masculinity is the characteristic that the majority of homosexuals value most in an erotic partner and that many homosexual relationships are more egalitarian than heterosexual relationships.

Older homosexual males (like heterosexual males) prefer attractive, younger partners. Consequently, many gay couples have an observable age difference. Harry and DeVall (1978) report that younger (18–29) and older (40+) homosexuals are more likely to be coupled. Although the general extent of coupleness is unknown, early studies clearly underrepresented the incidence of long-term relationships for male homosexuals and exaggerated the proportion whose lifestyles are based on free sex and pickups in gay bars. Clearly, however, homosexual couples are less sexually exclusive than heterosexuals. Sexual exclusivity is less common after the honeymoon stage of gay relationships, and there are major problems associated with the couple's arriving at an agreement about exclusivity. Indeed, Harry (1983) reviews data that suggest sexual exclusivity can interfere with a gay couple's relationship

and may be negatively associated with longerterm relationships. However, we must caution that little is known about norms or averages for the duration of gay relationships.

Lesbian couples are more likely to live together than male homosexual couples (Bell & Weinberg, 1978). Among lesbians, sexual exclusivity appears to be the norm rather than the exception. Little support can be found for a butch/femme dichotomy in lesbian couples' relationships. Unlike gay men, lesbian women tend to find their social network only marginally associated with gay bars. Lesbians are somewhat more likely to form close couple relationships than gay men. Further, lesbian women are only likely to move from one romantic involvement to another when another opportunity arises for a new intimate relationship. Finally, the nonexclusivity of sexual partners among lesbians tends to be associated with less traditional attitudes toward women and women's roles.

Considerable attention has recently been given to homosexuals as parents. Many gay men (14–25%) have a heterosexual marriage and children before becoming exclusively homosexual (Harry, 1983). As married gay men come to recognize their sexual preference they are likely to report fear of disclosure about their homosexuality to their children (Miller, 1979). A wife may allow her husband, on disclosure to her, to pursue an otherwise secret homosexual liaison. Many fathers reportedly agree to this arrangement and maintain their marriages because of love for their children. When fathers do disclose to their children, after the initial shock most children generally adjust and accept this new reality (Miller, 1979). On divorce, gay fathers rarely retain child custody. Little is known about the longterm consequences for heterosexual children reared in a homosexual household. However, Harry (1983) cites some incidents that suggest homosexual children may thrive by being reared in a homosexual home.

Many more children are found in the homes of lesbian individuals or couples. If lesbianism is not a cause of the divorce, it plays little or no role in child custody decisions. However, courts remain reluctant to place children in the homes of known lesbian mothers (or gay fathers). In many cases they deny visitation rights out of fear that the children will become homosexual. However, little evidence can be found to support this concern (Harry, 1983). Studies suggest no evidence that a disproportionate number of children born to or reared by lesbian mothers become homosexual. Some evidence does exist that these children experience more teasing and harassment by peers and neighbors. Once again, we have only a vague sketch of the developmental outcome for children reared by lesbian mothers. Although these children are more likely to be reared in nonsexist ways, there is some evidence that they experience more behavioral problems—particularly adolescent boys.

The primary strengths that professionals note when speaking of the homosexual couple are (1) the opportunity to develop an intimate and enduring relationship with a partner of the same sexual preference and (2) less focus on gender-stereotyped roles. The major limitations are concerns about societal acceptance of such relationships and of raising children in gay or lesbian households.

For excellent reading on the homosexual couple, we suggest McWhirter and Mattison (1984) and Blumstein and Schwartz (1983). These texts provide interesting interview responses by couples about the strengths and problems of living in a homosexual household.

*What implications does the growing number of people adopting alternative family lifestyles have for society at large? Can you think of other new family forms based on family composition?*

# CULTURALLY DIVERSE FAMILIES

In years past substantial social stigma was associated with a "mixed" marriage. Church doctrine and even legal prohibitions against interfaith and interracial marriages were prevalent into the middle 1960s. Not until June 12, 1967, did the U. S. Supreme Court overturn the remaining 16 state statutes making interracial marriages illegal (Crester & Leon, 1982). American Blacks, West Indians, Mongolians, Malayans, Japanese, Chinese, and Native Americans were among the many racial groups that were targeted as unacceptable for Caucasians to marry. To this day, some churches place social sanctions on individuals wishing to marry a person of another faith or race.

## *Interfaith Marriages*

Of the two most basic types of "mixed" marriages, the more common is marriage outside one's religion. Given that there are several hundred denominations, cults, and unorganized religions, it is no surprise that a large number of persons marry someone from another faith. Even within the most prominent faiths in the United States there are very wide ranges in doctrines and practices. Hence, differences, rather than similarities, are more likely the norm in religious practices and beliefs.

Research has shown that parents of the same faith are likely to disapprove of an interfaith marriage for their child (for example, see Heiss, 1980). Parents in interfaith marriages are less resistive to their children's entering such relationships.

There has been relatively little new research on this alternative family lifestyle. For example, the 1980 *Journal of Marriage and the Family* decade review focusing on aspects of marriage and the family does not include a single article on this topic. While an article on nontraditional family forms (Macklin, 1980) documents the gradual increase in pluralism over the last ten years in such family types as never-married singles, cohabitation, childlessness, stepfamilies, and open family forms, nothing is said about interfaith marriages. We suspect this is, in part, a reflection of the commonness of such marriages and the social acceptance of this family type.

Interfaith marriages have several possible strengths and limitations. The most obvious limitation is the problem of which faith will dominate the rearing of the children. Will children be confused about what they are to believe? Will disciplinary practices differ between spouses with fundamentalist and liberal religious orientations? More positively, can children profit from seeing more than one religious viewpoint? Will interpersonal and religious tolerance be more likely to emerge in children reared in a family with two religious orientations? We suspect that if parents are flexible and adaptable, children can profit from experiencing the complexity of an interfaith family.

## Interracial/Interethnic Marriages

Interracial marriages have received considerably more attention than interfaith marriages. By the early 1980s, about 1.2% of married couples in the United States had an interracial marriage (U.S. Bureau of the Census, 1970, 1981). In particular, Black/White intermarriages have been given considerable attention even though they represent only 20–21% of all interracial marriages in the United States. All minority racial groups, however, are associated with approximately a doubling of interracial marriages in the last decade; a large proportion of such marriages involve military personnel.

According to a comprehensive report on intermarriage in the United States, interracial mar-

*Over the next several years, what is the likelihood that interracial marriages will increase? In your opinion, what factors will either encourage or discourage this marital form?*

riages will "have a more congenial climate for success as society continues to become more attuned to individual freedom and personal rights regardless of race, color, creed, or religion" (Porterfield, 1982, p. 13). Further, it has been argued that general racial relations in our country might be improved by interracial marriages. Indeed, some suggest use of interracial marriages as an index of the degree to which a racial group is achieving equality with mainstream White culture. In a study of mate selection and divorce in Hawaii, one of the nation's most racially mixed states, Schwertfeger (1982) reports that even though some evidence suggests the divorce rate is higher for interracial marriages, the pattern is less clear in a societal context like Hawaii where interethnic marriage is relatively common.

Contrary to general expectations, interracial and interethnic couples generally hold conservative rather than liberal views. Most ethnic minorities are strongly influenced by local church groups as primary support systems and therefore internalize conservative attitudes on the family, the community, and politics (Peters & McAdoo, 1983). Further, most ethnic minorities are more involved with extended kin networks. For example, Billingsley (1968) identified four basic family structures in the Black community, associated with four types of extended kin households. McAdoo (1978) summarized these four types: (1) **simple extended** families where married couples, their children, and one or more relatives live in the same household, (2) **incipient extended** families consisting of a married childfree couple and relatives, (3) **attenuated extended** families consisting of a single mother (or father) with children and relatives, and (4) **modified extended** families that include two or more nuclear families living in a household and sharing emotional and/or economic bonds. Similar versions of such extended kin networks can be found for other ethnic families. One must assume that interracial marriages will bring couples into closer involvement with extended kin network patterns.

One notable strength of an interracial marriage is that it is very likely to be based on strong personal feelings between the couple that overcome any social sanctions by society. Further, a racial synergism is likely to emerge for children of an interracial marriage: strengths from each parent's ethnic background may provide an enriched knowledge and enjoyment of two ethnic heritages. There are risks associated with interracial marriages as well. If social stigma, prejudice, or cultural biases emerge, children of interracial marriages may experience difficulties in peer relations and find themselves confused and frustrated by prejudicial treatment. These problems can be minimized and turned toward beneficial results with careful planning, mutual love and concern in the family, and tolerance for individuals who are themselves intolerant.

As a "melting pot" society, we can expect an expanded number of interracial marriages. The stigma once associated with such a marriage has decreased, although subtle social sanctions still exist and interracial couples will continue to find some degree of intolerance.

 *How can interfaith and interracial couples maximize their ability to avoid divorce due to conflict of values or backgrounds?*

## EMPLOYMENT AND FAMILY LIFESTYLES

Families and work have been and probably always will be highly integrated social institutions. Indeed, every ten years the government census assesses the current status of these two institutions because of their importance. Can you imagine completing a census interview without providing detailed information on household employment characteristics? It would probably put half the census takers out of a job! In days past, and probably no less today, a family's status, resources, and residence were determined by the type of employment undertaken by the family. Comparisons between families based on employment characteristics have been central to such fields of study as family sociology, demography, economics, family management, and family relations.

As outlined in Figure 13-2, employment patterns are placing more and more husbands and wives in the job market. Fewer nonworking spouses are projected among married couples, more married persons with and without children are working, and changes in lifestyle patterns continue to unfold. This pattern raises issues not only of dual incomes but also of increased mobility associated with employment. To illustrate how employment affects families, we will examine both issues.

## Dual-Career Families

Aldous (1981a) writes that it is misleading to think of the dual-earner family as a new family form. It is true that the majority (about 51%) of families are now dual-earner households and that only 33% have a husband as the only breadwinner. However, women have been providing economic support for the family for decades. Indeed, dual-earner families increased by only about 5% from the 1960s to the late 1970s. And although women's participation in the labor force has increased substantially since World War II, before that time women were earning incomes from numerous home-based industries—for example, providing meals, boarding guests, selling homemade clothing, making toys.

The most dramatic change that we can focus on is not the gradual increase in the dual-earner family but the growth in the still relatively small number of dual-*career* families (estimated to be fewer than 100,000) where both spouses have

very demanding, competitive jobs like corporate executive, lawyer, physician, research scientist, and politician. Societal interest in such families is reflected in the array of books written about the dual-career family. Illustrations of these important contributions are *American Couples* (Blumstein & Schwartz, 1983), *Dual-Career Couples* (Pepitone-Rockwell, 1980), *Two Paychecks* (Aldous, 1981b), *Making It Together as a Two-Career Couple* (Shaevitz & Shaevitz, 1980), and *Families in a Working World* (M. R. Davis, 1982).

Although these popular books provide useful information, surprisingly little research has actually been conducted on the dual-career family (Aldous, 1981a), and definitional problems have limited the usefulness of several studies. For example, clear distinctions are seldom made between dual-earner and dual-career households. Further, since many married couples are dual earners but about half the wives are employed for only a few years (Masnick & Bane, 1980), many studies underestimate the incidence of dual-earner families.

But what are the general characteristics of a dual-career family? Foremost, both husband and wife have careers that are integrally part of their identities. Their work requires substantial training and prolonged commitment (Hicks, Hansen, & Christie, 1983). Both spouses must adjust their time to cooperate and balance household-task demands, child-care responsibilities, and time management (Pepitone-Rockwell, 1980). Each spouse must be able to compete in his or her own employment and yet provide support and understanding of the other spouse's time and energy demands. Career role strains and interpersonal conflict must be managed. The two earners must decide whether to pool all family income or maintain separate resources. Above all else, the dual-career family must learn to cope with the intrusion of work into family life.

*Like all marriage forms, dual-career marriages have advantages and disadvantages. Can you list some of them? How do you think Geraldine Ferraro, John Zaccaro, and their family (pictured here) would answer this question?*

Fortunately, some evidence suggests that happiness in employment is associated with the perception of one's happiness in marriage (Blumstein & Schwartz, 1983). In short, a career demands a great deal of mental and physical energy and long hours of work. Two spouses who are involved in careers will necessarily have less leisure time for each other or for household tasks.

Like employment as a homemaker, a career for a wife has both benefits and liabilities. Both husband and wife may benefit from the increased status of a wife's involvement in a career (Blumstein & Schwartz, 1983). She may receive more satisfaction from a career than from a job, making her happier at work and at home. A career may increase her feelings of self-worth and competence. And, of course, a career is likely to pay more than a job, increasing her ability to contribute to the family. Mothers with careers are less overprotective and self-sacrificing (Birnbaum, 1975), thereby encouraging confidence and self-esteem in their children. Their children see that employment is important in the lives of men and women and see both parents as role models (Nadelson & Nadelson, 1980). Thus, a mother's career can contribute positively to each family member's well-being and development, particularly if the spouses can resolve problems of role strain and interpersonal conflicts associated with time management and can balance the intrusion of work demands against the fulfillment of family needs.

Several studies suggest that dual-career families promote positive social adjustment for the spouses. Both spouses can take a certain pride and self-satisfaction in balancing their professional and family interests (for example, Blumstein & Schwartz, 1983); women in dual-career families report positive social adjustment and good mental health (Piotrkowski & Crits-Christoph, 1981); marital solidarity is high (Simpson & England, 1981); and dual-career husbands share slightly more in the demands of household maintenance and tasks (Model, 1981). However, liabilities are also evident. In particular, the care of children may be difficult. Unfortunately, most evidence suggests that women retain primary responsibility for this need, entering and leaving the work force as unusual child-rearing demands dictate (Aldous, 1981b). A rivalry may emerge in which husband and wife compete, each trying to make more money than the other (Marsh, 1981). This may lead to escalating hours on the job, conflict between the spouses, reducing parenting time, or psychological power plays

between the spouses in money management issues (Shaevitz & Shaevitz, 1980).

## Commuter Marriages

In addition to dual-career families that reside in the same household, many contemporary families have developed a lifestyle dubbed "commuter," "long-distance," or "two-location" families (Gerstel & Gross, 1982). Though not new to the 1980s, this lifestyle reflects societal changes in employment patterns. Research on such families is limited; five empirical studies provide the basis for our understanding of this form of marriage (Farris, 1978; Gerstel, 1979; Gross, 1978; Kirschner & Walum, 1978; Orton & Crossman, 1980).

Because of data-collection limitations, we have no accurate estimate of the number of commuter marriages in America. Further, definitional problems abound among studies on commuter marriage. However, researchers use several social trends to argue that commuter marriages must be increasing: (1) the entry of more women into professional jobs with high mobility demands, (2) employment patterns that force relocation, (3) greater acceptance of wives' career interests and demands, and (4) an increasing emphasis on individualism and self-fulfillment (Gerstel & Gross, 1982).

Commuter marriages seem to be primarily a middle-class phenomenon motivated more by high career commitment than by increased income. A commuter marriage typically involves the establishment of two households and the costs of travel and long-distance phone calls between them. Several studies indicate that little is gained financially and that the decision is seldom based on financial considerations but, rather, focuses on professional commitments and personal fulfillment.

Most commuter marriages have several common features. The majority consists of older couples—few newlyweds and few couples with young children. When fathers are absent because of a commuter marriage arrangement, they tend to report a sense of loss and guilt (Gerstel & Gross, 1982). However, longer-duration marriages have been found to be associated with less guilt or stress. Most couples arrange to reunite on occasion. Regular reunions on weekends and holidays have been shown to be associated with greater reported success and satisfaction with a commuter marriage arrangement. In sum, Gerstel and Gross (1982, p. 78) conclude from their analysis of commuter marriage research that five basic conditions enhance the success of the marriage: (1) couples have adequate, if not high, incomes or financial resources, (2) spouses have intense career motivations or view work as a central life commitment, (3) couples have been married long enough to share a history that provides a "taken for granted" stability, (4) children are not yet or no longer in the home, and (5) spouses reunite regularly on weekends.

The consequences of commuter marriages are various. Strengths include the obvious benefit of career development and mobility. Greater equity is available for both spouses' needs for career fulfillment. Living apart may enhance the relationship during periods of reunion; the partners' sensitivity and excitement about each other may be renewed. The couple can enjoy the benefits of living in two different locations. Liabilities can, but need not, be substantial. The costs of having two residences can be a financial burden. Having little leisure time for shared activities may cause the couple to grow apart. Spouses may miss the daily intimacy associated with living together and experience periods of loneliness. It may be difficult to develop friendships at one or both locations, and the urge or opportunity for extramarital affairs may be increased.

 *Can you think of other problems that dual-career and commuter marriages might encounter? How might couples meet these challenges?*

## Corporate and Military Families

Tennessee Ernie Ford used to sing a song about a coal miner who lamented "I owe my soul to the company store." Many mining operators paid employees in certificates that could be traded in for food and other goods at the company-owned general store. Little or no cash was exchanged. When miners needed something they couldn't pay for, the company provided them with a loan through a credit line. As you can probably guess, this resulted in a catch-22: the more the miners owed the company, the more the company actually owned them. Still, there is a security in working for an organization that promises the family will be cared for as long as the employee is faithful to the company.

In today's world, the **corporate family** functions much like the old mining family. The worker is guaranteed a comfortable living and good benefits in exchange for willingness to respond without question to the company's needs. This often means job promotions tied to frequent moves.

The moves may have many benefits for the family: more money, new adventures, sometimes better schools and recreational facilities. However, frequent moves can be frustrating, lonely, and stressful (Gullotta & Donohue, 1981a, 1981b). Children may develop signs of emotional stress, problems in school, or problems with peers. Spouses (usually wives) may feel lonely, alienated, or depressed. The corporate employee may overwork to establish competence in the new job, and family members may perceive that the only person who has profited is father. As our nation's economy develops, the corporate family will increasingly be a common family form in almost any middle-class neighborhood. Many moves in future years may be as much for a wife's career as for her husband's.

Distinct parallels in stress reactions to family disruptions are found between corporate and military families. As husbands are preparing to depart for an assignment, family tension builds, and military wives place greater emotional distance between themselves and their husbands. During the husband's absence, the wife idealizes her marital relationship, and rules are relaxed with the children. As the father reenters, family tension remounts, idealizations are confronted with reality, and rules are reestablished with the children. Thus, military assignments are associated with tensions during departure, idealization during absence, and renewed tension and readjustments on return of the husband/father (or possibly wife/mother).

For the corporate family, disruption comes most strikingly in a family move. Some husbands and wives cope with this distress by drinking, using drugs, considering divorce, or having extramarital affairs. As in the military family, anxiety and tension build before the move. Loneliness, depression, insomnia, and irritability are common for all family members. Many individuals actually manifest a grief reaction. Children may feel resentment and anger, and their school performance may drop.

Families can deal with the dysfunctional responses to moving. One educational prevention program is showing promise—*Plain Talk about Moving* (Donohue & Gullotta, 1981), a two-part series that uses newsletters to offer practical advice about moving, managing family stress, finding time for the family, and meeting the family's emotional needs. By obtaining basic information on stress management, maintaining open communications about the move, and helping the

children adjust to a new location, the family can reduce the dysfunctional behaviors associated with military and corporate family life. In fact, for many families the benefits of travel, promotion, and salary increases offset the costs of moving. Indeed, corporate and military families are not so dissimilar from many American households: more than 17% of households move each year.

*How can we help the corporate or military family cope with its lifestyle problems?*

# ALTERNATIVE SEXUAL LIFESTYLES

Central to the traditional nuclear family is the idea of sexual exclusivity between married partners. Among family forms varying from this perspective, the least extreme are cohabitating couples, somewhat more liberal are swinging couples, and even more extreme are group marriages.

## *Cohabitation*

Recent evidence indicates that about 2.3% of all U. S. households that include a man and a woman consist of nonmarried cohabiting couples. This is a twofold increase in the last ten years. For couples under age 25, it represents an eightfold increase in just one decade (Stein, 1981). There is no definitive explanation for this dramatic change, although society's increasing tolerance of varying lifestyles is almost certainly a factor.

Recent demographic research provides a general profile of cohabitants (Glick & Spanier, 1981). About 85% are under age 35. This finding may reflect a generational tolerance for cohabitation. Never-married cohabitating couples and married couples have very similar educational levels. Most live in urban communities. Although more cohabiting couples are White than Black, the cohabitation rate among Blacks is three times that of Whites.

Research by Macklin (1981) and other pioneers in the study of cohabitation suggests several advantages of this lifestyle. It allows a couple to develop sexual experience, love, caring, sharing, and understanding. Without the bonds of "commitment" or "permanence," it allows two persons to satisfy each other's needs in a close and intimate relationship while maintaining a sense of independence. On the practical side, it can reduce housing costs and living-arrangement problems.

There are limitations too. Macklin (1981) identifies four major categories: emotional problems, sexual problems, problems with parents, and problems related to the living arrangement. Emotional problems include feelings of being used or jealousy about a partner's involvement with others. Cohabitants may feel guilty about beginning, maintaining, or ending the relationship. Because of the feeling of temporariness, some feel they don't "belong." Sexual problems range from lack of orgasm, impotence, and fear of pregnancy to discomfort during intercourse. Living-arrangement problems include lack of privacy, inadequate space, and conflicts with other housemates.

Garrett (1982) concludes that cohabitation can strengthen emotional bonds, provide an opportunity for enhancing social skills, and foster interpersonal relationships, but there are numerous potential costs, too. Cohabiting couples may initially perceive that because their relationship has no legal status, it will be an easy matter to end it. However, Macklin's research suggests that such couples usually do not escape the psychological pain and adjustment associated with the ending of a meaningful relationship. Another

difficulty in cohabitation is conflict with parents. If told, many parents become upset, and conflict resolution becomes necessary. If parents are not told, the young people may try to hide the living arrangement from them and suffer from the fear of being discovered. Fear of an accidental disclosure during a conversation with parents may lead the offspring to avoid parents or constrain their style of communication with them.

Finally, legal difficulties can result. Accumulation of personal property or real estate by cohabitants may end in litigation if the couple can't decide how to set joint ownership. Even though cohabitation is illegal in some states, numerous suits have set precedents for "palimony" litigation. A pregnancy may lead to other legal problems by raising issues of child support and custody. Further, the gray areas of the law may result in substantial legal and psychological costs in the ending of a cohabitation.

## Swinging

When swinging came into the public eye, it was first called "wife swapping" and then "comarital relationships" (Murstein, 1978). Murstein (1978, p. 110) defines swinging as "a form of extramarital behavior involving legally married or pairbonded couples sharing coitus or other sexual pleasures with one or more persons in a social context defined by all participants as a form of recreational-convivial play." According to Murstein, several popular polls suggest that 1.5–2.0% of our married population have tried swinging at least once.

What are swinging couples like? Many are rather conservative. They oppose using drugs, support conservative political leaders, and describe themselves as highly traditional and religious. Others are extremely liberal and antiestablishment in attitudes and opinions. According to research summarized by Murstein (1978), perhaps the most outstanding characteristics of swingers are their acceptance of sex and interest in sexual experiences. Many people assume that swinging couples must be emotionally disturbed. However, most research suggests that they show relatively normal profiles on standard personality tests (Schupp, 1970; Twichell, 1974).

Many of the advantages of swinging parallel those of the extramarital affair. However, in this case, the activity is known about and approved (and participated in) by both partners. Murstein (1978) notes several advantages of swinging: it is less time-consuming and less emotionally demanding than an affair; it may rejuvenate sexual interest in one's spouse; it is basically equitable and honest; and it provides satisfaction, novelty, and expression of individual sexual drives. Disadvantages that lead people to drop out of swinging include jealousy, guilt, development of an intense emotional attachment to someone else's spouse, fear of discovery by children or community, spread of venereal disease, and perceived superficiality of relationships (Murstein, 1978; Stinnett & Birdsong, 1978).

## Group Marriage

In a group marriage three or more individuals form a union and live together on some type of communal basis. In the past, this form of marriage has been called "tribal marriage" or "communal marriage." One notable historical example was the Oneida Community, established in New York State in the middle 1800s. Popular contemporary interest in the idea of group marriage was stimulated by a series of novels written by Robert Rimmer entitled *The Harrad Experiment, Proposition 31,* and *You and I Searching for Tomorrow.*

What advantages might group marriage have? A classic work by Constantine and Constantine (1973) and reviews by others (for example, Murstein, 1978; Stinnett & Birdsong, 1978) suggest that this lifestyle increases one's loving and intimate relationships, establishes a sense of communal life, offers economic or social advantages in the home, and is a way for some to express their antiestablishment attitudes. Some see a group marriage as an opportunity to express idealism and find a utopian lifestyle.

A group marriage provides a variety of sexual experiences and partners, but jealousy, conflict, differences in the closeness of relationships between various participants, and related problems may make it difficult to achieve a fully shared sexual lifestyle. Parenthood and care of children are reportedly shared by all, and many group-marriage members perceive greater involvement by the husbands in caring for the children. Limitations of group marriage include differences in philosophies, diffusion of responsibility, and problems with compatibility of partners, sleeping arrangements, fulfilling daily responsibilities, or financial management.

It appears that group marriages, like extramarital relations and swinging, are highly unstable and seldom long-term. We suspect this reality is due to the unacceptability to society of these three forms of marital experimentation. In most states these three forms of sexually based social relations are illegal. Charges of fornication, adultery, keeping a disorderly house, or lewdness can be brought against participants. Many communities have developed zoning laws to limit the number of unrelated adults of mixed sexes who can live in the same dwelling. Nonetheless, a significant number of persons will probably continue to experiment and, at least for a brief period in their lives, attempt to find fulfillment through these three types of social relationships.

 *How do cohabitation, swinging, and group marriage differ from extramarital relationships? How are they all similar?*

In a diverse and changing society, alternative family lifestyles are likely to emerge. As individuals interested in the humane treatment of all members of society, we believe it is essential to promote tolerance for differences in family lifestyles.

# EDUCATION

All of us—children and adults alike—need to be aware of alternative family types, of the contributions made by individuals from diverse lifestyles, and of the numerous lifestyle choices that exist in this country. We must understand that the traditional nuclear family is just one family form; that certain family lifestyle differences are based on economic realities; and that singleness is a reality for all of us for some portion of our lives and that this lifestyle can be rich and fulfilling. Dual-career and commuter marriages reflect the reality that work patterns are changing and both members of a couple are likely to work. Moreover, our society is slowly accepting cohabitation and emerging sexual alternatives in family relationships. Interfaith and interracial marriages are increasing.

Within our own families, we can discuss these lifestyle patterns. We can clarify our personal and parental values about each of these alternative lifestyles. Awareness, recognition, and values clarification should enhance understanding by all family members of our changing society and of the lifestyles emerging from change.

# COMMUNITY ORGANIZATION/ SYSTEMS INTERVENTION

Each lifestyle we have discussed has its own social and legal advocates. To gain acceptance, members of each lifestyle need to organize and promote a positive image of that lifestyle. A lifestyle group should function as a representative for the rights and needs of its members. Group members' openness, honesty, and willingness to recognize the family type's limitations while promoting its strengths should enhance societal tolerance for that lifestyle. Tolerance for differences is based on a group's willingness to maintain an open and honest representation of itself while resisting attacking others. Above all else, in a society of special-interest groups, members of various family lifestyles should organize and help to represent their interests in political decision making, resource management, and government provision of services.

# COMPETENCY PROMOTION

Each lifestyle alternative has its strengths and limitations, and we have tried to describe what family-life specialists have thought these to be. In learning about these alternatives, discussion about variation and choice can enhance effective decision making. There may be no better issue to help young people clarify their values, opinions, or attitudes than that of establishing a moral perspective within the context of tolerance for other people's lifestyle choices. Indeed, we all can profit—children and adults—from an examination of alternative family lifestyles. In the process, we can explore and clarify morality, values, and ideals and learn effective decision-making practices. Discussing alternative lifestyles is an excellent way to develop effective decision-making strategies for life in general.

## NATURAL CAREGIVING

In helping others to help themselves, we need to recognize the strengths and limitations of all family lifestyles. All family forms, including the traditional nuclear family, have limitations in providing for the needs and interests of family members. If we recognize where the strengths of a family type end and where its limitations begin, we can, through tolerance and understanding, help all concerned to recognize and use effective caregiving, to utilize available resources, and to enhance the family's social support network.

 *Is tolerance something that adults can learn? What other things can be done to encourage tolerance of alternative lifestyles?*

# SUMMARY

Although the traditional nuclear family receives considerable political attention and is the focus of much research, there are many lifestyle variations based on family composition, sexual preference, cultural diversity, employment, and degree of sexual exclusivity. As we move into the next century, such variability in family lifestyle and household composition will likely increase and broaden. Given this variation, our nation must increase its tolerance and acceptance of such groups.

# MAJOR POINTS TO REMEMBER

1. Social change over the last 30 years has brought liberalization and changes in family lifestyles.
2. Alternatives to the nuclear family exist and are expected to expand in the future. Increased numbers of singles, employed couples, and childless families will emerge.
3. Variations on family relations can be seen in household composition: single persons, married and childfree couples, never-married families, and homosexual couples. Each family composition has both strengths and limitations.
4. Families can also be characterized by their degree of cultural diversity. Interfaith marriages bring individuals of different religions together; interracial marriages unite individuals of different races.
5. Employment patterns of men and women have created some unique family types. Current lifestyles of dual-earner families include dual-career and commuter marriages. Families that move often because of employment include corporate and military families. These two family types have similar problems, strengths, and liabilities.
6. Other alternative family lifestyles are distinguished by degree of commitment and sexual exclusivity. Couples can live together unmarried, or they can marry and engage in swinging, or they can form group marriages.
7. Promoting tolerance of alternative lifestyles is an important primary prevention objective that enhances family members' well-being.

# ADDITIONAL SOURCES OF INFORMATION

Alternatives to traditional family living. (1982). *Marriage and Family Review, 5*(2). [Adults]

Blumstein, P., & Schwartz, P. W. (1983). *American couples: Money, work, sex.* New York: William Morrow. [Adolescents, adults]

Davis, M. R. (1982). *Families in a working world: The impact of organization on domestic life.* New York: Praeger. [Adults]

Lobsenz, N. (1974, June). Living together. *Redbook,* p. 86. [Children, adolescents, adults]

Macklin, E. D., & Rubin, R. H. (1983). *Contemporary families and alternative lifestyles.* Beverly Hills, CA: Sage. [Adults]

Masnick, G., & Bane, M. J. (1980). *The nation's families: 1960–1990.* Boston, MA: Auburn House. [Adults]

Shaevitz, M. H., & Shaevitz, M. H. (1980). *Making it together as a two-career couple.* Boston: Houghton Mifflin. [Adolescents, adults]

Stinnett, N., Chesser, B., & DeFrain, J. (1979). *Building family strengths: Blueprints for action.* Lincoln: University of Nebraska Press. [Adults]

*Part Four*

# FAMILY MATTERS
# OF CONCERN

# 14

# FAMILY ECONOMICS: IN GOOD TIMES AND BAD

1. What is a "freewiller"?

2. Was it a wise decision to have purchased this book? What does that decision have to do with your future?

3. This country's population is moving.
Where is it going? What does that shift
mean for employment?

4. What are fixed expenses? What are flexible expenses?

5. Why is inflation feared?

6. What percentage of your income will
probably be spent on housing?

7. Why are there more kinds of mortgage
loans today than there were 20 years
ago?

8. Are there safe ways to build a retirement income?

9. Why can economists claim full employment when the unemployment rate is
3%, 5%, or even 7%?

10. How is technology changing the job
market?

11. How does unemployment hurt individuals and their families?

You can tell whether times are good or bad in a
family by the way they shop in a grocery store. I
mean, if things aren't going too good for a family, they look at prices more and argue more
over whether some item is needed. It's really sad
to see couples fighting over whether a can of
furniture polish should be purchased and then
to see one of them leave either angry or in tears.
It's not money that's the root of all evil—it's
poverty [Comments made to one of the authors].

The importance of having adequate financial resources has already been made abundantly clear
in this text. The management of those financial
resources is equally important. As the opening
story to this chapter suggests, financial disagreements can cause marital strife. We have organized this chapter to cover both good economic
times and bad. The section on good times describes the advantages of remaining in school,
career planning, and learning to budget, and it
considers such issues as the economy, credit,
shelter, loans, insurance, and retirement. In the
section on bad times, we examine the impact of
unemployment on the individual and the family.
The chapter concludes with suggestions for easing the distress that accompanies unemployment.

## IN GOOD TIMES
## OF EMPLOYMENT:
## A BRIEF HISTORY

Most of us probably remember from our American history courses that indentured servitude
was a form of bound labor present in North
America until the late 18th century. Indentured
servants, or "freewillers," as they were called,
exchanged their labor for some period of time
(often years) for passage to America. What those

history courses may have failed to tell us is that these "freewillers" did not always embark for America of their own free will and that an amazing 80% of White immigrants to North America before the colonial revolution arrived as indentured servants (Marris, 1976).

Why were so many "freewillers" kidnapped and sent to the New World? The reason, Marris (1976) suggests, was the New World's need for labor. In a land that stretched endlessly, the demand for a labor force far outstripped the supply. Consequently, inducements such as land grants and wages at least twice as high as those available in England were offered to new arrivals. And if that failed, "crimps" would recruit imprisoned debtors or in other (often illegal) ways find immigrants for the colonies. Although living conditions for indentured servants were poor, the opinion of most foreign visitors to the colonies was that, in comparison with Europe, poverty scarcely existed in America (Marris, 1976).

Times have changed. Since the Great Depression of the 1930s, the belief that labor opportunities are limitless no longer exists in most people's minds. As industry approaches the day when machines will be able to program machines, young people are pushed ever earlier into making decisions that will affect their lives for years to come.

# THE BEGINNING YEARS: TO AGE 18

We can assume that if you are reading this book, you have made one wise decision already. No, that decision is not having purchased this book, although we do appreciate it. The wise decision you made was to remain in school. As Table 14-1 shows, earnings significantly increase as education increases. The college graduate can expect to earn almost twice the grade school graduate's income each working year.

## Setting Occupational Goals

The decision that now faces you is determining your career and financial goals. Your success in attaining those goals depends not only on education and on your career choice but on variables such as the population shift in this country. How does a population shift affect career choice? Well, the population of the United States is shifting from the Northeast and the industrial states

**TABLE 14-1.** *1980–1981 median incomes for men and women by educational level*

| Educational Level | Men | Women | Women's Incomes as a Percentage of Men's |
|---|---|---|---|
| Elementary school | $13,117 | $ 8,216 | 62.6% |
| 1–3 years high school | 16,101 | 9,676 | 60.1 |
| High school graduate | 19,469 | 11,537 | 59.3 |
| 1–3 years college | 20,909 | 12,954 | 61.9 |
| College graduate (4 years) | 24,311 | 15,143 | 62.3 |
| Postgraduate (1 or more years) | 27,690 | 18,100 | 65.4 |

around the Great Lakes to the South and West. The U. S. Department of Labor (1980) estimates that by 1990 half of this country's population will live in those areas. One can predict that employment prospects will decline in areas that drop in population and will increase in areas that experience growth. Equally important is the "graying" of American society. The babies of the "baby boom" of the 1940s and 1950s are now between 28 and 43 years of age. As they continue to grow older, opportunities in areas that serve the elderly will grow dramatically (U. S. Department of Labor, 1980).

Other factors such as an individual's interests, talents, academic ability, and financial resources all enter into occupational choice. Now that rapidly changing technology is altering the way we conceive of possible careers, it would be advisable for all students to look closely at the United States Labor Department's *Occupational Outlook Handbook* (Bureau of Labor Statistics, 1982b). Published every two years, this book forecasts the employment outlook and salary ranges for more than 850 jobs. It provides a description of each, including educational and/or training requirements. (Table 14-2 shows a projection of the major occupational groupings for the remainder of this decade.)

Determining one's interests and setting sights on an occupation establish a person's goals. These goals are not only personal satisfaction goals but imply financial goals as well, and the individual will need to resolve any conflicts between the two. For example, debt collection may be financially rewarding, but it may not be the wisest choice for someone who likes to avoid conflict. As another example, it is unlikely that a decision to become an author will ever result in great wealth. The average book author earned $4775 in 1979 from writing. It is true that some authors had incomes in excess of $100,000 a year—but only 4% of those who had published a book recently. Most earned much less. In fact,

38% earned less than $2500 a year ("Author's Income," 1982).

 *Look at Tables 14-1 and 14-2. Why do you think gender affects employment opportunities and earnings?*

## Budgeting: Planning for the Future

Planning for the future suggests that you have an idea of where you would like to be at the end of this year, next year, and future years. What are your immediate financial goals? Where would you like to be five years from today, a decade from today? The first step in sensible planning is to establish flexible goals that enable you to judge your progress in managing your affairs. A simple way of doing this is to list your immediate, short-term, and long-term goals on paper (see Figure 14-1).

Goals for this year:

_____
_____
_____

Goals for the next five years:

_____
_____
_____

Long-term goals:

_____
_____
_____

**FIGURE 14-1.** *A goal list.*

Having done this, you are ready to follow an easy five-step plan to determine whether the goals you have set for yourself can be reached. The first step is to determine your total income

**TABLE 14-2.** Projected change in employment by major occupational group, 1978–1990

| Occupational Group | Employment, 1978 (in thousands) | No. of Women, 1978 (in thousands) | Women as Percentage of Total Employment | Projected Employment, 1990 (in thousands) | Percent Change[a] | Openings (in thousands) | | |
|---|---|---|---|---|---|---|---|---|
| | | | | | | Total | Growth | Replacements[b] |
| Total | 94,373 | 38,882 | 41.2 | 114,000 | 20.8 | 66,400 | 19,600 | 46,800 |
| White-collar workers | 47,205 | — | 52.1 | 58,400 | 23.6 | 36,800 | 11,200 | 25,600 |
| Professional and technical workers | 14,245 | 24,572 | 42.7 | 16,900 | 18.3 | 8,300 | 2,600 | 5,700 |
| Managers and administrators except farm | 10,105 | 2,361 | 23.4 | 12,200 | 20.8 | 7,100 | 2,100 | 5,000 |
| Sales workers | 5,951 | 2,666 | 44.8 | 7,600 | 27.7 | 4,800 | 1,700 | 3,100 |
| Clerical workers | 16,904 | 13,463 | 79.6 | 21,700 | 28.4 | 16,600 | 4,800 | 11,800 |
| Blue-collar workers | 31,531 | 5,767 | 18.3 | 36,600 | 16.1 | 16,200 | 5,100 | 11,100 |
| Craft workers | 12,386 | 697 | 5.6 | 14,900 | 20.0 | 7,000 | 2,500 | 4,500 |
| Operatives, except transport | 10,875 | 4,321 | 39.7 | 12,500 | 15.0 | 5,600 | 1,600 | 4,000 |
| Transport operatives | 3,541 | 257 | 7.3 | 4,100 | 16.2 | 1,700 | 600 | 1,100 |
| Nonfarm laborers | 4,729 | 491 | 10.4 | 5,100 | 8.1 | 2,000 | 400 | 1,600 |
| Service workers | 12,839 | 8,034 | 62.6 | 16,700 | 29.9 | 12,200 | 3,800 | 8,400 |
| Private household workers | 1,162 | 1,134 | 97.7 | 900 | -23.2 | 500 | -300 | 800 |
| Other service workers | 11,677 | 6,900 | 59.1 | 15,800 | 35.2 | 11,700 | 4,100 | 7,600 |
| Farm workers | 2,798 | 509 | 18.2 | 2,400 | -15.9 | 1,300 | -400 | 1,700 |

[a] Percentages were calculated using unrounded numbers.
[b] Replacements due to deaths, retirements, and other separations from the labor force. They do not include transfers out of occupations.

| Item | Amount |
|---|---|
| Salary | $ _____ |
| Dividends and interest | _____ |
| Allowance from parents | _____ |
| Social Security | _____ |
| Veterans' benefits | _____ |
| Other | _____ |

**FIGURE 14-2.** *Spendable income.*

after state and federal income taxes. Figure 14-2 lists several possible sources of income.

Step two is determining your total fixed expenses after taxes. These include such items as rent, utilities, insurance, and transportation costs. Figure 14-3 lists possible fixed expenses.

| Item | Amount |
|---|---|
| Housing | |
|   a. rent | $ _____ |
|   b. mortgage | _____ |
| Utilities | |
|   a. telephone | _____ |
|   b. gas | _____ |
|   c. electricity | _____ |
|   d. water | _____ |
|   e. fuel | _____ |
| Educational costs | |
|   a. books | _____ |
|   b. tuition | _____ |
|   c. other | _____ |
| Insurance | |
|   a. health | _____ |
|   b. automobile | _____ |
|   c. life | _____ |
|   d. property | _____ |
|   e. other | _____ |
| Transportation | |
|   a. gasoline | _____ |
|   b. motor vehicle costs | _____ |
|   c. commuting fares | _____ |
| Other | |
|   a. | _____ |
|   b. | _____ |
|   c. | _____ |

**FIGURE 14-3.** *Fixed expenses.*

The third step is to determine your flexible expenses. Flexible expenses are those that can be more easily controlled than fixed expenses. For example, it's easier to switch from steak to chicken (flexible expense) than to lower the price of a gallon of gasoline (fixed expense). Figure 14-4 lists flexible expenses. (See Box 14-1 for an idea of how well you may or may not be eating.)

Step four is to start a savings plan. A savings plan is crucial not only to cover the emergencies that occur in any calendar year but to make progress toward the five-year and longer-term goals you established for yourself earlier.

The final step in this budget plan is comparing expenses (adding steps two, three, and four) with income (step one). The two figures should be equal. Should expenses exceed income, reex-

| Item | Amount |
|---|---|
| Food | |
|   a. at home | $ _____ |
|   b. away from home | _____ |
| Clothing | _____ |
| Gifts | |
|   a. birthdays | _____ |
|   b. Christmas | _____ |
|   c. | _____ |
| Entertainment | |
|   a. movies | _____ |
|   b. hobbies | _____ |
|   c. sports events | _____ |
|   d. | _____ |
| Contributions | |
|   a. religious | _____ |
|   b. | _____ |
|   c. | _____ |
| Credit card loan payments | _____ |
| Miscellaneous | |
|   a. cable television | _____ |
|   b. magazines/papers | _____ |
|   c. tobacco | _____ |
|   d. alcohol | _____ |
|   e. grooming aids | _____ |
|   f. | _____ |
|   g. | _____ |
|   h. | _____ |

**FIGURE 14-4.** *Flexible expenses.*

## BOX 14-1
### *The Cost of Eating*

Did you ever wonder how well you were eating? The chart to the right assumes that all meals are eaten at home. To determine your standard, add the cost of weekly groceries to the cost of all meals and snacks eaten outside the home, and then compare that total with the figures below.

| | Cost for One Week | | | |
|---|---|---|---|---|
| **Sex/Age Group** | **Thrifty plan**[a] | **Low-cost plan** | **Moderate-cost plan** | **Liberal plan** |
| *Families* | | | | |
| Family of two:[b] | | | | |
| 20–54 years | $33.20 | $42.90 | $53.70 | $64.30 |
| 55 years and over | 29.80 | 38.20 | 47.30 | 56.40 |
| Family of four: | | | | |
| Couple, 20–54 years, and children— | | | | |
| 1–2 and 3–5 years | 47.20 | 60.30 | 75.00 | 89.90 |
| 6–8 and 9–11 years | 56.90 | 72.90 | 91.20 | 109.20 |
| *Individuals*[c] | | | | |
| Child: | | | | |
| 7 months to 1 year | 6.80 | 8.20 | 10.00 | 11.80 |
| 1–2 years | 7.70 | 9.70 | 11.90 | 14.20 |
| 3–5 years | 9.30 | 11.60 | 14.30 | 17.20 |
| 6–8 years | 11.80 | 15.10 | 18.80 | 22.50 |
| 9–11 years | 14.90 | 18.80 | 23.60 | 28.20 |
| Male: | | | | |
| 12–14 years | 15.80 | 20.00 | 25.00 | 29.80 |
| 15–19 years | 17.30 | 22.00 | 27.60 | 33.10 |
| 20–54 years | 16.70 | 21.60 | 27.20 | 32.70 |
| 55 years and over | 14.80 | 19.00 | 23.60 | 28.30 |
| Female: | | | | |
| 12–19 years | 14.00 | 17.80 | 22.00 | 26.30 |
| 20–54 years | 13.50 | 17.40 | 21.60 | 25.80 |
| 55 years and over | 12.30 | 15.70 | 19.40 | 23.00 |
| Pregnant | 17.00 | 21.50 | 26.50 | 31.40 |
| Nursing | 18.00 | 22.80 | 28.40 | 33.70 |

[a] The coupon allotment in the food-stamp program is based on this plan.

[b] Ten percent added for family-size adjustment. See footnote c.

[c] The costs given are for individuals in four-person families. For individuals in other-size families, the following adjustments are suggested: one person—add 20%; two persons—add 10%; three persons—add 5%; five or six persons—subtract 5%; seven or more persons—subtract 10%.

amine the items in steps three and four (flexible expenses and savings) that can be reduced to bring your budget into line. If you are exceptionally fortunate, income will exceed expenses. In this case you might consider increasing your savings or improving your lifestyle by increasing flexible expenses.

Finally, keep a record of your monthly expenses and assess your progress toward the flexible long-term goals you established for yourself.

Learning how to control your money and where it goes *now* will be of immense help as you enter that period of life known as the working years.

*Some might think financial planning is unnecessary at this stage of life. What is your opinion? Are there benefits to be gained by learning to budget your earnings at this time of life?*

## BOX 14-1
*Continued*

| Sex/Age Group | Cost for One Month | | | |
|---|---|---|---|---|
| | Thrifty plan[a] | Low-cost plan | Moderate-cost plan | Liberal plan |
| *Families* | | | | |
| Family of two:[b] | | | | |
| 20–54 years | $144.00 | $185.70 | $232.70 | $278.70 |
| 55 years and over | 129.30 | 165.70 | 205.00 | 244.60 |
| Family of four: | | | | |
| Couple, 20–54 years, and children— | | | | |
| 1–2 and 3–5 years | 204.40 | 260.80 | 325.10 | 389.10 |
| 6–8 and 9–11 years | 246.60 | 315.50 | 395.30 | 473.10 |
| *Individuals*[c] | | | | |
| Child: | | | | |
| 7 months to 1 year | 29.30 | 35.40 | 43.30 | 51.10 |
| 1–2 years | 33.20 | 41.90 | 51.60 | 61.30 |
| 3–5 years | 40.30 | 50.10 | 62.00 | 74.40 |
| 6–8 years | 51.30 | 65.20 | 81.60 | 97.60 |
| 9–11 years | 64.40 | 81.50 | 102.20 | 122.10 |
| Male: | | | | |
| 12–14 years | 68.60 | 86.50 | 108.20 | 129.30 |
| 15–19 years | 75.10 | 95.40 | 119.40 | 143.40 |
| 20–54 years | 72.20 | 93.40 | 117.80 | 141.60 |
| 55 years and over | 64.20 | 82.40 | 102.40 | 122.80 |
| Female: | | | | |
| 12–19 years | 60.70 | 77.10 | 95.50 | 113.80 |
| 20–54 years | 58.70 | 75.40 | 93.70 | 111.80 |
| 55 years and over | 53.30 | 68.20 | 84.00 | 99.60 |
| Pregnant | 73.50 | 93.20 | 114.70 | 136.20 |
| Nursing | 78.00 | 98.80 | 122.90 | 146.10 |

## THE WORKING YEARS: 18 TO 64

Earlier in this chapter we saw that the American economy is changing. Numerous authors looking at the growth of technology in the workplace have nearly all concluded that by the early part of the next century as many as half of the industrial jobs in this country may no longer exist (Shane, 1982; see Abelson, 1982a, 1982b).

Accompanying this technological revolution in the workplace is the impact of the post–World War II baby boom and the high price of energy. As a result, since the 1970s, this country has experienced inflation, recession, or both simultaneously. During your working years, as you strive to achieve your mid- and long-range goals, you too will probably be a victim of both. It is therefore important to understand them.

## Inflation

**Inflation** can be defined as a "general upward price movement of all goods and services that results in the decline in the value of a dollar" (Mittra, 1977, p. 633). In other words, prices go up and the value of money goes down. A glance at an old newspaper will show the effects of inflation on the dollar. For instance, a one-pound loaf of bread, which in the 1960s could be purchased for 20¢, increased to 59¢ in 1974 and to 90¢ in 1983. In 1969 you could have bought a brand-new Rambler American, a Volkswagen Beetle, or several other car models for less than $2000. In fact, in 1969, for $5534 you could have bought a Jaguar XK-E roadster. Those days clearly no longer exist.

Why do we have inflation? Economists offer a chicken-and-egg explanation. The demand for greater salaries pushes the cost of goods and services higher. Likewise, the rising cost of goods and services increases the demands of workers for salary increases. Inflation is inevitable in a growing economy.

If inflation is inevitable, why is it so feared? It is feared (and properly so) by workers who believe that their income will not increase as fast as the cost of living. That is why we hear so much about "real wages"—that is, the purchasing power of a paycheck after inflation has been taken into account (Juster, 1978–79).

In recent times these fears have been substantiated. Double-digit inflation rates have caused workers to lose purchasing power (Table 14-3).

According to one study, families respond to inflationary conditions by having additional family members enter the labor force, by having one or more family members increase their work hours, or by adjusting their flexible expenses (Converse, Curtin, & Kallick, 1980). It also appears that families are saving less and using those formerly saved dollars for living expenses ("What People Do to Adjust to Inflation," 1981).

**TABLE 14-3.** *Median family income and gains in real income, 1950–1981*

| Year | In Current Dollars | In Constant 1981 Dollars |
|---|---|---|
| Median family income | | |
| 1950 | $3,310 | $12,549 |
| 1955 | 4,418 | 15,003 |
| 1960 | 5,620 | 17,259 |
| 1965 | 6,957 | 20,054 |
| 1970 | 9,867 | 23,111 |
| 1973 | 12,051 | 24,663 |
| 1980 | 21,023 | 23,204 |
| 1981 | 22,388 | 22,388 |
| Gains in real income | | |
| 1950–1960 | 4,710 | 37.5% |
| 1960–1970 | 5,852 | 33.9% |
| 1970–1973 | 1,552 | 6.7% |
| 1973–1981 | −2,275 | −9.2% |

## Recession

In recent years inflation has often been accompanied by recession. A recession occurs when society produces more goods and services than it can absorb. The period of readjustment in which plants close, unemployment rises, and the prices of goods and services may fall (although they may not) is called a **recession.** The recessions of recent years are not necessarily the products of simple supply and demand; they have been influenced by other factors—the increasing price of energy, for instance.

Additionally, the postwar "baby boom" has significantly stressed the economy for the last four decades. Thousands of additional schools had to be built to educate these children. Colleges grew like weeds to accommodate their educational needs as young adults. But the labor market for them as adults has not grown as fast, and unemployment has increased as a result.

Finally, technology is reshaping the labor market. Jobs once held by people are now performed by robots. Although the product of the robot, such as welds on cars, may be uniform and errorless, the impact on welders is devastating. These and other factors have contributed to **stagflation**—an economic condition in which the economy is in recession but prices continue to rise. Stagflation affects decisions on credit use, housing choice, insurance and health care choices, and retirement planning.

## Credit

The authors of this book dream of the day when they will be free of debt. And the three of us, like many others, will probably be able to enjoy this same dream for years to come. Given the universal desire to achieve a life without debt, why would anyone want credit? For all its curses, credit does offer some benefits. Credit allows us to buy large items like cars, furniture, or an education and spread their cost over several months or years. Thus, it gives us the use of the item purchased before that item is paid for in full. Credit also provides a way of handling financial emergencies, such as car repairs.

Along with these advantages go disadvantages. The first, of course, is **debt.** Debt includes not only the purchase price of goods or services but also the interest being paid for the funds loaned to buy them. **Interest** is the fee charged for borrowing money. Interest rates vary, as do repayment schedules. Before buying anything on credit, it is imperative to find out what the total finance charges will be. Horror stories abound of unsuspecting buyers who have lost their shirts in their ignorance of the actual cost of a financed item. Beyond certain fixed costs (mortgage payments or rent, car payments, educational loans) a safe rule of thumb is never to be in debt greater than one month's take-home pay.

## The Cost of Shelter

"Gimme shelter" might well be the battle cry of this generation's young people. With the average selling price of a house over $76,000, the dream of owning a home is remaining for many just that—a dream (see Table 14-4).

As recently as a decade ago, families who spent as much as 25% of their income on housing were the exception. Today, it is the rule to see one fourth to one third or more of a new family's income go to housing (Hartman, 1984). This state of affairs has been called "the housing equivalent of the dark ages" (Sternlieb & Hughes, 1984, p. 32).

Nearly 65% of this nation's householders presently own their homes. Inflation and high interest rates are making it very unlikely that the figure will remain at this level much longer. Increasing numbers of families are finding it impossible to save enough money for a down payment on a home.

Not surprisingly, the purchase of a dwelling unit, whether a free-standing house or a condominium, is no longer quite the same. Most lending institutions expect a down payment of 20%

**TABLE 14-4.** *Average selling price of new single-family dwellings, 1964–1980 price[a]*

| Year | Price[a] |
|------|----------|
| 1964 | $20,500 |
| 1966 | 23,300 |
| 1968 | 26,600 |
| 1970 | 26,600 |
| 1972 | 30,500 |
| 1974 | 38,900 |
| 1976 | 48,000 |
| 1978 | 62,500 |
| 1980 | 76,300 |

[a] Includes the land on which the home is situated.

*With the median price of an average home well exceeding $75,000 in the 1980s, many of us may never achieve the "great American dream" of home ownership.*

of the purchase price. The old rule that a mortgage should not exceed 2½ times the borrower's salary has also changed. Reflecting the increased cost of housing, most lending institutions judge a borrower's worth by multiplying his or her salary 3 times, and a spouse's salary is now given full rather than partial credit.

The **fixed mortgage,** a home loan with a fixed interest rate, is still available but harder to obtain. (Figure 14-5 shows a fixed-mortgage rate schedule on a home loan of $60,000.) In recent years other mortgage plans have appeared that make it somewhat easier to buy a home. These new plans all carry the risk of higher payments than a fixed loan, but they begin at payment levels beneath that of a fixed loan. One of these new plans is the **graduated-payment loan:** payments increase by a predetermined amount each year for the first few years of the loan and then remain constant. A variation on the fixed- or graduated-payment loan is the **seller-assisted** or **creative mortgage,** in which the seller of the home finances its sale. A variation of the

seller-assisted loan is a **buydown mortgage,** in which the seller subsidizes the purchase by reducing the interest rate on the mortgage for the first few years.

The fourth type of loan available today is the **adjustable-rate loan.** The interest rate is pegged to the going market rate and may therefore rise and fall over the life of the loan. Because there is no cap on this type of loan, a word of caution is in order. It is conceivable that a borrower could pay far beyond the initial term of the loan for the money borrowed.

Finally, one other type of loan available to borrowers has so many drawbacks that we strongly discourage its consideration. It is called a **balloon loan** and works this way: Let's say you were to borrow $1000 at an interest rate of 15% with payments calculated for 20 years, ballooning after 1 year. You would pay $13.17 a month for 11 months. You would then owe the lender $991, because all but $9 of the money you had paid over those 11 months would have gone for interest charges. In the 12th month of the loan, the entire balance of $991 would come due. If you could not pay it, the lender would have the right to pursue legal action against you to recover his or her loaned funds.

## Insurance

The question is not so much whether to buy insurance as how much and what type. Insurance can be purchased to protect oneself from almost any mishap. Film studios have been known to insure a movie star's legs (Betty Grable's) or composers to insure their ears (Richard Stokler), believing that this particular part of their anatomy was priceless (Willis, 1982). The insurance protection that most of us consider falls into three rather broad categories.

The first is health insurance, which can cover such expenses as hospital bills, surgical fees, and physicians' charges. Today many Americans are covered under group medical insurance plans through their employers. Some health insurance plans cover dentistry and orthodonture, prescribed medicines, and even prescribed eyeglasses. Individuals not covered or inadequately covered by group insurance should acquire individual protection, especially if they are 65 or over. Medicare does provide health insurance

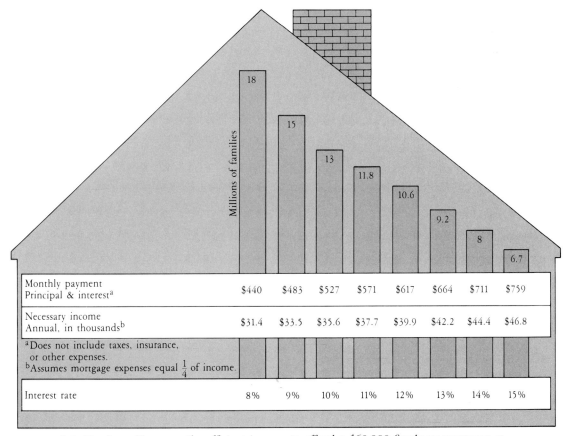

| | 8% | 9% | 10% | 11% | 12% | 13% | 14% | 15% |
|---|---|---|---|---|---|---|---|---|
| Monthly payment Principal & interest[a] | $440 | $483 | $527 | $571 | $617 | $664 | $711 | $759 |
| Necessary income Annual, in thousands[b] | $31.4 | $33.5 | $35.6 | $37.7 | $39.9 | $42.2 | $44.4 | $46.8 |

[a]Does not include taxes, insurance, or other expenses.
[b]Assumes mortgage expenses equal $\frac{1}{4}$ of income.

**FIGURE 14-5.** *Number of buyers with sufficient income to afford a $60,000 fixed-rate mortgage at varying interest rates.*

coverage for senior citizens, but that coverage is *not* comprehensive, and the elderly should carefully consider supplemental health-care coverage (New York Institute of Life Insurance, 1976).

The second type of insurance to consider is property insurance. This category of coverage includes homeowners' or tenants' policies to protect against theft, loss, or damage of personal property. Another type of property insurance is automobile insurance. Because cars are so expensive, the wisdom of protecting oneself from auto repair costs (and the car's occupants from medical expenses) should an accident occur is obvious. Property insurance also exists for all types of items—boats, a worker's tools, and the like.

The last type of insurance to consider is life insurance. The purpose of life insurance is to provide funds to someone in the event of your death.

There are two types of life insurance policies. Term insurance offers coverage for a specified period of time. Term insurance has advantages and disadvantages. Its primary advantage is its low cost for dollar coverage. It is possible to insure one's life for hundreds of thousands of dollars for only a few hundred dollars a year. Disadvantages are that renewal of the policy may depend on passing a physical examination, premiums (payments for coverage) rise as age increases, most plans do not allow renewal after age 65, and the policyholder has no cash equity.

Whole life insurance is much, much more expensive than term insurance. For that additional cost, coverage extends till death if premiums are paid. Premiums do not increase, and the policy acquires cash value. Whole life insurance is an investment that can be used in later life to supplement retirement income.

If the working years seem filled with expenses, gray hairs, and an occasional ulcer, they are. With successful planning, however, workers can hope to retire with sufficient financial resources to enjoy their senior years.

*Invite a local banker to attend class. Explore with that person the subjects discussed in this last section. Ask what the present market conditions for borrowers are. Find out how a credit rating is determined.*

## THE RETIREMENT YEARS: 65+

It used to be that the federal government occasionally issued cost-of-living predictions, but no longer. These publications have fallen under the budget ax. In one of the last reports, in fall 1982, the Bureau of Labor Statistics suggested that a retired couple in good health needed, at a low budget level, $7226 a year (after taxes) on which to live. At an intermediate budget level they needed $10,226, and at a high budget level $15,078 (Goodale, 1982; see Table 14-5).

In this section, we look at the steps people need to take during their working years to pro-

**TABLE 14-5.** *Annual budgets for a retired couple at three standards of living, urban United States, autumn 1981*

| Item | Budget Level | | |
|---|---|---|---|
| | **Low** | **Moderate** | **High** |
| Total budget | $7,266 | $10,226 | $15,078 |
| Total family consumption | 6,914 | 9,611 | 13,960 |
| Food | 2,183 | 2,898 | 3,642 |
| Housing | 2,377 | 3,393 | 5,307 |
| Transportation | 553 | 1,073 | 1,960 |
| Clothing | 244 | 409 | 629 |
| Personal care | 198 | 290 | 424 |
| Medical care | 1,085 | 1,091 | 1,098 |
| Other family consumption | 275 | 457 | 901 |
| Other items | 311 | 615 | 1,118 |

*Note:* Income taxes are not included. Because of rounding, sums of individual items may not equal totals.

vide for retirement. There are several ways of ensuring an adequate retirement income that satisfy the requirements that it be a safe investment. We will describe four safe and insured ways of putting away money for retirement.

The first of these is highly unlikely for most of us but helps to illustrate how money, when left alone, multiplies. The left half of Figure 14-6 shows the growth of a single deposit of $10,000 over 35 years at 15% interest. The resulting savings of $1,331,800 is truly impressive, but many people never have such a lump sum to deposit.

Our second and third methods are within more people's reach and are depicted in the right half of Figure 14-6. By depositing $1000 each year for 35 years at 15% interest, one can still become a millionaire. And even should interest rates drop, the total will be substantial. But how does an individual avoid paying taxes on the interest accruing in such an account?

Our second and third methods involve the opening of either an IRA (Individual Retirement Account) or a Keogh plan. An IRA is an insured account in a bank or other financial institution in which a working person may deposit up to $2000 a year toward retirement. No federal income tax is paid on the amount contributed to an IRA. Furthermore, interest earned on the in-

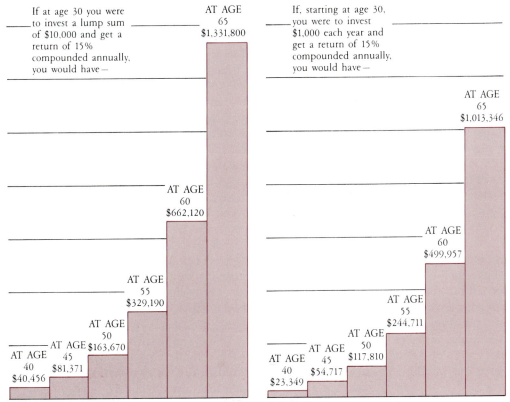

Note: Examples assume reinvestment of all dividends and payment from other income of taxes due on annual dividends.

**FIGURE 14-6.** *Two ways to pile up a million.*

*Proper financial planning earlier in life can provide retired persons with the financial security they need to enable them to continue with favorite activities or to explore new interests, such as computer programming.*

vested money accumulates tax-free until the money is withdrawn at retirement (between the ages of 59½ and 70). A working couple may contribute up to $4000 each year. A couple with one working spouse can contribute up to $2250 each year.

A Keogh plan permits the deposit of up to 15% of earnings or $15,000 each year into an insured retirement account for individuals who are in business for themselves or have a significant second income. Again, earnings on the invested money are tax-free until retirement, and the funds deposited can be deducted from one's earnings for tax purposes.

Either an IRA or a Keogh retirement account is an excellent safe investment for later years. However, both have minor drawbacks. The biggest of these is lack of access to funds deposited.

Money can be withdrawn, but there are heavy financial penalties for doing so. A second caution is that an individual cannot make contributions to both a Keogh and an IRA plan in the same year. Third, there are restrictions on moving a retirement account from one financial institution to another. As the laws change, regulations may be added or dropped. We encourage readers to fully discuss the advantages and disadvantages of each plan with their financial adviser before entering into either plan.

Our final safe plan for retirement is a money-market fund insured by the Federal Deposit Insurance Corporation (FDIC), available through savings institutions. Funds in such an account not only earn interest that varies with market conditions but are accessible to the investor without penalty. But even money-market accounts have minor drawbacks. The interest is taxable. Deposits cannot be deducted from one's earnings for tax purposes. A minimum deposit of $500 is currently required to open this type of account (minimums on IRAs and Keogh plans, for practical purposes, do not exist), and withdrawals that bring an account below $2500 subject the account to normal bank interest rates, not money-market rates. And the temptation to delve into savings may impede the growth of those savings for retirement purposes. Even so, if you believe ready access to savings may be necessary, then this type of account may be ideal for you.

We conclude this section without mentioning other investments such as stocks, bonds, whole life policies that can mature and pay dividends to their holders, or real estate—not because any of these investments should be avoided but because they either carry higher risk or require far more complicated decisions than we are prepared to discuss here. Nor have we discussed Social Security payments or pensions. The Social Security system is in such a state of flux that we

338

believe the wise person will not place too much emphasis on this monthly retirement payment, and we encourage readers to plan as if Social Security would not be a major source of income during their senior years. As for pensions, the multitude of variations that exist makes a meaningful discussion of their advantages and disadvantages impossible.

In good times of employment, one can formulate a budget, complain about inflation, debate whether to buy a home or life insurance, and save for retirement. In bad times, though, when you're out of work, out of money, and feeling out of society, your concerns lie elsewhere.

 *Invite a representative from a local Social Security office to class to discuss the present and future of Social Security. What effect might changes in the system have on you?*

# IN BAD TIMES OF UNEMPLOYMENT

[The federal work programs of the 1930s were] my salvation. I could just as easily have been in Sing Sing . . . . Hell, yes. Everybody was a criminal. You stole, you cheated through. You were getting by, survival. Stole clothes off lines, stole milk off back porches, you stole bread. I remember going through Tucumcari, New Mexico, on a freight. We made a brief stop. There was a grocery store, a supermarket kind of thing for those days. I beat it off the train and came back with rolls and crackers. This guy is standing in the window shaking his fist at you. It wasn't a big thing, but it created a coyote mentality. You were a predator. You had to be. The coyote is crafty. He can be fantastically coura-

geous and a coward at the same time. He'll run but when he's cornered, he'll fight. I grew up where they were hated, 'cause they'd kill sheep. They'll kill a calf, get in the chicken pen. They're mean. But how else does a coyote stay alive? He's not as powerful as a wolf. He has a small body. He's in such bad condition, a dog can run him down. He's not like a fox. A coyote is nature's victim as well as man's. We were coyotes in the Thirties, the jobless [Ed Paulsen, cited in Terkel, 1970, p. 246].

Without the means to support themselves or their families, individuals have behaved like coyotes for centuries. In France during the Industrial Revolution, for example, textile workers, angry over losing their jobs to the development of spinning looms, sought to protect themselves by inserting their wooden shoes, called "sabots," into the machinery. Although these futile attempts did not make the mills grind to a permanent halt, they did introduce a new word into our vocabulary—*saboteur* (Shane, 1982).

Today, when it will soon be possible to store 200 billion bits of information (the equivalent of nearly a half million textbook pages) on an optical disk, a new revolution is occurring (Abelson, 1982a) that will dwarf the "Great Industrial Revolution." Its light casts into shadows people who might have been workers but never will be. This technological revolution cannot be halted, and as it unfolds, it will have a dramatic impact on people. Their lives will be shaken, the courses they would have traveled altered. In this section we will examine how cruel unemployment is to individuals and their families.

## *Unemployment: Definition and Causes*

Unemployment will always exist. Even in a robust economy there will be some able-bodied people who, for a variety of reasons, will not be able to find employment. Thus, even though we define full employment as the opportunity for those able to work and wanting work to be able to acquire it, we are admitting that there will be those who will be excluded. The issue becomes, What is an acceptable rate of unemployment?

Most of us will agree that an unemployment rate of 25% like the one found in 1933, during the Great Depression, is far too high (Maurer, 1979). But what is acceptable? Interestingly, as times have changed, perceptions of acceptable unemployment rates have changed also. During the 1940s 3% unemployment was considered full employment; in the 1960s, 4%; in the 1970s, 5%. Today, with rates at times in two-digit figures, some economists say a 6% or 7% unemployment rate should represent full employment (Maurer, 1979). To further complicate matters, the official unemployment rate does not reflect all those actually unemployed. It omits people who are too discouraged to continue to search for employment, people who work part-time but would like to work full-time, and students who remain in school because there are no opportunities in the marketplace. Maurer (1979, p. 2) suggests that "true unemployment is approximately double the official rate."

Unemployment is not color-blind. Nationally, in 1980, the unemployment rate for Blacks and other minorities was about 7 percentage points higher than for Whites. In some states (Mississippi, for example) these minorities accounted for more than 50% of the unemployed.

Earlier in this chapter, we commented on the impact that the "baby boom" and the increasing price of energy have had on the economy. The employment picture might brighten considerably if either factor could be better controlled, not to mention the technological revolution now underway. Before we continue much further, we should note that the authors of this text are not modern-day equivalents of the French mill workers, inserting wooden phrases into word processors hoping to bring them to a grinding halt. Rather, our point is that the way technology is reshaping the workplace will have a powerful effect on the future of *all* of us as workers.

For example, Shane (1982) predicts that by the turn of the century half of all manufacturing jobs may be performed by "smart machines." Levitan and Johnson (1982, p. 11) report that "the current generation of robots has the technical capacity to perform nearly 7 million existing factory jobs—one third of all manufacturing em-

PART FOUR  FAMILY MATTERS OF CONCERN

## BOX 14-2
### *The Origin of the Word* Robot

The word *robot,* from the Czech word *robata* ("forced labor"), came into the English language in the early 1920s when a Czech playwright, Karel Capek, wrote about a future society in which chemically constructed ma- chines performed the work of humans. As an aside, the Holly- wood film *Blade Runner* has several similarities to Capek's play *R.U.R.* ("Rossum's Universal Robots"). In both the play and the film, the robots (or, if you prefer, humanoids) become more human and eventually turn against the human race because of its inhumanity. *R.U.R.* can be found in Arthur Lewis, *Of Men and Machines* (New York: Dutton, 1963).

ployment—and . . . sometime after 1990, it will become technically possible to replace all manu- facturing operatives in the automotive, electrical equipment, machinery, and fabricated-metals in- dustries."

Levitan and Johnson (1982) believe that the costs of automation will slow its introduction. We are not so certain. We remember not so long ago (in 1973, to be exact) rushing out to pay $89 for a calculator with a square-root key. "Miracles of technology!" we said to ourselves. "A square- root key for only $89." Today, for $89 we could buy a computer. A robot that now costs $150,000 might, within the next decade, cost only $10,000, while labor costs could run $25 to $30 an hour (Abelson, 1982b). In that market environment the decline of manufacturing jobs shown in Fig- ure 14-7 would give way to an outright plunge. The time may well come when

earning a living may no longer be a necessity but a privilege; services may have to be protected

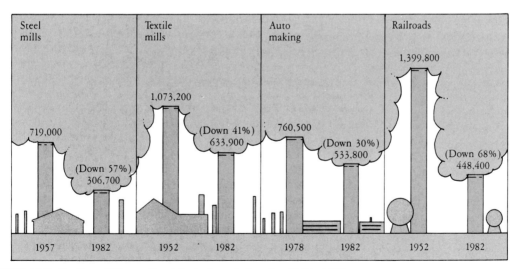

**FIGURE 14-7.** *Decline of blue-collar jobs in four industries, 1952–1982.*

from automation, and given certain social status; leisure time activities may have to be invented in order to give new meaning to a mode of life that may have become economically useless for a majority of the populace [Gordon & Hemer, cited in Levitan & Johnson, 1982, p. 13].

Some might argue, as people peer into video-game terminals trying to get a score high enough for their initials to take their place in the machine's memory, that the time has already come.

## Effects of Unemployment on Individuals and Families

Those bastards. They think this is a welfare check they're giving me. I earned this [unemployment] money. . . . Some people even refuse benefits. Well, I'm not proud. I want to live. I want to live like a human being, not like a beggar. And it doesn't get me down because I know it's not my doing. I didn't lose my job because I was a screw-up guy and got fired. I lost my job because of economic conditions [Frank Capek, cited in Maurer, 1979, p. 89].

The man speaking is a chemist holding his doctorate. His anger, his bitterness, and his pain clearly come through to the reader. His statements dispel the popular misconception that unemployment is painless. This misconception, Riegle (1982) believes, has contributed to the public's willingness to accept recession as a fact of life.

Unemployment damages one's image of oneself (Cohn, 1978), particularly for males, for whom paid employment has been described as their "strongest tie to reality" (Freud, cited in Hagen, 1983, p. 438). Unemployed males suffer significantly in terms of lowered self-esteem. They report feeling insignificant, unimportant, and like excess baggage. Disturbingly, even those reemployed never completely regain prior

levels of self-esteem (Hagen, 1983). Unemployment damages one's health. It can contribute to a fatalistic attitude that increases rates of physical illness, depression, and other forms of suffering ("Economic Decline . . . ," 1982; Fortin, 1984; Hayes & Nutman, 1981; Kirsh, 1983).

This last point has been extensively documented by Brenner's (1973, 1977) work on the undeniable connection between unemployment and illness. Brenner estimates that a 1% rise in unemployment sustained over six years results in 22,303 deaths—20,240 deaths due to cardiovascular diseases, 495 due to cirrhosis of the liver, 920 suicides, and 648 homicides. In addition, he predicts 4227 first-time admissions to state mental hospitals and 3340 admissions to state prisons as a result of this sustained 1% of unemployment. Brenner (1977) has estimated the costs of unemployment to society during 1970 as $6.6 billion in lost income due to illness and mortality and in added state prison and mental hospital outlays. The link between employment and health has been documented elsewhere (Ahr, Goradezky, & Cho, 1981; Liem & Rayman, 1982), as has the impact of unemployment on suicide rates (Ahlburg & Schapiro, 1983; Stack, 1981; Vigderhous & Fishman, 1978).

Powerful as these figures are, they cannot convey the anguish unemployment brings to a family. Unemployment increases family violence (Justice & Duncan, 1975; Straus, Gelles, & Steinmetz, 1980) and has a damaging impact on the marital relationship (Larson, 1984). Loss of employment is particularly devastating to single-female-headed households, to Blacks, to the working poor, and to young families (Corcoran & Hill, 1980; Moen, 1980, 1983)—groups that lack the economic resources to withstand a prolonged period of unemployment. New families, in particular, lack the job seniority, experience, and skills that are often necessary to reenter the job market quickly (Moen, 1983).

*Unemployment is a cruel life event for any family, but it is particularly difficult for single female heads-of-household, Blacks, the working poor, and families early in the life cycle.*

Unemployment forces families to struggle constantly to stretch limited assets to meet ever-growing financial demands. For some there is help in the form of Aid to Families with Dependent Children. For others there is help in the form of unemployment benefits. But for nearly half the unemployed there is nothing[1] (Moen, 1983). In Moen's study, families that handled the financial hardship of unemployment best were those that received unemployment benefits, were unemployed briefly, and had more than one wage earner.

Using Brenner's formulas, one author has estimated that the cost of human suffering from the 1980–1982 recession will exceed $100 billion before this decade is over (Brown, 1983). The issue becomes whether anything can be done about this suffering.

 *Invite to class a state labor department representative to discuss unemployment in your area. What is the present rate? Who is most likely to be unemployed? What services are available to the unemployed in your area? How effective are those services?*

---

[1] This figure is from the 1975 recession.

The obvious solution to unemployment would be to ensure that everyone desiring work would have it. In fact, such a statement (though without the means of implementing it) already exists in the Full Employment and Balanced Growth Act of 1978 (the Humphrey-Hawkins Act). This act calls on government to intercede to provide employment opportunities when the private sector cannot. Given that the action best suited for curing unemployment cannot be or has not been taken, how might our interest in prevention modify, eliminate, or avoid the stresses associated with this depressing life event?

## EDUCATION

It is clear that the future belongs to the educated. Their lifetime earnings are significantly greater than those of workers with less than a college degree. We expect that the well educated will be better able to adjust their careers to meet the changing demands of the new economy that will exist in this country by the year 2000. Consequently, one step a person can take to reduce the chance of unemployment is to acquire a good education. This same educational opportunity needs to be extended to retrain presently displaced workers (Briar, 1983). We believe the responsibility for providing this opportunity belongs to both industry and government. But in the absence of the private sector's ability to carry its share, government must assume the responsibility.

Some preventionists have recommended that anticipatory guidance in combination with behavioral techniques could moderate the distress accompanying unemployment. Such a program would offer information about the reactions others have experienced in this situation (change in social role, loss of self-esteem, loss of income) with information on available social supports (unemployment benefits, job retraining programs, employment opportunities). The behavioral training component of the program would teach stress-reduction strategies like physical exercise, yoga, deep breathing, and progressive relaxation (Catalano & Dooley, 1980; Hess, 1983).

 *What other educational approaches would you use to moderate the distress associated with unemployment?*

## COMMUNITY ORGANIZATION/ SYSTEMS INTERVENTION

What structural changes would you advocate to ease the distress of unemployment on families? Would you encourage political activism (Gullotta, 1983)? Increase support programs to families? Increase employment programs? Shorten the work week? Make a period of government service in programs like the Peace Corps, VISTA, or the Armed Forces mandatory for all young people? Lower the minimum wage for teenaged workers? Lower import quotas to reduce the influx of foreign goods into this country? Each of these ideas has been proposed in recent years. Each has its advantages and disadvantages. As you debate the foregoing proposals, we would encourage you also to consider three ideas.

The first would be provisions to ensure adequate notice before a plant closes. Presently, most states have no requirement that an industry provide a prior warning to employees. Advance notice of, say, three months would enable workers to anticipate and plan for a period of unemployment. It would permit a period of job searching or alternative career exploration in a less frenzied atmosphere.

The next proposal for your consideration is the provision of retraining for displaced workers. Presently, there is no systematic nationwide approach to retraining. Such a service could be funded through a payroll deduction similar to the one that provides for unemployment compensation.

The third possibility is to provide local, state, and federal funds to permit employee and/or community purchase of closing industries. As Catalano and Dooley (1980) point out, profitability is a nebulous concept. For a corporation, a plant that is breaking even may be considered unprofitable, while to the employees of that plant and to the communities in which they live, the maintenance of jobs is reason enough for continuing plant operation.

 *What are the advantages and disadvantages of the proposals listed in this section? Select one proposal and, from an ecological perspective, trace the effects that that idea might have on a system. Are all of them positive?*

## COMPETENCY PROMOTION

Lack of work damages one's self-esteem and one's ties to society. Work strengthens them (Hayes & Nutman, 1981). Thus, promoting opportunities for employment will promote competency. In the absence of work, some preventionists have encouraged programs directed at a "cognitive restructuring" of the life event of unemployment (Catalano & Dooley, 1980). Cognitive restructuring involves identifying negative self-statements and replacing them with positive ones. The purpose of this exercise is to help unemployed individuals who are the victims of economic forces beyond their control to avoid feelings of having failed personally.

Consideration also needs to be given to the traditional Calvinist attitudes that most Americans have about work. The predominant American belief is that those who want to work can. This belief flies in the face of evidence offered earlier in this chapter that there will *always* be unemployment. Societal attitudes change as a result of individual attitudinal change. Thus, it will not be until individuals reassess their own values and stop blaming the unemployed for their unemployment that societal values will change.

 *How else might you promote competency in the unemployed?*

## NATURAL CAREGIVING

Social support moderates the suffering that accompanies unemployment (Gore, 1978; Jones, 1979). Typically, job loss entails loss of friendships at the workplace, thus creating feelings of being ostracized. Expressions of caring—from a family member, a friend, a pastor, or a self-help group—help to bind an unemployed person to society. Settings where such support could be encouraged include churches, unemployment offices, unions, and social agencies.

*Can you identify the three subcomponents of natural caregiving in the preceding passage?*

# SUMMARY

Before the American Revolution, labor was so much in demand that great numbers of Europeans were brought here unwillingly as indentured servants. Conditions have reversed—the supply of labor now exceeds the demand—and young people now have to give serious attention to their employment prospects. It is wise to get an education, to consider the effects of technological advances and demographic trends on job opportunities, and to base occupational choice on financial realities as well as on one's interests. And, learning personal budgeting when young will help you manage your money during the working years.

In this all too brief chapter, we have carried you from the classroom to retirement, from work to joblessness. It certainly remains true that money cannot buy happiness. However, its absence, as we have seen in this chapter, can lead to misery. This misery can be avoided if you are prepared not only for today but for tomorrow.

# MAJOR POINTS TO REMEMBER

1. Before the revolution, the United States was settled mainly by indentured servants because of this country's need for labor.
2. Each of us will make many career and financial decisions throughout life. Learning to plan early in life can help us make the right choices.
3. Inflation, recession, and stagflation are three phases of a fluctuating economy. Each has a direct impact on consumers' ability to get credit, afford housing, and buy goods and services.
4. Most of us will acquire in our lifetime three general types of insurance—health, property, and life.

5. There are several safe and sensible ways to save for retirement. Two of the best ways are to make yearly deposits in an IRA or a Keogh account at a savings institution. Although Social Security will continue into the next century, it is unwise to expect to rely totally on that retirement benefit.
6. Even in a "full employment" economy, unemployment exists.
7. Technology is changing the shape and size of the labor force. It is likely that an increasing number of manufacturing jobs will be performed by "smart machines."
8. Unemployment damages not only emotional health but physical health as well.
9. Studies find that the families that best survived a period of unemployment received unemployment benefits, were unemployed briefly, and had more than one wage earner.
10. Several steps can be taken to assist the unemployed, from providing retraining opportunities and social support to allowing employee ownership of businesses.

# ADDITIONAL SOURCES OF INFORMATION

## *Publications*

The American Council of Life Insurance issues a number of free booklets covering a wide range of financial and legal matters. Ask for a current listing of materials by writing to 1850 K St., NW, Washington, D. C. 20006.

We would like to encourage you to take the time to read the works of three authors mentioned in this chapter: Harvey Brenner, Studs Terkel, and Harry Maurer. Exposing yourself to the writings of these three individuals will give you a good idea of the damage unemployment does to the human body, mind, and soul.

Cetron, M. J. (1983, June). Getting ready for the jobs of the future. *Futurist,* pp. 15–20.

Controversy over the Humphrey-Hawkins proposal to control unemployment: Pro and con. (1976, June–July). *Congressional Digest, 55,* 161–192.

Ehrbar, A. F. (1983, May 16). Unemployment. *Fortune,* pp. 107–112.

Jobs of the 1990's. (1983, May 16). *Fortune,* pp. 116–123.

## Organizations

Checks Anonymous
P.O. Box 81248
Lincoln, NB 68501
A self-help organization for individuals in debt.

Gamblers Anonymous
P.O. Box 4549
Downey, CA 90241
A self-help group for gamblers and their families.

# 15

# ON BEING A MINORITY IN A MAJORITY

## Questions
## to Guide Your Reading

1. What does the term *minority* mean?

2. Are prejudice and discrimination the same thing?

3. Why were Quaker missionaries hung in the Massachusetts Bay Colony in 1656?

4. Before the Civil War, was educational discrimination against Blacks exercised only in the South?

5. What three factors explain bigotry?

6. Do prejudice and discrimination serve useful functions?

7. Why is the Black youth unemployment rate so disturbing?

8. What is the "downward-drift hypothesis"?

9. What factors help minority families overcome prejudice and discrimination in our society?

It was 24 years ago, but I can still remember as if it were yesterday—sitting in a second-grade classroom, desks bolted to the floor, with a teacher passing out pictures to color. I can remember that when she turned her back on the class, we all lifted those freshly inked sheets of paper close to our faces and inhaled the intoxicating vapors rising from the blue ink on them. I'll never forget one day. It was in the early fall. The teacher passed out a picture of the "typical" American family and asked us to color it. I can remember the care and patience I exercised in coloring that picture, and I might remark that it was no small feat, for those fat crayons were not easy to hold. You can imagine my displeasure when the teacher seized this work of art, crumpled it, and told me to start over. This I did, despite my confusion over her reaction, only to see the same scene reenacted a second and then a third time. I failed art for that day. And my budding career as an artist, I maintain to this day, was destroyed forever. My parents were called and were asked to speak to me. My crime had been to color the faces of the people in the first picture brown, in the second picture yellow, and in the third picture red. When asked by my parents why I had done this, I said, in complete innocence, "Because the world is not all White" [the experience of one of the authors].

This chapter is about families—families of color—and their experiences in living in a society in which they are a minority. It is about the distress these families experience because of their minority status. And it is about what can be done to reduce—or, preferably, remove—that distress.

But what does the term **minority** mean? At one time or another, we probably have all used that term to describe our own situation. Is this chapter, then, about all of us? No; the occasional experience of nearly everyone of being a minority in a majority may help people appreciate the discomfort of minority status, but it does not mean that one is a minority. Wagley and Harris (1958, p. 10) associate the following five characteristics with minorities:

1. Minorities are subordinate segments of a complex society.
2. Minorities tend to have special physical or cultural traits that are seen as undesirable by the dominant segments of the society.
3. Minorities develop a group consciousness, or "we-feeling."
4. Membership in a minority is transmitted by descent—one is born into it—so that the minority status is imposed on future generations, even if by then the special physical or cultural traits of the minority have disappeared.
5. Members of a minority, whether by choice or by necessity, tend to practice endogamy—that is, to marry within the group.

Being noticeably different in race, ethnicity, sex, or age from the dominant segments of society subjects a minority group to prejudice and discrimination from the dominant group. **Prejudice** is an inaccurate, emotionally rigid attitude toward members of a particular group. **Discrimination** is the behavioral demonstration of that attitude expressed in the different treatment given to members of the group. For example, maintaining the inaccurate belief that all men are insensitive is holding a prejudice; denying men the custody of children solely on the basis of this belief is discrimination. In the section that follows we will explore the historical roots in this nation of prejudicial and discriminatory behavior against minorities and a theoretical explanation of why these attitudes and behaviors exist.

 *By the foregoing definition of* minority, *are divorced men a minority?*

# A HISTORICAL/THEORETICAL PERSPECTIVE ON PREJUDICE AND DISCRIMINATION

At the entrance to New York City's harbor stands the Statue of Liberty, given by the people of France to the people of the United States in appreciation of this nation's willingness to accept immigrants. The population of the United States presently exceeds 240 million people whose ancestral roots extend over the globe. This nation has been described as a melting pot capable of receiving every national, ethnic, and religious group and blending these groups into a homogeneous mixture from which a uniquely American personality emerges. This description suggests that our nation has a history of tolerance toward groups whose religious beliefs, ethnic backgrounds, or racial characteristics differed from those of the central group. And yet even a cursory review of American history offers substantial evidence to the contrary.

## The Myth of the Melting Pot

To understand prejudice and discrimination, it is important to appreciate the vital function they serve in society. To illustrate this function, we have arbitrarily selected, from hundreds of historical incidents, two that suggest America's early settlers were rarely willing to accept those different from themselves.

*Religious tolerance and the Puritan community.* At each Thanksgiving Day parade, sandwiched between the floats, marching bands, and toy commercials, there is a small program segment in which the parade's host retells the story of the first Thanksgiving. The television viewer is told that the very survival of the Puritan community was in doubt that first year but that the Puritans nevertheless gave thanks on that day for their blessings—one of which was the free-

*A person judged guilty in the Massachusetts Bay colony could be publicly humiliated, flogged, branded, imprisoned, or put to death in any number of painful ways, depending on the court's attitude toward the seriousness of that offense.*

dom to worship without fear of persecution. Almost without fail, this Thanksgiving story ends by crediting the Puritan community with establishing religious freedom in the United States. Interestingly, the historical evidence differs a wee bit from this idealized script.

The year was 1656. Many of the original leaders of the Massachusetts Bay Colony were no longer alive, and a new generation had assumed responsibility for leadership of the community. Accompanying these internal changes were changes in the attitude of the homeland English Puritan community toward New England. No longer was the colony viewed as an experiment attracting "saints . . . to the new world to pro-

vide an object lesson for the rest of mankind" (Erikson, 1966, p. 112). Events in England (Cromwell and the English Civil War) had thrown the colony into relative obscurity, leaving the Puritans with, as Erikson (1966) has termed it, an identity crisis:

> The settlers had stepped outside the historical momentum which was slowly drawing the rest of the English-speaking world into a general era of tolerance, and for that reason they were no longer able to look to the Puritan movement in England for help in assessing their place in the universe. The appearance of Quakers in America, then, had special meaning for the settlers; what-

ever else New England might be in these uncertain times, it was most assuredly not a place which encouraged freedom of religion, and this was a distinguishing trait which the settlers meant to publicize, literally, for all they were worth. For the moment, at least, this was almost the only identity they could claim [Erikson, 1966, p. 113].

For nine years (1656–1665) the missionary efforts of Quakers and the practice of Quaker beliefs in the Massachusetts Bay Colony were dealt with harshly. A convicted Quaker male missionary could expect, for example, to lose an ear for his first offense and the other ear for his second offense, to have "his tongue bored through with a hot iron" for a third conviction, and, perhaps as a welcome change of pace, to be hanged on the fourth offense (Erikson, 1966, p. 117). Convicted female missionaries could look forward to severe floggings and, for repeated violations, eventual hanging. This decided lack of Christian tolerance continued until Charles II ordered the colony to cease its oppression of religious minorities and to extend to them the same opportunity the Puritans had to practice their religious beliefs freely.

*Education and racial discrimination.* Racial discrimination in education is nothing new. Before the American Civil War educating a free Black or slave in many parts of the South was punishable by death. But discrimination was not confined to that corner of the United States, as the failure of Prudence Crandall's school for girls in Canterbury, Connecticut, illustrates.

In 1831 Prudence Crandall established a boarding school for young women in her home in Canterbury. In its first year of operation, the school, its students, and its Quaker headmistress were accepted by the townsfolk. This acceptance was short-lived, however. The following year, Miss Crandall, an abolitionist, admitted a Black

student. The reaction of this sleepy New England community was swift and hostile. Within weeks the school was closed. Miss Crandall was not so easily deterred, however, and with the support and financial backing of other abolitionists, she reopened her school in 1833 as a school for young Black women.

The response of the community was again swift and hostile. Residents expressed fears that property values would go down, that these Blacks would not be comfortable being away from their own kind, and that other "incalculable evils" would result. Miss Crandall and her supporters remained undeterred, and the community turned from rhetoric to action. Supplies for the school could no longer be purchased at village stores; its drinking well was poisoned; its students and headmistress were shunned, insulted, and threatened.

Still unable to make Miss Crandall close her school, the community intensified action against her legally and physically. In August 1833 she was brought before the Windham court and was found guilty of breaking a new Connecticut law prohibiting "any school academy, or literary institution, for the instruction or education of colored persons who are not inhabitants of this State" (Litwack, 1973, p. 258). The presiding chief justice, David Daggett, reluctantly declared that the Blacks living at Crandall's school were not residents. Nevertheless, Miss Crandall refused to shut down the school, hoping that eventually the community would come to accept her pupils. But after school windows were repeatedly broken, guns fired at the building, and an attempt made to set it on fire, she closed her institution and moved out of the state (Litwack, 1973).

*Factors contributing to bigotry.* The two incidents we have reported are not isolated episodes in American history. We could have chosen hundreds of other incidents involving nearly every immigrant group that has ever landed on these shores, from the "heathen Roman Catholic Irish" who have the distinction of being the very first occupants of America's city slums to the Eastern European immigrants slaughtered in the 1890s by cattle ranchers for homesteading on grazing lands in Johnson County, Wyoming. Is it possible to distill from these incidents the factors that contribute to bigotry? We believe three factors emerge to explain the intolerance of others that constitutes bigotry.

The first of these is *change.* Whether the incident involves the Quakers in 1656 or minority schoolchildren in Canterbury, Connecticut, in 1831, in Little Rock, Arkansas, in 1956, or in Boston, Massachusetts, in 1975, there is present in each incident the threat of change. This threat produces *fear,* fueled by a perceived loss of *resources*—and resources represent power.

The struggle over the practice of Quaker beliefs in the Massachusetts Bay Colony has long since subsided, but other conflicts continue in this country. For example, jobs in an ever-tightening economy are a resource, and the minority and majority groups in American society struggle over issues of hiring and affirmative action. Housing is a resource, and these groups struggle over issues of integrating the suburbs and the gentrification of the cities. Education is a resource, and these groups struggle over issues of busing and de facto segregation. Tax dollars are a resource, and these groups struggle over whether those dollars should be spent on social programs or returned to the taxpayer in the form of tax cuts (Walters, 1982). Prejudice and discrimination are the by-products of this struggle over resources. They represent the attempts of the majority to maintain the status quo while the minorities of the society try to alter that status quo. In the following section we will examine a theoretical perspective that attempts to explain the majority's need to maintain homeostasis.

 *In what way was religion a resource to the Puritans? Why do you think change brings fear?*

## A Theoretical Perspective: Structural Functionalism

The structural functionalist maintains that all behavior serves a useful and necessary purpose in maintaining the existing society. What useful purpose do prejudice and discrimination against minority groups serve? They are necessary to maintain the health and integrity of the majority in society.

Earlier in this chapter we noted that one distinguishing characteristic of minority groups is that they differ physically or culturally from the majority. These differences enable society to function by permitting both the majority and minority groups to establish a "we/they" perspective in which the perceived faults of the other group are magnified and inaccurate generalizations, called "stereotypes," are projected onto the "they." Values such as "good" and "bad," "correct" and "incorrect," "acceptable" and "unacceptable" are then attached to these differences. Traits or behaviors that are considered dangerous to the continuation of the present majority in society are labeled deviant, and sanctions are brought against minority members displaying those differences in an attempt to halt the spread of those undesirable traits or behaviors. Interestingly, Durkheim believed that even minor differences in appearance or cultural practices will provoke this reaction, so that even in a society of saints deviants will emerge: "Imagine a society of saints, a perfect cloister of exemplary individuals. Crimes properly so called, will there be unknown; but faults which appear venial to a layman will create there the same scandal that the ordinary offence does in ordinary consciousness" (1958, pp. 68–69).

Does society need deviance, then, in order to maintain homeostasis (stability)? The structural functionalist would say that it does. Deviance permits the "we" to unite collectively to express its fear of the "they." While the society of the majority thrives in such an environment, however, the minority invariably suffers. The distress that minorities experience in a nation dedicated in principle to the concept of "equality of opportunity" concerns us next.

> **?** *Use a different theoretical perspective to explain the presence of prejudice and discrimination in society. What are the similarities and differences between the two perspectives?*

# THE STRESS OF BELONGING TO A MINORITY

Belonging to a racial or ethnic minority is a chronic stressor (a stressor is a condition that causes stress). It cannot be escaped. Black authors have gone so far as to describe the United States as a "racist climate" similar in harshness to the cold, barren environments found in the more inhospitable corners of the globe. These authors note that, like people living in those barren environments, families of color expend enormous amounts of energy in a constant struggle to feed, clothe, and house themselves. And yet, despite all their efforts, their success often pales in comparison with the standard of living that the majority culture enjoys (McAdoo, 1983; Peters, 1981; Pierce, 1975). This holds true over such areas as employment, education, and health.

## Employment

Blame the Puritans and their work ethic or a preoccupation with Freud—Americans expect and want to work.[1] Work enables individuals to support the material needs of their families. Throughout the history of the United States, work has been a major entry card for gaining acceptance into the mainstream of society. Historically, those unable or unwilling to work have been lumped together and stereotyped as shiftless, irresponsible, and lazy.

Historically, minority groups have been unable to find work or have taken menial positions at the lowest possible pay. The stereotypes created by prejudice and maintained by discriminatory practices against minorities have deprived them of the opportunity to improve their economic condition. There is a good deal of evidence to support this last statement:

- Although unemployment rates vary with economic conditions, the relative rates of unemployment for Whites, Blacks, and Hispanics have remained relatively constant over the years. Whites usually experience an unemployment rate slightly less than the national average. The rate for Hispanics is 1.5 times the average, and the rate for Blacks is nearly 2 times the average. Teenagers of all ethnic groups are more likely to be unemployed than adults. But while White adolescents are without

---

[1] When asked to define psychological maturity, Freud is said to have replied that it meant to have the capacity "to love and to work."

## BOX 15-1
### Life in Suburbia as a Black Youngster

We have a wealth of information on the living conditions of lower-income Black youth but virtually no knowledge, outside of an occasional newspaper story, about middle-class Black youth. Accordingly, a recent article on this subject by James Banks in the *Journal of Negro Education* was warmly received by family sociologists. After studying 98 middle-class children, aged 4 to 18, in 64 families living in predominantly White suburbs, Banks reported:

- The vast majority developed "positive attitudes toward themselves, their communities, and their schools. These children . . . had positive attitudes toward both Blacks and Whites" (p. 16).

- For some youth in this study, a complex relationship between pride in their race and lowered self-esteem existed. It appears that "children who evaluated Blacks more positively on the [test measures] might be more culturally Black, have a stronger Black identity, be more external, and may have experienced more discriminatory situations that have negatively influenced their self-esteem than the children who evaluated Blacks less positively" (p. 15).

- Children evaluating Blacks less positively identified more with their schools and neighborhoods and displayed an internal locus of control.

- It appears that living in a predominantly White suburban community may be harder on older youth than younger ones and harder on girls than boys.

These results, though encouraging in many respects, suggest that even middle-class minority youth are not immune from the pressures associated with their color.

---

work at about twice the national unemployment rate, Black adolescent unemployment rates are more than 5 times the national average (Hacker, 1983). Census data help us fully appreciate the Black youth unemployment figure. In 1980 there were 10.5 million Black youth under age 19 in the United States. Of these young people, 3 million were of employable age (15–19). Another 3 million were between 20 and 24. Together these young people constituted 50% of the Black population in this country. The median age of Blacks was 25, compared with 41 for Whites. In short, a large segment of this minority group remains unable to find employment though able, ready, and willing to work.

- Blacks and Hispanics are more likely to be service workers and laborers than Whites and less likely to be salespeople or white-collar workers. For example, Blacks accounted for 11.2% of the employment force in 1980 but 53.4% of the domestic help and only 8.7% of the bank tellers (Hacker, 1983). While the career path of a bank teller can lead to positions of higher responsibility and pay, the career path of a domestic servant is decidedly more limited.

- In 1981 the average weekly earnings of Black high school graduates were 74% of White workers'. The weekly paycheck of Black college graduates was 80% of their White co-workers' (Hacker, 1983).

- In 1980 the median family income of White families was $21,094. It was $14,717 for Hispanic families and $12,674 for Black families (McAdoo, 1982a).

• In 1978 one fifth of the population of the United States was of Black (12%), Hispanic (6%), or Asian or Native American (2%) descent. With the exception of Asian Americans, roughly 6% of these citizens were able to achieve economic parity with Whites. The families able to achieve parity were most often young and childless and had both partners working (McAdoo, 1982a).

Low wages, menial positions, and limited opportunities for job advancement make providing for a family more difficult. For example, even if restrictive housing practices did not exist, housing choices would be limited by the income available to minorities. In 1980, 60% of the Black American population (the largest minority group in the United States) lived in the central cities in substandard housing (Barbarin, 1981; Hacker, 1983). When the poor (and often the poor are the unemployed, and the unemployed are minorities) spend 35% of their income on food, in comparison with the 10% the middle class spends, choices are limited (McAdoo, 1982a). Thus, families struggle with decisions that affect not only present standards of living but, as when deciding whether to keep a child in school or whether to get medical care, future standards of living as well.

 *How are stereotypes important to the continuation of prejudicial attitudes?*

## Education

Education holds a special place in the hearts of most Americans. It is considered a primary means of achieving a higher standard of living. We might understand the reaction of Canterbury residents in 1831 to Miss Crandall's school for Black girls as an attempt to reserve that precious resource for their own children. In the minds of Canterbury's residents and those across the nation who have followed in their footsteps since 1831, education translates into career opportunities, and career opportunities translate into a higher standard of living. It is this same desire to provide one's own children with a competitive edge in the marketplace that has motivated majority groups in the nation to practice de jure and de facto educational segregation. This unwillingness to share educational resources arises from a belief that educating minority children will either weaken the educational experience of majority children or increase competition in the marketplace for a limited number of jobs. **De jure segregation,** segregation enforced by law, has been replaced by more subtle forms of separating minority groups from the majority. Educational segregation resulting from exclusionary housing practices and the gerrymandering of school districts is called **de facto segregation.**

Attempts to address this form of segregation by transporting minority students from one part of a community to another—"busing"—generally have failed. These attempts have fallen victim to the movement of White families out of areas where minorities live. This "White flight" has contributed, some contend, to the failure to achieve the elusive goal of "equality of educational opportunity" (Coleman, 1975). Others suggest that educational inequality will continue until economic inequality is corrected (Jencks et al., 1972). Regardless of the causes, more than 30 years after the historic *Brown* v. *Board of Education* decision declaring "separate but equal" educational experiences inherently unequal, significant differences in the achievements of Whites and minorities continue to exist.

For example, fewer minority students finish high school than Whites. In 1980 nearly 70% of

Whites over age 25 had completed at least a high school education, while only 50% of Blacks had gone that far (U. S. Bureau of the Census, 1982). Although the number of Black students attending college has risen dramatically in recent years in proportion to their numbers in society, they remain underrepresented. In 1980 Black students accounted for 9.9% of college enrollments. Fewer than 8% of Blacks and Hispanics had completed four or more years of college, compared with nearly 18% of the White population (Hacker, 1983).

As we learned in the last chapter, in today's high-technology society education is a must if one hopes for a well-paying job. Without an education, minority heads of households struggle to make ends meet. Without education, equality of opportunity in the job market can never be achieved.

> **?** *Do you agree with the authors' contention that without an education equality of opportunity in the job market can never be achieved, or do you agree with the contention of Jencks and his colleagues that educational inequality will continue until economic inequality is corrected?*

## Health

Remembering that Harvey Brenner's work (see Chapter 14) links unemployment to a host of such personal and social problems as heart disease, suicide, and admissions to mental hospitals and prisons, we should not be surprised to learn that minorities disproportionately experience these problems. When unemployment is complicated by prejudice and discrimination, the effects are compounded and the results are devastating:

- The infant mortality rate is 11.4 per 1000 for Whites and 21.8 per 1000 for Blacks (Select Committee on Children, Youth, and Their Families, 1983, p. 31).

- Black infants (12.5%) are twice as likely as White infants (5.7%) to have a low birth weight—5 pounds, 8 ounces or less (Select Committee on Children, Youth, and Their Families, 1983, p. 29).

- Racial minorities are more likely to die of homicide, strokes, heart disease, and cancer than Whites (U. S. Public Health Service, 1977, p. 23).

- A minority woman is four times as likely as a White woman to die in childbirth (U. S. Public Health Service, 1977, p. 29).

- Blacks have a 66% greater chance of suffering from hypertension (high blood pressure) than Whites (U. S. Public Health Service, 1977, p. 30).

- Racial minorities suffer a rate of tuberculosis five times that of Whites (U. S. Public Health Service, 1977, p. 31).

- For the major notifiable diseases (strep throat, influenza, pneumonia, mumps, chicken pox, etc.), Native Americans experience rates 3 to 13 times the rate nationwide. Data suggest the same risk for Hispanics (U. S. Public Health Service, 1977, p. 33).

- Despite Medicaid and Medicare, racial minorities use health-care services less often than Whites. When they do use health services, their wait for service is longer and their health conditions more impaired than for Whites (U. S. Public Health Service, 1977, pp. 37, 38, 44).

Deprived of the opportunity to participate as equals in this society, minorities can be expected

Institutional Populations

Persons in Institutions, United States, 1970 and 1960
Rate per 100,000 Population, by Race

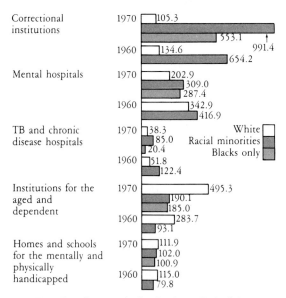

**FIGURE 15-1.** *Persons in institutions, United States, 1970 and 1960: Rate per 100,000 population, by race.*

to be disproportionately represented in the various categories of dysfunctional disorders—and, in fact, they are. Racial minorities occupy correctional institutions at nine times the White rate. The proportion of Blacks in institutions for the emotionally ill exceeds that of Whites by 52% (U. S. Public Health Service, 1977, p. 45; see Figure 15-1). Minorities are three times as likely as Whites to be diagnosed as schizophrenic, twice as likely to have alcohol disorders, and nearly six times as likely to have drug problems (U. S. Public Health Service, 1977, p. 48). With the exception of suicidal behavior, racial and ethnic minorities experience a greater incidence of emotional disorders than Whites.

And even suicide is nearly twice as common

among Native Americans (21.6 per 100,000) as among Whites (13.2 per 100,000) (Frederick, 1978). Additionally, several authors note that Black suicide rates (6.1 per 100,000) may be misleading (Braucht, Loya, & Jamieson, 1980; Gibbs, 1984; Holinger, 1979). As Durkheim (1951, p. 98) once observed, "If there are countries which accumulate suicides and homicides, it is never in the same proportions; the two manifestations never reach their maximum intensity at the same point. It is even a general rule that where homicide is very common it confers a sort of immunity against suicide." Several authors following this lead have pointed out that if we combine other violent deaths (particularly homicide) and suicide, the figures change radically. For example, according to one study (Erhardt & Berlin, 1974), homicide rates are 10 times as high for minorities as for Whites.

We offer for your consideration the argument that the present employment, educational, and health conditions of racial and ethnic minorities result largely from centuries of biased and unwarranted discrimination against them. However, not everyone agrees with this position. Critics of this position admit that racial and ethnic background correlate with impoverishment, educational deprivation, and physical and emotional ill health but suggest that one cannot infer causation from such data. They offer the "downward-drift hypothesis": "that the high rate of psychopathology among poor people may mean that disturbed people from higher classes drift downward—and wind up on skid row and/or rooming houses in the center of the city, thereby inflating the rate among the poor" (Albee, 1983, p. 25). It is genes, they argue, not poverty, that accounts for the conditions described in this chapter. As Albee and Gullotta (see Box 2-2 in Chapter 2) point out, this hypothesis fails to account for the movement of past minority groups such as the Irish, Italians, and Swedes into the

**BOX 15-2**
*The Single-Parent Black Family*

The resiliency that has enabled the Black family to survive and in many instances prosper in this nation is nowhere better illustrated than in the Black single-parent family. In a recent study on work and family life among female-headed Anglo, Mexican American, and Black single-parent families, Espinoza and Naron (1983) found the flexibility of the Black single-parent family structure better able to respond to the needs of individuals in those families.

For example, Black mothers experienced significantly fewer child-rearing problems than either Anglo or Mexican American mothers. The authors attrib-uted this finding to the tendency for Black mothers to be strong disciplinarians who are confident about their parenting ability and who expect their children to share in the responsibility of caring for their home. Further, because employment outside the home is not unusual in Black families, these women were better able to manage the dual roles of mother and worker. For instance, Black mothers were more involved in their children's school activities and more likely to have discussed career plans with their children than either Anglo or Mexican American mothers. Finally, the family and friend-ship support networks of Black women were least disrupted by divorce, enabling these women to receive the help necessary to raise their children.

These findings do not mean there is no distress associated with a divorce for this or any group of people. Rather, they tell us that because of environmental factors some groups are better able to manage a distressful life event than others. The "pathology" (see Chapter 1) that appeared so damaging to Black families in the 1960s appears in the 1980s an asset for many of them.

mainstream of North American society. As Albee (1983, p. 25) notes, if the downward-drift hypothesis is correct, "one must puzzle about what happened to all the bad genes that allegedly caused high rates of idiocy and lunacy among the Irish in 1855."

 *Do you agree or disagree with the downward-drift hypothesis?*

## The Struggle of the Minority Family for Survival

Despite the stresses on them, minority families have survived and some have prospered. In contrast to Moynihan's view (see Chapter 1) that the Black family is trapped in a tangled matriarchal web of pathology, it appears to many authors that Blacks (and minority groups in general) have created highly adaptable family structures (Delgado & Delgado, 1982; Pinderhughes, 1982; Siskind, 1981). These family structures, with their open boundaries (to borrow a term from general systems theory), enable minority families to respond creatively to crisis. A good illustration is the Puerto Rican practice of *hijo de crianza,* which allows a child to be raised by a godparent, relative, or family friend without stigma or time limit. This highly flexible child-caring arrangement in Puerto Rican society permits a child in a family experiencing severe financial or emotional problems to have a better chance at life (Ghali, 1982). Further, even though Blacks do experience a higher rate of

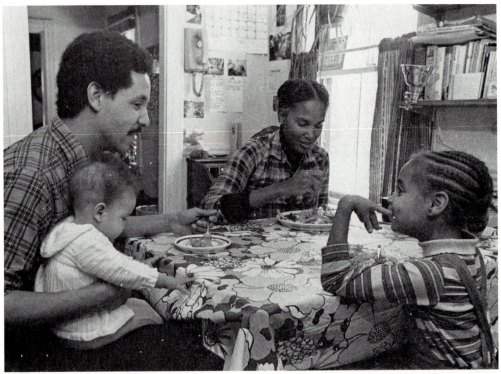

*Despite racist attitudes and prejudicial acts against them, many Black families have prospered in American society.*

marital dissolution than Whites, it should be noted that the majority of Black families with children in 1978 (59.3%) were two-parent families (Gary & Leashore, 1982).

Finally, in one of the earliest published papers on the strengths of Black families, Hill (1971) described five characteristics that enabled these families to withstand the withering effects of racism. First, roles in Black families are flexible. An uncle, grandfather, or family friend can easily assume within the Black culture the vacated position of a father; a grandmother, sister, or aunt can assume the vacated role of a mother. Second, strong kinship bonds exist and are nurtured through the extended and the modified extended family. Next, Black individ-

uals have a strong work orientation and have demonstrated their willingness on numerous occasions to accept positions no one else was willing to take in order to work. Fourth, this strong work orientation is coupled with a strong achievement orientation. Last, the church in the Black culture is not only a source of religious support but a source of concrete aid in times of real need.

 *If prejudice and discrimination were to disappear tomorrow, do you think minority families would be able to maintain "open family boundaries," or do you think those boundaries would gradually disappear?*

# PROMOTING FAMILY WELLNESS
## *Preventing Prejudice and Discrimination*

The struggle of minority families in a majority society is a battle "to be accorded equal dignity and opportunity in the organization of community life" (Longres, 1982, p. 11). How can the technology of prevention be used to offer these individuals and their families the same guarantees extended to the majority—not a chicken in every pot and a car in every garage but an equal chance at that chicken and that car?

## EDUCATION

One goal of education is to enlarge our understanding of ourselves and our environment. The preventionist uses education in its various forms—print, film, and the spoken word—to awaken, alert, and sensitize individuals. For example, the film *West Side Story* can be viewed as a touching tale of tragic love or as a statement of the harm that can come from ethnic hatred. The preventionist, in working with groups of people, would not deny the "touching" aspects of this film but would help people examine and discuss the basis of ethnic hatred that causes such unnecessary suffering in society.

Such efforts are not limited to adults. For example, Rooney-Rebeck and Jason (1980) designed a set of structured classroom exercises to promote interracial cooperation in first- and third-grade classes. They found that their exercises promoted interracial play in the first grade but not the third. This means that educational efforts to reduce prejudice and promote interracial cooperation ideally should begin before prejudicial stereotypes are established.

The National Institute on Drug Abuse publication *Growing Up and Feeling Powerful as an American Indian* (Mason & Baker, 1983) illustrates how the printed word can be used to promote competency. This publication encourages American Indian children to respect themselves and their heritage, as the following passage illustrates:

> I am an Eagle. I am powerful, bold and brave.
> I spread my wings and soar proudly and free in the skies.
> I feel good when I share my feathers with my Indian brothers.
> They respect me and pray that I give them my feathers.
> With my feathers, they dance and sing proudly.
> Some make pretty fans with colorful beads to hold my wings and tail.
> With my feathers and wings, they give praise and thanks to the Great Spirit.
> You too are important and powerful as Indian children.
> You can be powerful by carrying on the Indian ways and traditions of our people. You must always be proud and honoured people and I will always respect you [p. 21].

Education can do more than sensitize. It can do more than promote interracial cooperation and promote competency. As the incident of Prudence Crandall's school illustrates, education is power. And for a people who are seen by society and see themselves as powerless, education is vital to changing this inequality. One of the most ambitious educational prevention efforts has been Head Start. Begun in the mid-1960s, this program offered underprivileged preschool children an enriched program of educational experiences to narrow and, ideally, overcome the cognitive/developmental gap between the haves and have-nots in our society. Despite a disastrous initial evaluation of its failure to achieve

*"I am an eagle. I am powerful, bold and brave. I can be what I want to be. I can control my destiny if only given the opportunity."*

these goals (itself filled with methodological problems), the program continued—and fortunately so. Two recent papers demonstrate Head Start's success.

The first, by Royce, Lazar, and Darlington (1983), is a follow-up evaluation of a group of Head Start programs. Their findings are impressive. In comparison with controls, Head Start participants improved their school performance by 12% to 19% and maintained that level of achievement throughout their school careers. Head Start graduates were 15% more likely to finish high school. Gains in IQ, math ability, and attitudes toward school, as well as higher vocational aspirations, were observed. Finally, Head

Start students were less likely than controls to be either retained or placed in special education classes. The authors concluded that the program had long-term positive effects.

Examining more than 1500 Head Start evaluations, Collins and Deloria (1983) again demonstrate this program's success. For example, in the area of cognitive development, they conclude that "Head Start produces substantial gains in children's cognitive and language development" (p. 16). They note that dramatic improvements in students' learning in the 1970s followed programmatic changes earlier in that decade that included a year-round rather than a seasonal effort, increased parental involvement, initiation of program performance standards, and staff training. Head Start youth maintained their cognitive superiority over controls through high school.

Despite these impressive gains, Head Start cannot alone enable young people to equal the performance of middle-class youth on standardized tests—nor should it. The prevention of distress and the promotion of health can rarely, if ever, be achieved by using only one tool. Other techniques must be applied to this problem if equality of opportunity is to be achieved.

 *What other educational approaches might you use to reduce prejudicial attitudes toward minorities or build minorities' personal resources?*

# COMMUNITY ORGANIZATION/ SYSTEMS INTERVENTION

What can be done to change the social structures that contribute to dysfunctional behavior in minority groups, which, Hillard (1981, p. 138) believes, stems "less from psychogenic factors and more from political and social oppression?" According to Joffe and Albee (1981, p. 323), to "prevent psychopathology we should not alleviate feelings of powerlessness by altering perceptions but by altering reality." Joffe and Albee drive to the crux of the issue when they state:

> There is a strong tendency in our society to separate and isolate social problems. We have a social problem labeled violence against children in the family, and others labeled battered wives, sexism, racism, abuse of elderly persons, family disruption, poverty and unemployment, the incarceration and decarceration of persons we call mentally ill, the neglect of the mentally retarded, and the isolation of the physically handicapped, to name just a few. What do all these

> problems involving different groups have in common? . . . It is their powerlessness. People without power are commonly exploited by powerful economic groups who explain the resulting psychopathology by pointing to the defectiveness of the victims [1981, p. 322].

The community organization/systems intervention (CO/SI) proposals that follow are not by any stretch of the imagination revolutionary. Rather, these actions extend this nation's system of justice to protect the rights of minorities or to allow those minorities the opportunity to succeed. For example, one CO/SI method is removal of institutional practices that impede an individual's right to live his or her life effectively. Programs like affirmative action that remove past discriminatory practices in hiring or in admission to graduate school are excellent examples of this tool in action.

Activities that promote community resource development are a second possibility. One example is the Local Initiatives Support Corporation (LISC), started with a $5 million seed grant from the Ford Foundation. LISC's purpose is to stimulate private-sector investments in areas hard hit by poverty. LISC uses its money, most often in the form of low-interest loans, to attract additional capital to such community ventures as low-income housing and minority-owned businesses (Lodge & Glass, 1982; Porter, 1983).

CO/SI initiatives include political, legislative, and judicial actions. The voter registration drives of recent years are one example of a political CO/SI effort. The legal activities of the National Association for the Advancement of Colored People and the National Organization for Women illustrate the efforts that groups can take in court to ensure their equal protection and opportunity under the law. The 1964 Civil Rights Act and the ERA (Equal Rights Amendment) exemplify legislation aimed at guaranteeing the rights of minorities and women. One of these pieces of legislation passed into law; the other failed for want of sufficient support. Under this nation's system of government the failure of the ERA need not be permanent. Women and men have the right to organize and seek to have this legislation reintroduced in Congress and, if passed, ratified by the necessary number of state legislatures. Their efforts on behalf of the ERA are one form of CO/SI efforts.

 *What other CO/SI actions would you take to reduce discrimination in society?*

## COMPETENCY PROMOTION

Competency involves pride—pride in oneself, one's people, and one's community. Efforts that promote self-esteem, an internal locus of control, and community-interested rather than self-interested individuals form the basis of all competency promotion activities. In Chapter 2 we described such activities as involving either "active" or "passive" approaches.

An example of the active approach is the programs of the Alaskan Chevak Village Youth Association (CVYA). This organization was formed several years ago in an Eskimo village to combat the high rates of alcoholism and drug abuse found in many Native American communities (Manson, Tatum, & Dinges, 1982). CVYA uses task-oriented activities like dances, athletic events, educational programs, and special celebrations (a Winterfest in March, a Tundrafest in August) to encourage positive youth development. Like other youth competency programs described earlier in this text, this program is committed to creating

> close working relationships between a network of youth and young adults. These adults . . .

serve as role models . . . members were viewed in the village as responsible and reliable people who got things done. CVYA also presents to youth, character ideals, serving the village, being self-reliant, and taking responsibility for community affairs. CVYA also provides the opportunity for youth to perform roles where they act out these values and learn organizational skills [Kleinfeld, 1982, p. 362].

The second competency promotion approach is "passive." This means that the program's agenda is controlled by the program leader, not the participants. For instance, a school curriculum is passive in that the students do not design it. An example of a curriculum designed to promote ethnic pride is found in *Enhancing Self-Concept in Early Childhood* (Samuels, 1977). The author encourages teachers to promote children's ethnic and racial pride by, for instance, displaying a birthday chart with each child's birthday on it, decorating the classroom with photos of the children with their families, encouraging movement to music, role-playing feelings, discouraging sexism, and encouraging cultural diversity by means of ethnic songs, foods, and class visitors.

 *How else might competency be promoted?*

## NATURAL CAREGIVING

Considering the oppression that minority families have experienced, it is surprising to find that many succeed. If one reason were to be singled out to explain this phenomenon, it would be social support. Attacked from the outside, Hispanic, Native American, and Black families have formed strong networks of support in the family and in the community.

Numerous authors have described the important functions that the extended and modified extended family serve for minorities (Comer & Hamilton-Lee, 1982; Keefe & Casas, 1980; McAdoo, 1982b, 1983). Within these families child care is exchanged, food shared, and limited financial resources often pooled. Such support has significantly moderated the potentially devastating effects of prejudice and discrimination. This form of indigenous caregiving is transformed into mutual self-help groups in many minority cultures through their involvement with the church.

Historically, for many ethnic groups the church has served religious and social support functions. The church is a community. It is bonded together by a belief in God that is expressed in the church's caring for its members. This caring has found itself expressed over the centuries in food banks, soup kitchens, clothing drives, and sheltering the homeless. Recently, in some Black churches this caring has extended beyond sharing food and clothing to include the successful development of Black business enterprises (Bloom, 1983).

 *In your opinion, should any church take an active role in politics and the development of financial capital?*

# SUMMARY

In this chapter we have detailed some of the unnecessary stresses minority families experience in this country. We have outlined some of the steps that can be taken to moderate those stresses. Those steps will not be fully successful, however, until we commit ourselves to ensuring that opportunity is made available without regard to race, color, creed, or sex.

# MAJOR POINTS TO REMEMBER

1. Five characteristics are associated with being a minority: minorities are subordinate segments of society, they tend to have special traits, they develop a group consciousness, membership is transmitted by descent, and members tend to marry within the group.
2. Prejudice is an inaccurate, emotionally rigid attitude toward members of a particular group. Discrimination is the behavioral demonstration of that attitude expressed in the different treatment given to members of that group.
3. American history provides many examples that contradict the myth that this nation has a history of tolerance toward groups who differ in religious beliefs, ethnic background, or racial characteristics from the central group.
4. Three factors contribute to bigotry: the threat of change, fear of that change, and a perceived loss of resources.
5. Structural functionalism suggests that prejudice and discrimination exist because they serve a useful function.
6. Belonging to a racial or ethnic minority is a chronic stressor that cannot be escaped.

7. Minorities suffer from discrimination in such areas as employment, education, and access to health care.
8. Despite prejudice and discrimination, some minority families have prospered. In contrast to Moynihan's view that the Black family is trapped in a tangled matriarchal web of pathology, it appears to many authors that Black families (and minority families in general) have created highly adaptable family structures, enabling them to respond creatively to crisis.
9. According to one author, the Black family has five strengths: adaptability, strong kinship bonds, work orientation, achievement orientation, and religious ties.
10. Prevention efforts like Head Start are intended to help minority individuals overcome the educational deprivation that has resulted from years of discrimination.
11. Prevention efforts like the Civil Rights Act of 1964 are intended to guarantee the constitutional rights of all, but especially those of minorities.

# ADDITIONAL SOURCES OF INFORMATION

Davis, A. Y. (1981). *Women, race, and class.* New York: Random House.

Higham, J. (1955). *Strangers in the land: Patterns of American nativism, 1860–1925.* New Brunswick, NJ: Rutgers University Press.

Sebestyen, O. (1979). *Words by heart.* Boston: Little, Brown.

Wright, R. (1975). *White man listen.* Garden City, NY: Doubleday.

# 16

# SUBSTANCE USE, ABUSE, AND DEPENDENCE AND THE FAMILY

## Questions to Guide Your Reading

1. Does age have a bearing on alcohol consumption? Does race?

2. What are the medical risks associated with the misuse of alcohol?

3. What is fetal alcohol syndrome?

4. What evidence do we have that ties substance abuse by adolescents to failure of parents to fulfill their family roles?

5. How do families cope with an alcohol-abusing member?

6. What effect, if any, does an alcoholic parent have on a child?

7. Do people who occasionally use marijuana differ in other ways from people who never use it?

8. Why should we be cautious about attributing poor personal functioning among marijuana abusers to marijuana?

9. What did Pope Leo XIII, Freud, and the Incan emperors have in common?

10. What are "cocaine bugs"?

I guess my dad's OK. . . . Well, sometimes, anyways. That is, except when he's drinking. When he's drinking, he gets real mean and sometimes he hits me. My mom, she tries to protect me, but it doesn't work all the time. I sometimes wonder why she stays with him [the comments of an early adolescent to one of the authors].

I've discovered that my 14-year-old daughter is using marijuana. I confronted her with her behavior last night, to be told by her that marijuana was not a drug and that several states had decriminalized possession of one ounce of marijuana or less. Could that be true? [the comments of a mother to a drug counselor].

I've been using coke on a recreational basis for several years. I'd like to use more, but it's so damn expensive I can't afford to. To have a coke habit, I figure you either got to be rich or a dealer [the comments of a cocaine user to one of the authors].

This chapter is about three substances—alcohol, marijuana, and cocaine. In recent years each of these substances has been the focus of tremendous societal concern. Two of these substances (marijuana and cocaine) are widely feared to have ruinous effects on individual and family emotional health in any amount, while the third (alcohol) is thought to be harmful only when used excessively. In this chapter we shall look at the accuracy of these public beliefs. We shall examine, when possible, the effects each substance has on individuals, their families, and society. Finally, we shall see what efforts can be taken to ease the distress of children of alcoholics.

But before we examine individual substances, we need to clarify three terms: *substance use, abuse,* and *dependence.* By **substance use** we mean the infrequent and limited intake of alcohol or drugs. **Substance abuse** is the frequent and excessive use of alcohol or drugs so that physical, mental, or social functioning is impaired. **Substance dependence** is synonymous with addiction—the need to use alcohol or another drug continually to meet psychological or physical needs and to avoid the discomfort of its absence (withdrawal).

# ALCOHOL

Since the beginning of time, humans have consumed beverages made by fermenting grains or the juices of vine-ripened fruits. Accompanying this behavior have been warnings that overindulgence might have disastrous effects. Even the home medicine books of the 1800s, though filled with "recipes" liberally laced with opiates, urged temperance in the consumption of alcoholic beverages, as the following passage from *Dr. Chase's Recipes; or, Information for Everybody: An Invaluable Collection of about Eight Hundred Practical Recipes* (Chase, 1866) illustrates:

> So it will be seen that every quart of fruit wine not made for medicine, or sacramental purposes, helps to build up the cause [intemperance] which we all so much desire not to encourage. And for those who take any kind of spirits for the *sake* of the spirit, let me give you the following:
>
> 2. "SPIRITUAL FACTS.—That whis-*key* is the key by which many gain entrance into our prisons and almshouses.
> 3. That *brandy brands* the noses of all those who cannot govern their appetites.
> 4. That *punch* is the cause of many *un*friendly punches.

> 5. That *ale* causes many *ailings,* while *beer* brings to the *bier.*[1]
> 6. That *wine* causes many to take to a *winding* way home.
> 7. That *cham*-pagne is the source of many real pains.
> 8. That *gin slings* have "slewed" more than *slings* of old" [p. 77].

Is the good Dr. Chase correct in his counsel that alcohol, if misused, is a dangerous substance? The answer is found in the sections that follow.

## *Alcohol Use and Misuse in American Society*

*Consumption patterns.* Since 1850, with a few exceptions, the yearly American consumption of alcohol has exceeded two gallons per person (see Table 16-1). In recent years this figure has approached the three-gallon mark (2.73 gallons). When this 2.73 gallons is divided into individual beverages, beer accounts for 49% of the alcohol consumed by Americans, wine accounts for 12%, and distilled spirits (brandy, whisky, and so on) for 39%.

The National Institute of Alcohol and Alcoholism (NIAAA) reports that heavy drinking[2] appears to peak for males between ages 21 and 34, while for females this happens at a later age (35–49 years). Men in business and professional positions and women in service positions are the most likely to be heavy drinkers. Alcohol consumption also differs by race. Hispanics of both sexes have higher rates of heavy drinking than Whites, while large numbers of Black men and women refrain from drinking. Blacks who do drink report consumption levels similar to those of Whites. Finally, increasing numbers of young people are reporting heavier drinking by middle

---

[1] A bier is a frame on which a corpse is laid.

[2] A heavy drinker is defined as someone who once a week drinks 60 ounces of beer, 20 ounces of wine, or 5 ounces of distilled spirits at one sitting (DeLuca, 1981).

**TABLE 16-1.** *Apparent U.S. consumption of alcoholic beverages in gallons of ethanol (pure alcohol) per capita for the drinking-age population, 1850–1978*

| Year | Distilled Spirits Beverage Volume | Distilled Spirits Ethanol Volume | Wine Beverage Volume | Wine Ethanol Volume | Beer Beverage Volume | Beer Ethanol Volume | Total |
|---|---|---|---|---|---|---|---|
| (Based on population 15 years of age +) | | | | | | | |
| 1850 | 4.17 | 1.88 | 0.46 | 0.03 | 2.70 | 0.14 | 2.10 |
| 1860 | 4.79 | 2.16 | 0.57 | 0.10 | 5.39 | 0.27 | 2.53 |
| 1870 | 3.40 | 1.53 | 0.53 | 0.10 | 8.7 | 0.44 | 2.07 |
| 1871–80 | 2.27 | 1.02 | 0.77 | 0.14 | 11.26 | 0.56 | 1.72 |
| 1881–90 | 2.12 | 0.95 | 0.76 | 0.14 | 17.94 | 0.90 | 1.99 |
| 1891–95 | 2.12 | 0.95 | 0.60 | 0.11 | 23.42 | 1.17 | 2.23 |
| 1896–1900 | 1.72 | 0.77 | 0.55 | 0.10 | 23.72 | 1.19 | 2.06 |
| 1901–05 | 2.11 | 0.95 | 0.71 | 0.13 | 26.20 | 1.31 | 2.39 |
| 1906–10 | 2.14 | 0.96 | 0.92 | 0.12 | 29.27 | 1.47 | 2.60 |
| 1911–15 | 2.09 | 0.94 | 0.79 | 0.14 | 29.53 | 1.48 | 2.56 |
| 1916–19 | 1.68 | 0.76 | 0.69 | 0.12 | 21.63 | 1.08 | 1.96 |
| PROHIBITION | | | | | | | |
| 1934 | 0.64 | 0.29 | 0.36 | 0.07 | 13.58 | 0.61 | 0.97 |
| 1935 | 0.96 | 0.43 | 0.50 | 0.09 | 15.13 | 0.68 | 1.20 |
| 1936 | 1.20 | 0.59 | 0.64 | 0.12 | 17.53 | 0.79 | 1.50 |
| 1937 | 1.43 | 0.64 | 0.71 | 0.13 | 18.21 | 0.82 | 1.59 |
| 1938 | 1.32 | 0.59 | 0.70 | 0.13 | 16.58 | 0.75 | 1.47 |
| 1939 | 1.38 | 0.62 | 0.79 | 0.14 | 16.77 | 0.75 | 1.51 |
| 1940 | 1.43 | 0.67 | 0.01 | 0.16 | 16.29 | 0.73 | 1.56 |
| 1941 | 1.58 | 0.71 | 1.02 | 0.18 | 17.97 | 0.81 | 1.70 |
| 1942 | 1.89 | 0.85 | 1.11 | 0.20 | 20.00 | 0.90 | 1.95 |
| 1943 | 1.46 | 0.66 | 0.94 | 0.17 | 22.26 | 1.00 | 1.83 |
| 1944 | 1.00 | 0.76 | 0.02 | 0.17 | 25.22 | 1.13 | 2.06 |
| 1945 | 1.95 | 0.88 | 1.13 | 0.20 | 25.97 | 1.17 | 2.25 |
| 1946 | 2.20 | 0.99 | 1.34 | 0.24 | 23.75 | 1.07 | 2.30 |
| 1947 | 1.69 | 0.76 | 0.90 | 0.16 | 24.56 | 1.11 | 2.03 |
| 1948 | 1.56 | 0.70 | 1.11 | 0.20 | 23.77 | 1.07 | 1.97 |
| 1949 | 1.55 | 0.70 | 1.21 | 0.22 | 23.48 | 1.06 | 1.98 |
| 1950 | 1.72 | 0.77 | 1.27 | 0.23 | 23.21 | 1.04 | 2.04 |

| Year | Distilled Spirits Beverage Volume | Distilled Spirits Ethanol Volume | Wine Beverage Volume | Wine Ethanol Volume | Beer Beverage Volume | Beer Ethanol Volume | Total |
|---|---|---|---|---|---|---|---|
| 1951 | 1.73 | 0.78 | 1.13 | 0.20 | 22.92 | 1.03 | 2.01 |
| 1952 | 1.63 | 0.73 | 1.22 | 0.21 | 23.20 | 1.04 | 1.98 |
| 1953 | 1.70 | 0.77 | 1.19 | 0.20 | 23.04 | 1.04 | 2.01 |
| 1954 | 1.66 | 0.74 | 1.21 | 0.21 | 22.41 | 1.01 | 1.96 |
| 1955 | 1.71 | 0.77 | 1.25 | 0.22 | 22.39 | 1.01 | 2.00 |
| 1956 | 1.31 | 0.81 | 1.27 | 0.22 | 22.18 | 1.00 | 2.03 |
| 1957 | 1.77 | 0.80 | 1.26 | 0.22 | 21.44 | 0.97 | 1.99 |
| 1958 | 1.77 | 0.80 | 1.27 | 0.22 | 21.35 | 0.96 | 1.98 |
| 1959 | 1.86 | 0.84 | 1.28 | 0.22 | 22.15 | 1.00 | 2.06 |
| 1960 | 1.90 | 0.86 | 1.32 | 0.22 | 21.95 | 0.99 | 2.07 |
| 1961 | 1.91 | 0.86 | 1.36 | 0.23 | 21.47 | 0.97 | 2.06 |
| 1962 | 1.99 | 0.90 | 1.32 | 0.22 | 21.98 | 0.99 | 2.11 |
| 1963 | 2.02 | 0.91 | 1.37 | 0.23 | 22.51 | 1.01 | 2.15 |
| 1964 | 2.01 | 0.95 | 1.41 | 0.24 | 23.08 | 1.04 | 2.23 |
| 1965 | 2.21 | 0.99 | 1.42 | 0.24 | 23.07 | 1.04 | 2.27 |
| 1966 | 2.26 | 1.02 | 1.40 | 0.24 | 23.52 | 1.06 | 2.32 |
| 1967 | 2.34 | 1.05 | 1.46 | 0.25 | 23.81 | 1.07 | 2.37 |
| 1968 | 2.44 | 1.10 | 1.51 | 0.26 | 24.33 | 1.09 | 2.45 |
| 1969 | 2.51 | 1.13 | 1.62 | 0.26 | 24.90 | 1.12 | 2.51 |
| (Based on population 14 years of age +) | | | | | | | |
| 1970 | 2.48 | 1.12 | 1.71 | 0.27 | 25.23 | 1.14 | 2.53 |
| 1971 | 2.50 | 1.13 | 1.93 | 0.31 | 25.63 | 1.15 | 2.59 |
| 1972 | 2.52 | 1.08 | 2.10 | 0.30 | 25.90 | 1.17 | 2.55 |
| 1973 | 2.57 | 1.11 | 2.14 | 0.31 | 26.77 | 1.20 | 2.62 |
| 1974 | 2.59 | 1.10 | 2.13 | 0.31 | 27.76 | 1.25 | 2.66 |
| 1975 | 2.58 | 1.11 | 2.22 | 0.32 | 28.09 | 1.26 | 2.69 |
| 1976 | 2.56 | 1.10 | 2.24 | 0.32 | 28.09 | 1.26 | 2.68 |
| 1977 | 2.56 | 1.05 | 2.37 | 0.31 | 29.05 | 1.31 | 2.67 |
| 1978 | 2.60 | 1.07 | 2.51 | 0.32 | 29.78 | 1.34 | 2.73 |

adolescence (age 15). Consumption of alcohol by young people increases until age 17 and then levels off (DeLuca, 1981).

*Medical consequences of alcohol abuse.* In 1981 John DeLuca, then director of NIAAA, reported to the U. S. Congress the damage that uncontrolled alcohol consumption can have on the body. Among the findings was that long-term alcohol abuse increases the chances of unexplained heart-muscle disease. This condition can be reversed in patients who abstain from further drinking.

Heavy drinking is also a significant contributor to high blood pressure. It is associated with stroke, phlebitis, and varicose veins. In males, heavy alcohol consumption lowers testosterone levels. (Reduced testosterone levels can cause impotence, loss of interest in sex, breast enlargement, and testicular atrophy.) Long-term alcohol abusers and the alcohol-dependent suffer a high probability of brain atrophy. Depending on the sample, 50% to 100% of them experience some degree of brain dysfunction. Further, alcohol-abusing and alcohol-dependent people are at increased risk of mouth, pharynx, larynx, and esophagus cancers (DeLuca, 1981). Collectively, these findings explain why alcohol-abusing and dependent people have a life expectancy 10 to 12 years less than nondrinkers (Kihss, 1982).

Finally, it appears that even moderate use of alcohol during pregnancy can be hazardous to the unborn baby (see Table 16-2). Women averaging one ounce of absolute alcohol per day (two standard drinks) have twice the risk of low birth weight of nondrinkers. As little as one ounce of absolute alcohol a week doubles the chances of a spontaneous abortion. Alcohol-dependent women who continue drinking heavily during a pregnancy run the risk of severely damaging the unborn child with a disorder called **fetal alcohol syndrome.** This syndrome is characterized by mental retardation, central nervous system disorders, facial deformities, and growth deficiencies. Use of alcohol by nursing mothers is unhealthful for infants because alcohol enters the milk and is passed on to the child. Further, heavy drinking by a nursing mother reduces the amount of breast milk available to her child (DeLuca, 1981; National Institute on Alcohol Abuse and Alcoholism, 1981).

*Social consequences of alcohol misuse.* Depending on the source, one third to two thirds of all fatal motor vehicle accidents involve alcohol, as do 45% to 60% of adolescent motor vehicle fatalities. Alcohol is a factor in half of the falling accidents that prove fatal. Half of adult deaths due to fire and drownings involve alcohol (DeLuca, 1981).

**TABLE 16-2.** *Maternal alcohol abuse and risk to infant*

| Abnormality | Number of Times Risk Is Increased in Alcohol-Abusing Pregnancy | Percentage of Alcohol-Abusing Pregnancies in Which Abnormality Is Observed |
|---|---|---|
| Spontaneous abortion | 2 | 30 |
| Neonatal depression | 1.5 | 20 |
| Low birth weight | 2 | 25 |
| Intrauterine growth retardation | 2.5 | 20 |
| Anomalies | 4 | 40 |
| Fetal alcohol syndrome | — | 2.5 |
| Any abnormality | — | 50 |

*Young people who drink and drive often think they are immortal: accidents only happen to others. The sobering reality is that 45% to 60% of adolescent motor fatalities involve alcohol.*

Alcohol-dependent individuals are at high risk of suicide. They are 30 times as likely as the general population to take their own lives. Findings suggest that 80% of those who commit suicide were drinking before the event. Of the ten leading causes of premature death among Native Americans, half are directly related to alcohol abuse—accidents, cirrhosis of the liver, suicide, and homicide (DeLuca, 1981).

Statistics can give us some grasp of the dimensions of America's drinking problem. In 1977, 1.4 million people were treated for alcohol problems in the 5900 inpatient and outpatient treatment centers around the United States. Another 660,000 participated in Alcoholics Anonymous (AA) programs. It is estimated that 7% of American adults (10 million) and 19% of American adolescents (3.3 million) have an alcohol problem (Vischi, Jones, & Lima, 1980). The cost of alcohol abuse and dependence in the United States in the form of lost production, health care, accidents, crime, and fire has been placed at nearly $90 billion a year (see Table 16-3).

Given these statistics, why do many Americans think drinking is harmless? At one time alcohol consumption was prohibited in the United States, but that well-known 13-year experiment in sobriety failed. It failed because the simple truth is that drinking makes most people feel good. Further, most people do not abuse alcohol or become dependent on it. Given its unique status in our society (the cocktail party, the Sunday champagne brunch, the corner bar of countless television shows), it is understandable, but not pardonable, that most Americans consider other substances like marijuana or cocaine evil and corrupting, and alcohol acceptable, despite overwhelming evidence to the contrary. The damage this substance does to individuals' and families' lives concerns us next.

**TABLE 16-3.** *Costs to society of alcohol abuse, drug abuse, and mental illness, in millions of dollars, 1980*

| Cost | Alcohol Abuse | Drug Abuse | Mental Illness | Total |
|---|---|---|---|---|
| Core costs | $79,607 | $29,451 | $52,418 | $161,476 |
| Direct | | | | |
| Treatment | 9,487 | 1,200 | 20,961 | 31,647 |
| Support | 984 | 243 | 2,597 | 3,823 |
| Indirect | | | | |
| Mortality[a] | 14,456 | 1,980 | 7,196 | 23,632 |
| Morbidity[b] | 54,680 | 26,028 | 21,664 | 102,372 |
| Reduced productivity | (50,575)[c] | (25,716)[c] | (3,122)[c] | (79,413) |
| Lost employment | (4,105) | (312) | (18,542) | (22,959) |
| Other related costs | 9,919 | 17,485 | 1,818 | 29,222 |
| Direct | | | | |
| Motor vehicle crashes (property loss) | 2,185 | [d] | — | 2,185 |
| Crime[b] | 2,347 | 5,910 | 870 | 9,127 |
| Public | (2,062) | (4,454) | (635) | (7,151) |
| Private | (261) | (1,345) | (235) | (1,841) |
| Property loss/damage | (24) | (111) | (—) | (135) |
| Social welfare programs | 38 | 2 | 201 | 241 |
| Other | 2,912 | 537 | 659 | 4,108 |
| Indirect | | | | |
| Victims of crime | 172 | 845 | — | 1,017 |
| Crime careers | — | 8,725 | — | 8,725 |
| Incarceration | 1,801 | 1,466 | 88 | 3,356 |
| Motor vehicle crashes (time loss) | 464 | [d] | — | 464 |
| Total | $89,526[c] | $46,936[c] | $54,236[c] | $190,698 |

[a] At a 6% discount rate. The present value of lost future productivity due to premature mortality was also calculated using discount rates of 10% and 4%. Use of a 10% rate decreases indirect costs by the following amounts: alcohol abuse, $4881 million; drug abuse, $704 million; and mental illness, $2444 million. Use of a 4% rate increases indirect costs by the following amounts: alcohol abuse, $4455 million; drug abuse, $638 million; and mental illness, $2177 million.
[b] Components are shown in parentheses.
[c] The total costs to society for each of the three ADM disorders are not comparable, since the completeness of data available for each cost category varied significantly. For example, the estimate of reduced productivity is relatively complete for alcohol abuse, only partly complete for drug abuse, and incomplete for mental illness.
[d] Although costs are hypothesized to occur in this category, sufficient data are not available to develop a reliable estimate.
*Note:* Totals may not add because of rounding.

*Why do you think drinking peaks for women at a later age than for men? Why do you think Americans have been so lenient in their attitudes toward alcohol?*

## Misuse of Alcohol and Family Life

*A theoretical perspective: Developmental theory.* As discussed earlier in this book, developmental theory borrows several concepts from other family perspectives to explain human behavior. It proposes that families serve particular institutional functions, that family members fill certain role positions (mother, wife, husband, son, and so on) and play those roles against some societal ideal, and that family life follows a predictable life cycle. In a developmental model, an individual's alcohol abuse can be explained by the family's failure to perform its institutional functions and by its members' failure to play their roles appropriately or to facilitate, rather than arrest, progress through the life cycle.

For example, the developmentalist assumes that one of the family's functions is to provide a caring and nurturing environment for offspring. The family is expected to shelter but not over-protect its members. This theoretical assumption implies that domineering parents would impede the emotional growth of young family members, making it difficult for them to attain adult status. This supposition has been supported by the observations of numerous clinicians and researchers who have found the opposite-sex parent of a substance-abusing individual to be symbiotically tied to that child. This excessively close attachment smothers any effort by the offspring to free themselves from their parents (Harbin & Maziar, 1975; Stanton, 1979, 1980).

Further, the developmentalist assumes that each family member has several positions to fill and roles to perform in a family. For example, married men with children are supposed to behave as husbands and fathers. Certain societal expectations go with these roles. Two of these expectations are that fathers will love their children and will be involved in their lives (particularly with boys) as role models, teaching them the difference between acceptable and unacceptable behavior. Emerging from this set of assumptions is a hypothesis that congruity between role expectations and actual behavior results in functional family behavior, while incongruity between role expectations and actual behavior results in dysfunctional family behavior.

Several major reviews of the literature on alcohol and drug abuse have found evidence that incongruity does indeed contribute to dysfunctional behavior (Baither, 1978; Harbin & Maziar, 1975; Klagsburn & Davis, 1977). These reviews report parents of substance abusers to have fulfilled less than ideal roles as parents. For example, a significant number of substance-abusing males had no contact as children with their fathers. Where contact did occur, fathers were likely to be either weak and ineffectual or hostile and belligerent. These parents' failure to appropriately fill the parental role is further illustrated in the role models they provided to their children.

Using a role perspective and the available research on adolescent drinking, Barnes (1977, p. 573) proposes that "problem drinking is a manifestation of incomplete, inadequate socialization within the family." Citing recent studies, she states:

> The abstaining teenager is more likely to come from an abstaining home, the moderate drinker is more likely to come from a home where the parents are also moderate users of alcohol, while heavy drinkers in a disproportionate number of cases have parents who are likely to be heavy drinkers [p. 573].

The profile of the substance-abusing adolescent's family that emerges from studies is of a family in which parental control over the adolescent is lax and the relationship between teenager and parents distant (Barnes, 1977; Tudor, Peterson, & Elifson, 1980). Adolescents with affectionate, child-centered parents are much less likely to use illegal substances (Auerswald, 1980; Brook, Gordon, & Brook, 1980).

Many researchers have found that parents of an alcohol-dependent adolescent often condone, if not encourage, the adolescent's drinking. Mitchell, Hong, and Corman (1979), for example, found that "alcohol was freely available in the homes of most and a number of parents seemed tacitly to accept their children's drinking" (p. 512).

Finally, some developmentalists contend that the life cycle of the family with an alcohol-abusing member has been arrested (Stanton, 1979, 1980). Developmental theory suggests that in order for the family to evolve, it must successfully accomplish certain tasks. One of its most important tasks is allowing the child to become his or her own person—that is, releasing the child from the family to enable the child to create his or her own family. When the family refuses to engage in this process, it becomes fixated, the developmentalist believes, forcing family members into inappropriate behavior patterns. One of these inappropriate patterns is substance abuse. Several authors have speculated that the adolescent's misuse of alcohol and drugs is a feeble attempt to declare adulthood to parents who desire to keep the abusing individual in a perpetual state of childhood (Stanton, 1979, 1980).

From the perspective of a developmentalist, many interacting factors set the scene for misuse of substances (also see Box 16-1, page 376). We have briefly touched on three of these. In the next section we will examine more closely a family's reaction to a member's alcohol abuse.

**?** *Try using another theoretical perspective to explain alcohol abuse. What are the similarities and differences between that theory and developmental theory?*

*Family reactions to the misuse of alcohol.* While individual and societal losses to alcohol abuse and dependence are considerable, the impact of alcoholism on the family is tremendous. It is estimated that half the divorces and half the juvenile arrests for delinquency in this country occur in families with at least one alcohol-abus-

*It is estimated that 28 million young people live in homes with an alcohol-abusing individual.*

ing member. It is also estimated that 28 million young people live in homes with an alcohol abuser and that 80% of these young people will someday experience emotional difficulties serious enough to warrant intervention (Booz, Allen, & Hamilton, 1974; McCabe, 1978).

In a classic article, Jackson (1954) first described the attempts of families to live with an alcohol-abusing husband. Using a sample of families of Alcoholics Anonymous members, she outlined the following seven stages:

1. *The family attempts to deny the problem.* In this stage the spouse confronts the problem drinker with his behavior, to be assured by him that no problem exists. The family accepts

BOX 16-1
*Is There a Genetic Predisposition to Alcoholism?*

Are people who misuse alcohol genetically predisposed—that is, biologically hypersensitive to the substance? This question is hard to answer. Certainly, the theoretical explanation and the research to support that explanation offered earlier in this chapter provide a convincing account of excessive drinking without resorting to genes. Nevertheless, several studies support the claim that alcoholism has a genetic component. For example, Fox (1968) found that 52% of the alcoholics she studied had had an alcoholic parent. Goodwin's (1976, 1979) work with adopted children showed that 25% of the children from alcoholic families who were placed in nonalcoholic families still became alcoholics. Additional research lends support to the general finding that children of alcoholic parents stand a 25% to 50% greater chance of becoming alcoholics than children whose parents are not alcoholic (Chafetz, 1979; Cotton, 1979). What is your opinion? Is alcoholism genetic, or can you think of other possible reasons for these findings?

this assurance as it tries to maintain equilibrium by rationalizing his behavior.

2. *The family tries to eliminate the problem.* No longer able to ignore the problem drinker's behavior, his wife tries to control his drinking through threats, bribes, and/or hiding his alcohol, and marital conflicts increase. Family members increasingly isolate themselves from friends in a continued futile attempt to conceal the drinking.

3. *The family becomes disorganized.* At this stage the problem drinker's wife is no longer able to rationalize her husband's drinking behavior. Attempts to conceal his drinking from the children, make excuses for his poor work performance, and curtail his alcohol intake are given up as lost causes. Marital conflict increases, and the couple's children often find themselves caught between the arguing parents.

4. *The family makes a first attempt at reorganization.* As the problem drinker remains unable to manage family affairs, his spouse decides to take action. The decision to act can occur for several reasons, including misman-

agement of the family's money or violence toward the children or herself. Courses of action available to the spouse range from assuming her husband's role in the family to leaving him.

During this stage, the problem drinker bargains with family members for the return of his role in the family. His success in reattaining that role despite his continuing abuse of alcohol perpetuates a destructive cycle for the family, filled with pain.

5. *The family attempts to escape the problem.* Unable to tolerate her husband's excessive drinking any longer, the wife may seek a legal separation or initiate divorce proceedings. In either case his unstable behavior makes questionable her ability to rely on him for financial assistance.

6. *The family makes a second attempt at reorganization.* After a legal separation or a divorce, the family reorganizes for a second time, the mother assuming the roles formerly held by her spouse. Although she may feel guilty over having left her sick husband, the process of adjustment is not particularly diffi-

## BOX 16-2
### *Is Controlled Drinking Possible?*

Can an alcohol-dependent person be taught to control his or her drinking? No, says Alcoholics Anonymous (AA). Once an alcoholic, always an alcoholic, and the only way to a functional life is sobriety through abstinence, AA believes.

Can an alcohol-dependent person be taught to control his or her drinking? Yes, say Sobell and Sobell (1978). From 1970 to 1971, this research team worked with 40 severely dependent alcoholics (the technical term is *gamma alcoholics*) in a controlled study to determine whether they could be taught to

moderate their drinking. Using a variety of behavioral techniques over 17 training sessions, the authors demonstrated very positive results with 20 experimental subjects. These results continued to be maintained at a follow-up two years later.

Recently, another group of researchers (Pendery, Maltzman, & West, 1982) conducted a ten-year follow-up study of those 20 experimental subjects who had supposedly learned to moderate their drinking. Their findings seriously question whether alcohol-dependent individuals

can be taught to control their drinking.

Of the 20 original experimental subjects (19 of whom were located), only one had learned to "control" his drinking habit. Eight were drinking heavily at the time of the follow-up and had been for the last ten years. Six more were now abstaining from alcohol, but in each case this had resulted "only after repeated hospitalization" for their alcohol addiction (p. 174). Four of the experimental subjects had died over the ten-year period for reasons related to alcohol.

---

cult except when the alcohol-abusing spouse makes a continued effort to reenter the family.

7. *The family reorganizes with the substance-abusing member seeking help.* Should the alcohol-abusing spouse seek help for his problem and learn to control his drinking, it is possible for the family to reunite. Should this happen, the family must once again reassign family roles, and members must reassess their feelings toward the problem drinker.

More recently the work of James and Goldman (1971) has substantiated Jackson's research. Additionally, these authors outline five coping behaviors used by women with alcohol-abusing husbands: emotionally withdrawing from the marriage; infantilization of the husband; expressing anger in such ways as threatening separation or divorce or locking the husband out of the house; trying to avoid family conflict but nevertheless assuming control of the family's financial

matters in an attempt to avert economic disaster; and acting out in such ways as drinking, threatening suicide, or becoming involved with other men.

It is clear that abuse of alcohol is destructive of the very fabric of the marital relationship. It is also destructive for the children of the couple, as Cork's (1969) classic work *The Forgotten Children* has illustrated. Interviewing 115 young people between ages 10 and 16, Cork found that her subjects felt rejected by both the alcohol-abusing and the nonabusing parent. Forced to mature quickly, these young people reported problems with peer relationships. They expressed a reluctance to form friendships for fear that the "family's secret" might get out or that their alcohol-abusing parent might embarrass them in front of their friends. They often found themselves caught between their parents as the marital couple quarreled, seemingly forever, over the problem drinker's behavior.

Collectively, the literature on alcohol abuse and dependence paints a dismal picture of family life. Many young people survive this ordeal and prosper in their own adult and family lives, but few will ever attribute their success to the examples found in their own homes.

 *What do you think motivates a family with an alcoholic member to change?*

# MARIJUANA

*Some facts about marijuana:*

- In 1990 it is estimated that more than 17 million people between ages 18 and 25 will admit to some use of marijuana (Richards, 1981).

- Marijuana abuse (defined as daily use) among graduating high school seniors has declined each year from 10.7% in 1978 to 7% in 1981 (Johnston, Bachman, & O'Malley, 1981).

- Presently 11 states have decriminalized the possession of approximately one ounce or less of marijuana. These states treat marijuana possession as a misdemeanor or a civil offense.

- In 1977 President Carter stated that, although "we can and should discourage the use of marijuana . . . [I support] legislation amending Federal law to eliminate all Federal criminal penalties for the possession of up to one ounce of marijuana" ("President Carter's Address . . . ," 1977, p. 6).

The history of marijuana (*Cannabis sativa*) in North America is a curious one involving a king, an American president, ethnic prejudice, and the Great Depression. To begin at the beginning, the earliest English settlements in America raised marijuana (then called "hemp") as a cash crop. The hemp plant was extremely useful. Its fibers could be turned into sails, linens, blankets, clothing, flags, and, most important of all, rope. So important was this commodity to England that King James I ordered the settlers of Virginia to produce hemp for the mother country (Austin, 1979; Grinspoon, 1971, Sloman, 1979).

Production of marijuana continued after the revolution of 1776 without concern for its intoxicating qualities. In fact, George Washington cultivated the plant. Like many other gentlemen of the time, he raised hemp to be sold for making cloth and rope. At the time of the Civil War, the growing of marijuana as a cash crop declined. Other parts of the world, notably Russia and the Phillipines, produced a product superior to what could be grown here.

Like many now illegal substances, marijuana was used from the 1800s to the 1930s for medicinal purposes. However, it never captured the support other drugs were able to attract. The lack of medical enthusiasm for marijuana was due to the variable quality of the psychoactive substance found in the plant, THC (delta-9-tetra-hydrocannabinol).

Several social histories of marijuana published in recent years suggest that the events that moved marijuana from being considered a relatively harmless plant to the status of "killer weed" began with the Great Depression. The circumstances surrounding this redefinition include the migration of Mexicans into the United States and the scarcity of work. It appears that in the late 1920s and early 1930s the largest group of users of marijuana for recreational purposes was Mexican Americans. Ethnic prejudices against this immigrant group fueled by the high unemployment of the Great Depression evidently encouraged federal authorities to label marijuana a narcotic (Austin, 1979; Grinspoon, 1971; Sloman, 1979).

Does marijuana offer "one moment of bliss and a lifetime of regret"? Is it "the new drug menace destroying the youth of America" or "a violent narcotic. . . . the real Public Enemy Number One"? In the 1938 cult movie classic *Reefer Madness,* the answer to these questions was an unqualified "Yes!" What is the truth?

## Characteristics

Although it can be ingested, marijuana is usually smoked. The effects range from mild euphoria to shifting sensory images to hallucinations. Depending on the potency of the sample, the effects are usually experienced within a few minutes and can last several hours. The potency of marijuana depends on the concentration of THC in the plant. It is this chemical that gives marijuana its psychedelic qualities. Historically, much of the marijuana grown in the United States has contained a low concentration of THC. However, in recent years the THC content of American-grown plants has been increasing. Hashish and hashish oil, both derived from the marijuana plant, contain far more THC, so that the mind-altering effects of these two drugs are substantially greater. Marijuana is considered to have a low to moderate potential for creating a psychological dependence. Tolerance (the need for increasing amounts of a drug to maintain its effects) can occur (Jones, 1980; Petersen, 1980).

## The User/Abuser and the Family

Studies of the motivations and personal characteristics of marijuana users and nonusers show no differences. Occasional marijuana users are not seen as maladjusted or psychopathological in their use of this substance (Jessor, 1979; Pascale, Hurd, & Primavera, 1980).

In contrast, according to a recent study funded by the National Institute of Drug Abuse (NIDA), the homes and personal lives of mari-juana-*abusing* adolescents are conflict-ridden

(Hendin, Pollinger, Ulman, & Carr, 1981). The study said the relationships between parents and adolescent were strained to the breaking point. Marijuana-abusing adolescents acted out, often violently, at home and were frequently disruptive in school and other settings.

These young people viewed their parents as insensitive and uncaring toward them. Although all the families participating in this study were intact, each appeared to have a history of marital turmoil dating back to the early childhood of the marijuana-abusing adolescent. Of the 17 young people and their families involved in the study, "several . . . had at least one parent who was alcoholic, a characteristic which has been shown to be significantly correlated with adolescent substance abuse" (p. 71). These young people expressed a "high degree of self-hatred," indicative of low self-esteem (p. 20). Many appeared depressed, and at least one was suicidal.

In the opinion of the researchers, marijuana served several important functions in these young people's lives. The first was public expression of defiance against parental and community authority. Second was the self-destructiveness that seemed to mark the life of each participant. Third was the use of marijuana to numb the intense anger these young people felt toward their parents. Next, it appeared to the authors that these young people used marijuana to compensate for feeling "that they amounted to nothing within the context of their own families" (p. 76). Finally, marijuana permitted these adolescents to escape the competitive academic and peer pressures around them.

We can infer that, in those situations in which marijuana use becomes abuse, it is very difficult to attribute the decrease in personal functioning solely to the drug. Additional research findings that marijuana-abusing adolescents express a sense of alienation (Jessor, Chase, & Donovan, 1980) and experience weak parental control, affection, and support (Prendergast, 1974) raise a real question of whether it is the drug or the

**BOX 16-3**
*Does Marijuana Have Legitimate Medicinal Uses?*

In the 1851 edition of the *United States Dispensary* (cited in Sloman, 1979), marijuana was recommended as a treatment for more than a dozen ailments, from gout to insanity. In the 130+ years since the publication of that manual, other uses, associated more with pleasure than with medicine, have been found for this plant. Does marijuana have legitimate medicinal uses?

In recent years marijuana has found proponents praising its therapeutic qualities for open-angle glaucoma, asthma, vomiting in cancer therapy, epilepsy, tumor growth, depression, and alcoholism. It has also been suggested that marijuana may have an antibiotic action, reduce anxiety and pain, and be useful as a preanesthetic. In a recent review of the medical literature, Cohen (1980) has found enough evidence to support two of these claims and warrant further exploration of a third. The active ingredient in marijuana, THC, has proved effective in reducing the intraocular pressure associated with open-angle glaucoma. Additionally, many cancer patients undergoing chemotherapy seem to benefit from the use of marijuana. It appears that marijuana controls the vomiting caused by their treatments. Finally, the existing evidence warrants continued study to determine the effectiveness of marijuana as an anticonvulsant in the treatment of epilepsy.

young person's life environment that precipitates increased use. Further, since the marijuana-abusing individual is likely to be abusing other drugs, attributing decreased personal functioning to marijuana alone is highly unrealistic (Jessor et al., 1980).

Such a position does not mean that marijuana is without negative effects. Quite the contrary; it has been clearly shown, for instance, that marijuana and driving do not mix (Pace, 1981). Marijuana has been shown to impair short-term memory, and in persons with a history of emotional illness it may produce an acute toxic psychosis, including delusions, hallucinations, and agitated behavior (Jones, 1980). More research needs to be conducted to see whether there are long-term health effects similar to those of cigarette smoking before any move beyond decriminalization is considered.

 *Do you agree with the authors that the behavioral problems associated with marijuana abuse cannot be directly linked to marijuana?*

# COCAINE

*Some facts about cocaine:*

- It is estimated that in 1990 nearly 5.5 million young adults between ages 18 and 25 will admit to some use of cocaine (Richards, 1981).

- The number of graduating high school seniors who say they have ever used cocaine rose from 9% in 1975 to 16.5% in 1981 (Johnston et al., 1981).

- Cocaine abuse (daily use) among high school seniors in the graduating class of 1981 was reported to be 1/10 of 1% for that year (Johnston et al., 1981).

With the recent published reports of its abuse by athletes, movie stars, and the very wealthy, cocaine has acquired a degree of notoriety. Its history is particularly fascinating, for its use reaches back hundreds of years, to before the Incan Empire, and involves a pope, a soft-drink company, and the founder of the psychoanalytic movement.

Cocaine is found in the leaves of a South American plant, the coca shrub (*Erythroxylon coca*). Possessing religious significance for the Incans, coca was controlled directly by the Incan emperor, and its use was limited to the privileged nobility of that society. This custom changed with the invasion of the Spanish, who more freely distributed coca among the South American natives because they had discovered that its stimulant effect raised workers' productivity (Inglis, 1975).

Coca did not become popular in Europe until the mid-1850s, when it was introduced into a number of products ranging from patent medicines to wine. The wine, in particular a variety called Mariani's Wine, won a number of high endorsements, including one from Pope Leo XIII. The popularity of coca spread back overseas, this time to North America, where in Atlanta in 1886 a druggist introduced a patent medicine containing coca. Claimed to be a remedy for a number of ailments, Coca-Cola, as it was called, gained widespread popularity (Grinspoon & Bakalar, 1976).

Cocaine, the "kick" in coca, was chemically isolated in Germany, where it was used as a stimulant and as an anesthetic in eye surgery. The medical popularity of cocaine as an anesthetic, a reliever of depression, and a substitute for morphine in treating morphine addiction spread quickly. With no less an authority than Sigmund Freud describing it as a "magical drug," the popularity of cocaine moved from the medical to the public arena (Brecher, 1972).

Portrayed as a quick pick-me-up for the tired of mind or body, more enjoyable than alcohol and without the side effects, cocaine was widely used by the public for several years. Interest in cocaine diminished as reports began to come in that it produced strong psychological dependence, severe mental disturbances, and in some cases even death. Freud's own defense of cocaine abruptly ended with the emotional breakdown of a close friend, Dr. Ernst von Fleischl-

Marxow. Marxow was addicted to morphine, the result of treating nerve pain in the stump of a thumb amputated years before. It was Freud who struck on the idea of treating his friend with cocaine to end his morphine addiction. Freud succeeded in ending Marxow's morphine addiction, but Marxow quickly replaced his craving for morphine with a craving for cocaine, and his use of that drug soon reached such proportions that he developed a paranoid psychosis uniquely associated with severe cocaine abuse called the "cocaine bugs." An individual suffering from the "bugs" believes that insects and/or snakes are crawling on and under the skin. The sufferer of such hallucinations feverishly tries to dig through his skin in a futile attempt to rid himself of the creatures. This understandably unpleasant incident had such a profound effect on Freud that he forswore the use of cocaine from that time forward in his personal life and in his medical practice (Grinspoon & Bakalar, 1976; Petersen, 1977).

## Characteristics

Cocaine can be injected but is more frequently inhaled ("snorted"). Its effects on the user range from excitement and increased alertness to, in very large doses or with prolonged use, hallucinations and convulsions. Death can result from an overdose of 1.2 grams after oral ingestion or after applying 20 milligrams to the mucous membranes (Gay, Sheppard, Inaba, & Newmeyer, 1973).

Although the probability of a psychological dependence is considered high and tolerance builds rapidly, the high cost of cocaine ($125 a gram, or 1/30 ounce, at bargain-basement prices) makes it difficult to develop a habit (dependence). The abusing/dependent person must have access to large amounts of money or be dealing in the drug to support a habit. (This may change as increasing amounts of cocaine find their way into the country.) The most likely scenario to be found in so-called cocaine dependence is polydrug abuse; that is, the "coke" abuser is really abusing several drugs, of which cocaine is but one.

## The User/Abuser and the Family

Most of the published studies on pure cocaine abusers are more than four decades old and reflect a "reefer madness" attitude toward cocaine. For instance, according to one study (Seevers, 1939/1977), both cocaine and marijuana abusers

*While the media is filled with stories of the epidemic spread of cocaine abuse in the United States, the extent of the problem has yet to be accurately determined.*

have a deep "psychopathic desire to escape reality or a need to build up the personality. The addict to cocaine may be subjectively depressed, desire the drug intensely, and may commit murder to obtain it upon withdrawal. . . . The term 'psychopathic habituation' is posed to describe this type of condition."

Beyond the media reports describing cocaine abuse by celebrities, virtually no evidence exists to state with any degree of certainty the risks associated with the use of this drug. The few studies and commentaries that do exist portray users either as emotionally as healthy as the next person (Grinspoon & Bakalar, 1976) or as "presenting basic personality and maturational problems" (Connell, 1977). And next to nothing is known about the cocaine abuser's family life. What little is known suggests that cocaine abuse leads to serious individual and family problems. For example, Gold's (1984) study of 500 cocaine abusers using a toll-free hotline found most cocaine abusers to be in serious financial trouble. Nearly 26% were divorced or had lost a loved one because of their cocaine abuse. Another 28% were being threatened with divorce or separation. Given the high cost of cocaine, it is not surprising that abusers experience financial problems. Still, many questions remain unanswered, and additional research in this area is badly needed. We suspect that if there is such a thing as a pure cocaine abuser, the same family dynamics that move people to abuse other drugs are at work here too.

 *Why do you think cocaine has excited such concern among the public? Do you think that concern is warranted?*

# PROMOTING FAMILY WELLNESS
## Easing the Distress of Living with an Alcoholic Parent

It is clear from the material presented earlier in this chapter that young people living with one or more alcoholic parents are vulnerable. The preventionist believes that young people can be helped to survive this unfortunate situation.

## EDUCATION

To be a child in an alcoholic family is to feel alone, to feel forgotten, to feel sad. Prevention technology cannot change a child's family, but it can help that child realize that he or she is not alone and not forgotten and that people do care about his or her sadness. Alcohol and drug education courses in the school curriculum can help young people realize that others share the same problem.

In-service training for teachers to sensitize them to the needs of such children and to help them identify these young people is vital—not only to encourage teachers to extend themselves as caring and understanding people but to emphasize that young children should not be stigmatized for their parents' behavior.

Finally, thought needs to be given to sensitizing alcoholics to how their behavior affects their children. Such an educational program may not decrease parental abuse of alcohol, but it may at least encourage parents to support their children's efforts to seek help.

 *What other educational approaches would you use to help the children of alcoholic parents?*

## COMMUNITY ORGANIZATION/ SYSTEMS INTERVENTION

The CO/SI prevention technology assumes that structural changes in society will reduce the inci-
dence of some dysfunctional behavior. In this case the dysfunctional behavior is the pain the children of alcoholic parents experience. What causes that pain? The answer is clear—their parents' drinking. The solution is equally clear—stop the drinking. But can that be accomplished? This nation has experimented once with prohibition, and that experiment was a total failure.

In recent years interest has grown in the **distribution-of-consumption model.** This model states that there is a positive relationship between the amount of alcohol available in society and the number of alcoholics in that society (Parker & Harman, 1980; Smart, 1980). Proponents of this model direct their efforts not at eliminating alcohol from society but at better controlling its distribution. Recently passed federal legislation encouraging states to raise their drinking age to 21 is one example of this approach. Other applications would be to increase the cost of alcoholic beverages, prohibit the advertising of alcoholic beverages, or reduce their alcohol content (Gullotta & Adams, 1982).

 *Do you think the distribution-of-consumption model should be tried? Do you see any potential dangers in this model?*

## COMPETENCY PROMOTION

Powerlessness is a common feeling among children living with an alcoholic parent (Ackerman, 1983). Promoting positive self-esteem and an internal locus of control for this group of young people is important. Social competency can be promoted through activities such as values clarification and the encouragement of sensory awareness to increase self-understanding and self-acceptance. It can be promoted through programs conducted by the YMCA, YWCA, YMHA, and YWHA, by youth service agencies, and by church groups that involve young people in theater, wilderness courses, and other recreational or sports activities concerned with the individual's emotional growth.

 *How else might competency be promoted for this group of young people?*

## NATURAL CAREGIVING

Caring for oneself, for another, for each other—that is the essence of natural caregiving. For young people that spring of emotional support and strength can flow from several sources. Caring actions by the nonalcoholic parent can alter the family's destructive pattern of behavior. Friends, teachers, and the clergy can offer their ears as reflective listeners and provide the emotional support necessary to live with an alcoholic parent. Another form of care is the self-help group Alateen, founded on the AA model. Young people attend weekly meetings to discuss their problems and learn from others in similar situations how to live with an alcoholic parent.

The principle behind each of these caregiving actions is that people are interested, concerned, and willing to become involved in the life of another individual.

 *Invite a representative from AA or Alateen into class to learn more about how a self-help group functions and the importance that group has for its members.*

# SUMMARY

In this chapter we have looked at three substances and their effect on the lives of people who abuse these drugs or live with someone who does. Heavy drinking causes a multitude of medical problems that together lower life expectancy by 10–12 years and can be devastating to families, causing divorce, juvenile delinquency, and emotional problems in offspring. Marijuana, originally cultivated as a source of fiber, is grown today for its mind-altering effects. Although occasional users show no personality differences from nonusers, adolescents who abuse marijuana typically come from troubled homes and have serious personality problems. Cocaine was used medicinally until its undesirable effects became known—addiction, hallucinations and other mental disturbances, and sometimes death. Although dependence is easily established, the cost of this drug often discourages it.

Of the three drugs, alcohol causes the most harm, despite its social acceptability. Whether that would continue to be true if the other two were legally available is a question that we suspect will never be answered.

# MAJOR POINTS TO REMEMBER

1. Substance use is the infrequent and limited intake of alcohol or drugs. Substance abuse is frequent and excessive use of alcohol or drugs, impairing physical, mental, or social functioning. Substance dependence is addiction.
2. Americans consume almost three gallons of alcohol a year. Heavier drinking peaks at an earlier age for men than for women.
3. Hispanics have higher rates of heavy drinking than Whites. Many Blacks do not drink at all. Blacks who do drink closely match the drinking patterns of Whites.
4. Alcohol abuse has been linked to a number of health disorders, including heart-muscle disease, high blood pressure, stroke, reduced testosterone levels in males, and cancer. Alcohol use during pregnancy can harm the fetus.
5. Alcohol misuse is a major factor in motor vehicle, fire, suicide, and drowning fatalities. The cost of alcohol abuse each year in the United States has been placed at roughly $90 billion.
6. Developmental theory suggests that individuals abuse alcohol because their families failed to perform certain institutional functions, to play certain roles appropriately, or to facilitate passage through the life cycle.
7. Studies find that the abuse of alcohol by a family member hurts other members of the family socially and emotionally.
8. Marijuana was grown as a cash crop in the United States until the Civil War.
9. There are estimates that more than 17 million people between the ages of 18 and 25 will use marijuana in 1990. Occasional users show no personality differences from nonusers, but adolescents who abuse marijuana come from troubled homes and have serious personality problems. It is unclear, however, whether the problems that abusers experience can be traced solely to marijuana.
10. Cocaine was used in many patent drugs until the early 20th century.
11. It is estimated that 5.5 million young adults between ages 18 and 25 will use cocaine in 1990. Cocaine is a very expensive habit, leading to severe financial problems for those who cannot control their use of the substance.

# ADDITIONAL SOURCES OF INFORMATION

## Publications

Al-anon. (1973). *Alateen: Hope for the children of alcoholics*. New York: Al-Anon. [Early adolescents and older]

Al-Anon. (1977). *What's "drunk" mama?* New York: Al-Anon. [Late-elementary-school-age children whose parents are members of AA]

Griffin, J. H. (1977). *A time to be human*. New York: Macmillan. [Early adolescents]

Manning, W. O., & Vinton, S. (1978). *Harmfully involved*. Center City, MN: Hazelden Foundation. [Adults]

Seixas, J. S. (1979). *Living with a parent who drinks too much*. New York: Greenwillow Books. [Older children and early adolescents]

Woodward, N. H. (1981). *If your child is drinking*. New York: Putnam. [Parents]

## Organizations

Alcoholics Anonymous
468 Park Ave. South
New York, NY 10016
A self-help group for people who cannot control their alcohol use.

Narcotics Anonymous
P.O. Box 622
Sun Valley, CA 91352
A self-help group for recovered addicts.

Al-Anon Headquarters
P.O. Box 182
Madison Square Station
New York, NY 10159-0182
This organization sponsors self-help groups for alcoholics, their spouses, and their children.

# 17

# FAMILY VIOLENCE

1. What do Huck Finn, Pip, and Smike, have in common?

2. What are some characteristics of abusive parents?

3. What are some characteristics of abused children?

4. How is family violence related to unemployment?

5. What effect does a crying infant have on an adult?

6. How is family violence related to alcoholism?

7. Why do many women remain in abusing relationships?

8. Why is elder abuse unique?

9. Are Parents Anonymous programs effective?

[Nancy] was lying, half dressed. . . . "Get up!" said [Sikes]. "It is you, Bill!" said [Nancy], with an expression of pleasure at his return. "It is . . . Get up . . ." "Bill," said [Nancy] in the low voice of alarm, "why do you look like that at me!" [Sikes] sat regarding her, for a few seconds, with dilated nostrils and heaving breast; and then, grasping her by the head and throat, dragged her into the middle of the room, and looking once towards the door, placed his heavy hand upon her mouth. "Bill, Bill"! . . . gasped [Nancy]. . . . [Sikes] freed one arm, and grasped his pistol. The certainty of immediate detection if he fired, flashed across his mind even in the midst of his fury; and he beat it twice with all the force he could summon, upon [Nancy's] upturned face. . . . She staggered and fell, nearly blinded with the blood that rained down from a deep gash in her forehead. [Nancy struggled to raise herself, whereupon Sikes], shutting out the sight [of her] with his hand, seized a heavy club and struck her down [Dickens, 1894d, pp. 383–384].

Sikes' violence against Nancy (in what many would consider their common-law marriage) in *Oliver Twist* is not a rare incident in literature. For centuries, writers have recorded the violent times in which they lived, expressing their outrage at these conditions through their works. For this reason, it is hard to understand why, until a little more than a decade ago, family violence was not mentioned in the professional literature (Gelles, 1980), particularly considering that estimates of child, spousal, and elder abuse range from thousands to millions of incidents in each category every year (Bybee, 1979b; Gelles, 1980; Gelles & Straus, 1979a; Scott, 1977; Star, 1980; Starr, 1979). We may well wonder why this failure to see violence in the family existed, when, as Gelles and Straus (1979b) observe, no more violent social unit than the family can be found, with the possible exceptions of the armed forces and the police. In this chapter we will look at literature, history, theory, research, and the experience of mental health workers in trying to find explanations for why family members abuse one another. In this chapter we will also see what can be done to help the abused and the abuser and to end this pattern of violence.

## A LITERARY-HISTORICAL PERSPECTIVE

Literature is filled with examples of violence between family members, from the Bible to children's stories like "Cinderella," "Hansel and Gretel," and "Snow White." Even Shakespeare writes about cruelty against elderly parents (*King Lear*), spouses (*Othello, Cymbeline*), and children (*Titus Andronicus*).

When we remember the position of children and women in premodern times (see Chapter 1), violence toward them should not be surprising. Children were considered the property of their parents, and society rarely intervened in parent/child relationships even when the child was being abused. This same attitude of neglect, indifference, even resentment, was extended to women.

Premodern values, however, cannot explain the prevalence of family violence in literature of modern family times. To illustrate that prevalence, we have chosen two authors regarded as social commentators on their time—Charles Dickens and Mark Twain. Curiously enough, both lived during the period described in Chapter 1 as the "cult of domesticity." This was supposedly a time in society when apple pie, mom, and children were valued. They were valued in comparison with prior times, but as TV's Captain Kangaroo, Bob Keeshan, once observed, "In reality we can't eat very much apple pie, we divorce mother, and we usually ignore children" (Keeshan, 1983, p. A2). Both these remarkable writers illustrated this point throughout their long careers. Their novels abound with abuse

and neglect meeting the definition established by the National Center on Child Abuse and Neglect: "Abuse refers to an act of commission by a parent or caretaker resulting in harm to the child; while neglect refers to an act of omission by a parent or caretaker producing harm" (cited in Kinard, 1979, p. 83).

For example, consider the plight of Pip, living with his sister, the wife of the village blacksmith, in *Great Expectations:* "My sister, Mrs. Joe Gargery, was more than twenty years older than I, and had established a great reputation with herself and the neighbors because she had brought me up 'by hand'" (Dickens, 1894b, p. 6).

"By hand" often translated into the liberal application of a waxed piece of cane called a "tickler" to Pip's body:

> "Mrs. Joe has been out a dozen times, looking for you, Pip. And she's out now, making it a baker's dozen."
> "Is she?"
> "Yes Pip," said Joe; "and what's worse, she's got tickler with her. . . . She sat down," said Joe, "and she got up, and she made a grab at tickler, and she Ram-paged out. That's what she did . . . she Ram-paged out, Pip."
> "Has she been gone long, Joe?"
> "Well . . . she's been on the Ram-page, this last spell, about five minutes, Pip. She's a coming! Get behind the door, old chap, and have the jack-towel betwixt you."
> I took the advice. My sister, Mrs. Joe, throwing the door wide open, and finding an obstruction behind it, immediately divined the cause, and applied tickler to its further investigation. She concluded by throwing me—I often served her as a connubial missile—at Joe, who glad to get hold of me on any terms, passed me on into the chimney and quietly fenced me up there [protecting me] with his great leg [Dickens, 1894b, p. 7].

But *Great Expectations* is not Dickens' only comment on a caretaker's inhumanity to a child.

*Pip's sister—the Mrs. Joe Gargery—had "established a great reputation with . . . the neighbors [as a good parent] because she had brought [Pip] up 'by hand'"*

In *Oliver Twist* (1894d), Bumble, the parish beadle, cruelly mistreats the young waif. Smike is no better treated by the infamous Wachford Squeers, headmaster of Dotheboys Hall, in *Nicholas Nickleby* (1894c). Further, the poor and working class are not alone in their mistreatment of others, as Florence's treatment by her father in *Dombey and Son* (1894a) or David Copperfield's treatment by his stepfather Murdstone, ably assisted by his sister, Miss Murdstone, and a tyrannical headmaster named Creakle, amply demonstrate.

In fact, we believe parental neglect helps to explain why Ebenezer Scrooge, in *A Christmas Carol* (1843/1967), became a cruel, mean-spirited man:

"The school is not quite deserted," said the ghost. "A solitary child, neglected by his friends, is left there still."

Scrooge said he knew it. And he sobbed. . . .

[The boy, Scrooge, in his loneliness glanced at a door when] it opened; and a little girl, much younger than the boy, came darting in, and putting her arms about his neck, and often kissing him, addressed him as her "Dear, dear brother."

"I have come to bring you home, dear brother!" said the child, clapping her tiny hands, and bending down to laugh. "To bring you home, home, home!"

"Home, little Fan?" returned the boy.

"Yes!" said the child, brimful of glee. "Home for good and all. Home, for ever and ever. Father is so much kinder than he used to be, that home's like heaven! He spoke so gently to me one dear night when I was going to bed, that I was not afraid to ask him once more if you might come home; and he said yes, you should; and sent me in a coach to bring you" [pp. 48, 51–52].

By Dickens' time the value of women and children had improved from an earlier age when Romans operating under the principle of *patria potestas* permitted the male head of the household to sell, disfigure, or kill his wife and children (Bybee, 1979b; Dobash & Dobash, 1979). But not enough progress had been made to prevent passage of laws like the one in 1824 in Mississippi giving husbands immunity from prosecution for physically assaulting their wives (Davidson, 1977; Star, 1980). Nor was the 17th-century concept of *parens patriae* yet strong enough to protect a child from mistreatment (Brown, 1979–80). Children were still chattel (Bross, 1979) who, like one young child named Mary Ellen, might be saved from mistreatment not because they were human beings but because they were animals. It was with this argument that the Society for the Prevention of Cruelty to Animals interceded on Mary Ellen's behalf to save her from starvation and physical abuse. They argued that, as a member of the animal

**BOX 17-1**
*Premarital Violence*

Consider the words *romance, courtship,* and *love.* What images do these words convey to you? Are they images of two lovers walking hand in hand, of kindness and gentleness, of caring and concern? Or are your images of a couple pushing, grabbing, shoving, slapping, kicking, biting, and hitting each other? Most of us have assumed that courtship violence was a rare event. Only recently has society begun to realize that violence is not a stranger to courtship. Although the extent of courtship violence is uncer-

tain, two studies, one of college students and the other of high school students, found that 22.3% of the 355 college students and 13.1% of the 644 high school students admitted to some form of violence (Cate, Henton, Koval, Christopher, & Lloyd, 1982; Henton, Cate, Koyal, Lloyd, & Christopher, 1983).

Preliminary findings suggest that many of the patterns of abuse evident in other forms of family violence also appear to be present in courtship violence. For example, it appears that the abuser and the abused

often share the belief that the violent act was spontaneous, not premeditated. Violence does not necessarily end the relationship—many relationships continue. Finally, preliminary evidence suggests that individuals in violent relationships view themselves as "handicapped"— that is, as having "fewer alternative partners than those who broke up" their violent courtship (Cate et al., 1982, p. 88). The issue that we would like you to address is: How might courtship violence be prevented?

kingdom, she was protected by laws prohibiting cruelty to animals (Bybee, 1979b).

About this same time, Mark Twain was working on *Huckleberry Finn* (1884). Huck cannot escape his father's drunken rages through legal avenues. To survive, he must engage in deception and flee:

> The judge and the widow went to the law to get the court to take me away from him and let one of them be my guardian; but it was a new judge that had just come, and he didn't know the old man; so he said courts mustn't interfere and separate families if they could help it; he said he druther not take a child away from its father [p. 42].

In short, violence of one family member toward another did not cease with the advent of the modern family or the age of domesticity. The historical and literary evidence suggests an acceptance of this situation and a reluctance to intervene.

 *Identify with your classmates and instructor other passages from literature or scenes from films containing family violence. Can you identify the factors that caused this violence?*

## THEORETICAL EXPLANATIONS OF FAMILY VIOLENCE

There are scores of theories that attempt to explain family violence. We will examine these many competing schools of thought by separating them into two more manageable groups. The first group of explanations suggests that the problem of family violence essentially resides within the abuser and the abused. These we will call "psychological explanations." The second group sees family violence as originating not from within but as a reaction to forces surrounding the abuser and the abused. These we will call "sociocultural explanations."

## Psychological Explanations

In two recent surveys of the literature, Sweet and Resick (1979) and Gelles (1980) reviewed many of the explanations that might be labeled psychological, psychiatric, psychoanalytic, or behavioral understandings of family violence. Many authors using these psychodynamic perspectives have theorized that a defect in personality structure permits abuse to occur. For example, a parent's unresolved dependency needs may contribute to child abuse (Starr, 1979).

Terr (1970), for example, speculates that abusive parents fantasize about their child and that those fantasies originate from the parents' own childhoods. When this occurs in a relationship that is excessively dominant/submissive and the child is less than ideal in appearance or behavior, abuse occurs. Others believe that inability to control one's anger, low self-esteem, and low tolerance for frustration contribute to family violence (Starr, 1979).

Gillman (1980) suggests that women who remain with abusive husbands are those whose personality involves a split in their self-image. The abused woman has "two separate and quite distinct . . . representations; her lovable self in a warm, friendly relation to a good, providing husband-mother, and her helpless, worthless self who is in a hateful, destructive relation to a persecuting, damaging husband-mother" (p. 349). That is, women remain in violent relationships because they split the relationship into two parts. The first is rewarding; the second acts out unresolved issues in which the abusing husband represents the abused's mother.

Vasta and Copitch (1981) and Friedrich and Boriskin (1976) suggest that individuals contribute to the abuse they receive. The abused child, they note, is often flawed. The child may be pre-mature, retarded, handicapped, grouchy, or irritable—a far cry from the perfect "Gerber baby." If such children have caretakers who themselves are flawed by low frustration tolerance, low self-esteem, and so on, they are at high risk for abuse.

Learning theorists emphasize the importance of role modeling in explaining family violence. They suggest that abusers learned their violent behavior from others in early life (Sweet & Resick, 1979).

## Sociocultural Explanations

A second set of explanations places the causes of family violence outside the individual. Although sociologists do not deny that human beings are flawed, they are more interested in how society's structure and its operation aggravate these flaws, encouraging family violence. Some authors (for example, Brown 1979–80; Dobash & Dobash, 1979; Gil, 1973, 1975; Giovannoni, 1971) see family violence as emerging from a culture that permits—indeed, encourages—the use of physical force to control a loved one. As we pointed out in Chapter 1, historically husbands were (perhaps still are) expected to maintain family order, and the means and methods for maintaining order were left up to them.

Others such as Goode (1971) speculate that violence is the result of a loss of other options in the family. This view suggests that males, in particular, unable to adapt to a society that is redefining sex roles, retreat to more primitive responses and substitute force for reason and brutality for compassion and understanding.

Finally, other authors (Daniel, Hampton, & Newberger, 1983; Gil, 1973, 1975; Steinberg, Catalano, & Dooley, 1981) find evidence that society's inability to provide adequate employment opportunities encourages violence. The stress of unemployment or job dissatisfaction interacts with other elements to cause mistreatment.

The evidence that can be mustered in defense of these arguments will be examined next as we divide family violence into its three components—violence against children, against spouses, and against the aged.

*In your opinion, which perspective best explains family violence? Do you think husbands are, in today's society, still expected to maintain family order?*

# VIOLENCE AGAINST CHILDREN

The extent of child abuse still remains unknown nearly a quarter century after Kempe, Silverman, Steele, Droegemuller, and Silver (1962) introduced the possibility that the "battered-child syndrome" was not the figment of some over-imaginative author's mind. Estimates of abuse vary for countries reporting it, and ranges extend from thousands to millions. For example, Gil (1973) estimated that between 2.5 and 4 million young people in this country are abused each year. Light (1973), using Gil's data, esti-

mated the figure to be between 200,000 and 300,000. Nagi (1975), Cohen and Sussman (1975), and Kempe and Helfer (1972), counting actual reported cases, claim between 41,000 and 67,000 cases for the years studied. What are the dimensions of child abuse?

Gelles (1978) addressed this question in a study that involved a national probability sample consisting of 2143 respondents. Of these families, 1146 had members between ages 3 and 17 living at home. Defining violence as "an act carried out with the intention, or perceived intention, of physically injuring another person" (p. 584), Gelles reports that 63% of those families with children had exercised some form of violence against those children in the past year (see Table 17-1).

According to Gelles (1978), violence comes to reflect "a pattern of parent-child relations rather than an isolated event" (p. 587). Extrapolating from his findings to a national level, he estimates that as many as 1 to 1.9 million young people were "kicked, bitten, or punched in 1975" (p. 586). Somewhere between one fourth and three fourths of a million were beaten up, and perhaps 46,000 were confronted by parents attempting to use either a firearm or a knife against them. If these projections are even roughly close, it forces one to ask: How can this

**TABLE 17-1.** *Types of parent-to-child violence in a sample of 1146 families*

| | Occurrence in Past Year | | | | Occurrence ever |
|---|---|---|---|---|---|
| | Once | Twice | More than twice | Total | |
| Threw something | 1.3% | 1.8% | 2.3% | 5.4% | 9.6% |
| Pushed/grabbed/shoved | 4.3 | 9.0 | 27.2 | 40.5 | 46.4 |
| Slapped or spanked | 5.2 | 9.4 | 43.6 | 58.2 | 71.0 |
| Kicked/bit/hit with fist | 0.7 | 0.8 | 1.7 | 3.2 | 7.7 |
| Hit with something | 1.0 | 2.6 | 9.8 | 13.4 | 20.0 |
| Beat up | 0.4 | 0.3 | 0.6 | 1.3 | 4.2 |
| Threatened with knife/gun | 0.1 | 0.0 | 0.0 | 0.1 | 2.8 |
| Used knife or gun | 0.1 | 0.0 | 0.0 | 0.1 | 2.9 |

be? What clinical or research findings exist to explain this behavior?

With a skeptic's eye and properly heeding the caution of Bolton, Laner, Gai, and Kane (1981) that as many as 84% of the studies in this area are of an ex post facto design[1] with fewer than 10% of these having random samples, we will cluster certain findings that recur in observations and studies of child abuse.

One finding is that children of alcoholic parents are at greater risk of abuse[2] (DeLuca, 1981). Another is that child abusers were often themselves abused as children (Fontana, 1975; Kinard, 1980; Webster-Stratton, 1985). In addition, abusers are generally found to have an external locus of control (that is, to feel controlled by events rather than in control of events), to have poor self-esteem, and to be easily frustrated (Ellis & Milner, 1981; Frodi & Lamb, 1980; Starr, 1979; Vasta & Copitch, 1981). One of these studies, in particular, focusing on patience, tolerance, and frustration, deserves closer examination.

This study (Frodi & Lamb, 1980) used a small sample consisting of parents belonging to Parents Anonymous (PA)—a self-help group for parents at risk of abusing their children—and a control group. Both groups were shown brief videotapes of an infant who was either crying or calm and smiling. Measures of heart rate, blood pressure, and skin conductance were taken as signs of physical arousal indicative of tolerance. Both groups showed signs of irritation when viewing the crying infant. Interestingly, however, the PA group also showed these signs when watching the smiling infant. Frodi and Lamb (1980) conclude that the low frustration tolerances of abusing parents may gradually lead

them to perceive their child as an "aversive stimulus" that makes that child vulnerable to abuse.

A second and related body of research suggests that the bond between the abusive parent and the abused child was incompletely forged. This research is based on observations of species-specific maternal behavior patterns in the animal kingdom. Evidence suggests that children untimely removed at birth from their parents may be at greater risk of abuse (Yost, 1979).

Other clinical studies of abusers find that they may be depressed and at higher risk of psychosomatic complaints and of suicide (Carroll, Schaffer, Spensley, & Abramowitz, 1980; Ellis & Milner, 1981; Kinard, 1982b; Mogielnicki, Poffenberger, Chandler, & Weissberg, 1977; Roberts & Hawton, 1980).

Still other observations find that abusing parents either have low IQs or have highly unrealistic expectations for the behavior of their young children (Borgman, cited in Polansky, Hally, Lewis, & Wormer, 1977; Egeland & Sroufe, 1981; Elmer, 1979; Jones & McNeely, 1980; Newberger & Cook, 1983). Elmer (1979), for instance, reports the findings of several studies in which parents relied on their infants for emotional support and care. She mentions one study in which most abusive "mothers believed that infants should know right from wrong by twelve months, one third specified six months, and one mother thought a baby was born knowing right from wrong" (p. 63).

Other studies focus on the abused. Not surprisingly, since abusers tend to have been abused as children, these studies find characteristics in abused children that have also been observed in abusive parents. The children have been described as unhappy and depressed

---

[1] Ex post facto research designs examine the effects of naturalistically occurring events after the event has occurred. They differ from experimental designs in that there is no control group.

[2] It should be noted that Orme and Rimmer (1981) disagree with this position and argue that too little is known to make such a generalization.

## BOX 17-2
*The Molested Child*

The thought of using young children as sex objects is disturbing to many. And yet such exploitation is not uncommon. Before 1874, for instance, young people could legally enter into prostitution in England at the age of 12 (Baizerman, Thompson, & Stafford-White, 1979). In this century, although we don't openly violate young people, we still sexually exploit them. The authors suspect that a voyeuristic enjoyment, even among people who would never dream of molesting children, partly accounts for the popularity of the films *Taxi Driver, Hard Core,* and *Pretty Baby.* We also believe this same interest is what motivates manufacturers to produce, advertisers to market, and adults to buy form-fitting clothing for young children that, to our minds, offers them as sex objects.

Research on incestuous families describes the father as the dominant figure in the family, using his physical strength to hold other members in submission. He is often a heavy drinker. His marital and sexual relationship with his wife is unfulfilling (Taubman, 1984; Vander-May & Neff, 1982). It has been suggested that this flawed marital relationship may be due to his weak passive-aggressive personality and fear of heterosexual relationships with adults (Blumberg, 1981). Disturbingly, it appears that many wives of incestuous husbands are aware of the incest but do not act to stop it (Vander-May & Neff, 1982).

The victims of an incestuous assault are often passive participants. We use the word *often* deliberately: two rather different pictures of the victim's role in an incestuous relationship emerge from a review of the literature. The first describes the abused as passively cooperating with the assailant out of fear that he or she will be physically harmed or that the family will dissolve. The second position views the abused as a more active participant who may have encouraged or initiated the relationship (Vander-May & Neff, 1982; Yates, 1982). In either case, the abuser uses threats, deception, enticements, and manipulation to control the relationship with the molested child (Burgess, Groth, & McCausland, 1981; Perlmutter, Engel, & Sager, 1982).

As one might expect, the impact of sexual abuse on the child is often devastating. Particularly when a parent is aware of the molestation, the child "feels rejected, used, trapped, confused, humiliated, betrayed, disgraced, and fearful" (Vander-May & Neff, 1982, p. 726). The long-term effects of incest on children are unclear. Some escape permanent emotional harm and lead successful adult lives. Others are not so fortunate and experience emotional problems ranging from substance abuse to depression (Vander-May & Neff, 1982).

(Blumberg, 1981; Hjorth & Harway, 1981; Kinard, 1980; Yates, 1981). They are described as aggressive against other children or family members (Hughes & Barad, 1983; Kinard, 1982a, 1982c; Kratcoski, 1982). They may have lower IQs and an external locus of control (Barahal, Waterman, & Martin, 1981; Herzberger, Potts, & Dillon, 1981).

Evidence exists that child abuse is an outcome of the stress unemployed families feel. Steinberg et al. (1981, p. 982) found in their sample that "declines in the work force are significantly related to reported child abuse." In support of these findings, Kinard and Klerman (1980) found that the link between teenaged parents and child abuse does not exist except for *low-income* teenaged parents. Although Kinard and Klerman were unable to distinguish whether this abuse results from poverty or from a "disturbed family life" (p. 487), the evidence suggests that a lack of financial resources can measurably contribute to abusive behavior.

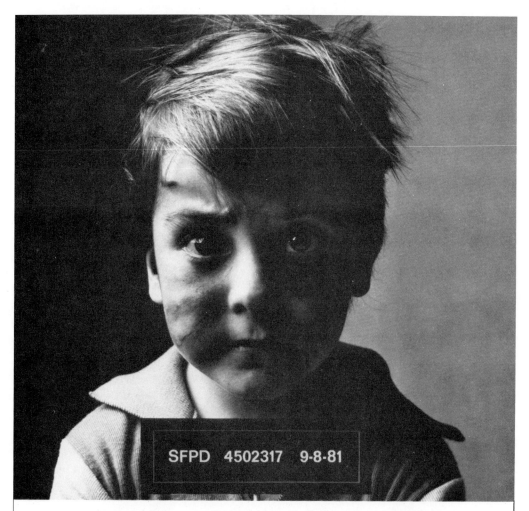

SFPD 4502317 9-8-81

## 4 out of 5 convicts were abused children.

In the United States, an average of 80% of our prisoners were abused children. That is why we are working so hard to help these children today, before they develop into a threat to others tomorrow.

With your support, we can have a full staff of trained people available 24 hours a day. Abused children desperately need us. Please let us be there to help. Write for our free brochure, or send in your tax-deductible donation today.

### San Francisco Child Abuse Council, Inc.
4093 24th Street, San Francisco, CA 94114

*This picture needs little explanation. It is estimated that perhaps as many as four million children are abused each year.*

Gelles and Hargreaves (1981) further explored this issue of the relation of stress to finances in a study of maternal employment and child abuse. Drawing their data from the national probability sample mentioned earlier (Gelles, 1978), these researchers interviewed 623 mothers and 523 fathers to uncover the level of violence present in their homes. They found that working mothers are not more likely to injure a child. Levels of child abuse were similar for women employed full-time, those employed part-time, and homemakers (Table 17-2). Interestingly, overall violence—all acts of violence whether they result in injury or not—against children in this study was significantly less for mothers employed full-time than for mothers employed part-time or staying home. Gelles and Hargreaves caution that this finding alone cannot be used to argue for increased employment opportunities for women. Rather, they point out that a woman at greatest risk for abuse is one who finds herself overburdened with family responsibilities and in a home with an unemployed husband. Gelles and Hargreaves (1981) conclude:

Gender equality in the home and in society can lessen the level of family violence . . . women need to have a major role in the decisions affecting their employment either in the paid labor force or as housewives. . . . Last our data provide additional evidence that unemployment among men has serious noneconomic, negative consequences for their families [p. 525].

 *Invite a child protection worker to class and explore with that person the factors contributing to child abuse in your area.*

# VIOLENCE AGAINST SPOUSES

The extent of spousal abuse in this country is unknown. Part of the problem is that it was not until the last decade that violence against one's spouse was even seen as a problem (Tierney, 1982). Since that time estimates of spousal abuse have ranged from thousands to millions (Gelles, 1980). Estimates suggest that some level of abuse is present in 30% (Rosenbaum & O'Leary, 1981) to 56% (Gelles, 1974) of marriages and cohabiting relationships and is a chronic problem in 13% of them (Rosenbaum & O'Leary, 1981). Ninety-five percent of those abused are women (Byles, 1982), and many are assaulted not once in the relationship but repeatedly (Byles, 1982;

**TABLE 17-2.** *Mother-to-child violence by maternal employment (percent of families who in the last year were violent toward their children)*

| Mother's Employment | Overall Violence[a] | Child Abuse[b] |
|---|---|---|
| Employed full-time ($N = 140$) | 57.6 | 17.1 |
| Employed part-time ($N = 102$) | 70.3 | 19.6 |
| Homemaker ($N = 373$) | 71.0 | 17.4 |
| | $\chi^2 = 8.684$ | $\chi^2 = 0.303$ |
| | $p < .05$ | $p$ N.S. |

[a] Defined as "all acts of physical violence ranging from slapping and spanking to using a knife or gun [p. 512]."
[b] Defined as "those items from the overall [violence] index where there was a high probability [of] causing an injury to the child [p. 512]."

**BOX 17-3**
*Violence against Women: Rape*

"Sexual relations with another person obtained through physical force, threat, or intimidation" constitute rape (Groth & Burgess, 1977, p. 400). It is an act that may be committed against either sex but is usually directed against women. Old understandings that the individual who commits the crime of rape is releasing pent-up sexual energy have given way in recent years to the view that rape is a violent, hostile act by one person against another (Groth & Burgess, 1977; Holmstrom & Burgess, 1983).

This understanding of rape as a violent act has led to a new interest in helping the victim and her family cope with this family crisis. It has also generated a new awareness and sensitivity to sexual relations within a marriage wherein one member is forced to participate (that is, marital rape).

In recent years several authors have described the suffering experienced by husbands, boyfriends, and other family members when a loved one is raped (White & Rollins, 1981). Holmstrom and Burgess (1979, p. 322) suggest that rape has an "enormous psychological impact" on husbands or boyfriends that generates many conflicting feelings within them. Some men, the authors report, identified with the rape victim and focused their concern on

her hurt. Others, "feeling betrayed or ashamed or repulsed" (p. 323), were able to focus only on their own hurt. Revenge was a common theme in these men's thoughts.

The relationship between husband and wife or between girlfriend and boyfriend is often strained after the crime. Many women experience a period of emotional disorganization, somatic complaints, fear, and desires (often acted on) to alter their lifestyle (Holmstrom & Burgess, 1979). Because their partner's reaction to this crime can vary from empathy to blame or repulsion, communication problems and sexual problems are common. Silverman (1978)

Gelles, 1974; Rounsaville, 1978). These estimates almost defy imagination when one considers that spousal abuse was "discovered" only recently. Who abuses and why are questions that deserve closer examination.

The cautions expressed earlier about the quality of child abuse research apply here as well. Problems in the design and conduct of studies of spousal abuse limit the credibility of research in this area (Gelles, 1982; Schumm, Martin, Bollman, & Jurich, 1982). We compared published research and clinical reports with our own clinical experiences and report here on results we found to be congruent.

Thus, we can report that men who abuse women either were themselves abused as children or witnessed abuse in their families (Gelles, 1980; Hilberman & Munson, 1977–78; LaBell, 1979; Petersen, 1980; Ponzetti, Cate, &

Koval, 1982; Rosenbaum & O'Leary, 1981). In particular, Rosenbaum and O'Leary (1981) found in their study of the children of 52 self-referred abused women that

the impact of spouse abuse in the husband's family of origin was highly significant. Abusive husbands were much more likely to come from families characterized by marital violence. . . . Of the husbands who were witnesses to parental spouse abuse, 82% were also victims of child abuse. . . . This highly significant result clearly indicated a tendency for husbands who had witnessed parental abuse to repeat the pattern [p. 697].

Many report that wives of alcoholics are at higher risk of abuse (Hanks & Rosenbaum, 1977; Koval, Ponzetti, & Cate, 1982; Ponzetti et al.,

**BOX 17-3**
*Continued*

encourages in his counseling interventions with such couples that families be educated to understand that rape is a violent, not a sexual, act. Anticipatory guidance can be helpful in explaining to family members the readjustment the rape victim must make to life after experiencing this brutalizing event. Family members need to let the victim mobilize her own coping resources and ventilate her anger, hurt, and suffering.

Sexual abuse at the hands of another is intolerable—even more so when that person is your marriage partner. Bowker (1983, p. 350) finds that, in comparison with violent marriages, "raping marriages are of significantly lower quality." It appears that marital rape is a feeble attempt to exercise power in the relationship. In large part this occurs, we suspect, because many men are caught in a masculine sex-role stereotype that is no longer (if it ever was) appropriate in our society. These individuals are vestiges of the past who desperately exercise their strength against those less strong. As Griffin (cited in Holmstrom & Burgess, 1983, p. 34) has disturbingly pointed out,

Many men appear to take sexual pleasure from nearly all forms of violence. Whatever the motivation, male sexuality and violence in our culture seem to be inseparable. James Bond alternately whips out his revolver and his cock, and though there is no known connection between the skills of gunfighting and love-making, pacifism seems suspiciously effeminate.

Holmstrom and Burgess (1983) suggest, and we concur, that rape, whether inside or outside marriage, will not be stopped until society changes its manner of socializing children and dispenses criminal penalties that communicate the revulsion society has for the rapist.

1982; Roy, 1977). It is important to note here that alcohol itself may not be the causal factor. Rather, as Ponzetti et al. (1982) point out, it reflects a style of coping and adaptation to stress. The sober drinker may be as abusive as the intoxicated drinker.

Numerous reports find the couple caught in the abusive cycle to be insecure, unfulfilled individuals. Rigid sex-role expectations combine with feelings of insecurity, jealousy, and possessiveness (Elbow, 1982; Hilberman & Munson, 1977–78; Ponzetti et al., 1982; Roy, 1977). The couple are isolated, with few outside friendships (Elbow, 1982; Gelles, 1980; Ponzetti et al., 1982). Finally, studies suggest that the abused woman views herself as helpless and controlled rather than in control (Elbow, 1982; Hendricks-Matthews, 1982; Weitzman & Dreen, 1982).

Drawing from this work and a sample of women admitted to a battered women's shelter, Snyder and Fruchtman (1981) have developed a five-type taxonomy that illustrates the complexity of human relationships caught in abusive cycles. Women labeled "type 1" in their sample have a stable relationship with the abuser; abuse is infrequent, rarely involving child abuse or sexual assault on the woman. Women in this type rarely make up with the abuser by having sexual intercourse after an abusive episode. Most rationalize the attack by attributing it to the abuser's drinking or "pressures" on him. Thus, it is not surprising to see that 90% of this type return to live with the abuser. Type 2 individuals live in very unstable and highly explosive relationships. They experience frequent separations. Violence, when it occurs, results in injuries. Sexual assault during the abuse is common, and sexual relations to make up afterward are common. These

*Battered women's shelters provide a temporary respite for the abused woman and her children, allowing a break in the cycle in which she often views herself as helpless and controlled.*

women are the least likely of the five types to return home once they have decided to enter a shelter. Of the five types, type 3 women live in the most fear of violence, and when violence does occur, it is the most severe. These women are the least likely to defend themselves. Child abuse is also present in these families. Type 3 women do not indicate a history of either abuse or neglect by their parents. Type 4 women are distinguished by the fact that they experience little abuse. It is their children who are abused, and so they enter the safety of a shelter in behalf of the children. The decision to leave home for these women is often permanent. The final type Snyder and Fruchtman describe have lived in violent homes most, if not all, of their lives. Having experienced abuse as a child and now as an

adult, type 5 women accept it as a part of their life. Often they enter a shelter only to temporarily escape the punishment they receive. Regrettably, these women are very likely to return to the abusing situation.

More than these internal factors are at work in spousal abuse. The stresses of unemployment, underemployment, and job dissatisfaction have also been linked to spousal abuse (Gelles, 1980; Ponzetti et al., 1982). Many authors point to a society whose basic structure has historically encouraged such violence. They argue that our society, with its continued sexual inequality, permits this abuse to occur (Dobash & Dobash, 1979; Gelles, 1980; Klein, 1981; M. Martin, personal communication, January 24, 1983; Sabo & Runfola, 1980). For example, Dobash and Do-

## BOX 17-4
## *Pornography and Violence*

Earlier in this chapter we expressed our indignation over the thrusting of children into roles in which they become sex objects. One might suppose that we oppose pornography as well. There is indeed, evidence that pornography is socially destructive. Diamond (1980), for example, argues that violence in pornography is a patriarchal response for the purpose of increasing social control over woman. Meyer (1972) and Baron (1974, 1978) find evidence that pornography increases levels of aggression in already angry males.

And yet, as Susan Gray (1982) has pointed out, the issue is more complex. Contrary to the beliefs of many, the typical consumers of pornographic material are not sick, twisted freaks wearing dirty raincoats; they are young, college-educated men who use "pornography most often as a means of enhancing the responsiveness and enjoyment of sexual intercourse with a stable partner. Younger [teenage] consumers without a stable partner usually use pornography to masturbate" (p. 388). Nor does Gray (1982) find that pornography generally incites violence. In fact, her review of the literature suggests that rapists and pedophiles (child molesters) were exposed to less pornography than the male population in general. We agree with her in part that society might be better served by focusing on power issues between the sexes than by restricting pornography. We will go so far as to say that *nonviolent* acts of whatever nature between two consenting adults are not offensive to us, but acts of violence or between nonconsenting adults or involving minors are. What is your position? Gray notes that some authors argue "that women have their own distinct pornographic genre in escapist romantic fiction whose heroines are often alternately raped and seduced" (p. 395). What do you think?

bash (1979) argue that times have changed very little since 1878, when Susannah Palmer assaulted her husband to find sanctuary from him in prison:

Her husband was a drunken costermonger, who took to thieving and tried to induce her to do likewise. He turned her out into the streets at night, in order to make room for another woman; in the morning he gave her two black eyes and knocked out five of her teeth. After a repetition of such scenes she left him, taking the children with her; but he pursued her, took her earnings from her, and sold her bed, all of which he had a legal right to do. At last, she took a knife and slightly wounded him. She had previously applied to the law for protection, but had been told that the law could do nothing as her husband had not deserted her. For assaulting her husband *she* [our emphasis] was sent to Newgate prison, where she expressed perfect contentment, because her husband could not get at her [Russell, 1935, cited in Dobash & Dobash, 1979, p. 5].

Evidence to support this position continues to abound, we feel, in a society that fills its airwaves, newspapers, and magazines with images of violence of one sex toward another.

 *Invite a worker from a local battered women's shelter to class and explore with that person the factors contributing to spousal abuse in your area.*

# VIOLENCE AGAINST THE AGED

As if we were traveling through an ever-narrowing corridor of knowledge, the information available in the professional literature on elder abuse is even more limited. There is no question that the aged in our society are at risk of abuse. Whether this almost never happens, occasionally happens, or frequently happens is uncertain. Steinmetz (1981) has estimated that 10% of the aged are at risk of abuse. Hickey and Douglass (1981), asking 228 professionals whether they had ever encountered elder abuse, found that 61.3% of those questioned had observed evidence of such violence. In another retrospective study of 404 older people admitted to a clinic for treatment, 39 cases (9.7%) were identified as having been abused (Lau & Kosberg, 1979). These threads of evidence are clearly not sufficient to determine the actual prevalence of elder abuse, and the urging of Rathbone-McCuan and Voyles (1982) for health-care professionals to search for additional evidence needs to be heeded. As Pedrick-Cornell and Gelles (1982) have pointed out, current estimates, including their own, are essentially guesses at the dimensions of this problem.

It has been suggested from the little knowledge we do have that elder abuse is a unique form of family violence. It is unique in that the victims may have once abused the abusers (Giordano & Giordano, 1984; Rathbone-McCuan, 1980; Steinmetz, 1981). It is unique in that the caregivers of the abused are likely to be women, and it is likely that these women will be abusing other women (Giordano & Giordano, 1984; Pedrick-Cornell & Gelles, 1982; Steinmetz, 1981). Reports suggest that caretakers may be overburdened with family responsibilities, and the additional stress of caring for a parent, particularly an ill parent, triggers violence (Douglas, 1983; Giordano & Giordano, 1984; Rathbone-McCuan, 1980). A 60-year-old son or daughter may be car-

ing for an 85-year-old parent while trying to help his or her children and grandchildren at the same time (Pedrick-Cornell & Gelles, 1982; Steinmetz, 1981). And as Steinmetz (1981) points out, the abused elderly may also be abusing their caretakers.

Lau and Kosberg's (1979) retrospective study provides some additional understanding of Steinmetz's observations. Of the 39 cases of elder abuse, 30 were women. Most of these (21 women) were widows. Eighty-six percent of those abused had been harmed by a family member. Lau and Kosberg suggest three possible reasons that such harm occurs. The first is that the abuser was himself or herself harmed. A second reason for inflicting physical or emotional harm on the aged may be to acquire their financial resources. A third possibility is found in the very fabric of our society, which places very little value on the aged. Whether this will change when one in eight of us will be 65 or older in the year 2000, we do not know.

> **?** *Do you agree with the authors' contention that society places little value on the aged? Do you agree with the authors' observation that societal factors may be more important than individual factors in explaining family violence?*

# IMPLICATIONS FOR TREATMENT

Several years ago a major mental health association devoted its annual meeting to the rise of new therapeutic techniques. By its count the number hovered around 500 approaches to solving the problems people experience in life. If our review of the treatment literature directed at family violence is any indication, we believe that number has grown by a hundred more. Numerous styles of individual, family, and group approaches have been suggested.

Many of the papers we reviewed proposed that the goals of treatment include establishing trust between the client and the therapist, improving client self-esteem, and assisting the client in placing his or her own painful childhood into the perspective of events unfolding today (Breton, 1981; Wodarski, 1981). Many of these papers also stressed the importance of immediately responding to calls for help, the need for group support in changing behavior, and the need for emergency shelter when the risk of physical harm is present (Brown, 1979; DePanfilis, 1982; Garbarino & Jacobson, 1978; Ostbloom & Crase, 1980).

Among the myriad treatment approaches ranging from play therapy for abused children (Eaddy & Gentry, 1981) to family therapy to transactional analysis (Shorkey, 1979), two often cited methods were behavior modification and group approaches. Interventions that emphasized a behavioral approach tended to combine conditioning techniques with extensive reeducation (Cautley, 1980) or with education alone (Burch & Mohr, 1980; Wolfe, Sandler, & Kaufman, 1981). Otto and Smith (1980) suggest that programs based on crisis intervention (that is, responding at the time of crisis) and using a behavioral model (that is, a group approach and a focus on cognitive restructuring of the client's sense of loneliness) have the greatest chance for success. They feel strongly that education programs must include attempts to change sex-role stereotyping and societal indifference to family violence. Cautley (1980), Burch and Mohr (1980), and Wolfe et al. (1981) have each re-

ported success with their particular variations of this general model.

Group therapy alone or in concert with other techniques is frequently mentioned in the literature (Courtois & Leehan, 1982; Edelson, 1984; Kruger, Moore, Schmidt, & Wiens, 1979; McNeil & McBride, 1979; Shorkey, 1979). Because the studies just cited lacked proper evaluation components to determine the success of treatment, these reports must be considered cautiously, and there is good evidence for exercising caution. A major evaluation study by the federal government suggests that the stopping of incidents of mistreatment depends not so much on the therapeutic approach as on the skill of the worker assigned to the case (Cohn, 1979). Of special interest is Cohn's report that individual counseling models were least effective in reducing the "future propensity toward child abuse and neglect" (p. 517): they worked in about 38% of the cases treated. Group therapy and/or parent education classes fared only marginally better, producing a 39% rate of reduced propensity. Significantly for prevention, the most successful approach combined lay counseling or Parents Anonymous programs with group, educational, and individual services. Disturbingly, even this "comprehensive approach" (Resick & Sweet, 1979) was effective little better than half the time (53%).

 *Why do you think Cohn found a combination of approaches more successful than individual counseling, group counseling, or parent education alone?*

## PROMOTING FAMILY WELLNESS
### Preventing Family Violence

As we have discussed throughout this book, successful prevention approaches cut across theoretical lines and apply each of the tools of prevention to the problem. The initiatives described here, when combined and applied to a population before family violence has occurred, will accomplish the preventionist's goal of reducing the incidence of new cases of violence in families.

## EDUCATION

The radio, television, and newspaper spots that awaken each of us to the existence of family violence in this country are all examples of the use of education to promote community awareness. Such efforts increase public and professional awareness of the problem and begin to influence opinion so as to discourage the future use of force against family members (Bybee, 1979a).

Education not only awakens our conscience to injustice but informs us as well. It can take as simple a form as NIMH's *Plain talk* series, explaining in Spanish and English why children become angry (Fried, 1980) or what women and men can do about spousal abuse (Kay, 1983). Educational programs to prevent family violence can occur in a number of settings, including schools. Of course, schools cannot make up for either a society or a family that deprives a child of a loving, protected, secure environment, and making family-life education an integral part of all school curricula is not a panacea. But helping young people understand family life, child development, and marital relationships will increase knowledge, and knowledge is a necessary ingredient in change (Marion, 1982). One example of a curriculum that has been developed to

do this is "Exploring Childhood" (Kruger, 1973). This series of lessons seeks to equip young people with some of the knowledge necessary for parenthood.

Another education effort would be prenatal programs to increase parent/infant contact by educating hospital personnel in the importance of such interaction and encouraging changes in hospital routine. These efforts to encourage parent/infant bonding extend also to encouraging parents to interact earlier and more frequently with their newborn (E. B. Gray, 1982).

*Explore with your class visitors (see "For Discussion" suggestions earlier in this chapter) what educational approaches they feel would work best to prevent child, spousal, and elder abuse.*

## COMMUNITY ORGANIZATION/ SYSTEMS INTERVENTION

Gil (1976, p. 33) once expressed the position of many of us when he observed that the primary prevention of family violence is "a political issue rather than a professional one." The purpose of community organization/systems intervention is to ensure that past societal inequities are stopped and not carried into the future. Many authors have argued forcefully, for instance, that the greatest contributor to family violence is poverty. The stresses associated with joblessness, housing unfit for habitation, inadequate clothing, and food are the causes of family violence, they argue. Until these issues are addressed and resolved, misery and cruelty will prevail (Daniel et al., 1983; Fanshel, 1981; Gil, 1976; Pelton, 1978).

An equally powerful argument is made by those who examine the cultural heritage of this nation and its treatment of children and women. This heritage of violence continues not only in overt physical abuse but in attitudes that continue to relegate women and children to inferior positions (Brown, 1979–80; M. Martin, personal communication, January 24, 1983). The view that these injustices can be corrected only on a societal level where family violence is treated as a crime and is resolved in a criminal court (Brown, 1979–80) is shared by many (Attorney General's Task Force on Family Violence, 1984; Costantino, 1981; Hemmons, 1981; Klein, 1981).

> It is our view that family violence must be combatted at the societal and not the interpersonal level. Combatting it at the societal level would be viewed as preventive; combatting it at the interpersonal level is essentially rehabilitative. Attacking the roots appears more beneficial than attacking the branches of a problem that has its foundation in the social structure and not in an individual's psychological make-up. Socialization patterns need to be analyzed for their contribution to violent behavior, and sex role expectations must become more fluid [Brown, 1979–80, p. 23].

Ford (1983) wisely cautions that this last course is filled with potholes. In his study of 325 abused Indiana women, the criminal justice system was less than responsive in prosecuting abusers. Until the historic reluctance of our legal and judicial systems to intercede changes, the prosecution process will remain "governed as much by chance as by rational procedures" (Ford, 1983, p. 463).

 *Do you agree or disagree with the authors' activist stance? Why do you maintain the position you do?*

## COMPETENCY PROMOTION

What suggestions might be offered to promote one's identification with a nonviolent society, to increase feelings of self-esteem and self-worth? One of the best actions that could be taken is proposed by Kempe (1976) and echoed by others (Alvy, 1975; Coolsen, 1980; Friedrich & Boriskin, 1978; Schmitt, 1980)—a mandatory national health visitor system. This system would be tax-supported and available to all new parents, who would be visited regularly by other "successful" parents and given help and advice on problems as needed. These lay workers, drawn from one's own community, would serve as links between families and the larger health-care systems, Kempe believes. Additionally, Martin (personal communication, January 24, 1983) argues that a healthy dose of feminism in the form of assertiveness training would have beneficial effects in raising the consciousness of all (but especially women) to the oppression women experience at the hands of an unjust society.

 *What possible dangers can you see rising from a mandatory national health visitor system?*

*Some authors caution that assertiveness training may increase violence against the victim. Explore with your guests in class their opinions on this subject.*

## NATURAL CAREGIVING

Natural caregiving helps people cope with the stresses of life. Evidence suggests that such lay care is important in treatment (Cohn, 1979; Hunter & Kilstrom, 1979). It is even more important in prevention. As discussed throughout this book, self-help works most effectively in natural, voluntary settings. The development of battered

In September 1984 the Attorney General's Task Force on Family Violence submitted its final report to the president. The first sentence of that report states that "progress against the problem of family violence must begin with the criminal justice system" (p. 10). The first recommendation of the report states that "family violence should be recognized and responded to as a criminal activity" (p. 10). In the following passage from the report, the task force discusses that recommendation. We ask that you read it carefully and then consider the following questions: How active should the government be in monitoring family behavior? Is family violence a crime against the individual, the community, or the state?

Family violence occurs in this country in staggering proportions. Each year thousands of men, women and children must deal with the tragedy of family violence. Although comprehensive and uniform statistics are not available, estimates from Task Force testimony indicate that family violence is a crime problem of shocking magnitude. Battery is a major cause of injury to women in America. Nearly a third of female homicide victims are killed by their husbands or boyfriends. Almost 20 percent of all murders involve family relationships. Ascertainable reported cases of child abuse and neglect have doubled from 1976 to 1981. In addition to the one million reported cases of child maltreatment, there may be yet another million unreported cases. Untold numbers of children are victims of sexual abuse, and uncounted older persons suffer abuse.

These intentional, purposeful acts of physical and sexual abuse by one family member against another must be defined and recognized by the criminal justice system as serious criminal offenses. A strong commitment by law enforcement officials, prosecutors, and courts in responding to family violence as a crime can aid in deterring, preventing and reducing violence against family members.

Contrary to popular myths, family violence cuts across all racial and economic lines. Victims of physical and sexual abuse come from all types of homes, even the very "best" of families. Violence has shattered the lives of men and women of all ages, representing every occupation and profession. The only major distinction between family violence and other criminal acts of violence is the relationship between the victim and the assailant.

The criminal justice system has responded inconsistently to acts of violence. Violence commited by a stranger is classified as an assault. If a person is apprehended after beating up a stranger, the usual result is an arrest and prosecution for assault and battery. Yet when one family member assaults another, it is commonly viewed as a family squabble, something less than a real crime. This disparity in the legal response to assaults

women's shelters by indigenous feminist volunteer organizations provides an excellent example of the help that can occur when people see a need and are moved to action. Many of the first shelters in the United States were totally volunteer efforts, providing assistance when many in our society still denied the existence of a problem.

A second example is Parents Anonymous, a self-help movement dedicated to helping parents not abuse their children. This organization uses the principles described in Chapter 2 of sharing both successful and unsuccessful parenting experiences in a group setting. From this sharing, parents learn from one another and gain, during and between meetings, the emo-

**BOX 17-5**
*Continued*

must be eliminated. The problem for too long has been viewed as a private matter best resolved by the parties themselves without resort to the legal system. Today, with increasing public awareness of the seriousness and pervasiveness of family violence, there is a growing demand for an effective response from all community agencies, particularly the criminal justice system. An assault is a crime, regardless of the relationship of the parties. A person beaten in the home is no less a victim than the person beaten on the sidewalk in front of the home. The law should not stop at the front door of the family home.

Traditional criminal justice practice in family violence cases has been to view an assault as a family disturbance, not requiring arrest. When an arrest does occur, law enforcement officers and prosecutors may fail to acknowledge the seriousness of the offense believing that the victim will be hesistant to cooperate. Penalties imposed by the court generally

do not reflect the severity of the injury or the number of prior convictions. . . . This under-enforcement of the law tells victims and assailants alike that family violence is not really a serious crime, if a crime at all. It is this widespread perception that has contributed to the perpetuation of violence within the family.

Assaults against family members are not only crimes against the individual but also crimes against the state and the community. Intervention by the criminal justice system can effectively restrain assailants and make them responsible for their violence like any other perpetrator of crime. Arrest by law enforcement officers sends a clear signal to the assailant: abusive behavior is a serious criminal act and will not be condoned or tolerated. Prosecution policies that are not dependent upon a signed complaint from the victim reinforce that message. Courts confirm it by imposing sanctions commensurate with the crime. Such measures not

only have a deterrent effect on the abuser but also provide protection for the victim.

Intervention by the criminal justice system must also recognize and be sensitive to the trauma suffered by the victim. . . . Reporting and successful prosecution requires victim cooperation. To achieve that cooperation after the initial call by the victim, law enforcement officials, prosecutors and judges, not the victim, must proceed with and monitor the criminal justice process. This not only reinforces the notion that abuse is a serious criminal act but also provides the victim the support necessary to participate in the criminal justice process.

The response of the criminal justice system, punishing the offender and protecting the victim, is a critical element of a community effort to reduce family violence. That response must be decisive and expeditious and, most importantly, guided by the nature of the abusive act and not the relationship of the victim and abuser.

tional support necessary to change their hurting behavior. Another example of such care is described by Sister Vincentia Joseph and Sister Ann Conrad (1980), who view the church as an ideal site for informal helping networks. They describe the efforts of many parishes to improve the quality of life of church members by increasing the feeling of community among these individuals. Besides the direct services that are an integral part of parish service, the authors emphasize the importance of informal neighborhood, family, church, and volunteer groupings. These groups are essential in fostering community-interested individuals. Such groups adopt a view of collective responsibility for individuals within the community in which they live. This is the very essence of self-help. In such environments cruelty to another is not condoned but condemned.

Finally, how can the efforts described in this chapter be financed? Acting on an idea first offered by Ray E. Helfer, the state of Kansas in 1980 created a Family and Children's Trust Fund. From a $7 surcharge on marriage licenses, the state raises more than $130,000 each year, which it distributes in grants up to $15,000 to projects working to prevent child abuse (Birch, 1983). Since 1980, 13 other states have followed Kansas' lead and passed similar legislation (Rowe, 1983–84). Those states (California, Iowa, Arizona, Michigan, Virginia, Washington, Alabama, Illinois, Mississippi, North Carolina, Oregon, Rhode Island, and Wisconsin) will, we hope, be joined by dozens more before this book appears in a revised edition.

 *How else might the programs described above be funded? Explore with your guests how their efforts are financed.*

# SUMMARY

Never has an area been so rich in observations but so barren in research as family violence. Explanations for family violence abound, and we suspect that all at some time or other are applicable. Clearly, no one theoretical explanation adequately explains all the cruelty humans do against their own kind. The existing evidence suggests that intrapsychic factors are at work in the family torn by violence, but equally powerful arguments suggest that societal factors are at least as important. The approach one must take is eclectic and involves fashioning initiatives that are not wedded to any one approach. Disturbingly, treatment approaches have been less than fully effective, and the hope of the future, prevention, has so far been applied only in partial doses using one or two of the four tools available.

# MAJOR POINTS TO REMEMBER

1. Family violence is not of recent origin. Numerous historical and literary examples of violence against children, spouses, and the elderly can be identified.
2. Psychological explanations of family violence suggest that its causes can be found within the abuser or the abused; sociocultural explanations of family violence find the causes in society.
3. It has been roughly estimated that between 2.5 and 4 million young people are abused (along a continuum from throwing something to using a weapon) each year. The vagueness of such estimates underscores the point that the true extent of child, spousal, and elder abuse is unknown.
4. Research shows that child abusers were abused as children, have an external locus

of control and low self-esteem, are easily frustrated, and have highly unrealistic expectations for the behavior of their young children.
5. Studies find that men who abuse women were often abused as children, may abuse alcohol, and maintain rigid sex-role expectations in their relationships with the abused women.
6. Unemployment has been identified as a contributing factor in spousal and child abuse.
7. Unique features of elder abuse are that the abused may once have been an abuser, that women may be abusing other women, that a parent is being abused by his or her child, and that the abused may currently be an abuser.
8. A myriad of treatment approaches have been proposed to address the problems of family violence. Those approaches considered most effective are multifocused, combining skilled help with education and natural caregiving.
9. Although family-life education cannot alone prevent family violence, helping young people to understand family life, child development, and marital relationships will increase knowledge, and knowledge is necessary for change.

# ADDITIONAL SOURCES OF INFORMATION

## *Publications*

Justice, B., & Justice, R. (1976). *The abusing family*. New York: Human Sciences Press.

Justice, B., & Justice, R. (1979). *The broken taboo*. New York: Human Sciences Press.

Pelton, L. H. (1981). *The social context of child abuse and neglect.* New York: Human Sciences Press.

## Organizations

Parents Anonymous
22330 Hawthorne
Torrance, CA 90505
Toll-free number: 800-421-0353
A nationwide self-help organization dedicated to helping parents not abuse children.

National Committee for the Prevention of Child Abuse
322 South Michigan Ave., #1250
Chicago, IL 60604
A national organization engaging in research and dissemination of information to prevent child abuse.

National Coalition against Domestic Violence
1728 N St. NW
Washington, DC 20036
An organization devoted to the prevention of domestic violence.

National Center for the Prevention and Control of Rape
5600 Fishers Lane, Rm. 15-99
Rockville, MD 20857
A federally funded organization devoted to the prevention of rape.

National Center for Child Abuse and Neglect
400 Sixth St. SW
Washington, DC 20201
A federally funded organization devoted to the prevention of child abuse and neglect.

# 18

# DEATH, GRIEF, AND THE FAMILY

I guess I was 14. You know how years have a way of dulling exact details. One thing I can remember is that Margie—that's my sister—had prepared lunch for me the night before. It would be hard to forget that lunch—peanut butter and marshmallow fluff on rye, with a pickle slipped in between the marshmallow and the peanut butter. I can remember sitting with a few friends in our school lunchroom trying to negotiate a sandwich trade. I would have traded that sandwich for anything, but I never got that opportunity. A school official interrupted those negotiations to tell me that my father had been rushed to the hospital.

During the trip home I can remember my sense of disbelief and my self-assuredness that my mother was overreacting. I was sure this was some minor problem that could be corrected, but I was wrong. My father died, leaving a mother, a brother, and a widow with three children, ages 14, 12, and 7. I don't remember crying. I can remember shock and an other-than-worldly feeling that I was, with my family, playing some role in a dream turned sour.

As I think about it now, I wish death had arrived differently for my father—not that death can be denied. But if given again the opportunity, the things I could have said, should have said. But death is not always kind. Thoughts left unspoken and opportunities not seized are lost [the experience of one of the authors].

The feelings expressed in the preceding passage have been expressed by others who have lost a loved one (Brandt, 1982). In this chapter we examine this feeling called "grief" that brings sadness and loneliness and, if left unresolved, erodes mind and body. In this chapter we try to make sense of the apparent senselessness of death for those who lose a parent, a spouse, or a child. We explore what can be done to facilitate the expression of grief so that grief does not permanently overshadow life. In so doing we

## Parental Death in the 17th-Century New England Colonies

Hard as it may be to imagine 24% of young people in 1900 losing a parent before they reached age 15, life was even harder and death even more frequent a visitor in colonial times. Adults fortunate enough to survive into their sixties were likely to have had two or more spouses. Couple this with high birthrates, and some rather complicated kinship patterns could emerge:

A man who married at age twenty-five, for example, might lose his wife when he was thirty-five, after she had borne him four or five children. He might marry a young widow with one or two children who would then provide him with several more. He might then die and she herself might remarry and have children in that marriage. One such "chain of marriage and re-

marriage" in Virginia from about 1655 to 1692 made up of "six marriages among seven people," yielded at least twenty-five children. A visit to this household in 1680 would have found the presence of children (ranging from infancy to the early twenties) from four of the marriages, some of whom did not have any parents in common [Scott & Wishy, 1982, p. 4].

venture into an area that, in the opinion of some authors, has been too often overlooked in marriage and family textbooks (Dickinson & Fritz, 1981).

## A HISTORICAL OVERVIEW

In a monumental effort extending for more than 17 years, the great historian Philippe Ariès has penned a work that chronicles our changing attitudes toward death, *The Hour of Our Death* (1981). In that book Ariès concludes that the oft-mentioned "ideal death" of passing away quietly in one's sleep is a far cry from attitudes held as recently as the late 19th century, which would have viewed such a death as cursed.

Then, people did not perish in hospitals surrounded by machinery, tiled walls, glaring lights, and concerned but nonetheless unknown strangers. Today, the chances of dying at home in one's bed, surrounded by familiar faces, are slim. Of those dying in New York City in 1967, 73% did so in hospitals (Ariès, 1981, p. 584). No, clearly customs of past times were different.

Death was less feared in past times. It was, for many, embraced as a new birth into a world less filled with misery, sickness, and despair (Kalish, 1985). Until the mid-19th century, death was a public rather than a private affair, in large part, we believe, because death was so common among young and old alike. As late as 1900, families with three children had a 50% chance of seeing one of them die before age 15 (Uhlenberg, 1980). Further, nearly one quarter of young people would see a parent die before reaching age 15.

During the Middle Ages and until the 14th century, mourning was public and open, with no attempt to hold back the sorrow or misery the family felt. The thought of burial was given little attention until the middle of the 12th century. Interment, if that word can even be used, meant literally rotting in garbage heaps. As the centuries passed, however, attitudes toward death changed from tolerance of its presence to an increasing attempt to withdraw from it (Ariès, 1981).

Burial practices, for instance, began to emerge. Some were quite ghastly: corpses were

# BOX 18-2
## Origins of Some Mourning Rituals (and Hollywood Screenplays)

The pomp and circumstance associated today with burial has a strange and fascinating history. Ariès (1981) shares with his readers the finding that, beginning around 800 A.D., the belief rose that prayers for the deceased might act as credits helping them gain entry into heaven. As the popularity of this belief spread, the demands on the religious community to remember departed souls overwhelmed its capacity to recall their names. The solution was to create a registry providing the name and a short biographical description of the individual. The name given to these lists: obituaries.

As any fan of Vincent Price movies already knows, graveyards and dead bodies have magical properties. Recounting some of these beliefs, Ariès establishes that historical fact often exceeds the wildest imaginations of screenplay writers:

> [The] bones [of a dead person] have the power to pre-

vent disease. It is recommended that they be worn around the neck or sewn into one's clothing, not as a memento mori, but for their intrinsic virtues. . . . Soldiers who carry with them the finger of a dead comrade are protected from harm. The soil of graves, especially the graves of hanged men . . . is . . . rich in therapeutic properties. . . . The list of the beneficial properties of the cadaver includes an aphrodisiac potion made from the ashes of bones of happily married couples and lovers. Even a fragment of the clothing of the dead cures headaches and hemorrhoids [p. 358].

The list continues. Ariès reports that, lacking CAT scan devices, the scientists of the period used such diagnostic tools as "divine water":

> You take the whole body of a man who had been in good health but had died a violent death, cut it into very

small pieces—flesh, bones, and viscera—mix everything thoroughly, and reduce it to liquid in an alembic. The resulting liquid . . . enables one to determine accurately the chances of recovery of someone who is seriously ill. [To do this] add three to nine drops of the blood of the sick man and agitate gently over a flame. If the water and the blood mix well, it is a sign of life; if they remain separate, it is a sign of death [p. 358].

Finally, Ariès explains that the fear of being buried alive gave rise not only to many a fine Gothic tale and many a poor horror film but also to precautions for avoiding premature burials. One of these precautions was to establish places where the presumed deceased person would lie in wait until all question of life had been resolved. These "shelters for doubtful life" are today called funeral homes (p. 401).

---

boiled in large vats to separate bones for burial from flesh and organs, and bodies were buried within the confines of churches. The practice of "waking" a body moved from its origin in the family home to other locations. The smell of death could no longer be accepted. Still, until the late 1800s, the act of dying among one's friends, in familiar surroundings, conscious and aware of one's environment, was the ideal death (Ariès, 1981). Beginning with this century, how-

ever, a cloak of secrecy descended around death. Only in the last two decades has this cloak been lifted and death, once again, been confronted and humanized.

Why is it that until recently society has hidden death from the living? Longer life expectancies, particularly lower infant death rates, have much to do with it. With death no longer a constant companion, the desire to escape the pain of grief intensified. The "tame death" (Ariès, 1981, p.

603) of accepting its arrival, bidding farewell to loved ones, and permitting mourning evaporated as humanity shrank back from the inevitable to set apart places for the old and ill to die. In so doing, humans may have delayed the realization of death's presence, but they have not ignored and cannot ignore its outcome.

# TO GRIEVE AND TO MOURN

## A Theoretical Perspective: Psychoanalytic Theory

Freud (1959, p. 313) once observed that human beings could not imagine their own death, because "our unconscious does not believe in its own death; it behaves as if [we were] immortal." He believed that any attempts to conceptualize one's own death were doomed to failure, for as "we attempt to imagine it we can perceive that we really survive as spectators" (p. 305). One could, however, recognize the death of others. In fact, Freud suggested that all human behavior might be rooted in the emotional pain and triumph that we experience when a loved one dies—the pain of the loss and the triumph at our own continued survival.

In psychoanalytic theory, the loss of a loved one (called a "love object") initiates the grief reaction. Grief is considered a normal reaction to loss. It arises when an individual recognizes that the "love object" no longer exists and then struggles with this realization. During this period, people may turn away from reality in an attempt to remain with the "love object." Psychoanalytic theory suggests that with time the person becomes able to release the love object and return to reality.

 *Use a different theoretical perspective from Chapter 2 to explain grief. What are the differences and similarities between the two explanations?*

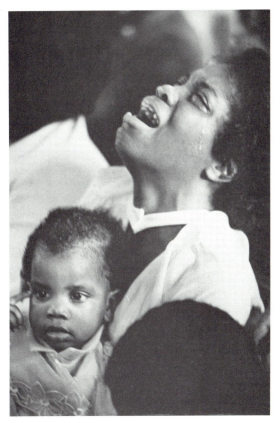

*A father expressed this woman's emotions nearly three centuries ago when he wrote, after the death of his children, "Lord, am I oppressed; undertake for me!" Centuries later the depth of that emotion remains unchanged.*

## The Phases of Grief and Mourning

Perhaps the most popularly accepted model of how an individual with a terminal illness responds to that realization and eventually comes to accept death (although acceptance does not always need to occur) is offered by Kübler-Ross (1969). She describes the grief process as unfolding in five phases: denial, anger, bargaining, depression, and acceptance.

In the first phase, denial, the ill person expresses disbelief at her condition and a rejection of that condition. A period of anger follows denial. Resentment, bitterness, and an urge to lash out may mark this period. The person asks "Why am I ill? Why me?" Having no satisfactory explanation of why God or fate should select her for this curse, she vents her emotions on those around her.

As anger exhausts itself, the period of bargaining begins. The person tries to negotiate with death for an extension of time, in the hope that if she does something differently, perhaps God will grant her a reprieve from her "sentence." Bargaining is a futile attempt to postpone the realization that the dying person is in fact slowly ceasing to exist.

The fourth phase, depression, occurs when the inevitable begins to become real. The prognosis is true. Bargaining does not change the outcome. In depression the person mourns her own loss of life. Helpless and hopeless, she struggles with the fact that soon she will no longer be.

In the final phase, acceptance, the ill person is neither angry nor depressed. This last phase is marked by resignation to her fate.

In a sensitive paper about her own impending death, O'Connell (1978), a graduate student at Rhode Island College, emphasizes the importance of hope throughout this entire process. Hope, she believes, must be permitted and should never be denied any ill person, no matter how poor the prognosis. Hope need not be for a miracle. It may be for a remission or for something as simple as one more day of life.

The work of Bowlby (1973, 1980) and Parkes (1972) is widely recognized as providing an understanding of the process of mourning a loved one's death (Balkwell, 1981; Greenblatt, 1978; Jacobs & Douglas, 1979). The mourning process begins, Bowlby (1973) believes, with shock and disbelief. The body reacts to the news of loss with denial and numbness as it grapples with the loss.

Next a period of yearning occurs in which the mourner searches for the deceased. In this phase anger, depression, fear, and physical changes such as weight loss or sleeplessness are common. As the mourner learns to readjust his life, he gradually comes to free himself from the loved one and readjust to the new environment. The bereaved works to reenter society and to participate in it. Finally, with the creation of new relationships and the establishment of a new role in life, the individual's identity is believed to have been reconstructed.

Parkes' (1972) model of mourning is similar to Bowlby's. This model identifies several commonly occurring behaviors during the process of mourning: denial, physiological arousal, searching for the lost person, anger, guilt, feelings of internal loss, and identifying with the lost one.

Each model presented is imperfect. As Metzer (1979–80) and Klass (1981–82) have discussed, the stage theory of Kübler-Ross (1969) does not withstand close examination. These explanations are subjective understandings of the grief and mourning process, not stage theories. Not everyone who is dying or bereaved follows each and every phase described. Some phases may last moments, some may never be experienced, some may linger in the person forever. However, despite their shortcomings, these models are helpful in structuring our thoughts about loss. They provide explanations of moments in time that, although they may not be experienced in totality, are felt at least in part by many of us.

## Excessive Grief

Normal grief, Freud (1959) believed, involved hurt, an inability to enter readily into new love relationships, and a loss of interest in activities not connected with the deceased. Normal grief may involve insomnia, guilt, hostility, and temporary inability to carry on with normal routines

(Jacobs & Douglas, 1979; Patterson, 1969). What separates "the gradual process of destroying the intense emotional ties to the dead person" (Patterson, 1969, p. 75) from pathological grief?

Excessive grief is protracted and involves complete despair, severe hopelessness, lost identity, impaired self-esteem, little interest in the future, and development of somatic complaints (Wahl, 1970). Such grief is more likely to be evident if the loss is sudden, if support systems are lacking, and if grief is delayed or suppressed (Greenblatt, 1978).

Why might grief be delayed or suppressed? Delayed grief may occur when a person is not sure the loved one is lost, as when a soldier is reported missing in action. Grief may be suppressed when, for example, the circumstances surrounding the loss are perceived by the mourner as embarrassing. The suicide of a loved one may violate a family's norms so that the death is not openly accepted. Since a normal part of grief is to make it "real" that the deceased will not be returning (Silverman & Silverman, 1979), grief that is suppressed or delayed can contribute to pathological grief.

Bugen (1977) has developed a model to predict the extent and severity of grief, based on the intimacy of the mourner's relationship with the deceased and the mourner's perception of how preventable the death was (see Table 18-1). If the relationship was important to the mourner and if the mourner perceives that death was pre-ventable, Bugen's model predicts a strong and extended period of mourning. The loss of a deeply loved husband from a heart attack who had complained of chest pains the night before would be an example. At the other end of the spectrum would be a relationship not central to the individual in which the loss was not preventable. The death of a distant relative, rarely a part of the mourner's life, after a long illness illustrates this second possibility. Using this model, we might suspect that the groups to be discussed in the rest of this chapter are at risk of pathological grief. The loss of a parent, a spouse, or a child suggests considerable pain during the mourning period. We will see in the next section whether this is really the case.

 *Why do you think we called this section "Phases," not "Stages"?*

## TO LOSE A LOVED ONE

The experience of death is not a single event in a person's life. It is true that each of us dies physically only once, but emotionally a little of us dies every time a loved one passes away.

### The Death of a Parent

> I think everybody knows that someday their parents are going to die, but it takes something to make it real. For me, I first realized my mom would die the day she asked if she could eat Thanksgiving dinner with us. You see, she always prepared the holiday meals and loved having the family over to her house. I knew then that she was getting old and would die [comments to one of the authors].

The death of a parent marks the end of a person's oldest relationship with another person. It

**TABLE 18-1.** *A model for the prediction of grief*

| Nature of Relationship | Nature of Death | |
|---|---|---|
| | Preventable | Unpreventable |
| Central | Intense and prolonged | Intense and brief |
| Peripheral | Mild and prolonged | Mild and brief |

is a sobering reminder of one's own mortality. For many, it is the loss of an individual who was unconditionally accepting and loving. It is an event that forces on many, perhaps for the first time, the realization that they are now adults and that they now constitute the older generation.

And yet, although this loss causes grief, the death of a parent is not associated in the research literature with excessive grief. Certainly, some individuals are emotionally devastated by the loss of a parent, but most adults cope with and eventually adapt to this event (Osterweis, Solomon, & Green, 1984).

What facilitates this coping process? As the comments opening this section suggest, the process may be assisted by anticipation of a parent's death. Advance acknowledgment that one's parents are growing older may moderate the severity of grief at the time of loss. Or, as another author has suggested, it may be that the death of a parent occurs at a time in the life cycle of adult offspring when they are so occupied with responsibilities that there is "little time to dwell upon the deceased parent" (Sanders, 1979–80, p. 318). In either case the hurt and sorrow accompanying an adult's loss of a parent are tempered, and the ability of most adults to go on living returns quickly. Typically, this is not so when a spouse or child dies.

> **?** *Do you agree that most offspring, sometime in their adult lives, come to admit and accept that their parents will die? Do you agree with Sanders' statement that an adult offspring's grief may be moderated by responsibilities to children, spouse, or job?*

## The Death of a Spouse

You've spent a good part of your life living with someone, caring for them, raising the children, sharing with them the sorrows and joys of your life—together. And then one day they're no longer there. You expect to hear them, see them, but they're no longer there. Sometimes I wish God would take me. I've so much I want to tell Mary [comments of a widower to one of the authors].

Numbers cannot express the feelings and emotions of this man. Numbers can, however, shape some impression of the dimension of spousal loss in North America, even though their sheer size may overwhelm our capacity to comprehend. In Canada, for instance, 20% of all new widows each year are under age 45 (Greenblatt, 1978). In the United States more than 12 million people are widowed, and 700,000 newly widowed people join this group every year. Ninety-two percent of people who lose spouses are women, and most of them are over 65 (see Table 18-2). Today, a married woman has a greater than 75% chance of becoming a widow sometime in her life (Balkwell, 1981; Gallagher, Thompson, & Peterson, 1981–82).

**TABLE 18-2.** *Widowhood among American females by age, March 1975*

| Age | Percentage Who Are Widowed |
| --- | --- |
| 14–17 | — |
| 18–19 | — |
| 20–24 | .3 |
| 25–29 | .4 |
| 30–34 | .7 |
| 35–39 | 1.4 |
| 40–44 | 3.0 |
| 45–54 | 7.7 |
| 55–64 | 19.4 |
| 65–74 | 40.8 |
| 75 and over | 68.9 |
| Total ($N$ = 10,104,000) | 12.1 |

Loss of a spouse affects one's life on three interrelated levels: physical, emotional, and economic. Physically, for instance, Parkes (1970) found that widows under 65 sought medical assistance three times as often as normally expected for their age group. They were hospitalized more often than the nonwidowed and received prescriptions for sedatives seven times as frequently as is typically expected. It has been suggested that the stress associated with spousal loss increases vulnerability to illness. Changes in the functioning of the endocrine system and neurotransmitters may help to explain the increased incidence of physical and emotional illness found in the bereaved (Jacobs & Douglas, 1979). Still more disturbing is evidence that grief can actually kill. There are several reports in the literature that mortality rates, particularly for men, are higher after the death of a spouse than would normally be expected. The most vulnerable time appears to be up to six months after the loss (Balkwell, 1981; Clayton, 1979; Lynch, 1979; McConnell, 1982). Although there are methodological problems with these studies (see Gallagher et al., 1981–82), the overwhelming weight of evidence points to the conclusion that widowhood is often damaging to one's health.

The widowed are also at risk of emotional illness. A number of studies find that loneliness increases substantially in widowed populations (Balkwell, 1981; Carey, 1979–80; Harvey & Bahr, 1980; Kivett, 1978; Scott & Kivett, 1980). Reports disagree over whether younger widowed persons are at greater risk (Blanchard, Blanchard, & Becker, 1976) or older ones are (Barrett & Schneweis, 1980–81; Sanders, 1980–81). Sanders suggests that increasing age diminishes opportunities, thus increasing feelings of hopelessness among the older widowed population. This position is supported by Barrett and Schneweis, who note that "the older person whose spouse died 16 years ago is just as unhappy, just as impoverished, and just as lonely as the recently widowed" (p. 102). Loneliness and hopelessness can

contribute not only to depression (Balkwell, 1981; Patterson, 1969) but even to suicide. The risk of suicide among widowed populations is 2.5 times as high as in nonwidowed groups during the first year after the loss and remains 1.5 times as high for the next few years (Clayton, 1979). In particular, the widowed man between ages 80 and 84 is at highest risk (McConnell, 1982). It is clear that grief, if unmanaged, can damage not only the body but the mind as well.

Compounding the physical and emotional elements of this life situation are the financial problems that often plague the widowed (Arens, 1982–83). Women are particularly affected. Many widows are living at or below the subsistence income levels set by the Social Security Administration (Balkwell, 1981). Those who appear to suffer the most are rural Black women, who, on average, see their husbands die seven years earlier than the White population (61 years for Black men, 68 years for White men). This group can only be described as the poorest of the poor (Scott & Kivett, 1980). The reduced living conditions of most widows force 60% of them to drastically reduce their standard of living. Many are forced into a labor market that often, because of their work inexperience, accepts them only at the lowest pay scale (Balkwell, 1981).

 *Why do you think the death of a spouse is not anticipated to the extent that the death of a parent is?*

*What factors do you think contribute to the higher suicide rate for aged widowers?*

### The Death of a Child

I didn't know anything was wrong. I had left him for only a few minutes. If I had known that

*Research studies suggest that the loss of a child is the most painful life event a married couple can experience.*

Timmy would—[soft sobbing begins, voice breaks] I would have never left him alone [comments to one of the authors by a mother whose child was a victim of sudden infant death syndrome (SIDS)].

*Grieving the loss of a child.* For one group in particular, there is no scale or rule of measurement that can adequately describe the suffering its members experience. These people are parents who have experienced a stillbirth or miscarriage or have lost an infant or a young child. In the case of a stillbirth or miscarriage, many authors believe a "conspiracy of silence" exists among the parties involved. This silence extends

beyond the parents to include friends, relatives, and medical staff. The suffering of the parents is particularly acute for mothers. According to several authors, mothers especially experience deep guilt and shame over their self-perceived failure. These writers suggest that to fill the void that contributes to the severity of the parents' depression, parents should be encouraged to mourn the dead child. They encourage hospital personnel to allow parents, should they wish, to look at and hold their deceased infant, to name the child, and to hold a burial service (Cohen, Zilkha, Middleton, & O'Donnohue, 1978; Kirkley-Best & Kellner, 1982; Lewis & Page, 1978; Stack, 1984; Stringham, Riley, & Ross, 1982).

The mourning process of parents, Chodoff, Friedman, and Hamburg (1963–64) find, is similar to the phases described earlier in this chapter. They observe that a worried anxiety precedes parents' shock and numbness on learning that their child will die or has died. A common feature of parents' grief is anger, expressed inwardly in depression or outwardly in resentment toward those who worked but failed to save the child. Coping mechanisms used by parents before the death of their child include intellectualization in an attempt to insulate their emotions from the unfolding events, denial of the actual situation, and physical activity. Physical activity includes walking, sewing, tapping fingers, and other "fidgety" behaviors. These "fidgety" behaviors are all desperate attempts to shed the physical anxiety that confronts parents who helplessly stand by, unable to assist their child.

*Sudden infant death syndrome (SIDS).* This helplessness is intensified when the child dies a victim of sudden infant death syndrome. In Chapter 1 we saw that infant care in premodern times was abysmally poor. The infant in Europe held the status of a nonperson. In large part this status can be traced to the reality that infants, even if well cared for, were very likely to die. It made little sense to become too attached to a child whose existence was, at best, an uncertain bet.

Today, these conditions have changed as infant deaths have become the exception rather than the rule. Children have gained partial recognition as human beings and a certain legal status in the eyes of society. Correspondingly, parents have come to bond sooner and more intensely to their offspring. Because family size is smaller and many births are now planned rather than chance events, each child holds a special status within the family constellation.

The demographics of this section apply, however, not to the rule but to the exceptions—those infants whose life has ended. Their numbers are small, only 8000 to 10,000, in comparison with the some 3½ million births each year. The leading killer of infants between the ages of 1 month and 1 year is sudden infant death syndrome (SIDS). It claims less than .3% of the infant population under age 1 (Aadalen, 1980; DeFrain, Taylor, & Ernst, 1982; Hawkins, 1980; Mackintosh, 1982; May & Breme, 1982–83; Weinstein, 1978). Statistically, this is a percentage that, when compared with earlier infant mortality rates, would be considered acceptable. But to the 8000 to 10,000 couples whose lives are shattered by this syndrome of uncertain origin, statistics do not matter. Nor do explanations that sudden infant death is an unavoidable chance death, possibly caused by amniotic-fluid infections, an underdeveloped carotid body, or a poorly developed heart, count for very much.

*The trauma of child loss.* The physical and emotional shock of losing a child is overwhelming. In a study comparing the intensity of grief experienced by persons who had lost a parent, spouse, or child, Sanders (1979–80) finds the loss of a child the most devastating. On every index except one, denial, parents show significantly elevated levels of anger, illness, despair, and poor health. Weinstein (1978) notes that this crisis is most often the first for young married couples. Moreover, in cases such as SIDS the unknown nature of the event tends to generate an atmosphere in which doubt, guilt, and anger lead to feelings of inadequacy. Young parents blame each other and then themselves for the sad and unavoidable death of their child. Despite assurances that they were powerless to save their child, each parent remains convinced that he or she could have prevented the event.

 *Can you explain the intensity of grief a parent feels after the death of a child using Bugen's model (see Table 18-1) and Hill's ABCX stress model (see Chapter 2)?*

**BOX 18-3**
*What We Know about SIDS*

Although the Bible provides evidence that SIDS existed in past times, not until recently have investigators tried to understand this syndrome. Epidemiological studies find that SIDS deaths occur most often in winter and spring, when respiratory illnesses are most frequent. Infants at greatest risk are Blacks, the poor, and those having teenaged mothers. Viral infections and botulism have been linked to some SIDS deaths, as have allergic reactions to milk (Valdes-Dapena, 1980). Recently, researchers have investigated with interest an organ located in our neck called the "carotid body" (see Figure 18-1). In many SIDS infants this organ is underdeveloped, which means it is not processing or is inadequately processing incoming nerve impulses from the respiratory-control centers of the brain. As Naeye (1980, p. 59) notes, "If this organ is not functioning normally, the infant may not be able to restart its breathing during a prolonged episode of apnea" (the cessation of breathing).

This work has led to the use of machines to monitor the breathing of high-risk infants while asleep. Results of these efforts are mixed: several babies have died while monitors were in use. One primary benefit of monitors seems to be the sense

of protection they offer parents who have lost a child to SIDS or have a high-risk child (DeFrain, Taylor, & Ernst, 1982).

Evidence suggests that SIDS may never be traced to one cause. The carotid-body explanation, though exciting tremendous interest, does not explain all SIDS deaths. As Naeye (1980, p. 61) points out, "At least one third of the victims have none of the postmortem signs that suggest underventilation of the lungs or chronic hypoxemia before death."

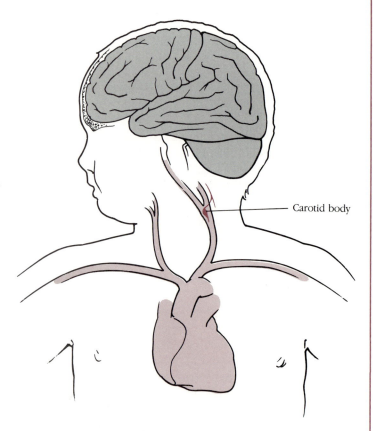

Carotid body

**FIGURE 18-1.** *Anatomical setting of the carotid body.*

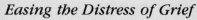

Most of the literature on counseling interventions to assist those experiencing excessive grief stresses the need for the counselor to facilitate the grief process. Counselors are encouraged to assist their clients in expressing their feelings about the deceased and examining and resolving feelings about their own mortality (Halligan, 1982). Clarke (1981) believes the most important characteristics for a counselor working with the bereaved are maturity, ability to listen, and willingness to be available when the bereaved need to share feelings.

Research on the effectiveness of such techniques with bereaved populations finds mixed results. Some work focusing on supporting the ego functioning of the bereaved finds that the grieving process can be assisted. Raphael (1977) reports that in an average of four counseling sessions she was successful in reducing client morbidity. Other attempts have not been so successful. Attempts to reduce acute grief using the therapeutic relationship as the means of intervention have, in some instances, increased client anxiety or extended dependence rather than diminished it (Williams, Lee, & Polak, 1976; Williams & Polak, 1979). These findings have led Williams and Polak (1979) to conclude:

> Most importantly, it appears that current intervention strategies are not effective nor appropriate and may even be harmful when utilized in major life crises. Certainly, those approaches that are predominantly person-centered, call for constant emotional release and conceptualize repression and denial as ineffective or harmful defenses are doomed to failure and possible harmful interference. . . . In this respect, [help] may be achieved more effectively by focusing upon basic education of the public of facts that involve major life crises and loss and the utilization of natural caregivers. The professional then becomes a consultant and educator rather than intruder [p. 44].

To this point let us add two more pieces of information. The first is the finding that many professionals are very poorly trained in bereavement counseling (Clarke, 1981; Stephenson, 1981). The second is that at least in two studies (Carey, 1979–80; Weber & Fournier, 1985) those professionals who might be imagined to be of most help frequently were not.

## EDUCATION

Williams and Polak's (1979) suggestion that education would be a useful effort is well taken. Educational activities could benefit not only the bereaved but professional helpers as well. One possible prevention strategy would be to sensitize doctors, nurses, and social workers to the process of death (Gullotta, 1982). Such efforts are called "death education" (Gibson, Roberts, & Buttery, 1982). Most death education courses use a dynamic group approach to help professionals become aware of their own feelings about death. It is believed that when individuals "can confront the meaning of their own death . . . death anxiety will diminish. With its decline the professional can extend the emotional care necessary not only to the patient but to that patient's family" (Gullotta, 1982, p. 12).

Education can also take the form of anticipatory guidance. For families that know a loved one is dying, help in the form of books such as *Questions and Answers on Death and Dying* (Kübler-Ross, 1974) or *The Chronically Ill Child* (McCollum, 1981) can assist the farewell process. Or anticipatory guidance can occur in group settings as family members work with others in similar situations to try to make sense of their circumstances.

A third educational strategy addresses the need for community information. Seminars providing factual information on such issues as life insurance, Social Security, veterans' benefits, food stamps, and probate court procedures could do much to allay the anxiety of the widowed (Gullotta, 1982). For instance, an excellent set of materials providing a framework for discussing many of these issues has been published by the Cooperative Extension Service at Pennsylvania State University. Entitled *The Family after 40 Series,* six booklets provide the basis for discussions in the areas of giving and receiving help, communication, finances, emotional changes, physical health, and living arrangements (Smyer, Davis, & Cohn, 1982).

 *What other educational approaches might be used to facilitate the expression of grief for each of the populations discussed in this chapter?*

## COMMUNITY ORGANIZATION/ SYSTEMS INTERVENTION

The second prevention tool acts to redress societal injustice that contributes to the distress a population is experiencing. The material reviewed in this chapter indicates several courses of action that could be pursued to ease the distress of the bereaved.

For instance, changes in Social Security regulations to end the reduction in benefits for those whose earnings exceed $4000 a year would ease the financial hardships of many widowed persons (Gullotta, 1982). Poor nutrition, lack of access to transportation (particularly in rural areas), adequate housing at affordable rents, and poor health care are other problem areas where change can be advocated.

One excellent example of advocacy leading to system change is the efforts of parents of SIDS children to encourage research into the causes of this syndrome and to sensitize the public to the plight of the bereaved parents. Reacting to the medical research community's lack of interest in the causes of SIDS (Naeye, 1980) and the often barbaric treatment parents were subjected to by hospital and police officials who assumed malfeasance without cause, groups of these parents organized to make the problem of SIDS visible to the community. They urged Congress to appropriate funds to stimulate medical research in this area and encouraged hospitals, police departments, and the wider community to develop services and procedures to spare future parents the additional agony of accusations by insensitive medical and police personnel who imply, with no evidence, that parental neglect was a cause of death (see Box 18-4).

 *Do you agree with the efforts proposed here? What other CO/SI efforts would you encourage?*

## COMPETENCY PROMOTION

To lose a loved one is to lose a part of one's own being. The bereaved experiences feelings of helplessness, worthlessness, and incompetence. Interventions that promote self-esteem and a sense of belonging are vital to counteracting Lynch's (1979, p. 8) observation that "loneliness and isolation can literally break your heart."

One possible intervention is to encourage consciousness-raising groups (Gullotta, 1982) to help the widowed make what Silverman (1970) calls the "three steps to recovery": making independent decisions, accepting the absence of the deceased spouse, and making new friends.

A second possible intervention is assertiveness training. The CO/SI actions taken by par-

BOX 18-4
## Suggested Interventions in a SIDS Situation

1. Every effort should be taken by those first arriving on the scene to save the infant's life.

2. On arriving at the hospital, the family should be provided with a private area equipped with a phone.

3. If the child dies, the family should be permitted to see their infant. The infant should be clothed and presented to the parents with tenderness and care, as one would a newborn infant.

4. An autopsy should be performed as soon as possible and all findings shared with the parents. The criteria for categorizing a death as SIDS should be standardized among pathologists in the area.

5. *Most important,* the hospital staff should be nonjudgmental and avoid any suggestion that the child has been harmed. Harm can be determined by an autopsy. Staff should be supportive, caring, and helpful. If SIDS is suspected, the family should be put in touch with the nearest SIDS organization. If no local organization exists, the hospital has the responsibility for helping to mobilize friends, relatives, members of the clergy, and other support systems to help the family cope with this painful loss.

ents of SIDS children could not have happened unless someone had been willing to protest the existing conditions. Assertiveness training develops people's ability to represent their own interests. For widows, who are often faced at the time of a spouse's death with numerous decisions, this ability to represent and defend one's own interests is crucial. Unfortunately, widows are too often the victims of high-pressure sales tactics by unscrupulous individuals regarding the purchase of goods and services or the sale of their own belongings. Assertiveness training offers the bereaved the skills to protect themselves from decisions that could endanger their emotional, physical, and financial health (Gullotta, 1982).

The final suggestion offered is a "widowline." Although this is really a self-help intervention, we include it here to illustrate how helping another promotes self-esteem. Widowlines are phone services staffed by volunteers who themselves are widowed, so that one bereaved person can help another. The widowline allows a widowed individual to be not only a recipient of service but a service provider as well. Mental health professionals report that such services have great therapeutic value in promoting health in the bereaved population (McCourt, Barnett, Brennen, & Becker, 1976).

*How else might competency be promoted in these populations?*

## NATURAL CAREGIVING

Extending oneself to assist another in a similar situation and, in turn, be assisted is one form of self-help. Evidence clearly suggests that those able to reach out to help others and to accept help themselves benefit in such areas as moderating the extent of depressive episodes and helping to resolve grief. One recent study, for example, finds that parents who participated in natural caregiving activities were better able to adapt to the loss of a child than those who did not (Videka-Sherman, 1982).

Silverman (1970), from her work with bereaved groups, disputes Lindemann's (1944) contention that grief lasts for four months. She suggests that it often extends for at least two years. Self-help groups acting on role-modeling principles permit those who have experienced the pain, the suffering, the loss of a loved one to assist others. Such help enables the widowed to accept the stigma of being widowed, Silverman believes, and to help others learn to live with that stigma. Encouragingly, studies are beginning to appear reporting the success of self-help group techniques in helping widows adjust to the bereavement process (Gartner, 1981).

One example of self-help can be found in the Ronald McDonald Houses. These community-sponsored homes, established with the help of the McDonald (fast food) Corporation, enable parents of very ill children to live near them during their hospitalization. More than simply being with their ill child, parents in these homes are brought into contact with other parents whose children are also very ill. From these contacts relationships emerge in which individuals share, listen, and provide emotional support to one another (Administration for Children, Youth, and Families, 1981).

Natural caregiving extends beyond the self-help movement to include each of us in helping others to live. One example of how this can translate into a prevention initiative is the "Carrier Watch" program developed by the United Way and the Letter Carriers Union of St. Louis, Missouri. This program is truly ingenious in its

*The Carrier Watch program is an example of natural caregiving and is an expression of concern and interest in other people.*

PART FOUR  FAMILY MATTERS OF CONCERN

approach to indigenous caregiving (H. A. Wright, personal communication, May 12, 1981).

Elderly or handicapped persons living alone are at particular risk of accidents and may suffer for days before being discovered. How might the incidence of undiscovered accidents and sicknesses be reduced? In St. Louis, people in these high-risk populations are encouraged to enroll in the "Carrier Watch" program. Participants provide basic information such as the persons to contact in an emergency, physician's name, and any special health problems. They receive a bright red sticker to attach to their mailbox. As letter carriers make their rounds delivering mail, should they find a "Carrier Watch" participant not picking up his or her mail, they report the omission to their immediate supervisor. This supervisor then contacts the social agency participating in this program. The social agency tries to reach the participant by phone or through friends or relatives. Should the social agency be unsuccessful, the authorities are contacted.

Programs like "Carrier Watch" assume that each of us has a responsibility for helping others.

This responsibility can be institutionalized in the form of a program like "Carrier Watch," or it can be individualized. For example, what can you do to help another who has lost a loved one? One thing you can do is to listen. Grieving persons need to be able to talk, to vent anger, to cry. Friends who allow grieving persons to express all their emotions without trying to restrain the emotions being expressed help them "put their confused worlds back into order" (DeFrain et al., 1982, p. 34).

What can you say to ease another's grief? No rehearsed or unrehearsed speech can ease the pain. "If we genuinely care, it will come through no matter how we fumble along" (DeFrain et al., 1982, p. 35). The important thing is to care and to accept the person and his or her grief.

 *Invite a hospice worker to class to discuss the approaches this program uses to promote caregiving between the dying patient and others.*

## SUMMARY

We have barely scratched the surface in describing interventions that could assist the bereaved in adapting to their new life situation. Much as we would like to deny it, death is inevitable for us all. We can learn about death and its impact on ourselves and others. But even with this understanding we cannot erase grief. Grief, sorrow, and mourning are all natural processes. What we can do in helping the bereaved is to ensure that grief does not permanently overshadow life.

## MAJOR POINTS TO REMEMBER

1. Over the last century, attitudes toward death have changed. In contrast to the past, when death's presence was openly acknowledged, modern society tries to hide or deny death.
2. According to psychoanalytic theory, we cannot imagine our own deaths but only the deaths of others. From this theoretical perspective grief is considered a normal reaction to loss.
3. In Kübler-Ross' theory of grief, a person comes to understand his or her impending death in five phases: denial, anger, bargaining, depression, and acceptance.
4. The mourning process of survivors can extend for months, even years. It involves several readjustment phases: shock or numbness on learning of the loved one's death, yearning for the deceased, freeing oneself from the deceased, and reentering society.
5. Normal grief involves pain, incapacity to readily adopt new love objects, and loss of interest in activities not associated with the deceased. Excessive grief involves complete despair, severe hopelessness, lost

identity, little interest in the future, and the development of somatic complaints.
6. Although the death of a parent is painful for adult offspring, it does not usually produce excessive grief. Two reasons have been offered—that as offspring grow older, they anticipate and prepare for their parents' death, and that adults are too busy with other responsibilities to dwell on the deceased parent.
7. The death of a spouse can affect the surviving spouse physically, emotionally, and financially.
8. The death of a child is a devastating life event for parents. Often it is the first major crisis a young couple face in their marriage.
9. Counseling interventions to reduce excessive grief have not always been successful and may do more harm than good.
10. Prevention initiatives cannot and should not eliminate grief, but they can ensure that grief does not permanently overshadow life.

## ADDITIONAL SOURCES OF INFORMATION

### *Publications*

Abbott, S. (1972). *Old dog.* New York: Coward, McCann & Geoghegan. [Young children]

Cleaver, V., & Cleaver, B. (1969). *Where the lilies bloom.* Philadelphia: Lippincott. [Adolescents]

Fassler, J. (1971). *My grandpa died today.* New York: Human Sciences Press. [Young children]

Grollman, E. A. (1967). *Explaining death to children.* Boston: Beacon Press. [Adults]

Langone, J. (1972). *Death is a noun: A view of the end of life.* Boston: Little, Brown. [Older youth]

McCollum, A. T. (1981). *The chronically ill child.* New Haven, CT: Yale University Press. [Adults]

Sargent, M. (1980). *Caring about kids: Talking to children about death.* NIMH, DHHS Pub. No. (ADM) 80-838. Washington, DC: U. S. Government Printing Office. [Adults]

## *Organizations*

Make Today Count
P.O. Box 303
Burlington, IA 52601
A national self-help organization for adult cancer victims.

Candlelighters
2025 I St. NW
Washington, DC 20006
A national lobbying and self-help organization for parents whose children have cancer.

National Sudden Infant Death Syndrome Foundation
310 South Michigan Ave.
Chicago, IL 60604
An organization dedicated to finding ways to prevent SIDS and to helping SIDS parents. Chapters are located in every state.

Widowed Persons Service
American Association of Retired Persons
1909 K St. NW
Washington, DC 20049
An informal clearinghouse able to provide information about how to start a self-help group for widowed individuals or where to find one.

Reach to Recovery
American Cancer Society
777 Third Ave.
New York, NY 10017
A program to assist women who have had a mastectomy.

Compassionate Friends
P.O. Box 1347
Oak Brook, IL 60521
For parents who have lost a child.

National Foundation for Sudden Infant Death
1501 Broadway
New York, NY 10017
For parents who have lost a child to SIDS.

Theos Foundation
Penn Hills Mall Office Bldg., Rm. 306
Pittsburgh, PA 15325
For the widowed and their families.

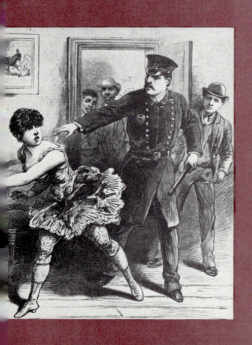

*Part Five*

# SOME FINAL
# OBSERVATIONS

# HERE TO STAY IN SEVERAL WAYS

## Questions to Guide Your Reading

1. Was society more caring in the past?

2. What was the practice of *vendue*?

3. In the past, could elderly parents rely on their children for help?

4. Have children, women, and men profited or suffered from recent changes in sex roles and responsibilities in the family?

5. What does the future hold for the traditional family?

6. Will birth rates continue to drop in the 21st century?

7. How might government react to a continued decline in the birth rate?

8. How might economic conditions affect the future of family life?

***Does the family*** have a future? Consider the following statement by Lasch (1977):

> Most of the writing on the modern family takes for granted the "isolation" of the nuclear family not only from the kinship system but from the world of work. It assumes that this isolation makes the family impervious to outside influences. In reality, the modern world intrudes at every point and obliterates its privacy. The sanctity of the home is a sham in a world dominated by giant corporations and by the apparatus of mass promotion. . . . Increasingly the same forces that have impoverished work and civic life invade the private realm and its last stronghold, the family [p. xvii].

Next, consider this statement by Bane (1976):

> The extended family is not, in fact, declining; it never existed. Family disruption has not increased but has only changed in character. The proportion of children living in single parent families results to a great extent from mothers keeping their children instead of farming them out. Mothers have changed the location and character of their work, but there is no evidence that this harms children. Nor is there any evidence that contemporary families have fewer neighbors and friends to call on for help and companionship now than in the past. In short, American families are "here to stay" [p. 70].

Finally, consider Shorter's (1977) view of the future of the family:

> The nuclear family is crumbling—to be replaced, I think, by the free floating couple, a marital dyad subject to dramatic fissions and fusions, and without the orbiting satellites of pubertal children, close friends, or neighbors . . . just the relatives, hovering in the background, friendly smiles on their faces [p. 280].

433

Three authors, all publishing their work within two years of one another—yet each has a different view of the future of family life. If the present strikes you as being uncertain, the future is even more so. If there is a lesson to be learned in either judging the present or predicting the future, it is that nothing is certain. Generalizations can be made and trends can be spotted, but for every generalization there is an exception. For every trend, contrary evidence exists to restrain the author's language from a word like *unquestionably* to a more modest phrase such as *it appears that.*

In previous chapters, we looked at families from both a historical and a contemporary perspective. In this chapter we intend to review some of the material presented earlier with an eye toward dispelling several myths. We also intend to look into our admittedly hazy crystal ball and speculate on what family life might be like in the 21st century.

# FAMILY MYTHS

Probably a day doesn't go by in which one of the authors doesn't hear someone saying "How I long for the good old days! Times were so much better then." The life of each of us consists of an accumulation of memories—memories of yesteryears when our problems and the problems of the world were, or at least appeared to be, manageable in comparison with the troubles we face today. But were the good old days really that good? Or is it that with each passing day we tend to forget the unkindnesses, the cruelties, and the injustices we experienced and remember, perhaps even cherish, only the laughter, the joy, and the excitement that in our minds belong to yesteryear?

In a time of change, a time filled with global threats of nuclear destruction, a time of growing international economic interdependence, and with all of us living in the throes of the second great industrial-technological revolution, the past as portrayed by Currier and Ives does indeed appear benign, comforting, and nurturing. But was it really that way? Was the family "a haven in a heartless world," as Lasch (1977) contends? Were homes sweeter, marriages stronger, and children happier? In the sections that follow, let's examine some of these commonly held beliefs and see whether the broad generalization "the good old days" applies.

## *The Myth of a Caring Society*

One common theme expressed by supporters of the good old days is that contemporary society is coming close to resembling the biblical Gomorrah. It is true that the present generation is more open in discussing sex than previous generations. And it is also true that this generation has shown a certain degree of tolerance for different sexual preferences or practices. But one does not have to search very hard to find that our ancestors engaged in a number of sexual practices and preferences that undoubtedly would shock many today.

For example, child prostitution was common throughout Western society. Indeed, it was not until 1874 that England first regulated the age at which an individual could enter into the practice of prostitution. After that year, children under the age of 12 were no longer permitted to be prostitutes (Baizerman et al., 1979). Should you consider the sexual exploitation of children a rare event or one found only in the lower strata of society, consider the diary of the 17th-century French court physician Heroard and his description of the early childhood of the future king of France, Louis XIII:

> Louis was also given complete freedom to express his curiosity about sex. He was allowed to explore what we would call pornographic picture books, and no one prevented him from

TAXI DRIVER © 1976

*The prostitution of children is not unique to our time. Remember that in England, prior to 1874, a child younger than 12 could legally engage in prostitution. Our world is not perfect today, but in the past it has been decidedly worse.*

Some die-hard proponents of yesteryear's virtue may argue that Europe was morally corrupt. Why, they might say, how can one be shocked about Louis XIII when that same society permitted women to wear dresses so low-cut and laced so tightly that a woman could balance a teacup on her bosom? And didn't Agnes Sorel, the mistress of Charles VII, introduce "the original topless gown," which "allowed the full charm of her left breast to be displayed while the right one remained modestly hidden away" (Murstein, 1974, p. 133)? Look instead, these moralists might say, to the settlers of the New World for virtue.

You may be smiling now as you recall the desire of the "pious" Reverend Michael Wigglesworth to leap into holy matrimony with his adolescent housekeeper. To that historical anecdote, we should add the observations of Morgan (1973) that even though Puritan society placed God before sex, the Puritans were no prudes. Rather, they viewed human sexuality from a practical standpoint, applying a liberal measure of understanding to instances of adultery and rape in the early days of the Massachusetts Bay Colony.

We offer for your consideration our observation that every society in history has explored and experimented with sex. Ours is no better or worse than those that came before us.

Another theme expressed by believers in the "good old days" is that back then we cared for one another. Society, they claim, had no need for social service agencies dispensing goods, services, and advice. Back then we needed no "Big Brother" in government to tell us what to do. Families were self-producing units that cared for themselves. When families needed help, they turned to their neighbors and found it there.

It's true the days of self-reliance are gone. The economy of the United States has shifted from many small, relatively independent producing units to a few large interconnected, interrelated, and interdependent units. And we agree with

playing sexually with his younger sister. When he was a little older [about 5] his forays became more ambitious: "Put to bed, he asks to play, plays with Mademoiselle Mercier [one of his ladies-in-waiting], calls me, saying the Mercier has a cunt as big as that, showing his two fists, and that there's a lot of water inside." As a result of these explorations, as well as of the marked outspokenness of the adults around him, Louis knew a great deal for a five year old. He was acquainted with prostitution, adultery, and sexual intercourse, which he had obviously been allowed to observe [Hunt, 1970, pp. 162–163].

*Many children spent their time working in the fields or the mills back during what some call "the good old days."*

those who call for a return to yesteryear that greater diversity in the marketplace would be nice. But although we may see some benefits in increasing the number of producing units in this nation, we shed no tears for a time in our society when children as young as 4 found themselves working in New England mills (Reynolds, 1977). Nor do we find a wealth of evidence to suggest that an earlier American society cared very much for the old, the poor, the orphaned, or the infirm.

Instead, examination of past land records and wills finds the older adult population protecting their estates in order to provide for their old age. Greven (1973) reports, for instance, that most young men in 17th-century Andover, Massachusetts, did not marry until after their 25th birthday. In large part, their delay in marriage can be traced to their fathers' unwillingness to provide them with land to enable them to achieve economic independence. By keeping their sons "down on the farm," the landowners of this community were able to avoid a fate that befell many a poor soul.

The fate we refer to was *vendue*. Vendue was the means by which many early New England communities cared for their indigent. In one community after another, those unable to care for themselves were auctioned off to the *lowest* bidder to be supervised at community expense.

The "caretaker" had a right to demand the services of auctioned individuals to help defray their keep (undoubtedly one of the first examples of workfare). As no profit was to be found in feeding the vendued individuals heaps of sausages, fowl, bread, and corn, they often went hungry. As no profit could be made by lavishing warm clothing and a pleasant, restful home on them, they often went ill-clothed and poorly housed.

No, self-sufficiency, for all the glamour and romance of the concept, meant, in the past, taking care of yourself before caring for someone else. Certainly, our present society can be faulted on many accounts for its lack of humanity, but in comparison with the past, present society is no worse (and, we might argue, is even better) than our ancestors in caring for the needy.

> **?** *Do you agree with the authors that today's society is no more sexually perverted than those that went before it?*
>
> *In your opinion, are the authors correct when they claim that modern society gives better care to the needy than past societies?*

## The Myth of a Caring Home

"Be it ever so humble, there's no place like home" is the cry of those who long for a return to past times. Now, don't get us wrong—we believe as much as anyone else that Dorothy (of *The Wizard of Oz*) was correct when she observed "There's no place like home." Our concern is with the era in which this home exists. Frankly, we see in the past little of redeeming virtue as it applies to the home. For one thing, the ages that came before the present time were sexist. Society insisted that women belonged before a stove, not out in the larger world. Little witticisms such as "A woman's place is in the home," "A wife should be kept barefoot and pregnant," and "Don't trouble your little mind with such worries" all contributed to a society in which it was absurd to imagine, even as late as 1858, that women could ever be expected to move beyond the kitchen stove. Thus the dialogue in *The World Upside Down: A Vision of the Future* (see Box 19-1) has the good Mrs. Poppington first desiring equality, attaining that equality in a dream, and then, once reawakened, thanking the heavens that women were in a subservient position to men.

Nor do we find much evidence to support the contention that children had it much better in the past. Certainly, practices such as swaddling and wet nursing do little to encourage the belief that infants were highly valued. The cruelty dispensed to women could be equally applied to offspring, and neither wife nor child had 're-course to the courts. Though never exercised, the Puritan statute permitting parents to take the life of a habitually disobedient child is a sobering reminder of the doctrine that children were the legal property of their parents. So strong was this doctrine that a child's mistreatment at the hands of her parents was halted only because she was an animal (see Chapter 17). When the court found in Mary Ellen's behalf, it did so not because she was a human being but because she deserved the protection extended to other animals. In fact, it was not until May 15, 1967, in the famous *In re Galt* decision, that the Supreme Court extended to children the protections guaranteed to all adult Americans by the Constitution and the Bill of Rights.

Granted, the proponents of yesteryear may concede, all family life was not rosy, but at least there was kinship. Families were extended, and support networks spanned three generations or more. But was this the case? Certainly, if one examines Hollywood's version of the American family, this understanding holds true, but the Hollywood image is flawed. The truth is that our

The schoolbooks of the early to mid-1800s contain many fascinating examples of the social mores of their time. The selection below is from a school play performed on July 27, 1858, at the Boylston School in Boston. As you read the dialogue, imagine the reaction of the audience to Mrs. Poppinton's "absurd" dream of women being equal to men. Consider also how this "vision of the future" appears today, more than a century after it was first performed.

THE WORLD UPSIDE DOWN
A VISION OF THE FUTURE
by W.T.A.
(Play)

Enter Mrs. Poppington

**Mrs. Pop.:**

*I will not stand for it! It will drive me mad!*
*No lady ever such a husband had!*
*To be a woman is to be a slave,*
*And crouch submissive to the wedded knave*
*Whom lord and master tyrant custom makes,*
*And all her manhood from the lady takes.*
*Adolphus treats me kindly, it is true,*
*Is sentimental, sweet, and loving, too;*
*He gives me money with a generous hand,*
*And every luxury of every land;*
*But after all, I'm not content with these—*
*I am his slave, and chains my spirit freeze.*
*Adolphus votes; but I, his wife, can't vote,*
*Or speak in caucus to a point of note.*
*Adolphus deals in stocks on 'Change to-day;*
*But I, his wife, must not in State Street stay.*
*Adolphus is a councilman this year,*
*Which I, his wife, may never be, I fear.*
*Adolphus is a member of the General Court.*
*Can make a speech and sign a state report;*
*But I, his wife, the general court must shun,*
*And my speeches and reports to one.*
*Adolphus yet may go to Congress, too,*
*Be governor, president, 'fore he gets through;*
*While I, his wife (the truth I dread to own),*
*Can only be plain Mrs. Poppington.*
*Why should not woman have her natural right,*
*And vote, make speeches, go to Congress, fight,*
*Be captain of a militia, or marine,*
*And run for office—run with the machine?*
*I should do well in Congress, I protest;*
*They only talk, and women do that best.*
*Upon my word, I vastly like the plan.*
*How fine to be a lady Congressman!*

ancestors were physically dirty. Their bodies were dirty. Their homes were dirty. Living in septic conditions and with primitive medical care, our ancestors considered themselves lucky if they lived to see 50.

Hollywood's images portraying children, both parents, and grandparents living together in the past do not reflect a common pattern. It was not divorces or relocations but death that separated biological family members. It is easy to forget the role death played in earlier times, as its visits today are rarer in early life and of greater predictability in the course of the life cycle. But in the past, death was a constant companion to all, regardless of age. Recall, if you will, that a woman's life expectancy in 1789 was about 36 years (Grabill et al., 1973). A man's life expectancy during the same period was about 45 years (Vogel, 1982). Recall also that as late as 1900 a family with three children had a 50%

438

**Box 19-1**
*Continued*

I'm sure I should make a first-
rate one—
. . . The Honorable Mrs. Poppington! (Gapes and yawns)
'Tis all in fancy—that's a sad
mishap;
I'm getting sleepy, and I'll take
a nap.

In her dream Mrs. Poppington's
wishes come true and the sexes
reverse their roles, as the following selection illustrates.

Enter Mr. Poppington in haste

**Mr.**
My dearest Julia, such a state
I'm in—
The baby's swallowed such a
monstrous pin!
I'm frightened out of half my
wits;
I fear that I shall shake myself
to bits.

**Mrs.**
Adolphus, where is all your
firmness gone?
(Sternly)
If you've no courage, put a
little on.

Run for the doctor; but be very
calm—
The pin can be removed, and
do no harm.

**Mr.**
He'll choke to death; I know he
will, my dear;
These women never know what
'tis to fear.

The dream continues with all of
Mrs.—or should we say Ms.?—
Poppington's wishes coming
true. Finally she awakens.

**Mrs.**
Dear me! Where am I? What a
funny dream.
What odd conceptions through
my fancy gleam.
Ah, woman's rights! I've enough
of that—
My husband acting like a frightened cat.

Enter Mr. Poppington

**Mr.**
Congratulate me, Julia; we have
won—
I'm Honorable Mr. Poppington.

**Mrs.**
I'm glad you are, and that it is
not I
Who go to Congress—from that
post I fly.

**Mr.**
You, Julia? Are you mad? On
mischief bent?
A woman never yet to Congress
went.

**Mrs.**
And never will, most earnestly I
trust;
I hope I may not be a candi-
date,
or come to any other dreadful
fate.

**Mr.**
Why, have you still your wits? I
almost doubt it.

**Mrs.**
(To audience) But, ladies, I
have come to this decision:
When we are sent to Congress,
in a vision,
That 'tis not real we should
thank our star—
Be thankful we are what and
where we are.
(Exeunt)

chance of seeing one of those children die before age 15, and nearly one quarter of young
people in 1900 would see a parent die before
reaching age 15 (Uhlenberg, 1980). These facts
of life gave rise to situations like those detailed
in Box 18-1 in which, through marriages and
remarriages, children could come to belong to
neither stepmother nor stepfather.

These circumstances inevitably lead to the
conclusion that the intact nuclear family so lov-
ingly depicted on television in the 1950s is of
recent vintage. The chances that a couple would
live together long enough to see all their children reach age 15 and that those children would
survive the birthing process and measles epidemics (see Chapter 1) and other childhood diseases were slim. The odds that these same parents would see their children reach adulthood
and have their own children as the parents settled into retirement were incredibly long.

No, the proponents of yesteryear are not remembering family life as it existed but as they wished it existed. Perhaps they will have greater success as we examine the third myth—that of the individual.

**?** *Do you agree with the authors' contention that home life was less than ideal 100 years ago? Should the state have a greater role in protecting children's rights? If the state were to assume a greater role in protecting children's rights, would that make a child the "property" of the state?*

## The Myth of the Individual

The final myth to command our attention is the belief that society has intruded into the area of individual rights, depriving man of the opportunity to fully realize his vision. We consciously use the word *man* here because this final myth contains at least one grain of truth. Until recent times, men have had tremendous latitude in their handling of women and children. This freedom to do as they wished also extended into the workplace in that they did not need to fear competition for employment from women. Thus, the proponents of this third myth are at least partly correct. The value judgment that must be made here is whether the redistribution of power to children and women has been of greater value than the loss of power to men.

As you may already have guessed, our position is that this redistribution of power has benefited all parties concerned. Women in the present age of equity have been able to act on Mrs. Poppington's dreams of escaping the kitchen and fulfilling their individual destinies, and society is the better for it. Children have escaped their historical role as chattel and in most of Western society now hold at least the

*The status of children within the family has improved significantly in the last half century. Some might even say that the child is now the center of the family.*

status of a junior member of the human race. The children's rights movement still has a long journey to make before children are extended full membership in society. Nevertheless, if you review the descriptions of childhood in past times that have filled the pages of this book, you can only conclude that progress has been made and that society is the better for it.

Finally, we believe that men too have profited from these changes. It is true that some men continue to long for the past when women "knew their place." But many more have come to appreciate the benefits that accrue from having two wage earners in the family, being able to share decision making in the family, and being able to express rather than conceal their emotions. As the past straitjacketed women into a narrow set of behaviors, so too did it confine men. The loosening of these restraints has enabled both men and women to grow as human beings. And, in our judgment, society is the better for it.

So much for our myths. We cannot escape them. They will always be with us. In fact, new myths will emerge as we grow older and view our own time and youth as the good old days. But what do all these changes hold for the future? What changes should we expect to see in the 21st century? These questions will be addressed in the rest of this chapter.

 *We feel men have profited from the increased power that children and women have gained over the last few decades. Do you agree?*

## FAMILY LIFE IN THE 21st CENTURY

It is with no little hesitancy that we venture into this last section. The prophecies of past soothsayers continue to haunt us. For example, at the turn of this century, some foresighted futurists predicted that every woman who wanted employment would find it, while others feared the literal burial of our cities. On the basis of the information available at that time, both predictions could have come true. First, the case of full employment for women. At the turn of the century, telephone operators were needed to complete every phone call made. As phone service was expected to grow and only women were phone operators, it made sense to predict a growth in the employment market for women. What about our compatriots who feared the bur-

ial of this country's great cities? They based their projections on the flow of horse-drawn traffic through metropolitan areas. These experts carefully calculated and recalculated a disturbing set of irrefutable statistics establishing the date at which metropolitan areas would be buried under an ocean of horse manure. Yes, that's right—horse manure.

These illustrations demonstrate the hazards of looking forward. Who in the 1890s, for example, could have predicted the invention of communication satellites, computers, lasers, and the host of other technologies that have revolutionized communications and limited employment opportunities for both women and men as phone operators? And can we really fault our turn-of-the-century futurists for not imagining a horseless carriage?

We must forgive these ancestral soothsayers, for as we now look forward a mere decade and a half to the beginning of the 21st century, who rightly knows whether the shadows we see are "the shadows of the things that WILL be, or are shadows of the things that MAY be" (Dickens, 1843/1967, p. 128)? For as the great novelist once observed in a magical and wondrous tale of an old skinflint he called Scrooge, "Men's courses will foreshadow certain ends, to which, if persevered in, they must lead. . . . But if the courses be departed from, the ends will change" (p. 128).

### Sexuality

We suspect that permissiveness with affection will continue to be the dominant form of sexual expression among young and old alike into the 21st century. The standard of abstinence has never been rigorously applied to males, and with changes in society's attitudes toward many sexual issues, coupled with the availability of safe, inexpensive contraceptives, women are emotionally freeing themselves from this standard. Inevitably, a decline in the abstinence-for-women standard will create a decline in the double standard. We do not see a significant rise in the sexual standard of permissiveness without affection, for two reasons. The first is a woman's apparent need for emotional intimacy in a relationship before physical intimacy occurs. Second is the fear of contracting genital herpes, a fear that has significantly reduced indiscriminate sexual relations for many. We suspect this fear will continue to depress the incidence of permissiveness without affection.

 *Do you agree with the contention that for most women emotional intimacy precedes physical intimacy?*

## Singlehood

The number of persons living alone has risen dramatically, from 1.4 million in 1970 to 4.3 million in 1978 (Bronfenbrenner, 1981). This growth is projected to continue at least through 1990 (Masnick & Bane, 1980). Will this trend continue into the 21st century? We believe it will, provided that society continues to express a neutral to benevolent attitude toward single people. Should this nation in the 1990s become alarmed over its shrinking youth population, social attitudes will produce a decrease in the number of people who remain single.

## Delayed Marriages

The phenomenon after World War II of late teenage marriages is a historical anomaly. The recent trend for couples to delay marriage until their midtwenties is, in fact, a return to earlier practices (Levitan & Belous, 1981). We believe this trend will continue, because women will continue to want the opportunity to receive a higher education and to develop a career before entering into marriage.

 *Do you think people can be pressured into having a child? Are only women delaying marriage? What reasons might men have for delaying marriage?*

## The Traditional Family

The image of the American family as pictured by Hollywood in the 1950s and early 1960s will apply to some families but not all. Joining the traditional nuclear family in equal numbers and acceptance will be the single-parent and remarried family (Cherlin & Furstenberg, 1982). Alternative family structures will remain just that, alternatives unable to attract much attention.

We believe family life and the government will be more closely linked in future years. We expect that before this century is over child care will be universally provided, supported by the tax dollar. Schools will admit children at the age of 4, and many children will have completed high school by their 16th birthday (Goodlad, 1984). Government interest in children will increase as the birthrate continues to decline. This interest will be motivated by the increased value each child will have in a rapidly aging society. The 17 federal agencies that presently administer 270 programs that affect families (Levitan & Belous, 1981) will remain, but policy will be less contradictory. A real possibility exists that the government will develop policies to encourage families to have children, as many European nations are already doing (Fuchs, 1983; Westoff, 1978; see Box 19-2, page 444). Incentives such as tax credits, free medical care, guaranteed "flex-time" work schedules, extended maternity and paternity leaves, and a shortened work week may be enacted before the 21st century to counter slumping birthrates (see Figure 19-1).

 *Do you see a danger in government's increased interest in the family?*

## Birthrates

If the present trend remains unaltered, the birth-rate will continue to decline (Masnick & Bane, 1980; see Figure 19-2). One reason is that the cost of raising children will keep rising, while the economic value of children to the family will keep slipping downward as technology continues to replace the labor functions they once served (Cohen, 1981). Other factors that suggest a declining birthrate are women's desire to work outside the home and their older age at the time of first marriage, the continued availability of and improvement in methods of birth control, and society's acceptance of a family's decision to remain childless.

As we indicated in the last section, this scenario may not be enacted. Government incentives in the form of benefits such as day care may increase the birthrate. Or the government may enact legislation limiting or removing access to abortions, contraceptives, and family-planning clinics. In fact, the pro-life movement has recently attempted to enact just such legislation in Congress. Finally, it may be that in a society with fewer people and more opportunities the disincentives for having children will not exist, and the companionship and love children provide to parents may encourage larger families.

Either of these two scenarios could prevail in the next century. We expect that legislation to encourage births will be passed and that its effect will be to stabilize the decline in the birthrate rather than to increase it.

 **We have used the word government several times in this section, but who is the government?**

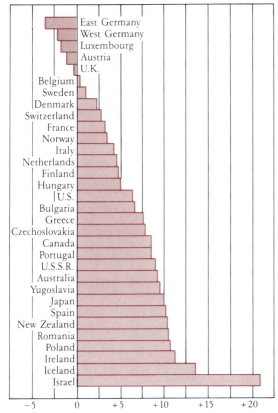

**FIGURE 19-1.** *The rate of natural increase (birthrate minus death rate) is below the zero-population-growth line in a few European countries, and it is approaching that level in most industrialized nations. Data are mostly for 1976; U. S. figure is for 12 months ending in May, 1978.*

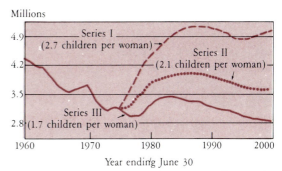

**FIGURE 19-2.** *Estimates and projections of annual number of births in U. S., 1960–2000.*

In the film *Logan's Run* an overpopulated contained colony on Earth handles the problem of crowding by "renewing"— that is, exterminating people over age 30. World birthrates are growing at an alarming pace, but many developed nations are approaching or have reached a zero population birthrate; that is, the death rate in those nations equals or exceeds the birthrate. This situation has led some of those nations to embark on campaigns to increase their birthrates, as the following newswire illustrates:

**ROMANIA SEEKING MORE BIRTHS**

Concerned about a stagnating national birth rate in Romania, communist officials Saturday announced a new campaign to urge citizens to have more children. The official news agency Agerpres, monitored in Vienna, said Saturday a resolution by the ruling Communist Party's political executive committee set "firm measures to boost the birth rate up to 19–20 per thousand inhabitants." The birthrate in 1981 was 7 births per 1,000 people. The measures also were designed to "firmly eradicate the causes preventing an appropriately high national growth," Agerpres said. Details of the measures were not revealed but the Yugoslav news agency Tanjug from Bucharest said, "It is to be inferred from the decision that abortion will be permitted only in some exceptionally strongly justified cases." Abortion is now allowed only if a woman is older than 40 or . . . has 4 children although reports say there are thousands of illegal abortions each year. Artificial means of birth control are virtually impossible to find in Romania. There are measures already on the books encouraging marriage and child-bearing and it is difficult to get a divorce in Romania.

## Divorce and Remarriage

The rapid growth in divorces and remarriages since the Second World War will not continue. The divorce rate has been stabilizing during the last decade. We expect that large numbers of marriages will continue to dissolve. We also expect that most of those individuals will remarry. With regard to the issue of joint custody, we agree with Cherlin and Furstenberg (1982) that the hostility that marks most divorces will discourage this form of parenting from being widely practiced.

## Sex Roles

Who sitting in the audience in 1858 watching *The World Upside Down: A Vision of the Future* would have ever imagined women in space, on the Supreme Court, occupying the highest political offices, and acting as leaders of the business community? The rapid changes we have witnessed in our lifetime will continue into the next century. We agree with many observers that women will continue to represent an increasing proportion of the labor force (Bronfenbrenner, 1981; Masnick & Bane, 1980).

Financial independence will increase women's power in female/male relationships. A rise in cohabitation can be expected (Bernard, 1981; Masnick & Bane, 1980). While a redistribution of power will facilitate the development of masculine behavior in women, it will also encourage feminine behavior in males. As a result of these changes, we believe androgyny will become the prevalent sex-role type in the next century.

*Do you think the number of male single-parent families will increase in the future? Why?*

*We have predicted an increase in women's power in their relationships with men. Do you agree with us that this increase in women's power will facilitate the development of feminine behavior in men?*

## The Economy and the Family

The most disturbing aspect of the future is not the status of the family. The family will survive, as it has for millions of years. The crucial question is: Will our environment be able to support families? If the pessimists are correct, the 21st century will be one of scarcity. Our world's natural resources will have been badly depleted. For example, the world's present "limitless" supply of oil, which contributed to the economic recovery of the mid-1980s, will vanish. The evidence is growing that the world's major oil deposits have all been discovered. If this is true, then at the present rates of consumption, the world's oil supply will be exhausted in 2044 A.D.—less than 60 years from now (Kerr, 1984).

One can expect that in such a world the gap between the haves and have-nots will grow. Inflation will return with a vengeance as the marketplace revalues limited goods. A return to the gas lines of a few years ago may occur for many more items than just gasoline. In such a world, the educated will have the advantage.

## SUMMARY

We desperately hope that this last scenario never happens and that the future is one of abundance. We hope that humanity exercises its wisdom and not its foolishness, exercises conservation and not wastefulness, and continues to develop technologies that contribute to a world of peace and abundance. In such a world, families, as they always have, will continue to evolve. Such a world is possible, however, only if individuals take an active role in shaping society. The promotion of health and the prevention of illness and even our very existence on this planet are responsibilities that each of us must carry into the future.

## MAJOR POINTS TO REMEMBER

1. Proponents of the "good old days" often describe modern society as a contemporary version of the biblical Gomorrah. Yet, history suggests that, no matter what time period, society has explored and experimented with sex.

2. The early New England practice of auctioning off the poor to the lowest bidder was called *vendue*.

3. Proponents of the "good old days" offer three arguments in defense of their position—that society, home, and individuals were more caring. Yet, historical evidence disputes each of these contentions.

4. In 1967 the Supreme Court decision *In re Galt* extended the protections guaranteed to all adult Americans by the Constitution and the Bill of Rights to children.

5. Major demographic changes are presently occurring in the United States. These changes include a declining birthrate for most racial and ethnic groups, a declining number of adolescents, and an increasing number of older people.

6. Concern over the slumping birthrate may encourage government in the 21st century to become more involved in the family.

7. The future may be one of abundance or scarcity. The choice belongs to the present generation.

## ADDITIONAL SOURCES OF INFORMATION

Council on Environmental Quality & U. S. Department of State. (1980). *Global 2000 report to the president: Entering the 21st century*. Washington, DC: U. S. Government Printing Office.

Future families. (1981). *Society, 18*(2), 38–78.

The future of advanced societies. (1984). *Society, 22*(1), 16–52.

Trend Analysis Program. (1981). *The uncertain future: Tap 20*. Washington, DC: American Council of Life Insurance.

# REFERENCES

Aadalen, S. (1980). Coping with sudden infant death syndrome: Intervention strategies and a case study. *Family Relations, 29,* 584–590.

Abarbanel, A. (1979). Shared parenting after separation and divorce. *American Journal of Orthopsychiatry, 49,* 320–329.

Abelson, P. H. (1982a). Computers and electronics. *Science, 215,* 750.

Abelson, P. H. (1982b). The revolution in computers and electronics. *Science, 215,* 751–753.

Abrahams, B., Feldman, S. S., & Nash, S. C. (1978). Sex role self-concept and sex role attitudes: Enduring personality characteristics of adaptations to changing life situations. *Developmental Psychology, 14,* 393–401.

Ackerman, R. J. (1983). *Children of alcoholics.* Holmes Beach, FL: Learning Publications.

Adams, B. N. (1968). *Kinship in an urban setting.* Chicago: Markham.

Adams, G. R. (1977). Physical attractiveness: Toward a developmental social psychology of beauty. *Human Development, 20,* 217–230.

Adams, G. R. (1982). Physical attractiveness. In A. G. Miller (Ed.), *In the eye of the beholder: Contemporary issues in stereotyping.* New York: Praeger.

Adams, G. R., & Gullotta, T. P. (1983). *Adolescent life experiences.* Monterey, CA: Brooks/Cole.

Adams, G. R., & Hicken, M. (1984). Historical-cultural change in the expression of vocational preference and expectation by preschool and elementary school-age children. *Family Relations, 33,* 301–307.

Adams, G. R., & Schvaneveldt, J. D. (1985). *Understanding research methods.* New York: Longman.

Administration for Children, Youth, and Families. (1981, May). *Promising practices: Reaching out to families.* Office of Human Development, DHHS Pub. No. (OHDS) 81-30324. Washington, DC: U. S. Government Printing Office.

Ahlburg, D. A., & Schapiro, M. O. (1983). The darker side of unemployment. *Hospital and Community Psychiatry, 34,* 389.

Ahr, P. R., Goradezky, M. J., & Cho, D. W. (1981). Measuring the relationship of public psychiatric admissions to rising unemployment. *Hospital and Community Psychiatry, 32,* 398–401.

Ahrons, C. R. (1981). The continuing coparental relationships between divorced spouses. *American Journal of Orthopsychiatry, 51,* 415–428.

*AIDS Information Bulletin.* (1983, November 22). Washington, DC: U.S. Public Health Service.

Alan Guttmacher Institute. (1981). *Teenage pregnancy: The problem that hasn't gone away.* New York: Alan Guttmacher Institute.

Albee, G. W. (1980). A competency model must replace the defect model. In L. A. Bond & J. C. Rosen (Eds.), *Competence and coping during adulthood.* Hanover, NH: University of New England Press.

Albee, G. W. (1981). The prevention of sexism. *Professional Psychology, 121,* 20–28.

Albee, G. W. (1983, April 26). Prevention and promotion in mental health. Testimony before the U. S. Senate Committee on Labor and Human Resources, Washington, DC.

Albee, G. W. (1985, February). The answer is prevention. *Psychology Today,* pp. 60–64.

Albee, G. W., & Gullotta, T. P. (in press). Fallacies and facts about primary prevention. *Journal of Primary Prevention.*

Albrecht, S. L. (1979). Correlates of marital happiness among the remarried. *Journal of Marriage and the Family, 41,* 857–866.

Albrecht, S. L. (1980). Reactions and adjustments to divorce: Differences in the experiences of males and females. *Family Relations, 29,* 59–68.

Albrecht, S. L., Bahr, H. M., & Chadwick, B. A. (1979). Changing family and sex roles: An assessment of age differences. *Journal of Marriage and the Family, 41,* 41–50.

Aldous, J. (1978). *Family careers: Developmental changes in families.* New York: Wiley.

Aldous, J. (1981a). From dual-earner to dual-career families and back again. *Journal of Family Issues, 2,* 115–125.

Aldous, J. (1981b). *Two paychecks: Life in dual-earner families.* Beverly Hills, CA: Sage.

Alexander, S. J. (1980). Influential factors on divorced parents in determining visitation arrangements. *Journal of Divorce, 3,* 223–239.

Alexander, S. J. (1981). Implications of the White House Conference on Families for family life education. *Family Relations, 30*(4), 643–650.

Alexander, S. J. (1984). Improving sex education programs for young adolescents: Parents' views. *Family Relations, 33*(2), 251–257.

Alexander, S. J., & Jorgensen, S. R. (1983). Sex education for early adolescents: A study of parents and students. *Journal of Early Adolescence, 3*(4), 315–325.

Alvarez, A. (1981). *Life after marriage: People in divorce.* New York: Simon & Schuster.

Alvy, K. T. (1975). Preventing child abuse. *American Psychologist, 30,* 921–928.

Anspach, D. F. (1976). Kinship and divorce. *Journal of Marriage and the Family, 38,* 323–330.

Arens, D. A. (1982–83). Widowhood and well-being: An examination of sex differences within a causal model. *International Journal of Aging and Human Development, 15,* 27–40.

Argyle, M., & Furnham, A. (1983). Sources of satisfaction and conflict in long-term relationships. *Journal of Marriage and the Family, 45*(3), 481–493.

Ariès, P. (1962). *Centuries of childhood.* New York: Knopf.

Ariès, P. (1979). The family and the city in the old world and the new. In V. Tufte & B. Myerhoff (Eds.), *Changing images of the family.* New Haven, CT: Yale University Press.

Ariès, P. (1981). *The hour of our death.* New York: Knopf.

Arling, G. (1976). The elderly widow and her family, neighbors and friends. *Journal of Marriage and the Family, 38,* 757–768.

Arnold, F., Bulato, R. A., Buripakdi, C., Cung, B. J., Fawcett, J. T., Iritani, T., Lee, S. J., & Wu, T. (1975). *The value of children: A cross-national study.* Vol. 1: *Introduction and comparative analysis.* Honolulu: East-West Population Institute, East-West Center.

Atchley, R. C. (1974). The meaning of retirement. *Journal of Communications, 24,* 97–101.

Atchley, R. C. (1983). *Aging: Continuity and change.* Belmont, CA: Wadsworth.

Atkinson, J., & Huston, T. L. (1984). Sex role orientation and division of labor early in marriage. *Journal of Personality and Social Psychology, 46,* 330–345.

Attorney General's Task Force on Family Violence. (1984). *Final Report.* Washington, DC: U. S. Government Printing Office.

Auerswald, E. H. (1980). Drug use and families. In B. G. Ellis (Ed.), *Drug abuse from the family perspective.* NIDA, DHHS Pub. No. (ADM) 80-910. Washington, DC: U. S. Government Printing Office.

Austin, G. A. (1979). *Research issues 24: Perspectives on the history of psychoactive substance use.* NIDA, DHHS Pub. No. (ADM) 79-810. Washington, DC: U. S. Government Printing Office.

Author's income. (1982). *Transaction, 19*(6), 2–3.

Avery, A. W., Rider, K., & Haynes-Clements, L. A. (in press). Communication skills training for adolescents: A five-month follow-up. *Adolescence.*

Avery, P. A. (1983, June 6). Surrogate mothers: Center of a new storm. *U. S. News and World Report,* p. 76.

Aznar, R. (1979). A clinical appraisal of a medicated polyurethane sponge used for contraception. *Vaginal Contraception: New Developments, 2,* 116–118.

Babbie, E. (1979). *The practice of social research* (2nd ed.). Belmont, CA: Wadsworth.

Bach, G. R., & Deutsch, R. M. (1969). *The intimate enemy.* New York: Avon Books.

Bach, G. R., & Deutsch, R. M. (1970). *Pairing.* New York: Avon Books.

Bach, G. R., & Deutsch, R. M. (1979). *Stop! You're driving me crazy.* New York: Putnam.

Bachrach, C. A. (1983). Children in families: Characteristics of biological, step- and adopted children. *Journal of Marriage and the Family, 45*(1), 171–179.

Bagarozzi, D. A., & Raven, P. (1981). Premarital counseling: Appraisal and status. *American Journal of Family Therapy, 9,* 13–28.

Bailey, J. M., & Prager, K. J. (1984, April). *Androgyny, ego development and psychosocial crisis resolution.* Paper presented at the annual meeting of the American Education Research Association, New Orleans.

Baither, R. C. (1978). Family therapy with adolescent drug abusers: A review. *Journal of Drug Education, 8*(4), 337–343.

Baizerman, M., Thompson, J., & Stafford-White, K. (1979). Adolescent prostitution. *Children Today, 8*(5), 20–24.

Baldwin, W., & Cain, V. S. (1980). The children of teenage parents. *Family Planning Perspectives, 12*(1), 34–43.

Balkwell, C. (1981). Transition to widowhood: A review of the literature. *Family Relations, 30,* 117–127.

Balswick, J. O., & Peek, C. W. (1971). The inexpressive male: A tragedy of American society. *Family Coordinator, 20*(4), 363–368.

Bandura, A. (1969). *Principles of behavior modification.* New York: Holt, Rinehart & Winston.

Bane, M. J. (1976). *Here to stay: American families in the 20th century.* New York: Basic Books.

Bane, M. J. (1979). Marital disruption and the lives of the children. In G. Levinger & O. C. Moles (Eds.), *Divorce and separation: Context, causes, and consequences.* New York: Basic Books.

Bankoff, E. A. (1983). Social support and adaptation to widowhood. *Journal of Marriage and the Family, 45*(4), 827–839.

Banks, J. A. (1984). Black youths in predominantly white suburbs: An exploratory study of their attitudes and self-concepts. *Journal of Negro Education, 53,* 3–17.

Barahal, R. M., Waterman, J., & Martin, H. P. (1981). The social cognitive development of abused children. *Journal of Consulting and Clinical Psychology, 49,* 508–516.

Barbarin, O. A. (1981). Community competence: An individual systems model of institutional racism. In O. A. Barbarin, P. R. Good, O. M. Pharr, & J. A. Siskind (Eds.), *Institutional racism and community competence.* DHHS Pub. No. (ADM) 81-907. Washington, DC: U. S. Government Printing Office.

Bardwick, J. M. (1971). *Psychology of women.* New York: Harper & Row.

Barnes, B. C., & Coplon, J. (1980). *The single-parent experience.* New York: Family Service Association of America.

Barnes, G. M. (1977). The development of adolescent drinking behavior: An evaluative review of the impact of the socialization process within the family. *Adolescence, 12,* 571–591.

Barnett, P., Gaudio, C. P., & Sumner, M. G. (1980). *Parenting children of divorce.* New York: Family Service Association of America.

Baron, R. A. (1974). Aggression-inhibiting influences on heightened sexual arousal. *Journal of Personality and Social Psychology, 30,* 318–322.

Baron, R. A. (1978). Aggression-inhibiting influences of sexual humor. *Journal of Personality and Social Psychology, 36,* 189–197.

Barrett, C. J., & Schneweis, K. M. (1980–81). An empirical search for stages of widowhood. *Omega, 11,* 94–104.

Bar-Tal, D., & Saxe, L. (1974, August). *Effect of physical attractiveness on the perception of couples.* Paper presented at the meeting of the American Psychological Association, New Orleans.

Bartz, K. W., & Levine, E. S. (1978). Child rearing by black parents: A description and comparison to Anglo and chicano parents. *Journal of Marriage and the Family, 40*(4), 709–719.

Battiata, M. (1983, July 6). Choosing a day-care center: Expert advice. *Washington Post,* p. Va. 1, 4.

Baumrind, D. (1972). An exploratory study of socialization effects on black children: Some black-white comparisons. *Child Development, 43,* 261–267.

Baumrind, D. (1982). Are androgynous individuals more effective persons and parents? *Child Development, 53,* 44–75.

Beck, D. F., & Jones, M. A. (1973). *Progress on family problems: A nationwide study of clients' and counselors' views on family agency services.* New York: Family Service Association of America.

Beck, S. (1982). Adjustment to and satisfaction with retirement. *Journal of Gerontology, 37*(5), 616–624.

Beckman, L. J., & Houser, B. B. (1982). The consequences of childlessness on the social-psychological well-being of older women. *Journal of Gerontology, 37*(2), 243–250.

Bell, A. P., & Weinberg, M. S. (1978). *Homosexualities: A study of diversity among men and women.* New York: Simon & Schuster.

Belsky, J., Spanier, G. B., & Rovine, M. (1983). Stability and change in marriage across the transition to parenthood. *Journal of Marriage and the Family, 45*(3), 567–577.

Bem, S. L. (1974). The measurement of psychological androgyny. *Journal of Consulting and Clinical Psychology, 42,* 155–162.

Bem, S. L. (1975). Sex role adaptability: One consequence of psychological androgyny. *Journal of Personality and Social Psychology, 31,* 634–643.

Bem, S. L. (1977). On the utility of alternative procedures for assessing psychological androgyny. *Journal of Consulting and Clinical Psychology, 45,* 196–205.

Bem, S. L. (1981). Gender schema theory: A cognitive account of sex typing. *Psychological Review, 88,* 354–364.

Bem, S. L., Martyna, W., & Watson, C. (1976). Sex typing and androgyny: Further explorations of the expressive domain. *Journal of Personality and Social Psychology, 34,* 1016–1023.

Benedek, R. S., & Benedek, E. P. (1979). Children of divorce: Can we meet their needs? *Journal of Social Issues, 35,* 155–169.

Benedict, R. (1946). *Patterns of culture.* New York: Penguin Books.

Benson, L. (1971). *The family bond.* New York: Random House.

Bentler, P. M., & Huba, G. J. (1979). Simple minitheories of love. *Journal of Personality and Social Psychology, 37,* 124–130.

Bereaud, S. R. (1975). Sex role images in French children's books. *Journal of Marriage and the Family, 37,* 194–207.

Berg, J. H., & Peplau, L. A. (1982). Loneliness: The relationship of self-disclosure and androgyny. *Personality and Social Psychology Bulletin, 8,* 624–630.

Bergler, E. (1948). *Divorce won't help.* New York: Harper & Row.

Bernard, J. (1972). *The future of marriage.* New York: World.

Bernard, J. (1974). The housewife: Between two worlds. In P. L. Stewart & M. G. Cantor (Eds.), *Varieties of work experience: The social control of occupational groups and roles.* Cambridge, MA: Schenkman.

Bernard, J. (1981). Facing the future. *Transaction, 18*(2), 53–59.

Bernard, J. M. (1981). The divorce myth. *Personnel and Guidance Journal, 60*(2), 67–71.

Berscheid, E., & Walster, E. (1974a). A little bit about love. In T. Huston (Ed.), *Foundations of interpersonal attraction.* New York: Academic Press.

Berscheid, E., & Walster, E. (1974b). Physical attractiveness. In L. Berkowitz (Ed.), *Advances in experimental social psychology* (Vol. 7). New York: Academic Press.

Bettoli, E. J. (1982). Herpes: Facts and fallacies. *Journal of Practical Nursing, 32*(8), 17–21, 42.

Biller, H. B. (1970). Father absence and the personality of the male child. *Developmental Psychology, 2,* 181–201.

Billingsley, A. (1968). *Black families in white America.* Englewood Cliffs, NJ: Prentice-Hall.

Birch, T. L. (1983). The children's trust fund. *Children Today, 12*(4), 25, 41.

Birnbaum, J. (1975). Life patterns and self-esteem in family oriented and career committed women. In M. Mednick (Ed.), *Women and achievement: Social and motivational analysis.* New York: Wiley.

Blanchard, C. G., Blanchard, E. B., & Becker, J. V. (1976). The young widow: Depressive symptomatology throughout the grief process. *Psychiatry, 39,* 394–399.

Blau, Z. S. (1972). Maternal aspirations, socialization and achievement of boys and girls in the white working class. *Journal of Youth and Adolescence, 1*(1), 32–57.

Bloch, D. (1979). Attitudes of mothers toward sex education. *American Journal of Public Health, 69,* 911–917.

Block, J., Von der Lippe, A., & Block, J. H. (1973). Sex role and socialization patterns: Some personality concomitants and environmental antecedents. *Journal of Consulting and Clinical Psychology, 41,* 321–341.

Blood, R. O. (1955). A test of Waller's rating-dating complex. *Marriage and Family Living, 17,* 41–47.

Blood, R. O. (1956). Uniformities and diversities in campus dating preferences. *Marriage and Family Living, 18,* 37–45.

Blood, R. O., & Wolfe, D. (1960). *Husbands and wives.* New York: Free Press.

Bloom, B. L., & Caldwell, R. A. (1981). Sex differences in adjustment during the process of marital separation. *Journal of Marriage and the Family, 43,* 693–701.

Bloom, B. L., Hodges, W. F., & Caldwell, R. A. (1982). A preventive program for the newly separated: Initial evaluation. *American Journal of Community Psychology, 10,* 251–264.

Bloom, B. L., Hodges, W. F., Kern, M. B., & McFaddin, S. C. (1985). A preventive intervention program for the newly separated: Final evaluations. *American Journal of Orthopsychiatry, 55,* 9–26.

Bloom, B. L., White, S. W., & Asher, S. J. (1978). Marital disruption as a stressful life event. *Psychological Bulletin, 85,* 867–894.

Bloom, M. (1983). Prevention/promotion with minorities. *Journal of Primary Prevention, 3,* 224–234.

Blumberg, M. L. (1981). Depression in abused and neglected children. *American Journal of Psychotherapy, 35,* 342–355.

Blumstein, P., & Schwartz, P. W. (1983). *American couples: Money, work, sex.* New York: Morrow.

Bohannon, P. (1970). *Divorce and after.* Garden City, NY: Doubleday.

Bolton, F. G., Jr., Laner, R. H., Gai, D. S., & Kane, S. P. (1981). The "study" of child maltreatment. *Journal of Family Issues, 2,* 531–539.

Booz, Allen, & Hamilton, Inc. (1974). *Final report of the needs and resources for children of alcoholic parents.* Washington, DC: U. S. Government Printing Office.

Boston Women's Health Book Collective. (1976). *Our bodies, ourselves.* New York: Simon & Schuster.

Bowen, G. B., & Orthner, D. K. (1983). Sex-role congruency and marital quality. *Journal of Marriage and the Family, 45*(1), 223–230.

Bower, T. (1981). Competent newborns. In L. Steinberg (Ed.), *The life cycle: Readings in human development.* New York: Columbia University Press.

Bowerman, C. E., & Irish, D. P. (1962). Some relationships of stepchildren to their parents. *Marriage and Family Living, 24,* 113–121.

Bowker, L. H. (1983). Marital rape: A distinct syndrome. *Social Casework, 64,* 347–352.

Bowlby, J. (1973). Pathological mourning and childhood mourning. *Journal of the American Psychoanalytic Association, 11,* 500–541.

Bowlby, J. (1980). *Attachment and loss.* Vol. 3: *Loss: Sadness and depression.* New York: Basic Books.

Braiker, H., & Kelley, H. (1979). Conflict in the development of close relationships. In R. L. Burgess & T. L. Huston (Eds.), *Social exchange in developing relationships.* New York: Academic Press.

Brandt, A. (1982, April). Last words for my father. *Psychology Today,* pp. 72-77.

Braucht, G. N., Loya, F., & Jamieson, K. J. (1980). Victims of violent death: A critical review. *Psychological Bulletin, 87,* 309–333.

Brazelton, T. B. (1981). *On becoming a family: The growth of attachment.* New York: Delacorte Press.

Brazelton, T. B. (1983, March 19). *Does the newborn baby shape its environment?* Speech presented at the conference of the Junior League of Washington, DC, "Parenting Issues of the '80s."

Brecher, E. (1972). *Licit and illicit drugs.* Boston: Little, Brown.

Bremner, R. H. (1970). *Children and youth in America.* Vol. 1: *1600–1865.* Cambridge, MA: Harvard University Press.

Brenner, H. M. (1973). *Mental illness and the economy.,* Cambridge, MA: Harvard University Press.

Brenner, H. M. (1977). Personal stability and economic security. *Social Policy, 8*(1), 2–4.

Breton, M. (1981). Resocialization of abusive parents. *Social Work, 26,* 119–122.

Briar, K. H. (1983). Unemployment: Toward a social work agenda. *Social Work, 28,* 211–216.

Brim, O. G., Jr. (1982). Theories of the male mid-life crisis. In J. Rosenfeld (Ed.), *Relationships: The marriage and family reader.* Glenview, IL: Scott, Foresman.

Brislin, R. W., & Lewis, S. A. (1968). Dating and physical attractiveness: Replication. *Psychological Reports, 22,* 976.

Broderick, C. B. (1976). Socio-sexual interests. *Adolescence, 11,* 487–496.

Broderick, C. B. (1982). Adult sexual development. In B. B. Wolman (Ed.), *Handbook of developmental psychology.* Englewood Cliffs, NJ: Prentice-Hall.

Broderick, C. B., & Smith, J. (1979). The general systems approach to the family. In W. R. Burr, R. Hill, F. I. Nye, & I. L. Reiss (Eds.), *Contemporary theories about the family* (Vol. 2). New York: Free Press.

Broderick, C. B., & Weaver, J. (1968). The perceptual context of boy/girl communication. *Journal of Marriage and the Family, 30*(4), 318–327.

Bronfenbrenner, U. (1974). The origins of alienation. *Scientific American, 231,* 53–61.

Bronfenbrenner, U. (1981). Children and families: 1984. *Transaction, 18*(2), 38–41.

Brook, J. S., Gordon, A. S., & Brook, D. W. (1980). Perceived paternal relationships, adolescent personality, and female marijuana use. *Journal of Psychology, 105,* 277–285.

Bross, D. C. (1979). Analysis of the protected status of maltreated children and youth. *Journal of Social Issues, 35,* 72–81.

Brown, B. S. (1983). The impact of political and economic changes upon mental health. *American Journal of Orthopsychiatry, 53,* 583–592.

Brown, H. F. (1979). Crisis intervention treatment in child abuse programs. *Social Casework, 60,* 430–433.

Brown, J. A. (1979–80). Combatting the roots of family violence. *Journal of Social Welfare, 6*(2), 17–24.

Bryant, F. B., & Veroff, J. (1982). The structure of psychological well-being: A socio-historical analysis. *Journal of Personality and Social Psychology, 43,* 653–673.

Bugen, L. A. (1977). Human grief: A model for prediction and intervention. *American Journal of Orthopsychiatry, 47,* 196–206.

Bumpass, L. (1984). Children and marital disruption: A replication and update. *Demography, 21,* 71–82.

Burch, G., & Mohr, V. (1980). Evaluating a child abuse intervention program. *Social Casework, 61,* 90–99.

Burchinal, L. G. (1964). Characteristics of adolescents from unbroken, broken, and reconstituted families. *Journal of Marriage and the Family, 26,* 44–51.

Burgess, A. W., Groth, A. N., & McCausland, M. P. (1981). Child sex initiation rings. *American Journal of Orthopsychiatry, 51,* 110–119.

Burr, W. R. (1971). An expansion and test of a role theory of marital satisfaction. *Journal of Marriage and the Family, 33,* 368.

Burr, W. R., Leigh, G. K., Day, R. D., & Constantine, J. (1979). Symbolic interaction and the family. In W. R. Burr, R. Hill, F. I. Nye, & I. L. Reiss (Eds.), *Contemporary theories about the family* (Vol. 1). New York: Free Press.

Burud, S. L., Collins, R. C., & Divine-Hawkins, P. (1983). Employer supported childcare: Everybody benefits. *Children Today, 12*(3), 2–7.

Bushman, R. L. (1981). Family security in the transition from farm to city, 1750–1850. *Journal of Family History, 6,* 238–256.

Buss, A. H. (1983). Social rewards and personality. *Journal of Personality and Social Psychology, 44,* 553–563.

Butler, R. N. (1975). *Why survive? Being old in America.* New York: Harper & Row.

Buunk, B. (1982). Anticipated sexual jealousy: Its relationship to self-esteem, dependency, and reciprocity. *Personality and Social Psychology Bulletin, 8,* 310–316.

Bybee, R. W. (1979a). Toward further understanding and reducing violence against youth in families. *Journal of Social Issues, 35,* 161–173.

Bybee, R. W. (1979b). Violence toward youth: A new perspective. *Journal of Social Issues, 1979, 35,* 1–14.

Byles, J. A. (1982). Family violence in Hamilton—revisited. *Canada's Mental Health, 30*(4), 10–11.

Byrne, D., Ervin, C., & Lamberth, J. (1970). Continuity between the experimental study of attraction and real-life computer dating. *Journal of Personality and Social Psychology, 16,* 157–165.

Calderone, M. S., & Johnson, E. W. (1981). *The family book about sexuality.* New York: Harper & Row.

Calhoun, L., & Selby, J. W. (1980). Voluntary childlessness, involuntary childlessness and having children: A study of social perceptions. *Family Relations, 29,* 181–183.

Callahan, B. N. (1979). *Separation and divorce.* New York: Family Service Association of America.

Cameron, C., Oskamp, S., & Sparks, W. (1977). Courtship American style: Newspaper ads. *Family Coordinator, 26,* 27–30.

Cannon, W. B. (1939). *The wisdom of the body.* New York: Norton.

Caplan, G. (Ed.). (1961). Prevention of mental disorders in children: Initial explorations. New York: Basic Books.

Caplan, G. (1964). *Principles of preventive psychiatry.* New York: Basic Books.

Caplan, G. (1974). *Support systems and community mental health.* New York: Behavioral Publications.

Card, J. J., & Wise, L. L. (1978). Teenage mothers and teenage fathers: The impact of early childbearing on the parents' personal and professional lives. *Family Planning Perspectives, 10*(4), 199–204.

Carey, R. G. (1979–80). Weathering widowhood: Problems and adjustment of the widowed during the first year. *Omega, 10,* 163–174.

Carrera, M. (1981). *Sex: The facts, the acts and your feelings.* New York: Crown.

Carroll, J., Schaffer, C., Spensley, J., & Abramowitz, S. I. (1980). Family experiences of self-mutilating patients. *American Journal of Psychiatry, 137,* 852–853.

Carter, D. B., & Patterson, C. J. (1982). Sex roles as social conventions: The development of children's conceptions of sex-role stereotypes. *Developmental Psychology, 18,* 812–824.

Cartwright, R. D., Lloyd, S., Nelson, J. B., & Bass, S. (1982). The traditional–liberated woman dimension: Social stereotype and self-concept. *Journal of Personality and Social Psychology, 44,* 581–588.

Cassell, C. (1983). Defining responsible sexuality. In G. Albee, S. Gordon, & H. Leitenberg (Eds), *Promoting sexual responsibility and preventing sexual problems.* Hanover, NH: University Press of New England.

Castle, S. (1977). *Face talk, hand talk, body talk.* New York: Doubleday.

Catalano, R., & Dooley, D. (1980). Economic change in primary prevention. In R. H. Price, R. F. Ketterer, B. C. Bader,

& J. Monaham (Eds.), *Prevention in mental health: Research, policy, and practice.* Beverly Hills, CA: Sage.

Cate, R. M., Henton, J. M., Koval, J., Christopher, F. S., & Lloyd, S. (1982). Premarital abuse. *Journal of Family Issues, 3,* 79–90.

Cate, R. M., Lloyd, S. A., Henton, J. M., & Larson, J. B. (1982). Fairness and reward level as predictors of relationship satisfaction. *Social Psychology Quarterly, 45,* 177–181.

Cates, W. (1982). Legal abortion: The public health record. *Science, 215,* 1586–1590.

Cautley, P. W. (1980). Treating dysfunctional families at home. *Social Work, 25,* 380–385.

Cavior, N., Jacobs, A., & Jacobs, M. (1974). *The stability and correlation of physical attractiveness and sex appeal ratings.* Unpublished manuscript, West Virginia University.

Centers for Disease Control. (1983a). Prevention of acquired immune deficiency syndrome (AIDS): Report of interagency recommendations. *Journal of the American Medical Association, 249*(12), 1544–1545.

Centers for Disease Control. (1983b). Acquired immune deficiency syndrome (AIDS) update: United States. *Journal of the American Medical Association, 250*(3), 335–336.

Chafetz, M. E. (1979, September). Children of alcoholics. *New York University Quarterly,* pp. 23–29.

Chang, P., & Deinard, A. S. (1982). Single-father caretakers: Demographic characteristics and adjustment processes. *American Journal of Orthopysychiatry, 52,* 236–243.

Chase, A. W. (1866). *Dr. Chase's recipes; or, information for everybody: An invaluable collection of about eight hundred practical recipes.* Ann Arbor, MI: A. W. Chase.

Cherlin, A. (1978–79). Remarriage as an incomplete institution. *American Journal of Sociology, 84*(3), 634–650.

Cherlin, A., & Furstenberg, F. F. (1982). *The shape of the family in the year 2000.* Washington, DC: American Council of Life Insurance.

Cherry, L., & Lewis, M. (1976). Mothers and two-year-olds: A study of sex-differentiated aspects of verbal interaction. *Developmental Psychology, 12,* 278–282.

Chess, S., Thomas, A., & Birch, H. (1959). Characteristics of the individual child's behavioral responses to the environment. *American Journal of Orthopsychiatry, 29,* 791–802.

Chilman, C. S. (1978). *Adolescent sexuality in a changing American society: Social and psychological perspectives.* NIH Pub. No. 80-1426 Washington, DC: U. S. Department of Health, Education and Welfare.

Chilman, C. S. (1983). Prologue: The 1970s and American families (a semitragedy). In E. D. Macklin & R. H. Rubin (Eds.), *Contemporary families and alternative lifestyles.* Beverly Hills, CA: Sage.

Chiriboga, D. A. (1980). Stress and coping—introduction. In L. W. Poon (Ed.), *Aging in the 1980s: Psychological issues.* Washington, DC: American Psychological Association.

Chiriboga, D. A. (1982). Adaptation to marital separation in later and earlier life. *Journal of Gerontology, 37*(1), 109–114.

Chodoff, P., Friedman, S. B., & Hamburg, D. A. (1963–64). Stress, defenses and coping behavior: Observations in parents of children with malignant disease. *American Journal of Psychiatry, 120,* 743–749.

Cicirelli, V. G. (1980). Sibling relationships in adulthood: A life span perspective. In L. W. Poon (Ed.), *Aging in the 1980s: Psychological issues.* Washington, DC: American Psychological Association.

Cicirelli, V. G. (1981). *Helping elderly parents: The role of adult children.* Boston: Auburn House.

Cicirelli, V. G. (1983). Adult children's attachment and helping behavior to elderly parents: A path model. *Journal of Marriage and the Family, 45*(4), 805–813.

Clarke, P. J. (1981). Exploration of countertransference toward the dying. *American Journal of Orthopsychiatry, 51,* 71–77.

Clarke-Stewart, K. A. (1978). And daddy makes three: The father's impact on mother and the young child. *Child Development, 49*(2), 466–478.

Clavan, S. (1978). The impact of social class and social trends on the role of grandparents. *Family Coordinator, 27*(4), 351–357.

Clayton, P. J. (1979). The sequelae and nonsequelae of conjugal bereavement. *American Journal of Psychiatry, 136,* 1530–1534.

Cohen, L., Zilkha, S., Middleton, J., & O'Donnohue, N. (1978). Perinatal mortality: Assisting parental affirmation. *American Journal of Orthopsychiatry, 48,* 727–731.

Cohen, S. (1980). Therapeutic aspects. In R. C. Petersen (Ed.), *Research 31: Marijuana research findings, 1980.* NIDA, DHHS, Pub. No. (ADM) 80-1001, Washington, DC: U. S. Government Printing Office.

Cohen, S., & Sussman, A. (1975). The incidence of child abuse in the U. S. *Child Welfare, 54,* 432–443.

Cohen, Y. A. (1981). Shrinking households. *Transaction, 18*(2), 48–52.

Cohn, A. H. (1979). Effective treatment of child abuse and neglect. *Social Casework, 60,* 513–519.

Cohn, R. M. (1978). The effect of employment status change on self-attitudes. *Social Psychology, 41,* 81–93.

Coleman, J. S. (1975). Racial segregation in the schools: New research with new policy implications. *Phi Delta Kappan, 57*(2), 75–78.

Collins, R. C., & Deloria, D. (1983). Head Start research: A new chapter. *Children Today, 12*(4), 15–19.

Comer, J. P., & Hamilton-Lee, M. E. (1982). Support systems in the black community. In D. E. Biegel & A. J. Naparstek (Eds.), *Community support systems and mental health.* New York: Springer.

Comfort, A. (1976). Sexuality and aging. *SIECUS Report, 4,* 7–9.

Connell, P. (1977). Drug taking in Great Britain: A growing problem. In *Research issues 15: Cocaine—summaries of psychosocial research.* NIDA, DHHS Pub. No. (ADM) 77–391. Washington, DC: U. S. Government Printing Office.

Constantine, L., & Constantine, J. M. (1973). *Group marriage.* New York: Collier Books.

Converse, M., Curtin, R. T., & Kallick, M. (1980). Coping with inflation. *Economic Outlook U. S. A., 7*(2), 35–38.

Coogler, O. J., Weber, R. E., & McKenry, P. C. (1979). Divorce mediation: A means of facilitating divorce and adjustment. *Family Coordinator, 28,* 255–259.

Cooley, C. H. (1964). *Human nature and the social order.* New York: Scribner's.

Coolsen, P. (1980). Community involvement in the prevention of child abuse and neglect. *Children Today, 9,* 5–8.

Corcoran, M., & Hill, M. S. (1980). Unemployment and poverty. *Social Science Review, 54,* 407–413.

Corey, L., & Holmes, K. K. (1983). Genital herpes virus infections: Current concepts in diagnosis, therapy, and prevention. *Annals of Internal Medicine, 98,* 973–983.

Cork, M. R. (1969). *The forgotten children.* Toronto: Addiction Research Foundation.

Costantino, C. (1981). Intervention with battered women: The lawyer–social worker team. *Social Work, 4,* 456–460.

Cotton, N. S. (1979). The familial incidence of alcoholism. *Journal of Studies on Alcohol, 40,* 89–116.

Courtois, C. A., & Leehan, J. (1982). Group treatment for grown-up abused children. *Personnel and Guidance Journal, 60,* 564–566.

Cowan, C. P., Cowan, P. A., Coie, L., & Coie, J. (1978). Becoming a family: The impact of a first child's birth on the couple's relationship. In W. B. Miller & L. F. Newman (Eds.), *The first child and family formation.* Chapel Hill, NC: Carolina Population Center.

Cowen, E. L. (1982a). Help is where you find it: Four informal helping groups. *American Psychologist, 37,* 385–395.

Cowen, E. L. (1982b). Primary prevention research: Barriers, needs, and opportunities. *Journal of Primary Prevention, 2,* 131–137.

Cowley, M. (1980). *The view from 80.* New York: Viking Press.

Crener, K. J., MacKett, M., Wohlenberg, C., Notkins, A. L., & Moss, B. (1985). Vaccinia virus recombinant expressing herpes simplex virus type 1 glycoprotein D prevents latent herpes in mice. *Science, 228,* 737–739.

Crester, G. A., & Leon, J. J. (1982). Intermarriage in the United States. *Marriage and Family Review, 5,* 3–16.

Critelli, J. W. (1975, September). *Physical attractiveness of dating couples.* Paper presented at the meeting of the American Psychological Association, Chicago.

Crosby, J. F. (1980). A critique of divorce statistics and their interpretation. *Family Relations, 29,* 51–58.

Cuber, J. F., & Harroff, P. B. (1965). *The significant Americans: A study of sexual behavior among the affluent.* New York: Appleton-Century-Crofts.

Culliton, B. J. (1984). Crash development of AIDS test nears goal. *Science, 225*(4667), 1128, 1130–1131.

Curran, J. P., & Lippold, S. (1975). The effects of physical attraction and attitude similarity on attraction in dating dyads. *Journal of Personality, 43,* 528–539.

Cytrynbaum, S., Blum, L., Patrick, R., Stein, J., Wadner, D., & Wilk, C. (1980). Midlife development: A personality and social systems perspective. In L. W. Poon (Ed.), *Aging in the 1980s: Psychological issues.* Washington, DC: American Psychological Association.

Dager, E. Z. (1964). Socialization and personality development in the child. In H. T. Christensen (Ed.), *Handbook of marriage and the family.* Chicago: Rand McNally.

Damon, W. (1983). *Social and personality development: Infancy through adolescence.* New York: Norton.

Daniel, J. H., Hampton, R. L., & Newberger, E. H. (1983). Child abuse and accidents in black families. *American Journal of Orthopsychiatry, 53,* 645–653.

Davidson, T. (1977). Wifebeating: A recurring phenomenon throughout history. In M. Roy (Ed.), *Battered women.* New York: Van Nostrand Reinhold.

Davis, M. R. (1982). *Families in a working world: The impact of organization on domestic life.* New York: Praeger.

Davis, N. J. (1982). Childless and single-childed women in early twentieth-century America. *Journal of Family Issues, 3,* 431–458.

Dawley, H. H., Winstead, D., Baxter, A., & Gay, J. R. (1979). An attitude survey of the effects of marijuana on sexual enjoyment. *Journal of Clinical Psychology, 35,* 212–217.

DeFleur, M. (1964). Occupational roles as portrayed on television. *Public Opinion Quarterly, 28,* 57–74.

Deford, F. (1983). *Alex: The life of a child.* New York: Viking Press.

DeFrain, J., & Eirick, R. (1981). Coping as divorced single parents: A comparative study of fathers and mothers. *Family Relations, 30,* 265–274.

DeFrain, J., Taylor, J., & Ernst, L. (1982). *Coping with sudden infant death.* Lexington, MA: Lexington Books.

Degler, C. N. (1969). Slavery and the genesis of American race prejudice. In A. Meier & E. Rudwick (Eds.), *The making of black America: Essays in Negro life and history* (Vol. 1). New York: Atheneum.

Delgado, M., & Delgado, D. H. (1982). Natural support systems: Sources of strength in Hispanic communities. *Social Work, 27,* 83–89.

deLissovoy, V. (1973). *Fourth special report to the U. S. Congress on alcohol and health.* National Institute on Alcohol Abuse and Alcoholism. DHHS Pub. No. (ADM) 81-1080. Washington, DC: U. S. Government Printing Office.

Demos, J. (1970). *A little commonwealth: Family life in Plymouth colony.* New York: Oxford University Press.

Demos, J. (1973). Infancy and childhood in the Plymouth colony. In M. Gordon (Ed.), *The American family in socio-historical perspective.* New York: St. Martin's Press.

Demos, J. (1979). Images of the American family, then and now. In V. Tufte & B. Myerhoff (Eds.), *Changing images of the family.* New Haven, CT: Yale University Press.

DePanfilis, D. (1982). Clients who refer themselves to child protective services. *Children Today, 11,* 21–25.

Dermer, M., & Pyszczynski, T. A. (1978). Effects of erotica upon men's loving and liking responses for women they love. *Journal of Personality and Social Psychology, 24,* 1–10.

Dermer, M., & Thiel, D. L. (1975). When beauty may fail. *Journal of Personality and Social Psychology, 31,* 1168–1176.

Desimone-Luis, J., O'Mahoney, K., & Hunt, D. (1979). Children of separation and divorce: Factors influencing adjustment. *Journal of Divorce, 3,* 37–42.

Diamond, I. (1980). Pornography and repression: A reconsideration. *Signs, 5,* 686–701.

Dick, T. (1847). *The works of Thomas Dick.* Hartford, CT: Sumner and Goodwin.

Dickens, C. (1894a). *Dombey and son.* Cambridge, MA: Houghton Mifflin.

Dickens, C. (1894b). *Great expectations.* Cambridge, MA: Houghton Mifflin.

Dickens, C. (1894c). *Nicholas Nickleby.* Cambridge, MA: Houghton Mifflin.

Dickens, C. (1894d). *Oliver Twist.* Cambridge, MA: Houghton Mifflin.

Dickens, C. (1967). *A Christmas carol.* New York: Heineman. (Originally published 1843)

Dickinson, G. E., & Fritz, J. L. (1981). Death in the family. *Journal of Family Issues, 2,* 379–384.

Dion, K., Berscheid, E., & Walster, E. (1972). What is beautiful is good. *Journal of Personality and Social Psychology, 24,* 285–290.

Dion, K. L., & Dion, K. K. (1976). Love, liking, and trust in heterosexual relationships. *Personality and Social Psychology Bulletin, 2,* 187–190.

Djerassi, C. (1984). The making of the pill. *Science 84, 5*(9), 127–129.

Dobash, R. E., & Dobash, R. (1979). *Violence against wives.* New York: Free Press.

Dodson, F. (1970). *How to parent.* New York: New American Library.

Donohue, K., & Gullotta, T. P. (1981). *Plain talk about moving.* Glastonbury, CT: Families in Transition.

Douglas, R. L. (1983). Domestic neglect and abuse of the elderly: Implications for research and service. *Family Relations, 32,* 395–402.

Dowd, J. J., & Bengtson, V. L. (1978). Aging in minority populations: An examination of the double jeopardy hypothesis. *Journal of Gerontology, 33,* 427–436.

Downing, N. E. (1979). Theoretical and operational conceptualizations of psychological androgyny: Implications for measurement. *Psychology of Women Quarterly, 3,* 284–292.

Dreikurs, R. (1964). *Children: The challenge.* New York: Hawthorn Books.

Driscoll, R., Davis, K. E., & Lipetz, M. E. (1977). Parental interference and romantic love: The Romeo and Juliet effect. *Journal of Personality and Social Psychology, 35,* 381–391.

Drummond, H. (1983). Growing old absurd. In H. Cox (Ed.), *Aging* (3rd ed.). Guilford, CT: Dushkin.

Dunphy, D. C. (1963). The social structure of urban adolescent peer groups. *Sociometry, 26,* 230–246.

Dupold, J., & Young, D. (1979). Empirical studies of adolescent sexual behavior: A critical review. *Adolescence, 53,* 45–63.

Durbin, L. (1973, March–April). Mices and bears, robbers and barbers. *Children Today, 2,* 19–23.

Durkheim, E. (1951). *Suicide: A study in sociology.* New York: Free Press.

Durkheim, E. (1958). *The rules of sociological method* (S. A. Soloway & J. H. Mueller, Trans.). New York: Free Press.

Dyer, E. D. (1963). Parenthood as crisis: A re-study. *Marriage and Family Living, 25*(2), 196–201.

Dyer, W. W. (1976). *Your erroneous zones.* New York: Avon.

Eaddy, V. B., & Gentry, C. E. (1981, Winter). Play with a purpose: Interviewing abused or neglected children. *Public Welfare,* pp. 43–47.

Early, F. H. (1982). The French-Canadian family economy and standard of living in Lowell, Massachusetts, 1870. *Journal of Family History, 7,* 180–199.

Eckerman, C. O., Whatley, J. L., & Kutz, S. L. (1981). Growth of social play with peers. In L. Steinberg (Ed.), *The life cycle: Readings in human development.* New York: Columbia University Press.

Economic decline can stimulate growth in alcohol consumption. (1982). *Alcohol, Drug Abuse, and Mental Health Administration News* (ADAMHA), 8(4), 3–4.

Edelman, D. A. (1980). Nonprescription vaginal contraception. *International Journal of Gynaecological Obstetrics, 18,* 340–344.

Edelson, J. L. (1984). Working with men who batter. *Social Work, 29,* 237–242.

Edwards, C. S. (1981). *USDA estimates of the cost of raising a child: A guide to their use and interpretation.* Department of Agriculture, U. S. Govt. (misc. pub. 1411). Washington, DC: U. S. Government Printing Office.

Edwards, J. N., & Saunders, J. M. (1981). Coming apart: A model of the marital dissolution decision. *Journal of Marriage and the Family, 43,* 379–389.

Egeland, B., & Sroufe, L. A. (1981). Attachment and early maltreatment. *Child Development, 52,* 44–52.

Eidelson, R. J. (1980). Interpersonal satisfaction and level of involvement: A curvilinear relationship. *Journal of Personality and Social Psychology, 39,* 460–470.

Elbow, M. (1982). Children of violent marriages: The forgotten victims. *Social Casework, 63,* 465–471.

Elkin, S. (1981). Turning middle aged. *TWA Ambassador,* pp. 15–17. New York: Trans World Airlines.

Elliott, G. R., & Eisdorfer, C. (Eds.). (1982). *Stress and human health: Analysis and implications of research.* New York: Springer.

Ellis, R. H., & Milner, J. S. (1981). Child abuse and neglect. *Psychological Reports, 48,* 507–510.

Elmer, E. (1979). Child abuse and family stress. *Journal of Social Issues, 35,* 60–71.

Elvenstar, D. C. (1982). *Children: To have or have not?* San Francisco: Harbor.

Emery, R. E. (1982). Interparental conflict and the children of discord and divorce. *Psychological Bulletin, 92,* 310–330.

Engels, F. (1910). *The origin of the family, private property, and the state.* Chicago: Charles H. Kerr.

Englebardt, S. L. (1982, February). Herpes: Taming a runaway virus. *Reader's Digest,* pp. 115–118.

Erhardt, C. L., & Berlin, J. E. (1974). *Mortality and morbidity in the United States.* Cambridge, MA: Harvard University Press.

Erikson, E. H. (1963). *Childhood and society* (2nd ed.). New York: Norton.

Erikson, K. (1966). *The wayward Puritans.* New York: Wiley.

Espinoza, R., & Naron, N. (1983). Work and family life among Anglo, Black, and Mexican-American single parent families. Executive summary, Southwest Educational Development Laboratory, Austin, TX.

Evans, J., Selstad, G., & Welcher, W. (1976). Teenagers: Fertility control behavior and attitudes before and after abortion, childbearing or negative pregnancy test. *Family Planning Perspectives, 8*(4), 192–200.

*Facts about AIDS.* (1983, December). Washington, DC: U. S. Public Health Service, Department of Health and Human Services.

Fadiman, A. (1983). The unborn patient. *Life, 6*(4), 38–44.

Falbo, T., & Peplau, L. A. (1979, September). *Sex role self-concept and power in intimate relationships.* Paper presented at the 87th annual meeting of the American Psychological Association, New York.

Falbo, T., & Peplau, L. A. (1980). Power strategies in intimate relationships. *Journal of Personality and Social Psychology, 38,* 618–628.

Fallows, S. (1910). *Know thyself.* Marietta, OH: S. A. Mullikin.

Fanshel, D. (1981). Decision-making under uncertainty: Foster care for abused or neglected children. *American Journal of Public Health, 71,* 685–686.

Farris. A. (1978). Commuting. In R. Rapaport & R. Rapaport (Eds.), *Working couples.* New York: Harper & Row.

Fast, I., & Cain, A. C. (1966). The stepparent role: Potential for disturbances in family functioning. *American Journal of Orthopsychiatry, 36,* 485–491.

Fast, J. (1970). *Body language.* New York: Pocket Books.

Featherstone, H. (1980). *A difference in the family: Living with a disabled child.* New York: Penguin/Basic Books.

Feinman, J. A. (1979, September). *Growth disorders.* Presentation at a symposium entitled "Endocrine Disorders in Childhood and Adolescence: Psychosocial Management," at the 87th annual meeting of the American Psychological Association, New York.

Feldman, H. (1971). The effect of children on the family. In A. Michel (Ed.), *Family issues of employed women in Europe and America*. Leiden, The Netherlands: Brill.

Feldman, H. (1974). Changes in marriage and parenthood: A methodological design. In E. Peck & J. Senderowitz (Eds.), *Pronatalism: The myth of mom and apple pie*. New York: Thomas Y. Crowell.

Feldman, P., & MacCulloch, M. (1980). *Human sexual behavior*. New York: Wiley.

Felner, R. D., Farber, S. S., Ginter, M. A., Boike, M. F., & Cowen, E. L. (1980). Family stress and organization following parental divorce or death. *Journal of Divorce, 4*, 67–76.

Felner, R. D., Primavera, J., Farber, S. S., & Bishop, T. A. (1982). Attorneys as caregivers during divorce. *American Journal of Orthopsychiatry, 52*, 323–336.

Feminists on Children's Media. (1971, January). A feminist look at children's books. *School Library Journal*, pp. 19–24.

Fine, S. (1980). Children in divorce, custody and access situations: The contribution of the mental health professional. *Journal of Child Psychology and Psychiatry, 21*, 353–361.

Fischer, J. L. (1981). Transitions in relationship style from adolescence to young adulthood. *Journal of Youth and Adolescence, 10*, 11–23.

Fischer, J. L. (1983). Mothers living apart from their children. *Family Relations, 32*, 351–357.

Fisher, W. (1969). Physicians and slavery in the antebellum southern medical journal. In A. Meier & E. Rudwick (Eds.), *The making of black America: Essays in Negro life and history*. New York: Atheneum.

Fishman, K. B. (1983). The economic behavior of step families. *Family Relations, 32*, 359–366.

Fitch, S. A., & Adams, G. R. (1983). Ego-identity and intimacy status: Replication and extension. *Developmental Psychology, 19*, 839–845.

Flake-Hobson, C., Skeen, P., & Robinson, B. (1980). Review of theories and research concerning sex-role development and androgyny with suggestions for teachers. *Family Relations, 24*, 155–162.

Foa, U. G., & Foa, E. B. (1974). *Societal structures of the mind*. Springfield, IL: Charles C Thomas.

Fontana, V. J. (1975). Children become what parents make them. *Psychiatric Annals, 5*(12), 59–67.

Ford, C., & Beach, F. (1951). *Patterns of sexual behavior*. New York: Harper and Hoeber.

Ford, D. A. (1983). Wife battery and criminal justice: A study of victim decision-making. *Family Relations, 32*, 463–475.

Ford, M. E. (1981). *Androgyny as self-assertion and integration: Implications for psychological and social competence*. Paper submitted for publication, School of Education, Stanford University.

Fortin, D. (1984). Unemployment as an emotional experience: The process and the mediating factors. *Canada's Mental Health, 32*(3), 6–9.

Fox, D. R. (1969). The Negro vote in old New York. In A. Meier & E. Ruswick (Eds.), *The making of black America: Essays in Negro life and history* (Vol. 1). New York: Atheneum.

Fox, R. (1968). Treating the alcoholic's family. In R. J. Cantanzaro (Ed.), *Alcoholism: The total treatment approach*. Springfield, IL: Charles C Thomas.

Frazier, E. F. (1939). *The Negro family in the United States*. Chicago: University of Chicago Press.

Frederick, C. J. (1978). Current trends in suicidal behavior in the United States. *American Journal of Psychotherapy, 32*, 172–200.

Freeman, D. (1983). *Margaret Mead and Samoa*. Cambridge, MA: Harvard University Press.

French, J., & Raven, B. (1959). The bases of social power. In D. Cartwright (Ed.), *Studies in social power*. Ann Arbor, MI: Institute for Social Research.

Freud, S. (1947). *The ego and the id*. London: Hogarth Press.

Freud, S. (1959). *Collected papers* (Vol. 4). New York: Basic Books.

Freudiger, P. (1983). Life satisfaction among three categories of married women. *Journal of Marriage and the Family, 45*(1), 213–219.

Fried, H. (1980). *Plain talk about dealing with the angry child*. NIMH Pub. No. (ADM) 80-781. Washington, DC: U. S. Government Printing Office.

Friedman, H. J. L. (1980). The father's parenting experience in divorce. *American Journal of Psychiatry, 137*, 177–182.

Friedrich, W. N., & Boriskin, J. A. (1976). The role of the child in abuse: A review of the literature. *American Journal of Orthopsychiatry, 46*, 580–590.

Friedrich, W. N., & Boriskin, J. A. (1978). Primary prevention of child abuse: Focus on the special child. *Hospital and Community Psychiatry, 29*, 248–251.

Frodi, A. M., & Lamb, M. E. (1980). Child abusers' responses to infant smiles and cries. *Child Development, 51*, 238–241.

Fuchs, V. R. (1983). *How we live: An economic perspective on Americans from birth to death*. Cambridge, MA: Harvard University Press.

*Funk & Wagnalls Encyclopedic College Dictionary.* (1968). New York: Funk & Wagnalls.

Furstenberg, F. F., Jr. (1971). Birth control experience among pregnant adolescents: The process of unplanned parenthood. *Social Problems, 19,* 192–203.

Furstenberg, F. F., Jr. (1976). *Unplanned parenthood: The social consequences of teenage childbearing.* New York: Free Press.

Furstenberg, F. F., Jr. (1978). Family support: Helping teenage mothers to cope. *Family Planning Perspectives, 10*(6), 322–333.

Furstenberg, F. F., Jr. (1979). Recycling the family: Perspectives for a neglected family form. *Marriage and Family Review, 2*(3), 12–22.

Futterman, E. H. (1980). After the civilized divorce. *Journal of American Academy of Child Psychiatry, 19,* 525–530.

Gallagher, D. A., Thompson, L. W., & Peterson, J. A. (1981–82). Psychosocial factors affecting adaptation to bereavement in the elderly. *International Journal of Aging and Human Development, 14,* 79–95.

Garbarino, J., & Jacobson, N. (1978). Youth helping youth in cases of maltreatment of adolescents. *Child Welfare, 57,* 505–509.

Gardner, R. (1971). *The boys' and girls' book about divorce.* New York: Science House.

Garrett, W. (1982). *Seasons of marriage and family life.* New York: Holt, Rinehart & Winston.

Gartner, A. (1981, October/November). New findings on widow self-help groups. *Self-Help Reporter,* pp. 1–3.

Gary, L. E., & Leashore, B. R. (1982). High risk status of black men. *Social Work, 27,* 54–58.

Gay, G., Sheppard, C., Inaba, D., & Newmeyer, J. (1973). Cocaine in perspective: "Gift from the sun gods" to "the rich man's drug." *Drug Forum, 2,* 409–430.

Gelfand, D. E., Olsen, J. K., & Bloc, M. R. (1978). Two generations of elderly in the changing American family: Implications for family services. *Family Coordinator, 27*(4), 395–403.

Gelles, R. J. (1974). *The violent home: A study of physical aggression between husbands and wives.* Beverly Hills, CA: Sage.

Gelles, R. J. (1978). Violence toward children in the United States. *American Journal of Orthopsychiatry, 48,* 580–592.

Gelles, R. J. (1980). Violence in the family: A review of research in the seventies. *Journal of Marriage and the Family, 42,* 873–885.

Gelles, R. J. (1982). Applying research on family violence to clinical practice. *Journal of Marriage and the Family, 44,* 9–20.

Gelles, R. J., & Hargreaves, E. F. (1981). Maternal employment and violence toward children. *Journal of Family Issues, 2,* 509–530.

Gelles, R. J., & Straus, M. A. (1979a). Determinants of violence in the family: Toward a theoretical integration. In W. R. Burr, R. Hill, F. I. Nye, & I. L. Reiss (Eds.), *Contemporary theories about the family.* New York: Free Press.

Gelles, R. J., & Straus, M. A. (1979b). Violence in the American family. *Journal of Social Issues, 35,* 15–39.

Genovese, E. (1974). *Roll Jordan roll: The world the slaves made.* New York: Vintage Books.

Gergen, K. J. (1973). Social psychology as history. *Journal of Personality and Social Psychology, 26,* 309–320.

Gergen, K. J. (1976). Social psychology, science and history. *Personality and Social Psychology Bulletin, 2,* 373–383.

Gergen, K. J. (1980). The emerging crisis in life-span developmental theory. In P. B. Baltes & O. G. Brim, Jr. (Eds), *Life-span development and behavior.* New York: Academic Press.

Gerstel, N. (1979). Marital alternatives and the regulation of sex. *Alternative lifestyles, 2,* 145–176.

Gerstel, N., & Gross, H. E. (1982). Commuter marriages: A review. *Marriage and Family Review, 5,* 71–91.

Gesell, A., Ilg, F., & Ames, L. B. (1956). *Youth: The years from ten to sixteen.* New York: Harper & Row.

Ghali, S. B. (1982). Understanding Puerto Rican traditions. *Social Work, 27,* 98–102.

Gibbs, J. T. (1984). Black adolescents and youth: An endangered species. *American Journal of Orthopsychiatry, 54,* 6–21.

Gibson, A. B., Roberts, P. C., & Buttery, T. J. (1982). *Death education: A concern for the living.* Bloomington, IN: Phi Delta Kappan Educational Foundation.

Gil, D. G. (1973). *Violence against children.* Cambridge, MA: Harvard University Press.

Gil, D. G. (1975). Unraveling child abuse. *American Journal of Orthopsychiatry, 45,* 346–356.

Gil, D. G. (1976). Primary prevention of child abuse: A philosophical and political issue. *Psychiatric Opinion, 13,* 30–34.

Gilligan, C. (1982). *In a different voice.* Cambridge, MA: Harvard University Press.

Gillman, I. S. (1980). An object-relations approach to the phenomenon and treatment of battered women. *Psychiatry, 43,* 346–358.

Ginott, H. G. (1969). *Between parent and child.* New York: Avon Books.

Ginott, H. G. (1971). *Between parent and teenager.* New York: Avon Books.

Giordano, N. H., & Giordano, J. A. (1984). Elder abuse: A review of the literature. *Social Work, 29,* 232–236.

Giovannoni, J. M. (1971). Parental mistreatment: Perpetrators and victims. *Journal of Marriage and the Family, 33,* 649–657.

Gladieux, J. D. (1978). Pregnancy—a transition to parenthood: Satisfaction with the pregnancy experience as a function of sex role conceptions, marital relationships and social network. In W. B. Miller and L. F. Newman (Eds.), *The first child and family formation.* Chapel Hill, NC: Carolina Population Center.

Glazer, N. (1963). Introduction. In S. M. Elkins, *Slavery.* New York: Grosset & Dunlap.

Glenn, N. D. (1975). Psychological well-being in the postparental stage: Some evidence from national surveys. *Journal of Marriage and the Family, 37*(1), 105–110.

Glenn, N. D., & McLanahan, S. (1981). The effect of offspring on the psychological well-being of older adults. *Journal of Marriage and the Family, 43*(2), 409–421.

Glenn, N. D., & Weaver, C. N. (1977). The marital happiness of remarried divorced persons. *Journal of Marriage and the Family, 39,* 331–337.

Glick, P. C., & Spanier, G. B. (1981). Cohabitation in the United States. In P. J. Stein (Ed.), *Single life: Unmarried adults in social context.* New York: St. Martin's Press.

Goetting, A. (1981). Divorce outcome research. *Journal of Family Issues, 2,* 350–378.

Goetting, A. (1982). The six stations of remarriage: Developmental tasks of remarriage after divorce. *Family Relations, 31,* 213–222.

Gold, M. S. (1984). *800-COCAINE.* New York: Bantam Books.

Goldberg, S., & Lewis, M. (1969). Play behavior in the year old infant: Early sex differences. *Child Development, 40,* 21–31.

Goldenberg, S., & Perlman, D. (1984). *Social relations and loneliness during adolescence.* Unpublished manuscript, University of Manitoba.

Goldstein, H. S. (1974). Reconstituted families: The second marriage and its children. *Psychiatric Quarterly, 48,* 433–440.

Goodale, G. (1982, November 28). Retirement income: Don't underestimate. *Hartford Courant,* p. D4.

Goode, W. J. (1956). *Women in divorce.* New York: Free Press.

Goode, W. J. (1971). Force and violence in the family. *Journal of Marriage and the Family, 33,* 624–636.

Goodlad, J. I. (1984). *A place called school: Prospects for the future.* New York: McGraw-Hill.

Goodwin, D. W. (1976). *Is alcoholism hereditary?* New York: Oxford University Press.

Goodwin, D. W. (1979). Alcoholism and heredity. *Archives of General Psychiatry, 36,* 57–61.

Gordon, M. (1973). *The American family in socio-historical perspective.* New York: St. Martin's Press.

Gordon, M. (1981). Was Waller ever right? The rating and dating complex reconsidered. *Journal of Marriage and the Family, 43,* 67–76.

Gordon, S., Scales, P., & Everly, K. (1979). *The sexual adolescent: Communicating with teenagers about sex* (2nd ed.). North Scituate, MA: Duxbury Press.

Gordon, T. (1970). *P.E.T.: Parent Effectiveness Training.* New York: Peter H. Wyden.

Gore, S. (1978). The effect of social support in moderating the health consequences of unemployment. *Journal of Health and Social Behavior, 19,* 157–165.

Gottman, J. M. (1979). *Marital interaction: Experimental investigations.* New York: Academic Press.

Gottman, J. M., Markman, H., & Notarius, C. (1977). The topography of marital conflict: A study of verbal and nonverbal communication. *Journal of Marriage and the Family, 39,* 461–477.

Gottman, J. M., Notarius, C., Gonso, J., & Markman, J. (1976). *A couple's guide to communication.* Champaign, IL: Research Press.

Gould, R. E. (1974). The wrong reasons to have children. In E. Peck & J. Senderowitz (Eds.), *Pronatalism: The myth of mom and apple pie.* New York: Thomas Y. Crowell.

Grabill, W. H., Kiser, C. V., & Whelpton, P. K. (1973). A long view. In M. Gordon (Ed.), *The American family in socio-historical perspective.* New York: St. Martin's Press.

Gray, E. B. (1982). Perinatal support programs: A strategy for the primary prevention of child abuse. *Journal of Primary Prevention, 2,* 138–152.

Gray, S. H. (1982). Exposure to pornography and aggression toward women: The case of the angry male. *Social Problems, 29,* 387–398.

Greenblat, C. S. (1983). The salience of sexuality in the early years of marriage. *Journal of Marriage and the Family, 45*(2), 289–299.

Greenblatt, M. (1978). The grieving spouse. *American Journal of Psychiatry, 135,* 43–47.

Gregg, C. T. (1983). *A virus of love and other tales of medical detection.* New York: Scribner's.

Greif, J. B. (1979). Fathers, children, and joint custody. *American Journal of Orthopsychiatry, 49,* 311–319.

Greven, P. J. (1973). Family structure in seventeenth-century Andover, Massachusetts. In M. Gordon (Ed.), *The American family in socio-historical perspective.* New York: St. Martin's Press.

Grinspoon, L. (1971). *Marijuana reconsidered.* Cambridge, MA: Harvard University Press.

Grinspoon, L., & Bakalar, J. B. (1976). *Cocaine: A drug and its social evolution.* New York: Basic Books.

Gross, H. (1978, August). *Couples who live apart: The dual-career variant.* Paper presented at the 73rd annual meeting of the American Sociological Association, San Francisco.

Grossman, S. M., Shea, J. A., & Adams, G. R. (1980). Effects of parental divorce during early childhood on ego development and identity formation of college students. *Journal of Divorce, 3,* 263–272.

Grotevant, H. D., & Thorbecke, W. L. (1982). Sex differences in styles of occupational identity formation in late adolescence. *Developmental Psychology, 18,* 396–405.

Groth, A. N., & Burgess, A. W. (1977). Rape: A sexual deviation. *American Journal of Orthopsychiatry, 47,* 400–406.

Guerney, B. G. (1977). *Relationship enhancement: Skill training programs for therapy, problem prevention and enrichment.* San Francisco: Jossey-Bass.

Guerney, L. (1976). Filial therapy program. In D. H. Olson (Ed.), *Treating relationships.* Lake Mills, IA: Graphic.

Gullotta, T. P. (1981). Children of divorce: Easing the transition from a nuclear family. *Journal of Early Adolescence, 1,* 357–364.

Gullotta, T. P. (1982). Easing the distress of grief: A selected review of the literature with implications for prevention programs. *Journal of Primary Prevention, 3,* 6–17.

Gullotta, T. P. (1983). Unemployment and mental health. *Journal of Primary Prevention, 4*(1), 3–4.

Gullotta, T. P. (in press). Prevention's technology. In S. E. Goldston & M. Shore (Eds.), *A primary prevention primer.* NIMH DHEW Pub.

Gullotta, T. P., & Adams, G. R. (1982). Substance abuse minimization: Conceptualizing prevention in adolescent and youth programs. *Journal of Youth and Adolescence, 11,* 409–423.

Gullotta, T. P., & Donohue, K. C. (1981a). Corporate families: Implications for preventive intervention. *Social Casework, 62,* 109–114.

Gullotta, T. P., & Donohue, K. (1981b). The corporate family: Theory and treatment. *Journal of Marriage and Family Therapy, 7,* 151–158.

Gullotta, T. P., & Donohue, K. (1983). Families, relocation, and the corporation: The role of the mental health agency. In S. L. White (Ed.), *New directions for mental health services: Advances in occupational mental health,* (No. 20). San Francisco: Jossey-Bass.

Gunther, J. (1971). *Death be not proud.* New York: Harper & Row.

Gustavus, S. O., & Henley, J. R., Jr. (1971). Correlates of voluntary childlessness in a select population. *Social Biology, 18,* 277–284.

Gutmann, D. (1969). The country of old men: Cross-cultural studies in the psychology of later life. In W. Donahue (Ed.), *Occasional papers in gerontology.* Ann Arbor: University of Michigan.

Guttentag, M. (1977). The prevention of sexism. In G. W. Albee & J. M. Joffe (Eds.), *Primary prevention of psychopathology* (Vol. 1). Hanover, NH: University Press of New England.

Guttman, H. G. (1976). *The black family in slavery and freedom, 1750–1925.* New York: Pantheon Books.

Haas, L. (1980). Role-sharing couples: A study of egalitarian marriages. *Family Relations, 29,* 289–296.

Hacker, A. (1983). *U/S: A statistical portrait of the American people.* New York: Viking Press.

Hagen, D. Q. (1983). The relationship between job loss and physical and mental illness. *Hospital and Community Psychiatry, 34,* 438, 441.

Hall, E. (1983). Acting one's age: New rules for old. In H. Cox (Ed.), *Aging* (3rd ed.). Guilford, CT: Dushkin.

Hall, E. T. (1963). Proxemics: A study of man's spatial relationships. In Iago Galdstom (Ed.), *Man's image in medicine and anthropology.* New York: International Universities Press.

Halligan, F. G. (1982). Death in the family system . . . the ultimate confrontation. *The Family, 9,* 117–123.

Hancock, E. (1980). The dimensions of meaning and belonging in the process of divorce. *American Journal of Orthopsychiatry, 50,* 18–27.

Haney, B., & Gold, M. (1977). The juvenile delinquent nobody knows. In D. Rogers (Ed.), *Issues in adolescent psychology.* Englewood Cliffs, NJ: Prentice-Hall.

Hanks, S. E., & Rosenbaum, C. P. (1977). Battered women: A study of women who live with violent alcohol-abusing men. *American Journal of Orthopsychiatry, 47,* 291–306.

Hansen, G. L. (1982). Reactions to hypothetical, jealousy producing events. *Family Relations, 31,* 513–518.

Harbin, H. T., & Maziar, H. M. (1975). The families of drug abusers: A literature review. *Family Process, 14,* 411–431.

Hardy, T. (1966). *The life and death of the mayor of Casterbridge.* New York: St. Martin's Press. (Originally published 1886)

Harford, T. C., Willis, C. H., & Beabler, H. L. (1967). Personality correlates of masculinity-femininity. *Psychological Reports, 21,* 881–884.

Harkins, E. B. (1978). Effects of empty nest transition on self-report of psychological and physical well-being. *Journal of Marriage and the Family, 40*(3), 549–556.

Harris, T. A. (1967). *I'm OK, you're OK.* New York: Avon Books.

Harrison, A. A., & Saeed, L. (1977). Let's make a deal: An analysis of revelations and stipulations in lonely hearts advertisements. *Journal of Personality and Social Psychology, 35,* 257–264.

Harry, J. (1976). Evolving sources of happiness for men over the life cycle: A structural analysis. *Journal of Marriage and the Family, 38*(2), 289–296.

Harry, J. (1983). Gay male and lesbian relationships. In E. Macklin & R. Rubin (Eds.), *Contemporary families and alternative lifestyles.* Beverly Hills, CA: Sage.

Harry, J., & DeVall, W. (1978). Age and sexual culture among homosexually oriented males. *Archives of Sexual Behavior, 3,* 199–209.

Hartman, C. (1984). Shelter and community. *Society, 21*(3), 18–27.

Harvey, C. D. H., & Bahr, H. M. (1980). *The sunshine widows.* Lexington, MA: Lexington Books.

Harwood, H. J., Napolitano, D. M., Kristiansen, P. L., & Collins, J. J. (1984). *Economic costs to society of alcohol and drug abuse and mental illness: 1980.* Research Triangle Park, NC: Research Triangle Institute.

Hawkins, D. G. (1980). Enigma in swaddling clothes: Sudden infant death syndrome. *Health and Social Work, 5*(4), 21–26.

Hayakawa, S. I. (1979). *Through the communication barrier.* New York: Harper & Row.

Hayes, J., & Nutman, P. (1981). *Understanding the unemployed.* New York: Tavistock.

Hayes, M. P., Stinnett, N., & DeFrain, J. (1980). Learning about marriage from the divorce. *Journal of Divorce, 4,* 23–29.

Hazen, B. S. (1978). *Two homes to live in.* New York: Human Sciences Press.

Heider, F. (1958). *The psychology of interpersonal relations.* New York: Wiley.

Heiss, J. S. (1980). Premarital characteristics of religiously intermarried in an urban area. *American Sociological Review, 15,* 619–627.

Helmreich, R. L., Spence, J. T., & Wilhelm, J. A. (1981). A psychometric analysis of the Personal Attributes Questionnaire. *Sex Roles, 7,* 1097–1108.

Hemmons, W. M. (1981). The need for domestic violence laws with adequate legal and support services. *Journal of Divorce, 4,* 49–60.

Hendin, H., Pollinger, A., Ulman, R., & Carr, A. C. (1981). *Research 40: Adolescent marijuana abusers and their families.* NIDA, DHHS Pub. No. (ADM) 81-1168. Washington, DC: U. S. Government Printing Office.

Hendricks, S. S. (1981). Self-disclosure and marital satisfaction. *Journal of Personality and Social Psychology, 40,* 1150–1159.

Hendricks-Matthews, M. (1982). The battered woman: Is she ready for help? *Social Casework, 63,* 131–137.

Henshaw, S. K., Forrest, J. D., Sullivan, E., & Tietze, C. (1984). Abortion services in the United States, 1981–82. *Family Planning Perspectives, 16*(3), 119–127.

Henton, J. M., Cate, R., Koval, J., Lloyd, S., & Christopher, S. (1983). Romance and violence in dating relationships. *Journal of Family Issues, 4,* 467–482.

Herzberger, S. D., Potts, D. A., & Dillon, M. (1981). Abusive and nonabusive parental treatment from the child's perspective. *Journal of Consulting and Clinical Psychology, 49,* 81–90.

Herzig, A. C., & Mali, J. L. (1980). *Oh, boy! Babies!* Boston: Little, Brown.

Herzog, A. R., & Bachman, J. G. (1982). *Sex role attitudes among high school seniors: Views about work and family roles.* Ann Arbor: Survey Research Center, Institute for Social Research, University of Michigan.

Hess, B. (1972). Friendship. In M. Riley, M. Johnson, & A. Foner (Eds.), *Aging and society.* Vol. 3: *A sociology of age stratification.* New York: Russell Sage Foundation.

Hess, B. B., & Waring, J. M. (1982). Changing patterns of aging and family bonds in later life. In J. Rosenfeld (Ed.), *Relationships: The marriage and family reader.* Glenview, IL: Scott, Foresman.

Hess, R. (1983). Early intervention with the unemployed. *Journal of Primary Prevention, 4*(3), 129–131.

Hetherington, E. M. (1979). Divorce: A child's perspective. *American Psychologist, 34,* 851–858.

Hetherington, E. M., Cox, M., & Cox, R. (1978). The aftermath of divorce. In J. H. Stevens & M. Mathews (Eds.), *Mother-child, father-child relationships.* Washington, DC: NAEYC.

Hickey, T., & Douglass, R. L. (1981). Neglect and abuse of older family members: Professionals' perspectives and case experiences. *Gerontologist, 21,* 171–176.

Hicks, M. W., Hansen, S. L., & Christie, L. A. (1983). Dual-career/dual-work families: A systems approach. In E. Macklin & R. Rubin (Eds.), *Contemporary families and alternative lifestyles.* Beverly Hills, CA: Sage.

Hicks, M. W., & Williams, J. W. (1981). Current challenges in education for parenthood. *Family Relations, 30*(4), 579–584.

Higham, E. (1980). Variations in adolescent psychohormonal development. In J. Adelson (Ed.), *Handbook of adolescent psychology.* New York: Wiley.

Highlights. (1984, March). *Science 84,* p. 14.

Hilberman, E., & Munson, K. (1977–78). Sixty battered women. *Victimology, 2,* 460–470.

Hill, C. T., Rubin, Z., & Peplau, L. A. (1976). Breakups before marriage: The end of 103 affairs. *Journal of Social Issues, 32,* 147–168.

Hill, R. (1949). *Families under stress.* New York: Harper & Row.

Hill, R. (1958). Social stresses on the family. *Social Casework, 34,* 139–150.

Hill, R. (1971). *The strengths of the black family.* Washington, DC: National Urban League.

Hill, R., & Hansen, D. A. (1960). The identification of conceptual frameworks utilized in family study. *Marriage and Family Living, 22,* 299–311.

Hill, R., & Rodgers, R. H. (1964). The developmental approach. In H. T. Christensen (Ed.), *Handbook of marriage and the family.* Chicago: Rand McNally.

Hillard, T. O. (1981). Political and social action in the prevention of psychopathology of blacks: A mental health strategy for oppressed people. In J. M. Joffe & G. W. Albee (Eds.), *Prevention through political action and social change* (Vol. 5). Hanover, NH: University Press of New England.

Hingst, A. G. (1981). Children and divorce: The child's view. *Journal of Clinical Child Psychology, 10,* 161–164.

Hinkle, D. E., & Sporakowski, M. J. (1975). Attitudes toward love: A reexamination. *Journal of Marriage and the Family, 37,* 764–767.

Hjorth, C. W., & Harway, M. (1981). The body image of physically abused and normal adolescents. *Journal of Clinical Psychology, 37,* 863–866.

Hochschild, A. (1973). *The unexpected community.* Englewood Cliffs, NJ: Prentice-Hall.

Hock, Z., Safir, M. P., Peres, Y., & Shepher, J. (1981). An evaluation of sexual performance—comparison between sexually dysfunctional and functional couples. *Journal of Sex and Marital Therapy, 7,* 195–206.

Hodgson, J., & Fischer, J. L. (1979). Sex differences in identity and intimacy development in college youth. *Journal of Youth and Adolescence, 8,* 37–50.

Hoffman, L. (1972). Early childhood experiences and women's achievement motives. *Journal of Social Issues, 28,* 129–156.

Holinger, P. C. (1979). Violent deaths among the young: Recent trends in suicide, homicide, and accidents. *American Journal of Psychiatry, 136,* 1144–1147.

Hollister, W. G. (1977). Basic strategies in designing primary prevention programs. In D. C. Klein & S. E. Goldston (Eds.), *Primary prevention: An idea whose time has come.* NIMH, DHEW Pub. No. (ADM) 77-447. Washington, DC: U. S. Government Printing Office.

Holman, T. B., & Burr, W. R. (1980). Beyond the beyond: The growth of family theories in the 1970's. *Journal of Marriage and the Family, 42,* 729–740.

Holmes, T. H., & Rahe, R. H. (1967). The Social Readjustment Rating Scale. *Journal of Psychosomatic Research, 11,* 213–218.

Holmstrom, L. L., & Burgess, A. W. (1979). Rape: The husband's and boyfriend's initial reaction. *Family Coordinator, 28,* 321–327.

Holmstrom, L. L., & Burgess, A. W. (1983). Rape and everyday life. *Society, 20*(5), 33–40.

Holzman, T. (1984). Schools can provide help for the children of divorce. *American School Board Journal, 171*(5), 46–47.

Houseknecht, S. K. (1977). Reference group support for voluntary childlessness: Evidence for conformity. *Journal of Marriage and the Family, 39*(2), 285–292.

Houseknecht, S. K. (1979). Childlessness and marital adjustment. *Journal of Marriage and the Family, 41*(2), 259–265.

Houseknecht, S. K. (1982a). Childless and single-childed women in early twentieth-century America. *Journal of Family Issues, 3,* 421–458.

Houseknecht, S. K. (1982b). Voluntary childlessness in the 1980s: A significant increase? *Marriage and Family Review, 5,* 51–69.

Hughes, H. M., & Barad, S. J. (1983). Psychological functioning of children in a battered women's shelter: A preliminary investigation. *American Journal of Orthopsychiatry, 53,* 525–531.

Humphreys, L. (1970). Tearoom trade: Impersonal sex in public places. *Transaction, 7,* 10–25.

Hunt, D. (1970). *Parents and children in history: The psychology of family life in early modern France.* New York: Basic Books.

Hunt, M. (1974). *Sexual behavior in the 1970s*. Chicago: Playboy Press.

Hunter, R. S., & Kilstrom, N. (1979). Breaking the cycle in abusive families. *American Journal of Psychiatry, 136*, 1320–1322.

Huston, A. C. (1983). Sex-typing. In E. M. Hetherington (Ed.), *Handbook of child psychology* (Vol. 4). New York: Wiley.

Huston, T. L. (1984). Power. In H. H. Kelley, E. Berscheid, A. Christensen, J. Harvey, T. Huston, G. Levinger, E. McClintock, A. Peplau, & D. Peterson (Eds.), *Close relationships*. Salt Lake City: W. H. Freeman.

Huston, T. L., & Levinger, G. (1978). Interpersonal attraction and relationships. *Annual Review of Psychology, 29*, 115–156.

Huston, T. L. & Surra, C. A. (1981). Social transitions in young adulthood. In S. Messick (Ed.), *Development in young adulthood: Characteristics and competencies in education, work, and social life*. San Francisco: Jossey-Bass.

Huston, T. L., Surra, C. A., Fitzgerald, N. M., & Cate, R. M. (1981). From courtship to marriage: Mate selection as an interpersonal process. In S. Duck & R. Gilmore (Eds.), *Personal relationships*. Vol. 1: *Developing personal relationships*. London: Academic Press.

Huston-Stein, A., & Higgins-Trenk, A. (1978). A development of females from childhood through adulthood: Career and feminine role orientations. In P. B. Baltes (Ed.), *Lifespan development and behavior* (Vol. 1). New York: Academic Press.

Hutchison, I. W. (1975). The significance of marital status for morale and life satisfaction among lower income elderly. *Journal of Marriage and the Family, 37*(2), 287–293.

Ickes, W., & Barnes, R. D. (1979). Boys and girls together—and alienated: On enacting stereotyped sex roles in mixed-sex dyads. *Journal of Personality and Social Psychology, 36*, 669–683.

Ilg, F. L., & Ames, L. B. (1955). *Child behavior*. New York: Harper & Row.

Inglis, B. (1975). *The forbidden game: A social history of drugs*. New York: Scribner's.

Insko, C. A., & Wilson, M. (1977). Interpersonal attraction as a function of social interaction. *Journal of Personality and Social Psychology, 35*, 903–911.

Jackson, J. K. (1954). The adjustments of the family to the crisis of alcoholism. *Quarterly Journal of Studies on Alcohol, 15*, 562–586.

Jacobs, S., & Douglas, L. (1979). Grief: A mediating process between a loss and illness. *Comprehensive Psychiatry, 20*, 165–176.

Jacques, E. (1965). Death and the mid-life crisis. *International Journal of Psychoanalysis, 4*, 502–514.

James, J. E., & Goldman, M. (1971). Behavior trends of wives of alcoholics. *Quarterly Journal of Studies on Alcohol, 32*, 373–381.

Jedlicka, D. (1980). Formal mate selection networks in the United States. *Family Relations, 29*, 199–203.

Jencks, C. S., Smith, M., Acland, H., Bane, M. J., Cohen, D., Gintis, H., Heyns, B., & Michelson, S. (1972). *Inequality: A reassessment of the effect of family and schooling in America*. New York: Basic Books.

Jessor, R. (1979). Marijuana: A review of recent psychosocial research. In R. Dupont, A. Goldstein, & J. O'Donnell (Eds.), *Handbook on drug abuse*. Washington, DC: U. S. Government Printing Office.

Jessor, R., Chase, J. A., & Donovan, J. E. (1980). Psychosocial correlates of marijuana use and perhaps drinking in a national sample of adolescents. *American Journal of Public Health, 70*, 604–612.

Joffe, J. M., & Albee, G. W. (1981). Powerlessness and psychopathology. In J. M. Joffe & G. W. Albee (Eds.), *Prevention through political action and social change*. Hanover, NH: University Press of New England.

Johnson, E. S. (1981). Older mothers' perceptions of their child's divorce. *Gerontologist, 21*, 395–401.

Johnson, J. H. (1983). Vasectomy—an international appraisal. *Family Planning Perspectives, 15*, 45–48.

Johnson, M., & Shuman, S. (1983, October). *Courtship as the development of commitment to a relationship*. Paper presented at the annual meeting of the National Council on Family Relations, St. Paul, MN.

Johnston, L. D., Bachman, J. G., & O'Malley, P. M. (1981). *Highlights from student drug use in America, 1975–1981*. NIDA, DHHS Pub. No. (ADM) 82-1208. Washington, DC: U. S. Government Printing Office.

Jones, J. M., & McNeely, R. L. (1980). Mothers who neglect and those who do not: A comparative study. *Social Casework, 10*, 559–567.

Jones, R. T. (1980). Human effects: An overview. In R. C. Petersen (Ed.), *Research 31: Marijuana research findings, 1980*. NIDA, DHHS Pub. No. (ADM) 80-1001. Washington, DC: U. S. Government Printing Office.

Jones, W. H. (1979). Involuntary career change: Its implications for counseling. *Vocational Guidance Quarterly, 27*, 196–201.

Jones, W. H., Hobbs, S. A., & Hockenbury, D. (1982). Loneliness and social skill deficits. *Journal of Personality and Social Psychology, 42*, 682–689.

Jorgensen, S. R., & Alexander, S. (1981). Reducing the risk of adolescent pregnancy: Toward certification of family life educators. *High School Journal, 64*(6), 257–268.

Jorgensen, S. R., & Gaudy, J. C. (1980). Self-disclosure and satisfaction in marriage: The relation examined. *Family Relations, 29*(3), 281–287.

Jorgensen, S. R., King, S. L., & Torrey, B. A. (1980). Dyadic and social network influences on adolescent exposure to pregnancy risk. *Journal of Marriage and the Family, 42*(1), 141–155.

Joseph, M. V., & Conrad, A. P. (1980). A parish neighborhood model for social work practice. *Social Casework, 61,* 423–432.

Jourard, S. (1971). *The transparent self.* New York: Van Nostrand.

Jurich, A. P., & Jurich, J. A. (1974). The effect of cognitive moral development upon the selection of premarital sexual standards. *Journal of Marriage and the Family, 36,* 736–741.

Juster, T. F. (1978–79). The psychology of inflation. *Economic Outlook U. S. A., 6*(1), 16–18.

Justice, B., & Duncan, D. F. (1975, May). *Child abuse as a work related problem.* Paper presented at the annual meeting of the American Public Health Association, Atlanta, GA.

Kacerguis, M. A., & Adams, G. R. (1979). Implications of sex typed child rearing practices, toys, and mass media materials in restricting occupational choices of women. *Family Coordinator, 28,* 369–375.

Kacerguis, M. A., & Adams, G. R. (1980). Erikson stage resolution: The relationship between identity and intimacy. *Journal of Youth and Adolescence, 9,* 117–126.

Kagan, J. (1964). Acquisition and significance of sex typing and sex role identity. In M. Hoffman & L. W. Hoffman (Eds.), *Review of child development research* (Vol. 1). New York: Russell Sage Foundation.

Kalish, R. A. (1985). *Death, grief, and caring relationships* (2nd ed.). Monterey, CA: Brooks/Cole.

Kalter, N. (1977). Children of divorce in an outpatient setting. *American Journal of Orthopsychiatry, 47,* 40–51.

Kandel, D. B. (1978). Similarity in real-life adolescent friendship pairs. *Journal of Personality and Social Psychology, 36,* 306–312.

Kanter, J., & Zelnik, M. (1972). Sexual experiences of young unmarried women in the U. S. *Family Planning Perspectives, 4,* 9–17.

Kargman, M. W. (1983). Stepchild support obligations of stepparents. *Family Relations, 32,* 231–238.

Karweit, N., & Hansell, S. (in press). Sex differences in adolescent relationships: Friendship and status. In J. L. Epstein & N. Karweit (Eds.), *Friends in school.* New York: Academic Press.

Katchadourian, H. A., & Lunde, D. T. (1972). *Fundamentals of human sexuality.* New York: Holt, Rinehart & Winston.

Kay, R. (Ed.), (1983). *Plain talk about wife abuse.* DHHS, NIMH, Pub. No. (ADM) 83-1265. Washington, DC: U. S. Government Printing Office.

Keefe, S. E., & Casas, J. M. (1980). Mexican Americans and mental health: A selected review and recommendations for mental health service delivery. *American Journal of Community Psychology, 8,* 303–326.

Keeshan, B. (1983, January 30). [Untitled comments.] *Hartford Courant,* p. A2.

Kelly, J. G. (1968). Toward an ecological conception of preventive interventions. In J. W. Carter (Ed.), *Research contributions from psychology to community mental health.* New York: Behavioral Publications.

Kelly, J. G., & Levin, R. (1984). *The ecological paradigm: Key concepts.* Mimeo (adapted by the authors of this text). (Available from James G. Kelley, Psychology Dept., University of Illinois, Chicago, IL 60680)

Kempe, C. H. (1976). Approaches to preventing child abuse. *American Journal of Diseases of Children, 130,* 941–947.

Kempe, C. H., & Helfer, R. (1972). *Helping the battered child and his family.* Philadelphia: Lippincott.

Kempe, C. H., Silverman, F. H., Steele, B. F., Droegemuller, W., & Silver, H. K. (1962). The battered child syndrome. *Journal of the American Medical Association, 181,* 17–24.

Kendrick, D. T., & Cialdini, R. B. (1977). Romantic attraction: Misattribution versus reinforcement explanations. *Journal of Personality and Social Psychology, 35,* 381–391.

Keniston, K. (1977). *All our children.* New York: Harcourt Brace Jovanovich.

Kenkel, W. F., & Gage, B. A. (1983). The restricted and gender-typed occupational aspirations of young women: Can they be modified? *Family Relations, 32,* 129–138.

Kent, M. O. (1980). Remarriage: A family system perspective. *Social Casework, 61,* 146–153.

Kephart, W. M. (1973). Evaluation of romantic love. *Medical Aspects of Human Sexuality, 7,* 92–108.

Kerckhoff, A., & Davis, K. E. (1962). Value consensus and need complementarity in mate selection. *American Sociological Review, 27,* 295–303.

Kerr, R. A. (1984). Another oil resource warning. *Science, 223*(4634), 382

Kessler, M., & Albee, G. W. (1977). An overview of the literature of primary prevention. In G. W. Albee & J. M. Joffe (Eds.), *Primary prevention of psychopathology.* Vol. 1:

*The issues*. Hanover, NH: University Press of New England.

Kessler, R. C., & McRae, J. A. (1982). The effect of wives' employment on the mental health of married men and women. *American Sociological Review, 47,* 216–227.

Kihss, P. (1982, June 15). Califano cites 50 percent increases in heroin addiction in city. *New York Times,* pp. 81, 85.

Kinard, E. M. (1979). The psychological consequences of abuse for the child. *Journal of Social Issues, 35,* 82–100.

Kinard, E. M. (1980). Emotional development in physically abused chidren. *American Journal of Orthopsychiatry, 50,* 686–696.

Kinard, E. M. (1982a). Aggression in abused children: Differential responses to the Rosenzweig picture-frustration study. *Journal of Personality Assessment, 46,* 139–141.

Kinard, E. M. (1982b). Child abuse and depression: Cause or consequence. *Child Welfare, 61,* 403–413.

Kinard, E. M. (1982c). Experiencing child abuse: Effects on emotional adjustment. *American Journal of Orthopsychiatry, 52,* 82–91.

Kinard, E. M., & Klerman, L. V. (1980). Teenage parenting and child abuse. *American Journal of Orthopsychiatry, 50,* 481–488.

King, C. E., & Christensen, A. (1983). The relationship event scale: A Guttman scaling of progress in courtship. *Journal of Marriage and the Family, 45,* 671–678.

Kinsey, A. C., Pomeroy, W., & Martin, C. E. (1948). *Sexual behavior of the human male.* Philadelphia: Saunders.

Kinsey, A. C., Pomeroy, W., Martin, C. E., & Gebhard, P. H. (1953). *Sexual behavior in the human female.* Philadelphia: Saunders.

Kirkley-Best, E., & Kellner, K. R. (1982). The forgotten grief: A review of the psychology of stillbirth. *American Journal of Orthopsychiatry, 52,* 420–429.

Kirschner, B., & Walum, L. (1978). Two-location families: Married singles. *Alternative Lifestyles, 1,* 513–525.

Kirsh, S. (1983). *Unemployment: Its impact on body and soul.* Toronto: Canadian Mental Health Association.

Kitchin, S. B. (1912). *A history of divorce.* London: Chapman and Hall.

Kitson, G. C., Lopata, H. Z., Holmes, W. M., & Meyering, S. M. (1980). Divorcees and widows. *American Journal of Orthopsychiatry, 50,* 291–301.

Kitson, G. C., Moir, R. N., & Mason, P. R. (1982). Family social support in crises: The special case of divorce. *American Journal of Orthopsychiatry, 52,* 161–165.

Kitson, G. C., & Sussman, M. B. (1982). Marital complaints, demographic characteristics, and symptoms of mental distress in divorce. *Journal of Marriage and the Family, 44,* 87–101.

Kivett, V. R. (1978). Loneliness and the rural widow. *Family Coordinator, 27,* 389–394.

Klagsburn, M., & Davis, D. I. (1977). Substance abuse and family interaction. *Family Process, 16*(2), 149–164.

Klass, D. (1981–82). Elisabeth Kübler-Ross and the tradition of the private sphere: An analysis of symbols. *Omega, 12,* 241–267.

Klein, D. (1981). Violence against women: Some considerations regarding its causes and its elimination. *Crime and Delinquency, 27,* 64–80.

Klein, D. C., & Goldston, S. E. (Eds.). (1977). *Primary prevention: An idea whose time has come.* NIMH, DHEW Pub. No. (ADM) 77-447. Washington, DC: U.S. Government Printing Office.

Klein, J. F., Calvert, G. P., Garland, T. N., & Poloma, M. M. (1969). Pilgrim's progress I: Recent developments in family theory. *Journal of Marriage and the Family, 31,* 677–687.

Klein, L. (1978). Antecedents to teenage pregnancy. *Clinical Obstetrics and Gynecology, 32,* 1151–1159.

Kleinfeld, J. (1982). Getting it together in adolescence: Case studies of positive socializing environments for Eskimo youth. In S. M. Manson (Ed.), *New directions in prevention among American Indian and Alaska native communities.* Portland: Oregon Health Services University.

Knapp, M. L. (1984). *Interpersonal communication and human relationships.* Boston: Allyn & Bacon.

Knox, D., & Wilson, K. (1981). Dating behaviors of university students. *Family Relations, 30,* 255–258.

Knudson, R. M., Sommers, A. A., & Golding, S. L. (1980). Interpersonal perception and mode of resolution in marital conflict. *Journal of Personality and Social Psychology, 38,* 751–763.

Koblinsky, S., & Atkinson, J. (1979). *Final grant report of the early childhood sex education project.* Unpublished manuscript, San Diego State University, San Diego, CA.

Komarovsky, M. (1962). *Blue-collar marriage.* New York: Random House.

Komarovsky, M. (1964). *Blue-collar marriage* (2nd ed.). New York: Random House.

Kompara, D. R. (1980). Difficulties in the socialization process of stepparenting. *Family Relations, 29,* 69–73.

Koval, J. E., Ponzetti, J. J., & Cate, R. M. (1982). Programmatic intervention for men involved in conjugal violence. *Family Therapy, 9,* 147–154.

Kraine, M. (1975). Communication among premarital couples at three stages of dating. *Journal of Marriage and the Family, 37,* 609–618.

Kraine, M., Cannon, D., & Bagford, J. (1977). Rating-dating or simple prestige homogamy? Data on dating in the Greek system on a Midwestern campus. *Journal of Marriage and the Family, 39,* 663–674.

Kratcoski, P. C. (1982). Child abuse and violence against the family. *Child Welfare, 61,* 435–444.

Kreidberg, G., Butcher, A. L., & White, K. M. (1978). Vocational role choice in second- and sixth-grade children. *Sex Roles, 4,* 175–181.

Kruger, L., Moore, D., Schmidt, P., & Wiens, R. (1979). Group work with abusive parents. *Social Work, 24,* 337–338.

Kruger, W. S. (1973). Education for parenthood and the schools. *Children Today, 2,* 4–7.

Kübler-Ross, E. (1969). *On death and dying.* New York: Macmillan.

Kübler-Ross, E. (1974). *Questions and answers on death and dying.* New York: Macmillan.

Kulka, R. W., & Weingarten, H. (1979). The long term effects of parental divorce in childhood on adult adjustment. *Journal of Social Issues, 35,* 50–78.

Kurdek, L. A. (1981). An integrative perspective on children's divorce adjustment. *American Psychologist, 36,* 856–866.

Kurdek, L. A., Blisk, D., & Siesky, A. E. (1981). Correlates of children's long-term adjustment to their parents' divorce. *Developmental Psychology, 17,* 565–579.

Kurdek, L. A., & Siesky, A. E. (1980a). Sex role self-concepts of single divorce parents and their children. *Journal of Divorce, 3,* 249–261.

Kurdek, L. A., & Siesky, A. E. (1980b). Effects of divorce on children: The relationship between parent and child perspectives. *Journal of Divorce, 4,* 85–99.

L'Abate, L., & L'Abate, B. L. (1981). Marriage: The dream and the reality. *Family Relations, 30,* 131–136.

LaBell, L. S. (1979). Wife abuse: A sociological study of battered women and their mates. *Victimology, 4,* 258–267.

Lamb, M. E., & Lamb, J. E. (1976). The nature and importance of the father-infant relationship. *Family Coordinator, 25*(4), 379–385.

Lamb, R., & Zusman, J. (1979). Drs. Lamb and Zusman reply. *American Journal of Psychiatry, 136,* 1949.

Lamke, L. K. (1982). Adjustment and sex-role orientation in adolescence. *Journal of Youth and Adolescence, 11,* 247–259.

Landy, S., Schubert, J., Cleland, J. F., Clark, C., & Montgomery, J. S. (1983). Teen pregnancy: Family syndrome? *Adolescence, 18,* 679–694.

Lang, A. M., & Brody, E. M. (1983). Characteristics of middle-aged daughters and help to their elderly mothers. *Journal of Marriage and the Family, 1983, 45*(1), 193–202.

Langner, T. S., & Michael, S. T. (1963). *Life stress and mental health.* New York: Free Press.

Langston, D. P. (1983). *Living with herpes: The comprehensive and authoritative guide to the causes, symptoms, and treatment of herpes virus illnesses.* Garden City, NY: Dolphin Books.

LaRossa, R. (1983). The transition to parenthood and the social reality of time. *Journal of Marriage and the Family, 45*(3), 579–589.

Larson, J. H. (1984). The effect of husband's unemployment on marital and family relations in blue-collar families. *Family Relations, 33,* 503–511.

Lasch, C. (1977). *Haven in a heartless world.* New York: Basic Books.

Laslett, B. (1979). The significance of family membership. In V. Tufte & B. Myerhoff (Eds.), *Changing images of the family.* New Haven, CT: Yale University Press.

Latané, B., & Hothersall, D. (1972). Social attraction in animals. In P. C. Dodwell (Ed.), *New horizons in psychology II.* Harmondsworth, England: Penguin Books.

Latané, B., Meltzer, J., Joy, V., Lubell, B., & Cappell, H. (1972). Stimulus determinants of social attraction in rats. *Journal of Comparative and Physiological Psychology, 79,* 12–21.

Lau, E. E., & Kosberg, J. I. (1979, March–April). Abuse of the elderly by informal care providers. *Aging,* pp. 10–15.

Leboyer, F. (1975). *Birth without violence.* New York: Knopf.

Lederer, W. J., & Jackson, D. D. (1968). *The mirages of marriage.* New York: Norton.

Lee, G. R. (1978). Marriage and morale in later life. *Journal of Marriage and the Family, 40*(1), 131–139.

Lee, G. R., & Ellithorpe, E. (1982). Intergenerational exchange and subjective well-being among the elderly. *Journal of Marriage and the Family, 44*(1), 217–224.

Lee, J. A. (1977). A typology of styles of loving. *Personality and Social Psychology Bulletin, 3,* 173–182.

Lein, L. (1979). Male participation in home life: Impact of social supports and breadwinner responsibility on the allocation of tasks. *Family Coordinator, 28,* 489–495.

LeMasters, E. E. (1957). Parenthood in crisis. *The Journal of Marriage and Family Living, 19,* 352–355.

Lenard, L. (1982, November). The battle to wipe out herpes. *Science Digest,* pp. 36–38.

Levine, S. B. (1981). Overview of sex therapy. In G. P. Sholevar (Ed.), *Handbook of marriage and marital therapy.* New York: S. P. Medical and Scientific Books.

Levinger, G. (1974). A three-level approach to attraction: Toward an understanding of pair relatedness. In T. Huston (Ed.), *Foundations of interpersonal attraction*. New York: Academic Press.

Levinger, G., & Snoek, J. D. (1972). *Attraction in relationship: A new look at interpersonal attraction*. New York: General Learning Press.

Levinson, D. J., Darrow, C. N., Klein, E. B., Levinson, M. H., & McKee, B. (1978). *The seasons of a man's life*. New York: Knopf.

Levi-Strauss, C. (1969). *The elementary structure of kinship*. London: Eyre & Spottiswoode.

Levitan, S. A., & Belous, R. S. (1981). *What's happening to the American family?* Baltimore, MD: Johns Hopkins University Press.

Levitan, S. A., & Johnson, C. M. (1982). The future of work: Does it belong to us or to the robots? *Monthly Labor Review, 105*(9), 10–14.

Lewis, A. (1963). *Of men and machines*. New York: Dutton.

Lewis, E., & Page, A. (1978). Failure to mourn a stillbirth: An overlooked catastrophe. *British Journal of Medical Psychology, 51,* 237–241.

Lewis, G. L. (1978). Changes in women's role participation. In I. H. Frieze, J. E. Parsons, P. B. Johnson, D. N. Ruble, & G. L. Zellmen (Eds.), *Women and sex roles: A social psychological perspective*. New York: Norton.

Lewis, M. (1972). State as an infant-environment interaction: An analysis of mother-infant interaction as a function of sex. *Merrill-Palmer Quarterly, 18,* 95–121.

Lewis, M., & Weinraub, M. (1974). Sex of parents × sex of the child: Socioemotional development. In R. Friedman, R. Richart, & R. Wiele (Eds.), *Sex differences in behavior*. New York: Wiley.

Lewis, O. (1959). *Five families: Mexican case studies in the culture of poverty*. New York: Basic Books.

Lewis, R. A. (1972). A developmental framework for the analysis of premarital dyad formation. *Family Process, 11,* 17–48.

Lewis, R. A. (1973). A longitudinal test of a development framework for premarital dyadic formation. *Journal of Marriage and the Family, 35,* 16–25.

Liem, R., & Rayman, P. (1982). Health and social costs of unemployment. *American Psychologist, 37,* 1116–1123.

Light, R. (1973). Abused and neglected children in America: A study of alternative policies. *Harvard Educational Review, 43,* 556–598.

Lightman, A. (1983, May). Nothing but the truth. *Science 83,* pp. 24–26.

Lindemann, E. (1944). Symptomatology and management of acute grief. *American Journal of Psychiatry, 101,* 141–148.

Litwack, L. (1973). Education: Separate and unequal. In M. B. Katz (Ed.), *Education in American history: Readings on the social issues*. New York: Praeger.

Lodge, C. G., & Glass, W. R. (1982). The desperate plight of the underclass. *Harvard Business Review, 60*(4), 60–71.

Logan, D. D. (1980). The menarche experience in twenty-three foreign countries. *Adolescence, 15,* 247–256.

Longres, J. F. (1982). Minority groups: An interest-group perspective. *Social Work, 27,* 7–14.

Looft, W. R. (1971). Sex differences in the expression of vocational aspirations by elementary school children. *Developmental Psychology, 5,* 366.

Lowenthal, M. F., & Chiriboga, D. (1975). Responses to stress. In M. Lowenthal, M. Thurnher, & D. Chiriboga (Eds.), *The four stages of life*. San Francisco: Jossey-Bass.

Luepnitz, D. A. (1979). Which aspects of divorce affect children. *Family Coordinator, 28,* 79–85.

Lueptow, L. B. (1981). Sex-typing and change in the occupational choices of high school seniors: 1964–1976. *Sociology of Education, 54,* 16–24.

Lutz, P. (1983). The stepfamily: An adolescent perspective. *Family Relations, 32,* 367–375.

Lynch, J. L. (1979). *The broken heart: The medical consequences of loneliness*. New York: Basic Books.

Maccoby, E. E., & Jacklin, C. N. (1974). *The psychology of sex differences*. Stanford, CA: Stanford University Press.

Mackintosh, E. (1982, October). What causes crib death? *Science 82,* p. 108.

Macklin, E. D. (1980). Nontraditional family forms: A decade of research. *Journal of Marriage and the Family, 42,* 905–922.

Macklin, E. D. (1981). Cohabitating college students. In P. J. Stein (Ed.), *Single life: Unmarried adults in social context*. New York: St. Martin's Press.

Maier, R. A. (1984). *Human sexuality in perspective*. Chicago: Nelson–Hall.

Maloney, L. (1981, August 24). Hispanics make their move. *U. S. News & World Report,* pp. 60–64.

Manis, J. G., & Meltzer, B. N. (1978). *Symbolic interaction: A reader in social psychology*. Boston: Allyn & Bacon.

Manson, S. M., Tatum, E., & Dinges, N. G. (1982). Prevention research among American Indian and Alaska native communities: Charting future courses for theory and practice in mental health. In S. M. Manson (Ed.), *New directions in prevention among American Indian and Alaska native communities*. Portland: Oregon Health Services University.

Marcia, J. E. (1976). Identity six years after: A follow-up study. *Journal of Youth and Adolescence, 5,* 145–160.

Marcy, P. T. (1981). Factors affecting the fecundity and fertility of historical populations: A review. *Journal of Family History, 6,* 309–326.

Marion, M. (1982). Primary prevention of child abuse: The role of the family life educator. *Family Relations, 31,* 515–582.

Marris, R. (1976). *The American worker.* U. S. Dept. of Labor, Pub. No. 029-000-00256-8. Washington, DC: U. S. Government Printing Office.

Marsh, L. C. (1981). Hours worked by husbands and wives. *Journal of Family Issues, 2,* 164–179.

Marx, J. L. (1985). AIDS virus genomes. *Science, 227*(4686), 503.

Masnick, G., & Bane, M. J. (1980). *The nation's families: 1960–1990.* Boston, MA: Auburn House.

Mason, V. G., & Baker, G. (1983). *Growing up and feeling powerful as an American Indian.* NIDA, DHHS Pub. No. (ADM) 83-787. Washington, DC: U. S. Government Printing Office.

Masters, W. H., & Johnson, V. E. (1966). *Human sexual response.* Boston, MA: Little, Brown.

Mathes, E. W. (1975). The effects of physical attractiveness and anxiety on heterosexual attraction over a series of five encounters. *Journal of Marriage and the Family, 37,* 769–774.

Maurer, H. (1979). *Not working: An oral history of the unemployed.* New York: Holt, Rinehart & Winston.

May, H. J., & Breme, F. J. (1982–83). SIDS Family Adjustment Scale: A method of assessing family adjustment to sudden infant death syndrome. *Omega, 13,* 59–74.

McAdams, D. P. (1982). Experiences of intimacy and power: Relationships between social motives and autobiographical memory. *Journal of Personality and Social Psychology, 42,* 292–302.

McAdams, D. P., & Powers, J. (1981). Themes of intimacy in behavior and thought. *Journal of Personality and Social Psychology, 40,* 1150–1159.

McAdoo, H. P. (1978). Factors related to stability in upwardly mobile black families. *Journal of Marriage and the Family, 40,* 761–776.

McAdoo, H. P. (1982a). Demographic trends for people of color. *Social Work, 27,* 15–23.

McAdoo, H. P. (1982b). Levels of stress and family support in black families. In H. I. McCubbin, A. E. Cauble, & J. M.

Patterson (Eds.), *Family stress, coping, and social support.* Springfield, IL: Charles C Thomas.

McAdoo, H. P. (1983). Societal stress: The black family. In H. I. McCubbin & C. R. Figley (Eds.), *Stress and the family.* Vol. 1: *Coping with normative transitions.* New York: Brunner/Mazel.

McCabe, T. R. (1978). *Victims no more.* Center City, MN: Hazelden Foundation.

McCall, R. B., & Stocking, S. H. (1980). Divorce: A summary of research about the effects of divorce on families. Boys Town, NE: Boys Town Center for the Study of Youth Development.

McCollum, A. T. (1981). *The chronically ill child.* New Haven, CT: Yale University Press.

McConnell, K. (1982). The aged widower. *Social Work, 27,* 188–189.

McCourt, W. F., Barnett, R. D., Brennen, J., & Becker, A. (1976). We help each other: Primary prevention for the widowed. *American Journal of Psychiatry, 133,* 98–100.

McCubbin, H. I., Cauble, A. E., & Patterson, J. M. (1982). *Family stress, coping, and social support.* Springfield, IL: Charles C Thomas.

McCubbin, H. I., Joy, C. B., Cauble, A. E., Comeau, J. K., Patterson, J. M., & Needle, R. H. (1980). Family stress and coping: A decade review. *Journal of Marriage and the Family, 42,* 855–871.

McCubbin, H. I., & Patterson, J. M. (1983). Family transitions: Adaptations to stress. In H. I. McCubbin & C. R. Figley (Eds.), *Stress and the family.* Vol. 1: *Coping with normative transitions.* New York: Brunner/Mazel.

McDaniel, C. O. (1969). Dating roles and reasons for dating. *Journal of Marriage and the Family, 31,* 97–107.

McHale, S. M., & Huston, T. L. (1984). Men and women as parents: Sex role orientations, employment, and parental roles with infants. *Child Development, 55,* 1349–1361.

McKain, W. C. (1972). A new look at older marriages. *Family Coordinator, 21*(1), 61–69.

McKirdy, G., & Nissley, D. (1980). *A decade of voluntary childlessness: A bibliography.* Washington, DC: National Alliance for Optional Parenthood.

McLaughlin, T. (1971). *Dirt: A social history as seen through the uses and abuses of dirt.* New York: Stein & Day.

McNeil, J. S., & McBride, M. L. (1979). Group therapy with abusive parents. *Social Casework, 60,* 36–42.

McWhirter, D., & Mattison, A. (1984). *The male couple.* Englewood Cliffs, NJ: Prentice-Hall.

Mead, G. H. (1962). *Mind, self and society: From the standpoint of a social behaviorist*. Chicago: University of Chicago Press.

Mead, M. (1928). *Coming of age in Samoa*. New York: Blue Ribbon Books

Mehrabian, A. (1972). *Nonverbal communication*. Chicago: Aldine-Atherton.

Meissner, M., Humphreys, E. W., Meis, S. M., & Scheu, W. J. (1975). No exit for wives: Sexual division of labour and the accumulation of household demands. *Canadian Review of Sociology and Anthropology, 12*, 424–439.

Mendes, H. A. (1976). Single fathers. *Family Coordinator, 25*(4), 439–444.

Mennel, R. (1973). *Thorns and thistles: Juvenile delinquency in the United States*. Hanover, NH: University Press of New England.

Menning, B. E. (1977). *Infertility: A guide for childless couples*. Englewood Cliffs, NJ: Prentice-Hall.

Messinger, L., & Walker, K. N. (1981). From marriage breakdown to remarriage: Parental tasks and therapeutic guidelines. *American Journal of Orthopsychiatry, 51*, 429–438.

Messinger, L., Walker, K. N., & Freeman, S. J. J. (1978). Preparation for remarriage following divorce: The use of group techniques. *American Journal of Orthopsychiatry, 48*, 263–272.

Metzer, A. M. (1979–80). A Q-methodological study of the Kübler-Ross stage theory. *Omega, 10*, 291–301.

Meyer, T. (1972). The effects of sexually arousing and violent films on aggressive behavior. *Journal of Sex Research, 8*, 324–331.

Milardo, R. M. (1982). Friendship networks in developing relationships: Converging and diverging social environments. *Social Psychology Quarterly, 45*, 162–172.

Miller, B. (1979). Unpromised paternity: The lifestyles of gay fathers. In M. Levine (Ed.), *Gay men*. New York: Harper & Row.

Miller, B. C. (1976). A multivariate developmental model of marital satisfaction. *Journal of Marriage and the Family, 38*(3), 643–657.

Miller, B. C., & Sollie, D. (1980). Normal stresses during the transition to parenthood. *Family Relations, 29*, 459–465.

Mindel, C. H., & Wright, R., Jr. (1982). Satisfaction in multi-generational households. *Journal of Gerontology, 37*(4), 483–489.

Mitchell, J. E., Hong, M. K., & Corman, C. (1979). Childhood onset of alcohol abuse. *American Journal of Orthopsychiatry, 51*, 511–513.

Mittra, S. (1977). *Personal finance: Lifetime management by objectives*. New York: Harper & Row.

Model, S. (1981). Housework by husbands: Determinants and implications. *Journal of Family Issues, 2*, 180–204.

Moen, P. (1980). Measuring unemployment: Family consideration. *Human Relations, 33*(3), 183–192.

Moen, P. (1983). Unemployment, public policy, and families: Forecasts for the 1980s. *Journal of Marriage and the Family, 45*, 751–760.

Mogielnicki, R. P., Poffenberger, N., Chandler, J. E., & Weissberg, M. P. (1977). Impending child abuse: Psychosomatic symptoms in adults as a clue. *Journal of the American Medical Association, 237*, 1109–1111.

Montemayor, R., & Van Komen, R. (1983). The development of sex differences in friendships and peer group structure during adolescence. Paper submitted for publication, University of Utah.

Montgomery, B. M. (1981). The form and function of quality communication in marriage. *Family Relations, 30*, 21–30.

Moore, K. A. (1978). Teenage childbirth and welfare dependency. *Family Planning Perspectives, 10*(4), 233–235.

Morgan, E. S. (1973). The Puritans and sex. In M. Gordon (Ed.), *The American family in socio-historical perspective*. New York: St. Martin's Press.

Morgan, M. (1982). Television and adolescents' sex role stereotypes: A longitudinal study. *Journal of Personality and Social Psychology, 43*, 947–955.

Morton, B. M. (1976). *VD: A guide for nurses and counselors*. Boston: Little, Brown.

Mosher, W. D., & Bachrach, C. A. (1982). Childlessness in the United States: Estimates from the National Survey of Family Growth. *Journal of Family Issues, 3*, 517–544.

Moss, H. (1967). Sex, age, and state as determinants of mother-infant interaction. *Merrill-Palmer Quarterly, 113*, 19–35.

Motowidlo, S. J. (1982). Sex role orientation and behavior in a work setting. *Journal of Personality and Social Psychology, 42*, 935–945.

Moynihan, D. (1965). *The case for national action: The Negro family*. Department of Labor Pub. No. 0-794-628. Washington, DC: U. S. Government Printing Office.

Mueller, C. W., & Pope, H. (1977). Marital instability: A study of its transmission between generations. *Journal of Marriage and the Family, 39*(1), 83–93.

Mueller, C. W., & Pope, H. (1980). Divorce and female remarriage mobility: Data on marriage matches after divorce for white women. *Social Forces, 58*, 726–738.

Mukherjee, A. B., & Hodgen, G. D. (1982). Maternal ethanol exposure induces transient impairment of umbilical circulation and fetal hypoxia in monkeys. *Science, 218,* 700–702.

Munro, B., & Adams, G. R. (1978). Love American style: A test of role structure theory on changes in attitudes toward love. *Human Relations, 31,* 215–228.

Murstein, B. I. (1974). *Love, sex, and marriage through the ages.* New York: Springer.

Murstein, B. I. (1977). The stimulus-value-role (SVR) theory of dyadic relationships. In S. W. Duck (Ed.), *Theory and practice in interpersonal attraction.* London: Academic Press.

Murstein, B. I. (1978). *Exploring intimate life styles.* New York: Springer.

Murstein, B. I. (1980). Mate selection in the 1970s. *Journal of Marriage and the Family, 42,* 777–792.

Mussen, P. H. (1969). Early sex-role development. In D. A. Goslin (Ed.), *Handbook of socialization theory and research.* Chicago: Rand McNally.

Mussen, P., Honzik, M. P., & Eichorn, D. H. (1982). Early adult antecedents of life satisfaction at age 70. *Journal of Gerontology, 37*(3), 316–322.

Nadelson, C. C., & Nadelson, T. (1980). Dual-career marriages: Benefits and costs. In F. Pepitone-Rockwell (Ed.), *Dual-career couples.* Beverly Hills, CA: Sage.

Nadelson, C., & Notman, M. T. (1977). Treatment of the pregnant teenager and the putative father. *Current Psychiatric Therapy, 19,* 81.

Naeye, R. L. (1980). Sudden infant death. *Scientific American, 242*(4), 52–62.

Nagi, S. Z. (1975, March). *The structure and performance of programs on child abuse and neglect.* Report to the Office of Child Development, Department of Health, Education and Welfare.

National Advisory Council on Economic Opportunity. (1980). *Critical choices for the 1980s.* Washington, DC: U. S. Government Printing Office.

National Institute of Mental Health. (1978). *Yours, mine and ours: Tips for stepparents.* DHEW Pub. No. (ADM) 78-676. Washington, DC: U. S. Government Printing Office.

National Institute of Mental Health. (1981). *Caring about kids: When parents divorce.* DHEW Pub. No. (ADM) 81-1120. Washington, DC: U. S. Government Printing Office.

National Institute on Alcohol Abuse and Alcoholism. (1981). *Preventing fetal alcohol effects: A practical guide for ob/gyn physicians and nurses.* Public Health Service, DHHS Pub. No. (ADM) 81-1163. Washington, DC: U. S. Government Printing Office.

*National Statistical Survey on Runaway Youth.* (1976). Princeton, NJ: Opinion Research Corp.

Neiswender-Reedy, M., Birren, J. A., & Schaie, K. W. (1976, September). *Love in adulthood: Beliefs versus experience.* Paper presented at the meeting of the American Psychological Association, Washington, DC.

Nelson, G. (1982). Coping with the loss of father. *Journal of Family Issues, 3,* 41–60.

Nelson, M., & Nelson, G. K. (1982). Problems of equity in the reconstituted family: A social exchange analysis. *Family Relations, 31,* 223–231.

Neugarten, B. (Ed.). (1968). *Middle age and aging: A reader in social psychology.* Chicago: University of Chicago Press.

Neugarten, B., & Weinstein, K. (1964). The changing American grandparent. *Journal of Marriage and the Family, 26,* 199–204.

Newberger, C. M., & Cook, S. J. (1983). Parental awareness and child abuse: A cognitive-developmental analysis of urban and rural samples. *American Journal of Orthopsychiatry, 53,* 512–524.

Newcomb, T. (1937). Recent changes in attitude toward sex and marriage. *American Sociological Review, 2,* 659–667.

Newman, M., & Berkowitz, B. (1971). *How to be your own best friend.* Center City, MN: Hazelden Foundation.

New York Institute of Life Insurance. (1976). *Let's talk about money.* New York: New York Institute of Life Insurance.

Nieto, D. S. (1982). Aiding the single father. *Social Work, 27,* 473–478.

Nock, S. L. (1979). The family life cycle: Empirical or conceptual tool? *Journal of Marriage and the Family, 41,* 15–26.

Nye, I. F. (1957). Child adjustment in broken and in unhappy unbroken homes. *Marriage and Family Living, 19,* 356–361.

Nye, I. F. (1979). Choice, exchange, and the family. In W. R. Burr, R. Hill, F. I. Nye, & I. L. Reiss (Eds.), *Contemporary theories about the family* (Vol. 2). New York: Free Press.

O'Connell, C. (1978). Destined to die. *Journal of Sociology and Social Welfare, 5*(2), 3–15.

Offord, D. R., Abrams, N., Allen, N., & Poushinsky, M. (1979). Broken homes, parental psychiatric illness, and female delinquency. *American Journal of Orthopsychiatry, 49,* 252–264.

Olson, D. H., & Cromwell, R. E. (1975). Power in families. In R. E. Cromwell & D. H. Olson (Eds.), *Power in families.* Beverly Hills: Sage.

Olson, D. H., McCubbin, H. I., Barnes, H., Larsen, A., Muxen,

M., & Wilson, M. (1983). *Families: What makes them work.* Beverly Hills, CA: Sage.

Olson, D. H., & Ryder, R. G. (1970). Inventory of marital conflicts. *Journal of Marriage and the Family, 32*(3), 443–448.

O'Neill, N., & O'Neill, G. (1972). *Open marriage.* New York: M. Evans.

O'Neill, W. (1973). Divorce in the progressive era. In M. Gordon (Ed.), *The American family in socio-historical perspective.* New York: St. Martin's Press.

Orden, S. R., & Bradburn, N. M. (1968). Dimensions of marriage happiness. *American Journal of Sociology, 73,* 715–731.

Orlofsky, J. L. (1976). Intimacy status: Relationship to interpersonal perception. *Journal of Youth and Adolescence, 5,* 73–88.

Orlofsky, J. L., Aslin, A. L., & Ginsburg, S. D. (1977). Differential effectiveness of two classification procedures on the Bem Sex Role Inventory. *Journal of Personality Assessment, 41,* 414–416.

Orlofsky, J. L., Marcia, J. E., & Lesser, I. M. (1973). Ego identity status and the intimacy vs. isolation crisis of young adulthood. *Journal of Personality and Social Psychology, 27,* 211–219.

Orme, T. C., & Rimmer, J. (1981). Alcoholism and child abuse: A review. *Journal of Studies on Alcohol, 42,* 273–286.

Orthner, D. K., Brown, T., & Ferguson, D. (1976). Single-parent fatherhood: An emerging family life style. *Family Coordinator, 25*(4), 429–437.

Orton, J., & Crossman, S. M. (1980, September). *Long distance marriage: Disruptor of marital stability and satisfaction or solution to unequal career development of dual career couples?* Paper presented at the Bi-Annual meeting of the Utah Academy of Arts, Sciences, and Letters, Logan, UT.

Osofsky, J. D., & Osofsky, H. (1972). The psychological reaction of patients to legalized abortions. *American Journal of Orthopsychiatry, 42*(1), 48–60.

Osofsky, J. D., & Osofsky, H. S. (1978). Teenage pregnancy: Psychosocial considerations. *Clinical Obstetrics and Gynecology, 21,* 1161–1173.

Ostbloom, N., & Crase, S. J. (1980). A model for conceptualizing child abuse causation and intervention. *Social Casework, 61,* 164–172.

Osterweis, M., Solomon, F., & Green, M. (1984). *Bereavement: Reactions, consequences, and care.* Washington, DC: National Academy Press.

Otto, M. L., & Smith, D. G. (1980). Child abuse: A cognitive behavioral intervention model. *Journal of Marriage and Family Therapy, 42,* 425–429.

Pace, N. A. (1981). Driving on pot. In L. H. Gross (Ed.), *The parent's guide to teenagers.* New York: Macmillan.

Pais, J., & White, P. (1979). Family redefinition. *Journal of Divorce, 2,* 271–281.

Palermo, E. (1980). Remarriage: Parental perceptions of step-relations with children and adolescents. *Journal of Psychiatric Nursing, 18*(4), 9–13.

Parish, T. S. (1981). The impact of divorce on the family. *Adolescence, 16,* 577–580.

Parish, T. S., & Dostal, J. W. (1980). Evaluations of self and parent figures by children from intact, divorced, and reconstituted families. *Journal of Youth and Adolescence, 9,* 347–351.

Parish, T. S., & Taylor, J. C. (1979). The impact of divorce and subsequent father absence on children's and adolescents' self-concepts. *Journal of Youth and Adolescence, 8,* 351–427.

Parke, R. D., & Sawin, D. B. (1976). The father's role in infancy: A re-evaluation. *Family Coordinator, 25*(4), 365–371.

Parker, D. A., & Harman, M. S. (1980). A critique of the distribution of consumption model of prevention. In T. C. Hartford, D. A. Parker, & L. Light (Eds.), *Normative approaches to the prevention of alcohol abuse and alcoholism.* Research Monograph 3. DHEW Pub. No. (ADM) 79-847. Washington, DC: U. S. Government Printing Office.

Parkes, C. M. (1970). The first year of bereavement. *Psychiatry, 33,* 444–467.

Parkes, C. M. (1972). *Bereavement: Studies of grief in adult life.* New York: International Universities Press.

Parnes, H. S., Adams, A. V., Andrisani, P., Kohlen, A. I., & Nestel, G. (1975). *The pre-retirement years: Five years in the work lives of middle-aged men.* Manpower Research Monograph No. 15. Washington, DC: U. S. Department of Labor.

Pascale, R., Hurd, M., & Primavera, L. H. (1980). The effects of chronic marijuana use. *Journal of Social Psychology, 110,* 273–283.

Patterson, R. D. (1969). Grief and depression in old people. *Maryland State Medical Journal, 18,* 75–79.

Patzer, G. L. (1985). *The physical attractiveness phenomena.* New York: Plenum.

Paul, J. L. (1981). *Understanding and working with parents of children with special needs.* New York: Holt, Rinehart & Winston.

Peck, E. (1974). Television's romance with reproduction. In

E. Peck & J. Senderowitz (Eds.), *Pronatalism: The myth of mom and apple pie*. New York: Thomas Y. Crowell.

Pedrick-Cornell, C., & Gelles, R. J. (1982). Elder abuse: The state of current knowledge. *Family Relations, 31,* 457–465.

Pelton, L. H. (1978). Child abuse and neglect: The myth of classlessness. *American Journal of Orthopsychiatry, 48,* 608–617.

Pendery, M. L., Maltzman, I. M., & West, L. J. (1982). Controlled drinking by alcoholics: New findings and a reevaluation of a major affirmative study. *Science, 217,* 169–175.

Pepitone-Rockwell, F. (1980). *Dual-career couples.* Beverly Hills, CA: Sage.

Peplau, L. A. (1976, September). *Sex, love, and the double standard.* Paper presented at the meeting of the American Psychological Association, Washington, DC.

Perlmutter, L. H., Engel, T., & Sager, C. J. (1982). The incest taboo: Loosened sexual boundaries in remarried families. *Sex and Marital Therapy, 8,* 83–96.

Peters, M. F. (1981). Making it black family style: Building on the strength of black families. In N. Stinnett, J. DeFrain, K. King, P. Knaub, & G. Rowe (Eds.), *Family strengths 3: Roots of well-being.* Lincoln: University of Nebraska Press.

Peters, M. F., & McAdoo, H. P. (1983). The present and future of alternative lifestyles in ethnic American cultures. In E. Macklin & R. Rubin (Eds.), *Contemporary families and alternative lifestyles.* Beverly Hills, CA: Sage.

Petersen, A. (1979, April). *The psychological significance of pubertal changes to adolescent girls.* Paper presented at the biennial meeting of the Society for Research in Child Development, San Francisco.

Petersen, A., & Taylor, B. (1980). The biological approach to adolescence: Biological change and psychological adaptation. In J. Adelson (Ed.), *Handbook of adolescent psychology.* New York: Wiley.

Petersen, J. R. (1983, March) The *Playboy* readers' sex survey, part II. *Playboy,* pp. 90–92, 178, 180, 182, 184.

Petersen, R. (1980). Social class, social learning, and wife abuse. *Social Science Review, 54,* 390–406.

Petersen, R. C. (1977). History of cocaine. In R. C. Petersen & R. C. Stillman (Eds.), *Research 13: Cocaine, 1977.* NIDA, DHHS Pub. No. (ADM) 82-471. Washington, DC: U. S. Government Printing Office.

Petersen, R. C. (1980). Marijuana and health: 1980. In R. C. Petersen (Ed.), *Research 31: Marijuana research findings, 1980.* NIDA, DHHS Pub. No. (ADM) 80-1001. Washington, DC: U. S. Government Printing Office.

Physicians for Automotive Safety. (1985). *Don't risk your child's life!* (Available from P.A.S., P.O. Box 430, Armonk, NY 10504)

Pierce, C. (1975). The mundane extreme environment and its effects on learning. In S. C. Bainerd (Ed.), *Learning disabilities: Issues and recommendations for research.* Washington, DC: National Institute of Education.

Pierce, R. V. (1895). *The people's common sense medical advisor.* Buffalo, NY: World's Dispensary.

Pill, C. J. (1981). A family life education group for working with stepparents. *Social Casework, 62,* 159–166.

Pinderhughes, E. B. (1982). Family functioning of Afro-Americans. *Social Work, 27,* 91–96.

Piotrkowski, C. S., & Crits-Christoph, P. (1981). Women's jobs and family adjustment. *Journal of Family Issues, 2,* 126–147.

Pitts, J. R. (1964). The structural-functional approach. In H. T. Christensen (Ed.), *Handbook of marriage and the family.* Chicago: Rand McNally.

Plath, D. W. (1972). Japan: The after years. In D. O. Cowgill & L. D. Holmes (Eds.), *Aging and modernization.* New York: Appleton-Century-Crofts.

Pleck, J. H. (1979). Men's family work: Three perspectives and some new data. *Family Coordinator, 28,* 481–488.

Pogrebin, L. C. (1980). *Growing up free.* New York: McGraw-Hill.

Pohlman, E. (1974). Changes in views toward childlessness: 1965–1970. In E. Peck & J. Senderowitz (Eds.), *Pronatalism: Thy myth of mom and apple pie.* New York: Thomas Y. Crowell.

Polansky, N. A., Hally, C., Lewis, J., & Wormer, K. V. (1977). *Child neglect: An annotated bibliography.* DHEW Pub. No. (OHDS) 77-02005. Washington, DC: U. S. Government Printing Office.

Polsby, G. K. (1974). Unmarried parenthood: Potential for growth. *Adolescence, 9,* 273–284.

Ponzetti, J. J., Cate, R. M., & Koval, J. E. (1982). Violence between couples: Profiling the male abuser. *Personnel and Guidance Journal, 61,* 222–224.

Porter, B. (1983, June–July). LISC—a new approach to community development. *Human Development News,* pp. 1–12.

Porterfield, E. (1982). Black-American intermarriage in the United States. *Marriage and Family Review, 5,* 3–16.

Powell, J. A., & Arquitt, G. E. (1978). Getting the generations back together: A rationale for development of community-based intergenerational interaction programs. *Family Coordinator, 27*(4), 421–426.

Prendergast, T. (1974). Family characteristics associated with marijuana use among adolescents. *International Journal of the Addictions, 9,* 827–839.

President Carter's address to the U. S. Congress on drug use. (1977, September–October). *Drug Survival News,* p. 6.

Price-Bonham, S., & Balswick, J. O. (1980). The noninstitutions: Divorce, desertion, and remarriage. *Journal of Marriage and the Family, 42,* 959–972.

Prosen, S. S., & Farmer, J. H. (1982). Understanding stepfamilies: Issues and implications for counselors. *Personnel and Guidance Journal, 60,* 393–397.

Pursell, S. A., & Banikiotes, P. G. (1978). Androgyny and initial interpersonal attraction. *Personality and Social Psychology Bulletin, 4,* 235–239.

Quinn, W. H. (1983). Personal and family adjustment in later life. *Journal of Marriage and the Family, 45*(1), 57–73.

Rainwater, L., & Yancey, W. L. (1967). *The Moynihan Report and the politics of controversy.* Cambridge, MA: M.I.T. Press.

Ramsey, G. (1943). The sexual development of boys. *American Journal of Psychiatry, 56,* 217–234.

Randal, J. (1982, August). What every young woman should know about herpes. *Redbook,* p. 22.

Rankin, R. P., & Maneker, J. S. (1985). The duration of marriage in a divorcing population: The impact of children. *Journal of Marriage and the Family, 47*(1), 43–52.

Ransom, J. W., Schlesinger, S., & Derdeyn, A. P. (1979). A stepfamily in formation. *American Journal of Orthopsychiatry, 49,* 36–43.

Raphael, B. (1977). Preventive intervention with the recently bereaved. *Archives of General Psychiatry, 34,* 1450–1454.

Rapoport, R., & Rapoport, R. N. (1975). Men, women, and equity. *Family Coordinator, 24,* 421–432.

Rappaport, A. F. (1976). Conjugal relationship enhancement program. In D. H. Olson (Ed.), *Treating relationships.* Lake Mills, IA: Graphic.

Rathbone-McCuan, E. (1980). Elderly victims of family violence and neglect. *Social Casework, 61,* 296–304.

Rathbone-McCuan, E., & Voyles, B. (1982). Case detection of abused elderly parents. *American Journal of Psychiatry, 139,* 189–192.

Read, D. A. (1979). *Healthy sexuality.* New York: Macmillan.

Rebelsky, F., & Hawks, C. (1971). Fathers' verbal interaction with infants in the first three months of life. *Child Development, 42,* 63–68.

Reinhard, D. W. (1977). The reaction of adolescent boys and girls to the divorce of their parents. *Journal of Clinical Child Psychology, 6*(2), 21–23.

Reisinger, K. S., Williams, A. F., Wells, J. K., John, C. E., Roberts, T. R., & Podgainy, H. J. (1981). Effect of pediatrician's counseling on infant restraint use. *Pediatrics, 67*(2), 201–206.

Reiss, I. L. (1967). *The social context of premarital sexual permissiveness.* New York: Holt, Rinehart & Winston.

Rendina, I., & Dickerscheid, J. D. (1976). Father involvement with first-born infants. *Family Coordinator, 25*(4), 373–377.

Renne, K. S. (1970). Correlates of dissatisfaction in marriage. *Journal of Marriage and the Family, 32*(1), 54–66.

Resick, P. A., & Sweet, J. J. (1979). Child maltreatment intervention: Directions and issues. *Journal of Social Issues, 35,* 140–160.

Rettig, K. D., & Bubolz, M. M. (1983). Interpersonal resource exchanges as indicators of a quality marriage. *Journal of Marriage and the Family, 45*(3), 497–509.

Reynolds, J. (1977). Two hundred years of children's recreation. In E. G. Grotberg (Ed.), *200 years of children.* DHEW Pub. No. (OHD) 77-30103. Washington, DC: U. S. Government Printing Office.

Richards, L. G. (1981). *Research 35: Demographic trends and drug abuse, 1980–1995.* NIDA, DHHS Pub. No. (ADM) 81-1069. Washington, DC: U. S. Government Printing Office.

Ridley, C. A., & Bain, A. B. (1983). The effects of a premarital relationship enhancement program on self-disclosure. *Family Therapy, 10,* 13–24.

Riegle, D. W. (1982). The psychological and social effects of unemployment. *American Psychologist, 37,* 1113–1115.

Rierdan, J., & Koff, E. (1980). The psychological impact of menarche: Integrative versus disruptive change. *Journal of Youth and Adolescence, 9,* 49–58.

Riley, P. J. (1981). The influence of gender on occupational aspirations of kindergarten children. *Journal of Vocational Behavior, 19,* 244–250.

Rindfuss, R. R., & St. John, C. (1983). Social determinants of age at first birth. *Journal of Marriage and the Family, 45*(3), 553–565.

Ritzer, G. (1983). *Sociological theory.* New York: Knopf.

Roberts, E. J., & Holt, S. A. (1980). Parent-child communication about sexuality. *SIECUS Report, 8,* 1–2.

Roberts, J., & Hawton, K. (1980). Child abuse and attempted suicide. *British Journal of Psychiatry, 137,* 319–323.

Robertson, J. F. (1978). Women in midlife: Crises, reverberations, and support networks. *Family Coordinator, 27*(4), 375–382.

Rodgers, R. H. (1964). Toward a theory of family development. *Journal of Marriage and the Family, 26,* 262–270.

Rodgers, R. H. (1973). *Family interaction and transaction.* Englewood Cliffs, NJ: Prentice-Hall.

Rollins, B. C., & Cannon, K. L. (1974). Marital satisfaction over the life cycle: A re-evaluation. *Journal of Marriage and the Family, 36*(2), 271–283.

Rollins, B. C., & Feldman, H. (1970). Marital satisfaction over the life cycle. *Journal of Marriage and the Family, 32*(1), 20–28.

Rooney-Rebeck, P., & Jason, L. (1980). *Prevention of prejudice in elementary school children.* Paper presented at the meeting of the American Association for the Advancement of Behavior Therapy, New York.

Roper, B. C., & LaBeff, E. (1977). Sex roles and feminism revisited: An intergenerational attitude comparison. *Journal of Marriage and the Family, 39,* 113–120.

Rosenbaum, A., & O'Leary, K. D. (1981). Children: The unintended victims of marital violence. *American Journal of Orthopsychiatry, 51,* 692–699.

Rosenberg, M. (1965). *Society and the adolescent self-image.* Princeton, NJ: Princeton University Press.

Rossi, A. (1968). Transition to parenthood. *Journal of Marriage and the Family, 30*(2), 26–29.

Rounsaville, B. J. (1978). Battered wives: Barriers to identification and treatment. *American Journal of Orthopsychiatry, 48,* 487–494.

Rowe, P. (1983–84, December–January). Update: Kansas trust fund lays groundwork for nationwide system. *Human Development News,* p. 11.

Roy, M. (1977). A current survey of 150 cases. In M. Roy (Ed.), *Battered women.* New York: Van Nostrand Reinhold.

Royce, J. M., Lazar, I., & Darlington, R. B. (1983). Minority families, early education, and later life chances. *American Journal of Orthopsychiatry, 53,* 706–720.

Rubenstein, J., Watson, F., Drolette, M., & Rubenstein, H. (1976). Young adolescents' sexual interests. *Adolescence, 11,* 487–496.

Rubin, J., Provenzano, F., & Luria, A. (1974). The eye of the beholder: Parents' views on sex of newborns. *American Journal of Orthopsychiatry, 44,* 512–519.

Rubin, L. B. (1976). *Worlds of pain: Life in the working-class family.* New York: Basic Books.

Rubin, Z. (1970). Measurement of romantic love. *Journal of Personality and Social Psychology, 16,* 265–273.

Rubin, Z., Hill, C. T., Peplau, L. A., & Dunkel-Schetter, C. (1980). Self-disclosure in dating couples: Sex roles and the ethic of openness. *Journal of Marriage and the Family, 42,* 305–317.

Ruble, D. N., & Brooks-Gunn, J. (1982). The experience of menarche. *Child Development, 53,* 1557–1566.

Russell, C. S. (1974). Transition to parenthood: Problems and gratifications. *Journal of Marriage and the Family, 36*(2), 294–302.

Russell, D. W., Peplau, L. A., & Ferguson, M. L. (1978). Developing a measure of loneliness. *Journal of Personality Assessment, 42,* 290–294.

Russell, G. (1978). The father role and its relation to masculinity, femininity, and androgyny. *Child Development, 49,* 1174–1181.

Ryder, R. G. (1980). Dimensions of early marriage. *Family Process, 9,* 51–68.

Sabo, D. F., & Runfola, R. (1980). *Jock: Sports and male identity.* Englewood Cliffs, NJ: Prentice-Hall.

Safran, C. (1979, January). Troubles that pull couples apart: A *Redbook* report. *Redbook,* pp. 138–141.

Saghir, M., & Robins, E. (1973). *Male and female homosexuality.* Baltimore, MD: Williams & Wilkins.

Samuels, S. C. (1977). *Enhancing self-concepts in early childhood: Theory and practice.* New York: Human Sciences Press.

Sanders, C. M. (1979–80). A comparison of adult bereavement in the death of a spouse, child, and parent. *Omega, 10,* 303–322.

Sanders, C. M. (1980–81). Comparison of younger and older spouses in bereavement outcome. *Omega, 11,* 217–232.

Santrock, J. W., Warshak, R., Lindbergh, C., & Meadows, L. (1982). Children's and parents' observed social behavior in stepfather families. *Child Development, 53,* 472–480.

Satir, V. (1972). *Peoplemaking.* Palo Alto, CA: Science and Behavior Books.

Scales, P. (1977). Males and morals: Teenage contraceptive behavior amid the double standard. *Family Coordinator, 26,* 211–222.

Scanzoni, J. (1970). *Opportunity and the family.* New York: Free Press.

Scanzoni, J. (1975). *Sex roles, life styles and childrearing: Changing patterns in marriage and the family.* New York: Free Press.

Scanzoni, J. (1976). Sex role change and influences on birth intentions. *Journal of Marriage and the Family, 38,* 43–60.

Scanzoni, J. (1979). Social processes and power in families. In W. Burr, R. Hill, F. Nye, & I. Reiss (Eds.), *Contemporary theories about the family* (Vol. 1). New York: Free Press.

Scanzoni, J., & Fox, G. L. (1980). Sex roles, family and society: The seventies and beyond. *Journal of Marriage and the Family, 42,* 743–758.

Schaper, K. K. (1982). Towards a calm baby and relaxed parents. *Family Relations, 32,* 409–414.

Scharff, D. E. (1976). Sex is a family affair: Sources of discord and harmony. *Journal of Sex and Marital Therapy, 2,* 17–31.

Schmitt, B. D. (1980). The prevention of child abuse and neglect: A review of the literature with recommendations for application. *Child Abuse and Neglect, 4,* 171–177.

Schoettle, U. C., & Cantwell, D. P. (1980). Children of divorce: Demographic variables, symptoms, and diagnoses. *Journal of the American Academy of Child Psychiatry, 19,* 453–475.

Schramm, W. (1973). *Men, messages, and media: A look at human communication.* New York: Harper & Row.

Schulman, G. L. (1972). Myths that intrude on the adaptation of the stepfamily. *Social Casework, 52,* 131–139.

Schumm, W. R., Martin, M. J., Bollman, S. R., & Jurich, A. P. (1982). Classifying family violence. *Journal of Family Issues, 3,* 319–340.

Schupp, C. E. (1970). An analysis of some social-psychological factors which operate in the functioning of married couples who exchange mates for the purpose of sexual experience. *Dissertation Abstracts International, 31,* 5-A.

Schwertfeger, M. M. (1982). Interethnic marriage and divorce in Hawaii: A panel study of 1968 marriages. *Marriage and Family Review, 5,* 49–60.

Scott, D. M., & Wishy, B. (1982). *America's families: A documentary history.* New York: Harper & Row.

Scott, J. P., & Kivett, V. R. (1980). The widowed, black, older adult in the rural south: Implications for policy. *Family Relations, 29,* 83–90.

Scott, P. D. (1977). Non-accidental injury in children. *British Journal of Psychiatry, 131,* 366–380.

Sears, W. (1982). *Creative parenting.* New York: Everest House.

Seelbach, W. C. (1978). Correlates of aged parents' filial responsibility expectations and realizations. *Family Coordinator, 27*(4), 341–350.

Seevers, M. (1977). Drug addiction problems. In *Research issues 15: Cocaine—summaries of psychosocial research.* NIDA, DHHS Pub. No. (ADM) 77-391. Washington, DC: U. S. Government Printing Office. (Originally published 1939)

Select Committee on Children, Youth, and Their Families. (1983, May). *U. S. children and their feelings: Current conditions and recent trends.* 98th Congress, 1st session, House of Representatives.

Seligman, C., Fazio, R. H., & Zanna, M. P. (1980). Effects of salience of extrinsic rewards on liking and loving. *Journal of Personality and Social Psychology, 38,* 452–460.

Selye, H. (1974). *Stress without distress.* Philadelphia: Lippincott.

Shaevitz, M. H., & Shaevitz, M. H. (1980). *Making it together as a two-career couple.* Boston: Houghton Mifflin.

Shah, F., & Zelnik, M. (1980). Sexuality in adolescence. In B. Wolman & J. Money (Eds.), *Handbook of human sexuality.* Englewood Cliffs, NJ: Prentice-Hall.

Shakespeare, W. (1969). *William Shakespeare: The complete works.* Baltimore: Penguin Books.

Shanas, E. (1980). Older people and their families: The new pioneers. *Journal of Marriage and the Family, 42*(1), 9–15.

Shanas, E., Townsend, P., Wedderborn, D., Friis, H., Milhoj, P., & Stehouwer, J. (1968). *Old people in three industrial societies.* New York: Atherton Press.

Shane, H. G. (1982). The silicon age and education. *Phi Delta Kappan, 63,* 303–308.

Shea, J. A., & Adams, G. R. (1984). Correlates of male and female romantic attachments: A path analysis study. *Journal of Youth and Adolescence, 13,* 27–44.

Sheehy, G. (1974). *Passages.* New York: Dutton.

Shepherd-Look, D. L. (1982). Sex differentiation and the development of sex roles. In B. B. Walman (Ed.), *Handbook of developmental psychology.* Englewood Cliffs, NJ: Prentice-Hall.

Sherman, S. (1975). Patterns of contact for residents of age-segregated and age-integrated housing. *Journal of Gerontology, 1975, 30,* 103–107.

Shettel-Neuber, J., Bryson, J. B., & Young, L. E. (1978). Physical attractiveness of the "other person" and jealousy. *Personality and Social Psychology Bulletin, 4,* 612–615.

Shipman, G. (1968). The psychodynamics of sex education. *Family Coordinator, 17,* 3–12.

Shorkey, C. T. (1979). A review of methods used in the treatment of abusing parents. *Social Casework, 60,* 360–367.

Shorter, E. (1977). *The making of the modern family.* New York: Basic Books.

Shorter, E. (1982). *A history of women's bodies.* New York: Basic Books.

Sigall, H., & Landy, D. (1973). Radiating beauty: The effects of having a physically attractive partner on person perception. *Journal of Personality and Social Psychology, 28,* 218–224.

Silber, S. J. (1980). *How to get pregnant.* New York: Warner Books.

Silka, L., & Keisler, S. (1977). Couples who choose to remain childless. *Family Planning Perspectives, 9,* 16–25.

Silverman, D. C. (1978). Sharing the crisis of rape: Counseling the mates and families of victims. *American Journal of Orthopsychiatry, 48,* 166–173.

Silverman, P. R. (1970). The widow as caregiver in a program of preventive intervention with other widows. *Mental Hygiene, 54,* 540–547.

Silverman, S. M., & Silverman, P. R. (1979). Parent-child communication in widowed families. *American Journal of Psychotherapy, 33,* 428–441.

Simpson, I. H., & England, P. (1981). Conjugal work roles and marital solidarity. *Journal of Family Issues, 2,* 180–204.

Siskind, J. A. (1981). Cross-cultural issues in mental health: Minority perspectives. In O. A. Barbarin, P. R. Good, O. M. Pharr, & J. A. Siskind (Eds.), *Institutional racism and community competence.* DHHS Pub. No. (ADM) 81-907. Washington, DC: U. S. Government Printing Office.

Skolnick, A. (1979). Public images, private realities: The American family in popular culture and social science. In V. Tufte & B. Myerhoff (Eds.), *Changing images of the family.* New Haven, CT: Yale University Press.

Sloan, L., & Latané, B. (1974). Sex and sociability in rats. *Journal of Experimental Social Psychology, 10,* 147–158.

Sloman, L. (1979). *The history of marijuana in America: Reefer madness.* New York: Bobbs-Merrill.

Smart, R. C. (1980). Availability and the prevention of alcohol-related problems. In T. C. Hartford, D. A. Parker, & L. Light (Eds.), *Normative approaches to the prevention of alcohol abuse and alcoholism.* Research Monograph 3. DHEW Pub. No. (ADM) 79-847. Washington, DC: U. S. Government Printing Office.

Smith, A., Goodwin, R., Gullotta, C. F., & Gullotta, T. P. (1979). Community mental health and the arts. *Children Today, 8*(1), 17–20.

Smith, B. K. (1973). *Aging in America.* Boston: Beacon Press.

Smith, D. S. (1973). The dating of the American sexual revolution: Evidence and interpretation. In M. Gordon (Ed.), *The American family in socio-historical perspective.* New York: St. Martin's Press.

Smith, E. R. (1978). Specification and estimation of causal models in social psychology: Comment on Tesser and Paulhus. *Journal of Personality and Social Psychology, 36,* 34–38.

Smith, K. F., & Bengtson, V. L. (1979). Positive consequences of institutionalization: Solidarity between elderly patients and their middle-aged children. *Gerontologist, 19,* 438–447.

Smith, L. G., & Smith, J. R. (1974). Co-marital sex: The incorporation of extramarital sex into the marriage relationship. In J. R. Smith & L. G. Smith (Eds.), *Beyond monogamy.* Baltimore: Johns Hopkins University Press.

Smith, R. M., & Smith, C. W. (1981). Child rearing and single-parent fathers. *Family Relations, 30,* 411–417.

Smith, W. M. (1952). Rating and dating: A restudy. *Marriage and Family Living, 14,* 312–317.

Smyer, M. A., Davis, B. W., & Cohn, M. (1982). A prevention approach to critical life events of the elderly. *Journal of Primary Prevention, 2,* 195–204.

Snyder, D. K., & Fruchtman, L. A. (1981). Differential patterns of wife abuse: A data-based typology. *Journal of Consulting and Clinical Psychology, 4,* 878–885.

Sobell, M. B., & Sobell, L. C. (1978). *Behavioral treatment of alcohol problems.* New York: Plenum.

Sonenstein, F. L., & Pittman, K. (1983). *The what and why of sex education: Describing and explaining program content and coverage in city schools.* Washington, DC: Urban Institute.

Sorensen, A. (1983). Women's employment patterns after marriage. *Journal of Marriage and the Family, 45*(2), 323–338.

Sorensen, R. (1973). *Adolescent sexuality in contemporary America.* New York: World.

Spanier, G. B. (1978). Sex education and premarital sexual behavior among American college students. *Adolescence, 52,* 559–574.

Spanier, G. B., & Glick, P. C. (1980). Paths to remarriage. *Journal of Divorce, 3,* 283–298.

Spanier, G. B., & Glick, P. C. (1981). Marital instability in the United States: Some correlates and recent changes. *Family Relations, 31,* 329–338.

Spanier, G. B., & Lewis, R. A. (1980). Marital quality: A review of the seventies. *Journal of Marriage and the Family, 42*(4), 96–110.

Spanier, G. B., Lewis, R. A., & Cole, C. L. (1975). Marital adjustment over the family life cycle: The issue of curvilinearity. *Journal of Marriage and the Family, 37,* 263–275.

Spence, J. T., & Helmreich, R. L. (1979). On assessing "androgyny." *Sex Roles, 5,* 721–738.

Spence, J. T., Helmreich, R. L., & Stapp, J. (1975). Ratings of self and peers on sex-role attributes and their relation to self-esteem and conceptions of masculinity and femininity. *Journal of Personality and Social Psychology, 32,* 29–39.

Spock, B. M. (1961). *Dr. Spock talks with mothers: Growth and guidance.* Westport, CT: Greenwood Press.

Stack, J. M. (1984). The psychodynamics of spontaneous abortion. *American Journal of Orthopsychiatry, 54,* 162–167.

Stack, S. (1981). Divorce and suicide: A time series analysis 1933–1970. *Journal of Family Issues, 2,* 77–90.

Stannard, D. E. (1979). Changes in the American family: Fiction and reality. In V. Tufte & B. Myerhoff (Eds.), *Changing images of the family.* New Haven, CT: Yale University Press.

Stanton, M. D. (1979). Family treatment of drug problems: A review. In R. I. Dupont, A. Goldstein, & J. O'Donnell (Eds.), *Handbook on drug abuse.* Washington, DC: U. S. Government Printing Office.

Stanton, M. D. (1980). A family theory of drug abuse. In D. J. Lettieri, M. Sayers, & H. W. Pearson (Eds.), *Research 30: Theories on drug abuse.* NIDA, DHHS Pub. No. (ADM) 80-967. Washington, DC: U. S. Government Printing Office.

Staples, R., & Mirande, A. (1980). Racial and cultural variations among American families: A decennial review of the literature on minority families. *Journal of Marriage and the Family, 42*(4), 157–176.

Star, B. (1980). Patterns in family violence. *Social Casework, 61,* 339–346.

Starr, R. H. (1979). Child abuse. *American Psychologist, 34,* 872–878.

Steckel, R. H. (1980). Slave marriage and the family. *Journal of Family History, 5,* 406–421.

Steffensmeier, R. H. (1982). A role model of the transition to parenthood. *Journal of Marriage and the Family, 44*(2), 319–334.

Stein, P. J. (1976). *Single.* Englewood Cliffs, NJ: Prentice-Hall.

Stein, P. J. (1981). *Single life: Unmarried adults in social context.* New York: St. Martin's Press.

Stein, P. J. (1983). Singlehood. In E. Macklin & R. Rubin (Eds.), *Contemporary families and alternative lifestyles.* Beverly Hills, CA: Sage.

Stein, S. L., & Weston, L. C. (1982). College women's attitudes toward women and identity achievement. *Adolescence, 17,* 895–900.

Steinberg, J. L. (1980). Towards an interdisciplinary commitment: A divorce lawyer proposes attorney-therapist marriages or, at the least, an affair. *Journal of Marital and Family Therapy, 19,* 259–269.

Steinberg, L. D., Catalano, R., & Dooley, D. (1981). Economic antecedents of child abuse. *Child Development, 52,* 975–985.

Steinman, S. (1981). The experience of children in a joint-custody arrangement: A report of a study. *American Journal of Orthopsychiatry, 51,* 403–414.

Steinmetz, S. K. (1981, January–February). Elder abuse. *Aging,* 6–10.

Stephenson, J. S. (1981). The family therapist and death: A profile. *Family Relations, 30,* 459–462.

Sternglanz, S. H., & Serbin, L. A. (1974). Sex role stereotyping in children's television programs. *Developmental Psychology, 10,* 710–715.

Sternlieb, G., & Hughes, J. W. (1984). Structuring the future. *Society, 21*(3), 28–34.

Stevens, S. (1980). *Infant caregiving: The role of the father.* Unpublished manuscript, University of Connecticut.

Stewart, A. J., & Rubin, A. (1974). The power motive in the dating couple. *Journal of Personality and Social Psychology, 34,* 305–309.

Stewart, M. (1983). Supportive group action for women: A self-help strategy. *Canada's Mental Health, 31*(3), 11–13.

Stinnett, N., & Birdsong, C. W. (1978). *The family and alternate life styles.* Chicago: Nelson-Hall.

Stoller, E. P. (1983). Parental caregiving by adult children. *Journal of Marriage and the Family, 45*(4), 851–858.

Stone, L. (1977). *The family, sex and marriage in England, 1500–1800.* New York: Harper & Row.

Straus, M. A., Gelles, R. J., & Steinmetz, S. K. (1980). *Behind closed doors: Violence in the American family.* New York: Doubleday.

Streib, G. F., & Beck, R. W. (1980). Older families: A decade review. *Journal of Marriage and the Family, 42*(4), 205–224.

Stringham, J. G., Riley, J. H., & Ross, A. (1982). Silent birth: Mourning a stillborn baby. *Social Work, 27,* 322–327.

Stryker, S. (1964). The interactional and situational approaches. In H. T. Christensen (Ed.), *Handbook of marriage and the family.* Chicago: Rand McNally.

Stuart, F. M., & Hammond, D. C. (1980). Sex therapy. In R. B. Stuart (Ed.), *Helping couples change.* New York: Guilford Press.

Sullivan, K., & Sullivan, A. (1980). Adolescent-parent separation. *Developmental Psychology, 16,* 93–99.

Sussman, M. B., Cates, J., & Smith, D. (1970). *The family and inheritance.* New York: Russell Sage Foundation.

Sutherland, A. E., & Insko, C. A. (1973). Attraction and interestingness of anticipated interaction. *Journal of Personality, 41,* 234–243.

Sweet, J. J., & Resick, P. A. (1979). The maltreatment of children: A review of theories and research. *Journal of Social Issues, 35,* 40–59.

Tannahill, R. (1980). *Sex in history.* New York: Stein & Day.

Tatum, M. L. (1981). The Falls Church experience. *Journal of School Health, 51,* 223–225.

Taubman, S. (1984). Incest in context. *Social Work, 29,* 35–45.

Tavris, C., & Sadd, S. (1977). *The Redbook report on female sexuality.* New York: Delacorte Press.

Taylor, M. C., & Hall, J. A. (1982). Psychological androgyny: Theories, methods, and conclusions. *Psychological Bulletin, 92,* 347–366.

Teaff, J., Lawton, M., Nahemow, L., & Carlson, D. (1978). Impact of age integration on the well-being of elderly tenants in public housing. *Journal of Gerontology, 33,* 126–133.

Tennov, D. (1979). *Love and limerance.* New York: Stein & Day.

Terkel, S. (1970). *Hard times: An oral history of the Great Depression.* New York: Pantheon.

Terr, L. C. (1970). A family study of child abuse. *American Journal of Psychiatry, 127,* 665–671.

Tesch, S. A., & Whitbourne, S. K. (1982). Intimacy and identity status in young adults. *Journal of Personality and Social Psychology, 43,* 1041–1051.

Tesser, A., & Paulhus, D. L. (1976). Toward a causal model of love. *Journal of Personality and Social Psychology, 34,* 1095–1105.

Thoen, G. A., & Russell, M. G. (1979). The childfree option: A workshop model for making one of life's major decisions. In N. Stinnett, B. Chesser, & J. DeFrain (Eds.), *Building family strengths: Blueprints for action.* Lincoln: University of Nebraska Press.

Thomas, A., Chess, S., & Birch, H. G. (1970). The origin of personality. *Scientific American, 223*(2), 102–109.

Thomas, S. P. (1982). After divorce: Personality factors related to the process of adjustment. *Journal of Divorce, 5,* 19–36.

Thorbecke, W., & Grotevant, H. D. (1982). Gender differences in adolescent interpersonal identity formation. *Journal of Youth and Adolescence, 11,* 479–492.

Thornburg, H. D. (1981). Adolescent sources of information on sex. *Journal of School Health, 51,* 274–277.

Thornton, A., Alwin, D. F., & Camburn, D. (1983). Causes and consequences of sex-role attitudes and attitude change. *American Sociological Review, 48,* 211–227.

Tierney, K. J. (1982). The battered women movement and the creation of the wife beating problem. *Social Problems, 29,* 207–220.

Tomeh, A. K. (1978). Sex role orientation: An analysis of structural and attitudinal predictors. *Journal of Marriage and the Family, 40,* 341–354.

Trethowan, W. H., & Conlon, M. F. (1965). The couvade syndrome. *British Journal of Psychiatry, 111,* 57–66.

Troll, L. E. (1971). The family of later life: A decade review. *Journal of Marriage and the Family, 33,* 263–290.

Troll, L. E. (1980a). Grandparenting. In L. W. Poon (Ed.), *Aging in the 1980s: Psychological issues.* Washington, DC: American Psychological Association.

Troll, L. E. (1980b). Interpersonal relations—introduction. In L. W. Poon (Ed.), *Aging in the 1980s: Psychological issues.* Washington, DC: American Psychological Association.

Troll, L. E., & Smith, J. (1976). Attachment through the life span: Some questions about dyadic relationships in later life. *Human Development, 19,* 156–171.

Trussell, J., & Westoff, C. F. (1980). Contraceptive practice and trends in coital frequency. *Family Planning Perspectives, 12*(5), 246–249.

Tudor, C. G., Peterson, D. M., & Elifson, K. W. (1980). An examination of the relationship between peer and parental influence and adolescent drug use. *Adolescence, 15,* 783–797.

Turk, J. L. (1975). Uses and abuses of family power. In R. E. Cromwell & D. H. Olson, *Power in families.* Beverly Hills, CA: Sage.

Turnbill, S. K., & Turnbill, J. M. (1983). To dream the impossible dream. An agenda for discussion with stepparents. *Family Relations, 32,* 227–230.

Turner, R., Shehab, Z., Osborne, K., & Hendley, J. O. (1982). Shedding and survival of herpes simplex virus from "fever blisters." *Pediatrics, 70*(4), 547–549.

Twain, M. (1884). *The adventures of Huckleberry Finn.* New York: Little.

Twichell, J. (1974). Sexual liberality and personality: A pilot study. In J. R. Smith & L. G. Smith (Eds.), *Beyond monogamy.* Baltimore, MD: Johns Hopkins University Press.

Two ways to pile up a million. (1968, November 11). *U. S. News & World Report,* p. 57.

Twombley, R. C., & Moore, R. H. (1969). Black Puritan: The Negro in seventeenth-century Massachusetts. In A. Meier & E. Rudwick (Eds.), *The making of black America: Essays in Negro life and history* (Vol. 1). New York: Atheneum.

Uhlenberg, P. (1980). Death and the family. *Journal of Family History, 5,* 313–320.

Uhlenberg, P., & Meyers, M. A. P. (1981). Divorce and the elderly. *Gerontologist, 21,* 275–282.

U. S. Bureau of the Census. (1970). Marital status. *Subject reports.* PC(2)-4C. Washington, DC: U. S. Government Printing Office.

U. S. Bureau of the Census. (1975). *Historical statistics of the United States: Colonial times to 1970.* Stock No. 003-024-

00120-9. Washington, DC: U. S. Government Printing Office.

U. S. Bureau of the Census. (1980). Marital status and living arrangements: March 1979. *Current population reports,* Series P-20, No. 349. Washington, DC: U. S. Government Printing Office.

U. S. Bureau of the Census. (1981). Household and family characteristics: March, 1980. *Current population reports,* Series P-20, No. 366. Washington, DC: U. S. Government Printing Office.

U. S. Bureau of the Census. (1982). *1980 census of population and housing supplemental report: Provisional estimates of social, economic, and housing characteristics.* Pub. No. PHC 80-SL-1. Washington, DC: U. S. Government Printing Office.

U. S. Bureau of Labor Statistics. (1982a). *Geographic profile of employment and unemployment, 1980.* Bulletin 2111. Washington, DC: U. S. Government Printing Office.

U. S. Bureau of Labor Statistics. (1982b). *Occupational outlook handbook 1982–83.* Washington, DC: U. S. Government Printing Office.

U. S. Department of Labor. (1980). *Job options for women in the 80's.* DOL Pamphlet 18. Washington, DC: U. S. Government Printing Office.

U. S. Department of Labor. (1982). *Twenty facts on women workers.* Washington, DC: U. S. Department of Labor.

U. S. Public Health Service. (1977). *Health of the disadvantaged: Chartbook.* DHEW Pub. No. (HRA) 77-628. Washington, DC: U. S. Government Printing Office.

Valdes-Dapena, M. (1980). Sudden infant death syndrome: Review of the medical literature, 1974–1979. *Pediatrics, 66,* 597–613.

Vanderkooi, L., & Pearson, J. (1983). Mediating divorce disputes. *Family Relations, 32,* 557–566.

Vander-May, B. J., & Neff, R. L. (1982). Adult-child incest: A review of research and treatment. *Adolescence, 17,* 717–735.

Vasta, R., & Copitch, P. (1981). Simulating conditions of child abuse in the laboratory. *Child Development, 52,* 164–170.

Veevers, J. E. (1973). Voluntarily childless wives: An exploratory study. *Sociology and Social Research, 57,* 356–366.

Veevers, J. E. (1979). Voluntary childlessness: A review of issues and evidence. *Marriage and Family Review, 2*(1), 3–16.

Veevers, J. E. (1983). Voluntary childlessness: A critical assessment of the research. In E. Macklin & R. Rubin (Eds.), *Contemporary families and alternative lifestyles.* Beverly Hills, CA: Sage.

Vega, W. A., Hough, R. L., & Romero, A. (1983). Family-life patterns of Mexican-Americans. In G. J. Powell (Ed.), *The psychosocial development of minority group children.* New York: Brunner/Mazel.

Ventura, S. J., Taffel, S. M., & Spratley, E. (1976). *Selected vital and health statistics in poverty and nonpoverty areas of 19 large cities, United States, 1969–1971.* National Vital Statistics Systems, Vital and Health Statistics, Monograph Series 21, No. 26. Washington, DC: U. S. Government Printing Office.

Verderber, R. F. (1978). *Communicate!* Belmont, CA: Wadsworth.

Veroff, J., Depner, C., Kulka, R., & Douvan, E. (1980). Comparison of American motives: 1957 versus 1976. *Journal of Personality and Social Psychology, 39,* 1249–1262.

Videka-Sherman, L. (1982). Coping with the death of a child: A study over time. *American Journal of Orthopsychiatry, 52,* 688–698.

Vigderhous, G., & Fishman, G. (1978). The impact of unemployment and familial integration on changing suicide rates in the U. S. A., 1920–1969. *Social Psychiatry, 13,* 239–248.

Vinick, B. H. (1978). Remarriage in old age. *Family Coordinator, 27*(4), 359–363.

Vischi, T. R., Jones, K. R., & Lima, L. H. (1980). *The alcohol, drug abuse, and mental health national data book.* U. S. Public Health Service, DHHS Pub. No. (ADM) 80-933. Washington, DC: U. S. Government Printing Office.

Visher, E. B., & Visher, J. S. (1978). Common problems of stepparents and their spouses. *American Journal of Orthopsychiatry, 48,* 252–262.

Visher, E. B., & Visher, J. S. (1983). Step-parenting: Blending families. In H. I. McCubbin & C. R. Figley (Eds.), *Stress and the family: Coping with normative transitions* (Vol. 1). New York: Brunner/Mazel.

Vogel, F. G. (1982). Life-spans. In J. A. Fruehling (Ed.), *Sourcebook on death and dying.* Chicago: Marquis.

Vorhauer, B. W. (1980). Human reproduction: Bioengineering aspects of contraception applied to the development of a new female contraceptive. In D. J. Schneck (Ed.), *Biofluid Mechanics* (Vol. 2). New York: Plenum.

Wagley, C., & Harris, M. (1958). *Minorities in the new world.* New York: Columbia University Press.

Wahl, C. (1970). The differential diagnosis of normal and neurotic grief following bereavement. *Psychosomatics, 11,* 104–106.

Wainwright, W. H. (1966). Fatherhood as a precipitant of mental illness. *American Journal of Psychiatry, 123,* 40–44.

Wakil, S. P., Siddique, C. M., & Wakil, F. A. (1981). Between two cultures: A study of socialization of the children of immigrants. *Journal of Marriage and the Family, 43*(4), 929–940.

Walker, K. E., & Woods, M. E. (1976). *Time use: A measure of household production of family goods and services.* Washington, DC: American Home Economics Association.

Walker, K. N., & Messinger, L. (1979). Remarriage after divorce: Dissolution and reconstruction of family boundaries. *Family Process, 18,* 185–192.

Walker, K. N., Rogers, J., & Messinger, L. (1977). Remarriage after divorce: A review. *Social Casework, 58,* 276–285.

Waller, W. (1937). The rating and dating complex. *American Sociological Review, 2,* 727–734.

Wallerstein, J. S. (1983). Children of divorce: The psychological tasks of the child. *American Journal of Orthopsychiatry, 53,* 230–243.

Wallerstein, J. S., & Kelly, S. B. (1974). The effects of parental divorce: The adolescent experience. In J. Anthony & C. Koupernick (Eds.), *The child in his family: Children at psychiatric risk.* New York: Wiley.

Wallerstein, J. S., & Kelly, S. B. (1976). The effects of parental divorce: Experiences of the child in late latency. *American Journal of Orthopsychiatry, 46,* 256–269.

Wallerstein, J. S., & Kelly, S. B. (1980a, January). California's children of divorce. *Psychology Today,* pp. 67–76.

Wallerstein, J. S., & Kelly, S. B. (1980b). Effects of divorce on the visiting father-child relationship. *American Journal of Psychiatry, 137,* 1534–1539.

Wallerstein, J. S., & Kelly, S. B. (1980c). *Surviving the breakup: How children and parents cope with divorce.* New York: Basic Books.

Walster, E., Aronson, V., Abrahams, E., & Rottman, L. (1966). Importance of physical attractiveness in dating behavior. *Journal of Personality and Social Psychology, 31,* 1168–1176.

Walters, R. W. (1982). Race, resources, conflict. *Social Work, 27,* 24–30.

Ward, R. A. (1978). Limitations of the family as a supportive institution in the lives of the aged. *Family Relations, 27*(4), 365–373.

Watson, M. A. (1981). Custody alternatives: Defining the best interest of the children. *Family Relations, 30,* 474–479.

Watzlawick, P., Beavin, J. H., & Jackson, D. D. (1967). *Pragmatics of human communication.* New York: Norton.

Weber, J. A., & Fournier, D. G. (1985). Family support and a child's adjustment to death. *Family Relations, 34,* 43–49.

Webster-Stratton, C. (1985). Comparison of abusive and non-abusive families with conduct disordered children. *American Journal of Orthopsychiatry, 55,* 59–69.

Weinstein, S. E. (1978). Sudden infant death syndrome: Impact on families and a direction for change. *American Journal of Psychiatry, 137,* 831–834.

Weiss, R. S. (1975). *Marital separation.* New York: Basic Books.

Weitzman, J., & Dreen, K. (1982). Wife beating: A view of the marital dyad. *Social Casework, 63,* 259–265.

Weitzman, L. J. (1981). *The marriage contract: Spouses, lovers and the law.* New York: Free Press.

Wells, K. (1980). Gender-role identity and psychological adjustment in adolescence. *Journal of Youth and Adolescence, 9,* 59–64.

Welter, B. (1973). The cult of true womanhood: 1820–1860. In M. Gordon (Ed.), *The American family in socio-historical perspective.* New York: St. Martin's Press.

West, S. (1983). One step behind a killer. *Science 83, 4*(2), 36–45.

Westoff, C. F. (1978). Marriage and fertility in the developed countries. *Scientific American, 239*(6), 51–57.

Westwood, G. (1960). *A minority.* London: Longmans.

What people do to adjust to inflation. (1981, December 14). *U. S. News & World Report,* pp. 52–53.

Whitbourne, S. K., & Tesch, S. A. (in press). A comparison of identity and intimacy statuses in college students and alumni. *Developmental Psychology.*

White, D. G. (1983). Female slaves: Sex roles and status in the antebellum plantation South. *Journal of Family History, 8,* 248–261.

White, G. L. (1977, August). *Inequality of emotional involvement, power, and jealousy in romantic couples.* Paper presented at the meeting of the American Psychological Association, New Orleans.

White, G. L. (1980). Physical attractiveness and courtship progress. *Journal of Personality and Social Psychology, 39,* 660–668.

White, G. L., Fishbein, S., & Rutstein, J. (1981). Passionate love and the misattribution of arousal. *Journal of Personality and Social Psychology, 41,* 56–62.

White, L. K. (1979). Sex differentials in the effect of remariage on global happiness. *Journal of Marriage and the Family, 41,* 869–876.

White, L. K. (1983). Determinants of spousal interaction: Marital structure or marital happiness. *Journal of Marriage and the Family, 45*(3), 511–519.

White, P. N., & Rollins, J. C. (1981). Rape: A family crisis. *Family Relations, 30,* 103–109.

White, S. W., & Bloom, B. L. (1981). Factors related to the adjustment of divorcing men. *Family Relations, 30,* 349–360.

Whiteside, M. F. (1982). Remarriage: A family developmental process. *Journal of Marital and Family Therapy, 8*(2), 59–68.

Whitfield, E. L., & Freeland, K. (1981, November–December). Divorce and children: What teachers can do. *Childhood Education,* pp. 88–89.

Whitley, B. E. (1983). Sex role orientation and self-esteem: A critical meta-analytic review. *Journal of Personality and Social Psychology, 44,* 765–778.

Williams, J. (1980). Sexuality in marriage. In B. Wolman & J. Money (Eds.), *Handbook of human sexuality.* Englewood Cliffs, NJ: Prentice-Hall.

Williams, R. H., & Wirth, C. G. (1965). *Lives through the years: Styles of life and successful aging.* New York: Atherton.

Williams, W. V., Lee, J., & Polak, P. R. (1976). Crisis intervention: Effects of crisis intervention on family survivors of sudden death situations. *Community Mental Health Journal, 12,* 128–136.

Williams, W. V., & Polak, P. R. (1979). Follow-up research in primary prevention: A model of adjustment in acute grief. *Journal of Clinical Psychology, 35,* 35–45.

Willis, D. K. (1982, December 26). Insuring the impossible is everyday role. *Hartford Courant,* p. B9.

Wilson, K. L., Zurcher, L. A., McAdams, D. C., & Curtis, R. L. (1975). An exploratory analysis from two national surveys. *Journal of Marriage and the Family, 37,* 526–536.

Wince, J. P. (1981). Sexual dysfunction (distress and dissatisfaction). In S. M. Turner, K. S. Calhoun, & H. E. Adams (Eds.), *Handbook of clinical behavior therapy.* New York: Wiley.

Winch, R. F. (1943). The relationship between courtship behavior and attitudes toward parents among college men. *American Sociological Review, 8,* 164–174.

Winch, R. F. (1954). The theory of complementary needs in mate selection: Final results on the test of general hypotheses. *American Sociological Review, 19,* 241–249.

Winch, R. F., Ktsanes, T., & Ktsanes, V. (1955). Empirical elaboration of the theory of complementary needs in mate selection. *Journal of Abnormal and Social Psychology, 51,* 508–518.

Wise, M. J. (1980). The aftermath of divorce. *American Journal of Psychoanalysis, 40,* 149–158.

With help from families, friends and welfare, unwed mothers can overcome serious obstacles. (1979). *Family Planning Perspectives, 11*(1), 43–44.

Wodarski, J. S. (1981). Comprehensive treatment of parents who abuse their children. *Adolescence, 16,* 959–972.

Wolfe, D. A., Sandler, J., & Kaufman, K. (1981). A competency-based parent training program for child abusers. *Journal of Consulting and Clinical Psychology, 49,* 633–640.

Women on Words and Images. (1972). *Dick and Jane as victims.* Princeton, NJ: Women on Words and Images.

Wood, V., & Robertson, J. F. (1978). Friendship and kinship interaction: Differential effect on the morale of the elderly. *Journal of Marriage and the Family, 40*(2), 367–375.

Woodward, J. C., Zabel, J., & DeCosta, C. (1980). Loneliness and divorce. *Journal of Divorce, 4,* 73–83.

Yankelovich, D. (1981, April) A world turned upside down. *Psychology Today,* pp. 35–91.

Yankelovich, Skelly & White, Inc. (1979). *The General Mills American family report: Family health in an era of stress.* Minneapolis, MN: General Mills.

Yates, A. (1981). Narcissistic traits in certain abused children. *American Journal of Orthopsychiatry, 51,* 55–62.

Yates, A. (1982). Children eroticized by incest. *American Journal of Psychiatry, 139,* 482–485.

Yost, K. M. (1979). *Selected readings on mother-infant bonding.* DHEW Pub. No. (OHDS) 79-30225. Washington, DC: U. S. Government Printing Office.

Young, E. R., & Parish, T. S. (1977). Impact of father absence during childhood on the psychological adjustment of college females. *Sex Roles, 26,* 44–51.

Zeiss, A. M., Zeiss, R. A., & Johnson, S. M. (1980). Sex differences in initiation of and adjustment to divorce. *Journal of Divorce, 4,* 21–33.

Zellman, G., Johnson, P. B., Giarrusso, R., & Goodchilds, J. D. (1979, September). *Adolescent expectations for dating relationships: Consensus and conflict between the sexes.* Paper presented at the meeting of the American Psychological Association, New York.

Zelnik, M., & Kantner, J. F. (1980). Sexual activity, contraceptive use and pregnancy among metropolitan-area teenagers: 1971–1979. *Family Planning Perspectives, 12*(5), 230–237.

Zelnik, M., & Shah, F. (1983). First intercourse among young Americans. *Family Planning Perspectives, 15,* 64–70.

# NAME/AUTHOR INDEX

# SUBJECT INDEX*

* Boldface page number indicates text page on which indexed term is defined.

# LIST OF
# SUPPORT
# ORGANIZATIONS

AIDS Hotline, 123

Al-Anon Headquarters, 386

Alcoholics Anonymous, 386

American Association for Retired Persons, 298

American Social Health Association, 124

Association for Children and Adults with Learning Disabilities, 2

Association of Couples for Marriage Enrichment, 202

Big Brothers/Big Sisters, 254

Candlelighters, 429

Checks Anonymous, 347

Compassionate Friends, 429

Divorce Anonymous, 254

Families Anonymous, 229

Federation of AIDS-Related Organizations, 123

Gamblers Anonymous, 347

Gray Panthers, 298

Make Today Count, 429

MELD, 229

Mended Hearts, 298

Narcotics Anonymous, 386

National Center for Child Abuse and Neglect, 410

National Center for the Prevention and Control of Rape, 410

National Coalition against Domestic Violence, 410

National Committee for the Prevention of Child Abuse, 410

National Foundation for Sudden Infant Death, 429

National Gay Task Force, 123

National Marriage Encounter, 202

National Self-Help Clearinghouse, 47

National Sudden Infant Death Syndrome Foundation, 429

Parents Anonymous, 229

Parents Without Partners, 254

Planned Parenthood Federation of America, 124

# CREDITS

This page constitutes an extension
of the copyright page.

**CHAPTER 1.** **17:** Table 1-1 data from U. S. Bureau of the Census, *Historical Statistics of the United States: Colonial Times to 1970* (Washington, DC: U. S. Government Printing Office, 1975), p. 41; U. S. Bureau of the Census, *1980 Census of Population and Housing, Supplemental Report: Provisional Estimates of Social, Economic and Housing Characteristics* (Washington, DC: U. S. Government Printing Office, March, 1982). **18:** Table 1-2 data from U. S. Bureau of the Census, *Historical Statistics of the United States: Colonial Times to 1970* (Washington, DC: U. S. Government Printing Office, 1975), p. 42; U. S. Bureau of the Census, *1980 Census of Population and Housing, Supplemental Report: Provisional Estimates of Social, Economic and Housing Characteristics* (Washington, DC: U. S. Government Printing Office, March, 1982). **21:** Table 1-3 from "The French-Canadian Family Economy and Standard of Living in Lowell, Massachusetts, 1870," by F. H. Early, *Journal of Family History,* 1982, *7,* 180–199. Copyright © 1982 by the National Council on Family Relations. Reprinted by permission.

**CHAPTER 2.** **35:** Table 2-2 from "The Family Life Cycle: Empirical or Conceptual Tool?" by S. L. Nock, *Journal of Marriage and the Family,* 1979, *41,* 19. Copyright © 1979 by the National Council on Family Relations. Reprinted by permission. **36:** Figure 2-1 adapted from "How to Live with Stress," by H. Selye, *Blue Print for Health,* 1978, 27(1), 11. Copyright © 1978 by the Blue Cross Association, Chicago, Illinois. **37:** Figure 2-2 from "Social Stress on the Family," by R. Hill, *Social Casework,* 1958, *34,* 146. Copyright © 1958 by Family Service America. Reprinted by permission. **38:** Figure 2-3 from *Family Stress and Social Support,* by H. I. McCubbin, E. A. Cauble, and J. M. Patterson, p. 46. Copyright © 1982 by Charles C Thomas, Publisher. Reprinted by permission. **39:** Table 2-3 from *Family Stress and Social Support,* by H. I. McCubbin, E. A. Cauble, and J. M. Patterson, p. 47. Copyright © 1982 by Charles C Thomas, Publisher. Reprinted by permission.

**CHAPTER 3.** **58:** cartoon by Pete Mueller. Reprinted by permission.

**CHAPTER 4.** **72:** Box 4-2 from "The Traditional-liberated Woman Dimension: Social Stereotype and Self-concept," by R. D. Cartwright, et al., *Journal of Personality and Social Psychology,* 1982, *44,* 581–588. Copyright © 1982 by the American Psychological Association. Adapted by permission of the publisher and author. **75:** Figure 4-1 adapted from "A Cognitive-developmental Analysis of Children's Sex-role Concepts and Attitudes," by L. Kohlberg. In E. Maccoby (Ed.), *The Development of Sex Differences,* p. 128. Copyright © 1966 by Stanford University Press. Reprinted by permission.

CHAPTER 5.   94: Table 5-1 from *Human Sexual Behavior,* by P. Feldman and M. MacCulloch, p. 50. Copyright © 1980 by John Wiley & Sons, Ltd. Reprinted by permission. 96: Box 5-1 from *The People's Common Sense Medical Advisor,* by R. V. Pierce. Buffalo, NY: World's Dispensary Printing Office and Binding, 1895. 99: Box 5-2 from *Then Again Maybe I Won't,* by J. Blume, p. 93. Copyright © 1971 by Judy Blume. Reprinted with permission of Bradbury Press, an affiliate of Macmillan, Inc. 101: Table 5-2 from "Sexuality in Adolescence," by F. Shah and M. Zelnik. In. B. Wolman and J. Money (Eds.), *Handbook of Human Sexuality.* Copyright © 1980 by Prentice-Hall, Inc. Reprinted by permission. 102: Table 5-3 from "Sexual Activity, Contraceptive Use and Pregnancy among Metropolitan-area Teenagers: 1971–1979," by M. Zelnik and J. F. Kantner, *Family Planning Perspectives,* 1980, 12(5), 230–237. Reprinted by permission. 102: Tables 5-4 and 5-5 from "First Intercourse among Young Americans," by M. Zelnik and F. Shah, *Family Planning Perspectives,* 1983, 15(2), 64–70. Reprinted by permission. 106: Table 5-6 from "Overview of Sex Therapy," by S. Levine. In G. P. Sholevar (Ed.), *Handbook of Marriage and Martial Therapy.* Copyright © 1981 Spectrum Publications, Inc. 109: Table 5-7 from *Living with Herpes,* by D. P. Langston. Copyright © 1983 by Deborah P. Langston. Reprinted by permission of Doubleday & Company, Inc. 113–115: Table 5-8 from U. S. Public Health Service. *Family Planning Methods of Contraception.* DHEW Publication No. HSA 785646. (Washington, DC: U. S. Government Printing Office, 1978). 116–117: Box 5-3 from "Court Sets Teens' Abortion Rights," by Dr. R. Gottesman, *NASW NEWS,* 1983, 28(9), 20–21. Reprinted by permission. 118: Table 5-9 from "Characteristics of Abortion Patients in the United States, 1979 and 1980," by S. K. Henshaw and K. O'Reilly, *Family Planning Perspectives,* 1983, 15(1), 5–8. Reprinted by permission.

CHAPTER 6.   134: Figure 6-2 from *Progress on Family Problems: A Nationwide Study of Clients' and Counselors' Views on Family Agency Services,* by D. F. Beck and M. A. Jones. Copyright © 1983 Family Service America. Reprinted by permission. 140: cartoon, SALLY FORTH by Greg Howard. © News Group Chicago, Inc., 1984. Courtesy of News America Syndicate.

CHAPTER 7.   154, Figure 7-1 from *Adolescent Life Experiences,* by G. R. Adams and T. Gullotta. Copyright © 1983 by Wadsworth, Inc. Reprinted by permission of the publisher, Brooks/Cole Publishing Company. 161: cartoon, Copyright, 1983, Universal Press Syndicate. Reprinted with permission. All rights reserved. 163: Figure 7-2 from *Personal Relationships II: Developing Personal Relationships,* by S. W. Duck and R. Gilmour (Eds.), p. 67. Copyright © 1981 by Academic Press. Reprinted by permission. 164–165: list from "The Relationship Even Scale: A Guttman Scaling of Progress in Courtship," by A. Christensen and C. E. King, *Journal of Marriage and Family,* 1983, 45, 671–678. Copyright © 1983 by the National Council on Family Relations. Reprinted by

permission. 166: Figure 7-3 from "Transitions in Relationship Style from Adolescence to Young Adulthood," by J. L. Fischer, *Journal of Youth and Adolescence,* 1981, 10, 11–23. Reprinted by permission.

CHAPTER 8.   178, 191, 195: song lyrics © 1982 WB Music Corp. All rights reserved. Used by permission. 180–181: Box 8-1 adapted from *The Marriage Contract: Spouses, Lovers, and the Law,* by L. J. Weitzman. Copyright © 1981 by Lenore J. Weitzman. Reprinted by permission of Free Press, a Division of Macmillan, Inc. 185: Table 8-1 from *Husbands and Wives,* by R. O. Blood and D. M. Wolfe. Copyright © 1960 by The Free Press. Reprinted by permission of The Free Press, a Division of Macmillan, Inc. 186: Table 8-2 from *Sexual Behavior in the 1970's,* by M. Hunt. Copyright © 1974 by PLAYBOY. Reprinted with permission from Playboy Enterprises, Inc. 194: cartoon, Copyright, 1983, Universal Press Syndicate. Reprinted with permission. All rights reserved. 197: Figure 8-2 adapted from *American Couples,* by P. Blumstein and P. Schwartz. Copyright © 1983 by Philip Blumstein and Pepper W. Schwartz. Reprinted by permission of William Morrow & Company.

CHAPTER 9.   206: Table 9-1 from "Changes in Views Toward Childlessness: 1965–1970," by E. Pohlman. In E. Peck and J. Senderowitz (Eds.), *Pronatalism: The Myth of Mom and Apple Pie.* Copyright © 1974 by Thomas Cromwell Company. Reprinted by permission of the author. 209: Table 9-2 from *How to Get Pregnant,* by S. J. Silber. Copyright © 1980 by Sherman J. Silber. Reprinted by permission of Charles Scribner's Sons. 222: Box 9-4 from "Perceptions of Parental Role Responsibilities Among Working People: Development of a Comprehensive Measure," by L. A. Gilbert and G. R. Hanson, *Journal of Marriage and the Family,* 1983, 45, 205. Copyright © 1983 by the National Council on Family Relations. Reprinted by permission. 223: Table 9-3 based on data from C. S. Edwards, *USDA estimates of the cost of raising a child: A guide to their use and interpretation.* U. S. Dept. of Agriculture (Misc. pub. #1411), U. S. Government Printing Office, 1981, pp. 46–49. 225: Table 9-4 from *United States: A Statistical Portrait of the American People,* by A. Hacker, p. 164. Copyright © 1983 by Andrew Hacker. Reprinted by permission of Viking Penguin, Inc.

CHAPTER 10.   232: cartoon. Reprinted by permission of Chronicle Features, San Francisco, CA. 233: quote from *The Life and Death of the Mayor of Casterbridge,* by T. Hardy, pp. 8–11. Copyright © 1966 by St. Martin's Press. Reprinted by permission. 234: Figure 10-1 from *What's Happening to the American Family,* by S. A. Levitan and R. S. Belous, p. 31. Copyright © by Johns Hopkins University. Reprinted by permission. 235, 236: Table 10-1 and Box 10-1 from *United States: A Statistical Portrait of the American People,* by A. Hacker. Copyright © 1983 by Andrew Hacker. Reprinted by permission of Viking Penguin, Inc. 240: Figure 10-2 data from Hartford Courant.

**CHAPTER 11.** **262, 268:** Tables 11-1 and 11-2 from "Correlates of Marital Happiness Among the Remarried," by S. L. Albrecht, *Journal of Marriage and the Family,* 1979, *41,* 862. Copyright © the National Council on Family Relations. Reprinted by permission.

**CHAPTER 12.** **283:** Table 12-1 from "Senior Citizens in Great Cities: The Case of Chicago," by B. Bild and R. Havighurst, *The Gerontologist,* 1976, 16(1), 62. Reprinted by permission. **285–286:** quote from *Why Survive? Being Old in America,* by R. N. Butler, pp. ix–x. Copyright © 1975 by Robert N. Butler, M.D. Reprinted by permission of Harper & Row, Publishers, Inc. **291:** Figure 12-1 from *Mother Jones Magazine.* Diagram by Robert Haydock.

**CHAPTER 13.** **302:** Figures 13-1 and 13-2 from *The Nation's Families: 1960–1990,* by G. Masnick and M. J. Bane. Copyright © 1980 by Auburn House Publishing Company. Reprinted by permission. **304,** Table 13-1 from U. S. Bureau of the Census, "Marital Status and Living Arrangements: March 1979," *Current Population Reports,* Series P-20, No. 349. (Washington, DC: U. S. Government Printing Office, 1980).

**CHAPTER 14.** **326:** Tables 14-1 and 14-4 from *United States: A Statistical Portrait of the American People,* by A. Hacker. Copyright © 1983 by Andrew Hacker. Reprinted by permission of Viking Penguin, Inc. **327:** Figure 14-1 from U. S. Dept. of Agriculture. *A Guide to Budgeting for the Family.* Bulletin #108. (U. S. Government Printing Office, 1970). **328:** Table 14-2 from Bureau of Labor Statistics. *Job Options for Women in the 80's.* U. S. Dept. of Labor, Pamphlet 18. (U. S. Government Printing Office, 1980). **329:** Figures 14-2 and 14-4 from U. S. Dept. of Agriculture, 1970. **330–331:** Box 14-1 from U. S. Dept. of Agriculture, *Family Economic Review,* (U. S. Government Printing Office, Winter, 1982). **332:** Table 14-3 from "Structuring the Future," by G. Sternlieb and J. W. Hughes, *Society,* 1984, 21(3). Copyright © 1984 by Transaction, Inc. Reprinted by permission. **335:** Figure 14-5 from National Association of Home Builders, Economics Division. Courtesy of The Hartford Courant. **336.** Table 14-5 from "Budgets for a Retired Couple," *Family Economic Review,* 1983, *1,* 31. Reprinted by permission. **337:** Figure 14-6 from *U. S. News and World Report,* November 11, 1968, p. 57. Copyright © 1968 by U. S. News and World Report. Reprinted by permission. **339:** quote from *Hard Times: An Oral History of the Great Depression,* by S. Terkel, p. 246. Copyright © 1970 by Pantheon Books. Reprinted by permission. **340:** cartoon by Bud Grace, © 1984. **341:** Figure 14-7 from *U. S. News and World Report,* September 13, 1982, p. 55. Copyright © 1982 by U. S. News and World Report. Reprinted by permission.

**CHAPTER 15.** **358:** Figure 15-1 from Public Health Service. *Health of the Disadvantaged* (*Chartbook*). DHHS pub #HRA 77-628. (U. S. Government Printing Office, 1977).

**CHAPTER 16.** **370, 371:** Tables 16-1 and 16-2 from J. R. Deluca, *Fourth Special Report to the U. S. Congress on Alcohol and Health.* NIAAA, DHHS Publication No. ADM 81 1080. (U. S. Government Printing Office, 1981). **373:** Table 16-3 from *Economic Costs to Society of Alcohol and Drug Abuse and Mental Illness: 1980,* by H. J. Harwood and D. M. Napolitano, P. L. Kristiansen, and J. J. Collins. Copyright © 1984 by Research Triangle Press. Reprinted by permission.

**CHAPTER 17.** **393:** Table 17-1 from "Violence Toward Children in the United States," by R. J. Gelles, *American Journal of Orthopsychiatry,* 1978, 48(4), 586. Copyright © 1978 by the American Orthopsychiatric Association, Inc. Reprinted by permission. **397:** Table 17-2 from "Maternal Employment and Violence Toward Children," by R. J. Gelles and E. F. Hargreaves, *Journal of Family Issues,* 1981, *2,* 514. Reprinted by permission of Sage Publications, Inc.

**CHAPTER 18.** **414:** Box 18-2 from *The Hour of Our Death,* by P. Aries, p. 358. Copyright © 1981 by Alfred A. Knopf, Inc. Reprinted by permission. **417:** Table 18-1 from "Human Grief: A Model for Prediction and Intervention," by L. A. Bugen, *American Journal of Orthopsychiatry,* 1977, 47(2), 197. Copyright © 1977 by the American Orthopsychiatric Association, Inc. Reprinted by permission. **418:** Table 18-2 from "Divorcees and Widows: Similarities and Differences," by G. C. Kitson, et al., *American Journal of Orthopsychiatry,* 1980, 50(2), 295. Copyright © 1980 by the American Orthopsychiatric Association, Inc. Reprinted by permission. **422:** Figure 18-1 from "Sudden Infant Death," by R. L. Naeye, *Scientific American,* 1980, 242(4), 61. Copyright © 1980 by Scientific American, Inc. All rights reserved.

**CHAPTER 19.** **443:** Figure 19-1 from "Marriage and Fertility in the Developed Countries," by C. F. Westoff, *Scientific American,* 1978, 239(6), 52. Copyright © 1978 by Scientific American, Inc. All rights reserved. **443:** Figure 19-2 from U. S. Bureau of the Census, *Current Population Reports,* Series P-25, No. 889. Cited in Data Tract 8. *A Population Profile: The 1980's and Beyond.* (Washington, DC: American Council of Life Insurance, 1981). **444:** Box 19-2 from UPI, March 4, 1984. Reprinted with permission of United Press International, Inc.

PHOTO CREDITS

**CHAPTER 1.** **2** and **3:** (top) Erika Stone, Peter Arnold, Inc.; (middle left) The Granger Collection; (middle right) Gale Zucker, Stock Boston, Inc.; (bottom left) Hazel Hankin, Stock Boston, Inc.; (bottom right) Brown Brothers; **7:** Courtesy KBHK TV, San Francisco; **14:** The Bettmann Archive, Inc.; **19:** (top) The Bettmann Archive, Inc.; (bottom) Charles Gatewood, The Image Works, Inc.; **22:** Burk Uzzle, Woodfin Camp & Associates.

**CHAPTER 2.** **29:** © Carol Simowitz; **42:** Courtesy of The American Lung Association; **43:** Patricia Fisher.

**CHAPTER 3.** **55:** Louis Dematteis, Jeroboam, Inc.

**CHAPTER 4.** **62** and **63:** (top right) Stephen Shames, Visions; (bottom left) © Freda Leinwand; (bottom middle) The Bettmann Archive, Inc.; (bottom right) Erika Stone, Peter Arnold, Inc.; **66:** Anonymous American Artist: *The Sargent Family,* 1800, National Gallery Art, Washington. Gift of William and Bernice Chrysler Garbisch; **67:** The Last of the Mohicans, © 1936. Museum of Modern Art/Film Stills Archives; **71:** NASA.

**CHAPTER 5.** **91:** William J. Glackens: *Nude with Apple.* 1910 The Brooklyn Museum. Dick S. Ramsey Fund; **97:** Norman Rockwell: "The Saturday Evening Post" cover March 6, 1954; **100:** (top left) Frank Siteman, Jeroboam, Inc.; (top right) © Mark Chester; (bottom left) Steven Shames, Visions; (bottom right) Michael Hayman, Stock Boston, Inc.; **107:** Courtesy of the San Francisco City Clinic; **120:** © Cleo Freelance Photo.

**CHAPTER 6.** **128:** George Segal: Three People on Four Benches, 1980 Collection: Martin Z. Marguilies, Miami Florida. Photo: Malcolm Varon; **147:** Gayle Zucker, Stock Boston, Inc.; **150** and **151:** (top) Jim Harrison, Stock Boston, Inc.; (top left) Anestis Diakopoulos, Stock Boston, Inc.; (bottom left) Rose Skytta, Jeroboam, Inc.; (bottom right) Sybil Shelton, Peter Arnold, Inc.

**CHAPTER 7.** **155:** Peter Vilms, Jeroboam, Inc.; **172:** © Mark Chester.

**CHAPTER 8.** **179:** The Bettmann Archive; **196:** © Cleo Freelance Photo.

**CHAPTER 9.** **208:** © James L. Shaffer; **218:** James R. Holland, Stock Boston, Inc.; **221:** *Kramer vs Kramer,* © 1979 Columbia Pictures Industries, Inc.; **224:** Luke Fildes: *The Doctor,* The Bettmann Archive.

**CHAPTER 10.** **238:** Sepp Seitz, Woodfin Camp & Associates; **247:** Nicholas Sapieha, Stock Boston, Inc.

**CHAPTER 11.** **259:** Lynne Jaeger Weinstein, Woodfin Camp & Associates; **263:** "Ms." Magazine cover for February 1985. Courtesy of the Ms. Foundation for Education and Communication. Photo: Carl Fischer; **271:** © Carol Simowitz.

**CHAPTER 12.** **277:** Steve Schapiro, Sygma; **286:** Kent Reno, Jeroboam, Inc.; **289:** © Carol Simowitz; **296:** Courtesy of the Grey Panthers.

**CHAPTER 13.** **301:** *Freedom from Want,* 1943. Promotion for the "Four Freedoms" War Bond Series. Printed by permission of the Estate of Norman Rockwell. Copyright © 1943 Estate of Norman Rockwell.; **307:** Rose Skytta, Jeroboam, Inc.;

**310:** Alan Carey, The Image Works, Inc.; **313:** AP/Wide World Photos, Inc.; **322** and **323:** (upper left) Ken Graves, Jeroboam, Inc.; (top middle) Frederick Bodin, Stock Boston, Inc.; (middle left) James R. Holland, Stock Boston, Inc.; (bottom left) National Archives; (bottom right) © Joel Gordon.

**CHAPTER 14.** **334:** © James L. Shaffer; **338:** Sybil Shelton, Peter Arnold, Inc.; **343:** Michael Hayman, Stock Boston, Inc.

**CHAPTER 15.** **351:** The Bettmann Archive; **360:** Karen Rosenthal, Stock Boston, Inc.; **362:** Earl Dotter, Archive Pictures, Inc.

**CHAPTER 16.** **372:** Polly Brown, Archive Pictures, Inc.; **375:** Bruce Kliewe, Jeroboam, Inc.; **382:** © Joel Gordon.

**CHAPTER 17.** **390:** Great Expectations, © 1936 Museum of Modern Art/Film Stills Archive; **396:** Courtesy of San Francisco Child Abuse Council, Inc.; **400:** Mark Antman, The Image Works, Inc.

**CHAPTER 18.** **415:** Ellis Herwig, Stock Boston, Inc.; **420:** © Cleo Freelance Photo; **426:** Michael Weisbrot, Stock Boston, Inc.

**CHAPTER 19.** **430** and **431:** (top left) Elizabeth Crews, Stock Boston, Inc.; (top right) Joanne Leonard, Woodfin Camp & Associates; (middle) Mark Chester; (bottom left) The Bettmann Archive, Inc.; (bottom right) Library of Congress; **435:** Taxi Driver, © 1976 Museum of Modern Art/Film Stills Archive; **436:** Brown Brothers; **440:** Kent Reno, Jeroboam, Inc.